Children's Books
for Times of Stress

Children's Books for Times of Stress

An Annotated Bibliography

Ruth J. Gillis

With technical assistance by Louise S. Spear

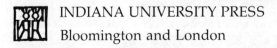
INDIANA UNIVERSITY PRESS
Bloomington and London

Library of Congress Cataloging in Publication Data

Gillis, Ruth J., 1921-
   Children's books for times of stress.

   Bibliography.
   Includes index.
   1. Children's literature--Bibliography.
I. Title.
Z1037 .A1G54 PN1009.A1 028.52 76-48517
ISBN 0-253-31348-1   2 3 4 5 82 81 80 79

Dedicated to all of the wonderful children at University
Elementary School, but especially to Khea Williams, who said,
"Make him say he's sorry, Mrs. Gillis, like in *The Sorely Trying
Day*!"

Contents

Preface

In recent years, there has been an increasing number of
books for young children dealing with the emotional aspects of a
child's life. Among them are books designed to help children
and their parents cope with a wide range of emotionally stressful
situations, from death, divorce, and hospitalization to everyday
problems like going to sleep, lack of self-confidence, shyness,
jealousy, and difficulty in getting along with other children.
Others concern happier experiences like friendship and expressions of love within the family. This bibliography is a guide
to those books in the affective area, and will be helpful to
teachers, parents, librarians, and others working with children
in the clinical setting, classroom, or social agency, as well as
to educators in higher education who prepare professionals in
that field.
   Criteria for the 261 books selected were established using
standards of excellence outlined by recognized authorities in the
field of children's literature: May Hill Arbuthnot and Zena
Sutherland, *Children and Books*, Charlotte Huck and Doris Young
Kuhn, *Children's Literature in the Elementary School*, Patricia J.
Cianciolo, *Illustrations in Children's Books*, and others. Each
book was examined, read with care, and selected if it met the
criteria of characterization, plot, theme, and style within the
context of a good story. Some titles, chosen because of the importance of their themes, did not meet the standards but were
deemed critical in order to provide material in an area of need.
By and large, however, the items selected reflect quality as a
prime concern.
   Three specific criteria were used in evaluating titles:
(1) the theme of the book was concerned with one of the identi-
fied topics in the affective area, (2) the book was appropriate
for children from preschool age to about the age of nine, and (3)
the title could be located in standard professional review
sources. For some few entries it was not possible to obtain a

review recommending the book. While many titles were published
in the seventies, including 1976, the imprint of the earliest
book cited is 1932.

Index to Subject Headings

The body of the work consists of an alphabetically arranged
subject index, and the entire bibliographic entry appears under
each relevant item in the subject index; thus a separate index
need not be consulted each time the reader searches for an item.
While the theme of the work and the model for the subject headings may be considered unique, it is the computer-assisted
indexing program that may be the more important aspect of the
bibliography. The program utilized is an adaptation of the
Selind Indexing Program, designed by Jean Nakhnikian, programer-
consultant at the Marshal H. Wrubel Computing Center at Indiana
University. The program will index, match, and select within
any field, i.e., author, publisher, and so forth, and will print
the entire input or just selected parts in any order specified.
In addition to the eight fields or categories that index the
bibliographic information, the program indexes in seven selected
major subject headings with as many subfields as desired, offering much flexibility and accessibility. The program allows for
constant revision, since additions and corrections may be made
for an individual item without dislocating other items in the
work.
Each citation contains the name of the author (no joint
authors are included), title of the book, publisher, copyright
date, and the name of the illustrator when known. This is followed by an acronym, in parentheses, for the review source or
selection aid. The annotation follows.
The annotation includes a description and evaluation of the
book, with occasional comments about the illustrations and a
statement about the reading level of the book if deemed important.
Comments concerning race and sex are included only when judged
to be pertinent to the theme. Following the annotation is a list
of all the subjects under which the book can be found.

Subject Headings

Seven broad categories, usually with subheadings, are used
for locating items in the bibliography:

EMOTIONS

Used for larger areas in the affective domain, such as
anger, jealousy, love.

BEHAVIOR

>   Used for specific areas in the affective domain, such
>   as quarreling, possessiveness, teasing.

FAMILY

>   Concerns basic interpersonal relationships, including
>   the extended family. Illustrates normal functional
>   relations as well as those that are less usual.

DIFFICULT SITUATION

>   Illustrates situations containing stress--personal and
>   environmental--such as death, divorce, illness, often
>   unplanned. Often overlaps with New Situation.

NEW SITUATION

>   Includes potentially stressful situations, personal and
>   in the environment, which may be predictable, therefore
>   prepared for, such as a move to a new home, new baby in
>   the household, need for eyeglasses. May overlap with
>   Difficult Situation.

SELF CONCEPT

>   Contains developmental concepts, such as Self-Confidence
>   and Self-Identity.

FRIENDSHIP

>   Allows for themes that present positive situations as
>   well as those containing abrasive encounters.

For example, *Monnie Hates Lydia*, by Susan Pearson, the story of
two sisters who live with their father, has the following nine
entries:

    ANGER
    DIFF(ICULT) SIT(UATION)--ONE PARENT
    EMOTIONS--ANGER
    FAM(ILY)--FATHERS
    FAM(ILY)--ONE PARENT
    FAM(ILY)--SIBLING RIVALRY
    FATHERS
    ONE PARENT

SIBLING RIVALRY

If the approach is through FAMILY, the reader will find the book
listed three times. If the reader's approach is through DIFFI-
CULT SITUATION, it will appear once. Under EMOTIONS, it will
appear once. It will also appear once under each of the four
subheadings ANGER, FATHERS, ONE PARENT, and SIBLING RIVALRY.
Many of the books have interrelated themes that suggest a wide
range of approaches.

The broad categories were devised after consulting a number of sources, all of which provided some useful guidelines, but
none of which provided the degree of specificity required. General reference tools for children's materials consulted were
Children's Catalog and *Elementary School Library Collection*. Books
dealing specifically with a subject approach were also examined:
Subject Index to Books for Primary Grades, *Subject Index to Books
for Intermediate Grades*, and *Subject Index to Children's Books in
Print*. Zena Sutherland, in *Best in Children's Books*, gave insight
into the possible groupings of the subject headings. *Bibliother-
apy: Methods and Materials* and *Reading Ladders for Human Relations*
were both helpful in suggesting the scope of the bibliography.
Other sources were also consulted.

Title Index

Each title is listed alphabetically by the first letter of
the first word, except when the title begins with an article.

Author Index

Authors are listed alphabetically by last name, and each
title that the author has written appears in alphabetical order
with the number of the page on which it first appears.

Illustration Index

Illustrators are listed alphabetically by last name, except
for Aliki and Ninon, which are *noms de plumes*. The titles follow
the name of the illustrator, and the page number where each first
appears is given. It was not possible to distinguish illustrations from photographs in the citation, although the distinction
is always made clear in the body of the annotation.

Opportunity to pursue this study came about through a sab-
batical leave granted by the Monroe County Consolidated School
Corporation for the school year 1975-76. The research topic
"Picture Books in the Affective Domain" was selected in response
to requests from teachers, students, and parents for an annotated
list of books for very young children. Thus a smaller-scale pre-

decessor of *Children's Books for Times of Stress* was distributed
to all elementary school libraries in the MCCSC in January 1977.

Much of the work on the books was completed at the Monroe
County Public Library with the assistance of librarians Ginnie
Richey and Dana Burton and their support staff. Their patient
assistance was invaluable; they provided bibliographies, shelf
space for materials, and constant moral support.

As the books were acquired and annotated, Jane Sarles, a
graduate student in the Graduate Library School at Indiana University searched and checked review sources and selection aids.
Ms. Sarles also coded the information on the summary sheet in preparation for the key-punched computer cards. Georgetta Bell,
under the auspices of the CETA program of the school system, was
hired to key-punch the computer cards during the summer of 1976.
Two other persons in the school system were helpful: Jeff Haas,
computer programer, who ran the program and was an adviser on the
early form of the printout, and Richard Engle, director of Data
Processing, who was instrumental in facilitating the program in
the form in which it was presented to the school board.

The decision to use a computer-assisted approach in the
study was originally facilitated by Louise Spear, librarian and
Assistant Director of the Archives of Traditional Music at Indiana
University, who felt that the information gathered for this book
could be organized, indexed, and adapted to the Selind Indexing
Program. It was largely through Ms. Spear's comprehension of the
holistic nature of the project that it eventually came to fruition.
When the initial obligation to the school corporation had been met,
it was she who engineered the format of the finished book, with
the assistance of R. Hunter Knight, graduate student computer programer at Indiana University, who made major format modifications
of the Selind Program.

Pauline Gough, sister teacher at University Elementary
School served in several ways: it was she who initially suggested
that the manuscript be submitted to Indiana University Press, and
who contributed editorial assistance with the completed manuscript.
Mona Sawyer, Unit Coordinator at the Marshal H. Wrubel Computing
Center, did much of the key punching in the latter phase, and Diane
Kliewer was proofreader at one juncture of the project.

For all assistance at the many and complex stages of this
book, thanks are tendered. I also wish to thank in a special way
the supportive role my husband, Frank, played from the beginning to
the end. The ultimate responsibility for the accuracy of the content rests with the author.

May 1977
Bloomington, Indiana

List of Subject Headings

BEHAVIOR

 BEHAVIOR--CONSIDERATION
 BEHAVIOR--DISLIKES
 BEHAVIOR--DISLIKES--BATH
 BEHAVIOR--DISLIKES--FOOD
 BEHAVIOR--DISLIKES--SLEEP
 BEHAVIOR--KINDNESS
 BEHAVIOR--LAZINESS
 BEHAVIOR--MANNERS
 BEHAVIOR--MISBEHAVIOR
 BEHAVIOR--POSSESSIVENESS
 BEHAVIOR--QUARRELING
 BEHAVIOR--RESPONSIBILITY
 BEHAVIOR--SAFETY
 BEHAVIOR--SELFISHNESS
 BEHAVIOR--SHARING
 BEHAVIOR--TEASING
 BEHAVIOR--THUMB SUCKING

DIFFICULT SITUATION

 DIFF SIT--ADOPTION
 DIFF SIT--ADOPTION--INTERRACIAL
 DIFF SIT--DEATH
 DIFF SIT--DEATH--PET
 DIFF SIT--DENTIST
 DIFF SIT--DIVORCE
 DIFF SIT--DOCTOR
 DIFF SIT--HANDICAPS
 DIFF SIT--HOSPITAL
 DIFF SIT--ILLNESS
 DIFF SIT--OLD AGE

NEW SITUATION

    NEW SIT--BABY
    NEW SIT--EYEGLASSES
    NEW SIT--HOSPITAL
    NEW SIT--MOVING
    NEW SIT--SCHOOL
    NEW SIT--TEACHER
    NEW SIT--TYING SHOELACES
    NEW SIT--WHISTLING

SELF CONCEPT

    SELF-CONFIDENCE
    SELF-CONSCIOUSNESS
    SELF-CONSCIOUSNESS--NAME
    SELF-CONSCIOUSNESS--SIZE
    SELF-DEVELOPMENT
    SELF-EVALUATION
    SELF-IDENTITY
    SELF-RELIANCE
    SELF-UNDERSTANDING

Key to Review Sources

BC   *Books for Children*, 1960-1965. Chicago: American Library Association, 1966.

Books for Children, 1965-- . Chicago: American Library Association, 1966-- . Annual. Selected and reviewed by the *Booklist and Subscription Books Bulletin*.

BCB   *Best in Children's Books, 1966-1972.* Edited by Zena Sutherland. Chicago: University of Chicago Press, 1973.

BECB   *The Black Experience in Children's Books.* Edited and compiled by Barbara Rollock. New York: The New York Public Library, 1974. 1971 edition edited and compiled by Augusta Baker.

BESL   *Books for Elementary School Libraries; an Initial Collection.* Edited and compiled by Elizabeth D. Hodges. Chicago: American Library Association, 1969.

BL   *Booklist.* Chicago: American Library Association, 1905-- . Semi-monthly.

CC   *Children's Catalog.* Towson, MD: Baltimore County Public Library, 1966.

CCC-B Center for Children's Books: *Bulletin.* Chicago: University of Chicago Press, 1945-- . Monthly (Sept.-July).

CSM   *Christian Science Monitor.* Boston, 1908-- . Daily, except Sat. and Sun.

ESLC   *Elementary School Library Collection*, Phases 1-2-3.
        Edited by Mary V. Gaver. Newark, NJ: Bro-Dart Foun-
        dation, 1965. Subsequent editions published annually,
        with supplements.

GBC   *Good Books for Children...; a Selection of Outstanding
        Children's Books Published in 1948-57.* By Mary K.
        Eakin. Chicago: University of Chicago Press, 1959.
        Revised and enlarged edition, 1962.

HB   *Horn Book Magazine.* Boston: Horn Book, Inc., 1924-- .
        Six times per year.

JMF   *Journal of Marriage and the Family.* Minneapolis:
        National Council of Family Relations, 1938-- . Quar-
        terly.

LJ   *Library Journal.* New York: R.R. Bowker, 1876-- .
        Semi-monthly (Sept.-June); monthly (July-Aug.).

NYTBR   *New York Times Book Review.* New York: New York Times
        Co., 1896-- . Weekly.

PBC   *Picture Books for Children.* Edited by Patricia J.
        Cianciola. Chicago: American Library Association,
        1973.

RLHR   *Reading Ladders for Human Relations.* 5th ed. Edited by
        Virginia M. Reid. Washington, D.C.: American Council
        on Education, 1972. Earlier editions by Margaret M.
        Heaton (1947, 1949, 1955) and Muriel E. Crosby (1963).

SLJ   *School Library Journal.* New York: R.R. Bowker, 1954-- .
        Monthly (Sept.-May).

TLS   *Times Literary Supplement.* London: Times Newspapers,
        Ltd., 1902-- . Weekly.

Key to Publishers

ABELARD   Abelard-Schuman, Ltd. (London)

ABINGDON   Abingdon Press (Nashville, TN)

AMERICAN   American Heritage Publishing Co. (New York)

ATHENEUM   Atheneum Publishers (New York)

BEACON   Beacon Press (Boston)

BEHAVIORAL   Behavioral Publications (New York)

BOWMAR   Bowmar (Glendale, CA)

BRADBURY   Bradbury Press, Inc. (Scarsdale, NY)

CHILDRENS   Childrens Press (Chicago)

COWARD   Coward, McCann & Geoghegan (New York)

CROWELL, T.   Thomas Y. Crowell Company (New York)

CROWN   Crown Publishers (New York)

DETERMINED   Determined Productions (San Francisco)

DIAL   The Dial Press (New York)

DOUBLEDAY   Doubleday & Company (New York)

DUTTON   E.P. Dutton & Co. (New York)

FARRAR   Farrar, Straus & Giroux (New York)

FOLLETT   Follett Publishing Company (Chicago)

FOUR   Four Winds Press (New York)

FUNK   Funk & Wagnalls Publishing Company (New York)

GREENWILLOW   Greenwillow Books (New York)

HARCOURT   Harcourt Brace Jovanovich (New York)

HARPER   Harper & Row (New York)

HARVEY   Harvey House (New York)

HASTINGS   Hastings House (New York)

HILL   Lawrence Hill & Company (Westport, CN)

HOLIDAY   Holiday House (New York)

HOLT   Holt, Rinehart and Winston (New York)

HOUGHTON   Houghton Mifflin Company (Boston)

JUDSON   Judson Press (Valley Forge, PA)

KNOPF   Alfred A. Knopf (New York)

LERNER   Lerner Publications Company (Minneapolis)

LION   Lion Books (New York)

LIPPINCOTT   J.B. Lippincott Company (Philadelphia)

LITTLE   Little, Brown and Company (Boston)

LOLLIPOP   Lollipop Power (Chapel Hill, NC)

LOTHROP   Lothrop, Lee & Shepard Company (New York)

MC GRAW   McGraw-Hill Book Company (New York)

MC KAY   David McKay Co. (New York)

MACMILLAN   Macmillan Publishing Company

MEREDITH   Meredith Corporation (Des Moines)

MORROW   William Morrow & Co. (New York)

NORTON   W.W. Norton & Company (New York)

OKPAKU   Joseph Okpaku Publishing Company (New York)

PANTHEON   Pantheon Books (New York)

PARENTS' MAG   Parents' Magazine Press (New York)

PLATT   Platt & Munk (Bronx, NY)

PRENTICE   Prentice-Hall (Englewood Cliffs, NJ)

PUTNAM   G.P. Putnam's Sons (New York)

RANDOM   Random House (New York)

REILLY   Reilly & Lee (Chicago)

SCIENCE   Science House (New York)

SCRIBNER   Charles Scribner's Sons (New York)

SEABURY   The Seabury Press (New York)

SIMON   Simon & Schuster (New York)

SPRINGFELLOW   Springfellow Books (New York)

VANGUARD   Vanguard Press (New York)

VIKING   The Viking Press (New York)

WALCK   Henry Z. Walck (New York)

WALKER   Walker & Company (New York)

WATTS   Franklin Watts (New York)

WHITMAN, A.   Albert Whitman & Company (New York)

WINDMILL   Windmill Books (New York)

Y. SCOTT   Young Scott Books (Reading, MA)

Children's Books
for Times of Stress

CAINES, JEANNETTE. ABBY. HARPER, 1973.
ILLUSTRATED BY STEVEN KELLOGG. (CC)

ABBY IS A ROUND-FACED BUNDLE OF CURIOSITY, WHO
ALWAYS WANTS TO HEAR THE STORY OF HER ADOPTION,
OVER AND OVER AGAIN. WHEN SHE PESTERS HER BROTHER
KEVIN, EMOTIONS SPILL OVER, WITH ABBY CRYING AND
BROTHER FEELING SORRY. THROUGHOUT THE STORY, THE
ILLUSTRATOR HAS PICTURED A COMFORTABLE HOME
FILLED WITH LOVE AND CONCERN. KEVIN PROMISES TO
TAKE ABBY TO SCHOOL FOR SHOW AND TELL, AND HIS
PRIDE IN HER IS VERY OBVIOUS. USEFUL IN VARIOUS
WAYS CONCERNING ADOPTION--THE OPEN CURIOSITY OF
THE CHILD, THE OPEN WILLINGNESS TO TALK OF IT,
THE PRIDE, IN THIS CASE, OF BEING ADOPTED.
(ADOPTION, BROTHERS & SISTERS, DIFF
SIT--ADOPTION, FAM--BROTHERS & SISTERS)

LAPSLEY, SUSAN. I AM ADOPTED. BRADBURY, 1974.
ILLUSTRATED BY MICHAEL CHARLTON. (CCB-B, TLS)

DELICATE WATERCOLORS TELL MUCH OF THIS STORY,
BUT THE SPARSE TEXT IN EXTRA LARGE TYPE PROVIDES
A BONUS TO THE THEME: "ADOPTION MEANS BELONGING."
IT IS A SIMPLY TOLD STORY WHICH SHOULD BE

REASSURING TO ADOPTED CHILDREN, BUT WILL HELP ALL
CHILDREN UNDERSTAND THE CONCEPT. THE PAINTINGS
ILLUSTRATE WELL A MIDDLE-CLASS, WHITE FAMILY
SHARING PETS, CRAFTS, COOKERY, AND CAR REPAIR.
(ADOPTION, DIFF SIT--ADOPTION)

ADOPTION--INTERRACIAL

BUNIN, SHERRY. IS THAT YOUR SISTER?. PANTHEON,
1976.

THIS IS SIX-YEAR-OLD CATHERINE BUNIN'S OWN
STORY AND THAT OF HER SISTER CARLA, IN A BOOK
ABOUT INTERRACIAL ADOPTION. OBVIOUSLY PROUD TO BE
LOVED AND CARED FOR BY HER FAMILY WHICH INCLUDES
TWO BROTHERS, CATHERINE RELATES THE STORY OF HER
ADOPTION BY ANSWERING MANY OF THE QUESTIONS PUT
TO HER BY CHILDREN AND ADULTS ALIKE. SHE TACKLES
EVEN VERY SUBSTANTIVE ANSWERS AS SHE DESCRIBES
THE WAY IN WHICH THE SOCIAL WORKER VISITED THEIR
HOME, AND THE CULMINATION OF THE PROCEEDINGS IN
THE FAMILY COURT. FILLED WITH MANY EXCELLENT,
INFORMAL PHOTOGRAPHS OF FAMILY LIFE, THIS SLIM
VOLUME WILL BE HELPFUL TO PARENTS ANTICIPATING OR
CONTEMPLATING THIS DIFFICULT SITUATION.
(ADOPTION--INTERRACIAL, BROTHERS & SISTERS, DIFF
SIT--ADOPTION--INTERRACIAL, FAM--BROTHERS &
SISTERS)

ANGER

BALDWIN, ANNE. JENNY'S REVENGE. FOUR, 1974.
ILLUSTRATED BY EMILY MC CULLY. (CCB-B)

JENNY HATES HER BABY-SITTER, AND EXPRESSES
HIDDEN ANGER TOWARD HER WORKING MOTHER WHO
APPARENTLY HAS WORKED ONLY SINCE A RECENT
DIVORCE. AFTER TRYING A NUMBER OF PLOYS TO FORCE
THE BABY-SITTER TO QUIT, SHE FINDS COMRADESHIP
WITH MRS. CRAMIE WHEN THEY DISCOVER A COMMON
INTEREST IN THE CIRCUS. A REALISTIC LOOK AT A
CHILD WHO NEEDS AND WANTS ATTENTION FROM HER
MOTHER. (ANGER, DIFF SIT--DIVORCE, DIFF SIT--ONE
PARENT, DIVORCE, EMOTIONS--ANGER, FAM--MOTHERS
WORKING, MOTHERS WORKING, ONE PARENT)

HITTE, KATHRYN. BOY WAS I MAD!. PARENTS' MAG,
1969. ILLUSTRATED BY MERCER MAYER. (CCB-B)

A SMALL BOY NAMED TEDDY GETS ANGRY ONE

MORNING, AND WE ARE INTRODUCED TO HIM SITTING IN
THE CORNER. HE DECIDES TO RUN AWAY, AND PACKS A
SANDWICH. ON HIS TRIP AROUND TOWN HE SEES A BIG
STEAM SHOVEL, RIDES ON A HORSE-DRAWN WAGON,
WATCHES ANTS IN A CRACK IN THE SIDEWALK. UP UNTIL
THIS TIME HE IS STILL MAD, BUT WHEN HE MEETS HIS
FRIEND TOM AND THEY PLAY IN THE PARK, HE
ABSENTMINDEDLY GOES HOME, AND FINDS HE'S NO
LONGER MAD. THE CONCLUSION ONE CAN COME TO IS
THAT WE CAN'T STAY MAD VERY LONG IF WE HAVE
INTERESTING THINGS TO DO, AND GOOD FRIENDS WITH
WHOM TO DO THEM. (ANGER, EMOTIONS--ANGER)

HOBAN, RUSSELL. TOM AND THE TWO HANDLES. HARPER,
1965. ILLUSTRATED BY LILLIAN HOBAN. (ESLC)

   KENNY AND TOM ARE ALWAYS FIGHTING, AND TOM
ALWAYS GETS A BLOODY NOSE. HIS DAD TELLS HIM THAT
THERE IS MORE THAN ONE WAY TO SOLVE THE PROBLEM.
YOU CAN FIGHT AGAIN, OR YOU CAN MAKE UP WITH
YOUR BEST FRIEND. TOM TRIES TO BE FRIENDS, BUT
THEY CONTINUE TO FIGHT UNTIL TOM'S FATHER GIVES
HIM SOME BOXING LESSONS. WHEN TOM WINS THE FIGHT,
THEN THEY MAKE UP, AND TOM FINDS THAT THERE WAS
ANOTHER WAY TO LOOK AT IT. (ANGER,
BEHAVIOR--QUARRELING, EMOTIONS--ANGER,
FRIENDSHIP, QUARRELING)

MC GOVERN, ANN. SCRAM, KID!. VIKING, 1974.
ILLUSTRATED BY NOLA LANGNER. (BL)

   IN AN INTERESTING ARRANGEMENT OF ILLUSTRATIONS
ON THE PAGE, PART BLACK AND WHITE AND PART
SEPIA, THE ILLUSTRATOR OF THIS BOOK HAS MANAGED
TO CAPTURE THE SIMULTANEITY OF REALITY AND
DAYDREAM. THE STORY OF A LITTLE BOY WHO FEELS
LEFT OUT AND HAS ANGRY FEELINGS ABOUT IT SHOULD
STRIKE A FEELING OF EMPATHY IN MANY READERS.
DON'T WE ALL WISH WE WERE BRAVE ENOUGH TO SAY,
"I'LL FIX YOUR WAGON!" AFTER VENTING HIS ANGER IN
THE DAYDREAM, JOE FINDS A FRIEND WHO WILL SAIL A
BOAT WITH HIM AND, TEMPORARILY AT LEAST, FORGETS
ABOUT THE KIDS WHO WON'T LET HIM PLAY BASEBALL.
(ANGER, EMOTIONS--ANGER, EMOTIONS--LONELINESS,
LONELINESS)

PEARSON, SUSAN. MONNIE HATES LYDIA. DIAL, 1975.
ILLUSTRATED BY DIANE PATERSON. (BL)

   INTERESTING BECAUSE A FATHER HEADS THIS

ONE-PARENT FAMILY CONSISTING OF MONNIE AND HER
THOROUGHLY OBNOXIOUS SISTER LYDIA. DADDY IS AN
IMPARTIAL ARBITER IN THE FAMILY SQUABBLE WHICH
ERUPTS ON LYDIA'S BIRTHDAY, SUPPORTIVE OF
MONNIE'S HURT FEELINGS, BUT NOT WILLING TO PUNISH
LYDIA. HE IS AN ATTRACTIVE, BEARDED CONTEMPORARY
FATHER WHO CAN BE ADMIRED FOR HIS COOL WHEN
MONNIE DUMPS THE BIRTHDAY CAKE IN LYDIA'S FACE.
ONE FEELS HE SHOULD BE CHEERING, BUT INSTEAD HE
HANDS LYDIA A TOWEL AND KISSES HER ON THE CHEEK.
USEFUL AS A PORTRAIT OF A NEW LIFE-STYLE FAMILY
COPING WITH OLD LIFE-STYLE PROBLEMS. (ANGER, DIFF
SIT--ONE PARENT, EMOTIONS--ANGER, FAM--FATHERS,
FAM--ONE PARENT, FAM--SIBLING RIVALRY, FATHERS,
ONE PARENT, SIBLING RIVALRY)

PRESTON, EDNA. THE TEMPER TANTRUM BOOK. VIKING,
1969. ILLUSTRATED BY RAINEY BENNETT. (HB)

   AN IMAGINATIVE WAY TO PORTRAY ALL OF THE
THINGS THAT BOTHER LITTLE KIDS--MOM GETS SOAP IN
YOUR EYES IN THE SHOWER, SHE HURTS YOU TRYING TO
GET SNARLS OUT OF YOUR HAIR--EXCEPT THAT ANIMALS
HUMOROUSLY ACT OUT ALL OF THESE HUMAN TEMPER
TANTRUMS. LIONS, TURTLES, AND PIGGISH PIGS MARCH
ACROSS THE PAGES, AND LEND A CERTAIN PERSPECTIVE
TO THE CHILD WHO MAY BE ABLE TO PUT HIMSELF INTO
THE BOOK. (ANGER, EMOTIONS--ANGER,
SELF-UNDERSTANDING)

SIMON, NORMA. I WAS SO MAD!. WHITMAN, A., 1974.
ILLUSTRATED BY DORA LEDER. (CCB-B)

   THE AUTHOR'S NOTE IN THE FOREWORD SPELLS OUT
THE INTENTION OF THIS BOOK: TO PICTURE SITUATIONS
WHICH PRODUCE ANGER AND SHOW THAT THIS HAPPENS
TO MANY PEOPLE. PERHAPS ONE OF THE STRENGTHS OF
THE BOOK IS THAT A DIFFERENT PERSON IS SHOWN IN
EACH SITUATION, INCLUDING A MOTHER. ENDS WITH A
FUNNY SONG ABOUT A MAN WHO WAS SO MAD HE "JUMPED
INTO A PUDDING BOG"--AND LEAVES THE READER WITH A
GOOD TASTE IN HIS MOUTH. (ANGER,
EMOTIONS--ANGER, SELF-UNDERSTANDING)

VIORST, JUDITH. I'LL FIX ANTHONY. HARPER, 1969.
ILLUSTRATED BY ARNOLD LOBEL. (BL)

   A CLASSIC RECITAL OF THE VENGEFUL JEALOUSY
SEETHING INSIDE A LITTLE BOY, WHO IS NOT YET
QUITE SIX. WE SEE A PORTRAIT OF THE OLDER BROTHER

THROUGH THE EYES OF THE ABUSED YOUNGER BROTHER:
THE OLDER BROTHER WHO IS CONSISTENTLY BIGGER AND
STRONGER, PHYSICALLY AND MENTALLY, BUT SELFISH,
PRIVILEGED, AND RATHER HORRID. ANTHONY ANNOUNCES
THAT HE'S GOING TO CLOBBER YOUNGER BROTHER, AND
SAYS, "YOU STINK." LITTLE BROTHER SAYS, "I'LL FIX
ANTHONY." (WHEN I'M SIX.) (ANGER,
EMOTIONS--ANGER, EMOTIONS--JEALOUSY, FAM--SIBLING
RIVALRY, JEALOUSY, SIBLING RIVALRY)

BEHAVIOR--CONSIDERATION

DAUGHERTY, JAMES. ANDY AND THE LION. VIKING,
1938. ILLUSTRATED BY JAMES DAUGHERTY. (CC)

   IN ROLLICKING, RHYTHMICAL DRAWINGS, JAMES
DAUGHERTY HAS SYNTHESIZED FEELINGS OF JOY IN
LIVING AND JOY IN HELPING OTHER PEOPLE. ANDY, WHO
BEFRIENDS A LION AND REMOVES A BIG THORN FROM
HIS PAW, LATER IS THE BENEFICIARY OF THE KIND
ACT. THE LION, WHO HAS ESCAPED FROM THE CIRCUS,
RECOGNIZES ANDY AND IS IMMEDIATELY FRIENDLY.
USEFUL BECAUSE IT DEMONSTRATES IN A VERY SIMPLE
WAY HOW ONE KIND ACT MAY BE REPAID, BUT FAR
BEYOND THAT, THE AFFECTIVE ASPECTS OF LIVING ARE
STRESSED--THE SENSUOUS EFFECT OF THE EXPRESSIONS
ON FACES, THE SUBTLE HUMOR IN THE DAILY FAMILY
LIFE, AND THE VIGOROUS FEELINGS DEPICTING THE JOY
OF LIVING. (BEHAVIOR--CONSIDERATION,
BEHAVIOR--KINDNESS, CONSIDERATION,
EMOTIONS--HAPPINESS, FAM, FRIENDSHIP, HAPPINESS,
KINDNESS)

GAEDDERT, LOU. NOISY NANCY NORRIS. DOUBLEDAY,
1965. ILLUSTRATED BY GIOIA FIAMMENGHI. (CC)

   NOT A MODEL GIRL, NANCY IS ABOUT THE NOISIEST
CHILD IMAGINABLE. WHEN THE NEIGHBOR COMPLAINS,
NANCY BECOMES SO VERY QUIET THAT EVERYONE THINKS
SHE IS ILL. THE LAST PICTURE IN THE BOOK IS TRULY
FUNNY, FOR NANCY HAS TIED A BIG SOFT RAG AROUND
HER STICK HORSE SO SHE WILL NOT BANG ON THE
FLOOR. USEFUL TO PRESENT A NON-STEREOTYPED LOOK
AT A LITTLE GIRL'S BEHAVIOR.
(BEHAVIOR--CONSIDERATION, BEHAVIOR--MISBEHAVIOR,
CONSIDERATION, MISBEHAVIOR)

HAWKINS, QUAIL. ANDROCLES AND THE LION. COWARD,
1970. ILLUSTRATED BY ROCCO NEGRI. (ESLC)

A SIMPLE RETELLING OF THIS AGE-OLD STORY
ILLUSTRATES FOR THE CHILDREN OF TODAY THE MORAL
THAT ONE SHOULD BE KIND TO PEOPLE IN NEED. WHEN
THE SLAVE ANDROCLES REMOVES A THORN FROM THE
LION'S PAW, AND THE LION LEADS HIM TO FOOD AND
DRINK, THERE IS A VIVID EXAMPLE OF THE BEGINNING
OF FRIENDSHIP. LATER ON WHEN THE LION MEETS
ANDROCLES IN THE ARENA AND REFUSES TO FIGHT HIM,
THE REWARDS OF FRIENDSHIP ARE SHOWN. A STORY FOR
OLDER CHILDREN RATHER THAN YOUNGER BECAUSE OF THE
CRUELTY IMPLIED IN THE COLOSSEUM.
(BEHAVIOR--CONSIDERATION, BEHAVIOR--KINDNESS,
CONSIDERATION, FRIENDSHIP, KINDNESS)

HOBAN, RUSSELL. THE SORELY TRYING DAY. HARPER,
1964.   ILLUSTRATED BY LILLIAN HOBAN.   (CC)

ALTHOUGH THIS IS A TONGUE-IN-CHEEK SPOOF, IT
WILL BE VALUABLE FOR POINTING OUT HOW ONE THING
LEADS TO ANOTHER IN A QUARREL, AND SHOWS IN A
VERY FUNNY WAY WHAT HAPPENS WHEN EVERYBODY
ACCEPTS THE BLAME. SHOWS THE BEAUTY OF THE PHRASE
"I AM SORRY." (BEHAVIOR--CONSIDERATION,
BEHAVIOR--QUARRELING, CONSIDERATION, FAM,
QUARRELING)

MARSHALL, JAMES. GEORGE AND MARTHA. HOUGHTON,
1972.   ILLUSTRATED BY JAMES MARSHALL.   (CC)

FIVE VERY SHORT STORIES FOR THE VERY YOUNG
ABOUT GEORGE AND MARTHA, HUGE HIPPOS WHO LIVE
LIKE HUMANS, GIVE THE READER SOME GOOD HUMAN
ADVICE: ALWAYS TELL THE TRUTH TO YOUR BEST
FRIEND, SO YOU DON'T HAVE TO POUR YOUR UNWANTED
SPLIT PEA SOUP IN YOUR SNEAKERS. ALSO, YOU MAY
GET THE BATHTUB DUMPED ON YOUR HEAD IF YOU PEEK
IN THE BATHROOM WINDOW WHEN YOU SHOULDN'T. BEING
TRUTHFUL, RESPECTING PRIVACY, LOOKING ON THE
BRIGHT SIDE OF THINGS, CHEERING YOU UP, THESE ARE
SOME OF THE THINGS THAT GOOD FRIENDS DO FOR ONE
ANOTHER. (BEHAVIOR--CONSIDERATION, CONSIDERATION,
FRIENDSHIP)

MARSHALL, JAMES. GEORGE AND MARTHA ENCORE.
HOUGHTON, 1973.   ILLUSTRATED BY JAMES MARSHALL.
(CC)

GOOD FRIENDS MARTHA AND GEORGE APPEAR IN FIVE
SHORT STORIES WHICH EXTOL THE BLESSINGS OF A GOOD
RELATIONSHIP: GEORGE DOESN'T SAY "I TOLD YOU SO"

WHEN MARTHA GETS SUNBURNED. WHEN MARTHA IS
FRUSTRATED OVER THE WEEDS IN HER GARDEN, GEORGE
IN A TRULY THOUGHTFUL ACT RUSHES OUT TO THE
FLORIST TO BUY TULIPS TO STICK IN THE GROUND AS A
SURPRISE. THOUGHTFULNESS AND PROTECTING THE
FEELINGS OF THE OTHER PERSON ARE TWO OF THE
IMPORTANT ELEMENTS IN THE BOOK.
(BEHAVIOR--CONSIDERATION, CONSIDERATION,
FRIENDSHIP)

MC LEOD, EMILIE. THE BEAR'S BICYCLE. LITTLE,
1975. ILLUSTRATED BY DAVID MC PHAIL. (BL)

   AN IMAGINATIVE STORY IN WHICH AN ENORMOUS
BEAR, ON A MINIATURE BICYCLE, BREAKS ALL THE
RULES. AS THE LITTLE BOY IN THE STORY
DEMONSTRATES THE CORRECT WAY TO STAY ON THE RIGHT
WHEN MEETING ANOTHER BIKER, THE LUMBERING BEAR
TAKES A SPILL IN THE MIDDLE OF THE PATH, CROWDING
A YOUNG BOY, CAUSING HIM TO CRASH. BEAUTIFUL
ILLUSTRATIONS AND HUMOROUS SITUATIONS TEACH A
LESSON OF SAFETY IN A PAINLESS WAY.
(BEHAVIOR--CONSIDERATION, BEHAVIOR--MISBEHAVIOR,
BEHAVIOR--SAFETY, CONSIDERATION, MISBEHAVIOR,
SAFETY)

NESS, EVALINE. DO YOU HAVE THE TIME, LYDIA?.
DUTTON, 1971. ILLUSTRATED BY EVALINE NESS. (CC,
ESLC)

   LYDIA IS A LITTLE GIRL WHO NEVER "HAS TIME" TO
FINISH ALL OF THE MANY THINGS IN WHICH SHE'S
INTERESTED. WHEN SHE NEGLECTS TO FINISH A RACING
CAR FOR HER YOUNGER BROTHER, HE IS DISAPPOINTED,
AND SHE BEGINS TO MAKE AMENDS. THE LESSON IS "IF
YOU TAKE TIME, YOU'LL HAVE TIME."
(BEHAVIOR--CONSIDERATION, BROTHERS & SISTERS,
CONSIDERATION, FAM--BROTHERS & SISTERS,
SELF-EVALUATION)

STEIG, WILLIAM. AMOS AND BORIS. FARRAR, 1971.
ILLUSTRATED BY WILLIAM STEIG. (BCB)

   IN A BEAUTIFUL SEA GREEN BOOK, STEIG HAS TOLD
A STORY SIMILAR TO ANDROCLES AND THE LION,
WHEREIN A WHALE SAVES THE LIFE OF AMOS THE MOUSE
WHEN HE IS SHIPWRECKED. LATER, BORIS THE WHALE IS
WASHED ASHORE DURING A HURRICANE, AND THE MOUSE
BRINGS TWO ELEPHANTS TO PUSH THE WHALE BACK INTO
THE WATER. POINTS OUT THE FACT THAT FRIENDSHIP

CAN BE BASED ON MUTUAL HELP--EVEN THOUGH THE
FRIENDS MIGHT NOT SEE EACH OTHER IN THE FUTURE.
(BEHAVIOR--CONSIDERATION, CONSIDERATION,
FRIENDSHIP)

WABER, BERNARD. LYLE AND THE BIRTHDAY PARTY.
HOUGHTON, 1966. ILLUSTRATED BY BERNARD WABER.
(CC)

  HELPFUL LYLE STEPS OUT OF HIS ROLE AS HE FINDS
HIMSELF BEING VERY JEALOUS OF JOSHUA'S BIRTHDAY
CELEBRATION. IN FACT HE BECOMES SO VERY JEALOUS
THAT HE MAKES HIMSELF SICK AND MOPES ABOUT THE
HOUSE, FINALLY LANDING IN THE HOSPITAL. HELPING
OTHER PATIENTS IS GOOD THERAPY FOR HIM, AND SOON
HE'S HOME--TO FIND THAT THE FAMILY IS PLANNING
HIS BIRTHDAY PARTY. LYLE'S FEELINGS OF JEALOUSY,
AND THE WAY THEY MADE HIM FEEL MEAN, ARE VERY
REAL AND WILL HELP CHILDREN KNOW THAT EVERYONE
HAS THESE KINDS OF FEELINGS--EVEN CROCODILES.
(BEHAVIOR--CONSIDERATION, CONSIDERATION,
EMOTIONS--JEALOUSY, JEALOUSY)

WINN, MARIE. SHIVER, GOBBLE AND SNORE. SIMON,
1971. ILLUSTRATED BY WHITNEY DARROW JR.. (ESLC)

  A BOOK FOR VERY YOUNG CHILDREN ABOUT WHY
PEOPLE NEED LAWS. THREE FRIENDS WHO DON'T LIKE
ALL OF THE LAWS WHICH THE KING MAKES DECIDE TO
MOVE AWAY AND NOT HAVE ANY LAWS. CHAOS REIGNS
HOWEVER--SHIVER MADE FIRES WHICH BOTHERED GOBBLE,
AND THE SNORING OF SNORE BOTHERED SHIVER. WHEN
THEY DECIDE THAT LIFE LIKE THIS IS NOT GOOD
EITHER, THEY SET UP NEW RULES. A GOOD WAY TO
INTRODUCE CHILDREN TO THE NECESSITY FOR LAWS.
THERE ARE FOUR PAGES AT THE END DEVOTED TO
ACTIVITIES TO REINFORCE THE CONCEPT.
(BEHAVIOR--CONSIDERATION, BEHAVIOR--MISBEHAVIOR,
BEHAVIOR--RESPONSIBILITY, CONSIDERATION,
MISBEHAVIOR, RESPONSIBILITY)

BEHAVIOR--DISLIKES

SIMON, NORMA. I KNOW WHAT I LIKE. WHITMAN, A.,
1971. ILLUSTRATED BY DORA LEDER. (CCB-B)

  LISTING MANY BEHAVIOR PREFERENCES IN SUCH
AREAS AS FOOD, PLAY, AND CERTAIN HOUSEHOLD
CHORES, THE BOOK ALSO GIVES INSIGHT INTO THE
DISLIKES OF INDIVIDUAL CHILDREN. AUTHOR SIMON IS

PARTICULARLY EFFECTIVE IN PRESENTING SITUATIONS
WHERE THE READER CAN EMPATHIZE, THUS GAINING IN
SELF-UNDERSTANDING IN THE AFFECTIVE AREAS SUCH AS
APPRECIATION OF BEAUTY IN THE STARS, AND THE
PLEASURES OF MUSIC. (BEHAVIOR--DISLIKES,
DISLIKES, EMOTIONS--HAPPINESS, HAPPINESS,
SELF-UNDERSTANDING)

ZOLOTOW, CHARLOTTE. WHEN I HAVE A SON. HARPER,
1967. ILLUSTRATED BY HILARY KNIGHT. (BCB)

IN AN IMAGINATIVE PROJECTION INTO THE FUTURE,
JOHN TELLS HOW HIS SON WOULD BE PERMITTED TO
BEHAVE AND, IN DOING SO, THE READER SEES A PARADE
OF FORBIDDEN BEHAVIOR: NOT SAYING THANK YOU FOR
PRESENTS HE HATES, AND HAVING A TRIPLE MALTED
JUST BEFORE DINNER. THE IDEAS THAT JOHN IS
REJECTING FALL INTO THE AREAS OF ETIQUETTE,
GROOMING, PARENTAL CONTROL, COMMON COURTESY, FOOD
DESIRES, AND HEALTH. SOME SEEM QUITE HARMLESS,
SUCH AS STAYING DOWN AT THE RAILROAD STATION ALL
DAY TO WATCH THE TRAINS. IN GENERAL, A MILD
GROUSING AGAINST RULES SET DOWN BY GROWN-UPS. IN
THE END, WE REALIZE JOHN IS ONLY DAYDREAMING OUT
LOUD TO HIS FRIEND: HE DUTIFULLY GOES IN THE
HOUSE FOR THE HATED PIANO LESSON.
(BEHAVIOR--DISLIKES, BEHAVIOR--MANNERS,
BEHAVIOR--MISBEHAVIOR, DISLIKES, MANNERS,
MISBEHAVIOR)

BEHAVIOR--DISLIKES--BATH

BARRETT, JUDI. I HATE TO TAKE A BATH. FOUR,
1975. ILLUSTRATED BY CHARLES SLACKMAN. (BL)

THE GOODS AND BADS ABOUT TAKING A BATH, WITH
DIFFERENT CHILDREN, BOTH BOYS AND GIRLS,
DEMONSTRATING EACH POINT. CERTAINLY NOT A CRUCIAL
BOOK--BUT A FUN ONE, WHICH MAY CHANGE A FEW
OPINIONS IN A FEW HOUSEHOLDS WHERE THIS MAY BE A
PROBLEM. ITS MAIN VALUE LIES IN ITS FRANKNESS,
AND THE REASONS FOR NOT WANTING TO TAKE A BATH
MAY STRIKE A CHORD IN MANY READERS.
(BEHAVIOR--DISLIKES--BATH, DISLIKES--BATH)

BEHAVIOR--DISLIKES--FOOD

HOBAN, RUSSELL. BREAD AND JAM FOR FRANCES.
HARPER, 1964. ILLUSTRATED BY LILLIAN HOBAN. (CC)

FRANCES CAN TELL YOU A NUMBER OF REASONS SHE
DISLIKES EGGS--"SUNNY-SIDE-UP EGGS LIE ON THE
PLATE AND LOOK UP AT YOU IN A FUNNY WAY."
FURTHERMORE, SHE TRADES AWAY HER CHICKEN SALAD
SANDWICH TO HER FRIEND ALBERT FOR A BREAD AND JAM
SANDWICH. BREAD AND JAM, INDEED, IS THE FAVORITE
FOOD OF FRANCES. HER WISE PARENTS, AFTER
TEMPTING HER WITH BREADED VEAL CUTLETS, STRING
BEANS, AND BAKED POTATOES DECIDED TO FEED HER A
STEADY DIET OF BREAD AND JAM. THE SLIGHTLY
CRESTFALLEN LOOK ON HER FACE DEEPENS TO TEARFUL
DISMAY WHEN SHE IS SERVED BREAD AND JAM ON THE
NIGHT THE FAMILY IS HAVING SPAGHETTI AND
MEATBALLS. SHE MAKES AN ABOUT-FACE, ENJOYS HER
DINNER, AND THE READER SEES HER ENJOYING A
SUMPTUOUS LUNCH NEXT DAY AT SCHOOL. ESPECIALLY
USEFUL FOR BOTH PARENTS AND CHILDREN, BECAUSE
THERE ARE NO ARGUING OR LOUD VOICES--JUST SUBTLE
ACTION, WHICH IS VERY EFFECTIVE, BECAUSE IN THE
END, THE CHILD MAKES THE DECISION.
(BEHAVIOR--DISLIKES--FOOD, DISLIKES--FOOD, FAM)

PATERSON, DIANE. EAT!. DIAL, 1975. ILLUSTRATED
BY DIANE PATERSON. (BL)

THE TABLES ARE TURNED WHEN MARTHA TRIES TO
COAX HER PET FROG TO EAT HIS FLIES. HERETOFORE
HER PARENTS HAD BEGGED HER TO EAT--SPAGHETTI,
SALAD, SOUP. WHEN MARTHA AND HER FROG BOTH EAT A
BIG BOWL OF SPAGHETTI, THE READER SEES THE HUMOR
IN THE STORY (AS WELL AS THE LESSON THAT THERE
ARE VARIOUS WAYS TO INDUCE CHILDREN TO EAT).
OR--ONE SHOULDN'T FORCE CHILDREN TO EAT? OR?
(BEHAVIOR--DISLIKES--FOOD, DISLIKES--FOOD)

BEHAVIOR--DISLIKES--SLEEP

HOBAN, RUSSELL. BEDTIME FOR FRANCES. HARPER,
1960. ILLUSTRATED BY GARTH WILLIAMS. (CC)

FATHER BADGER PLAYS AN IMPORTANT ROLE IN
HANDLING THE BEDTIME PROBLEMS OF HIS DAUGHTER
FRANCES WITH AN IMAGINATIVE EXPLANATION OF HER
FEARS. WHEN FRANCES, AN ENTRANCING LITTLE GIRL
WHO ONLY INCIDENTALLY HAPPENS TO BE A BADGER,
GOES THROUGH THE FAMILIAR BEDTIME ROUTINE OF
MILK, HUGS, KISSES, AND TEDDY BEAR, BUT STILL
DOES NOT FALL ASLEEP, FATHER GIVES REASSURING
ADVICE ABOUT THE IMAGINARY GIANTS AND THE
SOMETHING SCARY THAT MIGHT COME OUT OF THE CRACK

IN THE CEILING. HIS MOST CREATIVE SOLUTION,
HOWEVER, COMES WHEN FRANCES COMPLAINS OF THE
CURTAINS MOVING AT THE WINDOW--HE TELLS HER THAT
THE WIND'S JOB IS TO GO AROUND AND BLOW ALL THE
CURTAINS, THAT EVERYBODY HAS A JOB, AND THAT
FURTHERMORE, HER JOB IS TO GO TO SLEEP.
THROUGHOUT THE BOOK, FATHER IS THE PARENT WHO
RELATES TO THE CHILD, ALTHOUGH THE MOTHER IS
VISIBLE. (BEHAVIOR--DISLIKES--SLEEP,
DISLIKES--SLEEP, EMOTIONS--FEAR, FAM--FATHERS,
FATHERS, FEAR)

KRAUS, ROBERT. GOOD NIGHT, RICHARD RABBIT.
SPRINGFELLOW, 1972. ILLUSTRATED BY N.M.
BODECKER. (CCB-B)

   TINY FORMAT MAKES THIS A CHARMING BEDTIME
STORY FOR THE VERY YOUNG, AS MOST YOUNGSTERS WILL
IDENTIFY WITH RICHARD RABBIT. A MIX OF REAL AND
IMAGINARY FEARS, AND A LITTLE OF DOWNRIGHT
TEASING ARE SEEN AS THE YOUNG RABBIT PRETENDS
THERE IS A FACE LOOKING IN THE WINDOW. EVERY
OTHER PAGE DEALS WITH A QUESTION OR COMMENT, THE
FACING PAGE WITH MOTHER'S ANSWER. IN ALL OF THE
ILLUSTRATIONS, RICHARD IS VERY SMALL, AND MOTHER
LOOMS VERY LARGE AND SOLID, TRULY A SECURITY
FIGURE, AND ON THE FINAL PAGE RICHARD DRIFTS OFF
TO SLEEP. (BEHAVIOR--DISLIKES--SLEEP,
DISLIKES--SLEEP, EMOTIONS--FEAR,
EMOTIONS--SECURITY, FEAR, SECURITY)

BEHAVIOR--KINDNESS

DAUGHERTY, JAMES. ANDY AND THE LION. VIKING,
1938. ILLUSTRATED BY JAMES DAUGHERTY. (CC)

   IN ROLLICKING, RHYTHMICAL DRAWINGS, JAMES
DAUGHERTY HAS SYNTHESIZED FEELINGS OF JOY IN
LIVING AND JOY IN HELPING OTHER PEOPLE. ANDY, WHO
BEFRIENDS A LION AND REMOVES A BIG THORN FROM
HIS PAW, LATER IS THE BENEFICIARY OF THE KIND
ACT. THE LION, WHO HAS ESCAPED FROM THE CIRCUS,
RECOGNIZES ANDY AND IS IMMEDIATELY FRIENDLY.
USEFUL BECAUSE IT DEMONSTRATES IN A VERY SIMPLE
WAY HOW ONE KIND ACT MAY BE REPAID, BUT FAR
BEYOND THAT, THE AFFECTIVE ASPECTS OF LIVING ARE
STRESSED--THE SENSUOUS EFFECT OF THE EXPRESSIONS
ON FACES, THE SUBTLE HUMOR IN THE DAILY FAMILY
LIFE, AND THE VIGOROUS FEELINGS DEPICTING THE JOY
OF LIVING. (BEHAVIOR--CONSIDERATION,

BEHAVIOR--KINDNESS, CONSIDERATION,
EMOTIONS--HAPPINESS, FAM, FRIENDSHIP, HAPPINESS,
KINDNESS)

HAWKINS, QUAIL. ANDROCLES AND THE LION. COWARD,
1970. ILLUSTRATED BY ROCCO NEGRI. (ESLC)

A SIMPLE RETELLING OF THIS AGE-OLD STORY
ILLUSTRATES FOR THE CHILDREN OF TODAY THE MORAL
THAT ONE SHOULD BE KIND TO PEOPLE IN NEED. WHEN
THE SLAVE ANDROCLES REMOVES A THORN FROM THE
LION'S PAW, AND THE LION LEADS HIM TO FOOD AND
DRINK, THERE IS A VIVID EXAMPLE OF THE BEGINNING
OF FRIENDSHIP. LATER ON WHEN THE LION MEETS
ANDROCLES IN THE ARENA AND REFUSES TO FIGHT HIM,
THE REWARDS OF FRIENDSHIP ARE SHOWN. A STORY FOR
OLDER CHILDREN RATHER THAN YOUNGER BECAUSE OF THE
CRUELTY IMPLIED IN THE COLOSSEUM.
(BEHAVIOR--CONSIDERATION, BEHAVIOR--KINDNESS,
CONSIDERATION, FRIENDSHIP, KINDNESS)

BEHAVIOR--LAZINESS

DU BOIS, WILLIAM. LAZY TOMMY PUMPKINHEAD.
HARPER, 1966. ILLUSTRATED BY WILLIAM DU BOIS.
(BCB)

TOMMY WAS SO LAZY THAT HE HAD AN ELECTRIC
HOUSE WHICH GOT HIM UP IN THE MORNING, BATHED
HIM, AND FED HIM HIS BREAKFAST. HIS ELECTRIC
GADGETS GO HAYWIRE ONE DAY, AND EVERYTHING WORKS
BACKWARD, WITH TOOTHPASTE AND TOOTHBRUSH RUBBING
AWAY AT HIS TOES. TOMMY CONCLUDES BY SAYING "I
MUST TURN OVER A NEW LEAF...." A SPOOF ON THE
CHARACTERISTIC OF LAZINESS, THE HUMOR OF WHICH
WILL NOT BE LOST ON YOUNG READERS.
(BEHAVIOR--LAZINESS, LAZINESS)

BEHAVIOR--MANNERS

SLOBODKIN, LOUIS. THANK YOU--YOU'RE WELCOME.
VANGUARD, 1957. ILLUSTRATED BY LOUIS SLOBODKIN.
(CC)

IN SLOBODKIN'S SPARE STYLE, A LITTLE BOY IS
SHOWN HAPPILY SAYING THANK YOU IN THE PROPER
CIRCUMSTANCES. HE LEARNS THAT TO SAY "YOU'RE
WELCOME," HE MUST DO SOMETHING FOR SOMEONE ELSE.
A SIMPLE, HONEST STORY OF BASIC COURTESY.
(BEHAVIOR--MANNERS, MANNERS)

VIPONT, ELFRIDA. THE ELEPHANT AND THE BAD BABY.
COWARD, 1969. ILLUSTRATED BY RAYMOND BRIGGS.
(BCB)

EARLY RAYMOND BRIGGS ILLUSTRATIONS ADD TO THE
LIVELY VIGOR OF THIS STORY OF A BAD BABY WHO
NEVER SAID "PLEASE." MUCH PLEASING REPETITION IN
THE WAY THEY WENT RUNNING AROUND THE TOWN:
"RUMPETA, RUMPETA." BABY REALLY WAS BAD, BUT HE
TOO SHARED IN THE PANCAKES AT THE END, BEING SENT
TO BED ONLY AFTER THE FESTIVITIES WERE OVER.
RATHER A JOYOUS WAY TO LEARN MANNERS!
(BEHAVIOR--MANNERS, BEHAVIOR--MISBEHAVIOR,
MANNERS, MISBEHAVIOR)

ZOLOTOW, CHARLOTTE. WHEN I HAVE A SON. HARPER,
1967. ILLUSTRATED BY HILARY KNIGHT. (BCB)

IN AN IMAGINATIVE PROJECTION INTO THE FUTURE,
JOHN TELLS HOW HIS SON WOULD BE PERMITTED TO
BEHAVE AND, IN DOING SO, THE READER SEES A PARADE
OF FORBIDDEN BEHAVIOR: NOT SAYING THANK YOU FOR
PRESENTS HE HATES, AND HAVING A TRIPLE MALTED
JUST BEFORE DINNER. THE IDEAS THAT JOHN IS
REJECTING FALL INTO THE AREAS OF ETIQUETTE,
GROOMING, PARENTAL CONTROL, COMMON COURTESY, FOOD
DESIRES, AND HEALTH. SOME SEEM QUITE HARMLESS,
SUCH AS STAYING DOWN AT THE RAILROAD STATION ALL
DAY TO WATCH THE TRAINS. IN GENERAL, A MILD
GROUSING AGAINST RULES SET DOWN BY GROWN-UPS. IN
THE END, WE REALIZE JOHN IS ONLY DAYDREAMING OUT
LOUD TO HIS FRIEND: HE DUTIFULLY GOES IN THE
HOUSE FOR THE HATED PIANO LESSON.
(BEHAVIOR--DISLIKES, BEHAVIOR--MANNERS,
BEHAVIOR--MISBEHAVIOR, DISLIKES, MANNERS,
MISBEHAVIOR)

BEHAVIOR--MISBEHAVIOR

ETS, MARIE. BAD BOY, GOOD BOY!. CROWELL, T.,
1967. ILLUSTRATED BY MARIE ETS. (BCB)

ALTHOUGH THE STORY IS TOLD THROUGH THE
DESTRUCTIVE ACTIVITIES OF ROBERTO, A LITTLE
PRESCHOOLER ON HIS OWN AS HE ROAMS THE
NEIGHBORHOOD UNSUPERVISED, IT IS REALLY A
PORTRAIT OF A TROUBLED FAMILY, SEVEN SLEEPING IN
ONE BEDROOM, WITH A YOUNG INEXPERIENCED MOTHER
INCAPABLE OF COPING WITH THE FAMILY. WHEN ROBERTO
GOES TO DAY SCHOOL AT THE CHILDREN'S CENTER,

THINGS GET BETTER: HE LEARNS SOME ENGLISH BUT,
MORE IMPORTANTLY, PRINTS THE LETTER TO HIS MOTHER
WHICH BRINGS HER HOME. MOST CHILDREN WILL
UNDERSTAND THE "BAD" BEHAVIOR WHICH CAME ABOUT
BECAUSE ROBERTO NEEDED ATTENTION. THE TEXT IS
QUITE LONG, AND IT IS NOT PARTICULARLY EASY TO
READ. THEREFORE THIS IS PROBABLY MORE USEFUL AS A
BOOK TO BE SHARED. (BEHAVIOR--MISBEHAVIOR, DIFF
SIT--SEPARATION, MISBEHAVIOR, SEPARATION)

GAEDDERT, LOU. NOISY NANCY NORRIS. DOUBLEDAY,
1965. ILLUSTRATED BY GIOIA FIAMMENGHI. (CC)

   NOT A MODEL GIRL, NANCY IS ABOUT THE NOISIEST
CHILD IMAGINABLE. WHEN THE NEIGHBOR COMPLAINS,
NANCY BECOMES SO VERY QUIET THAT EVERYONE THINKS
SHE IS ILL. THE LAST PICTURE IN THE BOOK IS TRULY
FUNNY, FOR NANCY HAS TIED A BIG SOFT RAG AROUND
HER STICK HORSE SO SHE WILL NOT BANG ON THE
FLOOR. USEFUL TO PRESENT A NON-STEREOTYPED LOOK
AT A LITTLE GIRL'S BEHAVIOR.
(BEHAVIOR--CONSIDERATION, BEHAVIOR--MISBEHAVIOR,
CONSIDERATION, MISBEHAVIOR)

MC LEOD, EMILIE. THE BEAR'S BICYCLE. LITTLE,
1975. ILLUSTRATED BY DAVID MC PHAIL. (BL)

   AN IMAGINATIVE STORY IN WHICH AN ENORMOUS
BEAR, ON A MINIATURE BICYCLE, BREAKS ALL THE
RULES. AS THE LITTLE BOY IN THE STORY
DEMONSTRATES THE CORRECT WAY TO STAY ON THE RIGHT
WHEN MEETING ANOTHER BIKER, THE LUMBERING BEAR
TAKES A SPILL IN THE MIDDLE OF THE PATH, CROWDING
A YOUNG BOY, CAUSING HIM TO CRASH. BEAUTIFUL
ILLUSTRATIONS AND HUMOROUS SITUATIONS TEACH A
LESSON OF SAFETY IN A PAINLESS WAY.
(BEHAVIOR--CONSIDERATION, BEHAVIOR--MISBEHAVIOR,
BEHAVIOR--SAFETY, CONSIDERATION, MISBEHAVIOR,
SAFETY)

NESS, EVALINE. SAM, BANGS, AND MOONSHINE. HOLT,
1966. ILLUSTRATED BY EVALINE NESS. (BCB)

   DESPITE HER FATHER'S CAUTIONS, SAMANTHA IS NOT
ABLE TO KEEP STRAIGHT HER IMAGINARY LIFE FROM
HER REAL LIFE, AND TELLS PRETTY BIG WHOPPERS
TRIGGERED BY HER LONELINESS AND AN INSPIRED
IMAGINATION. WHEN SHE TELLS HER FRIEND THOMAS
THAT HER PET KANGAROO LIVES OUT IN A CAVE, THOMAS
BECOMES MAROONED AND ALMOST LOSES HIS LIFE. SAM

IS DISTRAUGHT WHEN SHE REALIZES THAT HER LIE, FOR
THAT IS WHAT IT IS, IS RESPONSIBLE. HER FATHER
TELLS HER TO THINK ABOUT THE DIFFERENCE BETWEEN
REAL AND MOONSHINE AND, AT THE END, HE ALSO TELLS
HER THAT THERE ARE TWO KINDS OF MOONSHINE: THE
GOOD KIND, WHICH IS HEALTHY IMAGINATIVE PLAY, AND
THE BAD KIND, THAT WHICH CAN BE HARMFUL.
(BEHAVIOR--MISBEHAVIOR, DIFF SIT--ONE PARENT,
EMOTIONS--LONELINESS, FAM--ONE PARENT,
LONELINESS, MISBEHAVIOR, ONE PARENT)

SENDAK, MAURICE. WHERE THE WILD THINGS ARE.
HARPER, 1963. ILLUSTRATED BY MAURICE SENDAK.
(BC, BESL, CC, CCB-B, GBC)

   MAX MISBEHAVES ONE NIGHT, NAILING A SPIKE INTO
THE WALL AND CRACKING THE PLASTER, CHASING THE
DOG WITH A FORK, AND HIS MOTHER SENDS HIM TO HIS
ROOM, TO BED WITHOUT ANY SUPPER. MAX DREAMS A
FANTASTIC DREAM, IN WHICH HE TURNS THE SITUATION
AROUND, AND HE IS THE BOSS. WHEN HE TELLS THE
WILD ANIMALS TO "BE STILL"--THEY OBEY, AND WHEN
HE IS CROWNED KING, HE REVELS IN HIS CONTROL OVER
THE BEASTS. OVERCOME WITH LONELINESS, THE SMELL
OF FOOD, AND WANTING TO BE SAFE AT HOME, MAX ENDS
UP IN HIS ROOM, WHERE HIS SUPPER IS WAITING. THE
AMBIVALENCE OF INDEPENDENCE/DEPENDENCE, THE
QUALITIES OF SECURITY AND LOVE ARE STRESSED IN
THIS BOOK. (BEHAVIOR--MISBEHAVIOR,
EMOTIONS--LONELINESS, EMOTIONS--LOVE,
EMOTIONS--SECURITY, LONELINESS, LOVE,
MISBEHAVIOR, SECURITY)

VIPONT, ELFRIDA. THE ELEPHANT AND THE BAD BABY.
COWARD, 1969. ILLUSTRATED BY RAYMOND BRIGGS.
(BCB)

   EARLY RAYMOND BRIGGS ILLUSTRATIONS ADD TO THE
LIVELY VIGOR OF THIS STORY OF A BAD BABY WHO
NEVER SAID "PLEASE." MUCH PLEASING REPETITION IN
THE WAY THEY WENT RUNNING AROUND THE TOWN:
"RUMPETA, RUMPETA." BABY REALLY WAS BAD, BUT HE
TOO SHARED IN THE PANCAKES AT THE END, BEING SENT
TO BED ONLY AFTER THE FESTIVITIES WERE OVER.
RATHER A JOYOUS WAY TO LEARN MANNERS!
(BEHAVIOR--MANNERS, BEHAVIOR--MISBEHAVIOR,
MANNERS, MISBEHAVIOR)

WABER, BERNARD. NOBODY IS PERFICK. HOUGHTON,
1971. ILLUSTRATED BY BERNARD WABER. (CCB-B)

A HARD-TO-DESCRIBE BOOK BECAUSE OF ITS
UNCONVENTIONAL FORMAT. IT IS DIVIDED INTO SEVEN
SECTIONS DEALING WITH IMPERFECTNESS: THE CHILD
WHO CAN'T SIT UP STRAIGHT, ONE WHO DAYDREAMS,
ANOTHER WHO SQUEALS THE CONTENTS OF SOMEONE'S
DIARY, AND ENDING WITH A PORTRAIT OF A PERFECT
BOY (WHO TURNS OUT TO BE A ROBOT WITH A WIND-UP
KEY IN HIS BACK). (BEHAVIOR--MISBEHAVIOR,
MISBEHAVIOR, SELF-EVALUATION)

WILLARD, BARBARA. HULLABALOO!. MEREDITH, 1969.
ILLUSTRATED BY FRITZ WAGNER. (ESLC)

A BEAUTIFUL COLLECTION OF POETRY AND STORIES
WHICH IS DIFFICULT TO CATEGORIZE OR DESCRIBE, BUT
THE EDITOR SAYS ONE OF THE GOOD THINGS ABOUT IT
IS THAT WE OUGHT TO BE GLAD WE ARE LIVING TODAY,
BECAUSE MANY OF THE OLDER POEMS INCLUDED SHOW
DIRE CONSEQUENCES OF MISBEHAVIOR, SUCH AS MAY, A
WISP OF A "FLIBBETIGIBBET," WHO WAS SWALLOWED UP
WHOLE BY THE GIANT NAMED MUST. NOT EVERYONE'S CUP
OF TEA, THIS ANTHOLOGY NEEDS TO BE PERUSED
LEISURELY BY THE READER, AND WILL PROBABLY REWARD
HIM/HER WITH A JUST RIGHT STORY. MANY OF THE
SELECTIONS ARE HUMOROUS. TRY THE LAST SELECTION
IN THE BOOK, "NURSE MATILDA," FOR A SPLENDID
EXAMPLE OF MISBEHAVING CHILDREN.
(BEHAVIOR--MISBEHAVIOR, MISBEHAVIOR)

WINN, MARIE. SHIVER, GOBBLE AND SNORE. SIMON,
1971. ILLUSTRATED BY WHITNEY DARROW JR.. (ESLC)

A BOOK FOR VERY YOUNG CHILDREN ABOUT WHY
PEOPLE NEED LAWS. THREE FRIENDS WHO DON'T LIKE
ALL OF THE LAWS WHICH THE KING MAKES DECIDE TO
MOVE AWAY AND NOT HAVE ANY LAWS. CHAOS REIGNS
HOWEVER--SHIVER MADE FIRES WHICH BOTHERED GOBBLE,
AND THE SNORING OF SNORE BOTHERED SHIVER. WHEN
THEY DECIDE THAT LIFE LIKE THIS IS NOT GOOD
EITHER, THEY SET UP NEW RULES. A GOOD WAY TO
INTRODUCE CHILDREN TO THE NECESSITY FOR LAWS.
THERE ARE FOUR PAGES AT THE END DEVOTED TO
ACTIVITIES TO REINFORCE THE CONCEPT.
(BEHAVIOR--CONSIDERATION, BEHAVIOR--MISBEHAVIOR,
BEHAVIOR--RESPONSIBILITY, CONSIDERATION,
MISBEHAVIOR, RESPONSIBILITY)

ZOLOTOW, CHARLOTTE. WHEN I HAVE A SON. HARPER,
1967. ILLUSTRATED BY HILARY KNIGHT. (BCB)

IN AN IMAGINATIVE PROJECTION INTO THE FUTURE, JOHN TELLS HOW HIS SON WOULD BE PERMITTED TO BEHAVE AND, IN DOING SO, THE READER SEES A PARADE OF FORBIDDEN BEHAVIOR: NOT SAYING THANK YOU FOR PRESENTS HE HATES, AND HAVING A TRIPLE MALTED JUST BEFORE DINNER. THE IDEAS THAT JOHN IS REJECTING FALL INTO THE AREAS OF ETIQUETTE, GROOMING, PARENTAL CONTROL, COMMON COURTESY, FOOD DESIRES, AND HEALTH. SOME SEEM QUITE HARMLESS, SUCH AS STAYING DOWN AT THE RAILROAD STATION ALL DAY TO WATCH THE TRAINS. IN GENERAL, A MILD GROUSING AGAINST RULES SET DOWN BY GROWN-UPS. IN THE END, WE REALIZE JOHN IS ONLY DAYDREAMING OUT LOUD TO HIS FRIEND: HE DUTIFULLY GOES IN THE HOUSE FOR THE HATED PIANO LESSON. (BEHAVIOR--DISLIKES, BEHAVIOR--MANNERS, BEHAVIOR--MISBEHAVIOR, DISLIKES, MANNERS, MISBEHAVIOR)

BEHAVIOR--POSSESSIVENESS

MAYER, MERCER. MINE!. SIMON, 1970.   ILLUSTRATED BY MERCER MAYER.   (LJ, PBC)

A VERY FUNNY STORY OF GREEDINESS AND POSSESSIVENESS, WHICH MOVES THROUGH SEVEN EPISODES OF A LITTLE BOY CLAIMING THINGS WHICH BELONG TO SOMEONE ELSE: SHOVEL, FISHING POLE, A DOG'S BONE. HE IS RATHER A BULLY--GIVING GROUND ONLY WHEN THE LITTLE GIRL HITS HIM OVER THE HEAD WITH HER DOLL, AND GRUDGINGLY GIVING BACK THE FISHLINE AFTER THE FISH HAS BEEN LOST. THE READER FEELS THAT HE REALLY GETS HIS JUST DUES WHEN HE FINDS HE MUST CLEAN HIS ROOM, WHICH HE ALSO CLAIMED AS "MINE"--AND HIS MOTHER HANDS HIM THE BROOM AND DUSTPAN WITH THE WORD "YOURS." (BEHAVIOR--POSSESSIVENESS, EMOTIONS--GREED, GREED, POSSESSIVENESS)

MC KEAN, ELLY. IT'S MINE. VANGUARD, 1951. ILLUSTRATED BY ELLY MC KEAN.   (GBC)

THOUGH PEDANTIC IN TONE AT TIMES, A USEFUL VOLUME FOR PARENTS OF CHILDREN WHO ARE FINDING IT DIFFICULT TO SHARE POSSESSIONS. ALSO INCLUDES A PREFACE DIRECTED TO ADULTS, BUT THE CHILD READER OR LISTENER WILL UNDERSTAND HOW OTHER PEOPLE FEEL ABOUT THEIR OWN TOYS, AND IN TURN MAY UNDERSTAND THE DIFFICULT BUT REWARDING PATH TOWARD LEARNING TO SHARE. (BEHAVIOR--POSSESSIVENESS,

BEHAVIOR--SHARING, POSSESSIVENESS, SHARING)

BEHAVIOR--QUARRELING

BRONIN, ANDREW. GUS AND BUSTER WORK THINGS OUT.
COWARD, 1975. ILLUSTRATED BY CYNDY SZEKERES.
(BL)

BROTHER RACCOONS ARE SHOWN IN FOUR STORIES OF
BROTHERLY SQUABBLES. GUS, WHO MAY BE A LITTLE
OLDER, TRICKS HIS SIBLING IN MANY
SITUATIONS--TRYING TO GET THE LOWER BUNK BED,
TRYING TO GET ALL THE BEST TOYS ON A RAINY DAY.
USEFUL FOR DISCUSSION BECAUSE SYMPATHY TENDS TO
LIE WITH BUSTER, THE PUT-UPON BROTHER, AND HE
SOMETIMES GETS THE BEST OF HIS WILY BIG BROTHER.
(BEHAVIOR--QUARRELING, BROTHERS, FAM--BROTHERS,
FAM--SIBLING RIVALRY, QUARRELING, SIBLING RIVALRY)

HOBAN, RUSSELL. THE SORELY TRYING DAY. HARPER,
1964. ILLUSTRATED BY LILLIAN HOBAN. (CC)

ALTHOUGH THIS IS A TONGUE-IN-CHEEK SPOOF, IT
WILL BE VALUABLE FOR POINTING OUT HOW ONE THING
LEADS TO ANOTHER IN A QUARREL, AND SHOWS IN A
VERY FUNNY WAY WHAT HAPPENS WHEN EVERYBODY
ACCEPTS THE BLAME. SHOWS THE BEAUTY OF THE PHRASE
"I AM SORRY." (BEHAVIOR--CONSIDERATION,
BEHAVIOR--QUARRELING, CONSIDERATION, FAM,
QUARRELING)

HOBAN, RUSSELL. TOM AND THE TWO HANDLES. HARPER,
1965. ILLUSTRATED BY LILLIAN HOBAN. (ESLC)

KENNY AND TOM ARE ALWAYS FIGHTING, AND TOM
ALWAYS GETS A BLOODY NOSE. HIS DAD TELLS HIM THAT
THERE IS MORE THAN ONE WAY TO SOLVE THE PROBLEM.
YOU CAN FIGHT AGAIN, OR YOU CAN MAKE UP WITH
YOUR BEST FRIEND. TOM TRIES TO BE FRIENDS, BUT
THEY CONTINUE TO FIGHT UNTIL TOM'S FATHER GIVES
HIM SOME BOXING LESSONS. WHEN TOM WINS THE FIGHT,
THEN THEY MAKE UP, AND TOM FINDS THAT THERE WAS
ANOTHER WAY TO LOOK AT IT. (ANGER,
BEHAVIOR--QUARRELING, EMOTIONS--ANGER,
FRIENDSHIP, QUARRELING)

UDRY, JANICE. LET'S BE ENEMIES. HARPER, 1961.
ILLUSTRATED BY MAURICE SENDAK. (CC)

DELICATE PINK AND GREEN WATERCOLORS BELIE

SENDAK'S VIGOROUS, BLOCKY LITTLE BOYS, BUT
SOMEHOW ARE HARMONIOUS WITH THE TEXT. THIS IS THE
STORY OF A FRIENDSHIP SO ENDURING THAT THE BOYS
EVEN HAVE CHICKEN POX TOGETHER--IN THE SAME BED.
BUT IN THE DAY-TO-DAY CONTACTS, THE BOYS END UP
IN SOME ABRASIVE SITUATIONS, AND THE NARRATOR
GROUSES ABOUT JAMES: HE ALWAYS WANTS TO BE BOSS.
IN THE CONCLUDING PAGES, HOWEVER, THE SUN BEGINS
TO SHINE, THE ARTIST'S BOYS BEGIN TO WALK INTO
THE FRAMES INSTEAD OF OUT OF THEM, AND THEY SKATE
OFF TOGETHER, JOINED BY A PRETZEL AND ONE PAIR
OF SKATES BETWEEN THEM. A COMFORTING STORY WHICH
IS APPEALING IN ITS REALISTIC VIEW OF THE
LOVE/HATE RELATIONSHIP WHICH CAN EXIST IN THE
BEST OF FRIENDSHIPS. (BEHAVIOR--QUARRELING,
BEHAVIOR--SHARING, FRIENDSHIP, QUARRELING,
SHARING)

ZOLOTOW, CHARLOTTE. THE QUARRELING BOOK. HARPER,
1963.   ILLUSTRATED BY ARNOLD LOBEL. (CC)

   THE GRAYNESS OF A RAINY DAY IS ECHOED IN THE
BLACK AND WHITE DRAWINGS OF ARNOLD LOBEL, AND THE
SLANTY LINES OF THE DRIVING RAIN ADD TENSION
THROUGHOUT. BEGINNING WITH A FATHER WHO FORGETS
HIS GOOD-BYE KISS, THE BOOK PROGESSES TO A CRANKY
MOTHER, A TEASING BOY CHILD, AND A SISTER SALLY
WITH HURT FEELINGS. IT TOOK THE DOG, WHO WASN'T
AFFECTED BY THE DEPRESSIVE DAY, TO SWEETEN UP
EVERYONE'S SPIRITS, AND IT IS A LESSON IN THE
CONTAGIOUSNESS OF FEELINGS, BOTH GOOD AND BAD.
(BEHAVIOR--QUARRELING, FAM, QUARRELING)

BEHAVIOR--RESPONSIBILITY

WINN, MARIE. SHIVER, GOBBLE AND SNORE. SIMON,
1971.   ILLUSTRATED BY WHITNEY DARROW JR.. (ESLC)

   A BOOK FOR VERY YOUNG CHILDREN ABOUT WHY
PEOPLE NEED LAWS. THREE FRIENDS WHO DON'T LIKE
ALL OF THE LAWS WHICH THE KING MAKES DECIDE TO
MOVE AWAY AND NOT HAVE ANY LAWS. CHAOS REIGNS
HOWEVER--SHIVER MADE FIRES WHICH BOTHERED GOBBLE,
AND THE SNORING OF SNORE BOTHERED SHIVER. WHEN
THEY DECIDE THAT LIFE LIKE THIS IS NOT GOOD
EITHER, THEY SET UP NEW RULES. A GOOD WAY TO
INTRODUCE CHILDREN TO THE NECESSITY FOR LAWS.
THERE ARE FOUR PAGES AT THE END DEVOTED TO
ACTIVITIES TO REINFORCE THE CONCEPT.
(BEHAVIOR--CONSIDERATION, BEHAVIOR--MISBEHAVIOR,

BEHAVIOR--RESPONSIBILITY, CONSIDERATION,
MISBEHAVIOR, RESPONSIBILITY)

BEHAVIOR--SAFETY

MC LEOD, EMILIE. THE BEAR'S BICYCLE. LITTLE,
1975. ILLUSTRATED BY DAVID MC PHAIL. (BL)

AN IMAGINATIVE STORY IN WHICH AN ENORMOUS
BEAR, ON A MINIATURE BICYCLE, BREAKS ALL THE
RULES. AS THE LITTLE BOY IN THE STORY
DEMONSTRATES THE CORRECT WAY TO STAY ON THE RIGHT
WHEN MEETING ANOTHER BIKER, THE LUMBERING BEAR
TAKES A SPILL IN THE MIDDLE OF THE PATH, CROWDING
A YOUNG BOY, CAUSING HIM TO CRASH. BEAUTIFUL
ILLUSTRATIONS AND HUMOROUS SITUATIONS TEACH A
LESSON OF SAFETY IN A PAINLESS WAY.
(BEHAVIOR--CONSIDERATION, BEHAVIOR--MISBEHAVIOR,
BEHAVIOR--SAFETY, CONSIDERATION, MISBEHAVIOR,
SAFETY)

BEHAVIOR--SELFISHNESS

ZOLOTOW, CHARLOTTE. IF IT WEREN'T FOR YOU.
HARPER, 1966. ILLUSTRATED BY BEN SHECTER. (BCB)

BIG BROTHER COMPLAINS THROUGHOUT THE BOOK
ABOUT THE THINGS HE MIGHT HAVE IF HE WERE AN ONLY
CHILD--HE'D GET ALL THE PRESENTS, THE TREE HOUSE
WOULD BE HIS ALONE, AND HE COULD ALWAYS SIT IN
THE FRONT SEAT OF THE CAR. A BASICALLY SELFISH
ATTITUDE IS EXPOSED, ALBEIT A NATURAL ONE. AT THE
END, HOWEVER, BIG BROTHER CONCEDES THAT IF IT
WEREN'T FOR LITTLE BROTHER, HE'D HAVE TO BE WITH
THE GROWN-UPS ALL THE TIME, AND THAT SEEMS A
WORSE FATE. (BEHAVIOR--SELFISHNESS, BROTHERS,
FAM--BROTHERS, SELFISHNESS)

BEHAVIOR--SHARING

BONSALL, CROSBY. IT'S MINE!--A GREEDY BOOK.
HARPER, 1964. ILLUSTRATED BY CROSBY BONSALL.
(ESLC)

MABEL ANN AND PATRICK ARE TWO PRESCHOOLERS WHO
PLAY TOGETHER EVERY DAY, WITH THEIR ASSORTED
FAVORITE TOYS. THEY REFUSE TO SHARE, AND GO HOME
MAD. BUT AT A PICNIC, WHILE THEY ARE QUARRELING
OVER A CARROT, A GOAT EATS THEIR LUNCH, AND WHAT
FOLLOWS IS AN AMAZING TURNABOUT. THE STORY ENDS

WITH "MINE" STILL THE MOST IMPORTANT WORD IN THE
STORY, BUT PATRICK IS PLAYING WITH MABEL ANN'S
RUBBER DUCK AND MABEL ANN IS WEARING PATRICK'S
FEATHER. DELICIOUS CHILD-APPEALING DRAWINGS MAKE
THE BOOK VERY ATTRACTIVE TO CHILDREN.
(BEHAVIOR--SHARING, EMOTIONS--GREED, FRIENDSHIP,
GREED, SHARING)

HILL, ELIZABETH. EVAN'S CORNER. HOLT, 1967.
ILLUSTRATED BY NANCY GROSSMAN. (BCB)

   EVAN, WHO WANTED A CORNER OF HIS OWN IN THE
TWO-ROOM APARTMENT HE SHARED WITH FIVE OTHER
CHILDREN AND HIS PARENTS, WAS SATISFIED TO FIND A
CORNER BY THE WINDOW WHICH HE FIXED UP WITH A
PICTURE HE PAINTED, AND A TURTLE. WHEN HE STILL
FELT UNHAPPY HIS MOTHER SUGGESTED HE HELP HIS
YOUNGER BROTHER ADAM, AND IMMEDIATELY HE FELT
BETTER AT THE THOUGHT OF HELPING ADAM FIX UP HIS
OWN CORNER. (BEHAVIOR--SHARING, BROTHERS &
SISTERS, FAM--BROTHERS & SISTERS,
SELF-UNDERSTANDING, SHARING)

HOBAN, RUSSELL. BEST FRIENDS FOR FRANCES.
HARPER, 1969. ILLUSTRATED BY LILLIAN HOBAN.
(BCB)

   THE LITTLE BADGERS IN THIS STORY DEMONSTRATE
THE POIGNANCY OF A LITTLE SISTER BEING LEFT OUT
WHEN OLDER BOYS AND GIRLS ARE PLAYING. A NO-GIRLS
AND NO-BOYS SITUATION FOLLOWS, BUT ALL IS
HAPPINESS WHEN FRANCES PACKS UP A SCRUMPTIOUS
PICNIC FOR ALBERT AND THE YOUNGER SISTER GLORIA.
(BEHAVIOR--SHARING, FAM--SISTERS, FRIENDSHIP,
SHARING, SISTERS)

JOHNSTON, TONY. MOLE AND TROLL TRIM THE TREE.
PUTNAM, 1974. ILLUSTRATED BY WALLACE TRIPP. (BL)

   CHRISTMASY RED AND GREEN COLORS SET THE STAGE
FOR THIS STORY OF TWO FRIENDS WHO WANTED TO SHARE
THEIR CHRISTMAS TREE BUT WHO FOUND IT VERY
DIFFICULT TO DECIDE SUCH THINGS AS WHETHER A STAR
OR ANGEL WAS BETTER FOR THE TOP OF THE TREE.
DIFFERENCES ARE RESOLVED AFTER A QUARREL AND THE
BOOK ENDS ON A POSITIVE NOTE OF SHARING, WITH THE
DECORATED TREE BEING TRANSPORTED OUT INTO THE
FOREST. OBSERVANT CHILDREN WILL WONDER HOW THE
ELECTRIC LIGHTS CAN FUNCTION OUT IN THE WOODS.
(BEHAVIOR--SHARING, FRIENDSHIP, SHARING)

KEATS, EZRA. LOUIE. GREENWILLOW, 1975.
ILLUSTRATED BY EZRA KEATS.   (CCB-B, CSM, HB, SLJ)

   LOUIE, A YOUNG BOY IN A SLUM NEIGHBORHOOD WHO
DOES NOT SPEAK, COMES ALIVE WHEN HE SEES A PUPPET
NAMED GUSSIE AT A PUPPET SHOW. THE READER SENSES
THE LONELINESS OF LOUIE IN A BEAUTIFUL DREAM
SEQUENCE, AND ALL CHILDREN WILL APPRECIATE THE
ENDING, WHEN LOUIE RECEIVES GUSSIE AS A GENEROUS
GIFT FROM THE CHILDREN WHO MADE HER.
(BEHAVIOR--SHARING, EMOTIONS--LONELINESS,
FRIENDSHIP, LONELINESS, SHARING)

MC KEAN, ELLY. IT'S MINE. VANGUARD, 1951.
ILLUSTRATED BY ELLY MC KEAN. (GBC)

   THOUGH PEDANTIC IN TONE AT TIMES, A USEFUL
VOLUME FOR PARENTS OF CHILDREN WHO ARE FINDING IT
DIFFICULT TO SHARE POSSESSIONS. ALSO INCLUDES A
PREFACE DIRECTED TO ADULTS, BUT THE CHILD READER
OR LISTENER WILL UNDERSTAND HOW OTHER PEOPLE FEEL
ABOUT THEIR OWN TOYS, AND IN TURN MAY UNDERSTAND
THE DIFFICULT BUT REWARDING PATH TOWARD LEARNING
TO SHARE. (BEHAVIOR--POSSESSIVENESS,
BEHAVIOR--SHARING, POSSESSIVENESS, SHARING)

UDRY, JANICE. LET'S BE ENEMIES. HARPER, 1961.
ILLUSTRATED BY MAURICE SENDAK. (CC)

   DELICATE PINK AND GREEN WATERCOLORS BELIE
SENDAK'S VIGOROUS, BLOCKY LITTLE BOYS, BUT
SOMEHOW ARE HARMONIOUS WITH THE TEXT. THIS IS THE
STORY OF A FRIENDSHIP SO ENDURING THAT THE BOYS
EVEN HAVE CHICKEN POX TOGETHER--IN THE SAME BED.
BUT IN THE DAY-TO-DAY CONTACTS, THE BOYS END UP
IN SOME ABRASIVE SITUATIONS, AND THE NARRATOR
GROUSES ABOUT JAMES: HE ALWAYS WANTS TO BE BOSS.
IN THE CONCLUDING PAGES, HOWEVER, THE SUN BEGINS
TO SHINE, THE ARTIST'S BOYS BEGIN TO WALK INTO
THE FRAMES INSTEAD OF OUT OF THEM, AND THEY SKATE
OFF TOGETHER, JOINED BY A PRETZEL AND ONE PAIR
OF SKATES BETWEEN THEM. A COMFORTING STORY WHICH
IS APPEALING IN ITS REALISTIC VIEW OF THE
LOVE/HATE RELATIONSHIP WHICH CAN EXIST IN THE
BEST OF FRIENDSHIPS. (BEHAVIOR--QUARRELING,
BEHAVIOR--SHARING, FRIENDSHIP, QUARRELING,
SHARING)

BEHAVIOR--TEASING

CARLSON, NATALIE. MARIE LOUISE AND CHRISTOPHE.
SCRIBNER, 1974. ILLUSTRATED BY JOSE ARUEGO. (BL)

IN THIS STORY OF FRIENDS WHO LIKE TO PLAY
TRICKS, A MONGOOSE AND A SPOTTED GREEN SNAKE GET
INTO BIG TROUBLE WHEN THEY ARE TRAPPED. AFTER
THEY ARE FREE, CHRISTOPHE, THE LITTLE GREEN
SNAKE, PROMISES NEVER TO PLAY TRICKS AGAIN.
ALTHOUGH THE SETTING IS THE ISLAND OF MARTINIQUE,
THE THEME IS UNIVERSAL. (BEHAVIOR--TEASING,
FRIENDSHIP, TEASING)

WILDSMITH, BRIAN. THE LITTLE WOOD DUCK. WATTS,
1973. ILLUSTRATED BY BRIAN WILDSMITH. (CC)

LITTLE WOOD DUCK LIVES IN A THICKET WITH HIS
MOTHER AND FIVE BROTHERS AND SISTERS. THE FIRST
TIME HE JUMPED IN THE WATER HE FOUND HE COULD
SWIM ONLY IN CIRCLES, AND HIS MOTHER BECAME
ANGRY, AND THE ANIMALS OF THE FOREST TEASED HIM.
WHEN WISE OLD OWL DIAGNOSED THE TROUBLE (ONE FOOT
WAS LARGER THAN THE OTHER), HE TOLD THE LITTLE
DUCKLING TO PAY NO ATTENTION TO THE TEASING.
LATER, WHEN WOOD DUCK'S EFFORTS AT SWIMMING IN
CIRCLES DIVERTED THE FOX, EVERYONE DECLARED HIM A
HERO, AND THEY PROMISED NEVER TO TEASE HIM
AGAIN. USEFUL BECAUSE IT ILLUMINATES THE WAY IN
WHICH A HANDICAP MAY BECOME A BLESSING, AND
DEMONSTRATES THAT MINDLESS TEASING IS
UNDESIRABLE. (BEHAVIOR--TEASING, DIFF
SIT--HANDICAPS, EMOTIONS--FRUSTRATION,
FRUSTRATION, HANDICAPS, TEASING)

BEHAVIOR--THUMB SUCKING

SCHULZ, CHARLES. SECURITY IS A THUMB AND A
BLANKET. DETERMINED, 1963. ILLUSTRATED BY
CHARLES SCHULZ.

THE EXEMPLAR OF DEFINITIONS OF SECURITY IN A
CHILD'S MIND, ALTHOUGH, AS IN MANY CHILDREN'S
BOOKS, THE PHILOSPHY IS UNIVERSAL. "SECURITY IS
RETURNING HOME AFTER A VACTION" IS A TRUISM FOR
GROWN-UPS, TOO, AS IS SNOOPY'S LINE THAT
"SECURITY IS OWNING YOUR OWN HOME," EVEN IF IT IS
ONLY A DOG HOUSE. BUT THE MORE TRULY CHILD-LIKE
EXPRESSIONS OF SECURITY ARE TO BE FOUND IN THOSE
RELATING TO FINDING YOUR MOTHER IN THE HOUSE WHEN

YOU COME HOME FROM SCHOOL, AND SALLY SAYING AS
SHE WALKS ALONG A HIGH CHAIN-LINK FENCE:
"SECURITY IS KNOWING THAT BIG DOG CAN'T REALLY
GET OUT." CURIOUSLY, THUMB SUCKING AND SECURITY
BLANKETS ARE MENTIONED ONLY IN THE TITLE, BUT
SERVE TO TUNE IN THE READER TO THE SUBJECT.
(BEHAVIOR--THUMB SUCKING, EMOTIONS--SECURITY,
SECURITY, THUMB SUCKING)

TOBIAS, TOBI. THE QUITTING DEAL. VIKING, 1975.
ILLUSTRATED BY TRINA HYMAN. (BL)

    IN REALISTIC DRAWINGS AND TEXT DEALING WITH A
CONTEMPORARY MOTHER AND DAUGHTER, EACH WEARING
LONG HAIR AND JEANS, THE AUTHOR AND ILLUSTRATOR
HAVE PRESENTED A SITUATION IN WHICH EACH
CHARACTER WISHES TO CONQUER A BAD HABIT: THUMB
SUCKING ON THE PART OF THE DAUGHTER, AND SMOKING
CIGARETTES ON THE PART OF THE MOTHER. THEY
PROGRESS THROUGH SEVERAL CURES, SUCH AS HOLDING
HANDS, AND THE CANDY CURE--EACH HAS ITS
DRAWBACKS. WHILE THEY SUCCEED FOR AWHILE, IN THE
END BOTH MOTHER AND DAUGHTER FIND THEY CANNOT
QUIT COLD. NOT THE USUAL ENDING FOR A CHILDREN'S
BOOK. (BEHAVIOR--THUMB SUCKING,
FAM--MOTHER-DAUGHTER, MOTHER-DAUGHTER, THUMB
SUCKING)

BOREDOM

ALEXANDER, MARTHA. WE NEVER GET TO DO ANYTHING.
DIAL, 1970. ILLUSTRATED BY MARTHA ALEXANDER.
(CC)

    A VERY BORED LITTLE BOY WHO WANTS TO GO
SWIMMING IS TIED TO THE CLOTHESLINE BY HIS BUSY
MOTHER, AND DECIDES TO DO SOMETHING ABOUT IT. HE
STEPS OUT OF HIS SUNSUIT, STILL TIED TO THE LINE,
AND SETS OUT IN THE ALTOGETHER FOR A WALK DOWN
THE STREET. AFTER HE IS RETRIEVED BY HIS MOTHER
HE TURNS HIS SANDBOX INTO A SWIMMING POOL,
DEMONSTRATING INGENUITY BOTH IN FULFILLING HIS
DESIRE TO GO SWIMMING AND IN RESOLVING HIS
PROBLEM ALL BY HIMSELF. (BOREDOM,
EMOTIONS--BOREDOM)

BERSON, HAROLD. I'M BORED, MA!. CROWN, 1976.
ILLUSTRATED BY HAROLD BERSON. (BL)

    AN ENGAGING, OVERPRIVILEGED RABBIT IS THE

CHARACTER WHO IS BORED, AS THE READER SEES HIM
KICK HIS TEDDY BEAR, THROW HIS TOY HORSE IN THE
CORNER, AND FINALLY THROW HIS LOVELY YELLOW
AIRPLANE IN THE TRASH CAN. STEVE RABBIT AND HIS
MOTHER ARE A COLORFUL PAIR IN AN URBAN APARTMENT
SETTING. MOTHER WEARS AN ANKLE LENGTH COAT AND A
HEAD SCARF TIED IN THE NEW LIFE-STYLE FASHION.
HER SON WEARS A PEAKED CAP IN THE FASHION OF TV'S
CAPTAIN AND TENNILLE AND A RAKISH LONG SCARF.
PARENTS WILL NOT FEEL SORRY FOR STEVE RABBIT, BUT
MANY CHILDREN WILL IDENTIFY WITH HIM. PACK RAT,
WHO SALVAGES THE YELLOW AIRPLANE FROM THE
GARBAGE, IS DRESSED JUST AS OUTRAGEOUSLY, AND
BETWEEN THE TWO FRIENDS THE PROBLEM OF BEING
BORED IS SOLVED IN A SATISFYING WAY. (BOREDOM,
EMOTIONS--BOREDOM, FRIENDSHIP)

HOBAN, RUSSELL. NOTHING TO DO. HARPER, 1964.
ILLUSTRATED BY LILLIAN HOBAN. (CC)

   WALTER, AN OPOSSUM, ALWAYS SAYS THERE IS
NOTHING TO DO UNTIL HIS FATHER GIVES HIM A
SOMETHING-TO-DO-STONE. WALTER USES HIS
SOMETHING-TO-DO-STONE VERY WELL, AND THINKS OF A
LOT OF WAYS FOR KENNETH AND HIMSELF TO PLAY. HE
LOSES THE STONE, BUT WHEN HIS PESTY SISTER
CHARLOTTE COMES AROUND BOTHERING HIM, HE GIVES
HER A PLAY-RIGHT-HERE STICK, WHICH WORKS MAGIC,
JUST THE WAY THE STONE WORKED FOR HIM. (BOREDOM,
EMOTIONS--BOREDOM, SELF-RELIANCE)

RASKIN, ELLEN. NOTHING EVER HAPPENS ON MY BLOCK.
ATHENEUM, 1967. ILLUSTRATED BY ELLEN RASKIN.
(BCB)

   CHESTER FILBERT, A BORED LITTLE BOY WHO SITS
ON THE CURB BEMOANING THE FACT THAT LIFE IS MORE
INTERESTING IN OTHER PLACES, IS STILL SITTING ON
THE CURB AT THE END OF THE BOOK WHILE ALL SORTS
OF EXCITING THINGS ARE HAPPENING: LIGHTNING
STRIKES THE ROOF OF A HOUSE SOON AFTER THE
CARPENTER FIXES IT--THAT WAS AFTER THE FIRE, OF
COURSE. POOR CHESTER IS OBLIVIOUS TO IT ALL, AND
CHILDREN WILL ENJOY PICKING OUT ALL THE DETAILS.
BY THE WAY, WHAT DID HAPPEN TO THE 34 WITCHES?
(BOREDOM, EMOTIONS--BOREDOM)

BRAVERY

   ALEXANDER, MARTHA. BOBO'S DREAM. DIAL, 1970.

ILLUSTRATED BY MARTHA ALEXANDER.   (CC)

AN ENGAGING RELATIONSHIP BETWEEN A LITTLE BOY,
WHO HAPPENS TO BE BLACK, WHO LIKES TO PLAY
FOOTBALL AS WELL AS READ BOOKS ABOUT MONSTERS,
AND HIS SAUSAGE DOG. ALTHOUGH THERE ARE NO WORDS,
THE READER KNOWS THE DOG'S NAME IS BOBO. THE
LITTLE BOY LOVES HIS DOG, BUYING HIM A BIG BONE
AND PROTECTING HIM AGAINST A BIG DOG, AND WHEN
BOBO DREAMS, HE DREAMS OF PROTECTING THE LITTLE
BOY. WHEN BOBO WAKES UP, HE FINDS THE COURAGE TO
BARK AT THE BIG SHAGGY DOG WHO IS AGAIN AFTER HIS
BONE, THUS PUTTING INTO PRACTICE THE BRAVERY IN
HIS DREAM. (BRAVERY, EMOTIONS--BRAVERY)

ANGLUND, JOAN. THE BRAVE COWBOY. HARCOURT, 1959.
   ILLUSTRATED BY JOAN ANGLUND.   (CC)

A LITTLE BOY OF PRESCHOOL AGE PRETENDS HE IS A
REAL COWBOY, WHO CAPTURES RUSTLERS AND CONFRONTS
ALL KINDS OF SCARY SITUATIONS IN HIS IMAGINARY
LIFE. THE PICTURES OF THE REAL LIFE OF THE LITTLE
BOY ARE IN BLACK AND WHITE AND HIS IMAGINARY
EXPLOITS IN RED, SO THE CHILD SEEING THE BOOK IS
WELL AWARE OF THE DIFFERENCE BETWEEN THE TWO
WORLDS. (BRAVERY, EMOTIONS--BRAVERY)

BUCKLEY, HELEN. MICHAEL IS BRAVE. LOTHROP, 1971.
   ILLUSTRATED BY EMILY MC CULLY.   (ESLC)

AN EXCELLENTLY REALISTIC STORY CONCERNING THE
FEAR THAT MICHAEL HAD ABOUT GOING DOWN THE SLIDE.
WHEN A NEW GIRL IN SCHOOL TRIES IT, AND FINDS
HERSELF IN TEARS, THE TEACHER SUGGESTS THAT
MICHAEL CLIMB THE LADDER AND STAND BEHIND HER.
THROUGH THIS ACT OF HELPING, MICHAEL IS ABLE TO
GO DOWN THE SLIDE ALONE. ILLUSTRATES THE POINT
THAT WHEN YOU HELP SOMEONE ELSE, YOU BECOME MORE
BRAVE YOURSELF. (BRAVERY, EMOTIONS--BRAVERY,
SELF-CONFIDENCE)

COHEN, MIRIAM. TOUGH JIM. MACMILLAN, 1974.
ILLUSTRATED BY LILLIAN HOBAN.   (CCB-B)

JIM IS THE RATHER QUIET, SELF-EFFACING FIRST
GRADER IN A MULTI-ETHNIC CLASSROOM WHO HAS
APPEARED IN EARLIER COHEN BOOKS, AND WE SEE HIS
INNER THOUGHTS IN THIS STORY OF A COSTUME PARTY.
HE WANTS TO BE "SOMEONE VERY STRONG, SOMEONE VERY
TOUGH." HE DRESSES AS THE STRONGEST MAN IN THE

WORLD AND, IN A VERY SUPPORTIVE CIRCLE OF
FRIENDS, GETS THE BEST OF AN OLDER BOY WHO WANTS
TO FIGHT. (BRAVERY, EMOTIONS--BRAVERY,
SELF-CONFIDENCE, SELF-IDENTITY)

HURLIMANN, BETTINA. BARRY. HARCOURT, 1967.
ILLUSTRATED BY PAUL NUSSBAUMER. (ESLC)

   CHILDREN WILL GRASP THE MEANING OF COURAGE
WHEN THEY HEAR THIS STORY, SET IN SWITZERLAND, OF
A ST. BERNARD RESCUE DOG. OF THE MANY RESCUES
THE DOG MADE, PERHAPS THE STORY OF HIS FINDING A
SMALL GIRL AND CARRYING HER ON HIS BACK TO THE
HOSPICE WHERE THE MONKS LIVED IS THE MOST
MEMORABLE. CHILDREN WILL ALSO EMPATHIZE WITH THIS
TRUE STORY, AS BARRY MEETS WITH AN ACCIDENT
WHICH EVENTUALLY LEADS TO HIS DEATH. THE
CONTINUITY OF BIRTH, LIFE, AND DEATH, AS YOUNG
ST. BERNARDS ARE TRAINED AS RESCUERS, ENLARGES
THE SCOPE OF THIS STORY. (BRAVERY,
EMOTIONS--BRAVERY, DEATH, DIFF SIT--DEATH)

MAYER, MERCER. YOU'RE THE SCAREDY-CAT. PARENTS'
MAG, 1974. ILLUSTRATED BY MERCER MAYER. (BL)

   OLDER BROTHER CONVINCES YOUNGER BROTHER TO
SLEEP OUT IN THE BACK YARD. THINKING TO SCARE THE
SMALLER YOUTH, HE TELLS STORIES OF THE GREEN
GARBAGE CAN MONSTER, WITH BEAUTIFULLY MONSTERISH
ILLUSTRATIONS. TURNS OUT HE'S THE ONE WHO HAS THE
NIGHTMARES, BUT WON'T ADMIT HE'S SCARED.
(BRAVERY, EMOTIONS--BRAVERY, EMOTIONS--FEAR, FEAR)

SHAY, ARTHUR. WHAT HAPPENS WHEN YOU GO TO THE
HOSPITAL. REILLY, 1969.   (CC)

   KAREN'S SHINY, SMILING FACE ON THE COLORFUL
COVER SETS THE TONE FOR A NON-THREATENING
EXPERIENCE IN THE HOSPITAL FOR ANY CHILD READER.
ALTHOUGH KAREN IS TEARFULLY APPREHENSIVE AT
TIMES, CHILDREN WILL UNDERSTAND THAT IT IS NORMAL
TO MISS YOUR PARENTS AND THAT YOU MIGHT BE A
LITTLE AFRAID OF THE X-RAY MACHINE. AUTHOR SHAY
HAS SAID THAT HIS PURPOSE IS TO SHOW THE JOBS AND
SERVICES THAT GO ON IN A HOSPITAL, AND TO HELP
CHILDREN UNDERSTAND IN ADVANCE WHAT WILL HAPPEN
TO THEM. HE HAS SUCCEEDED IN PRODUCING A VERY
USEFUL, SUCCESSFUL BOOK. (BRAVERY, DIFF
SIT--HOSPITAL, EMOTIONS--BRAVERY, HOSPITAL, NEW
SIT--HOSPITAL)

WILLIAMS, GWENEIRA. TIMID TIMOTHY. Y. SCOTT,
1944.   ILLUSTRATED BY LEONARD WEISGARD. (CC)

A LITTLE KITTEN IS TAUGHT BY HIS MOTHER TO BE
BRAVE, AND HOW TO SCARE OTHER ANIMALS. SHE TELLS
HIM TO ARCH HIS BACK, STICK OUT HIS WHISKERS, AND
GO P-SSS-T. TO BE SURE, MOST OF THE ANIMALS HE
SCARES ARE STUFFED ANIMALS, UNTIL HE MEETS UP
WITH A PUPPY. WHEN THE PUPPY RUNS AWAY, TIMOTHY
KNOWS HOW IT FEELS TO BE BRAVE. USEFUL BECAUSE IT
SHOWS THAT MANY YOUNG ANIMALS ARE AFRAID AT
TIMES. (BRAVERY, EMOTIONS--BRAVERY,
EMOTIONS--FEAR, FEAR)

BROTHERS

AMOSS, BERTHE. TOM IN THE MIDDLE. HARPER, 1968.
ILLUSTRATED BY BERTHE AMOSS. (CCB-B)

THE VERY REAL PLIGHT OF HAVING A YOUNGER
BROTHER WHO BUGS YOU AND AN OLDER BROTHER WHO
THINKS YOU'RE A PEST IS DEPICTED IN THIS
ATTRACTIVE LITTLE PICTURE BOOK. TOM THINKS HE
WILL RUN AWAY, BUT ALSO THINKS THAT HOME AND THE
SAFETY OF BREAD AND BUTTER AT BEDTIME IS THE
BETTER IDEA. (BROTHERS, FAM--BROTHERS,
FAM--SIBLING RIVALRY, SIBLING RIVALRY)

BRONIN, ANDREW. GUS AND BUSTER WORK THINGS OUT.
COWARD, 1975.   ILLUSTRATED BY CYNDY SZEKERES.
(BL)

BROTHER RACCOONS ARE SHOWN IN FOUR STORIES OF
BROTHERLY SQUABBLES. GUS, WHO MAY BE A LITTLE
OLDER, TRICKS HIS SIBLING IN MANY
SITUATIONS--TRYING TO GET THE LOWER BUNK BED,
TRYING TO GET ALL THE BEST TOYS ON A RAINY DAY.
USEFUL FOR DISCUSSION BECAUSE SYMPATHY TENDS TO
LIE WITH BUSTER, THE PUT-UPON BROTHER, AND HE
SOMETIMES GETS THE BEST OF HIS WILY BIG BROTHER.
(BEHAVIOR--QUARRELING, BROTHERS, FAM--BROTHERS,
FAM--SIBLING RIVALRY, QUARRELING, SIBLING RIVALRY)

FRIEDMAN, AILEEN. CASTLES OF THE TWO BROTHERS.
HOLT, 1972.   ILLUSTRATED BY STEVEN KELLOGG.
(ESLC)

AILEEN FRIEDMAN WAS INSPIRED TO WRITE THIS
STORY AFTER SHE VISITED TWO REAL CASTLES SITUATED
ON THE RHINE RIVER. IT HAS A FOLKTALE QUALITY

ABOUT IT WHICH IS MATCHED BY MEDIEVAL
ILLUSTRATIONS. BASICALLY IT IS THE STORY OF TWO
BROTHERS WHO WERE ORPHANED. HUBERT, THE OLDER
BROTHER, LOOKS AFTER HIS YOUNGER BROTHER KLAUS TO
SUCH AN EXTENT THAT THE YOUNGER BROTHER FINALLY
REBELS. AFTER BUILDING HIS OWN CASTLE AND A HUGE
WALL TO SEPARATE IT FROM HUBERT'S, KLAUS NARROWLY
AVOIDS DISASTER WHEN THE WALL CRUMBLES.
ILLUSTRATES VERY WELL THAT TOO MUCH "MOTHERING"
CAN BE BAD. (BROTHERS, FAM--BROTHERS,
FAM--SIBLING RIVALRY, SIBLING RIVALRY)

GUILFOILE, ELIZABETH. HAVE YOU SEEN MY BROTHER?.
FOLLETT, 1962. ILLUSTRATED BY MARY STEVENS.
(CC)

   A RELATIVELY EASY-TO-READ STORY FOR FIRST
GRADERS, IN WHICH A LITTLE BOY SEARCHES ALL OVER
THE NEIGHBORHOOD FOR HIS BIG BROTHER, WHO HAS RED
HAIR, FRECKLES, AND WEARS BLUE JEANS. ALL
THROUGH THE STORY THE READER THINKS THE BIG
BROTHER IS LOST: AT THE END WE REALIZE IT IS THE
LITTLE-BOY NARRATOR WHO IS LOST. A SLIGHT STORY
IN WHICH INTEREST IS MAINTAINED BY SUSPENSE.
USEFUL BECAUSE OF THE ROLE IN WHICH THE YOUNGER
BROTHER PUTS HIMSELF: LOOKING FOR THE OLDER
BROTHER WHO IS "LOST." (BROTHERS, FAM--BROTHERS)

HALLINAN, P.K.. WE'RE VERY GOOD FRIENDS.
CHILDRENS, 1973. ILLUSTRATED BY P.K. HALLINAN.
(CCB-B)

   TWO BROTHERS WHO REALLY ARE FRIENDS, WHO ENJOY
PLAYING TOGETHER, "ACTING CREEPY" TOGETHER,
BEING MAD AND SAD, ARE STILL GLAD TO BE BROTHERS,
AND THAT'S THE BEST REASON WHY "WE'RE VERY GOOD
FRIENDS, MY BROTHER AND I." SLIGHT STORY AND TEXT
USEFUL TO SEE THE RELATIONSHIP OF BROTHERHOOD
AND FRIENDSHIP. (BROTHERS, FAM--BROTHERS,
FRIENDSHIP)

ZOLOTOW, CHARLOTTE. IF IT WEREN'T FOR YOU.
HARPER, 1966. ILLUSTRATED BY BEN SHECTER. (BCB)

   BIG BROTHER COMPLAINS THROUGHOUT THE BOOK
ABOUT THE THINGS HE MIGHT HAVE IF HE WERE AN ONLY
CHILD--HE'D GET ALL THE PRESENTS, THE TREE HOUSE
WOULD BE HIS ALONE, AND HE COULD ALWAYS SIT IN
THE FRONT SEAT OF THE CAR. A BASICALLY SELFISH
ATTITUDE IS EXPOSED, ALBEIT A NATURAL ONE. AT THE

END, HOWEVER, BIG BROTHER CONCEDES THAT IF IT
WEREN'T FOR LITTLE BROTHER, HE'D HAVE TO BE WITH
THE GROWN-UPS ALL THE TIME, AND THAT SEEMS A
WORSE FATE. (BEHAVIOR--SELFISHNESS, BROTHERS,
FAM--BROTHERS, SELFISHNESS)

BROTHERS & SISTERS

ALEXANDER, MARTHA. NOBODY ASKED ME IF I WANTED A
BABY SISTER. DIAL, 1971. ILLUSTRATED BY MARTHA
ALEXANDER. (BCB)

   THE STORY OPENS WITH A SOUR-FACED LITTLE BOY
OVERHEARING GUSHY COMPLIMENTS ABOUT HIS NEW BABY
SISTER. HIS NEXT MOVE IS TO LOAD HER IN A WAGON
AND TRY TO GIVE HER AWAY. AFTER SEVERAL ABORTED
ATTEMPTS, HE ENDS UP AT HIS FRIEND'S HOUSE. BABY
BONNIE MISBEHAVES, HOWEVER, AND IN THE END IT IS
THE BROTHER WHO CAN PACIFY HER. WICKED THOUGHTS
GO THROUGH HIS HEAD AS HE IMAGINES HER GROWING UP
AND PULLING HIM IN THE WAGON. (BROTHERS &
SISTERS, EMOTIONS--JEALOUSY, FAM--BROTHERS &
SISTERS, JEALOUSY, NEW SIT--BABY)

BONSALL, CROSBY. THE DAY I HAD TO PLAY WITH MY
SISTER. HARPER, 1972. ILLUSTRATED BY CROSBY
BONSALL. (CC)

   WORDLESS LITTLE SISTER DOES PRETTY WELL
AMUSING HERSELF. WHEN THE STORY OPENS SHE IS
MAKING A VERY NICE PAPER HAT FOR HER BIG DOG, BUT
SHE IS NOT MUCH HELP WHEN HER BROTHER TRIES TO
TEACH HER HOW TO PLAY HIDE-AND-SEEK. HIS
EXASPERATION COMES TO A HIGH POINT WHEN, INSTEAD
OF LOOKING FOR HIS HIDING PLACE, SHE CURLS UP TO
TAKE A NAP IN A PILE OF LEAVES. ATTRACTIVE TO BOY
READERS WHO WILL COMMISERATE WITH THE BROTHER,
AND OTHER READERS WILL APPRECIATE THE HUMOR.
(BROTHERS & SISTERS, FAM--BROTHERS & SISTERS)

BRANDENBERG, FRANZ. I WISH I WAS SICK, TOO!.
MORROW, 1976. ILLUSTRATED BY ALIKI. (BL)

   THIS IS A BOOK IN WHICH ALL OF THE ACTION CAN
BE TRACED IN THE EXPRESSIONS IN THE EYES OF
EDWARD AND ELIZABETH, TWO ENDEARING CAT
PROTAGONISTS WITH ALL TOO HUMAN FOIBLES. EDWARD'S
EYES ARE AT HALF-MAST AS WE SEE HIM IN THE
SICKBED, AND ELIZABETH SHOOTS SIDEWISE GLANCES OF
ENVIOUS RAGE AS SHE RELUCTANTLY DOES HER CHORES

AND PRACTICES PIANO. CONCERN AND LOVE ARE
EXPRESSED IN THE EYES OF MOTHER AND FATHER AS
THEY MINISTER TO THE CHILDREN, FOR YES, ELIZABETH
ALSO BECOMES ILL. HER EYES ARE EVEN MORE
HELPLESSLY DROOPED, AND ONCE AGAIN SHE IS ENVIOUS
OF THE WELL BROTHER, WHOSE EYES ARE BY NOW ROUND
AND SPARKLY. THE STORY ENDS WITH EVERYONE
PROPERLY ROUND-EYED AND HAPPY. (BROTHERS &
SISTERS, DIFF SIT--ILLNESS, FAM--BROTHERS &
SISTERS, EMOTIONS--JEALOUSY, ILLNESS, JEALOUSY)

BUNIN, SHERRY. IS THAT YOUR SISTER?. PANTHEON,
1976.

   THIS IS SIX-YEAR-OLD CATHERINE BUNIN'S OWN
STORY AND THAT OF HER SISTER CARLA, IN A BOOK
ABOUT INTERRACIAL ADOPTION. OBVIOUSLY PROUD TO BE
LOVED AND CARED FOR BY HER FAMILY WHICH INCLUDES
TWO BROTHERS, CATHERINE RELATES THE STORY OF HER
ADOPTION BY ANSWERING MANY OF THE QUESTIONS PUT
TO HER BY CHILDREN AND ADULTS ALIKE. SHE TACKLES
EVEN VERY SUBSTANTIVE ANSWERS AS SHE DESCRIBES
THE WAY IN WHICH THE SOCIAL WORKER VISITED THEIR
HOME, AND THE CULMINATION OF THE PROCEEDINGS IN
THE FAMILY COURT. FILLED WITH MANY EXCELLENT,
INFORMAL PHOTOGRAPHS OF FAMILY LIFE, THIS SLIM
VOLUME WILL BE HELPFUL TO PARENTS ANTICIPATING OR
CONTEMPLATING THIS DIFFICULT SITUATION.
(ADOPTION--INTERRACIAL, BROTHERS & SISTERS, DIFF
SIT--ADOPTION--INTERRACIAL, FAM--BROTHERS &
SISTERS)

CAINES, JEANNETTE. ABBY. HARPER, 1973.
ILLUSTRATED BY STEVEN KELLOGG.   (CC)

   ABBY IS A ROUND-FACED BUNDLE OF CURIOSITY, WHO
ALWAYS WANTS TO HEAR THE STORY OF HER ADOPTION,
OVER AND OVER AGAIN. WHEN SHE PESTERS HER BROTHER
KEVIN, EMOTIONS SPILL OVER, WITH ABBY CRYING AND
BROTHER FEELING SORRY. THROUGHOUT THE STORY, THE
ILLUSTRATOR HAS PICTURED A COMFORTABLE HOME
FILLED WITH LOVE AND CONCERN. KEVIN PROMISES TO
TAKE ABBY TO SCHOOL FOR SHOW AND TELL, AND HIS
PRIDE IN HER IS VERY OBVIOUS. USEFUL IN VARIOUS
WAYS CONCERNING ADOPTION--THE OPEN CURIOSITY OF
THE CHILD, THE OPEN WILLINGNESS TO TALK OF IT,
THE PRIDE, IN THIS CASE, OF BEING ADOPTED.
(ADOPTION, BROTHERS & SISTERS, DIFF
SIT--ADOPTION, FAM--BROTHERS & SISTERS)

CONFORD, ELLEN. IMPOSSIBLE POSSUM. LITTLE, 1971.
ILLUSTRATED BY ROSEMARY WELLS.   (CC, ESLC)

   AN EXAMPLE OF SELF-FULFILLING PROPHECY OF
FAILURE. RANDOLPH, WHO COULDN'T HANG BY HIS TAIL
LIKE OTHER POSSUMS, BEGAN TO FEEL HE NEVER COULD
LEARN, AND THOSE AROUND HIM THOUGHT SO TOO.
GERALDINE, HIS INGENIOUS SISTER, FOUND THAT SAP
HELPED HIS TAIL STAY ON THE BRANCH, AND ALL WENT
WELL UNTIL THE SAP DRIED UP. SHE ALSO IS
INSTRUMENTAL IN PROVING TO HIM THAT HE REALLY
DOESN'T NEED THE SAP TO HANG UPSIDE DOWN.
(BROTHERS & SISTERS, FAM--BROTHERS & SISTERS,
SELF-CONFIDENCE)

ELLENTUCK, SHAN. MY BROTHER BERNARD. ABELARD,
1968. ILLUSTRATED BY SHAN ELLENTUCK. (CCB-B)

   TOLD BY A NAMELESS LITTLE SISTER, THIS IS A
PORTRAIT OF A KOOKY BROTHER WHO WANTS EVERYONE TO
THINK HE IS A PRINCE. IN ONE SENSE, HE BULLIES
HIS SISTER, AND THREATENS TO HIT HER IF SHE
DOESN'T PLAY AT THE GAME OF MAKE-BELIEVE. SHE,
HOWEVER, SECRETLY ADMIRES HIM AND HIS IMAGINARY
KINGDOM, AND IN THE END IS FLATTERED BY BEING
MADE A PRINCESS. THIS BOOK IS NOT A TRACT FOR
PERSONS LOOKING FOR BOOKS WITH STRONG IMAGES OF
WOMEN. (BROTHERS & SISTERS, FAM--BROTHERS &
SISTERS, FAM--SIBLING RIVALRY, SIBLING RIVALRY)

HEIDE, FLORENCE. SOUND OF SUNSHINE, SOUND OF
RAIN. PARENTS' MAG, 1970. ILLUSTRATED BY KENNETH
LONGTEMPS.

   THE BLIND CHILD WHO TELLS THIS STORY AND HIS
SISTER ARE NAMELESS, AND ONLY ABRAM, THE FRIENDLY
ICE CREAM MAN IN THE PARK, HAS A NAME.
NEVERTHELESS THE STORY IS ONE OF A DEVELOPING
SELF-AWARENESS IN A LITTLE BOY. HIS IS A WORLD OF
A TACTILE ENVIRONMENT, PERCEIVED AS BEING SMOOTH
OR ROUGH, AND OF SOUNDS, SOFT AND LOUD, AND OF
COLORS IMAGINED. IN THE TELLING, MANY THINGS ARE
LEARNED ABOUT THE WORLD OF THE BLIND, AND A CHILD
HEARING THIS STORY WILL HAVE AN UNDERSTANDING OF
THE GROWING INDEPENDENCE IN THIS SMALL DEPENDENT
CHILD. (BROTHERS & SISTERS, DIFF SIT--HANDICAPS,
FAM--BROTHERS & SISTERS, HANDICAPS,
SELF-IDENTITY, SELF-UNDERSTANDING)

HILL, ELIZABETH. EVAN'S CORNER. HOLT, 1967.

ILLUSTRATED BY NANCY GROSSMAN. (BCB)

EVAN, WHO WANTED A CORNER OF HIS OWN IN THE
TWO-ROOM APARTMENT HE SHARED WITH FIVE OTHER
CHILDREN AND HIS PARENTS, WAS SATISFIED TO FIND A
CORNER BY THE WINDOW WHICH HE FIXED UP WITH A
PICTURE HE PAINTED, AND A TURTLE. WHEN HE STILL
FELT UNHAPPY HIS MOTHER SUGGESTED HE HELP HIS
YOUNGER BROTHER ADAM, AND IMMEDIATELY HE FELT
BETTER AT THE THOUGHT OF HELPING ADAM FIX UP HIS
OWN CORNER. (BEHAVIOR--SHARING, BROTHERS &
SISTERS, FAM--BROTHERS & SISTERS,
SELF-UNDERSTANDING, SHARING)

HUTCHINS, PAT. TITCH. MACMILLAN, 1971.
ILLUSTRATED BY PAT HUTCHINS. (ESLC)

TITCH WAS TOO LITTLE, A PREDICAMENT COMMON TO
MANY PRESCHOOLERS. IN THIS LOVELY PICTURE BOOK
WITH LARGE COLORFUL PICTURES AND A SMALL AMOUNT
OF TEXT, PAT HUTCHINS HAS OUTLINED ALL OF THE
INEQUITIES--THE OLDER SIBLINGS HAVE BIGGER BIKES
AND TOYS. BUT JUSTICE PREVAILS IN THE END, FOR IT
IS TITCH WHO HAS THE TINY SEED, WHICH GROWS INTO
AN ENORMOUS PLANT, LARGER THAN ANYTHING HIS BIG
BROTHER PETE AND SISTER MARY OWN. (BROTHERS &
SISTERS, FAM--BROTHERS & SISTERS,
SELF-CONSCIOUSNESS--SIZE)

IWASAKI, CHIHIRO. NEW BABY IS COMING TO MY
HOUSE. MC GRAW, 1970. ILLUSTRATED BY CHIHIRO
IWASAKI. (LJ)

EXQUISITE WATERCOLORS EMPHASIZE THE HAPPINESS
THAT SISTER FEELS BECAUSE HER NEW BROTHER JOHN IS
COMING HOME FROM THE HOSPITAL TODAY. SIMPLE TEXT
MAKES THE BOOK VERY USEFUL FOR A PRESCHOOL
CHILD'S PREPARATION FOR A NEW BABY IN THE
HOUSEHOLD. (BROTHERS & SISTERS, FAM--BROTHERS &
SISTERS, NEW SIT--BABY)

JORDAN, JUNE. NEW LIFE, NEW ROOM. CROWELL, T.,
1975. ILLUSTRATED BY RAY CRUZ. (BL)

AN EXTENDED FORMAT TAKES THIS BOOK OUT OF THE
TRUE PICTURE-BOOK CATEGORY, AND THIRD GRADERS
WILL ENJOY READING IT ALONE, BUT THE
ILLUSTRATIONS AND STORY MAKE IT ENJOYABLE FOR
YOUNGER CHILDREN ALSO. A VERY REAL PROBLEM IS
DEALT WITH HERE--THAT OF REARRANGING A FAMILY'S

SLEEPING QUARTERS TO ACCOMMODATE A NEW BABY. A
PICTURE OF A WARM, FRIENDLY FAMILY DEALING
REALISTICALLY WITH AN EVERYDAY PROBLEM PROVIDES A
REASSURING, POSITIVE APPROACH. (BROTHERS &
SISTERS, FAM--BROTHERS & SISTERS, NEW SIT--BABY)

LEE, VIRGINIA. MAGIC MOTH. SEABURY, 1972.
ILLUSTRATED BY RICHARD CUFFARI. (BCB)

   ANOTHER BOOK WHICH FALLS OUT OF THE STRICT
CATEGORY OF A PICTURE BOOK, THIS TITLE IS
INCLUDED BECAUSE IT IS UNIQUE: IT TELLS THE
LOVING STORY OF THE DEATH OF A YOUNG CHILD AT
HOME. THE MAGIC MOTH ENTERS THE STORY JUST WHEN
MARYANNE STOPS BREATHING: "A HUGE WHITE MOTH ROSE
GENTLY FROM SOMEWHERE NEAR THE BED AND FLEW UP
TO THE CEILING." THIS ANALOGOUS DESCRIPTION ACTS
AS A BRIDGE BETWEEN THE COLD FACT OF DEATH, AND
THE WARM SPIRIT OF THE LITTLE GIRL AND HER
RELATIONSHIP WITHIN THE FAMILY. ALMOST EVERYONE
IS CURIOUS ABOUT CERTAIN ASPECTS OF DEATH, AND
THE AUTHOR HAS PROVIDED REALISTIC DIALOG AND
FEELINGS WHEN SHE DESCRIBES THE THOUGHTS OF A
YOUNGER BROTHER: "MARK-O, WHO WAS FULL OF
QUESTIONS, COULD NOT THINK JUST EXACTLY WHAT IT
WAS HE REALLY WANTED TO KNOW, SO HE TOO WAS
QUIET." THUS VIRGINIA LEE HAS WRITTEN A
COMPLETELY PLAUSIBLE STORY, BUT ONE TO WHICH
SECOND AND THIRD GRADERS CAN REALLY RESONATE.
(BROTHERS & SISTERS, DEATH, DIFF SIT--DEATH,
FAM--BROTHERS & SISTERS)

NESS, EVALINE. DO YOU HAVE THE TIME, LYDIA?.
DUTTON, 1971. ILLUSTRATED BY EVALINE NESS. (CC,
ESLC)

   LYDIA IS A LITTLE GIRL WHO NEVER "HAS TIME" TO
FINISH ALL OF THE MANY THINGS IN WHICH SHE'S
INTERESTED. WHEN SHE NEGLECTS TO FINISH A RACING
CAR FOR HER YOUNGER BROTHER, HE IS DISAPPOINTED,
AND SHE BEGINS TO MAKE AMENDS. THE LESSON IS "IF
YOU TAKE TIME, YOU'LL HAVE TIME."
(BEHAVIOR--CONSIDERATION, BROTHERS & SISTERS,
CONSIDERATION, FAM--BROTHERS & SISTERS,
SELF-EVALUATION)

SCOTT, ANN. SAM. MC GRAW, 1967. ILLUSTRATED BY
SYMEON SHIMIN. (BCB)

   THE ILLUSTRATIONS ARE PARAMOUNT IN THIS STORY

OF A LEFT-OUT BROTHER WHO IS REJECTED FIRST BY
MOTHER, BIG BROTHER GEORGE, SISTER MARCIA, AND
THEN HIS FATHER, WHO FORBIDS HIM TO TOUCH HIS
TYPEWRITER. THE BLACK, SEPIA, AND GOLDEN BROWN
WATERCOLORS INTENSIFY THE FEELINGS OF SADNESS IN
SAM'S HEART. SUDDENLY THE WHOLE FAMILY REALIZES
THAT HE NEEDS ATTENTION: HIS MOTHER HOLDS HIM AND
ROCKS HIM, AND AS EVERYONE RALLIES AROUND TO
KEEP HIM COMPANY, SAM HELPS BAKE A RASPBERRY
TART. (BROTHERS & SISTERS, EMOTIONS--REJECTION,
FAM--BROTHERS & SISTERS, REJECTION)

WELLS, ROSEMARY. NOISY NORA. DIAL, 1973.
ILLUSTRATED BY ROSEMARY WELLS. (CC, ESLC)

POOR NORA--SHE'S THE LEFT-OUT SISTER, AND
THREATENS TO RUN AWAY TO MAKE HER FAMILY FEEL
SORRY FOR HER AND GIVE HER SOME ATTENTION. WHEN
SHE SHOWS UP IN THE BROOM CLOSET, ALL IS WELL. A
CLEVER, FUNNY BOOK ABOUT A BUMPTIOUS LITTLE
MOUSE-GIRL WHICH WILL DELIGHT YOUNG CHILDREN AS
THEY CATALOG HER MISDEMEANORS. MANY CHILDREN MAY
SEE THEMSELVES. (BROTHERS & SISTERS,
EMOTIONS--JEALOUSY, FAM--BROTHERS & SISTERS,
FAM--SIBLING RIVALRY, JEALOUSY, SIBLING RIVALRY)

ZOLOTOW, CHARLOTTE. DO YOU KNOW WHAT I'LL DO?.
HARPER, 1958. ILLUSTRATED BY GARTH WILLIAMS.
(CC)

A LOVING PICTURE OF A GIRL ABOUT SEVEN YEARS
OLD, DREAMING ABOUT ALL OF THE WAYS SHE WILL BE
GOOD TO HER BABY BROTHER. GARTH WILLIAMS HAS
DRAWN LARGE FULL-PAGE ILLUSTRATIONS FILLED IN
WITH A DELICATE WATERCOLOR WASH TO ACCENTUATE THE
DREAMY QUALITY OF THE LITTLE GIRL'S THOUGHTS.
SHE PROMISES CONCRETE THINGS, SUCH AS BRINGING
HOME A PIECE OF BIRTHDAY CAKE, AND SHE PROMISES
THINGS THAT ARE IN THE AFFECTIVE DOMAIN: SHE
TELLS HIM THAT SHE'LL GET RID OF HIS NIGHTMARES
FOR HIM. IN DOING THIS, OF COURSE, SHE
DEMONSTRATES THE THINGS THAT ARE IMPORTANT AND
PROMINENT IN CHILDREN'S LIVES, THEIR EXPECTATIONS
AND FEARS. (BROTHERS & SISTERS, EMOTIONS--LOVE,
FAM--BROTHERS & SISTERS, LOVE)

CONSIDERATION

DAUGHERTY, JAMES. ANDY AND THE LION. VIKING,
1938. ILLUSTRATED BY JAMES DAUGHERTY. (CC)

IN ROLLICKING, RHYTHMICAL DRAWINGS, JAMES
DAUGHERTY HAS SYNTHESIZED FEELINGS OF JOY IN
LIVING AND JOY IN HELPING OTHER PEOPLE. ANDY, WHO
BEFRIENDS A LION AND REMOVES A BIG THORN FROM
HIS PAW, LATER IS THE BENEFICIARY OF THE KIND
ACT. THE LION, WHO HAS ESCAPED FROM THE CIRCUS,
RECOGNIZES ANDY AND IS IMMEDIATELY FRIENDLY.
USEFUL BECAUSE IT DEMONSTRATES IN A VERY SIMPLE
WAY HOW ONE KIND ACT MAY BE REPAID, BUT FAR
BEYOND THAT, THE AFFECTIVE ASPECTS OF LIVING ARE
STRESSED--THE SENSUOUS EFFECT OF THE EXPRESSIONS
ON FACES, THE SUBTLE HUMOR IN THE DAILY FAMILY
LIFE, AND THE VIGOROUS FEELINGS DEPICTING THE JOY
OF LIVING. (BEHAVIOR--CONSIDERATION,
BEHAVIOR--KINDNESS, CONSIDERATION,
EMOTIONS--HAPPINESS, FAM, FRIENDSHIP, HAPPINESS,
KINDNESS)

GAEDDERT, LOU. NOISY NANCY NORRIS. DOUBLEDAY,
1965. ILLUSTRATED BY GIOIA FIAMMENGHI. (CC)

NOT A MODEL GIRL, NANCY IS ABOUT THE NOISIEST
CHILD IMAGINABLE. WHEN THE NEIGHBOR COMPLAINS,
NANCY BECOMES SO VERY QUIET THAT EVERYONE THINKS
SHE IS ILL. THE LAST PICTURE IN THE BOOK IS TRULY
FUNNY, FOR NANCY HAS TIED A BIG SOFT RAG AROUND
HER STICK HORSE SO SHE WILL NOT BANG ON THE
FLOOR. USEFUL TO PRESENT A NON-STEREOTYPED LOOK
AT A LITTLE GIRL'S BEHAVIOR.
(BEHAVIOR--CONSIDERATION, BEHAVIOR--MISBEHAVIOR,
CONSIDERATION, MISBEHAVIOR)

HAWKINS, QUAIL. ANDROCLES AND THE LION. COWARD,
1970. ILLUSTRATED BY ROCCO NEGRI. (ESLC)

A SIMPLE RETELLING OF THIS AGE-OLD STORY
ILLUSTRATES FOR THE CHILDREN OF TODAY THE MORAL
THAT ONE SHOULD BE KIND TO PEOPLE IN NEED. WHEN
THE SLAVE ANDROCLES REMOVES A THORN FROM THE
LION'S PAW, AND THE LION LEADS HIM TO FOOD AND
DRINK, THERE IS A VIVID EXAMPLE OF THE BEGINNING
OF FRIENDSHIP. LATER ON WHEN THE LION MEETS
ANDROCLES IN THE ARENA AND REFUSES TO FIGHT HIM,
THE REWARDS OF FRIENDSHIP ARE SHOWN. A STORY FOR
OLDER CHILDREN RATHER THAN YOUNGER BECAUSE OF THE
CRUELTY IMPLIED IN THE COLOSSEUM.
(BEHAVIOR--CONSIDERATION, BEHAVIOR--KINDNESS,
CONSIDERATION, FRIENDSHIP, KINDNESS)

HOBAN, RUSSELL. THE SORELY TRYING DAY. HARPER,

1964. ILLUSTRATED BY LILLIAN HOBAN. (CC)

ALTHOUGH THIS IS A TONGUE-IN-CHEEK SPOOF, IT
WILL BE VALUABLE FOR POINTING OUT HOW ONE THING
LEADS TO ANOTHER IN A QUARREL, AND SHOWS IN A
VERY FUNNY WAY WHAT HAPPENS WHEN EVERYBODY
ACCEPTS THE BLAME. SHOWS THE BEAUTY OF THE PHRASE
"I AM SORRY." (BEHAVIOR--CONSIDERATION,
BEHAVIOR--QUARRELING, CONSIDERATION, FAM,
QUARRELING)

MARSHALL, JAMES. GEORGE AND MARTHA. HOUGHTON,
1972. ILLUSTRATED BY JAMES MARSHALL. (CC)

FIVE VERY SHORT STORIES FOR THE VERY YOUNG
ABOUT GEORGE AND MARTHA, HUGE HIPPOS WHO LIVE
LIKE HUMANS, GIVE THE READER SOME GOOD HUMAN
ADVICE: ALWAYS TELL THE TRUTH TO YOUR BEST
FRIEND, SO YOU DON'T HAVE TO POUR YOUR UNWANTED
SPLIT PEA SOUP IN YOUR SNEAKERS. ALSO, YOU MAY
GET THE BATHTUB DUMPED ON YOUR HEAD IF YOU PEEK
IN THE BATHROOM WINDOW WHEN YOU SHOULDN'T. BEING
TRUTHFUL, RESPECTING PRIVACY, LOOKING ON THE
BRIGHT SIDE OF THINGS, CHEERING YOU UP, THESE ARE
SOME OF THE THINGS THAT GOOD FRIENDS DO FOR ONE
ANOTHER. (BEHAVIOR--CONSIDERATION, CONSIDERATION,
FRIENDSHIP)

MARSHALL, JAMES. GEORGE AND MARTHA ENCORE.
HOUGHTON, 1973. ILLUSTRATED BY JAMES MARSHALL.
(CC)

GOOD FRIENDS MARTHA AND GEORGE APPEAR IN FIVE
SHORT STORIES WHICH EXTOL THE BLESSINGS OF A GOOD
RELATIONSHIP: GEORGE DOESN'T SAY "I TOLD YOU SO"
WHEN MARTHA GETS SUNBURNED. WHEN MARTHA IS
FRUSTRATED OVER THE WEEDS IN HER GARDEN, GEORGE
IN A TRULY THOUGHTFUL ACT RUSHES OUT TO THE
FLORIST TO BUY TULIPS TO STICK IN THE GROUND AS A
SURPRISE. THOUGHTFULNESS AND PROTECTING THE
FEELINGS OF THE OTHER PERSON ARE TWO OF THE
IMPORTANT ELEMENTS IN THE BOOK.
(BEHAVIOR--CONSIDERATION, CONSIDERATION,
FRIENDSHIP)

MC LEOD, EMILIE. THE BEAR'S BICYCLE. LITTLE,
1975. ILLUSTRATED BY DAVID MC PHAIL. (BL)

AN IMAGINATIVE STORY IN WHICH AN ENORMOUS
BEAR, ON A MINIATURE BICYCLE, BREAKS ALL THE

RULES. AS THE LITTLE BOY IN THE STORY
DEMONSTRATES THE CORRECT WAY TO STAY ON THE RIGHT
WHEN MEETING ANOTHER BIKER, THE LUMBERING BEAR
TAKES A SPILL IN THE MIDDLE OF THE PATH, CROWDING
A YOUNG BOY, CAUSING HIM TO CRASH. BEAUTIFUL
ILLUSTRATIONS AND HUMOROUS SITUATIONS TEACH A
LESSON OF SAFETY IN A PAINLESS WAY.
(BEHAVIOR--CONSIDERATION, BEHAVIOR--MISBEHAVIOR,
BEHAVIOR--SAFETY, CONSIDERATION, MISBEHAVIOR,
SAFETY)

NESS, EVALINE. DO YOU HAVE THE TIME, LYDIA?.
DUTTON, 1971. ILLUSTRATED BY EVALINE NESS. (CC,
ESLC)

   LYDIA IS A LITTLE GIRL WHO NEVER "HAS TIME" TO
FINISH ALL OF THE MANY THINGS IN WHICH SHE'S
INTERESTED. WHEN SHE NEGLECTS TO FINISH A RACING
CAR FOR HER YOUNGER BROTHER, HE IS DISAPPOINTED,
AND SHE BEGINS TO MAKE AMENDS. THE LESSON IS "IF
YOU TAKE TIME, YOU'LL HAVE TIME."
(BEHAVIOR--CONSIDERATION, BROTHERS & SISTERS,
CONSIDERATION, FAM--BROTHERS & SISTERS,
SELF-EVALUATION)

STEIG, WILLIAM. AMOS AND BORIS. FARRAR, 1971.
ILLUSTRATED BY WILLIAM STEIG. (BCB)

   IN A BEAUTIFUL SEA GREEN BOOK, STEIG HAS TOLD
A STORY SIMILAR TO ANDROCLES AND THE LION,
WHEREIN A WHALE SAVES THE LIFE OF AMOS THE MOUSE
WHEN HE IS SHIPWRECKED. LATER, BORIS THE WHALE IS
WASHED ASHORE DURING A HURRICANE, AND THE MOUSE
BRINGS TWO ELEPHANTS TO PUSH THE WHALE BACK INTO
THE WATER. POINTS OUT THE FACT THAT FRIENDSHIP
CAN BE BASED ON MUTUAL HELP--EVEN THOUGH THE
FRIENDS MIGHT NOT SEE EACH OTHER IN THE FUTURE.
(BEHAVIOR--CONSIDERATION, CONSIDERATION,
FRIENDSHIP)

WABER, BERNARD. LYLE AND THE BIRTHDAY PARTY.
HOUGHTON, 1966. ILLUSTRATED BY BERNARD WABER.
(CC)

   HELPFUL LYLE STEPS OUT OF HIS ROLE AS HE FINDS
HIMSELF BEING VERY JEALOUS OF JOSHUA'S BIRTHDAY
CELEBRATION. IN FACT HE BECOMES SO VERY JEALOUS
THAT HE MAKES HIMSELF SICK AND MOPES ABOUT THE
HOUSE, FINALLY LANDING IN THE HOSPITAL. HELPING
OTHER PATIENTS IS GOOD THERAPY FOR HIM, AND SOON

HE'S HOME--TO FIND THAT THE FAMILY IS PLANNING
HIS BIRTHDAY PARTY. LYLE'S FEELINGS OF JEALOUSY,
AND THE WAY THEY MADE HIM FEEL MEAN, ARE VERY
REAL AND WILL HELP CHILDREN KNOW THAT EVERYONE
HAS THESE KINDS OF FEELINGS--EVEN CROCODILES.
(BEHAVIOR--CONSIDERATION, CONSIDERATION,
EMOTIONS--JEALOUSY, JEALOUSY)

WINN, MARIE. SHIVER, GOBBLE AND SNORE. SIMON,
1971.   ILLUSTRATED BY WHITNEY DARROW JR..   (ESLC)

   A BOOK FOR VERY YOUNG CHILDREN ABOUT WHY
PEOPLE NEED LAWS. THREE FRIENDS WHO DON'T LIKE
ALL OF THE LAWS WHICH THE KING MAKES DECIDE TO
MOVE AWAY AND NOT HAVE ANY LAWS. CHAOS REIGNS
HOWEVER--SHIVER MADE FIRES WHICH BOTHERED GOBBLE,
AND THE SNORING OF SNORE BOTHERED SHIVER. WHEN
THEY DECIDE THAT LIFE LIKE THIS IS NOT GOOD
EITHER, THEY SET UP NEW RULES. A GOOD WAY TO
INTRODUCE CHILDREN TO THE NECESSITY FOR LAWS.
THERE ARE FOUR PAGES AT THE END DEVOTED TO
ACTIVITIES TO REINFORCE THE CONCEPT.
(BEHAVIOR--CONSIDERATION, BEHAVIOR--MISBEHAVIOR,
BEHAVIOR--RESPONSIBILITY, CONSIDERATION,
MISBEHAVIOR, RESPONSIBILITY)

DEATH

BARTOLI, JENNIFER. NONNA. HARVEY, 1975.
ILLUSTRATED BY JOAN DRESCHER.   (BL)

   AN INTERESTING, NON-THREATENING BOOK ABOUT THE
DEATH OF GRANDMOTHER TREATED FROM THE POINT OF
VIEW OF MEMORIES OF LIFE BEFORE HER DEATH AND
LIFE SEVERAL MONTHS LATER. NONNA'S COOKIES ARE
ONE MOTIF THAT REPEATS THROUGHOUT THE BOOK. IN
MEMORY, THE CHILDREN THINK ABOUT SOUP AND COOKIES
WITH NONNA ON SATURDAYS. ON THE DAY OF THE
FUNERAL, MOTHER BAKES NONNA'S COOKIES AND THE
CHILDREN EAT THEM FOR BREAKFAST, AND SIX MONTHS
LATER AT CHRISTMAS TIME, THE YOUNGEST DAUGHTER
BAKES THEM FOR THE ENTIRE FAMILY. USEFUL BECAUSE
ALTHOUGH IT SHOWS THE FUNERAL AND THE GRAVESIDE
SERVICE, IT ALSO USES A DEVICE TO SHOW HOW THE
LIVING COPE BY PERFORMING DAILY ROUTINES OF LIFE.
(DEATH, DIFF SIT--DEATH, FAM--GRANDMOTHERS,
GRANDMOTHERS)

DE PAOLA, TOMIE. NANA UPSTAIRS AND NANA
DOWNSTAIRS. PUTNAM, 1973.   ILLUSTRATED BY TOMIE

DE PAOLA. (BL)

   IN AN EASY BOOK FORMAT WITH LARGE PRINT AND
PICTURES ON EVERY PAGE, LITTLE TOMMY IS SHOWN IN
A CHARMING RELATIONSHIP WITH HIS 94-YEAR-OLD
GREAT-GRANDMOTHER, WHO IS NANA UPSTAIRS. HE
LEARNED THE MEANING OF DEATH ON THE DAY HIS
MOTHER TOLD HIM THAT NANA UPSTAIRS WOULD NOT BE
HERE ANY MORE, EXCEPT IN HIS MEMORY. TOMMY THINKS
OF HER WHEN HE SEES A FALLING STAR, AND THE BOOK
ENDS WITH HIM AS A YOUNG MAN, AGAIN SEEING A
FALLING STAR, AND THINKING OF BOTH GRANDMOTHERS.
A GENTLE, THOUGHTFUL WAY TO EXPLAIN DEATH TO THE
VERY YOUNG. (DEATH, DIFF SIT--DEATH,
FAM--GRANDMOTHERS, FAM--GREAT-GRANDMOTHERS,
GRANDMOTHERS, GREAT-GRANDMOTHERS)

HAZEN, NANCY. GROWNUPS CRY TOO. LOLLIPOP, 1973.
ILLUSTRATED BY NANCY HAZEN.

   IN THIS STARKLY ILLUSTRATED BOOK OF BLACK AND
WHITE LINE DRAWINGS ON OLIVE GREEN PAPER, THE
AUTHOR-ILLUSTRATOR HAS GIVEN A VERY LOW-KEY,
REALISTIC EXPLANATION OF THE EMOTIONS THAT MAY
MAKE GROWN-UPS CRY. PICTURES AND TEXT TELL THE
READER THAT SADNESS, MADNESS, FATIGUE, AND FEAR
SOMETIMES TRIGGER TEARS IN ADULTS. USEFUL TO SHOW
CHILDREN THAT ADULTS ALSO HAVE PROBLEMS.
PARTICULARLY USEFUL BECAUSE IT SHOWS A MAN IN
TEARS ALSO. (DEATH, DIFF SIT--DEATH, EMOTIONS)

HURLIMANN, BETTINA. BARRY. HARCOURT, 1967.
ILLUSTRATED BY PAUL NUSSBAUMER. (ESLC)

   CHILDREN WILL GRASP THE MEANING OF COURAGE
WHEN THEY HEAR THIS STORY, SET IN SWITZERLAND, OF
A ST. BERNARD RESCUE DOG. OF THE MANY RESCUES
THE DOG MADE, PERHAPS THE STORY OF HIS FINDING A
SMALL GIRL AND CARRYING HER ON HIS BACK TO THE
HOSPICE WHERE THE MONKS LIVED IS THE MOST
MEMORABLE. CHILDREN WILL ALSO EMPATHIZE WITH THIS
TRUE STORY, AS BARRY MEETS WITH AN ACCIDENT
WHICH EVENTUALLY LEADS TO HIS DEATH. THE
CONTINUITY OF BIRTH, LIFE, AND DEATH, AS YOUNG
ST. BERNARDS ARE TRAINED AS RESCUERS, ENLARGES
THE SCOPE OF THIS STORY. (BRAVERY,
EMOTIONS--BRAVERY, DEATH, DIFF SIT--DEATH)

LEE, VIRGINIA. MAGIC MOTH. SEABURY, 1972.
ILLUSTRATED BY RICHARD CUFFARI. (BCB)

ANOTHER BOOK WHICH FALLS OUT OF THE STRICT
CATEGORY OF A PICTURE BOOK, THIS TITLE IS
INCLUDED BECAUSE IT IS UNIQUE: IT TELLS THE
LOVING STORY OF THE DEATH OF A YOUNG CHILD AT
HOME. THE MAGIC MOTH ENTERS THE STORY JUST WHEN
MARYANNE STOPS BREATHING: "A HUGE WHITE MOTH ROSE
GENTLY FROM SOMEWHERE NEAR THE BED AND FLEW UP
TO THE CEILING." THIS ANALOGOUS DESCRIPTION ACTS
AS A BRIDGE BETWEEN THE COLD FACT OF DEATH, AND
THE WARM SPIRIT OF THE LITTLE GIRL AND HER
RELATIONSHIP WITHIN THE FAMILY. ALMOST EVERYONE
IS CURIOUS ABOUT CERTAIN ASPECTS OF DEATH, AND
THE AUTHOR HAS PROVIDED REALISTIC DIALOG AND
FEELINGS WHEN SHE DESCRIBES THE THOUGHTS OF A
YOUNGER BROTHER: "MARK-O, WHO WAS FULL OF
QUESTIONS, COULD NOT THINK JUST EXACTLY WHAT IT
WAS HE REALLY WANTED TO KNOW, SO HE TOO WAS
QUIET." THUS VIRGINIA LEE HAS WRITTEN A
COMPLETELY PLAUSIBLE STORY, BUT ONE TO WHICH
SECOND AND THIRD GRADERS CAN REALLY RESONATE.
(BROTHERS & SISTERS, DEATH, DIFF SIT--DEATH,
FAM--BROTHERS & SISTERS)

MILES, MISKA. ANNIE AND THE OLD ONE. LITTLE,
1971. ILLUSTRATED BY PETER PARNALL. (ESLC)

GOLDEN DESERT COLORS SPIKED WITH BLACK AND
WHITE LINE DRAWINGS CONTRIBUTE TO THE STARK
FEELINGS OF IMPENDING DEATH IN THIS DIALOG
BETWEEN A NAVAJO GRANDMOTHER AND HER SMALL
GRANDCHILD. ONE EVENING WHEN, SYMBOLICALLY, THE
FIRE IS DYING IN THE HOGAN, THE OLD ONE ANNOUNCED
THAT SHE WOULD GO TO MOTHER EARTH WHEN THE RUG
ON THE LOOM WAS FINISHED. ANNIE UNDERSTOOD,
ALTHOUGH SHE DID NOT UNDERSTAND WHY HER
GRANDMOTHER KNEW SHE WAS GOING TO DIE. IN THE
DAYS THAT FOLLOWED ANNIE DREAMED UP SCHEMES TO
DELAY THE COMPLETION OF THE RUG, AND IT IS ONLY
WHEN GRANDMOTHER EXPLAINS THE INEVITABILITY OF
DEATH IN ALL OF NATURE THAT ANNIE ACCEPTS THE
CONCEPT. INTERESTING VIEW OF DEATH FOR, WHILE A
VERY REALISTIC BOOK, IT RETAINS THE MYSTICAL
OUTLOOK OF THE NAVAJO WAY OF LIFE. (DEATH, DIFF
SIT--DEATH, FAM--GRANDMOTHERS, GRANDMOTHERS)

STEIN, SARA. ABOUT DYING. WALKER, 1974.
ILLUSTRATED BY DICK FRANK. (BL)

DRAWING THE ANALOGY BETWEEN THE DEATH OF A PET
PIGEON AND THE DEATH OF GRANDFATHER, THIS SIMPLY

WRITTEN BOOK PRESENTS DEATH IN A REALISTIC WAY,
YET IN A WAY THE YOUNG CHILD CAN UNDERSTAND,
SHOWING THAT THE BODY OF SNOW, THE PIGEON, WAS
COLD AND STIFF. BURIAL RITES FOR BOTH THE PET AND
GRANDFATHER ARE COMPARED. THE REACTION TO THE
DEATH OF THE GRANDFATHER IS EMPHASIZED, HOWEVER:
MOTHER CRIES AND JANE, A SIX-YEAR-OLD, IS ANGRY,
TEARS THINGS UP, AND CRIES. THE AUTHOR STATES
THAT ONE OF EVERY 20 CHILDREN WILL FACE THE DEATH
OF A PARENT DURING CHILDHOOD. THE BOOK GIVES
INSIGHT INTO WHAT CHILDREN MAY BE THINKING AND
FEELING, AND THROUGHOUT STRESSES HONESTY AND
COMPASSION. (DEATH, DEATH--PET, DIFF SIT--DEATH,
DIFF SIT--DEATH--PET, FAM--GRANDFATHERS,
GRANDFATHERS)

ZIM, HERBERT. LIFE AND DEATH. MORROW, 1970.
ILLUSTRATED BY RENE MARTIN. (BCB)

   ALTHOUGH NOT A PICTURE BOOK IN THE TRUE SENSE
OF THE WORD, THIS SLENDER VOLUME WILL BE USEFUL
FOR THIRD GRADERS BECAUSE OF THE DEARTH OF
MATERIAL ON THE SUBJECT. THE ILLUSTRATIONS, WHILE
NOT DYNAMIC, GIVE FACTUAL MATERIAL ABOUT
LIFESPANS IN GRAPH AND CHART FORM WHICH WILL BE
EASILY COMPREHENDED. THE MOST INTERESTING SECTION
IS THAT WHICH DISCUSSES THE CLINICAL MEANING OF
DEATH, AND DESCRIBES RIGOR MORTIS. TAKING THE
PROCEDURE ONE STEP FURTHER, THE BOOK DESCRIBES
THE EMBALMING PROCESS, BURIAL PROCEDURES, AND
FUNERAL RITUALS, SOME ANCIENT, SOME CONTEMPORARY,
AND SOME FROM CULTURES OTHER THAN THE UNITED
STATES. USEFUL BECAUSE THIS INFORMATION IS NOT
GENERALLY AVAILABLE IN A READILY ACCESSIBLE FORM
TO CHILDREN. AN EXCELLENT SOURCE TO SUPPLEMENT
THE PICTURE BOOKS WHICH DEAL WITH THE MORE
AFFECTIVE ELEMENTS INVOLVED IN FACING DEATH.
(DEATH, DIFF SIT--DEATH)

ZOLOTOW, CHARLOTTE. MY GRANDSON LEW. HARPER,
1974. ILLUSTRATED BY WILLIAM DU BOIS. (CC)

   A SMALL BOY WAKES UP IN THE NIGHT, AND TELLS
HIS MOTHER HE MISSES HIS GRANDFATHER. THEY CHAT,
AND THE LITTLE BOY RECALLS HOW HE WENT TO THE
MUSEUM WHEN HIS GRANDFATHER BABY-SAT HIM. THE
LITTLE BOY'S MOTHER IS TOUCHED BY THE MEMORIES,
AND SHE TOO REMEMBERS, GRATEFULLY, THE TIMES WHEN
GRANDPA WOULD COME TO VISIT. (DEATH, DIFF
SIT--DEATH, FAM--GRANDFATHERS, GRANDFATHERS)

DEATH--PET

BORACK, BARBARA. SOMEONE SMALL. HARPER, 1969.
ILLUSTRATED BY ANITA LOBEL. (BCB)

WHEN A NEW BABY ENTERS THE HOUSEHOLD, THE
YOUNG GIRL IN THE STORY ASKS FOR A BIRD. FLUFFY
BECOMES A GREAT FRIEND AND COMPANION, AND AS THE
NEW BABY JOYCE GROWS OLDER, FLUFFY GROWS OLDER,
TOO. THEN ONE DAY HE CATCHES A COLD AND DIES. THE
LITTLE GIRL AND HER SISTER BURY HIM UNDER A
TREE, SAY A LITTLE PRAYER, THEN GO INSIDE TO SEE
IF THEIR FATHER WILL TAKE THEM OUT FOR A RIDE IN
THEIR PAJAMAS AFTER SUPPER. ILLUSTRATES THE EBB
AND FLOW OF LIFE, BIRTH AND DEATH, IN A NATURAL
NON-TRAUMATIC WAY. (DEATH--PET, DIFF
SIT--DEATH--PET, NEW SIT--BABY)

BROWN, MARGARET. DEAD BIRD. Y. SCOTT, 1938,
1965. ILLUSTRATED BY REMY CHARLIP. (ESLC)

THIS BOOK IS A LANDMARK, SINCE IT IS PROBABLY
THE FIRST BOOK FOR YOUNG CHILDREN DEALING WITH
THE CONCEPT OF DEATH. POWERFUL ILLUSTRATIONS IN
THE GREENS, YELLOWS, AND BLUES OF NATURE
EMPHASIZE THE FOREST WHERE THE BIRD IS TO BE
BURIED. THE THEME OF NATURE IS CONTINUED AS THE
CHILDREN GATHER FERNS, FLOWERS, AND A GRAY ROCK
FOR A HEADSTONE, AND THE NOTION OF NEW LIFE IS
SUGGESTED AS THEY PLANT WHITE VIOLETS AND WILD
GERANIUMS. ON THE LAST PAGES, THE CHILDREN RETURN
TO THEIR LIFE OF GAMES AND PLAY, AND ONE SEES
THAT LIFE GOES ON, DESPITE DEATH. (DEATH--PET,
DIFF SIT--DEATH--PET)

SHECTER, BEN. ACROSS THE MEADOW. DOUBLEDAY,
1973. ILLUSTRATED BY BEN SHECTER. (LJ, NYTBR,
PBC)

IN A STORY WHICH DOES NOT MENTION DEATH OR
DYING, THE CONCEPT IS CARRIED FORWARD BY AN OLD
CAT WHO JOURNEYS INTO THE FOREST, SAYING GOOD-BYE
TO HIS FRIENDS, AND CURLING UP TO SLEEP IN AN
OLD ABANDONED CAR. THE FEELING OF DEATH IS
FINALIZED WHEN WE SEE THE OLD CAR COMPLETELY
COVERED BY CREEPING VINES, MUCH AS THE CASTLE IN
"SLEEPING BEAUTY." A SUBTLE WAY OF INDICATING
DEATH AND DECAY IS THE USE OF DEAD TWIGS IN THE
FRAMING MOTIF OF EACH PAGE, THOUGH ONE WHICH
CHILDREN MAY NOT RECOGNIZE. THE INTRODUCTION OF A

YOUNG KITTEN WHO IS SENT BACK TO THE FARM AS HIS
REPLACEMENT EMPHASIZES THE BIRTH/DEATH CYCLE.
(DEATH--PET, DIFF SIT--DEATH--PET, DIFF SIT--OLD
AGE, OLD AGE)

STEIN, SARA. ABOUT DYING. WALKER, 1974.
ILLUSTRATED BY DICK FRANK. (BL)

DRAWING THE ANALOGY BETWEEN THE DEATH OF A PET
PIGEON AND THE DEATH OF GRANDFATHER, THIS SIMPLY
WRITTEN BOOK PRESENTS DEATH IN A REALISTIC WAY,
YET IN A WAY THE YOUNG CHILD CAN UNDERSTAND,
SHOWING THAT THE BODY OF SNOW, THE PIGEON, WAS
COLD AND STIFF. BURIAL RITES FOR BOTH THE PET AND
GRANDFATHER ARE COMPARED. THE REACTION TO THE
DEATH OF THE GRANDFATHER IS EMPHASIZED, HOWEVER:
MOTHER CRIES AND JANE, A SIX-YEAR-OLD, IS ANGRY,
TEARS THINGS UP, AND CRIES. THE AUTHOR STATES
THAT ONE OF EVERY 20 CHILDREN WILL FACE THE DEATH
OF A PARENT DURING CHILDHOOD. THE BOOK GIVES
INSIGHT INTO WHAT CHILDREN MAY BE THINKING AND
FEELING, AND THROUGHOUT STRESSES HONESTY AND
COMPASSION. (DEATH, DEATH--PET, DIFF SIT--DEATH,
DIFF SIT--DEATH--PET, FAM--GRANDFATHERS,
GRANDFATHERS)

STULL, EDITH. MY TURTLE DIED TODAY. HOLT, 1964.
ILLUSTRATED BY MAMORU FUNAI. (ESLC)

THIS SLOWLY-PACED BOOK ABOUT THE DEATH OF ONE
PET ENDS WITH THE BIRTH OF KITTENS TO PATTY,
ANOTHER PET, SO THE STING OF LOSS IS REMOVED ON
THE ONE HAND, AND THE CYCLE OF LIFE IS EMPHASIZED
ON THE OTHER. THE REALISTIC, COLORFUL
ILLUSTRATIONS CONTRIBUTE TO THE URBAN SETTING,
YET MAMORU FUNAI HAS USED EARTH COLORS PLUS
UPBEAT ORANGES AND REDS TO FURTHER THE ATMOSPHERE
OF LIFE, RATHER THAN DEATH, MAKING THIS A
NON-THREATENING FIRST BOOK FOR THE YOUNG.
(DEATH--PET, DIFF SIT--DEATH--PET)

VIORST, JUDITH. THE TENTH GOOD THING ABOUT
BARNEY. ATHENEUM, 1973. ILLUSTRATED BY ERIK
BLEGVAD. (CC)

AN ABSOLUTELY CHARMING, JUST RIGHT BOOK THAT
DEALS WITH THE DEATH OF A CAT. MADE SO BY AN
UNDERSTANDING DAD, WHO SAID THAT IT WAS OK TO BE
SAD, AND AN INGENIOUS MOTHER WHO SUGGESTED THAT
THE LITTLE BOY SHOULD TRY TO THINK OF TEN "GOOD

THINGS" ABOUT BARNEY THAT THEY COULD TALK ABOUT
AT THE FUNERAL. TURNS OUT THAT THE TENTH GOOD
THING WAS THAT BARNEY'S GRAVE WAS A GOOD PLACE TO
GROW SOME FLOWERS, AND THAT BARNEY'S ROLE, AFTER
DEATH, WAS TO HELP THE FLOWERS GROW.
(DEATH--PET, DIFF SIT--DEATH--PET)

WARBURG, SANDOL. GROWING TIME. HOUGHTON, 1969.
ILLUSTRATED BY LEONARD WEISGARD. (ESLC)

   MEANT TO BE READ ALOUD, THE BOOK EMPHASIZES
NEW LIFE, AND THE "GROWING TIME" IS FOR THE
PUPPY, BEFORE IT CAN FILL THE VOID LEFT BY THE
OLDER DOG WHO DIES. JAMIE IS THE YOUNG BOY WHO IS
COMFORTED IN TURN BY HIS MOTHER, UNCLE JOHN, AND
HIS GRANDFATHER, EACH OF WHOM GIVE A DIFFERENT
EXPLANATION OF DEATH, AND EACH ANSWER HELPS WITH
UNDERSTANDING THE FACT OF DEATH. (DEATH--PET,
DIFF SIT--DEATH--PET)

DENTIST

ROCKWELL, HARLOW. MY DENTIST. MORROW, 1975.
ILLUSTRATED BY HARLOW ROCKWELL. (BL)

   FEAR OF THE DENTIST IS NOT CONFINED TO
CHILDREN, FOR MANY ADULTS GO THROUGH LIFE WITH AN
IRRATIONAL STATE OF APPREHENSION ABOUT SUCH
VISITS. EARLY EXPOSURE TO NON-THREATENING
SITUATIONS SUCH AS THE ONES PICTURED HERE SHOULD
DO MUCH TO REDUCE THESE FEARS, FOR THE ATTRACTIVE
PIG-TAILED YOUNGSTER IS SHOWN AS INTERESTED,
SMILING AT TIMES, AND THOROUGHLY COMFORTABLE
THROUGHOUT THE PROCESS OF TEETH CLEANING. WHILE
THE INSTRUMENTS (I.E., THE PICKS AND PROBES.) MAY
LOOK MENACING, THERE IS MUCH TO BE SAID FOR
SHOWING THEM IN DETAIL ALONG WITH THE X-RAY
CAMERA AND THE DRILLS. FEAR OF THE UNKNOWN IS
PERHAPS MORE THREATENING THAN FEAR OF THE KNOWN.
(DENTIST, DIFF SIT--DENTIST, EMOTIONS--FEAR, FEAR)

DIFF SIT--ADOPTION

CAINES, JEANNETTE. ABBY. HARPER, 1973.
ILLUSTRATED BY STEVEN KELLOGG. (CC)

   ABBY IS A ROUND-FACED BUNDLE OF CURIOSITY, WHO
ALWAYS WANTS TO HEAR THE STORY OF HER ADOPTION,
OVER AND OVER AGAIN. WHEN SHE PESTERS HER BROTHER
KEVIN, EMOTIONS SPILL OVER, WITH ABBY CRYING AND

BROTHER FEELING SORRY. THROUGHOUT THE STORY, THE
ILLUSTRATOR HAS PICTURED A COMFORTABLE HOME
FILLED WITH LOVE AND CONCERN. KEVIN PROMISES TO
TAKE ABBY TO SCHOOL FOR SHOW AND TELL, AND HIS
PRIDE IN HER IS VERY OBVIOUS. USEFUL IN VARIOUS
WAYS CONCERNING ADOPTION--THE OPEN CURIOSITY OF
THE CHILD, THE OPEN WILLINGNESS TO TALK OF IT,
THE PRIDE, IN THIS CASE, OF BEING ADOPTED.
(ADOPTION, BROTHERS & SISTERS, DIFF
SIT--ADOPTION, FAM--BROTHERS & SISTERS)

LAPSLEY, SUSAN. I AM ADOPTED. BRADBURY, 1974.
ILLUSTRATED BY MICHAEL CHARLTON. (CCB-B, TLS)

   DELICATE WATERCOLORS TELL MUCH OF THIS STORY,
BUT THE SPARSE TEXT IN EXTRA LARGE TYPE PROVIDES
A BONUS TO THE THEME: "ADOPTION MEANS BELONGING."
IT IS A SIMPLY TOLD STORY WHICH SHOULD BE
REASSURING TO ADOPTED CHILDREN, BUT WILL HELP ALL
CHILDREN UNDERSTAND THE CONCEPT. THE PAINTINGS
ILLUSTRATE WELL A MIDDLE-CLASS, WHITE FAMILY
SHARING PETS, CRAFTS, COOKERY, AND CAR REPAIR.
(ADOPTION, DIFF SIT--ADOPTION)

DIFF SIT--ADOPTION--INTER

BUNIN, SHERRY. IS THAT YOUR SISTER?. PANTHEON,
1976.

   THIS IS SIX-YEAR-OLD CATHERINE BUNIN'S OWN
STORY AND THAT OF HER SISTER CARLA, IN A BOOK
ABOUT INTERRACIAL ADOPTION. OBVIOUSLY PROUD TO BE
LOVED AND CARED FOR BY HER FAMILY WHICH INCLUDES
TWO BROTHERS, CATHERINE RELATES THE STORY OF HER
ADOPTION BY ANSWERING MANY OF THE QUESTIONS PUT
TO HER BY CHILDREN AND ADULTS ALIKE. SHE TACKLES
EVEN VERY SUBSTANTIVE ANSWERS AS SHE DESCRIBES
THE WAY IN WHICH THE SOCIAL WORKER VISITED THEIR
HOME, AND THE CULMINATION OF THE PROCEEDINGS IN
THE FAMILY COURT. FILLED WITH MANY EXCELLENT,
INFORMAL PHOTOGRAPHS OF FAMILY LIFE, THIS SLIM
VOLUME WILL BE HELPFUL TO PARENTS ANTICIPATING OR
CONTEMPLATING THIS DIFFICULT SITUATION.
(ADOPTION--INTERRACIAL, BROTHERS & SISTERS, DIFF
SIT--ADOPTION--INTERRACIAL, FAM--BROTHERS &
SISTERS)

DIFF SIT--DEATH

BARTOLI, JENNIFER. NONNA. HARVEY, 1975.

ILLUSTRATED BY JOAN DRESCHER. (BL)

AN INTERESTING, NON-THREATENING BOOK ABOUT THE
DEATH OF GRANDMOTHER TREATED FROM THE POINT OF
VIEW OF MEMORIES OF LIFE BEFORE HER DEATH AND
LIFE SEVERAL MONTHS LATER. NONNA'S COOKIES ARE
ONE MOTIF THAT REPEATS THROUGHOUT THE BOOK. IN
MEMORY, THE CHILDREN THINK ABOUT SOUP AND COOKIES
WITH NONNA ON SATURDAYS. ON THE DAY OF THE
FUNERAL, MOTHER BAKES NONNA'S COOKIES AND THE
CHILDREN EAT THEM FOR BREAKFAST, AND SIX MONTHS
LATER AT CHRISTMAS TIME, THE YOUNGEST DAUGHTER
BAKES THEM FOR THE ENTIRE FAMILY. USEFUL BECAUSE
ALTHOUGH IT SHOWS THE FUNERAL AND THE GRAVESIDE
SERVICE, IT ALSO USES A DEVICE TO SHOW HOW THE
LIVING COPE BY PERFORMING DAILY ROUTINES OF LIFE.
(DEATH, DIFF SIT--DEATH, FAM--GRANDMOTHERS,
GRANDMOTHERS)

DE PAOLA, TOMIE. NANA UPSTAIRS AND NANA
DOWNSTAIRS. PUTNAM, 1973. ILLUSTRATED BY TOMIE
DE PAOLA. (BL)

IN AN EASY BOOK FORMAT WITH LARGE PRINT AND
PICTURES ON EVERY PAGE, LITTLE TOMMY IS SHOWN IN
A CHARMING RELATIONSHIP WITH HIS 94-YEAR-OLD
GREAT-GRANDMOTHER, WHO IS NANA UPSTAIRS. HE
LEARNED THE MEANING OF DEATH ON THE DAY HIS
MOTHER TOLD HIM THAT NANA UPSTAIRS WOULD NOT BE
HERE ANY MORE, EXCEPT IN HIS MEMORY. TOMMY THINKS
OF HER WHEN HE SEES A FALLING STAR, AND THE BOOK
ENDS WITH HIM AS A YOUNG MAN, AGAIN SEEING A
FALLING STAR, AND THINKING OF BOTH GRANDMOTHERS.
A GENTLE, THOUGHTFUL WAY TO EXPLAIN DEATH TO THE
VERY YOUNG. (DEATH, DIFF SIT--DEATH,
FAM--GRANDMOTHERS, FAM--GREAT-GRANDMOTHERS,
GRANDMOTHERS, GREAT-GRANDMOTHERS)

HAZEN, NANCY. GROWNUPS CRY TOO. LOLLIPOP, 1973.
ILLUSTRATED BY NANCY HAZEN.

IN THIS STARKLY ILLUSTRATED BOOK OF BLACK AND
WHITE LINE DRAWINGS ON OLIVE GREEN PAPER, THE
AUTHOR-ILLUSTRATOR HAS GIVEN A VERY LOW-KEY,
REALISTIC EXPLANATION OF THE EMOTIONS THAT MAY
MAKE GROWN-UPS CRY. PICTURES AND TEXT TELL THE
READER THAT SADNESS, MADNESS, FATIGUE, AND FEAR
SOMETIMES TRIGGER TEARS IN ADULTS. USEFUL TO SHOW
CHILDREN THAT ADULTS ALSO HAVE PROBLEMS.
PARTICULARLY USEFUL BECAUSE IT SHOWS A MAN IN

TEARS ALSO. (DEATH, DIFF SIT--DEATH, EMOTIONS)

HURLIMANN, BETTINA. BARRY. HARCOURT, 1967.
ILLUSTRATED BY PAUL NUSSBAUMER. (ESLC)

   CHILDREN WILL GRASP THE MEANING OF COURAGE
WHEN THEY HEAR THIS STORY, SET IN SWITZERLAND, OF
A ST. BERNARD RESCUE DOG. OF THE MANY RESCUES
THE DOG MADE, PERHAPS THE STORY OF HIS FINDING A
SMALL GIRL AND CARRYING HER ON HIS BACK TO THE
HOSPICE WHERE THE MONKS LIVED IS THE MOST
MEMORABLE. CHILDREN WILL ALSO EMPATHIZE WITH THIS
TRUE STORY, AS BARRY MEETS WITH AN ACCIDENT
WHICH EVENTUALLY LEADS TO HIS DEATH. THE
CONTINUITY OF BIRTH, LIFE, AND DEATH, AS YOUNG
ST. BERNARDS ARE TRAINED AS RESCUERS, ENLARGES
THE SCOPE OF THIS STORY. (BRAVERY,
EMOTIONS--BRAVERY, DEATH, DIFF SIT--DEATH)

LEE, VIRGINIA. MAGIC MOTH. SEABURY, 1972.
ILLUSTRATED BY RICHARD CUFFARI. (BCB)

   ANOTHER BOOK WHICH FALLS OUT OF THE STRICT
CATEGORY OF A PICTURE BOOK, THIS TITLE IS
INCLUDED BECAUSE IT IS UNIQUE: IT TELLS THE
LOVING STORY OF THE DEATH OF A YOUNG CHILD AT
HOME. THE MAGIC MOTH ENTERS THE STORY JUST WHEN
MARYANNE STOPS BREATHING: "A HUGE WHITE MOTH ROSE
GENTLY FROM SOMEWHERE NEAR THE BED AND FLEW UP
TO THE CEILING." THIS ANALOGOUS DESCRIPTION ACTS
AS A BRIDGE BETWEEN THE COLD FACT OF DEATH, AND
THE WARM SPIRIT OF THE LITTLE GIRL AND HER
RELATIONSHIP WITHIN THE FAMILY. ALMOST EVERYONE
IS CURIOUS ABOUT CERTAIN ASPECTS OF DEATH, AND
THE AUTHOR HAS PROVIDED REALISTIC DIALOG AND
FEELINGS WHEN SHE DESCRIBES THE THOUGHTS OF A
YOUNGER BROTHER: "MARK-O, WHO WAS FULL OF
QUESTIONS, COULD NOT THINK JUST EXACTLY WHAT IT
WAS HE REALLY WANTED TO KNOW, SO HE TOO WAS
QUIET." THUS VIRGINIA LEE HAS WRITTEN A
COMPLETELY PLAUSIBLE STORY, BUT ONE TO WHICH
SECOND AND THIRD GRADERS CAN REALLY RESONATE.
(BROTHERS & SISTERS, DEATH, DIFF SIT--DEATH,
FAM--BROTHERS & SISTERS)

MILES, MISKA. ANNIE AND THE OLD ONE. LITTLE,
1971. ILLUSTRATED BY PETER PARNALL. (ESLC)

   GOLDEN DESERT COLORS SPIKED WITH BLACK AND
WHITE LINE DRAWINGS CONTRIBUTE TO THE STARK

FEELINGS OF IMPENDING DEATH IN THIS DIALOG
BETWEEN A NAVAJO GRANDMOTHER AND HER SMALL
GRANDCHILD. ONE EVENING WHEN, SYMBOLICALLY, THE
FIRE IS DYING IN THE HOGAN, THE OLD ONE ANNOUNCED
THAT SHE WOULD GO TO MOTHER EARTH WHEN THE RUG
ON THE LOOM WAS FINISHED. ANNIE UNDERSTOOD,
ALTHOUGH SHE DID NOT UNDERSTAND WHY HER
GRANDMOTHER KNEW SHE WAS GOING TO DIE. IN THE
DAYS THAT FOLLOWED ANNIE DREAMED UP SCHEMES TO
DELAY THE COMPLETION OF THE RUG, AND IT IS ONLY
WHEN GRANDMOTHER EXPLAINS THE INEVITABILITY OF
DEATH IN ALL OF NATURE THAT ANNIE ACCEPTS THE
CONCEPT. INTERESTING VIEW OF DEATH FOR, WHILE A
VERY REALISTIC BOOK, IT RETAINS THE MYSTICAL
OUTLOOK OF THE NAVAJO WAY OF LIFE. (DEATH, DIFF
SIT--DEATH, FAM--GRANDMOTHERS, GRANDMOTHERS)

STEIN, SARA. ABOUT DYING. WALKER, 1974.
ILLUSTRATED BY DICK FRANK.   (BL)

   DRAWING THE ANALOGY BETWEEN THE DEATH OF A PET
PIGEON AND THE DEATH OF GRANDFATHER, THIS SIMPLY
WRITTEN BOOK PRESENTS DEATH IN A REALISTIC WAY,
YET IN A WAY THE YOUNG CHILD CAN UNDERSTAND,
SHOWING THAT THE BODY OF SNOW, THE PIGEON, WAS
COLD AND STIFF. BURIAL RITES FOR BOTH THE PET AND
GRANDFATHER ARE COMPARED. THE REACTION TO THE
DEATH OF THE GRANDFATHER IS EMPHASIZED, HOWEVER:
MOTHER CRIES AND JANE, A SIX-YEAR-OLD, IS ANGRY,
TEARS THINGS UP, AND CRIES. THE AUTHOR STATES
THAT ONE OF EVERY 20 CHILDREN WILL FACE THE DEATH
OF A PARENT DURING CHILDHOOD. THE BOOK GIVES
INSIGHT INTO WHAT CHILDREN MAY BE THINKING AND
FEELING, AND THROUGHOUT STRESSES HONESTY AND
COMPASSION. (DEATH, DEATH--PET, DIFF SIT--DEATH,
DIFF SIT--DEATH--PET, FAM--GRANDFATHERS,
GRANDFATHERS)

ZIM, HERBERT. LIFE AND DEATH. MORROW, 1970.
ILLUSTRATED BY RENE MARTIN.   (BCB)

   ALTHOUGH NOT A PICTURE BOOK IN THE TRUE SENSE
OF THE WORD, THIS SLENDER VOLUME WILL BE USEFUL
FOR THIRD GRADERS BECAUSE OF THE DEARTH OF
MATERIAL ON THE SUBJECT. THE ILLUSTRATIONS, WHILE
NOT DYNAMIC, GIVE FACTUAL MATERIAL ABOUT
LIFESPANS IN GRAPH AND CHART FORM WHICH WILL BE
EASILY COMPREHENDED. THE MOST INTERESTING SECTION
IS THAT WHICH DISCUSSES THE CLINICAL MEANING OF
DEATH, AND DESCRIBES RIGOR MORTIS. TAKING THE

PROCEDURE ONE STEP FURTHER, THE BOOK DESCRIBES
THE EMBALMING PROCESS, BURIAL PROCEDURES, AND
FUNERAL RITUALS, SOME ANCIENT, SOME CONTEMPORARY,
AND SOME FROM CULTURES OTHER THAN THE UNITED
STATES. USEFUL BECAUSE THIS INFORMATION IS NOT
GENERALLY AVAILABLE IN A READILY ACCESSIBLE FORM
TO CHILDREN. AN EXCELLENT SOURCE TO SUPPLEMENT
THE PICTURE BOOKS WHICH DEAL WITH THE MORE
AFFECTIVE ELEMENTS INVOLVED IN FACING DEATH.
(DEATH, DIFF SIT--DEATH)

ZOLOTOW, CHARLOTTE. MY GRANDSON LEW. HARPER,
1974.   ILLUSTRATED BY WILLIAM DU BOIS. (CC)

   A SMALL BOY WAKES UP IN THE NIGHT, AND TELLS
HIS MOTHER HE MISSES HIS GRANDFATHER. THEY CHAT,
AND THE LITTLE BOY RECALLS HOW HE WENT TO THE
MUSEUM WHEN HIS GRANDFATHER BABY-SAT HIM. THE
LITTLE BOY'S MOTHER IS TOUCHED BY THE MEMORIES,
AND SHE TOO REMEMBERS, GRATEFULLY, THE TIMES WHEN
GRANDPA WOULD COME TO VISIT. (DEATH, DIFF
SIT--DEATH, FAM--GRANDFATHERS, GRANDFATHERS)

DIFF SIT--DEATH--PET

   BORACK, BARBARA. SOMEONE SMALL. HARPER, 1969.
   ILLUSTRATED BY ANITA LOBEL. (BCB)

   WHEN A NEW BABY ENTERS THE HOUSEHOLD, THE
YOUNG GIRL IN THE STORY ASKS FOR A BIRD. FLUFFY
BECOMES A GREAT FRIEND AND COMPANION, AND AS THE
NEW BABY JOYCE GROWS OLDER, FLUFFY GROWS OLDER,
TOO. THEN ONE DAY HE CATCHES A COLD AND DIES. THE
LITTLE GIRL AND HER SISTER BURY HIM UNDER A
TREE, SAY A LITTLE PRAYER, THEN GO INSIDE TO SEE
IF THEIR FATHER WILL TAKE THEM OUT FOR A RIDE IN
THEIR PAJAMAS AFTER SUPPER. ILLUSTRATES THE EBB
AND FLOW OF LIFE, BIRTH AND DEATH, IN A NATURAL
NON-TRAUMATIC WAY. (DEATH--PET, DIFF
SIT--DEATH--PET, NEW SIT--BABY)

BROWN, MARGARET. DEAD BIRD. Y. SCOTT, 1938,
1965.   ILLUSTRATED BY REMY CHARLIP. (ESLC)

   THIS BOOK IS A LANDMARK, SINCE IT IS PROBABLY
THE FIRST BOOK FOR YOUNG CHILDREN DEALING WITH
THE CONCEPT OF DEATH. POWERFUL ILLUSTRATIONS IN
THE GREENS, YELLOWS, AND BLUES OF NATURE
EMPHASIZE THE FOREST WHERE THE BIRD IS TO BE
BURIED. THE THEME OF NATURE IS CONTINUED AS THE

CHILDREN GATHER FERNS, FLOWERS, AND A GRAY ROCK
FOR A HEADSTONE, AND THE NOTION OF NEW LIFE IS
SUGGESTED AS THEY PLANT WHITE VIOLETS AND WILD
GERANIUMS. ON THE LAST PAGES, THE CHILDREN RETURN
TO THEIR LIFE OF GAMES AND PLAY, AND ONE SEES
THAT LIFE GOES ON, DESPITE DEATH. (DEATH--PET,
DIFF SIT--DEATH--PET)

SHECTER, BEN. ACROSS THE MEADOW. DOUBLEDAY,
1973. ILLUSTRATED BY BEN SHECTER. (LJ, NYTBR,
PBC)

   IN A STORY WHICH DOES NOT MENTION DEATH OR
DYING, THE CONCEPT IS CARRIED FORWARD BY AN OLD
CAT WHO JOURNEYS INTO THE FOREST, SAYING GOOD-BYE
TO HIS FRIENDS, AND CURLING UP TO SLEEP IN AN
OLD ABANDONED CAR. THE FEELING OF DEATH IS
FINALIZED WHEN WE SEE THE OLD CAR COMPLETELY
COVERED BY CREEPING VINES, MUCH AS THE CASTLE IN
"SLEEPING BEAUTY." A SUBTLE WAY OF INDICATING
DEATH AND DECAY IS THE USE OF DEAD TWIGS IN THE
FRAMING MOTIF OF EACH PAGE, THOUGH ONE WHICH
CHILDREN MAY NOT RECOGNIZE. THE INTRODUCTION OF A
YOUNG KITTEN WHO IS SENT BACK TO THE FARM AS HIS
REPLACEMENT EMPHASIZES THE BIRTH/DEATH CYCLE.
(DEATH--PET, DIFF SIT--DEATH--PET, DIFF SIT--OLD
AGE, OLD AGE)

STEIN, SARA. ABOUT DYING. WALKER, 1974.
ILLUSTRATED BY DICK FRANK. (BL)

   DRAWING THE ANALOGY BETWEEN THE DEATH OF A PET
PIGEON AND THE DEATH OF GRANDFATHER, THIS SIMPLY
WRITTEN BOOK PRESENTS DEATH IN A REALISTIC WAY,
YET IN A WAY THE YOUNG CHILD CAN UNDERSTAND,
SHOWING THAT THE BODY OF SNOW, THE PIGEON, WAS
COLD AND STIFF. BURIAL RITES FOR BOTH THE PET AND
GRANDFATHER ARE COMPARED. THE REACTION TO THE
DEATH OF THE GRANDFATHER IS EMPHASIZED, HOWEVER:
MOTHER CRIES AND JANE, A SIX-YEAR-OLD, IS ANGRY,
TEARS THINGS UP, AND CRIES. THE AUTHOR STATES
THAT ONE OF EVERY 20 CHILDREN WILL FACE THE DEATH
OF A PARENT DURING CHILDHOOD. THE BOOK GIVES
INSIGHT INTO WHAT CHILDREN MAY BE THINKING AND
FEELING, AND THROUGHOUT STRESSES HONESTY AND
COMPASSION. (DEATH, DEATH--PET, DIFF SIT--DEATH,
DIFF SIT--DEATH--PET, FAM--GRANDFATHERS,
GRANDFATHERS)

STULL, EDITH. MY TURTLE DIED TODAY. HOLT, 1964.

ILLUSTRATED BY MAMORU FUNAI.   (ESLC)

THIS SLOWLY-PACED BOOK ABOUT THE DEATH OF ONE
PET ENDS WITH THE BIRTH OF KITTENS TO PATTY,
ANOTHER PET, SO THE STING OF LOSS IS REMOVED ON
THE ONE HAND, AND THE CYCLE OF LIFE IS EMPHASIZED
ON THE OTHER. THE REALISTIC, COLORFUL
ILLUSTRATIONS CONTRIBUTE TO THE URBAN SETTING,
YET MAMORU FUNAI HAS USED EARTH COLORS PLUS
UPBEAT ORANGES AND REDS TO FURTHER THE ATMOSPHERE
OF LIFE, RATHER THAN DEATH, MAKING THIS A
NON-THREATENING FIRST BOOK FOR THE YOUNG.
(DEATH--PET, DIFF SIT--DEATH--PET)

VIORST, JUDITH. THE TENTH GOOD THING ABOUT
BARNEY. ATHENEUM, 1973. ILLUSTRATED BY ERIK
BLEGVAD. (CC)

AN ABSOLUTELY CHARMING, JUST RIGHT BOOK THAT
DEALS WITH THE DEATH OF A CAT. MADE SO BY AN
UNDERSTANDING DAD, WHO SAID THAT IT WAS OK TO BE
SAD, AND AN INGENIOUS MOTHER WHO SUGGESTED THAT
THE LITTLE BOY SHOULD TRY TO THINK OF TEN "GOOD
THINGS" ABOUT BARNEY THAT THEY COULD TALK ABOUT
AT THE FUNERAL. TURNS OUT THAT THE TENTH GOOD
THING WAS THAT BARNEY'S GRAVE WAS A GOOD PLACE TO
GROW SOME FLOWERS, AND THAT BARNEY'S ROLE, AFTER
DEATH, WAS TO HELP THE FLOWERS GROW.
(DEATH--PET, DIFF SIT--DEATH--PET)

WARBURG, SANDOL. GROWING TIME. HOUGHTON, 1969.
ILLUSTRATED BY LEONARD WEISGARD. (ESLC)

MEANT TO BE READ ALOUD, THE BOOK EMPHASIZES
NEW LIFE, AND THE "GROWING TIME" IS FOR THE
PUPPY, BEFORE IT CAN FILL THE VOID LEFT BY THE
OLDER DOG WHO DIES. JAMIE IS THE YOUNG BOY WHO IS
COMFORTED IN TURN BY HIS MOTHER, UNCLE JOHN, AND
HIS GRANDFATHER, EACH OF WHOM GIVE A DIFFERENT
EXPLANATION OF DEATH, AND EACH ANSWER HELPS WITH
UNDERSTANDING THE FACT OF DEATH. (DEATH--PET,
DIFF SIT--DEATH--PET)

DIFF SIT--DENTIST

ROCKWELL, HARLOW. MY DENTIST. MORROW, 1975.
ILLUSTRATED BY HARLOW ROCKWELL. (BL)

FEAR OF THE DENTIST IS NOT CONFINED TO
CHILDREN, FOR MANY ADULTS GO THROUGH LIFE WITH AN

IRRATIONAL STATE OF APPREHENSION ABOUT SUCH
VISITS. EARLY EXPOSURE TO NON-THREATENING
SITUATIONS SUCH AS THE ONES PICTURED HERE SHOULD
DO MUCH TO REDUCE THESE FEARS, FOR THE ATTRACTIVE
PIG-TAILED YOUNGSTER IS SHOWN AS INTERESTED,
SMILING AT TIMES, AND THOROUGHLY COMFORTABLE
THROUGHOUT THE PROCESS OF TEETH CLEANING. WHILE
THE INSTRUMENTS (I.E., THE PICKS AND PROBES) MAY
LOOK MENACING, THERE IS MUCH TO BE SAID FOR
SHOWING THEM IN DETAIL ALONG WITH THE X-RAY
CAMERA AND THE DRILLS. FEAR OF THE UNKNOWN IS
PERHAPS MORE THREATENING THAN FEAR OF THE KNOWN.
(DENTIST, DIFF SIT--DENTIST, EMOTIONS--FEAR, FEAR)

DIFF SIT--DIVORCE

BALDWIN, ANNE. JENNY'S REVENGE. FOUR, 1974.
ILLUSTRATED BY EMILY MC CULLY. (CCB-B)

JENNY HATES HER BABY-SITTER, AND EXPRESSES
HIDDEN ANGER TOWARD HER WORKING MOTHER WHO
APPARENTLY HAS WORKED ONLY SINCE A RECENT
DIVORCE. AFTER TRYING A NUMBER OF PLOYS TO FORCE
THE BABY-SITTER TO QUIT, SHE FINDS COMRADESHIP
WITH MRS. CRAMIE WHEN THEY DISCOVER A COMMON
INTEREST IN THE CIRCUS. A REALISTIC LOOK AT A
CHILD WHO NEEDS AND WANTS ATTENTION FROM HER
MOTHER. (ANGER, DIFF SIT--DIVORCE, DIFF SIT--ONE
PARENT, DIVORCE, EMOTIONS--ANGER, FAM--MOTHERS
WORKING, MOTHERS WORKING, ONE PARENT)

BLUE, ROSE. A MONTH OF SUNDAYS. WATTS, 1972.
ILLUSTRATED BY TED LEWIN. (CC)

IT WAS HARD HAVING A DAD WHO LOVED YOU ON
SUNDAYS WHEN HE USED TO LOVE YOU EVERY DAY. THIS
COMMENT EPITOMIZES THE UNHAPPY FEELINGS JEFFREY
HAS WHEN HE AND HIS MOTHER MOVE INTO AN APARTMENT
IN THE CITY. WHEN JEFF AND HIS DAD GET TOGETHER
IN THE OLD NEIGHBORHOOD, THINGS REALLY DON'T WORK
OUT. THE RELATIVES TALK AROUND HIM AS IF HE
WEREN'T PRESENT IN THE ROOM. THE MOTHER OF JEFF'S
BEST FRIEND MATTHEW TURNS OUT TO BE A GOOD
STRONG FRIEND WHO EXPLAINS SOME OF THE PROBLEMS
THAT JEFF'S MOM IS HAVING. GETTING INVOLVED IN A
GROUP PROJECT AT SCHOOL AND PARTICIPATING IN A
BIG BLOCK PARTY OVERFLOWING WITH DELICIOUS ETHNIC
FOODS, MUSIC, AND PEOPLE SEEM TO BE THE TWO
THINGS THAT BODE WELL FOR JEFF'S FUTURE. (DIFF
SIT--DIVORCE, DIVORCE, FAM--ONE PARENT, ONE

PARENT)

GARDNER, RICHARD. BOYS AND GIRLS BOOK ABOUT
DIVORCE. SCIENCE, 1970. ILLUSTRATED BY ALFRED
LOWENHEIM. (ESLC)

UNIQUE BOOK WRITTEN BY A PSYCHIATRIST FOR BOYS
AND GIRLS GOING THROUGH OR HAVING GONE THROUGH A
DIVORCE IN THE FAMILY. ILLUSTRATED WITH
CARTOON-LIKE FIGURES, THE BOOK IS FRANK AND
PRACTICAL ABOUT MATTERS SUCH AS HOW TO GET ALONG
BETTER WITH YOUR DIVORCED PARENTS, STEPFATHER,
AND STEPMOTHER. VERY REASSURING FOR THE CHILD WHO
HAS FEARS, GUILT, AND PROBLEMS IN THE DIVORCE
SITUATION. SOME OF THE STATEMENTS MAY BE
CONTROVERSIAL, SO IT WOULD BE WISE FOR AN ADULT
TO BE AWARE OF THE CONTENT OF THE BOOK BEFORE
SHARING IT WITH A CHILD. (DIFF SIT--DIVORCE,
DIVORCE)

GOFF, BETH. WHERE IS DADDY?. BEACON, 1969.
ILLUSTRATED BY SUSAN PERL. (CCB-B, JMF)

ALTHOUGH THE CHILD PORTRAYED IN THIS STORY IS
A VERY YOUNG PRESCHOOLER, AND A GIRL, A
FIFTH-GRADE BOY TUCKED THE COPY OF THIS BOOK IN
HIS DESK BECAUSE IT APPARENTLY FILLED A NEED IN
HIS LIFE. AT ONE POINT THE TEXT SAYS "THE ANGER
BETWEEN THEM (HER PARENTS) MADE A PAIN INSIDE
HER, AND SHE CRIED AND CRIED." IN THE CLASSIC
ATTITUDE OF MANY CHILDREN ABOUT DIVORCE, JANIE
FEELS THAT HER OCCASIONAL ANGER TOWARD HER DAD
CAUSED THE DIVORCE. AND SHE IS AFRAID TO SAY
ANYTHING UNPLEASANT TO HER MOTHER, WHO TAKES A
JOB, FOR FEAR HER MOTHER MIGHT ALSO ABANDON HER.
HAS AN EXCELLENT PAGE OF EXPLANATION BY AN M.D.
FROM THE CHILDREN'S PSYCHIATRIC HOSPITAL AT THE
UNIVERSITY OF MICHIGAN. (DIFF SIT--DIVORCE,
DIVORCE, EMOTIONS--GUILT, GUILT)

KINDRED, WENDY. LUCKY WILMA. DIAL, 1973.
ILLUSTRATED BY WENDY KINDRED. (LJ)

BEGINNING WITH A SERIES OF SATURDAYS WILMA AND
"CHARLIE," HER DAD, WALK TO MUSEUMS AND ZOOS,
AND FATHER AND DAUGHTER HAVE A UNIFORMLY GLUM
EXPRESSION. THE NEXT EIGHTEEN PAGES DEAL WITH
JOYOUS PICTURIZATION OF CLIMBING, JUMPING,
PIGGYBACKING, DANCING, AND REVELRY WITH THE
PIGEONS IN THE PARK. OBVIOUSLY THIS WAS THE

NEATEST SATURDAY THEY HAD SPENT TOGETHER, AND
THEY HUG AS THEY SEPARATE AND DAD SAYS: "WE'VE
GOT ALL THE SATURDAYS IN THE WORLD." CURIOUSLY
ENOUGH THE WORD DIVORCE IS NOT MENTIONED. WITH
VERY LITTLE TEXT, THIS BOOK CONVEYS THAT INDEED
WILMA IS LUCKY TO HAVE A WONDERFUL RELATIONSHIP
WITH HER FATHER. (DIFF SIT--DIVORCE, DIFF
SIT--ONE PARENT, DIVORCE, FAM--FATHERS, FATHERS,
ONE PARENT)

LEXAU, JOAN. EMILY AND THE KLUNKY BABY AND THE
NEXT DOOR DOG. DIAL, 1972. ILLUSTRATED BY MARTHA
ALEXANDER. (CC)

   CHARMINGLY ILLUSTRATED, THE BOOK IS A SLIGHT
EPISODE OF A SMALL GIRL ATTEMPTING TO RUN AWAY TO
HER FATHER, WHO LIVES IN AN APARTMENT NEAR BY.
EMILY FEELS HER MOTHER WAS IGNORING HER WHEN
DOING HER INCOME TAXES AND DIDN'T WANT TO BE
BOTHERED. EMILY TAKES THE BABY AND ALMOST GETS
LOST BUT INSTEAD GOES AROUND THE BLOCK (BECAUSE
SHE'S NOT ALLOWED TO CROSS THE STREET)--AND MAKES
IT HOME TO A LOVING MOTHER WHO THINKS SHE'S OUT
PLAYING. (DIFF SIT--DIVORCE, DIFF SIT--ONE
PARENT, DIVORCE, FAM--MOTHERS, FAM--ONE PARENT,
MOTHERS, ONE PARENT)

LEXAU, JOAN. ME DAY. DIAL, 1971. ILLUSTRATED BY
ROBERT WEAVER. (BCB)

   "ME DAY" IS RAFER'S BIRTHDAY, BUT IN A SLUM
FAMILY WHERE THERE IS NO MONEY FOR PRESENTS AND
THE TV IS BROKEN, WHAT MAKES A BOY HAPPY? THROUGH
THE TEXT WE LEARN THAT THE FATHER IS NOT AT
HOME, THE PARENTS BEING DIVORCED, APPARENTLY
BECAUSE THE FATHER COULD NOT FIND WORK. RAFER'S
DAY IS MADE PERFECT WHEN HIS FATHER SHOWS UP TO
SPEND THE ENTIRE DAY WITH HIM IN THE PARK, WITH
ICE CREAM AND HOT DOGS. (DIFF SIT--DIVORCE,
DIVORCE, FAM--FATHERS, FAM--ONE PARENT, FATHERS,
ONE PARENT, SELF-IDENTITY)

ZINDEL, PAUL. I LOVE MY MOTHER. HARPER, 1975.
ILLUSTRATED BY JOHN MELO. (CCB-B)

   STRIKING FULL-COLOR ILLUSTRATIONS EXPAND THE
LIMITED TEXT OF THIS STORY OF A BOY AND HIS
MOTHER, PRESUMABLY LIVING ALONE BECAUSE OF
DIVORCE OR SEPARATION. THE REASON IS NOT
EXPLICITLY STATED. COMPANIONSHIP AT THE ZOO, IN

THE KITCHEN, AND LATE AT NIGHT WHEN THE BAD
DREAMS COME, MAKES UP ONE PART OF THE BOOK. THERE
IS ALSO DEPICTED THE REALISM OF VULNERABLE
FEELINGS WHEN THE BOY WANTS TO RUN AWAY FROM
HOME, WHEN HIS MOTHER TRIES NOT TO LET HIM KNOW
WHEN THEY ARE SHORT OF MONEY, BUT THE MOST MOVING
SCENES ARE WHEN MOTHER ADMITS THAT SHE IS LONELY
AND WHEN THE BOY MISSES HIS FATHER. (DIFF
SIT--DIVORCE, DIVORCE, EMOTIONS--LONELINESS,
EMOTIONS--LOVE, FAM--MOTHERS, FAM--ONE PARENT,
LONELINESS, LOVE, MOTHERS, ONE PARENT)

DIFF SIT--DOCTOR

ROCKWELL, HARLOW. MY DOCTOR. MACMILLAN, 1973.
ILLUSTRATED BY HARLOW ROCKWELL. (BL)

FOR A CHILD WHO IS APPREHENSIVE ABOUT A VISIT
TO THE DOCTOR, THIS PICTURE BOOK MAY PROVE TO BE
A DE-SENSITIZING INSTRUMENT. LIKE THE OBSERVABLE
DETAIL ON THE THERMOMETER AND THE SYRINGE, THE
CALM, UNEMOTIONAL CLIMATE IN THE DOCTOR'S OFFICE
IS ALSO TANGIBLE, VISIBLE PROOF THAT THE OCCASION
IS NOT ONE TO FEAR. BY BRINGING OUT INTO THE
OPEN THE SECRETS OF THE JARS OF MEDICINE, AND BY
EXPLAINING VARIOUS INSTRUMENTS AND THEIR USES IN
A COLORFUL, FRIENDLY ATMOSPHERE, THE AUTHOR HAS
PROVIDED A NEEDED MEANS OF REDUCING TENSION IN
THE MIND OF A CHILD. (DIFF SIT--DOCTOR, DOCTOR,
EMOTIONS--FEAR, FEAR)

DIFF SIT--HANDICAPS

FASSLER, JOAN. HOWIE HELPS HIMSELF. WHITMAN, A.,
1975. ILLUSTRATED BY JOE LASKER. (BL)

IN A FOREWORD, THE AUTHOR LISTS THREE GROUPS
OF PEOPLE WHO MAY BE HELPED BY THIS BOOK: A CHILD
IN A WHEELCHAIR, THE SIBLINGS OF A HANDICAPPED
CHILD, AND NORMAL CHILDREN. THE AUTHOR HAS
ACHIEVED A VERY FINE PORTRAIT OF THE EFFORT HOWIE
MAKES TO PUSH HIS WHEELCHAIR, AND THE READER
REALLY WILL UNDERSTAND WHEN HE LOOKS AT THE SWEAT
RUNNING DOWN HOWIE'S FOREHEAD. AN EXCELLENT BOOK
WHICH WILL HELP ALL READERS DISCOVER THAT
HANDICAPPED PERSONS ARE REAL PEOPLE. (DIFF
SIT--HANDICAPS, HANDICAPS)

HEIDE, FLORENCE. SOUND OF SUNSHINE, SOUND OF
RAIN. PARENTS' MAG, 1970. ILLUSTRATED BY KENNETH

LONGTEMPS.

THE BLIND CHILD WHO TEL_S THIS STORY AND HIS
SISTER ARE NAMELESS, AND ONLY ABRAM, THE FRIENDLY
ICE CREAM MAN IN THE PARK, HAS A NAME.
NEVERTHELESS THE STORY IS ONE OF A DEVELOPING
SELF-AWARENESS IN A LITTLE BOY. HIS IS A WORLD OF
A TACTILE ENVIRONMENT, PERCEIVED AS BEING SMOOTH
OR ROUGH, AND OF SOUNDS, SOFT AND LOUD, AND OF
COLORS IMAGINED. IN THE TELLING, MANY THINGS ARE
LEARNED ABOUT THE WORLD OF THE BLIND, AND A CHILD
HEARING THIS STORY WILL HAVE AN UNDERSTANDING OF
THE GROWING INDEPENDENCE IN THIS SMALL DEPENDENT
CHILD. (BROTHERS & SISTERS, DIFF SIT--HANDICAPS,
FAM--BROTHERS & SISTERS, HANDICAPS,
SELF-IDENTITY, SELF-UNDERSTANDING)

KEATS, EZRA. APT. 3. MACMILLAN, 1971.
ILLUSTRATED BY EZRA KEATS. (ESLC)

TWO BROTHERS, SAM AND BEN, ARE LONELY AND
DECIDE TO INVESTIGATE THE SOURCE OF SOMEONE
PLAYING A HARMONICA. THE SETTING IS A GRIM GHETTO
APARTMENT BUILDING, AND VARIOUS MOODS ARE FELT
AS THE BOYS GO DOWN THE HALL. WHEN THEY FIND THE
BLIND MAN PLAYING THE HARMONICA IN APT. 3, HE
SHARES WITH THEM THE SECRETS HE KNOWS AND PLAYS
STRANGE MUSIC WHICH CONJURES UP SIGHTS, SOUNDS,
AND COLORS TO SAM. THE BOOK ENDS WITH SAM ASKING
THE OLD MAN TO TAKE A WALK WITH THEM. EVOCATIVE
ART WORK AND PROSE SHOW THE POWER OF MUSIC ON THE
EMOTIONS. (DIFF SIT--HANDICAPS, DIFF SIT--OLD
AGE, EMOTIONS--LONELINESS, HANDICAPS, LONELINESS,
OLD AGE)

KLEIN, GERDA. THE BLUE ROSE. HILL, 1974.
ILLUSTRATED BY NORMA HOLT.

MADE IN COOPERATION WITH THE KENNEDY CHILD
STUDY CENTER, THE BOOK IS A SYMPATHETIC VIEW OF
MENTAL RETARDATION. BLACK AND WHITE PHOTOGRAPHS
SHOW JENNY PLAYING, TRYING TO TIE HER SHOES.
CLOSES WITH JENNY BEING UNHAPPY BECAUSE OTHER
CHILDREN HAVE CALLED HER RETARDED, AND LAUGHED AT
HER. (DIFF SIT--HANDICAPS, EMOTIONS--REJECTION,
HANDICAPS, REJECTION)

LASKER, JOE. HE'S MY BROTHER. WHITMAN, A., 1974.
ILLUSTRATED BY JOE LASKER. (BL)

IN A PERCEPTIVE NOTE AT THE BACK OF THIS BOOK,
MILDRED AND JOE LASKER GIVE A DESCRIPTION OF
THIS "INVISIBLE HANDICAP," AS THEY TERM IT, WHERE
A CHILD MAY NOT BE RETARDED, BUT SUFFERS
DIFFICULTY IN LEARNING AND SOCIAL SITUATIONS.
WRITTEN SO THAT OTHER FAMILIES WILL BE ABLE TO
IDENTIFY WITH THE EXPERIENCES SHOWN AND THEREBY
TAKE COMFORT, THE BOOK IS DIVIDED INTO HALF, WITH
THE SECOND PART SHOWING THE POSITIVE QUALITIES
OF JAMIE: HIS RHYTHM ON HIS DRUM SET, AND HIS
INSIGHTFUL STATEMENTS ABOUT ANIMALS. THE FIRST
HALF SHOWS, WITH REALISTIC PICTURES, THE TRIALS
OF SUCH A CHILD BEING SHUNNED IN GAMES, THE
TRAVAILS THAT TEACHERS AND PARENTS FACE, AND THE
COMPASSION AND UNDERSTANDING HE IS SOMETIMES
SHOWN. ABOVE ALL, IT IS A HELPFUL BOOK, AND A
POSITIVE BOOK, SHOWING A CHILD, IF NOT LIVING
COMFORTABLY WITH HIS PEERS, AT LEAST INTEGRATED
INTO NORMAL FAMILY LIFE. (DIFF SIT--HANDICAPS,
HANDICAPS)

LITCHFIELD, ADA. A BUTTON IN HER EAR. WHITMAN,
A., 1976. ILLUSTRATED BY ELEANOR MILL. (BL)

DR. BROWN CALLED IT A MAGIC BUTTON BUT ANGELA
WEARS A HEARING AID TO HELP HER HEAR BETTER.
ANGELA NOT ONLY WEARS A HEARING AID, BUT WEARS IT
VERY VISIBLY, CARRYING A BACKPACK TYPE HARNESS
WHICH HOLDS HER BATTERIES. IN THE END, THE JAUNTY
HARNESS BECOMES A STATUS SYMBOL, A POSITIVE
ADDITION TO HER LIFE. ON THE LAST PAGE ANGELA
SAYS THAT SHE THINKS SOME OF THE OTHER CHILDREN
IN HER CLASS WISHED THEY COULD TRY A HEARING AID,
TOO. HANDSOME ILLUSTRATIONS SHOWING ANGELA TO BE
AN ACTIVE GIRL IN BLUE JEANS AND PONY TAIL MAKE
THIS A LANDMARK BOOK ON A SUBJECT NOT DEALT WITH
PREVIOUSLY FOR THIS AGE GROUP. (DIFF
SIT--HANDICAPS, HANDICAPS)

SOBOL, HARRIET. JEFF'S HOSPITAL BOOK. WALCK,
1975. ILLUSTRATED BY PATRICIA AGRE. (BL)

PHYSICIANS FROM TWO MAJOR MEDICAL INSTITUTIONS
WERE USED AS CONSULTANTS FOR THIS HELPFUL,
ACCURATE BOOK WHICH DESCRIBES A YOUNG BOY'S
EXPERIENCE AS HE UNDERGOES SURGERY TO CORRECT
CROSSED EYES. LARGE BLACK AND WHITE PHOTOGRAPHS
GIVE A STEP-BY-STEP NO NONSENSE APPROACH TO THIS
STORY BUT, THROUGHOUT, THE HUMAN ELEMENT IS
THERE, TOO, AS WE SEE JEFF FEELING SCARED AND

WORRIED BEFORE THE OPERATION. REASSURING PICTURES
OF MOTHER AND FATHER WITH HIM AFTERWARD, AND
HORSEPLAY WITH THE NEIGHBORHOOD KIDS LEND AN
UPBEAT FEELING TO THE BOOK. (DIFF SIT--HANDICAPS,
EMOTIONS--FEAR, FEAR, HANDICAPS, HOSPITAL, NEW
SIT--HOSPITAL)

STEIN, SARA. ABOUT HANDICAPS. WALKER, 1974.
ILLUSTRATED BY DICK FRANK. (BL)

   ILLUSTRATED WITH LIVELY PHOTOGRAPHS, SOME IN
COLOR, THIS BOOK ATTEMPTS TO BRING OUT INTO THE
OPEN A CHILD'S FEELINGS TOWARD HANDICAPPED
PEOPLE. SIGNIFICANT INCLUSION IS A PICTURE AND
EXPLANATION OF A MAN WITH AN ARTIFICIAL ARM WHICH
HAS A HOOK. ANOTHER USEFUL ASPECT OF THE BOOK IS
ITS VERY LARGE TYPE, AS WELL AS SECTIONS IN
SMALLER TYPE, FOR THE ADULT READER. THE BOOK
CONCLUDES WITH THE TWO YOUNG BOYS, JOE AND
MATTHEW, WORKING TOGETHER ON A BUILDING PROJECT.
(DIFF SIT--HANDICAPS, HANDICAPS)

WILDSMITH, BRIAN. THE LITTLE WOOD DUCK. WATTS,
1973. ILLUSTRATED BY BRIAN WILDSMITH. (CC)

   LITTLE WOOD DUCK LIVES IN A THICKET WITH HIS
MOTHER AND FIVE BROTHERS AND SISTERS. THE FIRST
TIME HE JUMPED IN THE WATER HE FOUND HE COULD
SWIM ONLY IN CIRCLES, AND HIS MOTHER BECAME
ANGRY, AND THE ANIMALS OF THE FOREST TEASED HIM.
WHEN WISE OLD OWL DIAGNOSED THE TROUBLE (ONE FOOT
WAS LARGER THAN THE OTHER), HE TOLD THE LITTLE
DUCKLING TO PAY NO ATTENTION TO THE TEASING.
LATER, WHEN WOOD DUCK'S EFFORTS AT SWIMMING IN
CIRCLES DIVERTED THE FOX, EVERYONE DECLARED HIM A
HERO, AND THEY PROMISED NEVER TO TEASE HIM
AGAIN. USEFUL BECAUSE IT ILLUMINATES THE WAY IN
WHICH A HANDICAP MAY BECOME A BLESSING, AND
DEMONSTRATES THAT MINDLESS TEASING IS
UNDESIRABLE. (BEHAVIOR--TEASING, DIFF
SIT--HANDICAPS, EMOTIONS--FRUSTRATION,
FRUSTRATION, HANDICAPS, TEASING)

DIFF SIT--HOSPITAL

REY, MARGRET. CURIOUS GEORGE GOES TO THE
HOSPITAL. HOUGHTON, 1966. ILLUSTRATED BY MARGRET
REY. (BCB)

   WRITTEN IN COLLABORATION WITH THE CHILDREN'S

HOSPITAL MEDICAL CENTER IN BOSTON, THIS ADVENTURE
HAS THE ADVANTAGE OF A CENTRAL CHARACTER WITH
WHOM ALL CHILDREN WILL IDENTIFY. LOVABLE GEORGE
LANDS IN THE HOSPITAL WITH AN AILMENT WHICH COULD
PLAGUE ANY CHILD, AND HIS TRIP THROUGH X-RAY AND
ADMISSIONS TO THE CHILDREN'S WARD IS COLORFULLY
REASSURING. ALTHOUGH THE TEXT DESCRIBES SOME OF
THE PAIN, AND THE PICTURES REALISTICALLY DEPICT
THE OPERATING ROOM, THERE IS A HAPPY, POSITIVE
NOTE THROUGHOUT, AND IRREPRESSIBLE GEORGE ENDS
HIS HOSPITAL VISIT WITH A WILD ADVENTURE IN A
RUNAWAY GO-CART. (DIFF SIT--HOSPITAL, HOSPITAL,
NEW SIT--HOSPITAL)

SHAY, ARTHUR. WHAT HAPPENS WHEN YOU GO TO THE
HOSPITAL. REILLY, 1969.   (CC)

   KAREN'S SHINY, SMILING FACE ON THE COLORFUL
COVER SETS THE TONE FOR A NON-THREATENING
EXPERIENCE IN THE HOSPITAL FOR ANY CHILD READER.
ALTHOUGH KAREN IS TEARFULLY APPREHENSIVE AT
TIMES, CHILDREN WILL UNDERSTAND THAT IT IS NORMAL
TO MISS YOUR PARENTS AND THAT YOU MIGHT BE A
LITTLE AFRAID OF THE X-RAY MACHINE. AUTHOR SHAY
HAS SAID THAT HIS PURPOSE IS TO SHOW THE JOBS AND
SERVICES THAT GO ON IN A HOSPITAL, AND TO HELP
CHILDREN UNDERSTAND IN ADVANCE WHAT WILL HAPPEN
TO THEM. HE HAS SUCCEEDED IN PRODUCING A VERY
USEFUL, SUCCESSFUL BOOK. (BRAVERY, DIFF
SIT--HOSPITAL, EMOTIONS--BRAVERY, HOSPITAL, NEW
SIT--HOSPITAL)

STEIN, SARA. A HOSPITAL STORY. WALKER, 1974.
ILLUSTRATED BY DORIS PINNEY.   (BL)

   LARGE REALISTIC PHOTOGRAPHS, SOME IN COLOR,
SET THE TONE FOR THIS HELPFUL BOOK. ACKNOWLEDGING
THAT SOME THINGS ARE SCARY, AND SOMETIMES
PAINFUL, THE AUTHOR, IN COOPERATION WITH STAFF AT
THE CENTER FOR PREVENTIVE PSYCHIATRY, HAS
ATTEMPTED TO HELP BOTH PARENT AND CHILD. VERY
LARGE PRINT IS USED IN THE TEXT FOR THE CHILD
WHILE, ON THE SAME PAGE, THERE IS AN EXTENSIVE
SECTION DIRECTED TO THE ADULT WHICH CONTAINS
EXCELLENT PRACTICAL ADVICE, SUCH AS TAKING A
CAMERA TO RECORD WHAT THE HOSPITAL IS REALLY
LIKE, AND ASKING ALL SORTS OF QUESTIONS IN
ADVANCE. (DIFF SIT--HOSPITAL, HOSPITAL, NEW
SIT--HOSPITAL)

DIFF SIT--ILLNESS

BRANDENBERG, FRANZ. I WISH I WAS SICK, TOO!.
MORROW, 1976. ILLUSTRATED BY ALIKI. (BL)

   THIS IS A BOOK IN WHICH ALL OF THE ACTION CAN
BE TRACED IN THE EXPRESSIONS IN THE EYES OF
EDWARD AND ELIZABETH, TWO ENDEARING CAT
PROTAGONISTS WITH ALL TOO HUMAN FOIBLES. EDWARD'S
EYES ARE AT HALF-MAST AS WE SEE HIM IN THE
SICKBED, AND ELIZABETH SHOOTS SIDEWISE GLANCES OF
ENVIOUS RAGE AS SHE RELUCTANTLY DOES HER CHORES
AND PRACTICES PIANO. CONCERN AND LOVE ARE
EXPRESSED IN THE EYES OF MOTHER AND FATHER AS
THEY MINISTER TO THE CHILDREN, FOR YES, ELIZABETH
ALSO BECOMES ILL. HER EYES ARE EVEN MORE
HELPLESSLY DROOPED, AND ONCE AGAIN SHE IS ENVIOUS
OF THE WELL BROTHER, WHOSE EYES ARE BY NOW ROUND
AND SPARKLY. THE STORY ENDS WITH EVERYONE
PROPERLY ROUND-EYED AND HAPPY. (BROTHERS &
SISTERS, DIFF SIT--ILLNESS, FAM--BROTHERS &
SISTERS, EMOTIONS--JEALOUSY, ILLNESS, JEALOUSY)

TOBIAS, TOBI. A DAY OFF. PUTNAM, 1973.
ILLUSTRATED BY RAY CRUZ. (CC)

   ALL CHILDREN WILL IMMEDIATELY RECOGNIZE THE
PREMISE IN THIS BOOK, THAT IT'S NICE TO STAY AT
HOME IF YOU DON'T FEEL WELL, AND ESPECIALLY IF
YOU'RE NOT ALL THAT SICK. CRUZ' ILLUSTRATIONS ARE
UNPRETTIFIED, YET MANAGE TO GIVE THE EFFECT OF A
SOLICITOUS FAMILY HOVERING AROUND, WILLING TO
CLOSE AN EYE TO BEHAVIOR WHICH MIGHT NOT NORMALLY
BE APPROVED. (DIFF SIT--ILLNESS, ILLNESS)

VIGNA, JUDITH. GREGORY'S STITCHES. WHITMAN, A.,
1974. ILLUSTRATED BY JUDITH VIGNA. (CCB-B, LJ)

   A HUMOROUS BOOK WHICH MAY BE USEFUL FOR A
CHILD WHO HAS HAD "STITCHES." WHILE ONE MAY FEEL
SORRY FOR GREGORY AT THE BEGINNING OF THE STORY,
BY THE END, WHEN HIS ACCIDENT IS MAGNIFIED AND
MAKES HIM OUT TO BE A HERO, RESCUING HIS PARENTS
FROM A LION, THE READER DOESN'T FEEL SORRY FOR
GREGORY. (DIFF SIT--ILLNESS, ILLNESS)

WILLIAMS, BARBARA. ALBERT'S TOOTHACHE. DUTTON,
1974. ILLUSTRATED BY KAY CHORAO. (CC)

   APPROPRIATE AS A BEDTIME STORY FOR YOUNGER

CHILDREN, THIS SLOWLY-PACED STORY ILLUSTRATED IN
SOFT PENCIL TONES STRIKES A SYMPATHETIC CHORD IN
CHILDREN WHO HAVE TRIED TO MAKE GROWN-UPS
UNDERSTAND THEM AND BELIEVE THEM. NO ONE BELIEVED
THAT ALBERT TURTLE WAS SICK WITH A TOOTHACHE
UNTIL HIS GRANDMOTHER CAME OVER THAT NIGHT. TURNS
OUT A GOPHER BIT HIM ON HIS LEFT TOE, BUT NO ONE
HAD BEEN WISE ENOUGH TO ASK HIM WHERE HIS
TOOTHACHE WAS. (DIFF SIT--ILLNESS,
FAM--GRANDMOTHERS, GRANDMOTHERS, ILLNESS)

WOLDE, GUNILLA. BETSY AND THE CHICKEN POX.
RANDOM, 1976. ILLUSTRATED BY GUNILLA WOLDE. (BL)

   WHEN BETSY'S BABY BROTHER BECOMES ILL AND
PARENTAL ATTENTION TURNS TOWARD HIM, BETSY'S
THUMB GOES IN HER MOUTH AS SHE WATCHES ROUND-EYED
IN THE BACKGROUND. BABY'S TEMPERATURE IS TAKEN,
THE DOCTOR IS CALLED AND, AMID ALL THE BUSTLE,
BETSY IS IGNORED. SHE PAINTS SPOTS ON HER FACE,
AND EVEN HER TONGUE, BUT STILL NO ONE NOTICES HER
AND WHEN SHE ERUPTS IN A TEMPER, BOTH PARENTS
ARE ANGRY. WHEN SHE HERSELF BREAKS OUT IN CHICKEN
POX, BETSY REALIZES SHE REALLY DOESN'T WANT THE
RED SPOTS AFTER ALL. A REALISTIC STORY WHICH IS
SIGNIFICANT FOR A NUMBER OF REASONS, IT WILL BE
USEFUL FOR PARENT AND CHILD BECAUSE IT DETAILS
THE TYPICALLY JEALOUS FEELINGS IN A CHILD WHO
FEELS NEGLECTED. A NO NONSENSE WOMAN DOCTOR, A
VIEW OF DADDY TAKING THE BABY'S TEMPERATURE WITH
A RECTAL THERMOMETER, AND LOW-KEY PASTEL AND
CRAYON DRAWINGS MAKE THIS A BOOK WHICH
DEMONSTRATES NON-STEREOTYPED SEX ROLES AS WELL AS
A RELEVANT FAMILY SITUATION. (DIFF SIT--ILLNESS,
FAM--SIBLING RIVALRY, ILLNESS, SIBLING RIVALRY)

DIFF SIT--OLD AGE

ARDIZONNE, EDWARD. LUCY BROWN AND MR. GRIMES.
WALCK, 1971. ILLUSTRATED BY EDWARD ARDIZONNE.
(CC)

   THIS BOOK HAS A FAIRY-TALE QUALITY WHICH MAKES
IT SOMETHING OF A FANTASY: A LONELY LITTLE
ORPHAN GIRL MEETS A LONELY OLD MAN AND THEY
BECOME GREAT FRIENDS. WHEN MR. GRIMES FALLS ILL
AND MUST MOVE TO THE COUNTRY, HE ASKS LUCY TO GO
WITH HIM, WITH LUCY'S AUNT'S PERMISSION. MR.
GRIMES, WHO IS VERY WEALTHY, IS GENEROUS WITH HIS
MONEY, AND LUCY BUYS NEW CLOTHING. ILLUSTRATES

THE POINT THAT THERE ARE THINGS IN COMMON FOR THE
YOUNG AND THE OLD. THE OLD MAN AND THE LITTLE
GIRL WALK TOGETHER, HAVE TEA TOGETHER, AND NEVER
FEEL LONELY. (DIFF SIT--OLD AGE,
EMOTIONS--LONELINESS, FRIENDSHIP--ADULTS,
LONELINESS, OLD AGE)

BLUE, ROSE. GRANDMA DIDN'T WAVE BACK. WATTS,
1972.   ILLUSTRATED BY TED LEWIN.   (CC)

   DEBBIE, TEN YEARS OLD, REALIZES THAT HER
BELOVED GRANDMOTHER IS CHANGING. SHE NO LONGER
WAVES AT DEBBIE FROM THE WINDOW, NOR DOES SHE
HAVE COOKIES FROM THE OVEN READY FOR HER. GRANDMA
EXHIBITS LOSS OF MEMORY, CONFUSION OVER NAMES,
AND OTHER EVIDENCE OF SENILITY, SUCH AS STAYING
IN HER NIGHT DRESS ALL DAY. AS THE GRANDMOTHER
DECLINES, DEBBIE MATURES, AND IS UPSET BY THE
RELATIVES' DECISION TO ENTER THE GRANDMOTHER IN A
NURSING HOME. THE BOOK ENDS ON A POSITIVE NOTE,
HOWEVER, AS THE OLDER WOMAN SPEAKS ENCOURAGINGLY
OF THE COMING OF SPRING. A USEFUL BOOK BECAUSE IT
DEALS WITH A PROBLEM FACING MANY FAMILIES TODAY.
APPROPRIATE FOR THIRD GRADERS TO READ
INDEPENDENTLY. (DIFF SIT--OLD AGE,
FAM--GRANDMOTHERS, GRANDMOTHERS, OLD AGE,
SELF-UNDERSTANDING)

KANTROWITZ, MILDRED. MAXIE. PARENTS' MAG, 1970.
ILLUSTRATED BY EMILY MC CULLY.   (ESLC)

   AN INTERESTING THEME FOR A CHILDREN'S
BOOK--THE LONELINESS OF A WHITE-HAIRED OLD WOMAN
WHO LIVES ALONE AND THINKS NO ONE NEEDS HER. ALL
THIS IS CHANGED ONE DAY WHEN SHE STAYS IN BED
INSTEAD OF GOING THROUGH HER USUAL ROUTINE. SHE
FINDS OUT THAT INDEED MANY PEOPLE WERE DEPENDING
ON HER: HER CANARY BIRD WOKE UP ONE FAMILY, HER
WHISTLING TEAKETTLE ANOTHER. ALTOGETHER THERE
WERE 53 PEOPLE WHO CAME TO HER DOOR LATER THAT
DAY...AND SHE SERVED THEM ALL A CUP OF TEA. (DIFF
SIT--OLD AGE, EMOTIONS--LONELINESS, LONELINESS,
OLD AGE)

KEATS, EZRA. APT. 3. MACMILLAN, 1971.
ILLUSTRATED BY EZRA KEATS.   (ESLC)

   TWO BROTHERS, SAM AND BEN, ARE LONELY AND
DECIDE TO INVESTIGATE THE SOURCE OF SOMEONE
PLAYING A HARMONICA. THE SETTING IS A GRIM GHETTO

APARTMENT BUILDING, AND VARIOUS MOODS ARE FELT
AS THE BOYS GO DOWN THE HALL. WHEN THEY FIND THE
BLIND MAN PLAYING THE HARMONICA IN APT. 3, HE
SHARES WITH THEM THE SECRETS HE KNOWS AND PLAYS
STRANGE MUSIC WHICH CONJURES UP SIGHTS, SOUNDS,
AND COLORS TO SAM. THE BOOK ENDS WITH SAM ASKING
THE OLD MAN TO TAKE A WALK WITH THEM. EVOCATIVE
ART WORK AND PROSE SHOW THE POWER OF MUSIC ON THE
EMOTIONS. (DIFF SIT--HANDICAPS, DIFF SIT--OLD
AGE, EMOTIONS--LONELINESS, HANDICAPS, LONELINESS,
OLD AGE)

LUNDGREN, MAX. MATT'S GRANDFATHER. PUTNAM, 1972.
 ILLUSTRATED BY FIBBEN HALD.   (CC)

   WRITTEN IN SWEDEN, THIS REFRESHINGLY HONEST
BOOK ABOUT AN OLD MAN IN AN OLD FOLKS' HOME
PRESENTS A POINT OF VIEW VERY DIFFERENT FROM
OTHER BOOKS ON THIS SUBJECT. WE SEE LIFE FROM THE
POINT OF VIEW OF THE GRANDFATHER: HE THINKS HE
LOOKS YOUNGER THAN HIS SON, AND HE THINKS THE SON
TALKS AS IF HE WERE THE FATHER. HE MAKES A GREAT
DEAL OF SENSE, AND IS FOXY ENOUGH TO MASQUERADE
IN A LINEN JACKET, SUNGLASSES, AND A BIG FLOPPY
STRAW HAT IN ORDER TO ESCAPE INTO THE OUTSIDE
WORLD FOR A FEW HOURS. THE BOOK DOES INCLUDE SOME
OF THE FOIBLES OF OLDER PEOPLE, SUCH AS
FORGETFULNESS AND SECRETIVENESS (HE HIDES HIS
SNUFF IN THE FLOWER POT), BUT TO THE LITTLE BOY
WHO IS VISITING, THESE MILD ABERRATIONS ARE TAKEN
IN STRIDE. LOVELY PASTEL ILLUSTRATIONS ACCENTING
HORIZONTAL LINES CONTRIBUTE TO A SENSE OF
PEACEFULNESS. A SENSE OF WELL-BEING PERMEATES THE
BOOK, AND THE READER HAS A FEELING OF PLEASURE
IN KNOWING THAT THE OLD GENTLEMAN IS BEING CARED
FOR IN A BUILDING AS BIG AS A CASTLE WITH TOWERS
AND SPIRES. PARTICULARLY USEFUL TO GIVE A CHILD A
POSITIVE, ALBEIT MINORITY REPORT ON OLDER
CITIZENS, MANY OF WHOM REMAIN CHIPPER AND IN
CHARGE OF THEIR SENSES. ()IFF SIT--OLD AGE,
FAM--GRANDFATHERS, GRANDFATHERS, OLD AGE)

SHARMAT, MARJORIE. REX. HARPER, 1967.
ILLUSTRATED BY EMILY MC CULLY. (HB)

   IN THIS HANDSOMELY ILLUSTRATED PICTURE BOOK,
REX GOES TO VISIT A NEIGHBOR, UNBEKNOWN TO HIS
MOTHER. THE OLD GENTLEMAN WELCOMES THE LITTLE BOY
(WHO PRETENDS HE IS A DOG) AND THE BEGINNINGS OF
A FINE FRIENDSHIP ARE SEEN. USEFUL BECAUSE OF

THE PLEASURE BOTH MAN AND BOY RECEIVE AS THEY
JOIN IN THE MAKE-BELIEVE PLAY. (DIFF SIT--OLD
AGE, FRIENDSHIP--ADULTS, OLD AGE)

SHECTER, BEN. ACROSS THE MEADOW. DOUBLEDAY,
1973. ILLUSTRATED BY BEN SHECTER. (LJ, NYTBR,
PBC)

IN A STORY WHICH DOES NOT MENTION DEATH OR
DYING, THE CONCEPT IS CARRIED FORWARD BY AN OLD
CAT WHO JOURNEYS INTO THE FOREST, SAYING GOOD-BYE
TO HIS FRIENDS, AND CURLING UP TO SLEEP IN AN
OLD ABANDONED CAR. THE FEELING OF DEATH IS
FINALIZED WHEN WE SEE THE OLD CAR COMPLETELY
COVERED BY CREEPING VINES, MUCH AS THE CASTLE IN
"SLEEPING BEAUTY." A SUBTLE WAY OF INDICATING
DEATH AND DECAY IS THE USE OF DEAD TWIGS IN THE
FRAMING MOTIF OF EACH PAGE, THOUGH ONE WHICH
CHILDREN MAY NOT RECOGNIZE. THE INTRODUCTION OF A
YOUNG KITTEN WHO IS SENT BACK TO THE FARM AS HIS
REPLACEMENT EMPHASIZES THE BIRTH/DEATH CYCLE.
(DEATH--PET, DIFF SIT--DEATH--PET, DIFF SIT--OLD
AGE, OLD AGE)

UDRY, JANICE. MARY JO'S GRANDMOTHER. WHITMAN,
A., 1970. ILLUSTRATED BY ELEANOR MILL. (BCB)

A SELF-RELIANT WOMAN WHO LIVES ALONE IN THE
COUNTRY GIVES A POSITIVE PICTURE OF AN OLDER
PERSON. RAISING CHICKENS AND MAKING GARDEN OCCUPY
THIS LADY'S TIME, AND MARY JO LOVES TO VISIT
HER. RESOURCEFUL MARY JO GOES FOR HELP WHEN
GRANDMA TAKES A FALL, BUT THE MAIN EMPHASIS IS ON
THE INDEPENDENT HOUSEHOLD OF THIS SPRIGHTLY
OLDSTER. (DIFF SIT--OLD AGE, FAM--GRANDMOTHERS,
GRANDMOTHERS, OLD AGE)

DIFF SIT--OLD AGE--PET

SKORPEN, LIESEL. OLD ARTHUR. HARPER, 1972.
ILLUSTRATED BY WALLACE TRIPP. (CC)

AS THE STORY OPENS, THE OLD DOG ARTHUR IS
HELPING TO BRING THE COWS HOME, AND HELPING THE
FARMER HUNT RABBITS, EXCEPT THAT HE IS SLOW AND
FORGETFUL. WHEN HE SENSES THAT THE FARMER IS
GOING TO GET RID OF HIM, HE SLIPS AWAY IN THE
NIGHT, AND ENDS UP IN THE POUND. WHEN HE IS
CLAIMED BY A LITTLE BOY, HIS LIFE TAKES A TURN
FOR THE BETTER, AND A SPLENDID RELATIONSHIP

DEVELOPS BETWEEN OLD ARTHUR AND THE BOY WILLIAM.
USEFUL BECAUSE OF HUMAN PARALLELS: OLD PEOPLE WHO
NO LONGER FEEL USEFUL ARE APT TO SLIP AWAY, OR
BE PUT AWAY, YET CAN LEAD HAPPY LIVES DOING
THINGS WITHIN THEIR ABILITIES. (DIFF SIT--OLD
AGE--PET, OLD AGE--PET)

DIFF SIT--ONE PARENT

BALDWIN, ANNE. JENNY'S REVENGE. FOUR, 1974.
ILLUSTRATED BY EMILY MC CULLY. (CCB-B)

JENNY HATES HER BABY-SITTER, AND EXPRESSES
HIDDEN ANGER TOWARD HER WORKING MOTHER WHO
APPARENTLY HAS WORKED ONLY SINCE A RECENT
DIVORCE. AFTER TRYING A NUMBER OF PLOYS TO FORCE
THE BABY-SITTER TO QUIT, SHE FINDS COMRADESHIP
WITH MRS. CRAMIE WHEN THEY DISCOVER A COMMON
INTEREST IN THE CIRCUS. A REALISTIC LOOK AT A
CHILD WHO NEEDS AND WANTS ATTENTION FROM HER
MOTHER. (ANGER, DIFF SIT--DIVORCE, DIFF SIT--ONE
PARENT, DIVORCE, EMOTIONS--ANGER, FAM--MOTHERS
WORKING, MOTHERS WORKING, ONE PARENT)

CLIFTON, LUCILLE. EVERETT ANDERSON'S YEAR. HOLT,
1974. ILLUSTRATED BY ANN GRIFALCONI. (CC)

"WALK TALL IN THE WORLD," HIS MOTHER TELLS
HIM. ALTHOUGH THIS IS, IN THE MAIN, A STORY OF A
SEVEN-YEAR-OLD BOY, THE INFLUENCE OF HIS MOTHER
SHINES THROUGH ON EVERY PAGE. EVERETT ANDERSON
REMEMBERS HIS DADDY ALTHOUGH HE DOES NOT KNOW
WHERE HE IS, AND READING THIS SERIES OF VERSES
ABOUT THE MONTHS OF THE YEAR, A CHILD CAN SHARE
THE SPECIAL LOVE THE YOUNG BOY FEELS FOR HIS
MOTHER. (DIFF SIT--ONE PARENT,
EMOTIONS--LONELINESS, FAM--MOTHERS WORKING,
LONELINESS, MOTHERS WORKING, ONE PARENT)

KINDRED, WENDY. LUCKY WILMA. DIAL, 1973.
ILLUSTRATED BY WENDY KINDRED. (LJ)

BEGINNING WITH A SERIES OF SATURDAYS WILMA AND
"CHARLIE," HER DAD, WALK TO MUSEUMS AND ZOOS,
AND FATHER AND DAUGHTER HAVE A UNIFORMLY GLUM
EXPRESSION. THE NEXT EIGHTEEN PAGES DEAL WITH
JOYOUS PICTURIZATION OF CLIMBING, JUMPING,
PIGGYBACKING, DANCING, AND REVELRY WITH THE
PIGEONS IN THE PARK. OBVIOUSLY THIS WAS THE
NEATEST SATURDAY THEY HAD SPENT TOGETHER, AND

THEY HUG AS THEY SEPARATE AND DAD SAYS: "WE'VE
GOT ALL THE SATURDAYS IN THE WORLD." CURIOUSLY
ENOUGH THE WORD DIVORCE IS NOT MENTIONED. WITH
VERY LITTLE TEXT, THIS BOOK CONVEYS THAT INDEED
WILMA IS LUCKY TO HAVE A WONDERFUL RELATIONSHIP
WITH HER FATHER. (DIFF SIT--DIVORCE, DIFF
SIT--ONE PARENT, DIVORCE, FAM--FATHERS, FATHERS,
ONE PARENT)

LEXAU, JOAN. EMILY AND THE KLUNKY BABY AND THE
NEXT DOOR DOG. DIAL, 1972.   ILLUSTRATED BY MARTHA
ALEXANDER. (CC)

   CHARMINGLY ILLUSTRATED, THE BOOK IS A SLIGHT
EPISODE OF A SMALL GIRL ATTEMPTING TO RUN AWAY TO
HER FATHER, WHO LIVES IN AN APARTMENT NEAR BY.
EMILY FEELS HER MOTHER WAS IGNORING HER WHEN
DOING HER INCOME TAXES AND DIDN'T WANT TO BE
BOTHERED. EMILY TAKES THE BABY AND ALMOST GETS
LOST BUT INSTEAD GOES AROUND THE BLOCK (BECAUSE
SHE'S NOT ALLOWED TO CROSS THE STREET)--AND MAKES
IT HOME TO A LOVING MOTHER WHO THINKS SHE'S OUT
PLAYING. (DIFF SIT--DIVORCE, DIFF SIT--ONE
PARENT, DIVORCE, FAM--MOTHERS, FAM--ONE PARENT,
MOTHERS, ONE PARENT)

NESS, EVALINE. SAM, BANGS, AND MOONSHINE. HOLT,
1966.   ILLUSTRATED BY EVALINE NESS. (BCB)

   DESPITE HER FATHER'S CAUTIONS, SAMANTHA IS NOT
ABLE TO KEEP STRAIGHT HER IMAGINARY LIFE FROM
HER REAL LIFE, AND TELLS PRETTY BIG WHOPPERS
TRIGGERED BY HER LONELINESS AND AN INSPIRED
IMAGINATION. WHEN SHE TELLS HER FRIEND THOMAS
THAT HER PET KANGAROO LIVES OUT IN A CAVE, THOMAS
BECOMES MAROONED AND ALMOST LOSES HIS LIFE. SAM
IS DISTRAUGHT WHEN SHE REALIZES THAT HER LIE, FOR
THAT IS WHAT IT IS, IS RESPONSIBLE. HER FATHER
TELLS HER TO THINK ABOUT THE DIFFERENCE BETWEEN
REAL AND MOONSHINE AND, AT THE END, HE ALSO TELLS
HER THAT THERE ARE TWO KINDS OF MOONSHINE: THE
GOOD KIND, WHICH IS HEALTHY IMAGINATIVE PLAY, AND
THE BAD KIND, THAT WHICH CAN BE HARMFUL.
(BEHAVIOR--MISBEHAVIOR, DIFF SIT--ONE PARENT,
EMOTIONS--LONELINESS, FAM--ONE PARENT,
LONELINESS, MISBEHAVIOR, ONE PARENT)

PEARSON, SUSAN. MONNIE HATES LYDIA. DIAL, 1975.
ILLUSTRATED BY DIANE PATERSON. (BL)

INTERESTING BECAUSE A FATHER HEADS THIS
ONE-PARENT FAMILY CONSISTING OF MONNIE AND HER
THOROUGHLY OBNOXIOUS SISTER LYDIA. DADDY IS AN
IMPARTIAL ARBITER IN THE FAMILY SQUABBLE WHICH
ERUPTS ON LYDIA'S BIRTHDAY, SUPPORTIVE OF
MONNIE'S HURT FEELINGS, BUT NOT WILLING TO PUNISH
LYDIA. HE IS AN ATTRACTIVE, BEARDED CONTEMPORARY
FATHER WHO CAN BE ADMIRED FOR HIS COOL WHEN
MONNIE DUMPS THE BIRTHDAY CAKE IN LYDIA'S FACE.
ONE FEELS HE SHOULD BE CHEERING, BUT INSTEAD HE
HANDS LYDIA A TOWEL AND KISSES HER ON THE CHEEK.
USEFUL AS A PORTRAIT OF A NEW LIFE-STYLE FAMILY
COPING WITH OLD LIFE-STYLE PROBLEMS. (ANGER, DIFF
SIT--ONE PARENT, EMOTIONS--ANGER, FAM--FATHERS,
FAM--ONE PARENT, FAM--SIBLING RIVALRY, FATHERS,
ONE PARENT, SIBLING RIVALRY)

STANEK, MURIEL. I WON'T GO WITHOUT A FATHER.
WHITMAN, A., 1972. ILLUSTRATED BY ELEANOR MILL.
(CCB-B, LJ)

THE READER IS NOT TOLD WHY STEVE DOESN'T HAVE
A FATHER. THE REASON MAY BE DEATH, DESERTION, OR
DIVORCE, BUT WHAT WE ARE SHOWN IS THE JEALOUSY
AND LONELINESS THAT STEVE FEELS WHEN HE SEES
SOMEONE ELSE WITH A FATHER. WHEN PARENTS ARE
INVITED TO AN OPEN-HOUSE AT SCHOOL, STEVE DOES
NOT WANT TO GO BECAUSE HE BELIEVES EVERYONE WILL
THINK HE'S A MAMA'S BOY, AND HE THINKS THEN
EVERYONE WILL SEE THAT HE DOES NOT HAVE A FATHER.
MANY VARIATIONS ON THE KINDS OF PARENTHOOD SERVE
TO GIVE STEVE SOME PERSPECTIVE: FIRST OF ALL,
ONE BOY'S FATHER WORKED NIGHTS AND HIS MOTHER WAS
ILL, SO A SISTER FILLED IN. ANOTHER BOY WAS
BRINGING TWO SETS OF PARENTS: HIS PARENTS WERE
DIVORCED. IN STEVE'S CASE, HIS GRANDPA, HIS
UNCLE, AND A NEIGHBOR SAT WITH HIM AND HIS
MOTHER. BUT WHAT STEVE REALLY FOUND OUT WAS THAT
NO ONE WAS LOOKING AT HIM. HE FINALLY LEARNS TO
ACCEPT THE STATEMENT HIS MOTHER MADE: "LOTS OF
CHILDREN DON'T HAVE BOTH PARENTS...THEY MUST
LEARN TO GET ALONG WITH THE FAMILY AND FRIENDS
THEY HAVE." (DIFF SIT--ONE PARENT, FAM--ONE
PARENT, ONE PARENT)

ZOLOTOW, CHARLOTTE. A FATHER LIKE THAT. HARPER,
1971. ILLUSTRATED BY BEN SHECTER. (BCB)

HOME WITHOUT A FATHER IS PICTURED AS A LITTLE
BOY PAINTS AN IMAGINARY PORTRAIT OF THE PERFECT

DAD. WE SEE A MOTHER WHO MAKES THE CHILD GO TO
BED AT BEDTIME, WHO READS WHEN THE BOY WOULD LIKE
TO PLAY CHECKERS. SHE IS A MOTHER WHO CAN'T
UNDERSTAND BECAUSE SHE NEVER WAS A BOY, AND WHO
SAYS THE BASEBALL GAME ON TV IS TOO LOUD. IT IS
THE MOTHER WHO, NERVOUSLY SEWING FASTER AND
FASTER BECAUSE OF THE GLOWING PICTURE HE
DESCRIBES OF THE MYTHICAL FATHER, SAYS THE
REALISTIC WORDS OF WISDOM: "IF HE NEVER COMES, "
TRYING TO MAKE THE CHILD UNDERSTAND THAT THIS
PARAGON IS PERHAPS EXAGGERATED. IN THE END,
MOTHER SAYS THAT HE CAN TRY TO BE THAT KIND OF
FATHER WHEN HE GROWS UP. USEFUL BECAUSE OF THE
EXEMPLAR ROLE OF THE FATHER. SOME CHILDREN MAY
NEED TO BE SHOWN WHAT THE ABSENCE OF THE FATHER
IN THE FAMILY MEANS. (DIFF SIT--ONE PARENT,
FAM--FATHERS, FAM--MOTHERS, FATHERS, MOTHERS, ONE
PARENT)

DIFF SIT--OVERWEIGHT

PINKWATER, MANUS. FAT ELLIOT AND THE GORILLA.
FOUR, 1974. ILLUSTRATED BY MANUS PINKWATER. (BL)

ELLIOT WAS A COMPULSIVE OVEREATER. HE WAS VERY
FAT. HIS DOCTOR GAVE HIM A DIET AND A LOLLIPOP
AND HIS FAMILY GAVE HIM ALL SORTS OF
RATIONALIZATIONS FOR BEING FAT. A PENNY SCALE
WHICH TALKED TO HIM AND GAVE OUT A MAGIC FORTUNE,
AND A BOOK ELLIOT BOUGHT FOR TEN CENTS, CHANGED
HIS LIFE. THE FORTUNE TOLD HIM HE DIDN'T HAVE TO
BE WHAT HE DIDN'T WANT TO BE, AND THE BOOK
SUGGESTED THAT HE CONJURE UP THE IMAGE OF
SOMETHING HE'D REALLY LIKE TO BE. A GORILLA?
ELLIOT'S GORILLA WAS HIS FRIEND AND CONSTANT
COMPANION. THE GORILLA SHOOK HIS HEAD WHEN ELLIOT
WANTED TO FINISH HIS EIGHTH DOUGHNUT, AND THE
GORILLA ALLOWED HIM ONLY GRAPEFRUIT AND EGG FOR
BREAKFAST THE NEXT DAY. WHEN ELLIOT STARTED
RUNNING ON THE TRACK, THE GORILLA GRABBED HIM BY
THE SHIRT AND HELPED HIM ALONG. IN A LONG,
COMPLEX STORY WHICH EXPLORES ALL OF THE PITFALLS
AND FRUSTRATION OF A DIETER, AUTHOR PINKWATER HAS
CREATED A CREDIBLE STORY WITH IMAGINATIVE
PICTURES FOR CHILDREN ON A SUBJECT NOT TACKLED
BEFORE. (DIFF SIT--OVERWEIGHT, OVERWEIGHT,
SELF-CONSCIOUSNESS--SIZE)

DIFF SIT--SEPARATION

ETS, MARIE. BAD BOY, GOOD BOY!. CROWELL, T.,
1967. ILLUSTRATED BY MARIE ETS. (BCB)

ALTHOUGH THE STORY IS TOLD THROUGH THE
DESTRUCTIVE ACTIVITIES OF ROBERTO, A LITTLE
PRESCHOOLER ON HIS OWN AS HE ROAMS THE
NEIGHBORHOOD UNSUPERVISED, IT IS REALLY A
PORTRAIT OF A TROUBLED FAMILY, SEVEN SLEEPING IN
ONE BEDROOM, WITH A YOUNG INEXPERIENCED MOTHER
INCAPABLE OF COPING WITH THE FAMILY. WHEN ROBERTO
GOES TO DAY SCHOOL AT THE CHILDREN'S CENTER,
THINGS GET BETTER: HE LEARNS SOME ENGLISH BUT,
MORE IMPORTANTLY, PRINTS THE LETTER TO HIS MOTHER
WHICH BRINGS HER HOME. MOST CHILDREN WILL
UNDERSTAND THE "BAD" BEHAVIOR WHICH CAME ABOUT
BECAUSE ROBERTO NEEDED ATTENTION. THE TEXT IS
QUITE LONG, AND IT IS NOT PARTICULARLY EASY TO
READ. THEREFORE THIS IS PROBABLY MORE USEFUL AS A
BOOK TO BE SHARED. (BEHAVIOR--MISBEHAVIOR, DIFF
SIT--SEPARATION, MISBEHAVIOR, SEPARATION)

DISLIKES

SIMON, NORMA. I KNOW WHAT I LIKE. WHITMAN, A.,
1971. ILLUSTRATED BY DORA LEDER. (CCB-B)

LISTING MANY BEHAVIOR PREFERENCES IN SUCH
AREAS AS FOOD, PLAY, AND CERTAIN HOUSEHOLD
CHORES, THE BOOK ALSO GIVES INSIGHT INTO THE
DISLIKES OF INDIVIDUAL CHILDREN. AUTHOR SIMON IS
PARTICULARLY EFFECTIVE IN PRESENTING SITUATIONS
WHERE THE READER CAN EMPATHIZE, THUS GAINING IN
SELF-UNDERSTANDING IN THE AFFECTIVE AREAS SUCH AS
APPRECIATION OF BEAUTY IN THE STARS, AND THE
PLEASURES OF MUSIC. (BEHAVIOR--DISLIKES,
DISLIKES, EMOTIONS--HAPPINESS, HAPPINESS,
SELF-UNDERSTANDING)

ZOLOTOW, CHARLOTTE. WHEN I HAVE A SON. HARPER,
1967. ILLUSTRATED BY HILARY KNIGHT. (BCB)

IN AN IMAGINATIVE PROJECTION INTO THE FUTURE,
JOHN TELLS HOW HIS SON WOULD BE PERMITTED TO
BEHAVE AND, IN DOING SO, THE READER SEES A PARADE
OF FORBIDDEN BEHAVIOR: NOT SAYING THANK YOU FOR
PRESENTS HE HATES, AND HAVING A TRIPLE MALTED
JUST BEFORE DINNER. THE IDEAS THAT JOHN IS
REJECTING FALL INTO THE AREAS OF ETIQUETTE,

GROOMING, PARENTAL CONTROL, COMMON COURTESY, FOOD
DESIRES, AND HEALTH. SOME SEEM QUITE HARMLESS,
SUCH AS STAYING DOWN AT THE RAILROAD STATION ALL
DAY TO WATCH THE TRAINS. IN GENERAL, A MILD
GROUSING AGAINST RULES SET DOWN BY GROWN-UPS. IN
THE END, WE REALIZE JOHN IS ONLY DAYDREAMING OUT
LOUD TO HIS FRIEND: HE DUTIFULLY GOES IN THE
HOUSE FOR THE HATED PIANO LESSON.
(BEHAVIOR--DISLIKES, BEHAVIOR--MANNERS,
BEHAVIOR--MISBEHAVIOR, DISLIKES, MANNERS,
MISBEHAVIOR)

DISLIKES--BATH

BARRETT, JUDI. I HATE TO TAKE A BATH. FOUR,
1975. ILLUSTRATED BY CHARLES SLACKMAN. (BL)

THE GOODS AND BADS ABOUT TAKING A BATH, WITH
DIFFERENT CHILDREN, BOTH BOYS AND GIRLS,
DEMONSTRATING EACH POINT. CERTAINLY NOT A CRUCIAL
BOOK--BUT A FUN ONE, WHICH MAY CHANGE A FEW
OPINIONS IN A FEW HOUSEHOLDS WHERE THIS MAY BE A
PROBLEM. ITS MAIN VALUE LIES IN ITS FRANKNESS,
AND THE REASONS FOR NOT WANTING TO TAKE A BATH
MAY STRIKE A CHORD IN MANY READERS.
(BEHAVIOR--DISLIKES--BATH, DISLIKES--BATH)

DISLIKES--FOOD

HOBAN, RUSSELL. BREAD AND JAM FOR FRANCES.
HARPER, 1964. ILLUSTRATED BY LILLIAN HOBAN. (CC)

FRANCES CAN TELL YOU A NUMBER OF REASONS SHE
DISLIKES EGGS--"SUNNY-SIDE-UP EGGS LIE ON THE
PLATE AND LOOK UP AT YOU IN A FUNNY WAY."
FURTHERMORE, SHE TRADES AWAY HER CHICKEN SALAD
SANDWICH TO HER FRIEND ALBERT FOR A BREAD AND JAM
SANDWICH. BREAD AND JAM, INDEED, IS THE FAVORITE
FOOD OF FRANCES. HER WISE PARENTS, AFTER
TEMPTING HER WITH BREADED VEAL CUTLETS, STRING
BEANS, AND BAKED POTATOES DECIDED TO FEED HER A
STEADY DIET OF BREAD AND JAM. THE SLIGHTLY
CRESTFALLEN LOOK ON HER FACE DEEPENS TO TEARFUL
DISMAY WHEN SHE IS SERVED BREAD AND JAM ON THE
NIGHT THE FAMILY IS HAVING SPAGHETTI AND
MEATBALLS. SHE MAKES AN ABOUT-FACE, ENJOYS HER
DINNER, AND THE READER SEES HER ENJOYING A
SUMPTUOUS LUNCH NEXT DAY AT SCHOOL. ESPECIALLY
USEFUL FOR BOTH PARENTS AND CHILDREN, BECAUSE
THERE ARE NO ARGUING OR LOUD VOICES--JUST SUBTLE

ACTION, WHICH IS VERY EFFECTIVE, BECAUSE IN THE
END, THE CHILD MAKES THE DECISION.
(BEHAVIOR--DISLIKES--FOOD, DISLIKES--FOOD, FAM)

PATERSON, DIANE. EAT!. DIAL, 1975. ILLUSTRATED
BY DIANE PATERSON. (BL)

THE TABLES ARE TURNED WHEN MARTHA TRIES TO
COAX HER PET FROG TO EAT HIS FLIES. HERETOFORE
HER PARENTS HAD BEGGED HER TO EAT--SPAGHETTI,
SALAD, SOUP. WHEN MARTHA AND HER FROG BOTH EAT A
BIG BOWL OF SPAGHETTI, THE READER SEES THE HUMOR
IN THE STORY (AS WELL AS THE LESSON THAT THERE
ARE VARIOUS WAYS TO INDUCE CHILDREN TO EAT).
OR--ONE SHOULDN'T FORCE CHILDREN TO EAT? OR?
(BEHAVIOR--DISLIKES--FOOD, DISLIKES--FOOD)

DISLIKES--SLEEP

HOBAN, RUSSELL. BEDTIME FOR FRANCES. HARPER,
1960. ILLUSTRATED BY GARTH WILLIAMS. (CC)

FATHER BADGER PLAYS AN IMPORTANT ROLE IN
HANDLING THE BEDTIME PROBLEMS OF HIS DAUGHTER
FRANCES WITH AN IMAGINATIVE EXPLANATION OF HER
FEARS. WHEN FRANCES, AN ENTRANCING LITTLE GIRL
WHO ONLY INCIDENTALLY HAPPENS TO BE A BADGER,
GOES THROUGH THE FAMILIAR BEDTIME ROUTINE OF
MILK, HUGS, KISSES, AND TEDDY BEAR, BUT STILL
DOES NOT FALL ASLEEP, FATHER GIVES REASSURING
ADVICE ABOUT THE IMAGINARY GIANTS AND THE
SOMETHING SCARY THAT MIGHT COME OUT OF THE CRACK
IN THE CEILING. HIS MOST CREATIVE SOLUTION,
HOWEVER, COMES WHEN FRANCES COMPLAINS OF THE
CURTAINS MOVING AT THE WINDOW--HE TELLS HER THAT
THE WIND'S JOB IS TO GO AROUND AND BLOW ALL THE
CURTAINS, THAT EVERYBODY HAS A JOB, AND THAT
FURTHERMORE, HER JOB IS TO GO TO SLEEP.
THROUGHOUT THE BOOK, FATHER IS THE PARENT WHO
RELATES TO THE CHILD, ALTHOUGH THE MOTHER IS
VISIBLE. (BEHAVIOR--DISLIKES--SLEEP,
DISLIKES--SLEEP, EMOTIONS--FEAR, FAM--FATHERS,
FATHERS, FEAR)

KRAUS, ROBERT. GOOD NIGHT, RICHARD RABBIT.
SPRINGFELLOW, 1972. ILLUSTRATED BY N.M.
BODECKER. (CCB-B)

TINY FORMAT MAKES THIS A CHARMING BEDTIME
STORY FOR THE VERY YOUNG, AS MOST YOUNGSTERS WILL

IDENTIFY WITH RICHARD RABBIT. A MIX OF REAL AND
IMAGINARY FEARS, AND A LITTLE OF DOWNRIGHT
TEASING ARE SEEN AS THE YOUNG RABBIT PRETENDS
THERE IS A FACE LOOKING IN THE WINDOW. EVERY
OTHER PAGE DEALS WITH A QUESTION OR COMMENT, THE
FACING PAGE WITH MOTHER'S ANSWER. IN ALL OF THE
ILLUSTRATIONS, RICHARD IS VERY SMALL, AND MOTHER
LOOMS VERY LARGE AND SOLID, TRULY A SECURITY
FIGURE, AND ON THE FINAL PAGE RICHARD DRIFTS OFF
TO SLEEP. (BEHAVIOR--DISLIKES--SLEEP,
DISLIKES--SLEEP, EMOTIONS--FEAR,
EMOTIONS--SECURITY, FEAR, SECURITY)

DIVORCE

BALDWIN, ANNE. JENNY'S REVENGE. FOUR, 1974.
ILLUSTRATED BY EMILY MC CULLY. (CCB-B)

JENNY HATES HER BABY-SITTER, AND EXPRESSES
HIDDEN ANGER TOWARD HER WORKING MOTHER WHO
APPARENTLY HAS WORKED ONLY SINCE A RECENT
DIVORCE. AFTER TRYING A NUMBER OF PLOYS TO FORCE
THE BABY-SITTER TO QUIT, SHE FINDS COMRADESHIP
WITH MRS. CRAMIE WHEN THEY DISCOVER A COMMON
INTEREST IN THE CIRCUS. A REALISTIC LOOK AT A
CHILD WHO NEEDS AND WANTS ATTENTION FROM HER
MOTHER. (ANGER, DIFF SIT--DIVORCE, DIFF SIT--ONE
PARENT, DIVORCE, EMOTIONS--ANGER, FAM--MOTHERS
WORKING, MOTHERS WORKING, ONE PARENT)

BLUE, ROSE. A MONTH OF SUNDAYS. WATTS, 1972.
ILLUSTRATED BY TED LEWIN. (CC)

IT WAS HARD HAVING A DAD WHO LOVED YOU ON
SUNDAYS WHEN HE USED TO LOVE YOU EVERY DAY. THIS
COMMENT EPITOMIZES THE UNHAPPY FEELINGS JEFFREY
HAS WHEN HE AND HIS MOTHER MOVE INTO AN APARTMENT
IN THE CITY. WHEN JEFF AND HIS DAD GET TOGETHER
IN THE OLD NEIGHBORHOOD, THINGS REALLY DON'T WORK
OUT. THE RELATIVES TALK AROUND HIM AS IF HE
WEREN'T PRESENT IN THE ROOM. THE MOTHER OF JEFF'S
BEST FRIEND MATTHEW TURNS OUT TO BE A GOOD
STRONG FRIEND WHO EXPLAINS SOME OF THE PROBLEMS
THAT JEFF'S MOM IS HAVING. GETTING INVOLVED IN A
GROUP PROJECT AT SCHOOL AND PARTICIPATING IN A
BIG BLOCK PARTY OVERFLOWING WITH DELICIOUS ETHNIC
FOODS, MUSIC, AND PEOPLE SEEM TO BE THE TWO
THINGS THAT BODE WELL FOR JEFF'S FUTURE. (DIFF
SIT--DIVORCE, DIVORCE, FAM--ONE PARENT, ONE
PARENT)

GARDNER, RICHARD. BOYS AND GIRLS BOOK ABOUT
DIVORCE. SCIENCE, 1970. ILLUSTRATED BY ALFRED
LOWENHEIM. (ESLC)

UNIQUE BOOK WRITTEN BY A PSYCHIATRIST FOR BOYS
AND GIRLS GOING THROUGH OR HAVING GONE THROUGH A
DIVORCE IN THE FAMILY. ILLUSTRATED WITH
CARTOON-LIKE FIGURES, THE BOOK IS FRANK AND
PRACTICAL ABOUT MATTERS SUCH AS HOW TO GET ALONG
BETTER WITH YOUR DIVORCED PARENTS, STEPFATHER,
AND STEPMOTHER. VERY REASSURING FOR THE CHILD WHO
HAS FEARS, GUILT, AND PROBLEMS IN THE DIVORCE
SITUATION. SOME OF THE STATEMENTS MAY BE
CONTROVERSIAL, SO IT WOULD BE WISE FOR AN ADULT
TO BE AWARE OF THE CONTENT OF THE BOOK BEFORE
SHARING IT WITH A CHILD. (DIFF SIT--DIVORCE,
DIVORCE)

GOFF, BETH. WHERE IS DADDY?. BEACON, 1969.
ILLUSTRATED BY SUSAN PERL. (CCB-B, JMF)

ALTHOUGH THE CHILD PORTRAYED IN THIS STORY IS
A VERY YOUNG PRESCHOOLER, AND A GIRL, A
FIFTH-GRADE BOY TUCKED THE COPY OF THIS BOOK IN
HIS DESK BECAUSE IT APPARENTLY FILLED A NEED IN
HIS LIFE. AT ONE POINT THE TEXT SAYS "THE ANGER
BETWEEN THEM (HER PARENTS) MADE A PAIN INSIDE
HER, AND SHE CRIED AND CRIED." IN THE CLASSIC
ATTITUDE OF MANY CHILDREN ABOUT DIVORCE, JANIE
FEELS THAT HER OCCASIONAL ANGER TOWARD HER DAD
CAUSED THE DIVORCE. AND SHE IS AFRAID TO SAY
ANYTHING UNPLEASANT TO HER MOTHER, WHO TAKES A
JOB, FOR FEAR HER MOTHER MIGHT ALSO ABANDON HER.
HAS AN EXCELLENT PAGE OF EXPLANATION BY AN M.D.
FROM THE CHILDREN'S PSYCHIATRIC HOSPITAL AT THE
UNIVERSITY OF MICHIGAN. (DIFF SIT--DIVORCE,
DIVORCE, EMOTIONS--GUILT, GUILT)

KINDRED, WENDY. LUCKY WILMA. DIAL, 1973.
ILLUSTRATED BY WENDY KINDRED. (LJ)

BEGINNING WITH A SERIES OF SATURDAYS WILMA AND
"CHARLIE," HER DAD, WALK TO MUSEUMS AND ZOOS,
AND FATHER AND DAUGHTER HAVE A UNIFORMLY GLUM
EXPRESSION. THE NEXT EIGHTEEN PAGES DEAL WITH
JOYOUS PICTURIZATION OF CLIMBING, JUMPING,
PIGGYBACKING, DANCING, AND REVELRY WITH THE
PIGEONS IN THE PARK. OBVIOUSLY THIS WAS THE
NEATEST SATURDAY THEY HAD SPENT TOGETHER, AND
THEY HUG AS THEY SEPARATE AND DAD SAYS: "WE'VE

GOT ALL THE SATURDAYS IN THE WORLD." CURIOUSLY
ENOUGH THE WORD DIVORCE IS NOT MENTIONED. WITH
VERY LITTLE TEXT, THIS BOOK CONVEYS THAT INDEED
WILMA IS LUCKY TO HAVE A WONDERFUL RELATIONSHIP
WITH HER FATHER. (DIFF SIT--DIVORCE, DIFF
SIT--ONE PARENT, DIVORCE, FAM--FATHERS, FATHERS,
ONE PARENT)

LEXAU, JOAN. EMILY AND THE KLUNKY BABY AND THE
NEXT DOOR DOG. DIAL, 1972. ILLUSTRATED BY MARTHA
ALEXANDER. (CC)

CHARMINGLY ILLUSTRATED, THE BOOK IS A SLIGHT
EPISODE OF A SMALL GIRL ATTEMPTING TO RUN AWAY TO
HER FATHER, WHO LIVES IN AN APARTMENT NEAR BY.
EMILY FEELS HER MOTHER WAS IGNORING HER WHEN
DOING HER INCOME TAXES AND DIDN'T WANT TO BE
BOTHERED. EMILY TAKES THE BABY AND ALMOST GETS
LOST BUT INSTEAD GOES AROUND THE BLOCK (BECAUSE
SHE'S NOT ALLOWED TO CROSS THE STREET)--AND MAKES
IT HOME TO A LOVING MOTHER WHO THINKS SHE'S OUT
PLAYING. (DIFF SIT--DIVORCE, DIFF SIT--ONE
PARENT, DIVORCE, FAM--MOTHERS, FAM--ONE PARENT,
MOTHERS, ONE PARENT)

LEXAU, JOAN. ME DAY. DIAL, 1971. ILLUSTRATED BY
ROBERT WEAVER. (BCB)

"ME DAY" IS RAFER'S BIRTHDAY, BUT IN A SLUM
FAMILY WHERE THERE IS NO MONEY FOR PRESENTS AND
THE TV IS BROKEN, WHAT MAKES A BOY HAPPY? THROUGH
THE TEXT WE LEARN THAT THE FATHER IS NOT AT
HOME, THE PARENTS BEING DIVORCED, APPARENTLY
BECAUSE THE FATHER COULD NOT FIND WORK. RAFER'S
DAY IS MADE PERFECT WHEN HIS FATHER SHOWS UP TO
SPEND THE ENTIRE DAY WITH HIM IN THE PARK, WITH
ICE CREAM AND HOT DOGS. (DIFF SIT--DIVORCE,
DIVORCE, FAM--FATHERS, FAM--ONE PARENT, FATHERS,
ONE PARENT, SELF-IDENTITY)

ZINDEL, PAUL. I LOVE MY MOTHER. HARPER, 1975.
ILLUSTRATED BY JOHN MELO. (CCB-B)

STRIKING FULL-COLOR ILLUSTRATIONS EXPAND THE
LIMITED TEXT OF THIS STORY OF A BOY AND HIS
MOTHER, PRESUMABLY LIVING ALONE BECAUSE OF
DIVORCE OR SEPARATION. THE REASON IS NOT
EXPLICITLY STATED. COMPANIONSHIP AT THE ZOO, IN
THE KITCHEN, AND LATE AT NIGHT WHEN THE BAD
DREAMS COME, MAKES UP ONE PART OF THE BOOK. THERE

IS ALSO DEPICTED THE REALISM OF VULNERABLE
FEELINGS WHEN THE BOY WANTS TO RUN AWAY FROM
HOME, WHEN HIS MOTHER TRIES NOT TO LET HIM KNOW
WHEN THEY ARE SHORT OF MONEY, BUT THE MOST MOVING
SCENES ARE WHEN MOTHER ADMITS THAT SHE IS LONELY
AND WHEN THE BOY MISSES HIS FATHER. (DIFF
SIT--DIVORCE, DIVORCE, EMOTIONS--LONELINESS,
EMOTIONS--LOVE, FAM--MOTHERS, FAM--ONE PARENT,
LONELINESS, LOVE, MOTHERS, ONE PARENT)

DOCTOR

ROCKWELL, HARLOW. MY DOCTOR. MACMILLAN, 1973.
ILLUSTRATED BY HARLOW ROCKWELL. (BL)

FOR A CHILD WHO IS APPREHENSIVE ABOUT A VISIT
TO THE DOCTOR, THIS PICTURE BOOK MAY PROVE TO BE
A DE-SENSITIZING INSTRUMENT. LIKE THE OBSERVABLE
DETAIL ON THE THERMOMETER AND THE SYRINGE, THE
CALM, UNEMOTIONAL CLIMATE IN THE DOCTOR'S OFFICE
IS ALSO TANGIBLE, VISIBLE PROOF THAT THE OCCASION
IS NOT ONE TO FEAR. BY BRINGING OUT INTO THE
OPEN THE SECRETS OF THE JARS OF MEDICINE, AND BY
EXPLAINING VARIOUS INSTRUMENTS AND THEIR USES IN
A COLORFUL, FRIENDLY ATMOSPHERE, THE AUTHOR HAS
PROVIDED A NEEDED MEANS OF REDUCING TENSION IN
THE MIND OF A CHILD. (DIFF SIT--DOCTOR, DOCTOR,
EMOTIONS--FEAR, FEAR)

EMOTIONS

BEHRENS, JUNE. HOW I FEEL. CHILDRENS, 1973.
ILLUSTRATED BY VINCE STREANO. (CCB-B)

A BOOK TO BE USED BY A PARENT OR TEACHER, WITH
ONE CHILD OR A GROUP. THE SIMPLE SENTENCES ARE
NOT DIFFICULT TO FOLLOW, AND CHILDREN WILL EASILY
COMPREHEND THE SEVERAL LINES DEVOTED TO VARIOUS
EMOTIONS: ANGER AND HATE, AS WELL AS PRIDE AND
HAPPINESS. EACH PAGE OF TEXT FACES A FULL-PAGE
COLOR PHOTOGRAPH SHOWING YOUNG CHILDREN IN THE
CLASSROOM, ON THE PLAYGROUND, AND AT HOME,
CAREFULLY CHOSEN TO INCLUDE CHILDREN OF VARIOUS
MINORITIES. (EMOTIONS, FRIENDSHIP,
SELF-UNDERSTANDING)

BEIM, JERROLD. LAUGH AND CRY. MORROW, 1955.
ILLUSTRATED BY RAY CAMPBELL. (ESLC)

ANGER, FEAR, LOVE, SORROW, AND JOY: IN ONE

AFTERNOON THE CHILDREN IN ONE FAMILY EXPERIENCE
THESE EMOTIONS. THE BOOK IS SOMEWHAT MARRED BY
CRASS, HEAVY LINE DRAWINGS WHICH OVER-EXAGGERATE
THE FACES AND BODIES OF THE CHILDREN PORTRAYED.
THE ILLUSTRATIONS ARE SOMEWHAT DATED AS WELL.
ANOTHER FAULT OF THE BOOK IS THAT IT TENDS TO
BLUR THE LINES OF MEANING, AS WHEN THE AUTHOR
CALLS JEALOUSY A KIND OF ANGER. DOCUMENTATION,
HOWEVER, IS PROVIDED IN THE FORM OF A PROFESSOR
OF PSYCHOLOGY AS AN AUTHORITATIVE READER.
(EMOTIONS)

BERGER, TERRY. I HAVE FEELINGS. BEHAVIORAL,
1971. ILLUSTRATED BY HOWARD SPIVAK. (CCB-B)

ONE LARGE BROWN TONE PHOTOGRAPH ACCOMPANIES
EACH EMOTION WHICH IS EXPLORED IN THIS VOLUME.
UNFORTUNATELY MOST OF THE EMOTIONS ARE NEGATIVE
ONES, AND THE SOMBER PHOTOGRAPHS CONTRIBUTE TO
THE ATMOSPHERE OF DOWNNESS, WHICH IS NOT
NECESSARILY STRESSED IN THE EXPLANATORY TEXT.
FACING EACH PHOTOGRAPH IS A POSSIBLE SOLUTION, OR
EXPLANATION, AS WHEN THE BABY-SITTER TELLS THE
BOY THAT BREAKING HIS MOTHER'S PLANT DOES NOT
MEAN HE IS BAD, ONLY THAT HE HAS MADE A MISTAKE.
OF LIMITED APPEAL TO CHILDREN, THE BOOK WILL BE
ESPECIALLY USEFUL WITH AN OLDER CHILD OF SEVEN OR
EIGHT CONFRONTING A SPECIFIC PROBLEM. (EMOTIONS,
SELF-EVALUATION)

BRENNER, BARBARA. FACES. DUTTON, 1970.
ILLUSTRATED BY GEORGE ANCONA. (CC)

ILLUSTRATED BY BLACK AND WHITE PHOTOGRAPHS,
THIS BOOK SHOWS MANY KINDS OF FACES, DIFFERENT
AGES, DIFFERENT RACES. WHILE IT DISCUSSES EYES,
NOSES, EARS, AND MOUTHS, THE BOOK ENDS BY SAYING
THAT A MOUTH IS AN IMPORTANT THING FOR "TELLING
HOW YOU FEEL, SPEAKING TO A FRIEND, FACE...TO
FACE...TO FACE." (EMOTIONS)

HAZEN, NANCY. GROWNUPS CRY TOO. LOLLIPOP, 1973.
ILLUSTRATED BY NANCY HAZEN.

IN THIS STARKLY ILLUSTRATED BOOK OF BLACK AND
WHITE LINE DRAWINGS ON OLIVE GREEN PAPER, THE
AUTHOR-ILLUSTRATOR HAS GIVEN A VERY LOW-KEY,
REALISTIC EXPLANATION OF THE EMOTIONS THAT MAY
MAKE GROWN-UPS CRY. PICTURES AND TEXT TELL THE
READER THAT SADNESS, MADNESS, FATIGUE, AND FEAR

SOMETIMES TRIGGER TEARS IN ADULTS. USEFUL TO SHOW
CHILDREN THAT ADULTS ALSO HAVE PROBLEMS.
PARTICULARLY USEFUL BECAUSE IT SHOWS A MAN IN
TEARS ALSO. (DEATH, DIFF SIT--DEATH, EMOTIONS)

LE SHAN, EDA. WHAT MAKES ME FEEL THIS WAY?.
MACMILLAN, 1972. ILLUSTRATED BY LISL WEIL. (CC)

IN A BOOK WHICH IS DIRECTED TOWARD CHILDREN,
BUT IS VERY, VERY HELPFUL FOR PARENTS AND
TEACHERS, THERE IS SOME PLAIN TALK REGARDING SOME
OF THE THINGS ABOUT WHICH CHILDREN ARE SHY AND
EMBARRASSED. THEREFORE ONE WOULD USE DISCRETION
WITH THE BOOK, EVEN WITH UPPER THIRD GRADERS, FOR
IT TOUCHES ON THE SUBJECTS OF MASTURBATION AND
OTHER MORE GROWN-UP MATTERS. THE VARIOUS CHAPTERS
ARE HELPFUL IN A MUCH BROADER SENSE, HOWEVER,
AND OFFER INSIGHTS INTO FEARS, TEACHERS' AND
PARENTS' BEHAVIOR, AND KNOWLEDGE OF SELF.
(EMOTIONS, SELF-UNDERSTANDING)

EMOTIONS--ANGER

BALDWIN, ANNE. JENNY'S REVENGE. FOUR, 1974.
ILLUSTRATED BY EMILY MC CULLY. (CCB-B)

JENNY HATES HER BABY-SITTER, AND EXPRESSES
HIDDEN ANGER TOWARD HER WORKING MOTHER WHO
APPARENTLY HAS WORKED ONLY SINCE A RECENT
DIVORCE. AFTER TRYING A NUMBER OF PLOYS TO FORCE
THE BABY-SITTER TO QUIT, SHE FINDS COMRADESHIP
WITH MRS. CRAMIE WHEN THEY DISCOVER A COMMON
INTEREST IN THE CIRCUS. A REALISTIC LOOK AT A
CHILD WHO NEEDS AND WANTS ATTENTION FROM HER
MOTHER. (ANGER, DIFF SIT--DIVORCE, DIFF SIT--ONE
PARENT, DIVORCE, EMOTIONS--ANGER, FAM--MOTHERS
WORKING, MOTHERS WORKING, ONE PARENT)

HITTE, KATHRYN. BOY WAS I MAD!. PARENTS' MAG,
1969. ILLUSTRATED BY MERCER MAYER. (CCB-B)

A SMALL BOY NAMED TEDDY GETS ANGRY ONE
MORNING, AND WE ARE INTRODUCED TO HIM SITTING IN
THE CORNER. HE DECIDES TO RUN AWAY, AND PACKS A
SANDWICH. ON HIS TRIP AROUND TOWN HE SEES A BIG
STEAM SHOVEL, RIDES ON A HORSE-DRAWN WAGON,
WATCHES ANTS IN A CRACK IN THE SIDEWALK. UP UNTIL
THIS TIME HE IS STILL MAD, BUT WHEN HE MEETS HIS
FRIEND TOM AND THEY PLAY IN THE PARK, HE
ABSENTMINDEDLY GOES HOME, AND FINDS HE'S NO

LONGER MAD. THE CONCLUSION ONE CAN COME TO IS
THAT WE CAN'T STAY MAD VERY LONG IF WE HAVE
INTERESTING THINGS TO DO, AND GOOD FRIENDS WITH
WHOM TO DO THEM. (ANGER, EMOTIONS--ANGER)

HOBAN, RUSSELL. TOM AND THE TWO HANDLES. HARPER,
1965.   ILLUSTRATED BY LILLIAN HOBAN.   (ESLC)

   KENNY AND TOM ARE ALWAYS FIGHTING, AND TOM
ALWAYS GETS A BLOODY NOSE. HIS DAD TELLS HIM THAT
THERE IS MORE THAN ONE WAY TO SOLVE THE PROBLEM.
YOU CAN FIGHT AGAIN, OR YOU CAN MAKE UP WITH
YOUR BEST FRIEND. TOM TRIES TO BE FRIENDS, BUT
THEY CONTINUE TO FIGHT UNTIL TOM'S FATHER GIVES
HIM SOME BOXING LESSONS. WHEN TOM WINS THE FIGHT,
THEN THEY MAKE UP, AND TOM FINDS THAT THERE WAS
ANOTHER WAY TO LOOK AT IT. (ANGER,
BEHAVIOR--QUARRELING, EMOTIONS--ANGER,
FRIENDSHIP, QUARRELING)

MC GOVERN, ANN. SCRAM, KID!. VIKING, 1974.
ILLUSTRATED BY NOLA LANGNER.   (BL)

   IN AN INTERESTING ARRANGEMENT OF ILLUSTRATIONS
ON THE PAGE, PART BLACK AND WHITE AND PART
SEPIA, THE ILLUSTRATOR OF THIS BOOK HAS MANAGED
TO CAPTURE THE SIMULTANEITY OF REALITY AND
DAYDREAM. THE STORY OF A LITTLE BOY WHO FEELS
LEFT OUT AND HAS ANGRY FEELINGS ABOUT IT SHOULD
STRIKE A FEELING OF EMPATHY IN MANY READERS.
DON'T WE ALL WISH WE WERE BRAVE ENOUGH TO SAY,
"I'LL FIX YOUR WAGON!" AFTER VENTING HIS ANGER IN
THE DAYDREAM, JOE FINDS A FRIEND WHO WILL SAIL A
BOAT WITH HIM AND, TEMPORARILY AT LEAST, FORGETS
ABOUT THE KIDS WHO WON'T LET HIM PLAY BASEBALL.
(ANGER, EMOTIONS--ANGER, EMOTIONS--LONELINESS,
LONELINESS)

PEARSON, SUSAN. MONNIE HATES LYDIA. DIAL, 1975.
ILLUSTRATED BY DIANE PATERSON.   (BL)

   INTERESTING BECAUSE A FATHER HEADS THIS
ONE-PARENT FAMILY CONSISTING OF MONNIE AND HER
THOROUGHLY OBNOXIOUS SISTER LYDIA. DADDY IS AN
IMPARTIAL ARBITER IN THE FAMILY SQUABBLE WHICH
ERUPTS ON LYDIA'S BIRTHDAY, SUPPORTIVE OF
MONNIE'S HURT FEELINGS, BUT NOT WILLING TO PUNISH
LYDIA. HE IS AN ATTRACTIVE, BEARDED CONTEMPORARY
FATHER WHO CAN BE ADMIRED FOR HIS COOL WHEN
MONNIE DUMPS THE BIRTHDAY CAKE IN LYDIA'S FACE.

ONE FEELS HE SHOULD BE CHEERING, BUT INSTEAD HE
HANDS LYDIA A TOWEL AND KISSES HER ON THE CHEEK.
USEFUL AS A PORTRAIT OF A NEW LIFE-STYLE FAMILY
COPING WITH OLD LIFE-STYLE PROBLEMS. (ANGER, DIFF
SIT--ONE PARENT, EMOTIONS--ANGER, FAM--FATHERS,
FAM--ONE PARENT, FAM--SIBLING RIVALRY, FATHERS,
ONE PARENT, SIBLING RIVALRY)

PRESTON, EDNA. THE TEMPER TANTRUM BOOK. VIKING,
1969.   ILLUSTRATED BY RAINEY BENNETT.   (HB)

   AN IMAGINATIVE WAY TO PORTRAY ALL OF THE
THINGS THAT BOTHER LITTLE KIDS--MOM GETS SOAP IN
YOUR EYES IN THE SHOWER, SHE HURTS YOU TRYING TO
GET SNARLS OUT OF YOUR HAIR--EXCEPT THAT ANIMALS
HUMOROUSLY ACT OUT ALL OF THESE HUMAN TEMPER
TANTRUMS. LIONS, TURTLES, AND PIGGISH PIGS MARCH
ACROSS THE PAGES, AND LEND A CERTAIN PERSPECTIVE
TO THE CHILD WHO MAY BE ABLE TO PUT HIMSELF INTO
THE BOOK. (ANGER, EMOTIONS--ANGER,
SELF-UNDERSTANDING)

SIMON, NORMA. I WAS SO MAD!. WHITMAN, A., 1974.
ILLUSTRATED BY DORA LEDER.   (CCB-B)

   THE AUTHOR'S NOTE IN THE FOREWORD SPELLS OUT
THE INTENTION OF THIS BOOK: TO PICTURE SITUATIONS
WHICH PRODUCE ANGER AND SHOW THAT THIS HAPPENS
TO MANY PEOPLE. PERHAPS ONE OF THE STRENGTHS OF
THE BOOK IS THAT A DIFFERENT PERSON IS SHOWN IN
EACH SITUATION, INCLUDING A MOTHER. ENDS WITH A
FUNNY SONG ABOUT A MAN WHO WAS SO MAD HE "JUMPED
INTO A PUDDING BOG"--AND LEAVES THE READER WITH A
GOOD TASTE IN HIS MOUTH. (ANGER,
EMOTIONS--ANGER, SELF-UNDERSTANDING)

VIORST, JUDITH. I'LL FIX ANTHONY. HARPER, 1969.
ILLUSTRATED BY ARNOLD LOBEL.   (BL)

   A CLASSIC RECITAL OF THE VENGEFUL JEALOUSY
SEETHING INSIDE A LITTLE BOY, WHO IS NOT YET
QUITE SIX. WE SEE A PORTRAIT OF THE OLDER BROTHER
THROUGH THE EYES OF THE ABUSED YOUNGER BROTHER:
THE OLDER BROTHER WHO IS CONSISTENTLY BIGGER AND
STRONGER, PHYSICALLY AND MENTALLY, BUT SELFISH,
PRIVILEGED, AND RATHER HORRID. ANTHONY ANNOUNCES
THAT HE'S GOING TO CLOBBER YOUNGER BROTHER, AND
SAYS, "YOU STINK." LITTLE BROTHER SAYS, "I'LL FIX
ANTHONY." (WHEN I'M SIX.) (ANGER,
EMOTIONS--ANGER, EMOTIONS--JEALOUSY, FAM--SIBLING

RIVALRY, JEALOUSY, SIBLING RIVALRY)

EMOTIONS--BOREDOM

ALEXANDER, MARTHA. WE NEVER GET TO DO ANYTHING.
DIAL, 1970. ILLUSTRATED BY MARTHA ALEXANDER.
(CC)

A VERY BORED LITTLE BOY WHO WANTS TO GO
SWIMMING IS TIED TO THE CLOTHESLINE BY HIS BUSY
MOTHER, AND DECIDES TO DO SOMETHING ABOUT IT. HE
STEPS OUT OF HIS SUNSUIT, STILL TIED TO THE LINE,
AND SETS OUT IN THE ALTOGETHER FOR A WALK DOWN
THE STREET. AFTER HE IS RETRIEVED BY HIS MOTHER
HE TURNS HIS SANDBOX INTO A SWIMMING POOL,
DEMONSTRATING INGENUITY BOTH IN FULFILLING HIS
DESIRE TO GO SWIMMING AND IN RESOLVING HIS
PROBLEM ALL BY HIMSELF. (BOREDOM,
EMOTIONS--BOREDOM)

BERSON, HAROLD. I'M BORED, MA!. CROWN, 1976.
ILLUSTRATED BY HAROLD BERSON. (BL)

AN ENGAGING, OVERPRIVILEGED RABBIT IS THE
CHARACTER WHO IS BORED, AS THE READER SEES HIM
KICK HIS TEDDY BEAR, THROW HIS TOY HORSE IN THE
CORNER, AND FINALLY THROW HIS LOVELY YELLOW
AIRPLANE IN THE TRASH CAN. STEVE RABBIT AND HIS
MOTHER ARE A COLORFUL PAIR IN AN URBAN APARTMENT
SETTING. MOTHER WEARS AN ANKLE LENGTH COAT AND A
HEAD SCARF TIED IN THE NEW LIFE-STYLE FASHION.
HER SON WEARS A PEAKED CAP IN THE FASHION OF TV'S
CAPTAIN AND TENNILLE AND A RAKISH LONG SCARF.
PARENTS WILL NOT FEEL SORRY FOR STEVE RABBIT, BUT
MANY CHILDREN WILL IDENTIFY WITH HIM. PACK RAT,
WHO SALVAGES THE YELLOW AIRPLANE FROM THE
GARBAGE, IS DRESSED JUST AS OUTRAGEOUSLY, AND
BETWEEN THE TWO FRIENDS THE PROBLEM OF BEING
BORED IS SOLVED IN A SATISFYING WAY. (BOREDOM,
EMOTIONS--BOREDOM, FRIENDSHIP)

HOBAN, RUSSELL. NOTHING TO DO. HARPER, 1964.
ILLUSTRATED BY LILLIAN HOBAN. (CC)

WALTER, AN OPOSSUM, ALWAYS SAYS THERE IS
NOTHING TO DO UNTIL HIS FATHER GIVES HIM A
SOMETHING-TO-DO-STONE. WALTER USES HIS
SOMETHING-TO-DO-STONE VERY WELL, AND THINKS OF A
LOT OF WAYS FOR KENNETH AND HIMSELF TO PLAY. HE
LOSES THE STONE, BUT WHEN HIS PESTY SISTER

CHARLOTTE COMES AROUND BOTHERING HIM, HE GIVES
HER A PLAY-RIGHT-HERE STICK, WHICH WORKS MAGIC,
JUST THE WAY THE STONE WORKED FOR HIM. (BOREDOM,
EMOTIONS--BOREDOM, SELF-RELIANCE)

RASKIN, ELLEN. NOTHING EVER HAPPENS ON MY BLOCK.
ATHENEUM, 1967. ILLUSTRATED BY ELLEN RASKIN.
(BCB)

   CHESTER FILBERT, A BORED LITTLE BOY WHO SITS
ON THE CURB BEMOANING THE FACT THAT LIFE IS MORE
INTERESTING IN OTHER PLACES, IS STILL SITTING ON
THE CURB AT THE END OF THE BOOK WHILE ALL SORTS
OF EXCITING THINGS ARE HAPPENING: LIGHTNING
STRIKES THE ROOF OF A HOUSE SOON AFTER THE
CARPENTER FIXES IT--THAT WAS AFTER THE FIRE, OF
COURSE. POOR CHESTER IS OBLIVIOUS TO IT ALL, AND
CHILDREN WILL ENJOY PICKING OUT ALL THE DETAILS.
BY THE WAY, WHAT DID HAPPEN TO THE 34 WITCHES?
(BOREDOM, EMOTIONS--BOREDOM)

EMOTIONS--BRAVERY

ALEXANDER, MARTHA. BOBO'S DREAM. DIAL, 1970.
ILLUSTRATED BY MARTHA ALEXANDER. (CC)

   AN ENGAGING RELATIONSHIP BETWEEN A LITTLE BOY,
WHO HAPPENS TO BE BLACK, WHO LIKES TO PLAY
FOOTBALL AS WELL AS READ BOOKS ABOUT MONSTERS,
AND HIS SAUSAGE DOG. ALTHOUGH THERE ARE NO WORDS,
THE READER KNOWS THE DOG'S NAME IS BOBO. THE
LITTLE BOY LOVES HIS DOG, BUYING HIM A BIG BONE
AND PROTECTING HIM AGAINST A BIG DOG, AND WHEN
BOBO DREAMS, HE DREAMS OF PROTECTING THE LITTLE
BOY. WHEN BOBO WAKES UP, HE FINDS THE COURAGE TO
BARK AT THE BIG SHAGGY DOG WHO IS AGAIN AFTER HIS
BONE, THUS PUTTING INTO PRACTICE THE BRAVERY IN
HIS DREAM. (BRAVERY, EMOTIONS--BRAVERY)

ANGLUND, JOAN. THE BRAVE COWBOY. HARCOURT, 1959.
ILLUSTRATED BY JOAN ANGLUND. (CC)

   A LITTLE BOY OF PRESCHOOL AGE PRETENDS HE IS A
REAL COWBOY, WHO CAPTURES RUSTLERS AND CONFRONTS
ALL KINDS OF SCARY SITUATIONS IN HIS IMAGINARY
LIFE. THE PICTURES OF THE REAL LIFE OF THE LITTLE
BOY ARE IN BLACK AND WHITE AND HIS IMAGINARY
EXPLOITS IN RED, SO THE CHILD SEEING THE BOOK IS
WELL AWARE OF THE DIFFERENCE BETWEEN THE TWO
WORLDS. (BRAVERY, EMOTIONS--BRAVERY)

BUCKLEY, HELEN. MICHAEL IS BRAVE. LOTHROP, 1971.
 ILLUSTRATED BY EMILY MC CULLY. (ESLC)

   AN EXCELLENTLY REALISTIC STORY CONCERNING THE
FEAR THAT MICHAEL HAD ABOUT GOING DOWN THE SLIDE.
WHEN A NEW GIRL IN SCHOOL TRIES IT, AND FINDS
HERSELF IN TEARS, THE TEACHER SUGGESTS THAT
MICHAEL CLIMB THE LADDER AND STAND BEHIND HER.
THROUGH THIS ACT OF HELPING, MICHAEL IS ABLE TO
GO DOWN THE SLIDE ALONE. ILLUSTRATES THE POINT
THAT WHEN YOU HELP SOMEONE ELSE, YOU BECOME MORE
BRAVE YOURSELF. (BRAVERY, EMOTIONS--BRAVERY,
SELF-CONFIDENCE)

COHEN, MIRIAM. TOUGH JIM. MACMILLAN, 1974.
 ILLUSTRATED BY LILLIAN HOBAN. (CCB-B)

   JIM IS THE RATHER QUIET, SELF-EFFACING FIRST
GRADER IN A MULTI-ETHNIC CLASSROOM WHO HAS
APPEARED IN EARLIER COHEN BOOKS, AND WE SEE HIS
INNER THOUGHTS IN THIS STORY OF A COSTUME PARTY.
HE WANTS TO BE "SOMEONE VERY STRONG, SOMEONE VERY
TOUGH." HE DRESSES AS THE STRONGEST MAN IN THE
WORLD AND, IN A VERY SUPPORTIVE CIRCLE OF
FRIENDS, GETS THE BEST OF AN OLDER BOY WHO WANTS
TO FIGHT. (BRAVERY, EMOTIONS--BRAVERY,
SELF-CONFIDENCE, SELF-IDENTITY)

HURLIMANN, BETTINA. BARRY. HARCOURT, 1967.
 ILLUSTRATED BY PAUL NUSSBAUMER. (ESLC)

   CHILDREN WILL GRASP THE MEANING OF COURAGE
WHEN THEY HEAR THIS STORY, SET IN SWITZERLAND, OF
A ST. BERNARD RESCUE DOG. OF THE MANY RESCUES
THE DOG MADE, PERHAPS THE STORY OF HIS FINDING A
SMALL GIRL AND CARRYING HER ON HIS BACK TO THE
HOSPICE WHERE THE MONKS LIVED IS THE MOST
MEMORABLE. CHILDREN WILL ALSO EMPATHIZE WITH THIS
TRUE STORY, AS BARRY MEETS WITH AN ACCIDENT
WHICH EVENTUALLY LEADS TO HIS DEATH. THE
CONTINUITY OF BIRTH, LIFE, AND DEATH, AS YOUNG
ST. BERNARDS ARE TRAINED AS RESCUERS, ENLARGES
THE SCOPE OF THIS STORY. (BRAVERY,
EMOTIONS--BRAVERY, DEATH, DIFF SIT--DEATH)

MAYER, MERCER. YOU'RE THE SCAREDY-CAT. PARENTS'
MAG, 1974. ILLUSTRATED BY MERCER MAYER. (BL)

   OLDER BROTHER CONVINCES YOUNGER BROTHER TO
SLEEP OUT IN THE BACK YARD. THINKING TO SCARE THE

SMALLER YOUTH, HE TELLS STORIES OF THE GREEN
GARBAGE CAN MONSTER, WITH BEAUTIFULLY MONSTERISH
ILLUSTRATIONS. TURNS OUT HE'S THE ONE WHO HAS THE
NIGHTMARES, BUT WON'T ADMIT HE'S SCARED.
(BRAVERY, EMOTIONS--BRAVERY, EMOTIONS--FEAR, FEAR)

SHAY, ARTHUR. WHAT HAPPENS WHEN YOU GO TO THE
HOSPITAL. REILLY, 1969.   (CC)

    KAREN'S SHINY, SMILING FACE ON THE COLORFUL
COVER SETS THE TONE FOR A NON-THREATENING
EXPERIENCE IN THE HOSPITAL FOR ANY CHILD READER.
ALTHOUGH KAREN IS TEARFULLY APPREHENSIVE AT
TIMES, CHILDREN WILL UNDERSTAND THAT IT IS NORMAL
TO MISS YOUR PARENTS AND THAT YOU MIGHT BE A
LITTLE AFRAID OF THE X-RAY MACHINE. AUTHOR SHAY
HAS SAID THAT HIS PURPOSE IS TO SHOW THE JOBS AND
SERVICES THAT GO ON IN A HOSPITAL, AND TO HELP
CHILDREN UNDERSTAND IN ADVANCE WHAT WILL HAPPEN
TO THEM. HE HAS SUCCEEDED IN PRODUCING A VERY
USEFUL, SUCCESSFUL BOOK. (BRAVERY, DIFF
SIT--HOSPITAL, EMOTIONS--BRAVERY, HOSPITAL, NEW
SIT--HOSPITAL)

WILLIAMS, GWENEIRA. TIMID TIMOTHY. Y. SCOTT,
1944.   ILLUSTRATED BY LEONARD WEISGARD.   (CC)

    A LITTLE KITTEN IS TAUGHT BY HIS MOTHER TO BE
BRAVE, AND HOW TO SCARE OTHER ANIMALS. SHE TELLS
HIM TO ARCH HIS BACK, STICK OUT HIS WHISKERS, AND
GO P-SSS-T. TO BE SURE, MOST OF THE ANIMALS HE
SCARES ARE STUFFED ANIMALS, UNTIL HE MEETS UP
WITH A PUPPY. WHEN THE PUPPY RUNS AWAY, TIMOTHY
KNOWS HOW IT FEELS TO BE BRAVE. USEFUL BECAUSE IT
SHOWS THAT MANY YOUNG ANIMALS ARE AFRAID AT
TIMES. (BRAVERY, EMOTIONS--BRAVERY,
EMOTIONS--FEAR, FEAR)

EMOTIONS--FEAR

COHEN, MIRIAM. WILL I HAVE A FRIEND?. MACMILLAN,
1967.   ILLUSTRATED BY LILLIAN HOBAN.   (BCB)

    A REALISTIC FEAR IN A YOUNG CHILD IS SHOWN IN
A TYPICAL PICTURE OF THE FIRST DAY OF
KINDERGARTEN. CHILDREN MILL ABOUT, EACH INTENT ON
HIS OWN BUSINESS, AND JIM DOESN'T FEEL INCLUDED
UNTIL AFTER REST TIME WHEN PAUL SHOWS HIM HIS
TINY TRUCK. THIS CHARACTER PAUL ALSO APPEARS IN
"BEST FRIEND" BY THE SAME AUTHOR.

(EMOTIONS--FEAR, FEAR, FRIENDSHIP, NEW
SIT--SCHOOL)

HOBAN, RUSSELL. BEDTIME FOR FRANCES. HARPER,
1960. ILLUSTRATED BY GARTH WILLIAMS. (CC)

   FATHER BADGER PLAYS AN IMPORTANT ROLE IN
HANDLING THE BEDTIME PROBLEMS OF HIS DAUGHTER
FRANCES WITH AN IMAGINATIVE EXPLANATION OF HER
FEARS. WHEN FRANCES, AN ENTRANCING LITTLE GIRL
WHO ONLY INCIDENTALLY HAPPENS TO BE A BADGER,
GOES THROUGH THE FAMILIAR BEDTIME ROUTINE OF
MILK, HUGS, KISSES, AND TEDDY BEAR, BUT STILL
DOES NOT FALL ASLEEP, FATHER GIVES REASSURING
ADVICE ABOUT THE IMAGINARY GIANTS AND THE
SOMETHING SCARY THAT MIGHT COME OUT OF THE CRACK
IN THE CEILING. HIS MOST CREATIVE SOLUTION,
HOWEVER, COMES WHEN FRANCES COMPLAINS OF THE
CURTAINS MOVING AT THE WINDOW--HE TELLS HER THAT
THE WIND'S JOB IS TO GO AROUND AND BLOW ALL THE
CURTAINS, THAT EVERYBODY HAS A JOB, AND THAT
FURTHERMORE, HER JOB IS TO GO TO SLEEP.
THROUGHOUT THE BOOK, FATHER IS THE PARENT WHO
RELATES TO THE CHILD, ALTHOUGH THE MOTHER IS
VISIBLE. (BEHAVIOR--DISLIKES--SLEEP,
DISLIKES--SLEEP, EMOTIONS--FEAR, FAM--FATHERS,
FATHERS, FEAR)

IWASAKI, CHIHIRO. STAYING HOME ALONE ON A RAINY
DAY. MC GRAW, 1968. ILLUSTRATED BY CHIHIRO
IWASAKI. (LJ)

   LONELINESS IS A SHARP PAIN FOR A CHILD LEFT
ALONE FOR THE FIRST TIME, AND ALLISON TRIES MANY
WAYS TO MAKE THOSE FEELINGS GO AWAY. SHE WANTS TO
HOLD HER KITTEN, SHE ENVIES THE BABY FISH
SWIMMING WITH ITS MOTHER, AND WHEN SHE TOUCHES
THE KEYS OF THE PIANO, IT ONLY REMINDS HER OF HER
MOTHER. AUTHOR-ARTIST IWASAKI HAS COMPLEMENTED
THESE FEELINGS OF FRUSTRATION WITH EXQUISITE,
WATERY, FREE-FORM WATERCOLORS, SUITING THE BROWN
AND GRAY TONES TO THE GRAY RAINY DAY SEEN THROUGH
THE WINDOW. CHILDREN IDENTIFY WITH THESE
SITUATIONS, ESPECIALLY THE TERROR OF THE PHONE
RINGING AND BEING AFRAID TO ANSWER IT. USEFUL
BECAUSE IT HELPS THE CHILD SEE THAT OTHER
CHILDREN ARE ALSO AFRAID, BUT THAT MOTHER DOES
RETURN, WHEN THE SUNSHINE RETURNS AT THE END OF
THE AFTERNOON. (EMOTIONS--FEAR,
EMOTIONS--LONELINESS, FEAR, LONELINESS)

KRAUS, ROBERT. GOOD NIGHT, RICHARD RABBIT.
SPRINGFELLOW, 1972. ILLUSTRATED BY N.M.
BODECKER. (CCB-B)

   TINY FORMAT MAKES THIS A CHARMING BEDTIME
STORY FOR THE VERY YOUNG, AS MOST YOUNGSTERS WILL
IDENTIFY WITH RICHARD RABBIT. A MIX OF REAL AND
IMAGINARY FEARS, AND A LITTLE OF DOWNRIGHT
TEASING ARE SEEN AS THE YOUNG RABBIT PRETENDS
THERE IS A FACE LOOKING IN THE WINDOW. EVERY
OTHER PAGE DEALS WITH A QUESTION OR COMMENT, THE
FACING PAGE WITH MOTHER'S ANSWER. IN ALL OF THE
ILLUSTRATIONS, RICHARD IS VERY SMALL, AND MOTHER
LOOMS VERY LARGE AND SOLID, TRULY A SECURITY
FIGURE, AND ON THE FINAL PAGE RICHARD DRIFTS OFF
TO SLEEP. (BEHAVIOR--DISLIKES--SLEEP,
DISLIKES--SLEEP, EMOTIONS--FEAR,
EMOTIONS--SECURITY, FEAR, SECURITY)

MAHY, MARGARET. A LION IN THE MEADOW. WATTS,
1969. ILLUSTRATED BY JENNY WILLIAMS. (BCB)

   FEARFUL THAT THERE IS A LION IN THE MEADOW,
THE LITTLE BOY TELLS HIS MOTHER. HER SOLUTION:
SHE SAYS HE IS MAKING UP STORIES, GIVES HIM A
LITTLE MATCH BOX, AND TELLS HIM THAT THERE IS A
TINY DRAGON IN IT WHICH WILL GROW BIG AND CHASE
THE LION AWAY. THE DRAGON MATERIALIZES AND CHASES
THE LION INTO THE HOUSE, WHERE HE AND THE BOY
BECOME FRIENDS. A CROSS BETWEEN FANTASY AND FAIRY
TALE, THE STORY CAN BE USED TO DEVELOP
IMAGINATION IN CHILDREN, AS WELL AS TO DISPEL
FEARS. HANDSOME, COLORFUL ILLUSTRATIONS TEND TO
DE-EMPHASIZE ANY FEARFUL ASPECTS OF THE BOOK.
(EMOTIONS--FEAR, FEAR)

MAYER, MERCER. YOU'RE THE SCAREDY-CAT. PARENTS'
MAG, 1974. ILLUSTRATED BY MERCER MAYER. (BL)

   OLDER BROTHER CONVINCES YOUNGER BROTHER TO
SLEEP OUT IN THE BACK YARD. THINKING TO SCARE THE
SMALLER YOUTH, HE TELLS STORIES OF THE GREEN
GARBAGE CAN MONSTER, WITH BEAUTIFULLY MONSTERISH
ILLUSTRATIONS. TURNS OUT HE'S THE ONE WHO HAS THE
NIGHTMARES, BUT WON'T ADMIT HE'S SCARED.
(BRAVERY, EMOTIONS--BRAVERY, EMOTIONS--FEAR, FEAR)

RESSNER, PHILIP. AT NIGHT. DUTTON, 1967.
ILLUSTRATED BY CHARLES PRATT. (ESLC)

A SERIES OF BLACK AND WHITE PHOTOGRAPHS,
APPROPRIATELY ENOUGH, LEAD THE READER'S EYE
THROUGH A NIGHT IN THE CITY. USEFUL BECAUSE IT
WILL GIVE THE READER A FEELING OF SECURITY,
KNOWING THAT THERE IS NOTHING TO FEAR FROM
DARKNESS IN ITSELF. IT SHOWS A LIFE THE CHILD
RARELY SEES, AND MAY NOT BE ABLE TO IMAGINE: THE
EMPTY SCHOOL ROOM, THE BUMPS IN THE SIDEWALK. AS
DAWN BREAKS, THE CHILD SEES THE MIRACLE OF A NEW
DAY, AS THE CIRCLE OF THE EARTH TURNS.
(EMOTIONS--FEAR, EMOTIONS--SECURITY, FEAR,
SECURITY)

ROCKWELL, HARLOW. MY DENTIST. MORROW, 1975.
ILLUSTRATED BY HARLOW ROCKWELL. (BL)

FEAR OF THE DENTIST IS NOT CONFINED TO
CHILDREN, FOR MANY ADULTS GO THROUGH LIFE WITH AN
IRRATIONAL STATE OF APPREHENSION ABOUT SUCH
VISITS. EARLY EXPOSURE TO NON-THREATENING
SITUATIONS SUCH AS THE ONES PICTURED HERE SHOULD
DO MUCH TO REDUCE THESE FEARS, FOR THE ATTRACTIVE
PIG-TAILED YOUNGSTER IS SHOWN AS INTERESTED,
SMILING AT TIMES, AND THOROUGHLY COMFORTABLE
THROUGHOUT THE PROCESS OF TEETH CLEANING. WHILE
THE INSTRUMENTS (I.E., THE PICKS AND PROBES) MAY
LOOK MENACING, THERE IS MUCH TO BE SAID FOR
SHOWING THEM IN DETAIL ALONG WITH THE X-RAY
CAMERA AND THE DRILLS. FEAR OF THE UNKNOWN IS
PERHAPS MORE THREATENING THAN FEAR OF THE KNOWN.
(DENTIST, DIFF SIT--DENTIST, EMOTIONS--FEAR, FEAR)

ROCKWELL, HARLOW. MY DOCTOR. MACMILLAN, 1973.
ILLUSTRATED BY HARLOW ROCKWELL. (BL)

FOR A CHILD WHO IS APPREHENSIVE ABOUT A VISIT
TO THE DOCTOR, THIS PICTURE BOOK MAY PROVE TO BE
A DE-SENSITIZING INSTRUMENT. LIKE THE OBSERVABLE
DETAIL ON THE THERMOMETER AND THE SYRINGE, THE
CALM, UNEMOTIONAL CLIMATE IN THE DOCTOR'S OFFICE
IS ALSO TANGIBLE, VISIBLE PROOF THAT THE OCCASION
IS NOT ONE TO FEAR. BY BRINGING OUT INTO THE
OPEN THE SECRETS OF THE JARS OF MEDICINE, AND BY
EXPLAINING VARIOUS INSTRUMENTS AND THEIR USES IN
A COLORFUL, FRIENDLY ATMOSPHERE, THE AUTHOR HAS
PROVIDED A NEEDED MEANS OF REDUCING TENSION IN
THE MIND OF A CHILD. (DIFF SIT--DOCTOR, DOCTOR,
EMOTIONS--FEAR, FEAR)

ROCKWELL, HARLOW. MY NURSERY SCHOOL. MORROW,

1976.   ILLUSTRATED BY HARLOW ROCKWELL. (BL)

WHILE THIS BOOK DOES NOT DEAL WITH THE
ADJUSTMENT TO THE NEWNESS OF NURSERY SCHOOL, THE
PLEASANT ENVIRONMENT OF BUILDING BLOCKS AND CLAY,
PETS AND PLANTS, AND EXCITING DRESS-UP CLOTHES
SETS A POSITIVE MOOD FOR ANY CHILD WHO MIGHT FEEL
APPREHENSIVE ABOUT GOING TO NURSERY SCHOOL.
CHILDREN OF DIFFERENT RACES ARE PICTURED IN THE
COLORFUL ACTIVITIES, AS IS MR. PAUL, A MALE
TEACHER. CLEAR, FRESH COLORS GIVE THE BOOK AN
UPBEAT FEELING, AND IT IS A PLUS FOR THOSE
PERSONS LOOKING FOR EXAMPLES OF NON-TRADITIONAL
ROLES FOR CHILDREN AND ADULTS. (EMOTIONS--FEAR,
FEAR, NEW SIT--SCHOOL)

SOBOL, HARRIET. JEFF'S HOSPITAL BOOK. WALCK,
1975. ILLUSTRATED BY PATRICIA AGRE. (BL)

PHYSICIANS FROM TWO MAJOR MEDICAL INSTITUTIONS
WERE USED AS CONSULTANTS FOR THIS HELPFUL,
ACCURATE BOOK WHICH DESCRIBES A YOUNG BOY'S
EXPERIENCE AS HE UNDERGOES SURGERY TO CORRECT
CROSSED EYES. LARGE BLACK AND WHITE PHOTOGRAPHS
GIVE A STEP-BY-STEP NO NONSENSE APPROACH TO THIS
STORY BUT, THROUGHOUT, THE HUMAN ELEMENT IS
THERE, TOO, AS WE SEE JEFF FEELING SCARED AND
WORRIED BEFORE THE OPERATION. REASSURING PICTURES
OF MOTHER AND FATHER WITH HIM AFTERWARD, AND
HORSEPLAY WITH THE NEIGHBORHOOD KIDS LEND AN
UPBEAT FEELING TO THE BOOK. (DIFF SIT--HANDICAPS,
EMOTIONS--FEAR, FEAR, HANDICAPS, HOSPITAL, NEW
SIT--HOSPITAL)

SONNEBORN, RUTH. THE LOLLIPOP PARTY. VIKING,
1967. ILLUSTRATED BY BRINTON TURKLE. (ESLC)

ONE DAY TOMAS IS LEFT ALONE IN THE APARTMENT
FOR THE FIRST TIME. HIS SISTER ANA, WHO USUALLY
CARED FOR HIM BEFORE GOING TO HER JOB, HAD TO
LEAVE HIM ALONE. STEP-BY-STEP THE READER
PARTICIPATES IN THE LITTLE BOY'S FEAR. HE WAS
CONCERNED ABOUT THE SOUND OF FOOTSTEPS ON THE
STAIRS, AND WISHED ONLY TO SIT QUIETLY AND HOLD
HIS CAT GATTO. WHEN HIS NURSERY SCHOOL TEACHER
COMES TO THE DOOR ON A VISIT, HOWEVER, THE
EMOTIONAL TONE OF THE BOOK CHANGES IMMEDIATELY.
HE IS HAPPY TO SEE HER, ACTS THE ROLE OF THE HOST
BY OFFERING HER A LOLLIPOP, AND THE STORY ENDS
WITH TOMAS FEELING A BIT GROWN-UP.

(EMOTIONS--FEAR, EMOTIONS--LONELINESS,
FAM--MOTHERS WORKING, FEAR, LONELINESS, MOTHERS
WORKING, SELF-RELIANCE)

TAMBURINE, JEAN. I THINK I WILL GO TO THE
HOSPITAL. ABINGDON, 1965.   ILLUSTRATED BY JEAN
TAMBURINE.   (CCB-B, LJ)

   AN EXCELLENT BOOK FOR A CHILD AND HIS PARENT
TO PREPARE FOR A HOSPITAL VISIT. WHEN SUSY
DECIDES SHE DOES NOT WANT TO GO TO THE HOSPITAL,
HER MOTHER TAKES HER TO THE WAITING ROOM OF THE
HOSPITAL, AND ON THE WAY SHE STOPS WITH GET-WELL
PRESENTS FOR PEOPLE JUST OUT OF THE HOSPITAL.
THESE ARE POSITIVE CONTACTS, AND SUSY ALSO MEETS
A FRIENDLY NURSE WHO TAKES TIME TO TALK ABOUT
WHAT WILL HAPPEN TO HER. AT HOME, SHE PLAYS
HOSPITAL WITH HER PETS, AND BY THE TIME SHE
ARRIVES AT THE HOSPITAL, SHE IS RELAXED AND READY
TO HAVE HER PARENTS LEAVE. THIS IS ONE OF THE
LONGEST STORIES ON THIS SUBJECT, AND IS A FUN
BOOK FOR READING ALOUD. (EMOTIONS--FEAR, FEAR,
HOSPITAL, NEW SIT--HOSPITAL)

VIORST, JUDITH. MY MOMMA SAYS THERE AREN'T ANY
ZOMBIES, GHOSTS, VAMPIRES, CREATURES, DEMONS,
MONSTERS, FIENDS, GOBLINS, OR THINGS. ATHENEUM,
1973.   ILLUSTRATED BY KAY CHORAO.   (CC)

   THE FEARSOME, SCARY PICTURES IN THIS PICTURE
BOOK WILL INTRIGUE CHILDREN WHO ARE LOOKING FOR A
SCARY BOOK, EVEN THOUGH THERE ARE REASSURING
LINES OF TEXT ON EVERY PAGE. DEMONSTRATES SOME OF
THE VERY REAL FEARS THAT CHILDREN HAVE IN THE
NIGHT ABOUT IMAGINARY THINGS. (EMOTIONS--FEAR,
FEAR)

WABER, BERNARD. IRA SLEEPS OVER. HOUGHTON, 1972.
 ILLUSTRATED BY BERNARD WABER.   (ESLC)

   IRA IS THE YOUNG CHILD IN A FAMILY WITH
UNDERSTANDING PARENTS, AND A SISTER FOND OF
PUT-DOWNS. WHEN HIS MOTHER AND FATHER TELL HIM
THAT IT WILL BE OK IF HE TAKES HIS TEDDY BEAR ON
HIS FIRST SLEEPOVER AT HIS FRIEND'S HOUSE, HIS
SISTER INSISTS THAT HIS FRIEND WILL LAUGH AND
THINK HE'S A BABY. HOW WILL HE FEEL SLEEPING
WITHOUT HIS TEDDY BEAR FOR THE VERY FIRST TIME?
LUCKILY IRA NEVER NEEDS TO FACE THAT SITUATION,
FOR THE CAPPER TO THE STORY IS THAT REGGIE SLEEPS

WITH HIS TEDDY BEAR, TOO, SO IRA FEELS CONFIDENT
ENOUGH TO MARCH OVER TO HIS OWN HOUSE, UP THE
STAIRS, WITH A SMUG EXPRESSION ON HIS FACE, TO
PICK UP TAH-TAH, HIS TEDDY BEAR. NOTABLE FOR ITS
RECOGNITION OF THE FACT THAT CHILDREN ENJOY
MILDLY SCARY SITUATIONS IF THERE IS AN UNDERLYING
BOLSTERING OF SECURITY, THE BOOK IS ALSO LIKELY
TO BE AROUND FOR AWHILE BECAUSE IT PICTURES AN
URBAN, CONTEMPORARY FAMILY WITH A FATHER COOKING
AT THE STOVE AND, IN ONE SCENE, A MOTHER CURLED
UP ON THE COUCH IN HER PAJAMAS. (EMOTIONS--FEAR,
EMOTIONS--SECURITY, FEAR, SECURITY)

WILLIAMS, GWENEIRA. TIMID TIMOTHY. Y. SCOTT,
1944. ILLUSTRATED BY LEONARD WEISGARD. (CC)

   A LITTLE KITTEN IS TAUGHT BY HIS MOTHER TO BE
BRAVE, AND HOW TO SCARE OTHER ANIMALS. SHE TELLS
HIM TO ARCH HIS BACK, STICK OUT HIS WHISKERS, AND
GO P-SSS-T. TO BE SURE, MOST OF THE ANIMALS HE
SCARES ARE STUFFED ANIMALS, UNTIL HE MEETS UP
WITH A PUPPY. WHEN THE PUPPY RUNS AWAY, TIMOTHY
KNOWS HOW IT FEELS TO BE BRAVE. USEFUL BECAUSE IT
SHOWS THAT MANY YOUNG ANIMALS ARE AFRAID AT
TIMES. (BRAVERY, EMOTIONS--BRAVERY,
EMOTIONS--FEAR, FEAR)

WOLDE, GUNILLA. BETSY'S FIRST DAY AT NURSERY
SCHOOL. RANDOM, 1976. ILLUSTRATED BY GUNILLA
WOLDE. (BL)

   THIS SMALL, CHILD-SIZE BOOK STRIKES JUST THE
RIGHT NOTE TO DISPEL FEARS ABOUT GOING OFF TO
NURSERY SCHOOL FOR THE FIRST TIME. MOTHER WISELY
SCHEDULES A SHORT VISIT WHICH BEGINS WITH ROBERT,
ONE OF THE TEACHERS, SHOWING THEM AROUND. BETSY
IS RELUCTANT TO JOIN IN THE ACTIVITIES, AND KEEPS
HER SNOWSUIT ON, BUT A LITTLE LATER FINDS A
FRIEND. BY THE TIME MOTHER GATHERS UP THE TWO
CHILDREN TO GO HOME, BETSY FEELS MORE RELAXED,
AND IS LOOKING FORWARD TO RETURNING THE NEXT DAY.
USEFUL BECAUSE IT SHOWS THE CHILD THAT OTHER
CHILDREN ARE ALSO A LITTLE CONCERNED ABOUT BEING
LEFT AT SCHOOL. SWEDISH AUTHOR WOLDE IS
CONSISTENT IN SHOWING MALES IN NON-TRADITIONAL
ROLES IN THIS SERIES ABOUT BETSY.
(EMOTIONS--FEAR, FEAR, NEW SIT--SCHOOL)

ZOLOTOW, CHARLOTTE. MY FRIEND JOHN. HARPER,
1968. ILLUSTRATED BY BEN SHECTER. (CC)

A STUDY IN FRIENDSHIP WHICH HIGHLIGHTS THE
DIFFERENCES AS WELL AS THE WAY THE BOYS ARE
ALIKE. ONE SLEEPS WITH THE LIGHT ON AT NIGHT, THE
OTHER IS AFRAID OF CATS. FRIENDSHIP IS KNOWING A
PERSON'S FAULTS AS WELL AS INTIMATE THOUGHTS,
AND THE AUTHOR HAS CAPTURED THIS PERFECTLY AS SHE
LETS US SEE THE SECRET CRUSHES THEY BOTH HAVE ON
GIRLS. (EMOTIONS--FEAR, FEAR, FRIENDSHIP)

EMOTIONS--FRUSTRATION

KLIMOWICZ, BARBARA. FRED, FRED, USE YOUR HEAD.
ABINGDON, 1966. ILLUSTRATED BY FRANK ALOISE.
(CCB-B)

AN OVERLY DIDACTIC BOOK WHICH NEVERTHELESS MAY
PROVE USEFUL TO SOME PARENTS AND SOME CHILDREN.
FRED LEARNS TO USE HIS HEAD TO HELP HIMSELF
RATHER THAN RELY ON HIS PARENTS TO FIND HIS TOYS,
TO OPEN THE DOOR, TO GET A DRINK. THE ULTIMATE
IN LEARNING IS PROVEN WHEN FRED SUGGESTS TO HIS
FRIEND MELISSA: "USE YOUR HEAD," IN ORDER TO
SOLVE THE PROBLEM OF HOW TO MAKE A SWING.
(EMOTIONS--FRUSTRATION, FRUSTRATION,
SELF-RELIANCE)

KRAUS, ROBERT. LEO THE LATE BLOOMER. WINDMILL,
1971. ILLUSTRATED BY JOSE ARUEGO. (BCB)

IMAGINATIVE ILLUSTRATIONS CARRY THE MESSAGE
AND EXTEND IT MIGHTILY IN THIS STORY OF A YOUNG
TIGER, WHO STILL HAS HIS BABY FAT, MAKING HIM A
VERY APPEALING PROTAGONIST. LEO HAS A GAGGLE OF
FRIENDS--OWL, ELEPHANT, SNAKE, BIRD, AND
CROCODILE--ALL OF WHOM CAN READ, WRITE, DRAW, EAT
NEATLY, AND HE FEELS VERY INADEQUATE. BUT,
BECAUSE LEO IS A LATE BLOOMER, HE EVENTUALLY
MAKES IT, AND GIVES REASSURANCE TO TEACHERS,
PARENTS, AND ALL "LATE BLOOMERS."
(EMOTIONS--FRUSTRATION, FRUSTRATION,
SELF-CONFIDENCE, SELF-CONSCIOUSNESS)

VIORST, JUDITH. ALEXANDER AND THE TERRIBLE,
HORRIBLE, NO GOOD, VERY BAD DAY. ATHENEUM, 1972.
ILLUSTRATED BY RAY CRUZ. (BCB)

ALEXANDER KNOWS HE'S GOING TO FEEL BAD ALL DAY
BECAUSE FROM THE TIME HE GETS OUT OF BED WITH
GUM IN HIS HAIR, PAST LUNCHTIME WHEN HIS FRIEND
GETS TWO CUPCAKES IN HIS LUNCH BUT ALEXANDER'S

MOM FORGETS HIS DESSERT ENTIRELY, THINGS GO
WRONG. BY EVENING HIS FRUSTRATIONS HAVE
MULTIPLIED, BUT HE SEEMS TO SETTLE DOWN TO SLEEP
WHEN HIS MOM TELLS HIM THAT "SOME DAYS ARE LIKE
THAT." A LITTLE HOMILY ON MAKING THE BEST OF
THINGS WHEN LIFE DOESN'T GO SMOOTHLY.
(EMOTIONS--FRUSTRATION, FRUSTRATION)

WILDSMITH, BRIAN. THE LITTLE WOOD DUCK. WATTS,
1973. ILLUSTRATED BY BRIAN WILDSMITH. (CC)

LITTLE WOOD DUCK LIVES IN A THICKET WITH HIS
MOTHER AND FIVE BROTHERS AND SISTERS. THE FIRST
TIME HE JUMPED IN THE WATER HE FOUND HE COULD
SWIM ONLY IN CIRCLES, AND HIS MOTHER BECAME
ANGRY, AND THE ANIMALS OF THE FOREST TEASED HIM.
WHEN WISE OLD OWL DIAGNOSED THE TROUBLE (ONE FOOT
WAS LARGER THAN THE OTHER), HE TOLD THE LITTLE
DUCKLING TO PAY NO ATTENTION TO THE TEASING.
LATER, WHEN WOOD DUCK'S EFFORTS AT SWIMMING IN
CIRCLES DIVERTED THE FOX, EVERYONE DECLARED HIM A
HERO, AND THEY PROMISED NEVER TO TEASE HIM
AGAIN. USEFUL BECAUSE IT ILLUMINATES THE WAY IN
WHICH A HANDICAP MAY BECOME A BLESSING, AND
DEMONSTRATES THAT MINDLESS TEASING IS
UNDESIRABLE. (BEHAVIOR--TEASING, DIFF
SIT--HANDICAPS, EMOTIONS--FRUSTRATION,
FRUSTRATION, HANDICAPS, TEASING)

EMOTIONS--GREED

BONSALL, CROSBY. IT'S MINE!--A GREEDY BOOK.
HARPER, 1964. ILLUSTRATED BY CROSBY BONSALL.
(ESLC)

MABEL ANN AND PATRICK ARE TWO PRESCHOOLERS WHO
PLAY TOGETHER EVERY DAY, WITH THEIR ASSORTED
FAVORITE TOYS. THEY REFUSE TO SHARE, AND GO HOME
MAD. BUT AT A PICNIC, WHILE THEY ARE QUARRELING
OVER A CARROT, A GOAT EATS THEIR LUNCH, AND WHAT
FOLLOWS IS AN AMAZING TURNABOUT. THE STORY ENDS
WITH "MINE" STILL THE MOST IMPORTANT WORD IN THE
STORY, BUT PATRICK IS PLAYING WITH MABEL ANN'S
RUBBER DUCK AND MABEL ANN IS WEARING PATRICK'S
FEATHER. DELICIOUS CHILD-APPEALING DRAWINGS MAKE
THE BOOK VERY ATTRACTIVE TO CHILDREN.
(BEHAVIOR--SHARING, EMOTIONS--GREED, FRIENDSHIP,
GREED, SHARING)

HOBAN, RUSSELL. A BIRTHDAY FOR FRANCES. HARPER,

1968.   ILLUSTRATED BY LILLIAN HOBAN.   (BCB)

USEFUL FOR DEMONSTRATING THE CONCEPT OF THE
BASIC FEELING OF SELFISHNESS THAT MAY BE IN ALL
OF US, THIS ATTRACTIVE VOLUME PRESENTS A HUMOROUS
PICTURE OF FRANCES NOT WANTING TO GIVE HER
SISTER A BIRTHDAY PRESENT, THEN ALMOST EATING IT
UP WHEN SHE DOES BUY IT. AFTER ONE LAST SQUEEZE
ON THE CHOMPO BAR, SHE PRESENTS IT TO HER SISTER
GLORIA, AND TELLS HER SHE "CAN EAT IT ALL."
(EMOTIONS--GREED, EMOTIONS--JEALOUSY, GREED,
JEALOUSY)

KUSKIN, KARLA. WHAT DID YOU BRING ME?. HARPER,
1973.   ILLUSTRATED BY KARLA KUSKIN.   (LJ)

EDWINA MOUSE WAS VERY GREEDY AND WANTED
SOMETHING NEW EVERY DAY. IF SHE WENT TO THE STORE
WITH HER MOTHER, SHE BEGGED FOR A NEW TOY, AND
SHE WAS VERY ANGRY AT HER FATHER IF HE DIDN'T
BRING HER A NEW TRINKET. A HELPFUL WITCH TURNS
THE TABLES, AND EDWINA PLAYS THE ROLE OF HER
MOTHER FOR A DAY, WITH HER MOTHER AS THE CHILD. A
HELPFUL BOOK WHICH NOT ONLY SHOWS EXCESSIVE
GREEDINESS, BUT THE ROLE REVERSAL GIVES THE
READER PERSPECTIVE ON A COMMON SITUATION.
(EMOTIONS--GREED, GREED, SELF-UNDERSTANDING)

MAYER, MERCER. MINE!. SIMON, 1970.   ILLUSTRATED
BY MERCER MAYER.   (LJ, PBC)

A VERY FUNNY STORY OF GREEDINESS AND
POSSESSIVENESS, WHICH MOVES THROUGH SEVEN
EPISODES OF A LITTLE BOY CLAIMING THINGS WHICH
BELONG TO SOMEONE ELSE: SHOVEL, FISHING POLE, A
DOG'S BONE. HE IS RATHER A BULLY--GIVING GROUND
ONLY WHEN THE LITTLE GIRL HITS HIM OVER THE HEAD
WITH HER DOLL, AND GRUDGINGLY GIVING BACK THE
FISHLINE AFTER THE FISH HAS BEEN LOST. THE READER
FEELS THAT HE REALLY GETS HIS JUST DUES WHEN HE
FINDS HE MUST CLEAN HIS ROOM, WHICH HE ALSO
CLAIMED AS "MINE"--AND HIS MOTHER HANDS HIM THE
BROOM AND DUSTPAN WITH THE WORD "YOURS."
(BEHAVIOR--POSSESSIVENESS, EMOTIONS--GREED,
GREED, POSSESSIVENESS)

EMOTIONS--GUILT

GOFF, BETH. WHERE IS DADDY?. BEACON, 1969.
ILLUSTRATED BY SUSAN PERL.   (CCB-B, JMF)

ALTHOUGH THE CHILD PORTRAYED IN THIS STORY IS
A VERY YOUNG PRESCHOOLER, AND A GIRL, A
FIFTH-GRADE BOY TUCKED THE COPY OF THIS BOOK IN
HIS DESK BECAUSE IT APPARENTLY FILLED A NEED IN
HIS LIFE. AT ONE POINT THE TEXT SAYS "THE ANGER
BETWEEN THEM (HER PARENTS) MADE A PAIN INSIDE
HER, AND SHE CRIED AND CRIED." IN THE CLASSIC
ATTITUDE OF MANY CHILDREN ABOUT DIVORCE, JANIE
FEELS THAT HER OCCASIONAL ANGER TOWARD HER DAD
CAUSED THE DIVORCE. AND SHE IS AFRAID TO SAY
ANYTHING UNPLEASANT TO HER MOTHER, WHO TAKES A
JOB, FOR FEAR HER MOTHER MIGHT ALSO ABANDON HER.
HAS AN EXCELLENT PAGE OF EXPLANATION BY AN M.D.
FROM THE CHILDREN'S PSYCHIATRIC HOSPITAL AT THE
UNIVERSITY OF MICHIGAN. (DIFF SIT--DIVORCE,
DIVORCE, EMOTIONS--GUILT, GUILT)

EMOTIONS--HAPPINESS

DAUGHERTY, JAMES. ANDY AND THE LION. VIKING,
1938. ILLUSTRATED BY JAMES DAUGHERTY. (CC)

IN ROLLICKING, RHYTHMICAL DRAWINGS, JAMES
DAUGHERTY HAS SYNTHESIZED FEELINGS OF JOY IN
LIVING AND JOY IN HELPING OTHER PEOPLE. ANDY, WHO
BEFRIENDS A LION AND REMOVES A BIG THORN FROM
HIS PAW, LATER IS THE BENEFICIARY OF THE KIND
ACT. THE LION, WHO HAS ESCAPED FROM THE CIRCUS,
RECOGNIZES ANDY AND IS IMMEDIATELY FRIENDLY.
USEFUL BECAUSE IT DEMONSTRATES IN A VERY SIMPLE
WAY HOW ONE KIND ACT MAY BE REPAID, BUT FAR
BEYOND THAT, THE AFFECTIVE ASPECTS OF LIVING ARE
STRESSED--THE SENSUOUS EFFECT OF THE EXPRESSIONS
ON FACES, THE SUBTLE HUMOR IN THE DAILY FAMILY
LIFE, AND THE VIGOROUS FEELINGS DEPICTING THE JOY
OF LIVING. (BEHAVIOR--CONSIDERATION,
BEHAVIOR--KINDNESS, CONSIDERATION,
EMOTIONS--HAPPINESS, FAM, FRIENDSHIP, HAPPINESS,
KINDNESS)

HOBAN, RUSSELL. LITTLE BRUTE FAMILY. MACMILLAN,
1966. ILLUSTRATED BY LILLIAN HOBAN. (CC)

THE LITTLE BRUTE FAMILY IS NOT A FAMILY WHICH
LOVES, NOR IS IT A FAMILY ONE COULD LOVE, AT
LEAST IN THE BEGINNING. THEY QUARREL, THEY NEVER
SAY THANK-YOU, THEY EAT STONES AND ARE THOROUGHLY
DISAGREEABLE, AS WELL AS BEING UGLY. BUT THE
POWER OF ONE LITTLE GOOD FEELING UPON THIS FAMILY
WORKS A MIRACLE. THEY CHANGE SO MUCH THAT IN THE

END THE LITTLE BRUTE FAMILY CHANGES ITS NAME TO
NICE. THIS IS A DRAMATIC WAY TO SHOW A CHILD THE
IMPORTANCE OF GOOD FEELINGS.
(EMOTIONS--HAPPINESS, EMOTIONS--LOVE, HAPPINESS,
LOVE)

SIMON, NORMA. I KNOW WHAT I LIKE. WHITMAN, A.,
1971. ILLUSTRATED BY DORA LEDER. (CCB-B)

   LISTING MANY BEHAVIOR PREFERENCES IN SUCH
AREAS AS FOOD, PLAY, AND CERTAIN HOUSEHOLD
CHORES, THE BOOK ALSO GIVES INSIGHT INTO THE
DISLIKES OF INDIVIDUAL CHILDREN. AUTHOR SIMON IS
PARTICULARLY EFFECTIVE IN PRESENTING SITUATIONS
WHERE THE READER CAN EMPATHIZE, THUS GAINING IN
SELF-UNDERSTANDING IN THE AFFECTIVE AREAS SUCH AS
APPRECIATION OF BEAUTY IN THE STARS, AND THE
PLEASURES OF MUSIC. (BEHAVIOR--DISLIKES,
DISLIKES, EMOTIONS--HAPPINESS, HAPPINESS,
SELF-UNDERSTANDING)

EMOTIONS--HATE

ZOLOTOW, CHARLOTTE. THE HATING BOOK. HARPER,
1969. ILLUSTRATED BY BEN SHECTER. (RLHR)

   A SMALL GIRL KNOWS SHE HATES HER FRIEND, BUT
CAN'T MUSTER UP HER COURAGE TO ASK HER WHY SHE IS
ACTING IN A MEAN WAY. WHEN SHE FINALLY DOES ASK,
SHE FINDS OUT THAT IT REALLY WAS A
MISUNDERSTANDING THAT STARTED ALL OF THE
UNFRIENDLINESS. MORAL IS THAT IT IS BETTER TO TRY
TO FIND OUT THE FACTS WHEN YOU FACE A PROBLEM.
(EMOTIONS--HATE, FRIENDSHIP, HATE)

EMOTIONS--JEALOUSY

ALEXANDER, MARTHA. NOBODY ASKED ME IF I WANTED A
BABY SISTER. DIAL, 1971. ILLUSTRATED BY MARTHA
ALEXANDER. (BCB)

   THE STORY OPENS WITH A SOUR-FACED LITTLE BOY
OVERHEARING GUSHY COMPLIMENTS ABOUT HIS NEW BABY
SISTER. HIS NEXT MOVE IS TO LOAD HER IN A WAGON
AND TRY TO GIVE HER AWAY. AFTER SEVERAL ABORTED
ATTEMPTS, HE ENDS UP AT HIS FRIEND'S HOUSE. BABY
BONNIE MISBEHAVES, HOWEVER, AND IN THE END IT IS
THE BROTHER WHO CAN PACIFY HER. WICKED THOUGHTS
GO THROUGH HIS HEAD AS HE IMAGINES HER GROWING UP
AND PULLING HIM IN THE WAGON. (BROTHERS &

SISTERS, EMOTIONS--JEALOUSY, FAM--BROTHERS &
SISTERS, JEALOUSY, NEW SIT--BABY)

BRANDENBERG, FRANZ. I WISH I WAS SICK, TOO!.
MORROW, 1976. ILLUSTRATED BY ALIKI. (BL)

   THIS IS A BOOK IN WHICH ALL OF THE ACTION CAN
BE TRACED IN THE EXPRESSIONS IN THE EYES OF
EDWARD AND ELIZABETH, TWO ENDEARING CAT
PROTAGONISTS WITH ALL TOO HUMAN FOIBLES. EDWARD'S
EYES ARE AT HALF-MAST AS WE SEE HIM IN THE
SICKBED, AND ELIZABETH SHOOTS SIDEWISE GLANCES OF
ENVIOUS RAGE AS SHE RELUCTANTLY DOES HER CHORES
AND PRACTICES PIANO. CONCERN AND LOVE ARE
EXPRESSED IN THE EYES OF MOTHER AND FATHER AS
THEY MINISTER TO THE CHILDREN, FOR YES, ELIZABETH
ALSO BECOMES ILL. HER EYES ARE EVEN MORE
HELPLESSLY DROOPED, AND ONCE AGAIN SHE IS ENVIOUS
OF THE WELL BROTHER, WHOSE EYES ARE BY NOW ROUND
AND SPARKLY. THE STORY ENDS WITH EVERYONE
PROPERLY ROUND-EYED AND HAPPY. (BROTHERS &
SISTERS, DIFF SIT--ILLNESS, FAM--BROTHERS &
SISTERS, EMOTIONS--JEALOUSY, ILLNESS, JEALOUSY)

HAZEN, BARBARA. WHY COULDN'T I BE AN ONLY KID
LIKE YOU, WIGGER. ATHENEUM, 1975. ILLUSTRATED BY
LEIGH GRANT. (HB)

   PLEASANT CLUTTER IN A LARGE FAMILY HOUSEHOLD
WHICH HAS SIX CHILDREN KEYNOTES THE FRUSTRATION
OF THE YOUNG BOY WHO TELLS THE STORY. WIGGER, HIS
FRIEND, DOESN'T HAVE TO MOP UP THE MILK THE BABY
SPILLED, OR STAND IN LINE FOR THE BATHROOM IN
THE MORNING, AND HE, THE NARRATOR, IS FRANKLY
QUITE JEALOUS. DURING HIS TIRADE HOWEVER, THE
ILLUSTRATIONS GIVE A DIFFERENT PICTURE OF WIGGER
WHO SEEMS TO LIKE WHEELING THE BABY CARRIAGE AND
BEING A PART OF THE ROUGH AND TUMBLE OF A LARGE
FAMILY. THE NARRATOR IS SURPRISED AT THE FACT
THAT AN ONLY CHILD CAN BE A LONELY CHILD. USEFUL
FOR THE CONTRASTING POINTS OF VIEW.
(EMOTIONS--JEALOUSY, FAM--ONLY CHILD, FRIENDSHIP,
JEALOUSY, ONLY CHILD)

HOBAN, RUSSELL. A BIRTHDAY FOR FRANCES. HARPER,
1968. ILLUSTRATED BY LILLIAN HOBAN. (BCB)

   USEFUL FOR DEMONSTRATING THE CONCEPT OF THE
BASIC FEELING OF SELFISHNESS THAT MAY BE IN ALL
OF US, THIS ATTRACTIVE VOLUME PRESENTS A HUMOROUS

PICTURE OF FRANCES NOT WANTING TO GIVE HER
SISTER A BIRTHDAY PRESENT, THEN ALMOST EATING IT
UP WHEN SHE DOES BUY IT. AFTER ONE LAST SQUEEZE
ON THE CHOMPO BAR, SHE PRESENTS IT TO HER SISTER
GLORIA, AND TELLS HER SHE "CAN EAT IT ALL."
(EMOTIONS--GREED, EMOTIONS--JEALOUSY, GREED,
JEALOUSY)

KEATS, EZRA. PETER'S CHAIR. HARPER, 1967.
ILLUSTRATED BY EZRA KEATS. (BCB)

   POOR PETER! HE WAS SO JEALOUS OF THE NEW BABY,
HE DECIDED TO RUN AWAY FROM HOME. WHEN HIS DAD
BEGAN TO PAINT ALL OF PETER'S FURNITURE, HE
GRABBED HIS LITTLE CHAIR, AND RAN OUTSIDE THE
DOOR. HE WAS VERY SURPRISED TO FIND THAT HE COULD
NOT FIT INTO IT ANYMORE BECAUSE HE HAD GROWN
BIGGER. USEFUL BECAUSE IT SHOWS THE RESOLVING OF
THE JEALOUS FEELINGS: PETER AND HIS FATHER PAINT
THE LITTLE CHAIR. ADDITIONALLY USEFUL BECAUSE IT
SHOWS A PRACTICAL EXAMPLE OF GROWTH IN A CHILD.
(EMOTIONS--JEALOUSY, FAM--SIBLING RIVALRY,
JEALOUSY, NEW SIT--BABY, SIBLING RIVALRY)

KLEIN, NORMA. IF I HAD MY WAY. PANTHEON, 1974.
ILLUSTRATED BY RAY CRUZ. (BL)

   ELLIE IS A LITTLE GIRL WHO GOES TO SCHOOL, BUT
IS YOUNG ENOUGH TO FEEL JEALOUS OF HER BABY
BROTHER--TO THE POINT WHERE SHE ASKS FOR A BOTTLE
HERSELF. SHE FEELS VERY PUT UPON, AND DREAMS ONE
NIGHT THAT THE ROLES ARE REVERSED, AND IT IS
SHE, THE CHILD, WHO HAS POWER OVER HER PARENTS.
IN THE INCIDENTS WHICH SHOW THIS URGE FOR
DOMINATION, ONE SEES THE ISSUES THAT MAKE
CHILDREN FEEL SO POWERLESS: HAVING TO GO TO BED
BEFORE THE GROWN-UPS, HAVING TO EAT CHILDREN'S
FOOD WHILE ADULTS HAVE SPECIAL ITEMS. HUMOR IS
PERVASIVE, AND ELLIE IS QUITE INGENIOUS IN
ORDERING UP A NEW BABY PERIODICALLY, ON APPROVAL,
TO BE KEPT ONLY IF HE'S "PERFECT," THAT IS, IF
HE DOESN'T CRY, ISN'T TOO FAT, AND DOESN'T EAT
TOO MUCH. THE NAKED BABY MAY BE THE ONE NOTE OF
UNREALITY IN THE STORY. EVERYONE ELSE IS DRESSED
WARMLY, BUT THE IRREPRESSIBLE FAT BABY NEVER
APPEARS WITH ONE STITCH OF CLOTHING.
(EMOTIONS--JEALOUSY, JEALOUSY, NEW SIT--BABY)

VIORST, JUDITH. I'LL FIX ANTHONY. HARPER, 1969.
ILLUSTRATED BY ARNOLD LOBEL. (BL)

A CLASSIC RECITAL OF THE VENGEFUL JEALOUSY
SEETHING INSIDE A LITTLE BOY, WHO IS NOT YET
QUITE SIX. WE SEE A PORTRAIT OF THE OLDER BROTHER
THROUGH THE EYES OF THE ABUSED YOUNGER BROTHER:
THE OLDER BROTHER WHO IS CONSISTENTLY BIGGER AND
STRONGER, PHYSICALLY AND MENTALLY, BUT SELFISH,
PRIVILEGED, AND RATHER HORRID. ANTHONY ANNOUNCES
THAT HE'S GOING TO CLOBBER YOUNGER BROTHER, AND
SAYS, "YOU STINK." LITTLE BROTHER SAYS, "I'LL FIX
ANTHONY." (WHEN I'M SIX.) (ANGER,
EMOTIONS--ANGER, EMOTIONS--JEALOUSY, FAM--SIBLING
RIVALRY, JEALOUSY, SIBLING RIVALRY)

WABER, BERNARD. LYLE AND THE BIRTHDAY PARTY.
HOUGHTON, 1966. ILLUSTRATED BY BERNARD WABER.
(CC)

HELPFUL LYLE STEPS OUT OF HIS ROLE AS HE FINDS
HIMSELF BEING VERY JEALOUS OF JOSHUA'S BIRTHDAY
CELEBRATION. IN FACT HE BECOMES SO VERY JEALOUS
THAT HE MAKES HIMSELF SICK AND MOPES ABOUT THE
HOUSE, FINALLY LANDING IN THE HOSPITAL. HELPING
OTHER PATIENTS IS GOOD THERAPY FOR HIM, AND SOON
HE'S HOME--TO FIND THAT THE FAMILY IS PLANNING
HIS BIRTHDAY PARTY. LYLE'S FEELINGS OF JEALOUSY,
AND THE WAY THEY MADE HIM FEEL MEAN, ARE VERY
REAL AND WILL HELP CHILDREN KNOW THAT EVERYONE
HAS THESE KINDS OF FEELINGS--EVEN CROCODILES.
(BEHAVIOR--CONSIDERATION, CONSIDERATION,
EMOTIONS--JEALOUSY, JEALOUSY)

WELLS, ROSEMARY. NOISY NORA. DIAL, 1973.
ILLUSTRATED BY ROSEMARY WELLS. (CC, ESLC)

POOR NORA--SHE'S THE LEFT-OUT SISTER, AND
THREATENS TO RUN AWAY TO MAKE HER FAMILY FEEL
SORRY FOR HER AND GIVE HER SOME ATTENTION. WHEN
SHE SHOWS UP IN THE BROOM CLOSET, ALL IS WELL. A
CLEVER, FUNNY BOOK ABOUT A BUMPTIOUS LITTLE
MOUSE-GIRL WHICH WILL DELIGHT YOUNG CHILDREN AS
THEY CATALOG HER MISDEMEANORS. MANY CHILDREN MAY
SEE THEMSELVES. (BROTHERS & SISTERS,
EMOTIONS--JEALOUSY, FAM--BROTHERS & SISTERS,
FAM--SIBLING RIVALRY, JEALOUSY, SIBLING RIVALRY)

EMOTIONS--LONELINESS

ARDIZONNE, EDWARD. LUCY BROWN AND MR. GRIMES.
WALCK, 1971. ILLUSTRATED BY EDWARD ARDIZONNE.
(CC)

THIS BOOK HAS A FAIRY-TALE QUALITY WHICH MAKES
IT SOMETHING OF A FANTASY: A LONELY LITTLE
ORPHAN GIRL MEETS A LONELY OLD MAN AND THEY
BECOME GREAT FRIENDS. WHEN MR. GRIMES FALLS ILL
AND MUST MOVE TO THE COUNTRY, HE ASKS LUCY TO GO
WITH HIM, WITH LUCY'S AUNT'S PERMISSION. MR.
GRIMES, WHO IS VERY WEALTHY, IS GENEROUS WITH HIS
MONEY, AND LUCY BUYS NEW CLOTHING. ILLUSTRATES
THE POINT THAT THERE ARE THINGS IN COMMON FOR THE
YOUNG AND THE OLD. THE OLD MAN AND THE LITTLE
GIRL WALK TOGETHER, HAVE TEA TOGETHER, AND NEVER
FEEL LONELY. (DIFF SIT--OLD AGE,
EMOTIONS--LONELINESS, FRIENDSHIP--ADULTS,
LONELINESS, OLD AGE)

CLIFTON, LUCILLE. EVERETT ANDERSON'S YEAR. HOLT,
1974.   ILLUSTRATED BY ANN GRIFALCONI. (CC)

"WALK TALL IN THE WORLD," HIS MOTHER TELLS
HIM. ALTHOUGH THIS IS, IN THE MAIN, A STORY OF A
SEVEN-YEAR-OLD BOY, THE INFLUENCE OF HIS MOTHER
SHINES THROUGH ON EVERY PAGE. EVERETT ANDERSON
REMEMBERS HIS DADDY ALTHOUGH HE DOES NOT KNOW
WHERE HE IS, AND READING THIS SERIES OF VERSES
ABOUT THE MONTHS OF THE YEAR, A CHILD CAN SHARE
THE SPECIAL LOVE THE YOUNG BOY FEELS FOR HIS
MOTHER. (DIFF SIT--ONE PARENT,
EMOTIONS--LONELINESS, FAM--MOTHERS WORKING,
LONELINESS, MOTHERS WORKING, ONE PARENT)

DEAN, LEIGH. LOOKING DOWN GAME. FUNK, 1968.
ILLUSTRATED BY PAUL GIOVANOPOULOS. (BECB)

A LONELY BOY SPENDS ALMOST A YEAR IN A NEW
NEIGHBORHOOD, LOOKING DOWN INSTEAD OF UP, TO
AVOID MAKING NEW FRIENDS. WHILE THE BONUSES ARE
MANY--THE DISCOVERY THAT HE LIKES ANTS, AND THE
BIRD'S NEST HE FOUND--THE READER IS RELIEVED WHEN
HE DISCOVERS A FRIEND UP IN A TREE AND DECIDES
TO FIND OUT "WHAT BEING UP WAS LIKE." THE SOMBER
BLACK AND WHITE DRAWINGS LEND THEMSELVES WELL TO
THE QUIET, INTROSPECTIVE MOOD OF THE STORY, AND
EDGAR IS SEEN AS A BASICALLY SHY PERSON, FAIRLY
CONTENT TO EXPLORE HIS LONELY WORLD. WHILE THE
READER IS GLAD TO SEE HIM MAKE A FRIEND, ONE ALSO
SENSES THIS IS A BOY WHO WILL ALWAYS BE A GOOD
OBSERVER OF LIFE. (EMOTIONS--LONELINESS,
EMOTIONS--SHYNESS, LONELIVESS, SHYNESS)

DUVOISIN, ROGER. LONELY VERONICA. KNOPF, 1963.

ILLUSTRATED BY ROGER DUVOISIN. (CC)

WHEN VERONICA THE HIPPOPOTAMUS IS MAROONED IN
NEW YORK CITY IN AN ELEVATOR SHAFT FOR AN ENTIRE
WEEKEND WITHOUT FOOD, SHE LEARNS THE MEANING OF
LONELINESS, AND SHE YEARNS FOR THE PEACEFUL RIVER
COUNTRY OF HER BIRTH. LONELY VERONICA
APPRECIATES THE CONSIDERATION SHOWN HER BY A
YOUNG PIGEON, WHO BRINGS HER FOOD, AND WHO
PROMISES TO VISIT VERONICA'S NEW HOME, A PEACEFUL
POND IN THE COUNTRY. (EMOTIONS--LONELINESS,
FRIENDSHIP, LONELINESS)

DUVOISIN, ROGER. TWO LONELY DUCKS. KNOPF, 1955.
ILLUSTRATED BY ROGER DUVOISIN. (CC)

A LOVELY COUNTING BOOK FOR YOUNG CHILDREN. THE
LITTLE WHITE DUCK AND THE LITTLE WHITE DRAKE
WERE LONELY IN THE POND. THEY DECIDED TO RAISE A
FAMILY, SO THE LITTLE DUCK BUILT A NEST, AND LAID
TEN EGGS IN ALL, SITTING ON THE EGGS FOR DAYS
AND WEEKS, AND ONE BY ONE HATCHED OUT TEN BABY
DUCKLINGS, AND NO ONE WAS LONELY ANY MORE.
UNDERSCORES COMPANIONSHIP IN FAMILY LIVING.
(EMOTIONS--LONELINESS, FAM, LONELINESS)

GORDON, SELMA. AMY LOVES GOODBYES. PLATT, 1966.
ILLUSTRATED BY JUNE GOLDSBOROUGH. (CCB-B)

AMY PLAYS THE GAME OF MAKING GOODBYES A VERY
FUN THING UNTIL HER PARENTS LEAVE FOR A SHORT
TRIP. WHEN THEY RETURN, SHE KNOWS HOW MUCH A
"HELLO" CAN MEAN. (EMOTIONS--LONELINESS,
LONELINESS)

IWASAKI, CHIHIRO. STAYING HOME ALONE ON A RAINY
DAY. MC GRAW, 1968. ILLUSTRATED BY CHIHIRO
IWASAKI. (LJ)

LONELINESS IS A SHARP PAIN FOR A CHILD LEFT
ALONE FOR THE FIRST TIME, AND ALLISON TRIES MANY
WAYS TO MAKE THOSE FEELINGS GO AWAY. SHE WANTS TO
HOLD HER KITTEN, SHE ENVIES THE BABY FISH
SWIMMING WITH ITS MOTHER, AND WHEN SHE TOUCHES
THE KEYS OF THE PIANO, IT ONLY REMINDS HER OF HER
MOTHER. AUTHOR-ARTIST IWASAKI HAS COMPLEMENTED
THESE FEELINGS OF FRUSTRATION WITH EXQUISITE,
WATERY, FREE-FORM WATERCOLORS, SUITING THE BROWN
AND GRAY TONES TO THE GRAY RAINY DAY SEEN THROUGH
THE WINDOW. CHILDREN IDENTIFY WITH THESE

SITUATIONS, ESPECIALLY THE TERROR OF THE PHONE
RINGING AND BEING AFRAID TO ANSWER IT. USEFUL
BECAUSE IT HELPS THE CHILD SEE THAT OTHER
CHILDREN ARE ALSO AFRAID, BUT THAT MOTHER DOES
RETURN, WHEN THE SUNSHINE RETURNS AT THE END OF
THE AFTERNOON. (EMOTIONS--FEAR,
EMOTIONS--LONELINESS, FEAR, LONELINESS)

JUSTUS, MAY. A NEW HOME FOR BILLY. HASTINGS,
1966. ILLUSTRATED BY JOAN PAYNE. (BCB)

   WHEN SIX-YEAR-OLD BILLY MOVES TO A NEW
NEIGHBORHOOD HE FINDS OUT THAT NOT ALL PEOPLE
WILL RENT TO NEGROES, AT LEAST NOT AT THE TIME
THIS BOOK WAS WRITTEN. A USEFUL FACT FOR ALL
CHILDREN TO KNOW. THE NEW HOUSE, THOUGH IN NEED
OF REPAIR, HAS AN APPLE TREE IN THE YARD AND IS A
GREAT IMPROVEMENT OVER THE DIRTY SLUM AREA HE
MOVED FROM. AFTER AN INITIAL PERIOD OF
LONELINESS, BILLY MAKES FRIENDS BECAUSE OF THE
SWING, A SLIDE, A JUMPING BAR, AND A SEESAW
CONSTRUCTED BY HIS FATHER. THE BOOK ENDS WITH
FRIENDS, BLACK AND WHITE, HELPING TO PAINT THE
HOUSE. (EMOTIONS--LONELINESS, FRIENDSHIP,
LONELINESS, MOVING, NEW SIT--MOVING)

KANTROWITZ, MILDRED. MAXIE. PARENTS' MAG, 1970.
ILLUSTRATED BY EMILY MC CULLY. (ESLC)

   AN INTERESTING THEME FOR A CHILDREN'S
BOOK--THE LONELINESS OF A WHITE-HAIRED OLD WOMAN
WHO LIVES ALONE AND THINKS NO ONE NEEDS HER. ALL
THIS IS CHANGED ONE DAY WHEN SHE STAYS IN BED
INSTEAD OF GOING THROUGH HER USUAL ROUTINE. SHE
FINDS OUT THAT INDEED MANY PEOPLE WERE DEPENDING
ON HER: HER CANARY BIRD WOKE UP ONE FAMILY, HER
WHISTLING TEAKETTLE ANOTHER. ALTOGETHER THERE
WERE 53 PEOPLE WHO CAME TO HER DOOR LATER THAT
DAY...AND SHE SERVED THEM ALL A CUP OF TEA. (DIFF
SIT--OLD AGE, EMOTIONS--LONELINESS, LONELINESS,
OLD AGE)

KEATS, EZRA. APT. 3. MACMILLAN, 1971.
ILLUSTRATED BY EZRA KEATS. (ESLC)

   TWO BROTHERS, SAM AND BEN, ARE LONELY AND
DECIDE TO INVESTIGATE THE SOURCE OF SOMEONE
PLAYING A HARMONICA. THE SETTING IS A GRIM GHETTO
APARTMENT BUILDING, AND VARIOUS MOODS ARE FELT
AS THE BOYS GO DOWN THE HALL. WHEN THEY FIND THE

BLIND MAN PLAYING THE HARMONICA IN APT. 3, HE
SHARES WITH THEM THE SECRETS HE KNOWS AND PLAYS
STRANGE MUSIC WHICH CONJURES UP SIGHTS, SOUNDS,
AND COLORS TO SAM. THE BOOK ENDS WITH SAM ASKING
THE OLD MAN TO TAKE A WALK WITH THEM. EVOCATIVE
ART WORK AND PROSE SHOW THE POWER OF MUSIC ON THE
EMOTIONS. (DIFF SIT--HANDICAPS, DIFF SIT--OLD
AGE, EMOTIONS--LONELINESS, HANDICAPS, LONELINESS,
OLD AGE)

KEATS, EZRA. LOUIE. GREENWILLOW, 1975.
ILLUSTRATED BY EZRA KEATS. (CCB-B, CSM, HB, SLJ)

   LOUIE, A YOUNG BOY IN A SLUM NEIGHBORHOOD WHO
DOES NOT SPEAK, COMES ALIVE WHEN HE SEES A PUPPET
NAMED GUSSIE AT A PUPPET SHOW. THE READER SENSES
THE LONELINESS OF LOUIE IN A BEAUTIFUL DREAM
SEQUENCE, AND ALL CHILDREN WILL APPRECIATE THE
ENDING, WHEN LOUIE RECEIVES GUSSIE AS A GENEROUS
GIFT FROM THE CHILDREN WHO MADE HER.
(BEHAVIOR--SHARING, EMOTIONS--LONELINESS,
FRIENDSHIP, LONELINESS, SHARING)

MC GOVERN, ANN. SCRAM, KID!. VIKING, 1974.
ILLUSTRATED BY NOLA LANGNER. (BL)

   IN AN INTERESTING ARRANGEMENT OF ILLUSTRATIONS
ON THE PAGE, PART BLACK AND WHITE AND PART
SEPIA, THE ILLUSTRATOR OF THIS BOOK HAS MANAGED
TO CAPTURE THE SIMULTANEITY OF REALITY AND
DAYDREAM. THE STORY OF A LITTLE BOY WHO FEELS
LEFT OUT AND HAS ANGRY FEELINGS ABOUT IT SHOULD
STRIKE A FEELING OF EMPATHY IN MANY READERS.
DON'T WE ALL WISH WE WERE BRAVE ENOUGH TO SAY,
"I'LL FIX YOUR WAGON!" AFTER VENTING HIS ANGER IN
THE DAYDREAM, JOE FINDS A FRIEND WHO WILL SAIL A
BOAT WITH HIM AND, TEMPORARILY AT LEAST, FORGETS
ABOUT THE KIDS WHO WON'T LET HIM PLAY BASEBALL.
(ANGER, EMOTIONS--ANGER, EMOTIONS--LONELINESS,
LONELINESS)

NESS, EVALINE. SAM, BANGS, AND MOONSHINE. HOLT,
1966. ILLUSTRATED BY EVALINE NESS. (BCB)

   DESPITE HER FATHER'S CAUTIONS, SAMANTHA IS NOT
ABLE TO KEEP STRAIGHT HER IMAGINARY LIFE FROM
HER REAL LIFE, AND TELLS PRETTY BIG WHOPPERS
TRIGGERED BY HER LONELINESS AND AN INSPIRED
IMAGINATION. WHEN SHE TELLS HER FRIEND THOMAS
THAT HER PET KANGAROO LIVES OUT IN A CAVE, THOMAS

BECOMES MAROONED AND ALMOST LOSES HIS LIFE. SAM
IS DISTRAUGHT WHEN SHE REALIZES THAT HER LIE, FOR
THAT IS WHAT IT IS, IS RESPONSIBLE. HER FATHER
TELLS HER TO THINK ABOUT THE DIFFERENCE BETWEEN
REAL AND MOONSHINE AND, AT THE END, HE ALSO TELLS
HER THAT THERE ARE TWO KINDS OF MOONSHINE: THE
GOOD KIND, WHICH IS HEALTHY IMAGINATIVE PLAY, AND
THE BAD KIND, THAT WHICH CAN BE HARMFUL.
(BEHAVIOR--MISBEHAVIOR, DIFF SIT--ONE PARENT,
EMOTIONS--LONELINESS, FAM--ONE PARENT,
LONELINESS, MISBEHAVIOR, ONE PARENT)

SENDAK, MAURICE. WHERE THE WILD THINGS ARE.
HARPER, 1963. ILLUSTRATED BY MAURICE SENDAK.
(BC, BESL, CC, CCB-B, GBC)

   MAX MISBEHAVES ONE NIGHT, NAILING A SPIKE INTO
THE WALL AND CRACKING THE PLASTER, CHASING THE
DOG WITH A FORK, AND HIS MOTHER SENDS HIM TO HIS
ROOM, TO BED WITHOUT ANY SUPPER. MAX DREAMS A
FANTASTIC DREAM, IN WHICH HE TURNS THE SITUATION
AROUND, AND HE IS THE BOSS. WHEN HE TELLS THE
WILD ANIMALS TO "BE STILL"--THEY OBEY, AND WHEN
HE IS CROWNED KING, HE REVELS IN HIS CONTROL OVER
THE BEASTS. OVERCOME WITH LONELINESS, THE SMELL
OF FOOD, AND WANTING TO BE SAFE AT HOME, MAX ENDS
UP IN HIS ROOM, WHERE HIS SUPPER IS WAITING. THE
AMBIVALENCE OF INDEPENDENCE/DEPENDENCE, THE
QUALITIES OF SECURITY AND LOVE ARE STRESSED IN
THIS BOOK. (BEHAVIOR--MISBEHAVIOR,
EMOTIONS--LONELINESS, EMOTIONS--LOVE,
EMOTIONS--SECURITY, LONELINESS, LOVE,
MISBEHAVIOR, SECURITY)

SHARMAT, MARJORIE. I WANT MAMA. HARPER, 1974.
ILLUSTRATED BY EMILY MC CULLY. (CCB-B, NYTBR)

   A LITTLE GIRL'S MOTHER GOES TO THE HOSPITAL
FOR AN OPERATION. IN CHILDLIKE PICTURES AND
DIALOG, THE READER LEARNS OF THE LONELINESS AND
CONCERN WITHIN THE LITTLE GIRL. USEFUL BECAUSE IT
SHOWS WHAT A CHILD CAN DO TO SPELL THE
LONELINESS, SUCH AS MAKE PRESENTS AND CLEAN THE
HOUSE. AN ESPECIALLY MOVING ILLUSTRATION AT THE
END OF THE BOOK SHOWS THE PEACE AND CONTENTMENT
IN THE HOUSEHOLD WHEN MOTHER COMES HOME.
(EMOTIONS--LONELINESS, FAM--MOTHERS, HOSPITAL,
LONELINESS, MOTHERS, NEW SIT--HOSPITAL)

SONNEBORN, RUTH. THE LOLLIPOP PARTY. VIKING,

1967.   ILLUSTRATED BY BRINTON TURKLE.   (ESLC)

ONE DAY TOMAS IS LEFT ALONE IN THE APARTMENT
FOR THE FIRST TIME. HIS SISTER ANA, WHO USUALLY
CARED FOR HIM BEFORE GOING TO HER JOB, HAD TO
LEAVE HIM ALONE. STEP-BY-STEP THE READER
PARTICIPATES IN THE LITTLE BOY'S FEAR. HE WAS
CONCERNED ABOUT THE SOUND OF FOOTSTEPS ON THE
STAIRS, AND WISHED ONLY TO SIT QUIETLY AND HOLD
HIS CAT GATTO. WHEN HIS NURSERY SCHOOL TEACHER
COMES TO THE DOOR ON A VISIT, HOWEVER, THE
EMOTIONAL TONE OF THE BOOK CHANGES IMMEDIATELY.
HE IS HAPPY TO SEE HER, ACTS THE ROLE OF THE HOST
BY OFFERING HER A LOLLIPOP, AND THE STORY ENDS
WITH TOMAS FEELING A BIT GROWN-UP.
(EMOTIONS--FEAR, EMOTIONS--LONELINESS,
FAM--MOTHERS WORKING, FEAR, LONELINESS, MOTHERS
WORKING, SELF-RELIANCE)

THOMPSON, VIVIAN. SAD DAY, GLAD DAY. HOLIDAY,
1962.   ILLUSTRATED BY LILIAN OBLIGADO.   (RLHR)

THE LARGE PRINT IS JUST RIGHT IN THIS BOOK FOR
NEW READERS WHO ARE BEGINNING TO PROGRESS TO
MORE DIFFICULT THINGS. KATHY MOVES TO A NEW
APARTMENT IN THE CITY FROM THE COUNTRY WHERE SHE
HAD A SWING ON AN APPLE TREE, AND FEELS VERY
LONELY. LUCKILY SHE FINDS A DOLL IN THE CLOSET OF
THE NEW HOUSE WHICH GOES A LONG WAY TOWARD
MAKING HER FEEL GOOD. EXPLAINS CHANGE AND HOW
PEOPLE ADJUST TO NEW PLACES.
(EMOTIONS--LONELINESS, LONELINESS, MOVING, NEW
SIT--MOVING)

ZINDEL, PAUL. I LOVE MY MOTHER. HARPER, 1975.
ILLUSTRATED BY JOHN MELO.   (CCB-B)

STRIKING FULL-COLOR ILLUSTRATIONS EXPAND THE
LIMITED TEXT OF THIS STORY OF A BOY AND HIS
MOTHER, PRESUMABLY LIVING ALONE BECAUSE OF
DIVORCE OR SEPARATION. THE REASON IS NOT
EXPLICITLY STATED. COMPANIONSHIP AT THE ZOO, IN
THE KITCHEN, AND LATE AT NIGHT WHEN THE BAD
DREAMS COME, MAKES UP ONE PART OF THE BOOK. THERE
IS ALSO DEPICTED THE REALISM OF VULNERABLE
FEELINGS WHEN THE BOY WANTS TO RUN AWAY FROM
HOME, WHEN HIS MOTHER TRIES NOT TO LET HIM KNOW
WHEN THEY ARE SHORT OF MONEY, BUT THE MOST MOVING
SCENES ARE WHEN MOTHER ADMITS THAT SHE IS LONELY
AND WHEN THE BOY MISSES HIS FATHER. (DIFF

SIT--DIVORCE, DIVORCE, EMOTIONS--LONELINESS,
EMOTIONS--LOVE, FAM--MOTHERS, FAM--ONE PARENT,
LONELINESS, LOVE, MOTHERS, ONE PARENT)

ZOLOTOW, CHARLOTTE. JANEY. HARPER, 1973.
ILLUSTRATED BY RONALD HIMLER. (CC)

   A PERCEPTIVE STORY OF THE LONELINESS THAT A
LITTLE GIRL FEELS AFTER HER FRIEND MOVES AWAY.
TOLD IN A MONOLOG, CATALOGING THE WAYS IN WHICH
SHE MISSES HER FRIEND JANEY, THE BOOK SHOWS
INCIDENTS IN THE PRESENT WHICH REMIND THE LITTLE
GIRL OF THE IMPORTANT MEMORIES IN THE PAST,
WALKING HOME TOGETHER FROM SCHOOL, CHRISTMAS
PRESENTS. THE SITUATIONS DESCRIBED ARE OFTEN
SENSUOUS. THE MEMORIES OF JANEY TOUCHING
EVERYTHING AS SHE WALKED ALONG THE STREET, THE
SOUND OF HER VOICE, THE MEMORIES OF THE SOUND OF
THE WIND BLOWING THROUGH THE TREES. IT IS A BOOK
WHICH ENDS ON A POSITIVE NOTE, AND ONE FEELS
GOOD, NOT SAD, ABOUT THE SHARED MEMORIES.
(EMOTIONS--LONELINESS, FRIENDSHIP, LONELINESS)

ZOLOTOW, CHARLOTTE. THE NEW FRIEND. ABELARD,
1968. ILLUSTRATED BY ARVIS STEWART. (ESLC)

   STRONG WATERCOLOR PAINTINGS IN DEEP PURPLES,
YELLOWS, AND GREENS COMPETE WITH THE RATHER QUIET
STORY OF FRIENDSHIP AND, SUBSEQUENTLY, A LOST
FRIEND. THE LITTLE GIRL CRIES ALL DAY, THEN
DREAMS OF A NEW FRIEND, AND CONSOLES HERSELF AS
SHE THINKS THAT SHE MIGHT FORGET, AND NOT CARE
ABOUT THE OLD FRIEND, THUS SOMEWHAT RESOLVING HER
HURT FEELINGS. (EMOTIONS--LONELINESS,
FRIENDSHIP, LONELINESS)

EMOTIONS--LOVE

ADOFF, ARNOLD. BLACK IS BROWN IS TAN. HARPER,
1973. ILLUSTRATED BY EMILY MC CULLY. (CC)

   DESCRIBING THIS FAMILY IN TERMS OF FREE VERSE
AND BEAUTIFUL WATERCOLORS DOES NOT BEGIN TO
INCLUDE THE NUANCES OF LOVE PORTRAYED AS THESE
CONTEMPORARY FAMILY MEMBERS CHOP THEIR OWN WOOD,
MAKE THEIR OWN MUSIC, COOK ON A BIG BLACK
COOKSTOVE. ALTHOUGH COLOR, THE VARYING SHADES OF
SKIN, IS THE THEME, CERTAINLY THE WARMTH OF
FAMILY LOVE IS THE MORE IMPORTANT MESSAGE.
(EMOTIONS--LOVE, FAM, LOVE)

ANGLUND, JOAN. LOVE IS A SPECIAL WAY OF FEELING.
HARCOURT, 1960. ILLUSTRATED BY JOAN ANGLUND.
(ESLC)

   SUBTLE ASPECTS OF LOVE ARE DEALT WITH IN THIS
TINY VOLUME--THE GOOD FEELINGS THAT COME WITH
HELPING AND SHARING, AND WITH THE SECURITY OF A
MOTHER'S LAP AND THE PEACEFULNESS OF HOME. A
WHOLESOME WAY TO EXPLORE THE FACETS OF LOVE
WITHOUT DEALING WITH ROMANTIC LOVE.
(EMOTIONS--LOVE, LOVE)

BROWNSTONE, CECILY. ALL KINDS OF MOTHERS. MC
KAY, 1969. ILLUSTRATED BY MIRIAM BROFSKY. (CSM,
LJ)

   THE ILLUSTRATIONS AND TEXT ILLUSTRATE THAT
MOTHERS COME IN ALL SHAPES AND SIZES, THAT SOME
ARE NEAT AND SOME MAY BE SLOPPY, BUT THE MAIN
MESSAGE THAT COMES THROUGH IS THAT "MOTHERS KEEP
RIGHT ON LOVING THEM"--THOSE MISBEHAVING
CHILDREN. WHEN THE BOOK DISCUSSES WHERE SOME
MOTHERS MIGHT WORK, THE LIST IS RATHER LIMITED,
AND WOULD SUGGEST A RATHER NARROW ROLE FOR WOMEN
OUTSIDE THE HOME. (EMOTIONS--LOVE, FAM--MOTHERS,
LOVE, MOTHERS)

EHRLICH, AMY. ZEEK SILVER MOON. DIAL, 1972.
ILLUSTRATED BY ROBERT PARKER. (ESLC)

   NOTABLE BECAUSE IT SHOWS AN ALTERNATIVE LIFE
STYLE OF A MUSICIAN, HIS WIFE, AND THEIR CHILD,
ZEEK SILVER MOON, THE BOOK IS GREATLY ENHANCED BY
STUNNINGLY BEAUTIFUL WATERCOLORS EVOKING THE
SOFTNESS OF LOVE. THIS IS A STORY OF
NON-CONFORMING, ALIVE, NEW LIFE-STYLE PEOPLE:
FATHER MADE THE BABY A CRADLE OF WOOD AFTER HE
WAS BORN AND LATER, WHEN ZEEK WAS FOUR YEARS OLD,
HIS FATHER, IN AN INCIDENT CALLED THE CARPET
RAISING, STAPLED THEIR LIVING ROOM RUG TO THE
CEILING BECAUSE A NEIGHBOR COMPLAINED OF NOISE.
WITHIN THE FRAMEWORK OF A FAMILY WHICH PLACES A
HIGH VALUE ON NATURAL FOODS, HOME-BAKED BREAD,
AND ENTERTAINMENT OTHER THAN TELEVISION, ZEEK IS
SHOWN TO BE A LOVED CHILD, ONE WHO RECEIVES
GENTLE LOVING CARE, IS TUCKED IN AT NIGHT AND
TOLD STORIES. (EMOTIONS--LOVE,
EMOTIONS--SECURITY, FAM, LOVE, SECURITY)

FLACK, MARJORIE. ASK MR. BEAR. MACMILLAN, 1932.

ILLUSTRATED BY MARJORIE FLACK. (CC)

THIS CLASSIC PICTURE BOOK WHICH PORTRAYS THE
DILEMMA OF WHAT TO GIVE MOTHER FOR HER BIRTHDAY
SUSTAINS THE BELIEF THAT AN EXPRESSION OF LOVE,
LIKE A BIG BEAR HUG, IS JUST AS GOOD, OR PERHAPS
BETTER, THAN ANY MATERIAL GIFT A CHILD COULD
GIVE. (EMOTIONS--LOVE, FAM, LOVE)

HOBAN, RUSSELL. LITTLE BRUTE FAMILY. MACMILLAN,
1966. ILLUSTRATED BY LILLIAN HOBAN. (CC)

THE LITTLE BRUTE FAMILY IS NOT A FAMILY WHICH
LOVES, NOR IS IT A FAMILY ONE COULD LOVE, AT
LEAST IN THE BEGINNING. THEY QUARREL, THEY NEVER
SAY THANK-YOU, THEY EAT STONES AND ARE THOROUGHLY
DISAGREEABLE, AS WELL AS BEING UGLY. BUT THE
POWER OF ONE LITTLE GOOD FEELING UPON THIS FAMILY
WORKS A MIRACLE. THEY CHANGE SO MUCH THAT IN THE
END THE LITTLE BRUTE FAMILY CHANGES ITS NAME TO
NICE. THIS IS A DRAMATIC WAY TO SHOW A CHILD THE
IMPORTANCE OF GOOD FEELINGS.
(EMOTIONS--HAPPINESS, EMOTIONS--LOVE, HAPPINESS,
LOVE)

LOBEL, ARNOLD. FROG AND TOAD ARE FRIENDS.
HARPER, 1970. ILLUSTRATED BY ARNOLD LOBEL. (BCB)

AN EASY-TO-READ FORMAT IS USED FOR FIVE
STORIES OF GENTLE RELATIONSHIPS BETWEEN TWO GOOD
FRIENDS: FROG HELPS TOAD LOOK FOR THE LOST
BUTTONS ON HIS JACKET, ROUSES TOAD FROM HIS LONG
WINTER SLEEP, AND LAUGHS AT HIS OLD-FASHIONED
STRIPED BATHING SUIT. THE QUALITIES OF FRIENDSHIP
ARE ILLUMINATED WELL: LOVING CARE FOR ANOTHER
PERSON, YET A HEALTHY HUMOR WHICH ALLOWS ONE
FRIEND TO LAUGH AT ANOTHER WITHOUT HARMING THE
FRIENDSHIP. (EMOTIONS--LOVE, FRIENDSHIP, LOVE)

MILES, BETTY. AROUND AND AROUND--LOVE. KNOPF,
1975. ILLUSTRATED BY BETTY MILES. (BL)

BLACK AND WHITE PHOTOGRAPHS OF LOVE IN AN
INFINITE VARIETY DOMINATE THIS PICTURE BOOK. THE
BRIEF TEXT READS LIKE POETRY, AND SERVES TO TIE
THE PICTURES TOGETHER IN A LOOSE MANNER, AS IN
THE ONE SEQUENCE OF FIVE PICTURES WHICH
ILLUSTRATE "WORKING AND SHARING ARE LOVE."
RELATIONSHIPS BETWEEN PETS AND CHILDREN, THE OLD
AND THE YOUNG, PARENT AND CHILD, GIRL/BOY LOVE,

INCLUDING ETHNIC GROUPS OTHER THAN WHITE, ARE
ONLY SOME OF THE WAYS LOVE IS DEPICTED. "IT'S
HARD TO TELL ABOUT, EASY TO SHOW."
(EMOTIONS--LOVE, LOVE)

MINARIK, ELSE. A KISS FOR LITTLE BEAR. HARPER,
1968. ILLUSTRATED BY MAURICE SENDAK. (BCB)

    AMUSING STORY BECAUSE OF THE HUMOROUS INCIDENT
IN WHICH LITTLE BEAR'S KISS ALMOST GETS LOST
WHEN LITTLE SKUNK GIVES IT TO HIS LADY FRIEND
INSTEAD OF PASSING IT ON, BUT THE UNDERLYING
MESSAGE IS THERE. LITTLE BEAR MAKES A PRESENT FOR
HIS GRANDMOTHER AND SHE, IN A LOVING GESTURE,
SENDS HIM A KISS. THE DELICATE ROUNDED LINES IN
THE ILLUSTRATIONS, FRAMED ON EACH PAGE, FURTHER
THE GENTLE, CARING MESSAGE. (EMOTIONS--LOVE,
FAM--GRANDMOTHERS, GRANDMOTHERS, LOVE)

RAYNOR, DORKA. THIS IS MY FATHER AND ME.
WHITMAN, A., 1973. ILLUSTRATED BY DORKA RAYNOR.
(BL)

    STRIKING BLACK AND WHITE PHOTOGRAPHS FROM ALL
OVER THE WORLD SHOW VARYING RELATIONSHIPS OF
FATHERS TO THEIR CHILDREN. WHILE NOT A BOOK WHICH
WILL BE READILY PICKED UP BY CHILDREN, IT
REVEALS THE ROLE OF LOVE, COOPERATION,
PROTECTION, CARE, DEVOTION, WORK, PLAY, AND PRIDE
WHICH CAN EXIST BETWEEN PARENT AND CHILD IN A
UNIVERSAL WAY. (EMOTIONS--LOVE, FAM--FATHERS,
FATHERS, LOVE)

SCOTT, ANN. ON MOTHER'S LAP. MC GRAW, 1972.
ILLUSTRATED BY GLO COALSON. (BCB)

    A LOVING STORY OF A LAP WITH UNLIMITED ROOM.
FIRST IT HAS MICHAEL, THEN HIS DOLL, THEN HIS
BOAT, THEN HIS PUPPY, THEN HIS REINDEER BLANKET.
THEY ALL ROCKED TOGETHER. WHEN THE BABY WAKES UP,
MICHAEL PUTS ON A SOUR FACE, AND SAYS THERE
ISN'T ANY ROOM. BUT MOTHER MAKES ROOM FOR ALL,
AND GIVES A SENSE OF SECURITY TO THE READER THAT
ONLY A LAP AND A ROCKING CHAIR CAN PROVIDE.
(EMOTIONS--LOVE, EMOTIONS--SECURITY,
FAM--MOTHERS, FAM--SIBLING RIVALRY, LOVE,
MOTHERS, SECURITY, SIBLING RIVALRY)

SEGAL, LORE. TELL ME A MITZI. FARRAR, 1970.
ILLUSTRATED BY HARRIET PINCUS. (BCB)

MARTHA IS A VERY LUCKY LITTLE GIRL: HER MOTHER
AND FATHER AND GRANDMOTHER ARE WONDERFUL
STORYTELLERS. THEY TELL HER "MITZIES," WHICH ARE
REALLY STORIES ABOUT HER AND HER BROTHER, SUCH AS
THE TIME SHE WOKE UP EARLY, GOT HER BABY BROTHER
UP AND DRESSED, AND PLANNED TO TAKE A TAXI TO
SEE HER GRANDPARENTS. EXCEPT THAT SHE DIDN'T KNOW
THE ADDRESS. SO THE TAXI DRIVER LET HER OUT AND
SHE AND JACOB WENT UPSTAIRS AND WENT BACK TO BED,
JUST AS MOTHER'S ALARM CLOCK WENT OFF. TWO OTHER
STORIES COMPLETE THE BOOK: ONE IS A HILARIOUS
ACCOUNT OF THE FAMILY FALLING ILL, ONE BY ONE,
THE OTHER AN IMAGINATIVE TALE OF THE PRESIDENT OF
THE UNITED STATES GIVING A PIECE OF GUM TO
JACOB. ILLUSTRATIONS ARE IN RICH, VIBRANT COLORS
WHICH REFLECT THE VIGOR OF THE FAMILY.
(EMOTIONS--LOVE, FAM, LOVE)

SENDAK, MAURICE. WHERE THE WILD THINGS ARE.
HARPER, 1963. ILLUSTRATED BY MAURICE SENDAK.
(BC, BESL, CC, CCB-B, GBC)

MAX MISBEHAVES ONE NIGHT, NAILING A SPIKE INTO
THE WALL AND CRACKING THE PLASTER, CHASING THE
DOG WITH A FORK, AND HIS MOTHER SENDS HIM TO HIS
ROOM, TO BED WITHOUT ANY SUPPER. MAX DREAMS A
FANTASTIC DREAM, IN WHICH HE TURNS THE SITUATION
AROUND, AND HE IS THE BOSS. WHEN HE TELLS THE
WILD ANIMALS TO "BE STILL"--THEY OBEY, AND WHEN
HE IS CROWNED KING, HE REVELS IN HIS CONTROL OVER
THE BEASTS. OVERCOME WITH LONELINESS, THE SMELL
OF FOOD, AND WANTING TO BE SAFE AT HOME, MAX ENDS
UP IN HIS ROOM, WHERE HIS SUPPER IS WAITING. THE
AMBIVALENCE OF INDEPENDENCE/DEPENDENCE, THE
QUALITIES OF SECURITY AND LOVE ARE STRESSED IN
THIS BOOK. (BEHAVIOR--MISBEHAVIOR,
EMOTIONS--LONELINESS, EMOTIONS--LOVE,
EMOTIONS--SECURITY, LONELINESS, LOVE,
MISBEHAVIOR, SECURITY)

SONNEBORN, RUTH. FRIDAY NIGHT IS PAPA NIGHT.
VIKING, 1970. ILLUSTRATED BY EMILY MC CULLY.
(BCB, CC)

A SYMPATHETIC PICTURE OF PUERTO RICAN LIFE IN
A CROWDED APARTMENT, WHERE PEDRO'S BED IS IN THE
KITCHEN, AND FATHER WORKS TWO JOBS TO PROVIDE FOR
HIS FAMILY. BROWN TONES COMPLEMENT THE WARMTH
AND SKIN COLOR OF THE CHARACTERS, AND LEND A
HARMONIOUS TONE TO THE THEME, WHICH IS THE

SPECIAL FEELING IN PEDRO'S MIND WHEN HIS FATHER
COMES HOME ON FRIDAY NIGHT. (EMOTIONS--LOVE,
FAM--FATHERS, FATHERS, LOVE)

STEPTOE, JOHN. STEVIE. HARPER, 1969.
ILLUSTRATED BY JOHN STEPTOE. (BCB)

   BRILLIANT PAINTINGS ENHANCE THIS INTERESTING
BOOK WRITTEN AND ILLUSTRATED BY A YOUNG BLACK
MAN. THE STORY OF STEVIE, WHO COMES TO STAY WITH
THE NARRATOR, BEGINS WHEN ROBERT'S MOTHER TAKES A
PRESCHOOLER INTO HER HOME FOR DAY CARE. ROBERT,
AN ONLY CHILD, IS BOTHERED BY HAVING A TAG-ALONG
WHEREVER HE GOES AND ONE WHO ALWAYS BREAKS THE
TOYS. ROBERT THINKS STEVIE IS SPOILED AND HE
THINKS HIS MOTHER ISN'T STRICT ENOUGH. BUT WHEN
STEVIE'S FAMILY MOVES AWAY, ROBERT REALIZES THE
VOID IN HIS LIFE AND, AS HE MUSES OVER THIS
THOUGHT, HE REALIZES HE ALMOST HAD A REAL-LIFE
LITTLE BROTHER. (EMOTIONS--LOVE, LOVE,
SELF-UNDERSTANDING)

TURKLE, BRINTON. THY FRIEND OBADIAH. VIKING,
1969. ILLUSTRATED BY BRINTON TURKLE. (BCB)

   OBADIAH, A YOUNG QUAKER BOY, IS ANGRY WHEN A
SEA GULL TRIES TO BE HIS FRIEND BY TAGGING ALONG
BEHIND HIM IN THIS EXCELLENT PORTRAYAL OF QUAKER
FAMILY LIFE. AS THE STORY PROGRESSES, THE GULL
GETS A LARGE RUSTY FISHHOOK CAUGHT IN HIS BEAK,
OBADIAH TAKES IT OUT, AND THE SEA GULL FLIES
AWAY. WHEN THE GULL RETURNS, OBADIAH REASONS:
"SINCE I HELPED HIM, I'M HIS FRIEND, TOO."
TURKLE'S WATERCOLORS EVOKE A POWERFUL FEELING OF
A COZY, SECURE LIFE IN THE DAYS WHEN THE FAMILY
GATHERED AROUND THE FIREPLACE WHILE THE BREAD WAS
BAKING. (EMOTIONS--LOVE, EMOTIONS--SECURITY,
FAM, FRIENDSHIP, LOVE, SECURITY)

YOLEN, JANE. IT ALL DEPENDS. FUNK, 1969.
ILLUSTRATED BY DON BOLOGNESE. (LJ)

   IN A ROUNDABOUT WAY, THIS IS A POETICAL STORY
OF THE VALUE OF LOVE. DAVID IS A LITTLE BOY WHO
QUESTIONS HIS MOTHER ABOUT A NUMBER OF THINGS.
"HOW TALL AM I?" AND SHE ANSWERS BY SAYING THAT
IT ALL DEPENDS UPON THE RELATIONSHIP OF THINGS.
THAT TO AN ANT, HE IS VERY LARGE, BUT THAT TO A
WHALE, HE IS VERY SMALL. IN AN IMAGINATIVE SERIES
OF ILLUSTRATIONS, BOLOGNESE HAS PRODUCED A BOOK

USEFUL TO TEACHERS AND PARENTS WHICH TEACHES
DIFFERING SIZE RELATIONSHIPS. IT IS NOT UNTIL
ALMOST THE END THAT DAVID ASKS, "WHAT IF I GROW,
AND CHANGE," AND SHE ANSWERS THAT HE WILL ALWAYS
BE JUST RIGHT, BECAUSE HIS PARENTS LOVE HIM.
(EMOTIONS--LOVE, FAM--MOTHERS, LOVE, MOTHERS,
SELF-CONSCIOUSNESS--SIZE)

ZINDEL, PAUL. I LOVE MY MOTHER. HARPER, 1975.
ILLUSTRATED BY JOHN MELO. (CCB-B)

STRIKING FULL-COLOR ILLUSTRATIONS EXPAND THE
LIMITED TEXT OF THIS STORY OF A BOY AND HIS
MOTHER, PRESUMABLY LIVING ALONE BECAUSE OF
DIVORCE OR SEPARATION. THE REASON IS NOT
EXPLICITLY STATED. COMPANIONSHIP AT THE ZOO, IN
THE KITCHEN, AND LATE AT NIGHT WHEN THE BAD
DREAMS COME, MAKES UP ONE PART OF THE BOOK. THERE
IS ALSO DEPICTED THE REALISM OF VULNERABLE
FEELINGS WHEN THE BOY WANTS TO RUN AWAY FROM
HOME, WHEN HIS MOTHER TRIES NOT TO LET HIM KNOW
WHEN THEY ARE SHORT OF MONEY, BUT THE MOST MOVING
SCENES ARE WHEN MOTHER ADMITS THAT SHE IS LONELY
AND WHEN THE BOY MISSES HIS FATHER. (DIFF
SIT--DIVORCE, DIVORCE, EMOTIONS--LONELINESS,
EMOTIONS--LOVE, FAM--MOTHERS, FAM--ONE PARENT,
LONELINESS, LOVE, MOTHERS, ONE PARENT)

ZOLOTOW, CHARLOTTE. DO YOU KNOW WHAT I'LL DO?.
HARPER, 1958. ILLUSTRATED BY GARTH WILLIAMS.
(CC)

A LOVING PICTURE OF A GIRL ABOUT SEVEN YEARS
OLD, DREAMING ABOUT ALL OF THE WAYS SHE WILL BE
GOOD TO HER BABY BROTHER. GARTH WILLIAMS HAS
DRAWN LARGE FULL-PAGE ILLUSTRATIONS FILLED IN
WITH A DELICATE WATERCOLOR WASH TO ACCENTUATE THE
DREAMY QUALITY OF THE LITTLE GIRL'S THOUGHTS.
SHE PROMISES CONCRETE THINGS, SUCH AS BRINGING
HOME A PIECE OF BIRTHDAY CAKE, AND SHE PROMISES
THINGS THAT ARE IN THE AFFECTIVE DOMAIN: SHE
TELLS HIM THAT SHE'LL GET RID OF HIS NIGHTMARES
FOR HIM. IN DOING THIS, OF COURSE, SHE
DEMONSTRATES THE THINGS THAT ARE IMPORTANT AND
PROMINENT IN CHILDREN'S LIVES, THEIR EXPECTATIONS
AND FEARS. (BROTHERS & SISTERS, EMOTIONS--LOVE,
FAM--BROTHERS & SISTERS, LOVE)

EMOTIONS--REJECTION

KLEIN, GERDA. THE BLUE ROSE. HILL, 1974.
ILLUSTRATED BY NORMA HOLT.

   MADE IN COOPERATION WITH THE KENNEDY CHILD
STUDY CENTER, THE BOOK IS A SYMPATHETIC VIEW OF
MENTAL RETARDATION. BLACK AND WHITE PHOTOGRAPHS
SHOW JENNY PLAYING, TRYING TO TIE HER SHOES.
CLOSES WITH JENNY BEING UNHAPPY BECAUSE OTHER
CHILDREN HAVE CALLED HER RETARDED, AND LAUGHED AT
HER. (DIFF SIT--HANDICAPS, EMOTIONS--REJECTION,
HANDICAPS, REJECTION)

SCOTT, ANN. SAM. MC GRAW, 1967.   ILLUSTRATED BY
SYMEON SHIMIN. (BCB)

   THE ILLUSTRATIONS ARE PARAMOUNT IN THIS STORY
OF A LEFT-OUT BROTHER WHO IS REJECTED FIRST BY
MOTHER, BIG BROTHER GEORGE, SISTER MARCIA, AND
THEN HIS FATHER, WHO FORBIDS HIM TO TOUCH HIS
TYPEWRITER. THE BLACK, SEPIA, AND GOLDEN BROWN
WATERCOLORS INTENSIFY THE FEELINGS OF SADNESS IN
SAM'S HEART. SUDDENLY THE WHOLE FAMILY REALIZES
THAT HE NEEDS ATTENTION: HIS MOTHER HOLDS HIM AND
ROCKS HIM, AND AS EVERYONE RALLIES AROUND TO
KEEP HIM COMPANY, SAM HELPS BAKE A RASPBERRY
TART. (BROTHERS & SISTERS, EMOTIONS--REJECTION,
FAM--BROTHERS & SISTERS, REJECTION)

EMOTIONS--SECURITY

BROWN, MARGARET. THE RUNAWAY BUNNY. HARPER,
1942.   ILLUSTRATED BY CLEMENT HURD. (CC)

   A THOROUGHLY SATISFYING STORY FOR A YOUNG
CHILD, FOR ALL CHILDREN DREAM OF RUNNING AWAY
FROM HOME. THIS MOTHER RABBIT, WHO ALWAYS THINKS
OF A WAY TO INTERCEPT HER YOUNG ONE, IS A PERFECT
PORTRAIT OF THE MOTHER WHO IS ALWAYS THERE, AND
WILL ALWAYS BE THERE, THE ULTIMATE IN SECURITY
AND LOVE. (EMOTIONS--SECURITY, FAM--MOTHERS,
MOTHERS, SECURITY)

BUCKLEY, HELEN. GRANDMOTHER AND I. LOTHROP,
1961.   ILLUSTRATED BY PAUL GALDONE. (CC)

   LARGE PRINT AND SHORT, RHYTHMIC SENTENCES
WHICH ECHO THE ROCKING CHAIR CHARACTERIZE THIS
BOOK OF OVERSIZE PICTURES. THE ILLUSTRATIONS,

WHICH ARE BRIGHT AND HOMEY IN THE FIRELIGHT, SET
THE SCENE FOR PEACE AND COMFORT AT THE BEGINNING
OF THE BOOK, PROGRESS TO A DRAMATIC PURPLE PAGE
WHEN THE LITTLE GIRL IS SECURE FROM THE LIGHTNING
OUTSIDE, AND END ON A CHEERFUL NOTE AFTER
GRANDMOTHER'S LAP HAS BEEN COMPARED TO THOSE
BELONGING TO MOTHER, FATHER, BROTHER, AND SISTER.
USEFUL BECAUSE THE UNIQUE ROLE OF GRANDMOTHER'S
LAP IS REINFORCED AGAIN AND AGAIN.
(EMOTIONS--SECURITY, FAM--GRANDMOTHERS,
GRANDMOTHERS, SECURITY)

CHALMERS, MARY. BE GOOD, HARRY. HARPER, 1967.
ILLUSTRATED BY MARY CHALMERS.   (BCB)

   A USEFUL BOOK, WITH SUBTLE HUMOR, FOR THE
SMALL CHILD WHO WILL EMPATHIZE WITH HARRY AS HE
GOES TO A BABY-SITTER FOR THE FIRST TIME, AND
SITS ON MRS. BREWSTER'S LAP ALL OF THE TIME WITH
ALL OF HIS TOYS AND BOOKS. PARTICULARLY
REASSURING FOR A CHILD WHO NEEDS THE SECURITY OF
HIS OWN THINGS, SUCH AS A BLANKET, SO THAT HE
KNOWS HE'S NOT THE ONLY ONE WITH NEEDS SUCH AS
THESE. (EMOTIONS--SECURITY, SECURITY)

EHRLICH, AMY. ZEEK SILVER MOON. DIAL, 1972.
ILLUSTRATED BY ROBERT PARKER.   (ESLC)

   NOTABLE BECAUSE IT SHOWS AN ALTERNATIVE LIFE
STYLE OF A MUSICIAN, HIS WIFE, AND THEIR CHILD,
ZEEK SILVER MOON, THE BOOK IS GREATLY ENHANCED BY
STUNNINGLY BEAUTIFUL WATERCOLORS EVOKING THE
SOFTNESS OF LOVE. THIS IS A STORY OF
NON-CONFORMING, ALIVE, NEW LIFE-STYLE PEOPLE:
FATHER MADE THE BABY A CRADLE OF WOOD AFTER HE
WAS BORN AND LATER, WHEN ZEEK WAS FOUR YEARS OLD,
HIS FATHER, IN AN INCIDENT CALLED THE CARPET
RAISING, STAPLED THEIR LIVING ROOM RUG TO THE
CEILING BECAUSE A NEIGHBOR COMPLAINED OF NOISE.
WITHIN THE FRAMEWORK OF A FAMILY WHICH PLACES A
HIGH VALUE ON NATURAL FOODS, HOME-BAKED BREAD,
AND ENTERTAINMENT OTHER THAN TELEVISION, ZEEK IS
SHOWN TO BE A LOVED CHILD, ONE WHO RECEIVES
GENTLE LOVING CARE, IS TUCKED IN AT NIGHT AND
TOLD STORIES. (EMOTIONS--LOVE,
EMOTIONS--SECURITY, FAM, LOVE, SECURITY)

KRAUS, ROBERT. GOOD NIGHT, RICHARD RABBIT.
SPRINGFELLOW, 1972. ILLUSTRATED BY N.M.
BODECKER. (CCB-B)

TINY FORMAT MAKES THIS A CHARMING BEDTIME
STORY FOR THE VERY YOUNG, AS MOST YOUNGSTERS WILL
IDENTIFY WITH RICHARD RABBIT. A MIX OF REAL AND
IMAGINARY FEARS, AND A LITTLE OF DOWNRIGHT
TEASING ARE SEEN AS THE YOUNG RABBIT PRETENDS
THERE IS A FACE LOOKING IN THE WINDOW. EVERY
OTHER PAGE DEALS WITH A QUESTION OR COMMENT, THE
FACING PAGE WITH MOTHER'S ANSWER. IN ALL OF THE
ILLUSTRATIONS, RICHARD IS VERY SMALL, AND MOTHER
LOOMS VERY LARGE AND SOLID, TRULY A SECURITY
FIGURE, AND ON THE FINAL PAGE RICHARD DRIFTS OFF
TO SLEEP. (BEHAVIOR--DISLIKES--SLEEP,
DISLIKES--SLEEP, EMOTIONS--FEAR,
EMOTIONS--SECURITY, FEAR, SECURITY)

RESSNER, PHILIP. AT NIGHT. DUTTON, 1967.
ILLUSTRATED BY CHARLES PRATT.   (ESLC)

A SERIES OF BLACK AND WHITE PHOTOGRAPHS,
APPROPRIATELY ENOUGH, LEAD THE READER'S EYE
THROUGH A NIGHT IN THE CITY. USEFUL BECAUSE IT
WILL GIVE THE READER A FEELING OF SECURITY,
KNOWING THAT THERE IS NOTHING TO FEAR FROM
DARKNESS IN ITSELF. IT SHOWS A LIFE THE CHILD
RARELY SEES, AND MAY NOT BE ABLE TO IMAGINE: THE
EMPTY SCHOOL ROOM, THE BUMPS IN THE SIDEWALK. AS
DAWN BREAKS, THE CHILD SEES THE MIRACLE OF A NEW
DAY, AS THE CIRCLE OF THE EARTH TURNS.
(EMOTIONS--FEAR, EMOTIONS--SECURITY, FEAR,
SECURITY)

SCHULZ, CHARLES. SECURITY IS A THUMB AND A
BLANKET. DETERMINED, 1963.   ILLUSTRATED BY
CHARLES SCHULZ.

THE EXEMPLAR OF DEFINITIONS OF SECURITY IN A
CHILD'S MIND, ALTHOUGH, AS IN MANY CHILDREN'S
BOOKS, THE PHILOSPHY IS UNIVERSAL. "SECURITY IS
RETURNING HOME AFTER A VACTION" IS A TRUISM FOR
GROWN-UPS, TOO, AS IS SNOOPY'S LINE THAT
"SECURITY IS OWNING YOUR OWN HOME," EVEN IF IT IS
ONLY A DOG HOUSE, BUT THE MORE TRULY CHILD-LIKE
EXPRESSIONS OF SECURITY ARE TO BE FOUND IN THOSE
RELATING TO FINDING YOUR MOTHER IN THE HOUSE WHEN
YOU COME HOME FROM SCHOOL, AND SALLY SAYING AS
SHE WALKS ALONG A HIGH CHAIN-LINK FENCE:
"SECURITY IS KNOWING THAT BIG DOG CAN'T REALLY
GET OUT." CURIOUSLY, THUMB SUCKING AND SECURITY
BLANKETS ARE MENTIONED ONLY IN THE TITLE, BUT
SERVE TO TUNE IN THE READER TO THE SUBJECT.

(BEHAVIOR--THUMB SUCKING, EMOTIONS--SECURITY,
SECURITY, THUMB SUCKING)

SCOTT, ANN. ON MOTHER'S LAP. MC GRAW, 1972.
ILLUSTRATED BY GLO COALSON. (BCB)

A LOVING STORY OF A LAP WITH UNLIMITED ROOM.
FIRST IT HAS MICHAEL, THEN HIS DOLL, THEN HIS
BOAT, THEN HIS PUPPY, THEN HIS REINDEER BLANKET.
THEY ALL ROCKED TOGETHER. WHEN THE BABY WAKES UP,
MICHAEL PUTS ON A SOUR FACE, AND SAYS THERE
ISN'T ANY ROOM. BUT MOTHER MAKES ROOM FOR ALL,
AND GIVES A SENSE OF SECURITY TO THE READER THAT
ONLY A LAP AND A ROCKING CHAIR CAN PROVIDE.
(EMOTIONS--LOVE, EMOTIONS--SECURITY,
FAM--MOTHERS, FAM--SIBLING RIVALRY, LOVE,
MOTHERS, SECURITY, SIBLING RIVALRY)

SENDAK, MAURICE. WHERE THE WILD THINGS ARE.
HARPER, 1963. ILLUSTRATED BY MAURICE SENDAK.
(BC, BESL, CC, CCB-B, GBC)

MAX MISBEHAVES ONE NIGHT, NAILING A SPIKE INTO
THE WALL AND CRACKING THE PLASTER, CHASING THE
DOG WITH A FORK, AND HIS MOTHER SENDS HIM TO HIS
ROOM, TO BED WITHOUT ANY SUPPER. MAX DREAMS A
FANTASTIC DREAM, IN WHICH HE TURNS THE SITUATION
AROUND, AND HE IS THE BOSS. WHEN HE TELLS THE
WILD ANIMALS TO "BE STILL"--THEY OBEY, AND WHEN
HE IS CROWNED KING, HE REVELS IN HIS CONTROL OVER
THE BEASTS. OVERCOME WITH LONELINESS, THE SMELL
OF FOOD, AND WANTING TO BE SAFE AT HOME, MAX ENDS
UP IN HIS ROOM, WHERE HIS SUPPER IS WAITING. THE
AMBIVALENCE OF INDEPENDENCE/DEPENDENCE, THE
QUALITIES OF SECURITY AND LOVE ARE STRESSED IN
THIS BOOK. (BEHAVIOR--MISBEHAVIOR,
EMOTIONS--LONELINESS, EMOTIONS--LOVE,
EMOTIONS--SECURITY, LONELINESS, LOVE,
MISBEHAVIOR, SECURITY)

TURKLE, BRINTON. THY FRIEND OBADIAH. VIKING,
1969. ILLUSTRATED BY BRINTON TURKLE. (BCB)

OBADIAH, A YOUNG QUAKER BOY, IS ANGRY WHEN A
SEA GULL TRIES TO BE HIS FRIEND BY TAGGING ALONG
BEHIND HIM IN THIS EXCELLENT PORTRAYAL OF QUAKER
FAMILY LIFE. AS THE STORY PROGRESSES, THE GULL
GETS A LARGE RUSTY FISHHOOK CAUGHT IN HIS BEAK,
OBADIAH TAKES IT OUT, AND THE SEA GULL FLIES
AWAY. WHEN THE GULL RETURNS, OBADIAH REASONS:

"SINCE I HELPED HIM, I'M HIS FRIEND, TOO."
TURKLE'S WATERCOLORS EVOKE A POWERFUL FEELING OF
A COZY, SECURE LIFE IN THE DAYS WHEN THE FAMILY
GATHERED AROUND THE FIREPLACE WHILE THE BREAD WAS
BAKING. (EMOTIONS--LOVE, EMOTIONS--SECURITY,
FAM, FRIENDSHIP, LOVE, SECURITY)

WABER, BERNARD. IRA SLEEPS OVER. HOUGHTON, 1972.
 ILLUSTRATED BY BERNARD WABER. (ESLC)

   IRA IS THE YOUNG CHILD IN A FAMILY WITH
UNDERSTANDING PARENTS, AND A SISTER FOND OF
PUT-DOWNS. WHEN HIS MOTHER AND FATHER TELL HIM
THAT IT WILL BE OK IF HE TAKES HIS TEDDY BEAR ON
HIS FIRST SLEEPOVER AT HIS FRIEND'S HOUSE, HIS
SISTER INSISTS THAT HIS FRIEND WILL LAUGH AND
THINK HE'S A BABY. HOW WILL HE FEEL SLEEPING
WITHOUT HIS TEDDY BEAR FOR THE VERY FIRST TIME?
LUCKILY IRA NEVER NEEDS TO FACE THAT SITUATION,
FOR THE CAPPER TO THE STORY IS THAT REGGIE SLEEPS
WITH HIS TEDDY BEAR, TOO, SO IRA FEELS CONFIDENT
ENOUGH TO MARCH OVER TO HIS OWN HOUSE, UP THE
STAIRS, WITH A SMUG EXPRESSION ON HIS FACE, TO
PICK UP TAH-TAH, HIS TEDDY BEAR. NOTABLE FOR ITS
RECOGNITION OF THE FACT THAT CHILDREN ENJOY
MILDLY SCARY SITUATIONS IF THERE IS AN UNDERLYING
BOLSTERING OF SECURITY, THE BOOK IS ALSO LIKELY
TO BE AROUND FOR AWHILE BECAUSE IT PICTURES AN
URBAN, CONTEMPORARY FAMILY WITH A FATHER COOKING
AT THE STOVE AND, IN ONE SCENE, A MOTHER CURLED
UP ON THE COUCH IN HER PAJAMAS. (EMOTIONS--FEAR,
EMOTIONS--SECURITY, FEAR, SECURITY)

EMOTIONS--SERENITY

GAUCH, PATRICIA. GRANDPA AND ME. COWARD, 1972.
ILLUSTRATED BY SYMEON SHIMIN. (CC)

   THE ILLUSTRATIONS ARE PARAMOUNT IN THIS STORY
OF A BOY, PERHAPS TEN OR ELEVEN, AND THE
COMPANIONSHIP HE AND HIS GRANDFATHER SHARE, AS
THE DELICATE WATERCOLORS WASH ACROSS THE PAGES IN
PASTELS OF SAND, SUN, AND WATER. SYMEON SHIMIN'S
ARTISTRY DOMINATES THE BOOK, YET IN A SUPPORTIVE
WAY, AND THE READER COMES AWAY FROM THE BOOK
WITH A FEELING OF CONTENTMENT, PEACE, AND
THOUGHTFUL REFLECTIONS ON THE VALUES OF GETTING
BACK TO NATURE AND BEING ALONE, AWAY FROM PEOPLE.
(EMOTIONS--SERENITY, FAM--GRANDFATHERS,
GRANDFATHERS, SERENITY)

EMOTIONS--SHYNESS

DEAN, LEIGH. LOOKING DOWN GAME. FUNK, 1968.
ILLUSTRATED BY PAUL GIOVANOPOULOS. (BECB)

A LONELY BOY SPENDS ALMOST A YEAR IN A NEW
NEIGHBORHOOD, LOOKING DOWN INSTEAD OF UP, TO
AVOID MAKING NEW FRIENDS. WHILE THE BONUSES ARE
MANY--THE DISCOVERY THAT HE LIKES ANTS, AND THE
BIRD'S NEST HE FOUND--THE READER IS RELIEVED WHEN
HE DISCOVERS A FRIEND UP IN A TREE AND DECIDES
TO FIND OUT "WHAT BEING UP WAS LIKE." THE SOMBER
BLACK AND WHITE DRAWINGS LEND THEMSELVES WELL TO
THE QUIET, INTROSPECTIVE MOOD OF THE STORY, AND
EDGAR IS SEEN AS A BASICALLY SHY PERSON, FAIRLY
CONTENT TO EXPLORE HIS LONELY WORLD. WHILE THE
READER IS GLAD TO SEE HIM MAKE A FRIEND, ONE ALSO
SENSES THIS IS A BOY WHO WILL ALWAYS BE A GOOD
OBSERVER OF LIFE. (EMOTIONS--LONELINESS,
EMOTIONS--SHYNESS, LONELINESS, SHYNESS)

KRASILOVSKY, PHYLLIS. THE SHY LITTLE GIRL.
HOUGHTON, 1970. ILLUSTRATED BY TRINA HYMAN.
(LJ, TLS)

ANNE WAS A LONER WHO SPOKE IN A VOICE NO ONE
COULD HEAR, WHO OFTEN PLAYED ALONE, AND WHO, WHEN
SHE DID PLAY, FOUND PLAYMATES YOUNGER THAN
HERSELF. WHEN CLAUDIA, A NEW GIRL, COMES TO
SCHOOL, THEY IMMEDIATELY STRIKE UP A FRIENDSHIP.
ANNE'S SELF-CONFIDENCE GROWS AS THE FRIENDSHIP
GROWS, AND WE SEE HER BLOSSOM INTO A
PARTICIPATING, SHARING YOUNG GIRL.
(EMOTIONS--SHYNESS, SELF-CONFIDENCE, SHYNESS)

LEXAU, JOAN. BENJIE. DIAL, 1964. ILLUSTRATED BY
DON BOLOGNESE. (CC)

A LIGHT GRAY WATERCOLOR WASH MATCHES THE
GRUBBY STREET SETTING OF THIS REALISTIC STORY.
ACTION TAKES PLACE ON THE STOOP, STREETS, AND
SHOPS OF THE INNER CITY, INCLUDING THE ONE ROOM
IN WHICH GRANNY AND BENJIE LIVE. HE IS A SMALL
BOY SO SHY THAT HE HIDES BEHIND HIS GRANNY'S
SKIRTS, AND IS TEASED BY THE NEIGHBORS. WHEN HIS
GRANDMOTHER LOSES A FAVORITE EARRING, BENJIE
OVERCOMES HIS SHYNESS TO HELP LOOK FOR IT, AND IN
ASSERTING HIMSELF MAKES PROGRESS TOWARD
INDEPENDENCE. USEFUL ALSO TO DEMONSTRATE A
LOVING, CARING RELATIONSHIP BETWEEN YOUNG AND

OLD. (EMOTIONS--SHYNESS, FAM--GRANDMOTHERS, GRANDMOTHERS, SELF-CONFIDENCE, SHYNESS)

ZOLOTOW, CHARLOTTE. A TIGER CALLED THOMAS. LOTHROP, 1963. ILLUSTRATED BY KURT WERTH. (CC)

SHY THOMAS SITS ON THE PORCH OF HIS NEW HOUSE AND REFUSES TO TRY TO MAKE NEW FRIENDS. HE IS VERY OBSERVANT, HOWEVER, AND IS AWARE OF GERALD, WHO PLAYS BALL ALONE, AND OF MARIE, AND OTHER PEOPLE IN THE NEIGHBORHOOD. GIVEN CONFIDENCE BY DRESSING UP IN A TIGER SUIT ON HALLOWEEN, HE TAKES ON SOME OF THE COURAGE OF THE BEAST, AND VISITS ALL OF THE HOUSES IN THE NEIGHBORHOOD. WHEN PEOPLE ASK HIM TO VISIT AND PLAY, HE REALIZES THAT THEY ALL LIKE HIM, AND HE DECIDES THAT HE ALSO LIKES THEM. (EMOTIONS--SHYNESS, FRIENDSHIP, MOVING, NEW SIT--MOVING, SELF-CONFIDENCE, SHYNESS)

EYEGLASSES

GOODSELL, JANE. KATIE'S MAGIC GLASSES. HOUGHTON, 1965. ILLUSTRATED BY BARBARA COONEY. (ESLC)

KATIE IS A YOUNG GIRL WHO DISCOVERS SHE NEEDS GLASSES WHEN SHE IS SIX YEARS OLD, BUT THINKS SHE DOES NOT WANT TO HAVE GLASSES. THE DOCTOR TELLS HER SHE'LL SEE "MAGIC." WHEN THEY FINALLY ARRIVE, SHE PUTS THEM ON, AND HOCUS-POCUS--THE BLUR IS GONE! AND SHE SEES EVERYTHING "JUST RIGHT." (EYEGLASSES, NEW SIT--EYEGLASSES)

RASKIN, ELLEN. SPECTACLES. ATHENEUM, 1968. ILLUSTRATED BY ELLEN RASKIN. (BCB)

IMAGINATIVE ILLUSTRATIONS SHOW THE READER THE FUNNY BUT CONFUSING IMAGES IRIS SEES IN HER NEARSIGHTED CONDITION: THE BIG FRIENDLY-LOOKING BULL DOG IN MRS. SCHMIDLAP'S PARLOR IS REALLY A VICTORIAN SOFA WITH LEGS WHICH RESEMBLE THE PAWS OF A DOG. IRIS DOES NOT WANT TO WEAR EYEGLASSES, BUT SHE IS EXAMINED, SHE TRIES ON MANY KINDS OF FRAMES, AND WHEN SHE WEARS THEM FOR THE FIRST TIME NO ONE NOTICES, EXCEPT HER FRIEND CHESTER. THE DRAMATIC DIFFERENCE IN WHAT SHE SEES IS EVIDENT ON THE LAST PAGE WHERE THE BOOK ENDS ON THE HUMOROUS NOTE IT HAS MAINTAINED THROUGHOUT. AN EXCELLENT NON-PREACHY BOOK. (EYEGLASSES, NEW SIT--EYEGLASSES)

SANDS, GEORGE. WHY GLASSES?. LERNER, 1960.
ILLUSTRATED BY ROV ANDRE. (ESLC)

   SOME THIRD GRADERS WILL BE ABLE TO ASSIMILATE
THE RATHER TECHNICAL INFORMATION IN THIS VOLUME,
AND FOR THE FACTUALLY-MINDED CHILD, IT WILL BE
HELPFUL TO KNOW TERMS SUCH AS RETINA, REFRACTION,
AND ASTIGMATISM. THIS STRAIGHTFORWARD APPROACH
MAY BE VERY USEFUL FOR THE CHILD WHO NEEDS, OR
ALREADY WEARS, EYEGLASSES, FOR IT REMOVES THE
DISCUSSION FROM THE AFFECTIVE DOMAIN INTO THE
COGNITIVE ASPECT OF THE SOMETIMES UNPLEASANT
EXPERIENCE OF WEARING EYEGLASSES. (EYEGLASSES,
NEW SIT--EYEGLASSES)

WOLFF, ANGELIKA. MOM! I NEED GLASSES!. LION,
1970. ILLUSTRATED BY DOROTHY HILL. (CC)

   SECOND-GRADER SUSAN KNOWS SHE NEEDS GLASSES
BECAUSE THE NUMBERS ON THE BLACKBOARD IN SCHOOL
ARE BLURRED, BUT SHE HAS VAGUE FEARS OF HAVING
HER EYES EXAMINED. SHE IS EXAMINED BY A VERY
BREEZY OCULIST. THERE IS A GREAT DEAL OF TEXT AND
A COMPLEX DIAGRAM OF HOW THE HUMAN EYE WORKS
(FAR TOO COMPLICATED FOR A SEVEN-YEAR-OLD). SUSAN
IS HAPPY WHEN SHE RECEIVES HER FASHIONABLE BLUE
SHADES AND CAN SEE ONCE AGAIN. (EYEGLASSES, NEW
SIT--EYEGLASSES)

FAM

ADOFF, ARNOLD. BLACK IS BROWN IS TAN. HARPER,
1973. ILLUSTRATED BY EMILY MC CULLY. (CC)

   DESCRIBING THIS FAMILY IN TERMS OF FREE VERSE
AND BEAUTIFUL WATERCOLORS DOES NOT BEGIN TO
INCLUDE THE NUANCES OF LOVE PORTRAYED AS THESE
CONTEMPORARY FAMILY MEMBERS CHOP THEIR OWN WOOD,
MAKE THEIR OWN MUSIC, COOK ON A BIG BLACK
COOKSTOVE. ALTHOUGH COLOR, THE VARYING SHADES OF
SKIN, IS THE THEME, CERTAINLY THE WARMTH OF
FAMILY LOVE IS THE MORE IMPORTANT MESSAGE.
(EMOTIONS--LOVE, FAM, LOVE)

ADOFF, ARNOLD. MA NDA LA. HARPER, 1971.
ILLUSTRATED BY EMILY MC CULLY. (BCB)

   A TONE POEM USING ONLY SYLLABLES, ILLUSTRATED
WITH HANDSOME WATERCOLOR PAINTINGS, THIS BOOK
CELEBRATES THE LOVE BETWEEN THE MEMBERS OF AN

AFRICAN FAMILY AS THEY PERFORM THEIR LABOR OF
HOEING, PLANTING, WATCHING THE CROPS GROW,
HARVESTING THE CORN, AND FINALLY EATING THE FRESH
ROASTING EARS. CHILDREN MAY "READ" THIS BOOK AS
A FIRST BOOK, OR SING THE SYLLABLES. IT OFFERS
MANY POSSIBILITIES FOR CHILDREN TO REACT IN
DIFFERENT WAYS. (FAM)

CHARLIP, REMY. HOORAY FOR ME!. PARENTS' MAG,
1975. ILLUSTRATED BY VERA WILLIAMS. (LJ, NYTBR)

IN WATERY, EVOCATIVE WATERCOLORS, THE
ILLUSTRATOR SETS THE TONE FOR THE THEME OF
INTERRELATEDNESS OF THE HUMAN FAMILY. THE BOOK,
WHILE STRESSING THAT THE INDIVIDUAL IS A "ME,"
EXPLORES THE RELATIONSHIP OF NIECES TO UNCLES,
AND COUSINS TO COUSINS, AND DEVELOPS
UNDERSTANDING OF GREAT-GRANDPARENTS TO
GREAT-GREAT-GRANDPARENTS IN A SEQUENCE WITH A
KITTEN WHICH CHILDREN WILL LIKE. A BOOK WHICH
DEFIES DESCRIPTION, IT IS LIKELY TO BE ONE WHICH
WILL BE ENDURINGLY USEFUL IN HELPING TO DEVELOP
THE CONCEPT OF SELF. (FAM, FAM--GRANDPARENTS,
FAM--GREAT-GRANDPARENTS, GRANDPARENTS,
GREAT-GRANDPARENTS, SELF-IDENTITY)

DAUGHERTY, JAMES. ANDY AND THE LION. VIKING,
1938. ILLUSTRATED BY JAMES DAUGHERTY. (CC)

IN ROLLICKING, RHYTHMICAL DRAWINGS, JAMES
DAUGHERTY HAS SYNTHESIZED FEELINGS OF JOY IN
LIVING AND JOY IN HELPING OTHER PEOPLE. ANDY, WHO
BEFRIENDS A LION AND REMOVES A BIG THORN FROM
HIS PAW, LATER IS THE BENEFICIARY OF THE KIND
ACT. THE LION, WHO HAS ESCAPED FROM THE CIRCUS,
RECOGNIZES ANDY AND IS IMMEDIATELY FRIENDLY.
USEFUL BECAUSE IT DEMONSTRATES IN A VERY SIMPLE
WAY HOW ONE KIND ACT MAY BE REPAID, BUT FAR
BEYOND THAT, THE AFFECTIVE ASPECTS OF LIVING ARE
STRESSED--THE SENSUOUS EFFECT OF THE EXPRESSIONS
ON FACES, THE SUBTLE HUMOR IN THE DAILY FAMILY
LIFE, AND THE VIGOROUS FEELINGS DEPICTING THE JOY
OF LIVING. (BEHAVIOR--CONSIDERATION,
BEHAVIOR--KINDNESS, CONSIDERATION,
EMOTIONS--HAPPINESS, FAM, FRIENDSHIP, HAPPINESS,
KINDNESS)

DUVOISIN, ROGER. TWO LONELY DUCKS. KNOPF, 1955.
ILLUSTRATED BY ROGER DUVOISIN. (CC)

A LOVELY COUNTING BOOK FOR YOUNG CHILDREN. THE
LITTLE WHITE DUCK AND THE LITTLE WHITE DRAKE
WERE LONELY IN THE POND. THEY DECIDED TO RAISE A
FAMILY, SO THE LITTLE DUCK BUILT A NEST, AND LAID
TEN EGGS IN ALL, SITTING ON THE EGGS FOR DAYS
AND WEEKS, AND ONE BY ONE HATCHED OUT TEN BABY
DUCKLINGS, AND NO ONE WAS LONELY ANY MORE.
UNDERSCORES COMPANIONSHIP IN FAMILY LIVING.
(EMOTIONS--LONELINESS, FAM, LONELINESS)

EHRLICH, AMY. ZEEK SILVER MOON. DIAL, 1972.
ILLUSTRATED BY ROBERT PARKER. (ESLC)

NOTABLE BECAUSE IT SHOWS AN ALTERNATIVE LIFE
STYLE OF A MUSICIAN, HIS WIFE, AND THEIR CHILD,
ZEEK SILVER MOON, THE BOOK IS GREATLY ENHANCED BY
STUNNINGLY BEAUTIFUL WATERCOLORS EVOKING THE
SOFTNESS OF LOVE. THIS IS A STORY OF
NON-CONFORMING, ALIVE, NEW LIFE-STYLE PEOPLE:
FATHER MADE THE BABY A CRADLE OF WOOD AFTER HE
WAS BORN AND LATER, WHEN ZEEK WAS FOUR YEARS OLD,
HIS FATHER, IN AN INCIDENT CALLED THE CARPET
RAISING, STAPLED THEIR LIVING ROOM RUG TO THE
CEILING BECAUSE A NEIGHBOR COMPLAINED OF NOISE.
WITHIN THE FRAMEWORK OF A FAMILY WHICH PLACES A
HIGH VALUE ON NATURAL FOODS, HOME-BAKED BREAD,
AND ENTERTAINMENT OTHER THAN TELEVISION, ZEEK IS
SHOWN TO BE A LOVED CHILD, ONE WHO RECEIVES
GENTLE LOVING CARE, IS TUCKED IN AT NIGHT AND
TOLD STORIES. (EMOTIONS--LOVE,
EMOTIONS--SECURITY, FAM, LOVE, SECURITY)

FLACK, MARJORIE. ASK MR. BEAR. MACMILLAN, 1932.
ILLUSTRATED BY MARJORIE FLACK. (CC)

THIS CLASSIC PICTURE BOOK WHICH PORTRAYS THE
DILEMMA OF WHAT TO GIVE MOTHER FOR HER BIRTHDAY
SUSTAINS THE BELIEF THAT AN EXPRESSION OF LOVE,
LIKE A BIG BEAR HUG, IS JUST AS GOOD, OR PERHAPS
BETTER, THAN ANY MATERIAL GIFT A CHILD COULD
GIVE. (EMOTIONS--LOVE, FAM, LOVE)

HOBAN, RUSSELL. BREAD AND JAM FOR FRANCES.
HARPER, 1964. ILLUSTRATED BY LILLIAN HOBAN. (CC)

FRANCES CAN TELL YOU A NUMBER OF REASONS SHE
DISLIKES EGGS--"SUNNY-SIDE-UP EGGS LIE ON THE
PLATE AND LOOK UP AT YOU IN A FUNNY WAY."
FURTHERMORE, SHE TRADES AWAY HER CHICKEN SALAD
SANDWICH TO HER FRIEND ALBERT FOR A BREAD AND JAM

SANDWICH. BREAD AND JAM, INDEED, IS THE FAVORITE
FOOD OF FRANCES. HER WISE PARENTS, AFTER
TEMPTING HER WITH BREADED VEAL CUTLETS, STRING
BEANS, AND BAKED POTATOES DECIDED TO FEED HER A
STEADY DIET OF BREAD AND JAM. THE SLIGHTLY
CRESTFALLEN LOOK ON HER FACE DEEPENS TO TEARFUL
DISMAY WHEN SHE IS SERVED BREAD AND JAM ON THE
NIGHT THE FAMILY IS HAVING SPAGHETTI AND
MEATBALLS. SHE MAKES AN ABOUT-FACE, ENJOYS HER
DINNER, AND THE READER SEES HER ENJOYING A
SUMPTUOUS LUNCH NEXT DAY AT SCHOOL. ESPECIALLY
USEFUL FOR BOTH PARENTS AND CHILDREN, BECAUSE
THERE ARE NO ARGUING OR LOUD VOICES--JUST SUBTLE
ACTION, WHICH IS VERY EFFECTIVE, BECAUSE IN THE
END, THE CHILD MAKES THE DECISION.
(BEHAVIOR--DISLIKES--FOOD, DISLIKES--FOOD, FAM)

HOBAN, RUSSELL. THE SORELY TRYING DAY. HARPER,
1964. ILLUSTRATED BY LILLIAN HOBAN. (CC)

   ALTHOUGH THIS IS A TONGUE-IN-CHEEK SPOOF, IT
WILL BE VALUABLE FOR POINTING OUT HOW ONE THING
LEADS TO ANOTHER IN A QUARREL, AND SHOWS IN A
VERY FUNNY WAY WHAT HAPPENS WHEN EVERYBODY
ACCEPTS THE BLAME. SHOWS THE BEAUTY OF THE PHRASE
"I AM SORRY." (BEHAVIOR--CONSIDERATION,
BEHAVIOR--QUARRELING, CONSIDERATION, FAM,
QUARRELING)

KEATS, EZRA. WHISTLE FOR WILLIE. VIKING, 1964.
ILLUSTRATED BY EZRA KEATS. (CC)

   THE UNDERSTANDING PARENTS OF YOUNG PETER
SUPPORT HIS EFFORTS TO TRY TO BE GROWN-UP. HE
WANTS TO LEARN TO WHISTLE, HE TRIES ON HIS
FATHER'S HAT, HE TRIES TO CATCH HIS SHADOW. HIS
MOTHER DOES NOT DEMEAN HIM, AND BOTH HIS PARENTS
PRAISE PETER WHEN HE LEARNS TO WHISTLE. THE SMILE
THAT PETER HAS ON HIS FACE TELLS THE WHOLE STORY
OF PRIDE IN ACCOMPLISHMENT. AS MOTHER AND FATHER
APPLAUD IN THE BACKGROUND, HIS DOG WILLIE SITS
UP ON HIS HIND LEGS. (FAM, NEW SIT--WHISTLING,
SELF-DEVELOPMENT, WHISTLING)

MEEKS, ESTHER. FAMILIES LIVE TOGETHER. FOLLETT,
1969.   (CC)

   BEGINNING WITH ATTRACTIVE PICTURES OF ANIMAL
FAMILIES, THE CONCEPT OF FAMILY LIFE IS
ILLUSTRATED IN MANY WAYS, FROM MOTHERS WITH NEW

BABIES IN HOSPITALS, TO FATHERS DISCIPLINING
THEIR CHILDREN AS WELL AS READING BEDTIME
STORIES. INTERRACIAL THROUGHOUT, THE BOOK IS
USEFUL IN THAT IT SHOWS MANY DIFFERENT FAMILIES
(IN HOME SITUATIONS, AT SCHOOL, PICNICKING IN THE
PARK) HAVING GOOD TIMES AND BAD TIMES, BUT
ALWAYS HELPING EACH OTHER. THE CONTEMPORARY
PHOTOS AND THE GOOD COLOR MAKE IT A VOLUME WHICH
IS NOT LIKELY TO BECOME DATED. (FAM)

SEGAL, LORE. TELL ME A MITZI. FARRAR, 1970.
ILLUSTRATED BY HARRIET PINCUS. (BCB)

  MARTHA IS A VERY LUCKY LITTLE GIRL: HER MOTHER
AND FATHER AND GRANDMOTHER ARE WONDERFUL
STORYTELLERS. THEY TELL HER "MITZIES," WHICH ARE
REALLY STORIES ABOUT HER AND HER BROTHER, SUCH AS
THE TIME SHE WOKE UP EARLY, GOT HER BABY BROTHER
UP AND DRESSED, AND PLANNED TO TAKE A TAXI TO
SEE HER GRANDPARENTS. EXCEPT THAT SHE DIDN'T KNOW
THE ADDRESS. SO THE TAXI DRIVER LET HER OUT AND
SHE AND JACOB WENT UPSTAIRS AND WENT BACK TO BED,
JUST AS MOTHER'S ALARM CLOCK WENT OFF. TWO OTHER
STORIES COMPLETE THE BOOK: ONE IS A HILARIOUS
ACCOUNT OF THE FAMILY FALLING ILL, ONE BY ONE,
THE OTHER AN IMAGINATIVE TALE OF THE PRESIDENT OF
THE UNITED STATES GIVING A PIECE OF GUM TO
JACOB. ILLUSTRATIONS ARE IN RICH, VIBRANT COLORS
WHICH REFLECT THE VIGOR OF THE FAMILY.
(EMOTIONS--LOVE, FAM, LOVE)

SONNEBORN, RUTH. SEVEN IN A BED. VIKING, 1968.
ILLUSTRATED BY DON FREEMAN. (BCB)

  A TRULY FUNNY BOOK OF PAPA'S PREDICAMENT IN
TRYING TO BED DOWN HIS FOUR CHILDREN, ONE NIECE
AND TWO NEPHEWS, HIMSELF, HIS WIFE, AND A NEW
BABY IN TWO BEDS. THEY HAVE JUST ARRIVED FROM
PUERTO RICO, AND THESE ARE TEMPORARY QUARTERS,
FORTUNATELY FOR THEM, FOR DON FREEMAN'S GRAPHIC
ILLUSTRATION SHOWS THE CHILDREN THE NEXT
MORNING--UPSIDE DOWN, FEET ON PILLOWS, LYING ON
TOP OF ONE ANOTHER, AND ONE ON THE FLOOR,
COMPLETE WITH PILLOW AND BUNNY RABBIT.
ILLUSTRATES THE GOOD HUMOR IN MAKING THE BEST OF
THE SITUATION. (FAM)

TURKLE, BRINTON. THY FRIEND OBADIAH. VIKING,
1969. ILLUSTRATED BY BRINTON TURKLE. (BCB)

OBADIAH, A YOUNG QUAKER BOY, IS ANGRY WHEN A
SEA GULL TRIES TO BE HIS FRIEND BY TAGGING ALONG
BEHIND HIM IN THIS EXCELLENT PORTRAYAL OF QUAKER
FAMILY LIFE. AS THE STORY PROGRESSES, THE GULL
GETS A LARGE RUSTY FISHHOOK CAUGHT IN HIS BEAK,
OBADIAH TAKES IT OUT, AND THE SEA GULL FLIES
AWAY. WHEN THE GULL RETURNS, OBADIAH REASONS:
"SINCE I HELPED HIM, I'M HIS FRIEND, TOO."
TURKLE'S WATERCOLORS EVOKE A POWERFUL FEELING OF
A COZY, SECURE LIFE IN THE DAYS WHEN THE FAMILY
GATHERED AROUND THE FIREPLACE WHILE THE BREAD WAS
BAKING. (EMOTIONS--LOVE, EMOTIONS--SECURITY,
FAM, FRIENDSHIP, LOVE, SECURITY)

ZOLOTOW, CHARLOTTE. THE QUARRELING BOOK. HARPER,
1963.   ILLUSTRATED BY ARNOLD LOBEL. (CC)

THE GRAYNESS OF A RAINY DAY IS ECHOED IN THE
BLACK AND WHITE DRAWINGS OF ARNOLD LOBEL, AND THE
SLANTY LINES OF THE DRIVING RAIN ADD TENSION
THROUGHOUT. BEGINNING WITH A FATHER WHO FORGETS
HIS GOOD-BYE KISS, THE BOOK PROGESSES TO A CRANKY
MOTHER, A TEASING BOY CHILD, AND A SISTER SALLY
WITH HURT FEELINGS. IT TOOK THE DOG, WHO WASN'T
AFFECTED BY THE DEPRESSIVE DAY, TO SWEETEN UP
EVERYONE'S SPIRITS, AND IT IS A LESSON IN THE
CONTAGIOUSNESS OF FEELINGS, BOTH GOOD AND BAD.
(BEHAVIOR--QUARRELING, FAM, QUARRELING)

FAM--BROTHERS

AMOSS, BERTHE. TOM IN THE MIDDLE. HARPER, 1968.
ILLUSTRATED BY BERTHE AMOSS. (CCB-B)

THE VERY REAL PLIGHT OF HAVING A YOUNGER
BROTHER WHO BUGS YOU AND AN OLDER BROTHER WHO
THINKS YOU'RE A PEST IS DEPICTED IN THIS
ATTRACTIVE LITTLE PICTURE BOOK. TOM THINKS HE
WILL RUN AWAY, BUT ALSO THINKS THAT HOME AND THE
SAFETY OF BREAD AND BUTTER AT BEDTIME IS THE
BETTER IDEA. (BROTHERS, FAM--BROTHERS,
FAM--SIBLING RIVALRY, SIBLING RIVALRY)

BRONIN, ANDREW. GUS AND BUSTER WORK THINGS OUT.
COWARD, 1975.   ILLUSTRATED BY CYNDY SZEKERES.
(BL)

BROTHER RACCOONS ARE SHOWN IN FOUR STORIES OF
BROTHERLY SQUABBLES. GUS, WHO MAY BE A LITTLE
OLDER, TRICKS HIS SIBLING IN MANY

SITUATIONS--TRYING TO GET THE LOWER BUNK BED,
TRYING TO GET ALL THE BEST TOYS ON A RAINY DAY.
USEFUL FOR DISCUSSION BECAUSE SYMPATHY TENDS TO
LIE WITH BUSTER, THE PUT-UPON BROTHER, AND HE
SOMETIMES GETS THE BEST OF HIS WILY BIG BROTHER.
(BEHAVIOR--QUARRELING, BROTHERS, FAM--BROTHERS,
FAM--SIBLING RIVALRY, QUARRELING, SIBLING RIVALRY)

FRIEDMAN, AILEEN. CASTLES OF THE TWO BROTHERS.
HOLT, 1972. ILLUSTRATED BY STEVEN KELLOGG.
(ESLC)

   AILEEN FRIEDMAN WAS INSPIRED TO WRITE THIS
STORY AFTER SHE VISITED TWO REAL CASTLES SITUATED
ON THE RHINE RIVER. IT HAS A FOLKTALE QUALITY
ABOUT IT WHICH IS MATCHED BY MEDIEVAL
ILLUSTRATIONS. BASICALLY IT IS THE STORY OF TWO
BROTHERS WHO WERE ORPHANED. HUBERT, THE OLDER
BROTHER, LOOKS AFTER HIS YOUNGER BROTHER KLAUS TO
SUCH AN EXTENT THAT THE YOUNGER BROTHER FINALLY
REBELS. AFTER BUILDING HIS OWN CASTLE AND A HUGE
WALL TO SEPARATE IT FROM HUBERT'S, KLAUS NARROWLY
AVOIDS DISASTER WHEN THE WALL CRUMBLES.
ILLUSTRATES VERY WELL THAT TOO MUCH "MOTHERING"
CAN BE BAD. (BROTHERS, FAM--BROTHERS,
FAM--SIBLING RIVALRY, SIBLING RIVALRY)

GUILFOILE, ELIZABETH. HAVE YOU SEEN MY BROTHER?.
FOLLETT, 1962. ILLUSTRATED BY MARY STEVENS.
(CC)

   A RELATIVELY EASY-TO-READ STORY FOR FIRST
GRADERS, IN WHICH A LITTLE BOY SEARCHES ALL OVER
THE NEIGHBORHOOD FOR HIS BIG BROTHER, WHO HAS RED
HAIR, FRECKLES, AND WEARS BLUE JEANS. ALL
THROUGH THE STORY THE READER THINKS THE BIG
BROTHER IS LOST: AT THE END WE REALIZE IT IS THE
LITTLE-BOY NARRATOR WHO IS LOST. A SLIGHT STORY
IN WHICH INTEREST IS MAINTAINED BY SUSPENSE.
USEFUL BECAUSE OF THE ROLE IN WHICH THE YOUNGER
BROTHER PUTS HIMSELF: LOOKING FOR THE OLDER
BROTHER WHO IS "LOST." (BROTHERS, FAM--BROTHERS)

HALLINAN, P.K.. WE'RE VERY GOOD FRIENDS.
CHILDRENS, 1973. ILLUSTRATED BY P.K. HALLINAN.
(CCB-B)

   TWO BROTHERS WHO REALLY ARE FRIENDS, WHO ENJOY
PLAYING TOGETHER, "ACTING CREEPY" TOGETHER,
BEING MAD AND SAD, ARE STILL GLAD TO BE BROTHERS,

AND THAT'S THE BEST REASON WHY "WE'RE VERY GOOD
FRIENDS, MY BROTHER AND I." SLIGHT STORY AND TEXT
USEFUL TO SEE THE RELATIONSHIP OF BROTHERHOOD
AND FRIENDSHIP. (BROTHERS, FAM--BROTHERS,
FRIENDSHIP)

ZOLOTOW, CHARLOTTE. IF IT WEREN'T FOR YOU.
HARPER, 1966.   ILLUSTRATED BY BEN SHECTER.   (BCB)

   BIG BROTHER COMPLAINS THROUGHOUT THE BOOK
ABOUT THE THINGS HE MIGHT HAVE IF HE WERE AN ONLY
CHILD--HE'D GET ALL THE PRESENTS, THE TREE HOUSE
WOULD BE HIS ALONE, AND HE COULD ALWAYS SIT IN
THE FRONT SEAT OF THE CAR. A BASICALLY SELFISH
ATTITUDE IS EXPOSED, ALBEIT A NATURAL ONE. AT THE
END, HOWEVER, BIG BROTHER CONCEDES THAT IF IT
WEREN'T FOR LITTLE BROTHER, HE'D HAVE TO BE WITH
THE GROWN-UPS ALL THE TIME, AND THAT SEEMS A
WORSE FATE. (BEHAVIOR--SELFISHNESS, BROTHERS,
FAM--BROTHERS, SELFISHNESS)

FAM--BROTHERS & SISTERS

ALEXANDER, MARTHA. NOBODY ASKED ME IF I WANTED A
BABY SISTER. DIAL, 1971.   ILLUSTRATED BY MARTHA
ALEXANDER.   (BCB)

   THE STORY OPENS WITH A SOUR-FACED LITTLE BOY
OVERHEARING GUSHY COMPLIMENTS ABOUT HIS NEW BABY
SISTER. HIS NEXT MOVE IS TO LOAD HER IN A WAGON
AND TRY TO GIVE HER AWAY. AFTER SEVERAL ABORTED
ATTEMPTS, HE ENDS UP AT HIS FRIEND'S HOUSE. BABY
BONNIE MISBEHAVES, HOWEVER, AND IN THE END IT IS
THE BROTHER WHO CAN PACIFY HER. WICKED THOUGHTS
GO THROUGH HIS HEAD AS HE IMAGINES HER GROWING UP
AND PULLING HIM IN THE WAGON. (BROTHERS &
SISTERS, EMOTIONS--JEALOUSY, FAM--BROTHERS &
SISTERS, JEALOUSY, NEW SIT--BABY)

BONSALL, CROSBY. THE DAY I HAD TO PLAY WITH MY
SISTER. HARPER, 1972.   ILLUSTRATED BY CROSBY
BONSALL.   (CC)

   WORDLESS LITTLE SISTER DOES PRETTY WELL
AMUSING HERSELF. WHEN THE STORY OPENS SHE IS
MAKING A VERY NICE PAPER HAT FOR HER BIG DOG, BUT
SHE IS NOT MUCH HELP WHEN HER BROTHER TRIES TO
TEACH HER HOW TO PLAY HIDE-AND-SEEK. HIS
EXASPERATION COMES TO A HIGH POINT WHEN, INSTEAD
OF LOOKING FOR HIS HIDING PLACE, SHE CURLS UP TO

TAKE A NAP IN A PILE OF LEAVES. ATTRACTIVE TO BOY
READERS WHO WILL COMMISERATE WITH THE BROTHER,
AND OTHER READERS WILL APPRECIATE THE HUMOR.
(BROTHERS & SISTERS, FAM--BROTHERS & SISTERS)

BRANDENBERG, FRANZ. I WISH I WAS SICK, TOO!.
MORROW, 1976. ILLUSTRATED BY ALIKI. (BL)

   THIS IS A BOOK IN WHICH ALL OF THE ACTION CAN
BE TRACED IN THE EXPRESSIONS IN THE EYES OF
EDWARD AND ELIZABETH, TWO ENDEARING CAT
PROTAGONISTS WITH ALL TOO HUMAN FOIBLES. EDWARD'S
EYES ARE AT HALF-MAST AS WE SEE HIM IN THE
SICKBED, AND ELIZABETH SHOOTS SIDEWISE GLANCES OF
ENVIOUS RAGE AS SHE RELUCTANTLY DOES HER CHORES
AND PRACTICES PIANO. CONCERN AND LOVE ARE
EXPRESSED IN THE EYES OF MOTHER AND FATHER AS
THEY MINISTER TO THE CHILDREN, FOR YES, ELIZABETH
ALSO BECOMES ILL. HER EYES ARE EVEN MORE
HELPLESSLY DROOPED, AND ONCE AGAIN SHE IS ENVIOUS
OF THE WELL BROTHER, WHOSE EYES ARE BY NOW ROUND
AND SPARKLY. THE STORY ENDS WITH EVERYONE
PROPERLY ROUND-EYED AND HAPPY. (BROTHERS &
SISTERS, DIFF SIT--ILLNESS, FAM--BROTHERS &
SISTERS, EMOTIONS--JEALOUSY, ILLNESS, JEALOUSY)

BUNIN, SHERRY. IS THAT YOUR SISTER?. PANTHEON,
1976.

   THIS IS SIX-YEAR-OLD CATHERINE BUNIN'S OWN
STORY AND THAT OF HER SISTER CARLA, IN A BOOK
ABOUT INTERRACIAL ADOPTION. OBVIOUSLY PROUD TO BE
LOVED AND CARED FOR BY HER FAMILY WHICH INCLUDES
TWO BROTHERS, CATHERINE RELATES THE STORY OF HER
ADOPTION BY ANSWERING MANY OF THE QUESTIONS PUT
TO HER BY CHILDREN AND ADULTS ALIKE. SHE TACKLES
EVEN VERY SUBSTANTIVE ANSWERS AS SHE DESCRIBES
THE WAY IN WHICH THE SOCIAL WORKER VISITED THEIR
HOME, AND THE CULMINATION OF THE PROCEEDINGS IN
THE FAMILY COURT. FILLED WITH MANY EXCELLENT,
INFORMAL PHOTOGRAPHS OF FAMILY LIFE, THIS SLIM
VOLUME WILL BE HELPFUL TO PARENTS ANTICIPATING OR
CONTEMPLATING THIS DIFFICULT SITUATION.
(ADOPTION--INTERRACIAL, BROTHERS & SISTERS, DIFF
SIT--ADOPTION--INTERRACIAL, FAM--BROTHERS &
SISTERS)

CAINES, JEANNETTE. ABBY. HARPER, 1973.
ILLUSTRATED BY STEVEN KELLOGG. (CC)

ABBY IS A ROUND-FACED BUNDLE OF CURIOSITY, WHO
ALWAYS WANTS TO HEAR THE STORY OF HER ADOPTION,
OVER AND OVER AGAIN. WHEN SHE PESTERS HER BROTHER
KEVIN, EMOTIONS SPILL OVER, WITH ABBY CRYING AND
BROTHER FEELING SORRY. THROUGHOUT THE STORY, THE
ILLUSTRATOR HAS PICTURED A COMFORTABLE HOME
FILLED WITH LOVE AND CONCERN. KEVIN PROMISES TO
TAKE ABBY TO SCHOOL FOR SHOW AND TELL, AND HIS
PRIDE IN HER IS VERY OBVIOUS. USEFUL IN VARIOUS
WAYS CONCERNING ADOPTION--THE OPEN CURIOSITY OF
THE CHILD, THE OPEN WILLINGNESS TO TALK OF IT,
THE PRIDE, IN THIS CASE, OF BEING ADOPTED.
(ADOPTION, BROTHERS & SISTERS, DIFF
SIT--ADOPTION, FAM--BROTHERS & SISTERS)

CONFORD, ELLEN. IMPOSSIBLE POSSUM. LITTLE, 1971.
  ILLUSTRATED BY ROSEMARY WELLS. (CC, ESLC)

AN EXAMPLE OF SELF-FULFILLING PROPHECY OF
FAILURE. RANDOLPH, WHO COULDN'T HANG BY HIS TAIL
LIKE OTHER POSSUMS, BEGAN TO FEEL HE NEVER COULD
LEARN, AND THOSE AROUND HIM THOUGHT SO TOO.
GERALDINE, HIS INGENIOUS SISTER, FOUND THAT SAP
HELPED HIS TAIL STAY ON THE BRANCH, AND ALL WENT
WELL UNTIL THE SAP DRIED UP. SHE ALSO IS
INSTRUMENTAL IN PROVING TO HIM THAT HE REALLY
DOESN'T NEED THE SAP TO HANG UPSIDE DOWN.
(BROTHERS & SISTERS, FAM--BROTHERS & SISTERS,
SELF-CONFIDENCE)

ELLENTUCK, SHAN. MY BROTHER BERNARD. ABELARD,
1968. ILLUSTRATED BY SHAN ELLENTUCK. (CCB-B)

TOLD BY A NAMELESS LITTLE SISTER, THIS IS A
PORTRAIT OF A KOOKY BROTHER WHO WANTS EVERYONE TO
THINK HE IS A PRINCE. IN ONE SENSE, HE BULLIES
HIS SISTER, AND THREATENS TO HIT HER IF SHE
DOESN'T PLAY AT THE GAME OF MAKE-BELIEVE. SHE,
HOWEVER, SECRETLY ADMIRES HIM AND HIS IMAGINARY
KINGDOM, AND IN THE END IS FLATTERED BY BEING
MADE A PRINCESS. THIS BOOK IS NOT A TRACT FOR
PERSONS LOOKING FOR BOOKS WITH STRONG IMAGES OF
WOMEN. (BROTHERS & SISTERS, FAM--BROTHERS &
SISTERS, FAM--SIBLING RIVALRY, SIBLING RIVALRY)

HEIDE, FLORENCE. SOUND OF SUNSHINE, SOUND OF
RAIN. PARENTS' MAG, 1970. ILLUSTRATED BY KENNETH
LONGTEMPS.

THE BLIND CHILD WHO TELLS THIS STORY AND HIS

SISTER ARE NAMELESS, AND ONLY ABRAM, THE FRIENDLY
ICE CREAM MAN IN THE PARK, HAS A NAME.
NEVERTHELESS THE STORY IS ONE OF A DEVELOPING
SELF-AWARENESS IN A LITTLE BOY. HIS IS A WORLD OF
A TACTILE ENVIRONMENT, PERCEIVED AS BEING SMOOTH
OR ROUGH, AND OF SOUNDS, SOFT AND LOUD, AND OF
COLORS IMAGINED. IN THE TELLING, MANY THINGS ARE
LEARNED ABOUT THE WORLD OF THE BLIND, AND A CHILD
HEARING THIS STORY WILL HAVE AN UNDERSTANDING OF
THE GROWING INDEPENDENCE IN THIS SMALL DEPENDENT
CHILD. (BROTHERS & SISTERS, DIFF SIT--HANDICAPS,
FAM--BROTHERS & SISTERS, HANDICAPS,
SELF-IDENTITY, SELF-UNDERSTANDING)

HILL, ELIZABETH. EVAN'S CORNER. HOLT, 1967.
ILLUSTRATED BY NANCY GROSSMAN. (BCB)

   EVAN, WHO WANTED A CORNER OF HIS OWN IN THE
TWO-ROOM APARTMENT HE SHARED WITH FIVE OTHER
CHILDREN AND HIS PARENTS, WAS SATISFIED TO FIND A
CORNER BY THE WINDOW WHICH HE FIXED UP WITH A
PICTURE HE PAINTED, AND A TURTLE. WHEN HE STILL
FELT UNHAPPY HIS MOTHER SUGGESTED HE HELP HIS
YOUNGER BROTHER ADAM, AND IMMEDIATELY HE FELT
BETTER AT THE THOUGHT OF HELPING ADAM FIX UP HIS
OWN CORNER. (BEHAVIOR--SHARING, BROTHERS &
SISTERS, FAM--BROTHERS & SISTERS,
SELF-UNDERSTANDING, SHARING)

HUTCHINS, PAT. TITCH. MACMILLAN, 1971.
ILLUSTRATED BY PAT HUTCHINS. (ESLC)

   TITCH WAS TOO LITTLE, A PREDICAMENT COMMON TO
MANY PRESCHOOLERS. IN THIS LOVELY PICTURE BOOK
WITH LARGE COLORFUL PICTURES AND A SMALL AMOUNT
OF TEXT, PAT HUTCHINS HAS OUTLINED ALL OF THE
INEQUITIES--THE OLDER SIBLINGS HAVE BIGGER BIKES
AND TOYS. BUT JUSTICE PREVAILS IN THE END, FOR IT
IS TITCH WHO HAS THE TINY SEED, WHICH GROWS INTO
AN ENORMOUS PLANT, LARGER THAN ANYTHING HIS BIG
BROTHER PETE AND SISTER MARY OWN. (BROTHERS &
SISTERS, FAM--BROTHERS & SISTERS,
SELF-CONSCIOUSNESS--SIZE)

IWASAKI, CHIHIRO. NEW BABY IS COMING TO MY
HOUSE. MC GRAW, 1970. ILLUSTRATED BY CHIHIRO
IWASAKI. (LJ)

   EXQUISITE WATERCOLORS EMPHASIZE THE HAPPINESS
THAT SISTER FEELS BECAUSE HER NEW BROTHER JOHN IS

COMING HOME FROM THE HOSPITAL TODAY. SIMPLE TEXT
MAKES THE BOOK VERY USEFUL FOR A PRESCHOOL
CHILD'S PREPARATION FOR A NEW BABY IN THE
HOUSEHOLD. (BROTHERS & SISTERS, FAM--BROTHERS &
SISTERS, NEW SIT--BABY)

JORDAN, JUNE. NEW LIFE, NEW ROOM. CROWELL, T.,
1975. ILLUSTRATED BY RAY CRUZ. (BL)

   AN EXTENDED FORMAT TAKES THIS BOOK OUT OF THE
TRUE PICTURE-BOOK CATEGORY, AND THIRD GRADERS
WILL ENJOY READING IT ALONE, BUT THE
ILLUSTRATIONS AND STORY MAKE IT ENJOYABLE FOR
YOUNGER CHILDREN ALSO. A VERY REAL PROBLEM IS
DEALT WITH HERE--THAT OF REARRANGING A FAMILY'S
SLEEPING QUARTERS TO ACCOMMODATE A NEW BABY. A
PICTURE OF A WARM, FRIENDLY FAMILY DEALING
REALISTICALLY WITH AN EVERYDAY PROBLEM PROVIDES A
REASSURING, POSITIVE APPROACH. (BROTHERS &
SISTERS, FAM--BROTHERS & SISTERS, NEW SIT--BABY)

LEE, VIRGINIA. MAGIC MOTH. SEABURY, 1972.
ILLUSTRATED BY RICHARD CUFFARI. (BCB)

   ANOTHER BOOK WHICH FALLS OUT OF THE STRICT
CATEGORY OF A PICTURE BOOK, THIS TITLE IS
INCLUDED BECAUSE IT IS UNIQUE: IT TELLS THE
LOVING STORY OF THE DEATH OF A YOUNG CHILD AT
HOME. THE MAGIC MOTH ENTERS THE STORY JUST WHEN
MARYANNE STOPS BREATHING: "A HUGE WHITE MOTH ROSE
GENTLY FROM SOMEWHERE NEAR THE BED AND FLEW UP
TO THE CEILING." THIS ANALOGOUS DESCRIPTION ACTS
AS A BRIDGE BETWEEN THE COLD FACT OF DEATH, AND
THE WARM SPIRIT OF THE LITTLE GIRL AND HER
RELATIONSHIP WITHIN THE FAMILY. ALMOST EVERYONE
IS CURIOUS ABOUT CERTAIN ASPECTS OF DEATH, AND
THE AUTHOR HAS PROVIDED REALISTIC DIALOG AND
FEELINGS WHEN SHE DESCRIBES THE THOUGHTS OF A
YOUNGER BROTHER: "MARK-O, WHO WAS FULL OF
QUESTIONS, COULD NOT THINK JUST EXACTLY WHAT IT
WAS HE REALLY WANTED TO KNOW, SO HE TOO WAS
QUIET." THUS VIRGINIA LEE HAS WRITTEN A
COMPLETELY PLAUSIBLE STORY, BUT ONE TO WHICH
SECOND AND THIRD GRADERS CAN REALLY RESONATE.
(BROTHERS & SISTERS, DEATH, DIFF SIT--DEATH,
FAM--BROTHERS & SISTERS)

NESS, EVALINE. DO YOU HAVE THE TIME, LYDIA?.
DUTTON, 1971. ILLUSTRATED BY EVALINE NESS. (CC,
ESLC)

LYDIA IS A LITTLE GIRL WHO NEVER "HAS TIME" TO
FINISH ALL OF THE MANY THINGS IN WHICH SHE'S
INTERESTED. WHEN SHE NEGLECTS TO FINISH A RACING
CAR FOR HER YOUNGER BROTHER, HE IS DISAPPOINTED,
AND SHE BEGINS TO MAKE AMENDS. THE LESSON IS "IF
YOU TAKE TIME, YOU'LL HAVE TIME."
(BEHAVIOR--CONSIDERATION, BROTHERS & SISTERS,
CONSIDERATION, FAM--BROTHERS & SISTERS,
SELF-EVALUATION)

SCOTT, ANN. SAM. MC GRAW, 1967.   ILLUSTRATED BY
SYMEON SHIMIN.   (BCB)

THE ILLUSTRATIONS ARE PARAMOUNT IN THIS STORY
OF A LEFT-OUT BROTHER WHO IS REJECTED FIRST BY
MOTHER, BIG BROTHER GEORGE, SISTER MARCIA, AND
THEN HIS FATHER, WHO FORBIDS HIM TO TOUCH HIS
TYPEWRITER. THE BLACK, SEPIA, AND GOLDEN BROWN
WATERCOLORS INTENSIFY THE FEELINGS OF SADNESS IN
SAM'S HEART. SUDDENLY THE WHOLE FAMILY REALIZES
THAT HE NEEDS ATTENTION: HIS MOTHER HOLDS HIM AND
ROCKS HIM, AND AS EVERYONE RALLIES AROUND TO
KEEP HIM COMPANY, SAM HELPS BAKE A RASPBERRY
TART. (BROTHERS & SISTERS, EMOTIONS--REJECTION,
FAM--BROTHERS & SISTERS, REJECTION)

WELLS, ROSEMARY. NOISY NORA. DIAL, 1973.
ILLUSTRATED BY ROSEMARY WELLS.   (CC, ESLC)

POOR NORA--SHE'S THE LEFT-OUT SISTER, AND
THREATENS TO RUN AWAY TO MAKE HER FAMILY FEEL
SORRY FOR HER AND GIVE HER SOME ATTENTION. WHEN
SHE SHOWS UP IN THE BROOM CLOSET, ALL IS WELL. A
CLEVER, FUNNY BOOK ABOUT A BUMPTIOUS LITTLE
MOUSE-GIRL WHICH WILL DELIGHT YOUNG CHILDREN AS
THEY CATALOG HER MISDEMEANORS. MANY CHILDREN MAY
SEE THEMSELVES. (BROTHERS & SISTERS,
EMOTIONS--JEALOUSY, FAM--BROTHERS & SISTERS,
FAM--SIBLING RIVALRY, JEALOUSY, SIBLING RIVALRY)

ZOLOTOW, CHARLOTTE. DO YOU KNOW WHAT I'LL DO?.
HARPER, 1958.   ILLUSTRATED BY GARTH WILLIAMS.
(CC)

A LOVING PICTURE OF A GIRL ABOUT SEVEN YEARS
OLD, DREAMING ABOUT ALL OF THE WAYS SHE WILL BE
GOOD TO HER BABY BROTHER. GARTH WILLIAMS HAS
DRAWN LARGE FULL-PAGE ILLUSTRATIONS FILLED IN
WITH A DELICATE WATERCOLOR WASH TO ACCENTUATE THE
DREAMY QUALITY OF THE LITTLE GIRL'S THOUGHTS.

SHE PROMISES CONCRETE THINGS, SUCH AS BRINGING
HOME A PIECE OF BIRTHDAY CAKE, AND SHE PROMISES
THINGS THAT ARE IN THE AFFECTIVE DOMAIN: SHE
TELLS HIM THAT SHE'LL GET RID OF HIS NIGHTMARES
FOR HIM. IN DOING THIS, OF COURSE, SHE
DEMONSTRATES THE THINGS THAT ARE IMPORTANT AND
PROMINENT IN CHILDREN'S LIVES, THEIR EXPECTATIONS
AND FEARS. (BROTHERS & SISTERS, EMOTIONS--LOVE,
FAM--BROTHERS & SISTERS, LOVE)

FAM--FATHERS

FLORA, JAMES. FISHING WITH DAD. HARCOURT, 1967.
ILLUSTRATED BY JAMES FLORA. (ESLC)

EXPLORES THE CONCEPT OF A LITTLE BOY GROWING
OLD ENOUGH TO PARTICIPATE IN AN ADULT'S WORLD,
AND IS A REALISTIC LOOK AT LIFE ON A DEEP-SEA
FISHING BOAT. THE FISHING NET PICKS UP A TORPEDO
WHICH MUST BE DISPOSED OF BY THE COAST GUARD, AND
THIS, PLUS THE DANGER OF FOG AND COLLISION WITH
LARGE SHIPS, GIVES AN UNUSUAL SENSE OF ADVENTURE.
A LONGER STORY THAN MANY, THE READING LEVEL
FALLS AT THE HIGH RANGE OF THIRD GRADE, BUT THE
BOOK WILL APPEAL TO A MUCH YOUNGER AUDIENCE.
(FAM--FATHERS, FATHERS, SELF-IDENTITY)

HOBAN, RUSSELL. BEDTIME FOR FRANCES. HARPER,
1960. ILLUSTRATED BY GARTH WILLIAMS. (CC)

FATHER BADGER PLAYS AN IMPORTANT ROLE IN
HANDLING THE BEDTIME PROBLEMS OF HIS DAUGHTER
FRANCES WITH AN IMAGINATIVE EXPLANATION OF HER
FEARS. WHEN FRANCES, AN ENTRANCING LITTLE GIRL
WHO ONLY INCIDENTALLY HAPPENS TO BE A BADGER,
GOES THROUGH THE FAMILIAR BEDTIME ROUTINE OF
MILK, HUGS, KISSES, AND TEDDY BEAR, BUT STILL
DOES NOT FALL ASLEEP, FATHER GIVES REASSURING
ADVICE ABOUT THE IMAGINARY GIANTS AND THE
SOMETHING SCARY THAT MIGHT COME OUT OF THE CRACK
IN THE CEILING. HIS MOST CREATIVE SOLUTION,
HOWEVER, COMES WHEN FRANCES COMPLAINS OF THE
CURTAINS MOVING AT THE WINDOW--HE TELLS HER THAT
THE WIND'S JOB IS TO GO AROUND AND BLOW ALL THE
CURTAINS, THAT EVERYBODY HAS A JOB, AND THAT
FURTHERMORE, HER JOB IS TO GO TO SLEEP.
THROUGHOUT THE BOOK, FATHER IS THE PARENT WHO
RELATES TO THE CHILD, ALTHOUGH THE MOTHER IS
VISIBLE. (BEHAVIOR--DISLIKES--SLEEP,
DISLIKES--SLEEP, EMOTIONS--FEAR, FAM--FATHERS,

FATHERS, FEAR)

KINDRED, WENDY. LUCKY WILMA. DIAL, 1973.
ILLUSTRATED BY WENDY KINDRED. (LJ)

   BEGINNING WITH A SERIES OF SATURDAYS WILMA AND
"CHARLIE," HER DAD, WALK TO MUSEUMS AND ZOOS,
AND FATHER AND DAUGHTER HAVE A UNIFORMLY GLUM
EXPRESSION. THE NEXT EIGHTEEN PAGES DEAL WITH
JOYOUS PICTURIZATION OF CLIMBING, JUMPING,
PIGGYBACKING, DANCING, AND REVELRY WITH THE
PIGEONS IN THE PARK. OBVIOUSLY THIS WAS THE
NEATEST SATURDAY THEY HAD SPENT TOGETHER, AND
THEY HUG AS THEY SEPARATE AND DAD SAYS: "WE'VE
GOT ALL THE SATURDAYS IN THE WORLD." CURIOUSLY
ENOUGH THE WORD DIVORCE IS NOT MENTIONED. WITH
VERY LITTLE TEXT, THIS BOOK CONVEYS THAT INDEED
WILMA IS LUCKY TO HAVE A WONDERFUL RELATIONSHIP
WITH HER FATHER. (DIFF SIT--DIVORCE, DIFF
SIT--ONE PARENT, DIVORCE, FAM--FATHERS, FATHERS,
ONE PARENT)

LEXAU, JOAN. ME DAY. DIAL, 1971. ILLUSTRATED BY
ROBERT WEAVER. (BCB)

   "ME DAY" IS RAFER'S BIRTHDAY, BUT IN A SLUM
FAMILY WHERE THERE IS NO MONEY FOR PRESENTS AND
THE TV IS BROKEN, WHAT MAKES A BOY HAPPY? THROUGH
THE TEXT WE LEARN THAT THE FATHER IS NOT AT
HOME, THE PARENTS BEING DIVORCED, APPARENTLY
BECAUSE THE FATHER COULD NOT FIND WORK. RAFER'S
DAY IS MADE PERFECT WHEN HIS FATHER SHOWS UP TO
SPEND THE ENTIRE DAY WITH HIM IN THE PARK, WITH
ICE CREAM AND HOT DOGS. (DIFF SIT--DIVORCE,
DIVORCE, FAM--FATHERS, FAM--ONE PARENT, FATHERS,
ONE PARENT, SELF-IDENTITY)

PEARSON, SUSAN. MONNIE HATES LYDIA. DIAL, 1975.
ILLUSTRATED BY DIANE PATERSON. (BL)

   INTERESTING BECAUSE A FATHER HEADS THIS
ONE-PARENT FAMILY CONSISTING OF MONNIE AND HER
THOROUGHLY OBNOXIOUS SISTER LYDIA. DADDY IS AN
IMPARTIAL ARBITER IN THE FAMILY SQUABBLE WHICH
ERUPTS ON LYDIA'S BIRTHDAY, SUPPORTIVE OF
MONNIE'S HURT FEELINGS, BUT NOT WILLING TO PUNISH
LYDIA. HE IS AN ATTRACTIVE, BEARDED CONTEMPORARY
FATHER WHO CAN BE ADMIRED FOR HIS COOL WHEN
MONNIE DUMPS THE BIRTHDAY CAKE IN LYDIA'S FACE.
ONE FEELS HE SHOULD BE CHEERING, BUT INSTEAD HE

HANDS LYDIA A TOWEL AND KISSES HER ON THE CHEEK.
USEFUL AS A PORTRAIT OF A NEW LIFE-STYLE FAMILY
COPING WITH OLD LIFE-STYLE PROBLEMS. (ANGER, DIFF
SIT--ONE PARENT, EMOTIONS--ANGER, FAM--FATHERS,
FAM--ONE PARENT, FAM--SIBLING RIVALRY, FATHERS,
ONE PARENT, SIBLING RIVALRY)

RADLAUER, RUTH. FATHER IS BIG. BOWMAR, 1967.
ILLUSTRATED BY HARVEY MANDLIN. (ESLC)

   SIMPLE TEXT, AND LARGE, FULL-PAGE COLOR
PHOTOGRAPHS TAKE THE READER THROUGH SIX
SITUATIONS DESCRIBING THE BIGNESS OF THE BOY'S
DAD. THE NEXT SIX ELEMENTS DEAL WITH FATHER/SON
COOPERATIVE RELATIONSHIPS, USING THE LAWN MOWER,
BIKE, AND JUNGLE GYM, ENDING WITH THE INTERESTING
STATEMENT THAT "FATHER CAN EVEN MAKE ME BIGGER
THAN HE IS." THE PICTURE OPPOSITE SHOWS THE BOY
ON HIS FATHER'S SHOULDERS. THE FAMILY SHOWN IS
DARK SKINNED. (FAM--FATHERS, FATHERS)

RAYNOR, DORKA. THIS IS MY FATHER AND ME.
WHITMAN, A., 1973. ILLUSTRATED BY DORKA RAYNOR.
(BL)

   STRIKING BLACK AND WHITE PHOTOGRAPHS FROM ALL
OVER THE WORLD SHOW VARYING RELATIONSHIPS OF
FATHERS TO THEIR CHILDREN. WHILE NOT A BOOK WHICH
WILL BE READILY PICKED UP BY CHILDREN, IT
REVEALS THE ROLE OF LOVE, COOPERATION,
PROTECTION, CARE, DEVOTION, WORK, PLAY, AND PRIDE
WHICH CAN EXIST BETWEEN PARENT AND CHILD IN A
UNIVERSAL WAY. (EMOTIONS--LOVE, FAM--FATHERS,
FATHERS, LOVE)

SONNEBORN, RUTH. FRIDAY NIGHT IS PAPA NIGHT.
VIKING, 1970. ILLUSTRATED BY EMILY MC CULLY.
(BCB, CC)

   A SYMPATHETIC PICTURE OF PUERTO RICAN LIFE IN
A CROWDED APARTMENT, WHERE PEDRO'S BED IS IN THE
KITCHEN, AND FATHER WORKS TWO JOBS TO PROVIDE FOR
HIS FAMILY. BROWN TONES COMPLEMENT THE WARMTH
AND SKIN COLOR OF THE CHARACTERS, AND LEND A
HARMONIOUS TONE TO THE THEME, WHICH IS THE
SPECIAL FEELING IN PEDRO'S MIND WHEN HIS FATHER
COMES HOME ON FRIDAY NIGHT. (EMOTIONS--LOVE,
FAM--FATHERS, FATHERS, LOVE)

STEWART, ROBERT. DADDY BOOK. AMERICAN, 1972.

ILLUSTRATED BY DON MADDEN.   (CCB-B, LJ)

ACCORDING TO THE AUTHOR, HE WROTE THIS BOOK
BECAUSE THERE WEREN'T VERY MANY DADDIES IN THE
CHILDREN'S BOOKS HE READ, AND HE HAS PROCEEDED TO
PRESENT AN ARRAY OF TALL, FAT, YELLOW, SHORT
DADDIES WHO HAVE ALL KINDS OF HOBBIES, DO ALL
KINDS OF JOBS, BUT WHO, MOST OF ALL, SHARE MANY,
MANY ACTIVITIES WITH THEIR CHILDREN, INCLUDING
SOME OF THE TASKS THAT MOMMIES DO. A THOROUGHLY
CONTEMPORARY, HELPFUL BOOK WHICH GIVES AN
EXCELLENT VIEW OF THE MANY-FACETED ROLES OF
FATHERS. (FAM--FATHERS, FATHERS)

ZOLOTOW, CHARLOTTE. A FATHER LIKE THAT. HARPER,
1971.   ILLUSTRATED BY BEN SHECTER.   (BCB)

HOME WITHOUT A FATHER IS PICTURED AS A LITTLE
BOY PAINTS AN IMAGINARY PORTRAIT OF THE PERFECT
DAD. WE SEE A MOTHER WHO MAKES THE CHILD GO TO
BED AT BEDTIME, WHO READS WHEN THE BOY WOULD LIKE
TO PLAY CHECKERS. SHE IS A MOTHER WHO CAN'T
UNDERSTAND BECAUSE SHE NEVER WAS A BOY, AND WHO
SAYS THE BASEBALL GAME ON TV IS TOO LOUD. IT IS
THE MOTHER WHO, NERVOUSLY SEWING FASTER AND
FASTER BECAUSE OF THE GLOWING PICTURE HE
DESCRIBES OF THE MYTHICAL FATHER, SAYS THE
REALISTIC WORDS OF WISDOM: "IF HE NEVER COMES, "
TRYING TO MAKE THE CHILD UNDERSTAND THAT THIS
PARAGON IS PERHAPS EXAGGERATED. IN THE END,
MOTHER SAYS THAT HE CAN TRY TO BE THAT KIND OF
FATHER WHEN HE GROWS UP. USEFUL BECAUSE OF THE
EXEMPLAR ROLE OF THE FATHER. SOME CHILDREN MAY
NEED TO BE SHOWN WHAT THE ABSENCE OF THE FATHER
IN THE FAMILY MEANS. (DIFF SIT--ONE PARENT,
FAM--FATHERS, FAM--MOTHERS, FATHERS, MOTHERS, ONE
PARENT)

FAM--GRANDFATHERS

BORACK, BARBARA. GRANDPA. HARPER, 1967.
ILLUSTRATED BY BEN SHECTER.   (BCB, BL)

THIS GRANDPA SEEMS ALMOST TOO GOOD TO BE TRUE.
WE'RE NOT SURE OF THE VINTAGE, BECAUSE HE
LISTENS TO THE RADIO AND RUNS A TINY STORE, BUT
WHATEVER THE VINTAGE, IT IS A LOVING PICTURE OF
THE RELATIONSHIP BETWEEN GRANDDAUGHTER, ABOUT AGE
FOUR, AND GRANDDAD, WHO IS A YOUNG OLDSTER. HE
ALWAYS HAS TIME TO PLAY HIDE-AND-SEEK, TO MAKE A

NOISE LIKE A CHICKEN, AND TO GIVE HER SYMPATHY
WHEN SHE NEEDS IT. USEFUL BECAUSE IT DEFINES THE
ROLE OF GRANDPARENTS, I.E., THEY DO PERFORM
FUNCTIONS THAT ARE DIFFERENT FROM PARENTS.
(FAM--GRANDFATHERS, GRANDFATHERS)

BUCKLEY, HELEN. GRANDFATHER AND I. LOTHROP,
1959. ILLUSTRATED BY PAUL GALDONE. (CC)

   HELEN BUCKLEY WROTE FAMILY STORIES ABOUT
GRANDPARENTS IN THE 1950'S AND THEY ARE AS VALID
NOW AS IN 1959. IN LARGE TYPE, AND LARGE COLORFUL
ILLUSTRATIONS, THE STORY IS TOLD OF THE JOYS OF
NOT HURRYING, OF A BOY AND HIS GRANDFATHER WHO
TAKE WALKS AND TAKE TIME TO LOOK FOR THINGS SUCH
AS BIRDS AND SQUIRRELS AND EVEN SNAILS.
CONTRASTING ARE EXAMPLES OF THE HUSTLE AND BUSTLE
OF HURRYING MOTHERS, DADS, TRAFFIC, AND OLDER
CHILDREN. "EVERYONE ELSE IS ALWAYS IN A HURRY BUT
WHEN A BOY AND HIS GRANDFATHER GO WALKING THEY
HAVE TIME TO STOP AND LOOK." (FAM--GRANDFATHERS,
FAM--OLD AGE, GRANDFATHERS, OLD AGE)

FLORA, JAMES. GRANDPA'S FARM. HARCOURT, 1965.
ILLUSTRATED BY JAMES FLORA. (CC)

   ALTHOUGH THIS IS A TALE ABOUT A GRANDPA WHO
TELLS STORIES, IT IS MORE A BOOK OF TALL TALES
THAN A BOOK ABOUT GRANDFATHER. THE SETTING IS
GRANDPA'S FARM, HOWEVER, AND THE READER LEARNS
STORIES OF HOW HE GOT HIS BLUE BARN, THE COW
SALVE THAT MADE EVERYTHING GROW, THE TERRIBLE
WINTER WHEN EVEN WORDS FROZE AND HAD TO BE THAWED
OUT IN THE FRYING PAN, AND LITTLE HATCHY HEN,
WHO HATCHED OUT WRISTWATCHES FROM ALARM CLOCKS.
ITS VALUE LIES IN THE CASTING OF GRANDPA IN THE
ROLE OF STORYTELLER, AND HIS RELATIONSHIP WITH
THE YOUNG CHILD LISTENING ON HIS LAP.
(FAM--GRANDFATHERS, GRANDFATHERS)

GAUCH, PATRICIA. GRANDPA AND ME. COWARD, 1972.
ILLUSTRATED BY SYMEON SHIMIN. (CC)

   THE ILLUSTRATIONS ARE PARAMOUNT IN THIS STORY
OF A BOY, PERHAPS TEN OR ELEVEN, AND THE
COMPANIONSHIP HE AND HIS GRANDFATHER SHARE, AS
THE DELICATE WATERCOLORS WASH ACROSS THE PAGES IN
PASTELS OF SAND, SUN, AND WATER. SYMEON SHIMIN'S
ARTISTRY DOMINATES THE BOOK, YET IN A SUPPORTIVE
WAY, AND THE READER COMES AWAY FROM THE BOOK

WITH A FEELING OF CONTENTMENT, PEACE, AND
THOUGHTFUL REFLECTIONS ON THE VALUES OF GETTING
BACK TO NATURE AND BEING ALONE, AWAY FROM PEOPLE.
(EMOTIONS--SERENITY, FAM--GRANDFATHERS,
GRANDFATHERS, SERENITY)

HORVATH, BETTY. JASPER MAKES MUSIC. WATTS, 1967.
   ILLUSTRATED BY FERMIN ROCKER. (CCB-B)

   JASPER WAS WILLING TO SHOVEL SNOW ALL WINTER
IN ORDER TO MAKE ENOUGH MONEY TO BUY A GUITAR.
BUT IT WAS GRANDPA WHO TOLD HIM ABOUT THE MAGIC
SHOVEL, AND THAT PART OF THE MAGIC DEPENDED UPON
THE PERSON WHO OWNED IT. CHILDREN WILL APPRECIATE
JASPER'S EFFORT TO LINE UP CUSTOMERS, AND HIS
DETERMINATION TO SAVE HIS MONEY IN A BAKING
POWDER CAN. (FAM--GRANDFATHERS, GRANDFATHERS,
SELF-RELIANCE)

LUNDGREN, MAX. MATT'S GRANDFATHER. PUTNAM, 1972.
   ILLUSTRATED BY FIBBEN HALD. (CC)

   WRITTEN IN SWEDEN, THIS REFRESHINGLY HONEST
BOOK ABOUT AN OLD MAN IN AN OLD FOLKS' HOME
PRESENTS A POINT OF VIEW VERY DIFFERENT FROM
OTHER BOOKS ON THIS SUBJECT. WE SEE LIFE FROM THE
POINT OF VIEW OF THE GRANDFATHER: HE THINKS HE
LOOKS YOUNGER THAN HIS SON, AND HE THINKS THE SON
TALKS AS IF HE WERE THE FATHER. HE MAKES A GREAT
DEAL OF SENSE, AND IS FOXY ENOUGH TO MASQUERADE
IN A LINEN JACKET, SUNGLASSES, AND A BIG FLOPPY
STRAW HAT IN ORDER TO ESCAPE INTO THE OUTSIDE
WORLD FOR A FEW HOURS. THE BOOK DOES INCLUDE SOME
OF THE FOIBLES OF OLDER PEOPLE, SUCH AS
FORGETFULNESS AND SECRETIVENESS (HE HIDES HIS
SNUFF IN THE FLOWER POT), BUT TO THE LITTLE BOY
WHO IS VISITING, THESE MILD ABERRATIONS ARE TAKEN
IN STRIDE. LOVELY PASTEL ILLUSTRATIONS ACCENTING
HORIZONTAL LINES CONTRIBUTE TO A SENSE OF
PEACEFULNESS. A SENSE OF WELL-BEING PERMEATES THE
BOOK, AND THE READER HAS A FEELING OF PLEASURE
IN KNOWING THAT THE OLD GENTLEMAN IS BEING CARED
FOR IN A BUILDING AS BIG AS A CASTLE WITH TOWERS
AND SPIRES. PARTICULARLY USEFUL TO GIVE A CHILD A
POSITIVE, ALBEIT MINORITY REPORT ON OLDER
CITIZENS, MANY OF WHOM REMAIN CHIPPER AND IN
CHARGE OF THEIR SENSES. (DIFF SIT--OLD AGE,
FAM--GRANDFATHERS, GRANDFATHERS, OLD AGE)

STEIN, SARA. ABOUT DYING. WALKER, 1974.

ILLUSTRATED BY DICK FRANK.   (BL)

DRAWING THE ANALOGY BETWEEN THE DEATH OF A PET
PIGEON AND THE DEATH OF GRANDFATHER, THIS SIMPLY
WRITTEN BOOK PRESENTS DEATH IN A REALISTIC WAY,
YET IN A WAY THE YOUNG CHILD CAN UNDERSTAND,
SHOWING THAT THE BODY OF SNOW, THE PIGEON, WAS
COLD AND STIFF. BURIAL RITES FOR BOTH THE PET AND
GRANDFATHER ARE COMPARED. THE REACTION TO THE
DEATH OF THE GRANDFATHER IS EMPHASIZED, HOWEVER:
MOTHER CRIES AND JANE, A SIX-YEAR-OLD, IS ANGRY,
TEARS THINGS UP, AND CRIES. THE AUTHOR STATES
THAT ONE OF EVERY 20 CHILDREN WILL FACE THE DEATH
OF A PARENT DURING CHILDHOOD. THE BOOK GIVES
INSIGHT INTO WHAT CHILDREN MAY BE THINKING AND
FEELING, AND THROUGHOUT STRESSES HONESTY AND
COMPASSION. (DEATH, DEATH--PET, DIFF SIT--DEATH,
DIFF SIT--DEATH--PET, FAM--GRANDFATHERS,
GRANDFATHERS)

ZOLOTOW, CHARLOTTE. MY GRANDSON LEW. HARPER,
1974.   ILLUSTRATED BY WILLIAM DU BOIS.   (CC)

A SMALL BOY WAKES UP IN THE NIGHT, AND TELLS
HIS MOTHER HE MISSES HIS GRANDFATHER. THEY CHAT,
AND THE LITTLE BOY RECALLS HOW HE WENT TO THE
MUSEUM WHEN HIS GRANDFATHER BABY-SAT HIM. THE
LITTLE BOY'S MOTHER IS TOUCHED BY THE MEMORIES,
AND SHE TOO REMEMBERS, GRATEFULLY, THE TIMES WHEN
GRANDPA WOULD COME TO VISIT. (DEATH, DIFF
SIT--DEATH, FAM--GRANDFATHERS, GRANDFATHERS)

FAM--GRANDMOTHERS

ALEXANDER, MARTHA. THE STORY GRANDMOTHER TOLD.
DIAL, 1969.   ILLUSTRATED BY MARTHA ALEXANDER.
(BCB)

A PRESCHOOL GIRL NAMED LISA BEGS "GRAMMA" FOR
A STORY AS SHE AND HER GRANDMOTHER FIX SUPPER IN
THE COZY KITCHEN WITH AN OLD-FASHIONED STOVE.
THEN FOR THE REST OF THE BOOK, LISA PROCEEDS TO
TELL THE STORY HERSELF, ABOUT HER CAT IVAN AND
THE BALLOON THEY BOUGHT. TOUCHES OF HUMOR IN THE
ILLUSTRATIONS MAKE THIS A BOOK THAT YOUNG
CHILDREN WILL ENJOY. (FAM--GRANDMOTHERS,
GRANDMOTHERS)

BALDWIN, ANNE. SUNFLOWERS FOR TINA. FOUR, 1970.
ILLUSTRATED BY ANN GRIFALCONI.   (CCB-B)

IN SUNFLOWER COLORS, THE ILLUSTRATOR HAS SHOWN
A CORNER OF A DIRTY CITY NEIGHBORHOOD WHERE THE
LAUNDRY HANGS BETWEEN THE BUILDINGS, WHERE TINA
TRIES TO GROW A GARDEN BY PLANTING CARROTS SHE
FINDS IN THE REFRIGERATOR. WHEN SHE DISCOVERS
SUNFLOWERS GROWING A FEW BLOCKS FROM HOME, SHE
DELIGHTS IN THEIR FRESHNESS AND THINKS OF HER
AGING GRANDMOTHER AT HOME IN HER DARK CORNER.
LATER SHE DANCES IN HER YELLOW DRESS, AND EVOKES
LAUGHTER FROM THE OLD WOMAN. A STORY OF CONTRASTS
BETWEEN OLD AND YOUNG, BEAUTY AND RUBBLE, THIS
IS A POSITIVE STATEMENT FOR THE NECESSITY OF
AESTHETIC PLEASURE IN LIFE. (FAM--GRANDMOTHERS,
FAM--OLD AGE, GRANDMOTHERS, OLD AGE)

BARTOLI, JENNIFER. NONNA. HARVEY, 1975.
ILLUSTRATED BY JOAN DRESCHER. (BL)

AN INTERESTING, NON-THREATENING BOOK ABOUT THE
DEATH OF GRANDMOTHER TREATED FROM THE POINT OF
VIEW OF MEMORIES OF LIFE BEFORE HER DEATH AND
LIFE SEVERAL MONTHS LATER. NONNA'S COOKIES ARE
ONE MOTIF THAT REPEATS THROUGHOUT THE BOOK. IN
MEMORY, THE CHILDREN THINK ABOUT SOUP AND COOKIES
WITH NONNA ON SATURDAYS. ON THE DAY OF THE
FUNERAL, MOTHER BAKES NONNA'S COOKIES AND THE
CHILDREN EAT THEM FOR BREAKFAST, AND SIX MONTHS
LATER AT CHRISTMAS TIME, THE YOUNGEST DAUGHTER
BAKES THEM FOR THE ENTIRE FAMILY. USEFUL BECAUSE
ALTHOUGH IT SHOWS THE FUNERAL AND THE GRAVESIDE
SERVICE, IT ALSO USES A DEVICE TO SHOW HOW THE
LIVING COPE BY PERFORMING DAILY ROUTINES OF LIFE.
(DEATH, DIFF SIT--DEATH, FAM--GRANDMOTHERS,
GRANDMOTHERS)

BLUE, ROSE. GRANDMA DIDN'T WAVE BACK. WATTS,
1972. ILLUSTRATED BY TED LEWIN. (CC)

DEBBIE, TEN YEARS OLD, REALIZES THAT HER
BELOVED GRANDMOTHER IS CHANGING. SHE NO LONGER
WAVES AT DEBBIE FROM THE WINDOW, NOR DOES SHE
HAVE COOKIES FROM THE OVEN READY FOR HER. GRANDMA
EXHIBITS LOSS OF MEMORY, CONFUSION OVER NAMES,
AND OTHER EVIDENCE OF SENILITY, SUCH AS STAYING
IN HER NIGHT DRESS ALL DAY. AS THE GRANDMOTHER
DECLINES, DEBBIE MATURES, AND IS UPSET BY THE
RELATIVES' DECISION TO ENTER THE GRANDMOTHER IN A
NURSING HOME. THE BOOK ENDS ON A POSITIVE NOTE,
HOWEVER, AS THE OLDER WOMAN SPEAKS ENCOURAGINGLY
OF THE COMING OF SPRING. A USEFUL BOOK BECAUSE IT

DEALS WITH A PROBLEM FACING MANY FAMILIES TODAY.
APPROPRIATE FOR THIRD GRADERS TO READ
INDEPENDENTLY. (DIFF SIT--OLD AGE,
FAM--GRANDMOTHERS, GRANDMOTHERS, OLD AGE,
SELF-UNDERSTANDING)

BUCKLEY, HELEN. GRANDMOTHER AND I. LOTHROP,
1961.   ILLUSTRATED BY PAUL GALDONE.   (CC)

   LARGE PRINT AND SHORT, RHYTHMIC SENTENCES
WHICH ECHO THE ROCKING CHAIR CHARACTERIZE THIS
BOOK OF OVERSIZE PICTURES. THE ILLUSTRATIONS,
WHICH ARE BRIGHT AND HOMEY IN THE FIRELIGHT, SET
THE SCENE FOR PEACE AND COMFORT AT THE BEGINNING
OF THE BOOK, PROGRESS TO A DRAMATIC PURPLE PAGE
WHEN THE LITTLE GIRL IS SECURE FROM THE LIGHTNING
OUTSIDE, AND END ON A CHEERFUL NOTE AFTER
GRANDMOTHER'S LAP HAS BEEN COMPARED TO THOSE
BELONGING TO MOTHER, FATHER, BROTHER, AND SISTER.
USEFUL BECAUSE THE UNIQUE ROLE OF GRANDMOTHER'S
LAP IS REINFORCED AGAIN AND AGAIN.
(EMOTIONS--SECURITY, FAM--GRANDMOTHERS,
GRANDMOTHERS, SECURITY)

DE PAOLA, TOMIE. NANA UPSTAIRS AND NANA
DOWNSTAIRS. PUTNAM, 1973.   ILLUSTRATED BY TOMIE
DE PAOLA. (BL)

   IN AN EASY BOOK FORMAT WITH LARGE PRINT AND
PICTURES ON EVERY PAGE, LITTLE TOMMY IS SHOWN IN
A CHARMING RELATIONSHIP WITH HIS 94-YEAR-OLD
GREAT-GRANDMOTHER, WHO IS NANA UPSTAIRS. HE
LEARNED THE MEANING OF DEATH ON THE DAY HIS
MOTHER TOLD HIM THAT NANA UPSTAIRS WOULD NOT BE
HERE ANY MORE, EXCEPT IN HIS MEMORY. TOMMY THINKS
OF HER WHEN HE SEES A FALLING STAR, AND THE BOOK
ENDS WITH HIM AS A YOUNG MAN, AGAIN SEEING A
FALLING STAR, AND THINKING OF BOTH GRANDMOTHERS.
A GENTLE, THOUGHTFUL WAY TO EXPLAIN DEATH TO THE
VERY YOUNG. (DEATH, DIFF SIT--DEATH,
FAM--GRANDMOTHERS, FAM--GREAT-GRANDMOTHERS,
GRANDMOTHERS, GREAT-GRANDMOTHERS)

DE PAOLA, TOMIE. WATCH OUT FOR THE CHICKEN FEET
IN YOUR SOUP. PRENTICE, 1974.   ILLUSTRATED BY
TOMIE DE PAOLA. (CC)

   LUSH COLORS MAKE THIS BOOK AN ATTRACTIVE
SETTING FOR INTRODUCING JOEY'S ITALIAN
GRANDMOTHER. JOEY BRINGS HIS FRIEND TO VISIT,

THINKING HE MAY BE EMBARRASSED BY OLD-COUNTRY
CUSTOMS, AND IS A LITTLE PUT OUT WHEN EUGENE IS
INVITED TO BAKE THE BREAD WITH GRANDMA.
DELICIOUS-SOUNDING RECIPE IS ALSO INCLUDED FOR
THE BRAIDED BREAD DOLLS. USEFUL BECAUSE OF THE
INTERACTION BETWEEN YOUNG AND OLD.
(FAM--GRANDMOTHERS, FRIENDSHIP, GRANDMOTHERS)

GILL, JOAN. SARA'S GRANNY AND THE GROODLE.
DOUBLEDAY, 1969. ILLUSTRATED BY SEYMOUR CHWAST.
(LJ)

   NONSENSICAL TEXT WHICH LOOKS LIKE PROSE, BUT
RHYMES, WITH SUCH AMUSING WORDS AS STRUDEL,
NOODLE, AND GROODLE, MAKE THIS A VERY ATTRACTIVE
BOOK TO READ ALOUD. IT SHOWS GRANNY AND YOUNG
SARA IN AN ADVENTURE WHICH MAY OR MAY NOT BE A
DREAM. THE PICTURE IT PORTRAYS OF GRANDMA IS A
VERY UNCONVENTIONAL ONE. ALTHOUGH SHE WEARS LONG
SKIRTS AND HIGH BUTTON BOOTS, SHE SHOUTS "OLE" AS
THEY RIDE DOWN THE STREET IN THE OYSTER SHELL
WHICH IS BEING DRAWN ALONG BY THE GOOSE. ITS
VALUE LIES PERHAPS IN THE VIEW IT GIVES OF OLD
AGE--THAT OLDER PEOPLE DON'T NEED TO SIT IN A
ROCKER AT HOME. (FAM--GRANDMOTHERS, FAM--OLD AGE,
GRANDMOTHERS, OLD AGE)

LEXAU, JOAN. BENJIE. DIAL, 1964. ILLUSTRATED BY
DON BOLOGNESE. (CC)

   A LIGHT GRAY WATERCOLOR WASH MATCHES THE
GRUBBY STREET SETTING OF THIS REALISTIC STORY.
ACTION TAKES PLACE ON THE STOOP, STREETS, AND
SHOPS OF THE INNER CITY, INCLUDING THE ONE ROOM
IN WHICH GRANNY AND BENJIE LIVE. HE IS A SMALL
BOY SO SHY THAT HE HIDES BEHIND HIS GRANNY'S
SKIRTS, AND IS TEASED BY THE NEIGHBORS. WHEN HIS
GRANDMOTHER LOSES A FAVORITE EARRING, BENJIE
OVERCOMES HIS SHYNESS TO HELP LOOK FOR IT, AND IN
ASSERTING HIMSELF MAKES PROGRESS TOWARD
INDEPENDENCE. USEFUL ALSO TO DEMONSTRATE A
LOVING, CARING RELATIONSHIP BETWEEN YOUNG AND
OLD. (EMOTIONS--SHYNESS, FAM--GRANDMOTHERS,
GRANDMOTHERS, SELF-CONFIDENCE, SHYNESS)

LEXAU, JOAN. BENJIE ON HIS OWN. DIAL, 1970.
ILLUSTRATED BY DON BOLOGNESE. (BCB)

   WHEN YOUNG BENJIE'S GRANDMOTHER IS SICK BENJIE
MUST WALK HOME FROM SCHOOL BY HIMSELF FOR THE

FIRST TIME. HE MEETS SOME TOUGH-LOOKING BOYS, BUT
FINALLY FINDS HIS WAY HOME. THIS IS THE STORY OF
HOW A GHETTO CHILD FUNCTIONS: NO PHONE IN THEIR
PLACE, SO HE USES THE POLICE BOX, EXCEPT THAT
HE'S TOO SHORT. PEOPLE AT FIRST DO NOT WISH TO
HELP, AND HE DOES NOT HAVE CLOSE FRIENDS TO CALL
UPON. WHEN HIS GRANDMOTHER GOES TO THE HOSPITAL,
HE WORRIES THAT NO ONE WILL BE AROUND TO TAKE HIM
TO SCHOOL, BUT IS HAPPY WHEN HE FINDS THAT RAY,
A NEIGHBOR HE'S STAYING WITH, WILL WALK HIM TO
SCHOOL. (FAM--GRANDMOTHERS, GRANDMOTHERS,
SELF-RELIANCE)

MILES, MISKA. ANNIE AND THE OLD ONE. LITTLE,
1971.   ILLUSTRATED BY PETER PARNALL.   (ESLC)

   GOLDEN DESERT COLORS SPIKED WITH BLACK AND
WHITE LINE DRAWINGS CONTRIBUTE TO THE STARK
FEELINGS OF IMPENDING DEATH IN THIS DIALOG
BETWEEN A NAVAJO GRANDMOTHER AND HER SMALL
GRANDCHILD. ONE EVENING WHEN, SYMBOLICALLY, THE
FIRE IS DYING IN THE HOGAN, THE OLD ONE ANNOUNCED
THAT SHE WOULD GO TO MOTHER EARTH WHEN THE RUG
ON THE LOOM WAS FINISHED. ANNIE UNDERSTOOD,
ALTHOUGH SHE DID NOT UNDERSTAND WHY HER
GRANDMOTHER KNEW SHE WAS GOING TO DIE. IN THE
DAYS THAT FOLLOWED ANNIE DREAMED UP SCHEMES TO
DELAY THE COMPLETION OF THE RUG, AND IT IS ONLY
WHEN GRANDMOTHER EXPLAINS THE INEVITABILITY OF
DEATH IN ALL OF NATURE THAT ANNIE ACCEPTS THE
CONCEPT. INTERESTING VIEW OF DEATH FOR, WHILE A
VERY REALISTIC BOOK, IT RETAINS THE MYSTICAL
OUTLOOK OF THE NAVAJO WAY OF LIFE. (DEATH, DIFF
SIT--DEATH, FAM--GRANDMOTHERS, GRANDMOTHERS)

MINARIK, ELSE. A KISS FOR LITTLE BEAR. HARPER,
1968.   ILLUSTRATED BY MAURICE SENDAK.   (BCB)

   AMUSING STORY BECAUSE OF THE HUMOROUS INCIDENT
IN WHICH LITTLE BEAR'S KISS ALMOST GETS LOST
WHEN LITTLE SKUNK GIVES IT TO HIS LADY FRIEND
INSTEAD OF PASSING IT ON, BUT THE UNDERLYING
MESSAGE IS THERE. LITTLE BEAR MAKES A PRESENT FOR
HIS GRANDMOTHER AND SHE, IN A LOVING GESTURE,
SENDS HIM A KISS. THE DELICATE ROUNDED LINES IN
THE ILLUSTRATIONS, FRAMED ON EACH PAGE, FURTHER
THE GENTLE, CARING MESSAGE. (EMOTIONS--LOVE,
FAM--GRANDMOTHERS, GRANDMOTHERS, LOVE)

SKORPEN, LIESEL. MANDY'S GRANDMOTHER. DIAL,

1975.   ILLUSTRATED BY MARTHA ALEXANDER.   (BL)

   MANDY THINKS GRANDMOTHERS ARE PRETTY
BORING--ESPECIALLY WHEN HER GRANDMOTHER 1) BRINGS
HER A FUSSY YELLOW DRESS FOR A PRESENT, 2)
DOESN'T LIKE HER PET TOAD, AND 3) WANTS TO GIVE
HER EGGS FOR BREAKFAST. MANDY BEGINS TO
APPRECIATE HER GRANDMOTHER AFTER A SESSION OF
LAP-SITTING. THEY DID MANY THINGS TOGETHER: THEY
TOLD STORIES, MANDY LEARNED TO KNIT. SYMBOLIC OF
THEIR RAPPORT IS THE FACT THAT MANDY IS WEARING
THE YELLOW DRESS WHEN GRANDMOTHER SAYS GOOD-BYE.
(FAM--GRANDMOTHERS, GRANDMOTHERS)

SONNEBORN, RUTH. I LOVE GRAM. VIKING, 1971.
ILLUSTRATED BY LEO CARTY.   (ESLC)

   A THIRD GRADER COULD READ THIS PICTURE-STORY
BOOK WHICH IS MORE TEXT THAN PICTURES, BUT IT CAN
BE ENJOYED BY YOUNGER CHILDREN AS A READ-ALOUD.
ELLIE'S GRANDMOTHER CARES FOR HER, AND COOKS FOR
THE FAMILY WHILE ELLIE'S MOTHER WORKS. WHEN GRAM
GOES TO THE HOSPITAL, ELLIE IS VERY LONELY, AND
INDEED EXPERIENCES A FEELING OF THE FORESHADOWING
OF DEATH. THE POSITIVE THINGS SHE DOES TO
PREPARE FOR GRAM'S HOMECOMING SHOW HER LOVE: A
PICTURE SHE DRAWS AND THE PARTY TABLE SHE
PREPARES. WE KNOW AT THE END OF THE STORY THE
STRONG BOND OF LOVE BETWEEN GRAM AND HER FAMILY.
(FAM--GRANDMOTHERS, FAM--MOTHERS WORKING,
FAM--OLD AGE, GRANDMOTHERS, MOTHERS WORKING, OLD
AGE)

UDRY, JANICE. MARY JO'S GRANDMOTHER. WHITMAN,
A., 1970. ILLUSTRATED BY ELEANOR MILL. (BCB)

   A SELF-RELIANT WOMAN WHO LIVES ALONE IN THE
COUNTRY GIVES A POSITIVE PICTURE OF AN OLDER
PERSON. RAISING CHICKENS AND MAKING GARDEN OCCUPY
THIS LADY'S TIME, AND MARY JO LOVES TO VISIT
HER. RESOURCEFUL MARY JO GOES FOR HELP WHEN
GRANDMA TAKES A FALL, BUT THE MAIN EMPHASIS IS ON
THE INDEPENDENT HOUSEHOLD OF THIS SPRIGHTLY
OLDSTER. (DIFF SIT--OLD AGE, FAM--GRANDMOTHERS,
GRANDMOTHERS, OLD AGE)

WAHL, JAN. GRANDMOTHER TOLD ME. LITTLE, 1972.
ILLUSTRATED BY MERCER MAYER. (LJ)

   AN IMAGINATIVE GRANDMOTHER WHO SEES DANCING

ALLIGATORS, MERMAIDS, AND TROLLS IN FAMILIAR
COUNTRYSIDE SCENES ENLIVENS HER GRANDSON'S
VISITS. THROUGH THE COMPANIONSHIP OF BAKING
BREAD, WASHING DISHES TOGETHER, AND SWEEPING THE
PORCH, GRANDMOTHER AND GRANDSON PROCEED THROUGH
THE DAYS WHICH END IN A CLIMACTIC VISION WHEN THE
LITTLE BOY SEES, OR DREAMS, OR IMAGINES ALL OF
THE THINGS HIS GRANDMOTHER HAS BEEN DESCRIBING.
ONE COMMENT: CHILDREN WILL NOT FORGIVE MERCER
MAYER FOR SHOWING PANCAKES ON A PAGE THAT REFERS
TO WAFFLES. (FAM--GRANDMOTHERS, GRANDMOTHERS)

WILLIAMS, BARBARA. ALBERT'S TOOTHACHE. DUTTON,
1974. ILLUSTRATED BY KAY CHORAO. (CC)

   APPROPRIATE AS A BEDTIME STORY FOR YOUNGER
CHILDREN, THIS SLOWLY-PACED STORY ILLUSTRATED IN
SOFT PENCIL TONES STRIKES A SYMPATHETIC CHORD IN
CHILDREN WHO HAVE TRIED TO MAKE GROWN-UPS
UNDERSTAND THEM AND BELIEVE THEM. NO ONE BELIEVED
THAT ALBERT TURTLE WAS SICK WITH A TOOTHACHE
UNTIL HIS GRANDMOTHER CAME OVER THAT NIGHT. TURNS
OUT A GOPHER BIT HIM ON HIS LEFT TOE, BUT NO ONE
HAD BEEN WISE ENOUGH TO ASK HIM WHERE HIS
TOOTHACHE WAS. (DIFF SIT--ILLNESS,
FAM--GRANDMOTHERS, GRANDMOTHERS, ILLNESS)

WILLIAMS, BARBARA. KEVIN'S GRANDMA. DUTTON,
1975. ILLUSTRATED BY KAY CHORAO. (BL)

   SPARKLY-EYED KEVIN MAY BE STRETCHING THE TRUTH
A BIT WHEN HE TELLS ABOUT HIS HONDA-RIDING
GRANDMOTHER, A VERY MUCH "WITH IT" LADY WHO IS
CONTRASTED WITH THE TRADITIONAL VIEW OF THE
NARRATOR'S GRANDMOTHER. A REFRESHING LOOK AT TWO
DIFFERENT CULTURES IN A BOOK WHICH REALLY DOESN'T
TAKE SIDES--AND AS SUCH IS A GOOD FORUM FOR
DISCUSSION. (FAM--GRANDMOTHERS, FAM--OLD AGE,
GRANDMOTHERS, OLD AGE)

FAM--GRANDPARENTS

   CHARLIP, REMY. HOORAY FOR ME!. PARENTS' MAG,
1975. ILLUSTRATED BY VERA WILLIAMS. (LJ, NYTBR)

   IN WATERY, EVOCATIVE WATERCOLORS, THE
ILLUSTRATOR SETS THE TONE FOR THE THEME OF
INTERRELATEDNESS OF THE HUMAN FAMILY. THE BOOK,
WHILE STRESSING THAT THE INDIVIDUAL IS A "ME,"
EXPLORES THE RELATIONSHIP OF NIECES TO UNCLES,

AND COUSINS TO COUSINS, AND DEVELOPS
UNDERSTANDING OF GREAT-GRANDPARENTS TO
GREAT-GREAT-GRANDPARENTS IN A SEQUENCE WITH A
KITTEN WHICH CHILDREN WILL LIKE. A BOOK WHICH
DEFIES DESCRIPTION, IT IS LIKELY TO BE ONE WHICH
WILL BE ENDURINGLY USEFUL IN HELPING TO DEVELOP
THE CONCEPT OF SELF. (FAM, FAM--GRANDPARENTS,
FAM--GREAT-GRANDPARENTS, GRANDPARENTS,
GREAT-GRANDPARENTS, SELF-IDENTITY)

CHILD, LYDIA. OVER THE RIVER AND THROUGH THE
WOOD. COWARD, 1974. ILLUSTRATED BY BRINTON
TURKLE. (CC)

   WRITTEN IN 1844, MS. CHILD'S POEM GIVES AN
AUTHENTIC PICTURE OF THANKSGIVING DAYS OF THE
PAST, AND MANY OF THE VERSES WILL BE NEW TO
CHILDREN. THE WORDS AND MUSIC, INCLUDING GUITAR
ACCOMPANIMENT, ARE FOUND AT THE END. THE DETAILS
WHICH ARTIST BRINTON TURKLE INCLUDES ARE VALUABLE
DOCUMENTATION. PICTURED ARE AN OLD WOOD
COOKSTOVE, AN INDOOR PUMP IN THE SINK, THE DUST
CAP WORN BY GRANDMOTHER, AND OTHER VALUABLE
ARTIFACTS OF THE PAST. (FAM--GRANDPARENTS,
GRANDPARENTS)

FAM--GREAT-GRANDMOTHERS

DE PAOLA, TOMIE. NANA UPSTAIRS AND NANA
DOWNSTAIRS. PUTNAM, 1973. ILLUSTRATED BY TOMIE
DE PAOLA. (BL)

   IN AN EASY BOOK FORMAT WITH LARGE PRINT AND
PICTURES ON EVERY PAGE, LITTLE TOMMY IS SHOWN IN
A CHARMING RELATIONSHIP WITH HIS 94-YEAR-OLD
GREAT-GRANDMOTHER, WHO IS NANA UPSTAIRS. HE
LEARNED THE MEANING OF DEATH ON THE DAY HIS
MOTHER TOLD HIM THAT NANA UPSTAIRS WOULD NOT BE
HERE ANY MORE, EXCEPT IN HIS MEMORY. TOMMY THINKS
OF HER WHEN HE SEES A FALLING STAR, AND THE BOOK
ENDS WITH HIM AS A YOUNG MAN, AGAIN SEEING A
FALLING STAR, AND THINKING OF BOTH GRANDMOTHERS.
A GENTLE, THOUGHTFUL WAY TO EXPLAIN DEATH TO THE
VERY YOUNG. (DEATH, DIFF SIT--DEATH,
FAM--GRANDMOTHERS, FAM--GREAT-GRANDMOTHERS,
GRANDMOTHERS, GREAT-GRANDMOTHERS)

HEIN, LUCILLE. MY VERY SPECIAL FRIEND. JUDSON,
1974. ILLUSTRATED BY JOAN ORFE. (CCB-B)

A FIVE-YEAR-OLD STAYS WITH HER GRANDMOTHER AND
GRANDFATHER WHILE HER MOTHER IS IN THE HOSPITAL,
BUT IT IS REALLY HER GREAT-GRANDMOTHER WITH WHOM
SHE SPENDS HER TIME. A HEALTHY RELATIONSHIP
DEVELOPS BETWEEN THE VERY OLD (85) AND THE VERY
YOUNG (5). THE CHILD HELPS THE OLD ONE, DOES
ERRANDS, AND IS A GENTLE COMPANION.
GREAT-GRANDMOTHER TEACHES THE CHILD TO TIE HER
SHOES, TO WHISTLE, AND SHARES OLD FAMILY
PHOTOGRAPHS TO GIVE THE CHILD A SENSE OF HISTORY
AND A SENSE OF BELONGING TO A FAMILY.
(FAM--GREAT-GRANDMOTHERS, FAM--OLD AGE,
GREAT-GRANDMOTHERS, OLD AGE)

FAM--GREAT-GRANDPARENTS

CHARLIP, REMY. HOORAY FOR ME!. PARENTS' MAG,
1975. ILLUSTRATED BY VERA WILLIAMS. (LJ, NYTBR)

IN WATERY, EVOCATIVE WATERCOLORS, THE
ILLUSTRATOR SETS THE TONE FOR THE THEME OF
INTERRELATEDNESS OF THE HUMAN FAMILY. THE BOOK,
WHILE STRESSING THAT THE INDIVIDUAL IS A "ME,"
EXPLORES THE RELATIONSHIP OF NIECES TO UNCLES,
AND COUSINS TO COUSINS, AND DEVELOPS
UNDERSTANDING OF GREAT-GRANDPARENTS TO
GREAT-GREAT-GRANDPARENTS IN A SEQUENCE WITH A
KITTEN WHICH CHILDREN WILL LIKE. A BOOK WHICH
DEFIES DESCRIPTION, IT IS LIKELY TO BE ONE WHICH
WILL BE ENDURINGLY USEFUL IN HELPING TO DEVELOP
THE CONCEPT OF SELF. (FAM, FAM--GRANDPARENTS,
FAM--GREAT-GRANDPARENTS, GRANDPARENTS,
GREAT-GRANDPARENTS, SELF-IDENTITY)

FAM--MOTHER-DAUGHTER

TOBIAS, TOBI. THE QUITTING DEAL. VIKING, 1975.
ILLUSTRATED BY TRINA HYMAN. (BL)

IN REALISTIC DRAWINGS AND TEXT DEALING WITH A
CONTEMPORARY MOTHER AND DAUGHTER, EACH WEARING
LONG HAIR AND JEANS, THE AUTHOR AND ILLUSTRATOR
HAVE PRESENTED A SITUATION IN WHICH EACH
CHARACTER WISHES TO CONQUER A BAD HABIT: THUMB
SUCKING ON THE PART OF THE DAUGHTER, AND SMOKING
CIGARETTES ON THE PART OF THE MOTHER. THEY
PROGRESS THROUGH SEVERAL CURES, SUCH AS HOLDING
HANDS, AND THE CANDY CURE--EACH HAS ITS
DRAWBACKS. WHILE THEY SUCCEED FOR AWHILE, IN THE
END BOTH MOTHER AND DAUGHTER FIND THEY CANNOT

QUIT COLD. NOT THE USUAL ENDING FOR A CHILDREN'S
BOOK. (BEHAVIOR--THUMB SUCKING,
FAM--MOTHER-DAUGHTER, MOTHER-DAUGHTER, THUMB
SUCKING)

FAM--MOTHERS

BLAINE, MARGE. THE TERRIBLE THING THAT HAPPENED
AT OUR HOUSE. PARENTS' MAG, 1975. ILLUSTRATED BY
JOHN WALLVER. (BL)

   A DEVASTATINGLY FUNNY/SAD BOOK ABOUT MOTHER
GOING BACK TO WORK AS A SCIENCE TEACHER. THE
ILLUSTRATIONS ARE VERY REALISTIC WHEN THEY
PORTRAY CHAOS IN THE MORNING AS ALL THE FAMILY
HAS TO DRESS AND LEAVE AT THE SAME TIME.
ACCUSTOMED TO COMING HOME FOR LUNCH, THE
BESPECTACLED LITTLE GIRL WHO NOW EATS IN THE
SCHOOL LUNCHROOM IS APPALLED AT THE NOISE AND
MESSINESS. WHILE THE FAMILY FINALLY ADJUSTS
SOMEWHAT, AND SOME VALUABLE LESSONS IN
COOPERATION ARE LEARNED, THE READER MAY BE LEFT
WITH THE FEELING THAT PERHAPS THERE ARE SOME VERY
POSITIVE VALUES IN HAVING A FULL-TIME MOTHER AT
HOME. (FAM--MOTHERS, FAM--MOTHERS WORKING,
MOTHERS WORKING)

BROWN, MARGARET. THE RUNAWAY BUNNY. HARPER,
1942. ILLUSTRATED BY CLEMENT HURD. (CC)

   A THOROUGHLY SATISFYING STORY FOR A YOUNG
CHILD, FOR ALL CHILDREN DREAM OF RUNNING AWAY
FROM HOME. THIS MOTHER RABBIT, WHO ALWAYS THINKS
OF A WAY TO INTERCEPT HER YOUNG ONE, IS A PERFECT
PORTRAIT OF THE MOTHER WHO IS ALWAYS THERE, AND
WILL ALWAYS BE THERE, THE ULTIMATE IN SECURITY
AND LOVE. (EMOTIONS--SECURITY, FAM--MOTHERS,
MOTHERS, SECURITY)

BROWNSTONE, CECILY. ALL KINDS OF MOTHERS. MC
KAY, 1969. ILLUSTRATED BY MIRIAM BROFSKY. (CSM,
LJ)

   THE ILLUSTRATIONS AND TEXT ILLUSTRATE THAT
MOTHERS COME IN ALL SHAPES AND SIZES, THAT SOME
ARE NEAT AND SOME MAY BE SLOPPY, BUT THE MAIN
MESSAGE THAT COMES THROUGH IS THAT "MOTHERS KEEP
RIGHT ON LOVING THEM"--THOSE MISBEHAVING
CHILDREN. WHEN THE BOOK DISCUSSES WHERE SOME
MOTHERS MIGHT WORK, THE LIST IS RATHER LIMITED,

AND WOULD SUGGEST A RATHER NARROW ROLE FOR WOMEN
OUTSIDE THE HOME. (EMOTIONS--LOVE, FAM--MOTHERS,
LOVE, MOTHERS)

LEXAU, JOAN. EMILY AND THE KLUNKY BABY AND THE
NEXT DOOR DOG. DIAL, 1972. ILLUSTRATED BY MARTHA
ALEXANDER. (CC)

   CHARMINGLY ILLUSTRATED, THE BOOK IS A SLIGHT
EPISODE OF A SMALL GIRL ATTEMPTING TO RUN AWAY TO
HER FATHER, WHO LIVES IN AN APARTMENT NEAR BY.
EMILY FEELS HER MOTHER WAS IGNORING HER WHEN
DOING HER INCOME TAXES AND DIDN'T WANT TO BE
BOTHERED. EMILY TAKES THE BABY AND ALMOST GETS
LOST BUT INSTEAD GOES AROUND THE BLOCK (BECAUSE
SHE'S NOT ALLOWED TO CROSS THE STREET)--AND MAKES
IT HOME TO A LOVING MOTHER WHO THINKS SHE'S OUT
PLAYING. (DIFF SIT--DIVORCE, DIFF SIT--ONE
PARENT, DIVORCE, FAM--MOTHERS, FAM--ONE PARENT,
MOTHERS, ONE PARENT)

MARINO, DOROTHY. WHERE ARE THE MOTHERS?.
LIPPINCOTT, 1959. ILLUSTRATED BY DOROTHY MARINO.
 (ESLC)

   DIFFERENT ROLES OF MOTHERS ARE EXPLORED, AND A
VARIETY OF ROLES OUTSIDE THE HOME ARE DEPICTED:
OFFICE WORKER, SCHOOL TEACHER, AND CHECK-OUT
PERSON IN A GROCERY STORE. SINCE THE BOOK WAS
WRITTEN IN 1959, THE ROLES TEND TO BE
TRADITIONAL. A BONUS TO THE BOOK IS THE SECTION
WHICH DEALS WITH THE FAMILY. IT INCLUDES
SIBLINGS, FATHERS, AND GRANDPARENTS INVOLVED IN
SUCH ACTIVITIES AS SWIMMING, PICNICKING, AND
GOING TO THE ZOO. (FAM--MOTHERS, MOTHERS)

SCOTT, ANN. ON MOTHER'S LAP. MC GRAW, 1972.
ILLUSTRATED BY GLO COALSON. (BCB)

   A LOVING STORY OF A LAP WITH UNLIMITED ROOM.
FIRST IT HAS MICHAEL, THEN HIS DOLL, THEN HIS
BOAT, THEN HIS PUPPY, THEN HIS REINDEER BLANKET.
THEY ALL ROCKED TOGETHER. WHEN THE BABY WAKES UP,
MICHAEL PUTS ON A SOUR FACE, AND SAYS THERE
ISN'T ANY ROOM. BUT MOTHER MAKES ROOM FOR ALL,
AND GIVES A SENSE OF SECURITY TO THE READER THAT
ONLY A LAP AND A ROCKING CHAIR CAN PROVIDE.
(EMOTIONS--LOVE, EMOTIONS--SECURITY,
FAM--MOTHERS, FAM--SIBLING RIVALRY, LOVE,
MOTHERS, SECURITY, SIBLING RIVALRY)

SHARMAT, MARJORIE. I WANT MAMA. HARPER, 1974.
ILLUSTRATED BY EMILY MC CULLY. (CCB-B, NYTBR)

A LITTLE GIRL'S MOTHER GOES TO THE HOSPITAL
FOR AN OPERATION. IN CHILDLIKE PICTURES AND
DIALOG, THE READER LEARNS OF THE LONELINESS AND
CONCERN WITHIN THE LITTLE GIRL. USEFUL BECAUSE IT
SHOWS WHAT A CHILD CAN DO TO SPELL THE
LONELINESS, SUCH AS MAKE PRESENTS AND CLEAN THE
HOUSE. AN ESPECIALLY MOVING ILLUSTRATION AT THE
END OF THE BOOK SHOWS THE PEACE AND CONTENTMENT
IN THE HOUSEHOLD WHEN MOTHER COMES HOME.
(EMOTIONS--LONELINESS, FAM--MOTHERS, HOSPITAL,
LONELINESS, MOTHERS, NEW SIT--HOSPITAL)

WELBER, ROBERT. THE WINTER PICNIC. PANTHEON,
1970. ILLUSTRATED BY DEBORAH RAY. (CC)

A YOUNG PRESCHOOLER CAN'T WAIT FOR SUMMER TO
COME IN ORDER TO HAVE A PICNIC. DESPITE HIS
MOTHER'S DISINTEREST, ADAM MAKES CUPS AND PLATES
OUT OF FROZEN SNOW, AND FILLS THEM WITH PEANUT
BUTTER SANDWICHES AND LEMONADE. HIS SURPRISED
MOTHER AGREES IN THE END THAT ONE CAN INDEED HAVE
A WINTER PICNIC. INTERESTING IN THAT THE CHILD'S
POINT OF VIEW IS ALLOWED TO PREVAIL OVER THAT OF
HIS MOTHER. (FAM--MOTHERS, MOTHERS)

YOLEN, JANE. IT ALL DEPENDS. FUNK, 1969.
ILLUSTRATED BY DON BOLOGNESE. (LJ)

IN A ROUNDABOUT WAY, THIS IS A POETICAL STORY
OF THE VALUE OF LOVE. DAVID IS A LITTLE BOY WHO
QUESTIONS HIS MOTHER ABOUT A NUMBER OF THINGS.
"HOW TALL AM I?" AND SHE ANSWERS BY SAYING THAT
IT ALL DEPENDS UPON THE RELATIONSHIP OF THINGS.
THAT TO AN ANT, HE IS VERY LARGE, BUT THAT TO A
WHALE, HE IS VERY SMALL. IN AN IMAGINATIVE SERIES
OF ILLUSTRATIONS, BOLOGNESE HAS PRODUCED A BOOK
USEFUL TO TEACHERS AND PARENTS WHICH TEACHES
DIFFERING SIZE RELATIONSHIPS. IT IS NOT UNTIL
ALMOST THE END THAT DAVID ASKS, "WHAT IF I GROW,
AND CHANGE," AND SHE ANSWERS THAT HE WILL ALWAYS
BE JUST RIGHT, BECAUSE HIS PARENTS LOVE HIM.
(EMOTIONS--LOVE, FAM--MOTHERS, LOVE, MOTHERS,
SELF-CONSCIOUSNESS--SIZE)

ZINDEL, PAUL. I LOVE MY MOTHER. HARPER, 1975.
ILLUSTRATED BY JOHN MELO. (CCB-B)

STRIKING FULL-COLOR ILLUSTRATIONS EXPAND THE
LIMITED TEXT OF THIS STORY OF A BOY AND HIS
MOTHER, PRESUMABLY LIVING ALONE BECAUSE OF
DIVORCE OR SEPARATION. THE REASON IS NOT
EXPLICITLY STATED. COMPANIONSHIP AT THE ZOO, IN
THE KITCHEN, AND LATE AT NIGHT WHEN THE BAD
DREAMS COME, MAKES UP ONE PART OF THE BOOK. THERE
IS ALSO DEPICTED THE REALISM OF VULNERABLE
FEELINGS WHEN THE BOY WANTS TO RUN AWAY FROM
HOME, WHEN HIS MOTHER TRIES NOT TO LET HIM KNOW
WHEN THEY ARE SHORT OF MONEY, BUT THE MOST MOVING
SCENES ARE WHEN MOTHER ADMITS THAT SHE IS LONELY
AND WHEN THE BOY MISSES HIS FATHER. (DIFF
SIT--DIVORCE, DIVORCE, EMOTIONS--LONELINESS,
EMOTIONS--LOVE, FAM--MOTHERS, FAM--ONE PARENT,
LONELINESS, LOVE, MOTHERS, ONE PARENT)

ZOLOTOW, CHARLOTTE. A FATHER LIKE THAT. HARPER,
1971. ILLUSTRATED BY BEN SHECTER. (BCB)

HOME WITHOUT A FATHER IS PICTURED AS A LITTLE
BOY PAINTS AN IMAGINARY PORTRAIT OF THE PERFECT
DAD. WE SEE A MOTHER WHO MAKES THE CHILD GO TO
BED AT BEDTIME, WHO READS WHEN THE BOY WOULD LIKE
TO PLAY CHECKERS. SHE IS A MOTHER WHO CAN'T
UNDERSTAND BECAUSE SHE NEVER WAS A BOY, AND WHO
SAYS THE BASEBALL GAME ON TV IS TOO LOUD. IT IS
THE MOTHER WHO, NERVOUSLY SEWING FASTER AND
FASTER BECAUSE OF THE GLOWING PICTURE HE
DESCRIBES OF THE MYTHICAL FATHER, SAYS THE
REALISTIC WORDS OF WISDOM: "IF HE NEVER COMES, "
TRYING TO MAKE THE CHILD UNDERSTAND THAT THIS
PARAGON IS PERHAPS EXAGGERATED. IN THE END,
MOTHER SAYS THAT HE CAN TRY TO BE THAT KIND OF
FATHER WHEN HE GROWS UP. USEFUL BECAUSE OF THE
EXEMPLAR ROLE OF THE FATHER. SOME CHILDREN MAY
NEED TO BE SHOWN WHAT THE ABSENCE OF THE FATHER
IN THE FAMILY MEANS. (DIFF SIT--ONE PARENT,
FAM--FATHERS, FAM--MOTHERS, FATHERS, MOTHERS, ONE
PARENT)

FAM--MOTHERS WORKING

BALDWIN, ANNE. JENNY'S REVENGE. FOUR, 1974.
ILLUSTRATED BY EMILY MC CULLY. (CCB-B)

JENNY HATES HER BABY-SITTER, AND EXPRESSES
HIDDEN ANGER TOWARD HER WORKING MOTHER WHO
APPARENTLY HAS WORKED ONLY SINCE A RECENT
DIVORCE. AFTER TRYING A NUMBER OF PLOYS TO FORCE

THE BABY-SITTER TO QUIT, SHE FINDS COMRADESHIP
WITH MRS. CRAMIE WHEN THEY DISCOVER A COMMON
INTEREST IN THE CIRCUS. A REALISTIC LOOK AT A
CHILD WHO NEEDS AND WANTS ATTENTION FROM HER
MOTHER. (ANGER, DIFF SIT--DIVORCE, DIFF SIT--ONE
PARENT, DIVORCE, EMOTIONS--ANGER, FAM--MOTHERS
WORKING, MOTHERS WORKING, ONE PARENT)

BLAINE, MARGE. THE TERRIBLE THING THAT HAPPENED
AT OUR HOUSE. PARENTS' MAG, 1975. ILLUSTRATED BY
JOHN WALLNER. (BL)

   A DEVASTATINGLY FUNNY/SAD BOOK ABOUT MOTHER
GOING BACK TO WORK AS A SCIENCE TEACHER. THE
ILLUSTRATIONS ARE VERY REALISTIC WHEN THEY
PORTRAY CHAOS IN THE MORNING AS ALL THE FAMILY
HAS TO DRESS AND LEAVE AT THE SAME TIME.
ACCUSTOMED TO COMING HOME FOR LUNCH, THE
BESPECTACLED LITTLE GIRL WHO NOW EATS IN THE
SCHOOL LUNCHROOM IS APPALLED AT THE NOISE AND
MESSINESS. WHILE THE FAMILY FINALLY ADJUSTS
SOMEWHAT, AND SOME VALUABLE LESSONS IN
COOPERATION ARE LEARNED, THE READER MAY BE LEFT
WITH THE FEELING THAT PERHAPS THERE ARE SOME VERY
POSITIVE VALUES IN HAVING A FULL-TIME MOTHER AT
HOME. (FAM--MOTHERS, FAM--MOTHERS WORKING,
MOTHERS WORKING)

CLIFTON, LUCILLE. EVERETT ANDERSON'S YEAR. HOLT,
1974. ILLUSTRATED BY ANN GRIFALCONI. (CC)

   "WALK TALL IN THE WORLD," HIS MOTHER TELLS
HIM. ALTHOUGH THIS IS, IN THE MAIN, A STORY OF A
SEVEN-YEAR-OLD BOY, THE INFLUENCE OF HIS MOTHER
SHINES THROUGH ON EVERY PAGE. EVERETT ANDERSON
REMEMBERS HIS DADDY ALTHOUGH HE DOES NOT KNOW
WHERE HE IS, AND READING THIS SERIES OF VERSES
ABOUT THE MONTHS OF THE YEAR, A CHILD CAN SHARE
THE SPECIAL LOVE THE YOUNG BOY FEELS FOR HIS
MOTHER. (DIFF SIT--ONE PARENT,
EMOTIONS--LONELINESS, FAM--MOTHERS WORKING,
LONELINESS, MOTHERS WORKING, ONE PARENT)

MERRIAM, EVE. MOMMIES AT WORK. KNOPF, 1961.
ILLUSTRATED BY BENI MONTRESOR. (ESLC)

   ROLES OF MOTHERS PROFUSELY ILLUSTRATED WITH
STRIKING PICTURES ACCOMPANIED BY A SPARSE TEXT.
MOMMIES ARE SHOWN IN TRADITIONAL AND
NON-TRADITIONAL ROLES, NOTABLE BEING THOSE OF

TELEVISION DIRECTOR, DOCTOR, AND ARCHITECT.
(FAM--MOTHERS WORKING, MOTHERS WORKING)

SONNEBORN, RUTH. I LOVE GRAM. VIKING, 1971.
ILLUSTRATED BY LEO CARTY. (ESLC)

A THIRD GRADER COULD READ THIS PICTURE-STORY
BOOK WHICH IS MORE TEXT THAN PICTURES, BUT IT CAN
BE ENJOYED BY YOUNGER CHILDREN AS A READ-ALOUD.
ELLIE'S GRANDMOTHER CARES FOR HER, AND COOKS FOR
THE FAMILY WHILE ELLIE'S MOTHER WORKS. WHEN GRAM
GOES TO THE HOSPITAL, ELLIE IS VERY LONELY, AND
INDEED EXPERIENCES A FEELING OF THE FORESHADOWING
OF DEATH. THE POSITIVE THINGS SHE DOES TO
PREPARE FOR GRAM'S HOMECOMING SHOW HER LOVE: A
PICTURE SHE DRAWS AND THE PARTY TABLE SHE
PREPARES. WE KNOW AT THE END OF THE STORY THE
STRONG BOND OF LOVE BETWEEN GRAM AND HER FAMILY.
(FAM--GRANDMOTHERS, FAM--MOTHERS WORKING,
FAM--OLD AGE, GRANDMOTHERS, MOTHERS WORKING, OLD
AGE)

SONNEBORN, RUTH. THE LOLLIPOP PARTY. VIKING,
1967. ILLUSTRATED BY BRINTON TURKLE. (ESLC)

ONE DAY TOMAS IS LEFT ALONE IN THE APARTMENT
FOR THE FIRST TIME. HIS SISTER ANA, WHO USUALLY
CARED FOR HIM BEFORE GOING TO HER JOB, HAD TO
LEAVE HIM ALONE. STEP-BY-STEP THE READER
PARTICIPATES IN THE LITTLE BOY'S FEAR. HE WAS
CONCERNED ABOUT THE SOUND OF FOOTSTEPS ON THE
STAIRS, AND WISHED ONLY TO SIT QUIETLY AND HOLD
HIS CAT GATTO. WHEN HIS NURSERY SCHOOL TEACHER
COMES TO THE DOOR ON A VISIT, HOWEVER, THE
EMOTIONAL TONE OF THE BOOK CHANGES IMMEDIATELY.
HE IS HAPPY TO SEE HER, ACTS THE ROLE OF THE HOST
BY OFFERING HER A LOLLIPOP, AND THE STORY ENDS
WITH TOMAS FEELING A BIT GROWN-UP.
(EMOTIONS--FEAR, EMOTIONS--LONELINESS,
FAM--MOTHERS WORKING, FEAR, LONELINESS, MOTHERS
WORKING, SELF-RELIANCE)

FAM--OLD AGE

BALDWIN, ANNE. SUNFLOWERS FOR TINA. FOUR, 1970.
ILLUSTRATED BY ANN GRIFALCONI. (CCB-B)

IN SUNFLOWER COLORS, THE ILLUSTRATOR HAS SHOWN
A CORNER OF A DIRTY CITY NEIGHBORHOOD WHERE THE
LAUNDRY HANGS BETWEEN THE BUILDINGS, WHERE TINA

TRIES TO GROW A GARDEN BY PLANTING CARROTS SHE
FINDS IN THE REFRIGERATOR. WHEN SHE DISCOVERS
SUNFLOWERS GROWING A FEW BLOCKS FROM HOME, SHE
DELIGHTS IN THEIR FRESHNESS AND THINKS OF HER
AGING GRANDMOTHER AT HOME IN HER DARK CORNER.
LATER SHE DANCES IN HER YELLOW DRESS, AND EVOKES
LAUGHTER FROM THE OLD WOMAN. A STORY OF CONTRASTS
BETWEEN OLD AND YOUNG, BEAUTY AND RUBBLE, THIS
IS A POSITIVE STATEMENT FOR THE NECESSITY OF
AESTHETIC PLEASURE IN LIFE. (FAM--GRANDMOTHERS,
FAM--OLD AGE, GRANDMOTHERS, OLD AGE)

BUCKLEY, HELEN. GRANDFATHER AND I. LOTHROP,
1959. ILLUSTRATED BY PAUL GALDONE. (CC)

   HELEN BUCKLEY WROTE FAMILY STORIES ABOUT
GRANDPARENTS IN THE 1950'S AND THEY ARE AS VALID
NOW AS IN 1959. IN LARGE TYPE, AND LARGE COLORFUL
ILLUSTRATIONS, THE STORY IS TOLD OF THE JOYS OF
NOT HURRYING, OF A BOY AND HIS GRANDFATHER WHO
TAKE WALKS AND TAKE TIME TO LOOK FOR THINGS SUCH
AS BIRDS AND SQUIRRELS AND EVEN SNAILS.
CONTRASTING ARE EXAMPLES OF THE HUSTLE AND BUSTLE
OF HURRYING MOTHERS, DADS, TRAFFIC, AND OLDER
CHILDREN. "EVERYONE ELSE IS ALWAYS IN A HURRY BUT
WHEN A BOY AND HIS GRANDFATHER GO WALKING THEY
HAVE TIME TO STOP AND LOOK." (FAM--GRANDFATHERS,
FAM--OLD AGE, GRANDFATHERS, OLD AGE)

GILL, JOAN. SARA'S GRANNY AND THE GROODLE.
DOUBLEDAY, 1969. ILLUSTRATED BY SEYMOUR CHWAST.
(LJ)

   NONSENSICAL TEXT WHICH LOOKS LIKE PROSE, BUT
RHYMES, WITH SUCH AMUSING WORDS AS STRUDEL,
NOODLE, AND GROODLE, MAKE THIS A VERY ATTRACTIVE
BOOK TO READ ALOUD. IT SHOWS GRANNY AND YOUNG
SARA IN AN ADVENTURE WHICH MAY OR MAY NOT BE A
DREAM. THE PICTURE IT PORTRAYS OF GRANDMA IS A
VERY UNCONVENTIONAL ONE. ALTHOUGH SHE WEARS LONG
SKIRTS AND HIGH BUTTON BOOTS, SHE SHOUTS "OLE" AS
THEY RIDE DOWN THE STREET IN THE OYSTER SHELL
WHICH IS BEING DRAWN ALONG BY THE GOOSE. ITS
VALUE LIES PERHAPS IN THE VIEW IT GIVES OF OLD
AGE--THAT OLDER PEOPLE DON'T NEED TO SIT IN A
ROCKER AT HOME. (FAM--GRANDMOTHERS, FAM--OLD AGE,
GRANDMOTHERS, OLD AGE)

HEIN, LUCILLE. MY VERY SPECIAL FRIEND. JUDSON,
1974. ILLUSTRATED BY JOAN ORFE. (CCB-B)

A FIVE-YEAR-OLD STAYS WITH HER GRANDMOTHER AND
GRANDFATHER WHILE HER MOTHER IS IN THE HOSPITAL,
BUT IT IS REALLY HER GREAT-GRANDMOTHER WITH WHOM
SHE SPENDS HER TIME. A HEALTHY RELATIONSHIP
DEVELOPS BETWEEN THE VERY OLD (85) AND THE VERY
YOUNG (5). THE CHILD HELPS THE OLD ONE, DOES
ERRANDS, AND IS A GENTLE COMPANION.
GREAT-GRANDMOTHER TEACHES THE CHILD TO TIE HER
SHOES, TO WHISTLE, AND SHARES OLD FAMILY
PHOTOGRAPHS TO GIVE THE CHILD A SENSE OF HISTORY
AND A SENSE OF BELONGING TO A FAMILY.
(FAM--GREAT-GRANDMOTHERS, FAM--OLD AGE,
GREAT-GRANDMOTHERS, OLD AGE)

SONNEBORN, RUTH. I LOVE GRAM. VIKING, 1971.
ILLUSTRATED BY LEO CARTY. (ESLC)

A THIRD GRADER COULD READ THIS PICTURE-STORY
BOOK WHICH IS MORE TEXT THAN PICTURES, BUT IT CAN
BE ENJOYED BY YOUNGER CHILDREN AS A READ-ALOUD.
ELLIE'S GRANDMOTHER CARES FOR HER, AND COOKS FOR
THE FAMILY WHILE ELLIE'S MOTHER WORKS. WHEN GRAM
GOES TO THE HOSPITAL, ELLIE IS VERY LONELY, AND
INDEED EXPERIENCES A FEELING OF THE FORESHADOWING
OF DEATH. THE POSITIVE THINGS SHE DOES TO
PREPARE FOR GRAM'S HOMECOMING SHOW HER LOVE: A
PICTURE SHE DRAWS AND THE PARTY TABLE SHE
PREPARES. WE KNOW AT THE END OF THE STORY THE
STRONG BOND OF LOVE BETWEEN GRAM AND HER FAMILY.
(FAM--GRANDMOTHERS, FAM--MOTHERS WORKING,
FAM--OLD AGE, GRANDMOTHERS, MOTHERS WORKING, OLD
AGE)

WILLIAMS, BARBARA. KEVIN'S GRANDMA. DUTTON,
1975. ILLUSTRATED BY KAY CHORAO. (BL)

SPARKLY-EYED KEVIN MAY BE STRETCHING THE TRUTH
A BIT WHEN HE TELLS ABOUT HIS HONDA-RIDING
GRANDMOTHER, A VERY MUCH "WITH IT" LADY WHO IS
CONTRASTED WITH THE TRADITIONAL VIEW OF THE
NARRATOR'S GRANDMOTHER. A REFRESHING LOOK AT TWO
DIFFERENT CULTURES IN A BOOK WHICH REALLY DOESN'T
TAKE SIDES--AND AS SUCH IS A GOOD FORUM FOR
DISCUSSION. (FAM--GRANDMOTHERS, FAM--OLD AGE,
GRANDMOTHERS, OLD AGE)

FAM--ONE PARENT

BLUE, ROSE. A MONTH OF SUNDAYS. WATTS, 1972.
ILLUSTRATED BY TED LEWIN. (CC)

IT WAS HARD HAVING A DAD WHO LOVED YOU ON
SUNDAYS WHEN HE USED TO LOVE YOU EVERY DAY. THIS
COMMENT EPITOMIZES THE UNHAPPY FEELINGS JEFFREY
HAS WHEN HE AND HIS MOTHER MOVE INTO AN APARTMENT
IN THE CITY. WHEN JEFF AND HIS DAD GET TOGETHER
IN THE OLD NEIGHBORHOOD, THINGS REALLY DON'T WORK
OUT. THE RELATIVES TALK AROUND HIM AS IF HE
WEREN'T PRESENT IN THE ROOM. THE MOTHER OF JEFF'S
BEST FRIEND MATTHEW TURNS OUT TO BE A GOOD
STRONG FRIEND WHO EXPLAINS SOME OF THE PROBLEMS
THAT JEFF'S MOM IS HAVING. GETTING INVOLVED IN A
GROUP PROJECT AT SCHOOL AND PARTICIPATING IN A
BIG BLOCK PARTY OVERFLOWING WITH DELICIOUS ETHNIC
FOODS, MUSIC, AND PEOPLE SEEM TO BE THE TWO
THINGS THAT BODE WELL FOR JEFF'S FUTURE. (DIFF
SIT--DIVORCE, DIVORCE, FAM--ONE PARENT, ONE
PARENT)

LEXAU, JOAN. EMILY AND THE KLUNKY BABY AND THE
NEXT DOOR DOG. DIAL, 1972. ILLUSTRATED BY MARTHA
ALEXANDER. (CC)

CHARMINGLY ILLUSTRATED, THE BOOK IS A SLIGHT
EPISODE OF A SMALL GIRL ATTEMPTING TO RUN AWAY TO
HER FATHER, WHO LIVES IN AN APARTMENT NEAR BY.
EMILY FEELS HER MOTHER WAS IGNORING HER WHEN
DOING HER INCOME TAXES AND DIDN'T WANT TO BE
BOTHERED. EMILY TAKES THE BABY AND ALMOST GETS
LOST BUT INSTEAD GOES AROUND THE BLOCK (BECAUSE
SHE'S NOT ALLOWED TO CROSS THE STREET)--AND MAKES
IT HOME TO A LOVING MOTHER WHO THINKS SHE'S OUT
PLAYING. (DIFF SIT--DIVORCE, DIFF SIT--ONE
PARENT, DIVORCE, FAM--MOTHERS, FAM--ONE PARENT,
MOTHERS, ONE PARENT)

LEXAU, JOAN. ME DAY. DIAL, 1971. ILLUSTRATED BY
ROBERT WEAVER. (BCB)

"ME DAY" IS RAFER'S BIRTHDAY, BUT IN A SLUM
FAMILY WHERE THERE IS NO MONEY FOR PRESENTS AND
THE TV IS BROKEN, WHAT MAKES A BOY HAPPY? THROUGH
THE TEXT WE LEARN THAT THE FATHER IS NOT AT
HOME, THE PARENTS BEING DIVORCED, APPARENTLY
BECAUSE THE FATHER COULD NOT FIND WORK. RAFER'S
DAY IS MADE PERFECT WHEN HIS FATHER SHOWS UP TO
SPEND THE ENTIRE DAY WITH HIM IN THE PARK, WITH
ICE CREAM AND HOT DOGS. (DIFF SIT--DIVORCE,
DIVORCE, FAM--FATHERS, FAM--ONE PARENT, FATHERS,
ONE PARENT, SELF-IDENTITY)

NESS, EVALINE. SAM, BANGS, AND MOONSHINE. HOLT,
1966. ILLUSTRATED BY EVALINE NESS. (BCB)

DESPITE HER FATHER'S CAUTIONS, SAMANTHA IS NOT
ABLE TO KEEP STRAIGHT HER IMAGINARY LIFE FROM
HER REAL LIFE, AND TELLS PRETTY BIG WHOPPERS
TRIGGERED BY HER LONELINESS AND AN INSPIRED
IMAGINATION. WHEN SHE TELLS HER FRIEND THOMAS
THAT HER PET KANGAROO LIVES OUT IN A CAVE, THOMAS
BECOMES MAROONED AND ALMOST LOSES HIS LIFE. SAM
IS DISTRAUGHT WHEN SHE REALIZES THAT HER LIE, FOR
THAT IS WHAT IT IS, IS RESPONSIBLE. HER FATHER
TELLS HER TO THINK ABOUT THE DIFFERENCE BETWEEN
REAL AND MOONSHINE AND, AT THE END, HE ALSO TELLS
HER THAT THERE ARE TWO KINDS OF MOONSHINE: THE
GOOD KIND, WHICH IS HEALTHY IMAGINATIVE PLAY, AND
THE BAD KIND, THAT WHICH CAN BE HARMFUL.
(BEHAVIOR--MISBEHAVIOR, DIFF SIT--ONE PARENT,
EMOTIONS--LONELINESS, FAM--ONE PARENT,
LONELINESS, MISBEHAVIOR, ONE PARENT)

PEARSON, SUSAN. MONNIE HATES LYDIA. DIAL, 1975.
ILLUSTRATED BY DIANE PATERSON. (BL)

INTERESTING BECAUSE A FATHER HEADS THIS
ONE-PARENT FAMILY CONSISTING OF MONNIE AND HER
THOROUGHLY OBNOXIOUS SISTER LYDIA. DADDY IS AN
IMPARTIAL ARBITER IN THE FAMILY SQUABBLE WHICH
ERUPTS ON LYDIA'S BIRTHDAY, SUPPORTIVE OF
MONNIE'S HURT FEELINGS, BUT NOT WILLING TO PUNISH
LYDIA. HE IS AN ATTRACTIVE, BEARDED CONTEMPORARY
FATHER WHO CAN BE ADMIRED FOR HIS COOL WHEN
MONNIE DUMPS THE BIRTHDAY CAKE IN LYDIA'S FACE.
ONE FEELS HE SHOULD BE CHEERING, BUT INSTEAD HE
HANDS LYDIA A TOWEL AND KISSES HER ON THE CHEEK.
USEFUL AS A PORTRAIT OF A NEW LIFE-STYLE FAMILY
COPING WITH OLD LIFE-STYLE PROBLEMS. (ANGER, DIFF
SIT--ONE PARENT, EMOTIONS--ANGER, FAM--FATHERS,
FAM--ONE PARENT, FAM--SIBLING RIVALRY, FATHERS,
ONE PARENT, SIBLING RIVALRY)

STANEK, MURIEL. I WON'T GO WITHOUT A FATHER.
WHITMAN, A., 1972. ILLUSTRATED BY ELEANOR MILL.
(CCB-B, LJ)

THE READER IS NOT TOLD WHY STEVE DOESN'T HAVE
A FATHER. THE REASON MAY BE DEATH, DESERTION, OR
DIVORCE, BUT WHAT WE ARE SHOWN IS THE JEALOUSY
AND LONELINESS THAT STEVE FEELS WHEN HE SEES
SOMEONE ELSE WITH A FATHER. WHEN PARENTS ARE

INVITED TO AN OPEN-HOUSE AT SCHOOL, STEVE DOES
NOT WANT TO GO BECAUSE HE BELIEVES EVERYONE WILL
THINK HE'S A MAMA'S BOY, AND HE THINKS THEN
EVERYONE WILL SEE THAT HE DOES NOT HAVE A FATHER.
MANY VARIATIONS ON THE KINDS OF PARENTHOOD SERVE
TO GIVE STEVE SOME PERSPECTIVE: FIRST OF ALL,
ONE BOY'S FATHER WORKED NIGHTS AND HIS MOTHER WAS
ILL, SO A SISTER FILLED IN. ANOTHER BOY WAS
BRINGING TWO SETS OF PARENTS: HIS PARENTS WERE
DIVORCED. IN STEVE'S CASE, HIS GRANDPA, HIS
UNCLE, AND A NEIGHBOR SAT WITH HIM AND HIS
MOTHER. BUT WHAT STEVE REALLY FOUND OUT WAS THAT
NO ONE WAS LOOKING AT HIM. HE FINALLY LEARNS TO
ACCEPT THE STATEMENT HIS MOTHER MADE: "LOTS OF
CHILDREN DON'T HAVE BOTH PARENTS...THEY MUST
LEARN TO GET ALONG WITH THE FAMILY AND FRIENDS
THEY HAVE." (DIFF SIT--ONE PARENT, FAM--ONE
PARENT, ONE PARENT)

ZINDEL, PAUL. I LOVE MY MOTHER. HARPER, 1975.
ILLUSTRATED BY JOHN MELO. (CCB-B)

   STRIKING FULL-COLOR ILLUSTRATIONS EXPAND THE
LIMITED TEXT OF THIS STORY OF A BOY AND HIS
MOTHER, PRESUMABLY LIVING ALONE BECAUSE OF
DIVORCE OR SEPARATION. THE REASON IS NOT
EXPLICITLY STATED. COMPANIONSHIP AT THE ZOO, IN
THE KITCHEN, AND LATE AT NIGHT WHEN THE BAD
DREAMS COME, MAKES UP ONE PART OF THE BOOK. THERE
IS ALSO DEPICTED THE REALISM OF VULNERABLE
FEELINGS WHEN THE BOY WANTS TO RUN AWAY FROM
HOME, WHEN HIS MOTHER TRIES NOT TO LET HIM KNOW
WHEN THEY ARE SHORT OF MONEY, BUT THE MOST MOVING
SCENES ARE WHEN MOTHER ADMITS THAT SHE IS LONELY
AND WHEN THE BOY MISSES HIS FATHER. (DIFF
SIT--DIVORCE, DIVORCE, EMOTIONS--LONELINESS,
EMOTIONS--LOVE, FAM--MOTHERS, FAM--ONE PARENT,
LONELINESS, LOVE, MOTHERS, ONE PARENT)

FAM--ONLY CHILD

   HAZEN, BARBARA. WHY COULDN'T I BE AN ONLY KID
LIKE YOU, WIGGER. ATHENEUM, 1975. ILLUSTRATED BY
LEIGH GRANT. (HB)

   PLEASANT CLUTTER IN A LARGE FAMILY HOUSEHOLD
WHICH HAS SIX CHILDREN KEYNOTES THE FRUSTRATION
OF THE YOUNG BOY WHO TELLS THE STORY. WIGGER, HIS
FRIEND, DOESN'T HAVE TO MOP UP THE MILK THE BABY
SPILLED, OR STAND IN LINE FOR THE BATHROOM IN

THE MORNING, AND HE, THE NARRATOR, IS FRANKLY
QUITE JEALOUS. DURING HIS TIRADE HOWEVER, THE
ILLUSTRATIONS GIVE A DIFFERENT PICTURE OF WIGGER
WHO SEEMS TO LIKE WHEELING THE BABY CARRIAGE AND
BEING A PART OF THE ROUGH AND TUMBLE OF A LARGE
FAMILY. THE NARRATOR IS SURPRISED AT THE FACT
THAT AN ONLY CHILD CAN BE A LONELY CHILD. USEFUL
FOR THE CONTRASTING POINTS OF VIEW.
(EMOTIONS--JEALOUSY, FAM--ONLY CHILD, FRIENDSHIP,
JEALOUSY, ONLY CHILD)

FAM--SIBLING RIVALRY

AMOSS, BERTHE. TOM IN THE MIDDLE. HARPER, 1968.
ILLUSTRATED BY BERTHE AMOSS. (CCB-B)

   THE VERY REAL PLIGHT OF HAVING A YOUNGER
BROTHER WHO BUGS YOU AND AN OLDER BROTHER WHO
THINKS YOU'RE A PEST IS DEPICTED IN THIS
ATTRACTIVE LITTLE PICTURE BOOK. TOM THINKS HE
WILL RUN AWAY, BUT ALSO THINKS THAT HOME AND THE
SAFETY OF BREAD AND BUTTER AT BEDTIME IS THE
BETTER IDEA. (BROTHERS, FAM--BROTHERS,
FAM--SIBLING RIVALRY, SIBLING RIVALRY)

ANDRY, ANDREW. HI, NEW BABY. SIMON, 1970.
ILLUSTRATED BY DI, THOMAS GRAZIA. (ESLC)

   IN WHAT APPEARS TO BE DARK CHARCOAL DRAWINGS
SUPERIMPOSED ON COLORED BACKGROUNDS, DI GRAZIA
HAS ACHIEVED AN ALMOST PHOTOGRAPHIC QUALITY IN
THIS BOOK TRACING THE MANY FACETS OF BABYHOOD.
BATHING, FEEDING, AND SLEEPING ARE SHOWN TO BE
ACTIVITIES WHICH ENCROACH ON THE OLDER SIBLING,
BUT WAYS OF HELPING ARE EXPLORED, AND THE BABY IS
SHOWN GROWING UP TO BE A COMPANION. POSITIVE
NOTE THROUGHOUT WILL MAKE THIS A USEFUL VOLUME.
(FAM--SIBLING RIVALRY, NEW SIT--BABY, SIBLING
RIVALRY)

BRONIN, ANDREW. GUS AND BUSTER WORK THINGS OUT.
COWARD, 1975. ILLUSTRATED BY CYNDY SZEKERES.
(BL)

   BROTHER RACCOONS ARE SHOWN IN FOUR STORIES OF
BROTHERLY SQUABBLES. GUS, WHO MAY BE A LITTLE
OLDER, TRICKS HIS SIBLING IN MANY
SITUATIONS--TRYING TO GET THE LOWER BUNK BED,
TRYING TO GET ALL THE BEST TOYS ON A RAINY DAY.
USEFUL FOR DISCUSSION BECAUSE SYMPATHY TENDS TO

LIE WITH BUSTER, THE PUT-UPON BROTHER, AND HE
SOMETIMES GETS THE BEST OF HIS WILY BIG BROTHER.
(BEHAVIOR--QUARRELING, BROTHERS, FAM--BROTHERS,
FAM--SIBLING RIVALRY, QUARRELING, SIBLING RIVALRY)

BROWN, MYRA. AMY AND THE NEW BABY. WATTS, 1965.
ILLUSTRATED BY HARRIET HUREWITZ. (RLHR)

  MOTHER WISELY BRINGS A PRESENT FOR AMY WHEN
NEW BROTHER RICKY COMES HOME. ALTHOUGH PALE BLUE
ILLUSTRATIONS ENHANCE THE SOFT TONE OF THE STORY,
JEALOUSY CREEPS IN TO SPOIL THE FAMILY
RELATIONSHIP. DADDY TAKES AMY TO THE PARK, JUST
THE TWO OF THEM, FOR A PONY RIDE AND AN ICE CREAM
CONE, TWO THINGS THE BABY CANNOT HAVE.
(FAM--SIBLING RIVALRY, NEW SIT--BABY, SIBLING
RIVALRY)

BURNINGHAM, JOHN. THE BABY. CROWELL, T., 1974.
ILLUSTRATED BY JOHN BURNINGHAM. (BL)

  IN NINE SHORT SENTENCES, THIS BRITISH AUTHOR
CAPTURES THE ESSENCE OF B-A-B-Y AND WHAT IT MEANS
TO A SLIGHTLY OLDER CHILD. THE FRONT COVER
DRAWING, CRAYONED IN A CHILDLIKE MANNER, CAPTURES
THE TONE OF THE BOOK: THE RATHER LARGE BABY WITH
THE RATHER LARGE HEAD IS ALMOST AS LARGE AS THE
BOY UPON WHOSE LAP IT SITS. YET THIS BABY CANNOT
DO ANYTHING TO GIVE THE YOUNG BOY REAL
COMPANIONSHIP, AND INDEED DEPRIVES HIM OF THE
COMPANY OF HIS MOTHER. AN EASY-TO-READ BOOK, AS
WELL AS ONE TO BE SHARED. (FAM--SIBLING RIVALRY,
NEW SIT--BABY, SIBLING RIVALRY)

ELLENTUCK, SHAN. MY BROTHER BERNARD. ABELARD,
1968. ILLUSTRATED BY SHAN ELLENTUCK. (CCB-B)

  TOLD BY A NAMELESS LITTLE SISTER, THIS IS A
PORTRAIT OF A KOOKY BROTHER WHO WANTS EVERYONE TO
THINK HE IS A PRINCE. IN ONE SENSE, HE BULLIES
HIS SISTER, AND THREATENS TO HIT HER IF SHE
DOESN'T PLAY AT THE GAME OF MAKE-BELIEVE. SHE,
HOWEVER, SECRETLY ADMIRES HIM AND HIS IMAGINARY
KINGDOM, AND IN THE END IS FLATTERED BY BEING
MADE A PRINCESS. THIS BOOK IS NOT A TRACT FOR
PERSONS LOOKING FOR BOOKS WITH STRONG IMAGES OF
WOMEN. (BROTHERS & SISTERS, FAM--BROTHERS &
SISTERS, FAM--SIBLING RIVALRY, SIBLING RIVALRY)

FRIEDMAN, AILEEN. CASTLES OF THE TWO BROTHERS.

HOLT, 1972. ILLUSTRATED BY STEVEN KELLOGG.
(ESLC)

    AILEEN FRIEDMAN WAS INSPIRED TO WRITE THIS
STORY AFTER SHE VISITED TWO REAL CASTLES SITUATED
ON THE RHINE RIVER. IT HAS A FOLKTALE QUALITY
ABOUT IT WHICH IS MATCHED BY MEDIEVAL
ILLUSTRATIONS. BASICALLY IT IS THE STORY OF TWO
BROTHERS WHO WERE ORPHANED. HUBERT, THE OLDER
BROTHER, LOOKS AFTER HIS YOUNGER BROTHER KLAUS TO
SUCH AN EXTENT THAT THE YOUNGER BROTHER FINALLY
REBELS. AFTER BUILDING HIS OWN CASTLE AND A HUGE
WALL TO SEPARATE IT FROM HUBERT'S, KLAUS NARROWLY
AVOIDS DISASTER WHEN THE WALL CRUMBLES.
ILLUSTRATES VERY WELL THAT TOO MUCH "MOTHERING"
CAN BE BAD. (BROTHERS, FAM--BROTHERS,
FAM--SIBLING RIVALRY, SIBLING RIVALRY)

GREENFIELD, ELOISE. SHE COME BRINGING ME THAT
LITTLE BABY GIRL. LIPPINCOTT, 1974. ILLUSTRATED
BY JOHN STEPTOE. (CC)

    "I DIDN'T LIKE THE WAY MAMA AND DADDY LOOKED
AT HER, LIKE SHE WAS THE ONLY BABY IN THE WORLD."
THIS WAS THE FEELING THAT KEVIN HAD WHEN THE NEW
BABY CAME HOME--AND RELATIVES AND NEIGHBORS CAME
TO CALL WITH PRESENTS FOR THE BABY BUT NOTHING
FOR KEVIN. WHEN HIS MOTHER TOLD HIM THAT SHE HAD
ONCE BEEN A BABY GIRL, KEVIN FELT MUCH BETTER,
AND WAS SATISFIED, AT THE END, TO SHARE ONE OF
HIS MOTHER'S ARMS WITH THE BABY. (FAM--SIBLING
RIVALRY, NEW SIT--BABY, SIBLING RIVALRY)

HOLLAND, VIKI. WE ARE HAVING A BABY. SCRIBNER,
1972. ILLUSTRATED BY VIKI HOLLAND. (RLHR)

    REALISTIC BLACK AND WHITE PHOTOGRAPHS
UNDERLINE THE AUTHENTICITY OF THIS VOLUME FOR
PARENTS AND SIBLINGS. THE BOOK OPENS WITH THE
CHILD AT HOME FEELING THE SIZE OF MOTHER'S
ABDOMEN, AND PROGRESSES THROUGH THE DAY MOTHER
LEAVES FOR THE HOSPITAL. AFTER DANA STRUGGLES TO
DRESS HERSELF, THE BOOK GIVES A STEP-BY-STEP
PICTURE OF WHAT IS HAPPENING TO THE MOTHER, MUCH
AS A FATHER MIGHT DESCRIBE IT TO THE CHILD AT
HOME. DANA HAS SOME FEELINGS OF REJECTION AFTER
THE BABY COMES HOME AND SHE REFUSES TO EAT LUNCH.
WHEN HER FATHER RETURNS IN THE EVENING THEY HAVE
A SHARING TIME TOGETHER AND SHE HELPS TO FEED
THE BABY. THERE IS A VERY SATISFIED EXPRESSION ON

DANA'S FACE IN THE LAST ILLUSTRATION AS SHE
SAYS: "HE'S MY BROTHER." (FAM--SIBLING RIVALRY,
NEW SIT--BABY, SIBLING RIVALRY)

KEATS, EZRA. PETER'S CHAIR. HARPER, 1967.
ILLUSTRATED BY EZRA KEATS.   (BCB)

   POOR PETER! HE WAS SO JEALOUS OF THE NEW BABY,
HE DECIDED TO RUN AWAY FROM HOME. WHEN HIS DAD
BEGAN TO PAINT ALL OF PETER'S FURNITURE, HE
GRABBED HIS LITTLE CHAIR, AND RAN OUTSIDE THE
DOOR. HE WAS VERY SURPRISED TO FIND THAT HE COULD
NOT FIT INTO IT ANYMORE BECAUSE HE HAD GROWN
BIGGER. USEFUL BECAUSE IT SHOWS THE RESOLVING OF
THE JEALOUS FEELINGS: PETER AND HIS FATHER PAINT
THE LITTLE CHAIR. ADDITIONALLY USEFUL BECAUSE IT
SHOWS A PRACTICAL EXAMPLE OF GROWTH IN A CHILD.
(EMOTIONS--JEALOUSY, FAM--SIBLING RIVALRY,
JEALOUSY, NEW SIT--BABY, SIBLING RIVALRY)

PEARSON, SUSAN. MONNIE HATES LYDIA. DIAL, 1975.
ILLUSTRATED BY DIANE PATERSON. (BL)

   INTERESTING BECAUSE A FATHER HEADS THIS
ONE-PARENT FAMILY CONSISTING OF MONNIE AND HER
THOROUGHLY OBNOXIOUS SISTER LYDIA. DADDY IS AN
IMPARTIAL ARBITER IN THE FAMILY SQUABBLE WHICH
ERUPTS ON LYDIA'S BIRTHDAY, SUPPORTIVE OF
MONNIE'S HURT FEELINGS, BUT NOT WILLING TO PUNISH
LYDIA. HE IS AN ATTRACTIVE, BEARDED CONTEMPORARY
FATHER WHO CAN BE ADMIRED FOR HIS COOL WHEN
MONNIE DUMPS THE BIRTHDAY CAKE IN LYDIA'S FACE.
ONE FEELS HE SHOULD BE CHEERING, BUT INSTEAD HE
HANDS LYDIA A TOWEL AND KISSES HER ON THE CHEEK.
USEFUL AS A PORTRAIT OF A NEW LIFE-STYLE FAMILY
COPING WITH OLD LIFE-STYLE PROBLEMS. (ANGER, DIFF
SIT--ONE PARENT, EMOTIONS--ANGER, FAM--FATHERS,
FAM--ONE PARENT, FAM--SIBLING RIVALRY, FATHERS,
ONE PARENT, SIBLING RIVALRY)

SCOTT, ANN. ON MOTHER'S LAP. MC GRAW, 1972.
ILLUSTRATED BY GLO COALSON. (BCB)

   A LOVING STORY OF A LAP WITH UNLIMITED ROOM.
FIRST IT HAS MICHAEL, THEN HIS DOLL, THEN HIS
BOAT, THEN HIS PUPPY, THEN HIS REINDEER BLANKET.
THEY ALL ROCKED TOGETHER. WHEN THE BABY WAKES UP,
MICHAEL PUTS ON A SOUR FACE, AND SAYS THERE
ISN'T ANY ROOM. BUT MOTHER MAKES ROOM FOR ALL,
AND GIVES A SENSE OF SECURITY TO THE READER THAT

ONLY A LAP AND A ROCKING CHAIR CAN PROVIDE.
(EMOTIONS--LOVE, EMOTIONS--SECURITY,
FAM--MOTHERS, FAM--SIBLING RIVALRY, LOVE,
MOTHERS, SECURITY, SIBLING RIVALRY)

VIORST, JUDITH. I'LL FIX ANTHONY. HARPER, 1969.
ILLUSTRATED BY ARNOLD LOBEL. (BL)

A CLASSIC RECITAL OF THE VENGEFUL JEALOUSY
SEETHING INSIDE A LITTLE BOY, WHO IS NOT YET
QUITE SIX. WE SEE A PORTRAIT OF THE OLDER BROTHER
THROUGH THE EYES OF THE ABUSED YOUNGER BROTHER:
THE OLDER BROTHER WHO IS CONSISTENTLY BIGGER AND
STRONGER, PHYSICALLY AND MENTALLY, BUT SELFISH,
PRIVILEGED, AND RATHER HORRID. ANTHONY ANNOUNCES
THAT HE'S GOING TO CLOBBER YOUNGER BROTHER, AND
SAYS, "YOU STINK." LITTLE BROTHER SAYS, "I'LL FIX
ANTHONY." (WHEN I'M SIX.) (ANGER,
EMOTIONS--ANGER, EMOTIONS--JEALOUSY, FAM--SIBLING
RIVALRY, JEALOUSY, SIBLING RIVALRY)

WELLS, ROSEMARY. NOISY NORA. DIAL, 1973.
ILLUSTRATED BY ROSEMARY WELLS. (CC, ESLC)

POOR NORA--SHE'S THE LEFT-OUT SISTER, AND
THREATENS TO RUN AWAY TO MAKE HER FAMILY FEEL
SORRY FOR HER AND GIVE HER SOME ATTENTION. WHEN
SHE SHOWS UP IN THE BROOM CLOSET, ALL IS WELL. A
CLEVER, FUNNY BOOK ABOUT A BUMPTIOUS LITTLE
MOUSE-GIRL WHICH WILL DELIGHT YOUNG CHILDREN AS
THEY CATALOG HER MISDEMEANORS. MANY CHILDREN MAY
SEE THEMSELVES. (BROTHERS & SISTERS,
EMOTIONS--JEALOUSY, FAM--BROTHERS & SISTERS,
FAM--SIBLING RIVALRY, JEALOUSY, SIBLING RIVALRY)

WOLDE, GUNILLA. BETSY AND THE CHICKEN POX.
RANDOM, 1976. ILLUSTRATED BY GUNILLA WOLDE. (BL)

WHEN BETSY'S BABY BROTHER BECOMES ILL AND
PARENTAL ATTENTION TURNS TOWARD HIM, BETSY'S
THUMB GOES IN HER MOUTH AS SHE WATCHES ROUND-EYED
IN THE BACKGROUND. BABY'S TEMPERATURE IS TAKEN,
THE DOCTOR IS CALLED AND, AMID ALL THE BUSTLE,
BETSY IS IGNORED. SHE PAINTS SPOTS ON HER FACE,
AND EVEN HER TONGUE, BUT STILL NO ONE NOTICES HER
AND WHEN SHE ERUPTS IN A TEMPER, BOTH PARENTS
ARE ANGRY. WHEN SHE HERSELF BREAKS OUT IN CHICKEN
POX, BETSY REALIZES SHE REALLY DOESN'T WANT THE
RED SPOTS AFTER ALL. A REALISTIC STORY WHICH IS
SIGNIFICANT FOR A NUMBER OF REASONS, IT WILL BE

USEFUL FOR PARENT AND CHILD BECAUSE IT DETAILS
THE TYPICALLY JEALOUS FEELINGS IN A CHILD WHO
FEELS NEGLECTED. A NO NONSENSE WOMAN DOCTOR, A
VIEW OF DADDY TAKING THE BABY'S TEMPERATURE WITH
A RECTAL THERMOMETER, AND LOW-KEY PASTEL AND
CRAYON DRAWINGS MAKE THIS A BOOK WHICH
DEMONSTRATES NON-STEREOTYPED SEX ROLES AS WELL AS
A RELEVANT FAMILY SITUATION. (DIFF SIT--ILLNESS,
FAM--SIBLING RIVALRY, ILLNESS, SIBLING RIVALRY)

FAM--SISTERS

HOBAN, RUSSELL. BEST FRIENDS FOR FRANCES.
HARPER, 1969. ILLUSTRATED BY LILLIAN HOBAN.
(BCB)

  THE LITTLE BADGERS IN THIS STORY DEMONSTRATE
THE POIGNANCY OF A LITTLE SISTER BEING LEFT OUT
WHEN OLDER BOYS AND GIRLS ARE PLAYING. A NO-GIRLS
AND NO-BOYS SITUATION FOLLOWS, BUT ALL IS
HAPPINESS WHEN FRANCES PACKS UP A SCRUMPTIOUS
PICNIC FOR ALBERT AND THE YOUNGER SISTER GLORIA.
(BEHAVIOR--SHARING, FAM--SISTERS, FRIENDSHIP,
SHARING, SISTERS)

ZOLOTOW, CHARLOTTE. BIG SISTER AND LITTLE
SISTER. HARPER, 1966. ILLUSTRATED BY MARTHA
ALEXANDER. (ESLC)

  FRETTING BECAUSE OF AN OVERLY SOLICITOUS BIG
SISTER WHO HOLDS HER HAND AND WATCHES OVER HER,
LITTLE SISTER DECIDES TO SLIP AWAY INTO THE
MEADOW TO BE ALONE. WHEN BIG SISTER CRIES BECAUSE
LITTLE SISTER IS LOST, LITTLE SISTER PUTS HER
ARMS AROUND BIG SISTER AND HELPS HER BLOW HER
NOSE, AND COMFORTS HER. THE LESSON IS THAT LITTLE
SISTER NEEDED TO LEARN TO GIVE AS WELL AS
RECEIVE, AND IN FACT BIG SISTER NEEDED TO LEARN
TO RECEIVE. (FAM--SISTERS, SISTERS)

FATHERS

FLORA, JAMES. FISHING WITH DAD. HARCOURT, 1967.
ILLUSTRATED BY JAMES FLORA. (ESLC)

  EXPLORES THE CONCEPT OF A LITTLE BOY GROWING
OLD ENOUGH TO PARTICIPATE IN AN ADULT'S WORLD,
AND IS A REALISTIC LOOK AT LIFE ON A DEEP-SEA
FISHING BOAT. THE FISHING NET PICKS UP A TORPEDO
WHICH MUST BE DISPOSED OF BY THE COAST GUARD, AND

THIS, PLUS THE DANGER OF FOG AND COLLISION WITH
LARGE SHIPS, GIVES AN UNUSUAL SENSE OF ADVENTURE.
A LONGER STORY THAN MANY, THE READING LEVEL
FALLS AT THE HIGH RANGE OF THIRD GRADE, BUT THE
BOOK WILL APPEAL TO A MUCH YOUNGER AUDIENCE.
(FAM--FATHERS, FATHERS, SELF-IDENTITY)

HOBAN, RUSSELL. BEDTIME FOR FRANCES. HARPER,
1960. ILLUSTRATED BY GARTH WILLIAMS. (CC)

   FATHER BADGER PLAYS AN IMPORTANT ROLE IN
HANDLING THE BEDTIME PROBLEMS OF HIS DAUGHTER
FRANCES WITH AN IMAGINATIVE EXPLANATION OF HER
FEARS. WHEN FRANCES, AN ENTRANCING LITTLE GIRL
WHO ONLY INCIDENTALLY HAPPENS TO BE A BADGER,
GOES THROUGH THE FAMILIAR BEDTIME ROUTINE OF
MILK, HUGS, KISSES, AND TEDDY BEAR, BUT STILL
DOES NOT FALL ASLEEP, FATHER GIVES REASSURING
ADVICE ABOUT THE IMAGINARY GIANTS AND THE
SOMETHING SCARY THAT MIGHT COME OUT OF THE CRACK
IN THE CEILING. HIS MOST CREATIVE SOLUTION,
HOWEVER, COMES WHEN FRANCES COMPLAINS OF THE
CURTAINS MOVING AT THE WINDOW--HE TELLS HER THAT
THE WIND'S JOB IS TO GO AROUND AND BLOW ALL THE
CURTAINS, THAT EVERYBODY HAS A JOB, AND THAT
FURTHERMORE, HER JOB IS TO GO TO SLEEP.
THROUGHOUT THE BOOK, FATHER IS THE PARENT WHO
RELATES TO THE CHILD, ALTHOUGH THE MOTHER IS
VISIBLE. (BEHAVIOR--DISLIKES--SLEEP,
DISLIKES--SLEEP, EMOTIONS--FEAR, FAM--FATHERS,
FATHERS, FEAR)

KINDRED, WENDY. LUCKY WILMA. DIAL, 1973.
ILLUSTRATED BY WENDY KINDRED. (LJ)

   BEGINNING WITH A SERIES OF SATURDAYS WILMA AND
"CHARLIE," HER DAD, WALK TO MUSEUMS AND ZOOS,
AND FATHER AND DAUGHTER HAVE A UNIFORMLY GLUM
EXPRESSION. THE NEXT EIGHTEEN PAGES DEAL WITH
JOYOUS PICTURIZATION OF CLIMBING, JUMPING,
PIGGYBACKING, DANCING, AND REVELRY WITH THE
PIGEONS IN THE PARK. OBVIOUSLY THIS WAS THE
NEATEST SATURDAY THEY HAD SPENT TOGETHER, AND
THEY HUG AS THEY SEPARATE AND DAD SAYS: "WE'VE
GOT ALL THE SATURDAYS IN THE WORLD." CURIOUSLY
ENOUGH THE WORD DIVORCE IS NOT MENTIONED. WITH
VERY LITTLE TEXT, THIS BOOK CONVEYS THAT INDEED
WILMA IS LUCKY TO HAVE A WONDERFUL RELATIONSHIP
WITH HER FATHER. (DIFF SIT--DIVORCE, DIFF
SIT--ONE PARENT, DIVORCE, FAM--FATHERS, FATHERS,

ONE PARENT)

LEXAU, JOAN. ME DAY. DIAL, 1971. ILLUSTRATED BY
ROBERT WEAVER. (BCB)

"ME DAY" IS RAFER'S BIRTHDAY, BUT IN A SLUM
FAMILY WHERE THERE IS NO MONEY FOR PRESENTS AND
THE TV IS BROKEN, WHAT MAKES A BOY HAPPY? THROUGH
THE TEXT WE LEARN THAT THE FATHER IS NOT AT
HOME, THE PARENTS BEING DIVORCED, APPARENTLY
BECAUSE THE FATHER COULD NOT FIND WORK. RAFER'S
DAY IS MADE PERFECT WHEN HIS FATHER SHOWS UP TO
SPEND THE ENTIRE DAY WITH HIM IN THE PARK, WITH
ICE CREAM AND HOT DOGS. (DIFF SIT--DIVORCE,
DIVORCE, FAM--FATHERS, FAM--ONE PARENT, FATHERS,
ONE PARENT, SELF-IDENTITY)

PEARSON, SUSAN. MONNIE HATES LYDIA. DIAL, 1975.
ILLUSTRATED BY DIANE PATERSON. (BL)

INTERESTING BECAUSE A FATHER HEADS THIS
ONE-PARENT FAMILY CONSISTING OF MONNIE AND HER
THOROUGHLY OBNOXIOUS SISTER LYDIA. DADDY IS AN
IMPARTIAL ARBITER IN THE FAMILY SQUABBLE WHICH
ERUPTS ON LYDIA'S BIRTHDAY, SUPPORTIVE OF
MONNIE'S HURT FEELINGS, BUT NOT WILLING TO PUNISH
LYDIA. HE IS AN ATTRACTIVE, BEARDED CONTEMPORARY
FATHER WHO CAN BE ADMIRED FOR HIS COOL WHEN
MONNIE DUMPS THE BIRTHDAY CAKE IN LYDIA'S FACE.
ONE FEELS HE SHOULD BE CHEERING, BUT INSTEAD HE
HANDS LYDIA A TOWEL AND KISSES HER ON THE CHEEK.
USEFUL AS A PORTRAIT OF A NEW LIFE-STYLE FAMILY
COPING WITH OLD LIFE-STYLE PROBLEMS. (ANGER, DIFF
SIT--ONE PARENT, EMOTIONS--ANGER, FAM--FATHERS,
FAM--ONE PARENT, FAM--SIBLING RIVALRY, FATHERS,
ONE PARENT, SIBLING RIVALRY)

RADLAUER, RUTH. FATHER IS BIG. BOWMAR, 1967.
ILLUSTRATED BY HARVEY MANDLIN. (ESLC)

SIMPLE TEXT, AND LARGE, FULL-PAGE COLOR
PHOTOGRAPHS TAKE THE READER THROUGH SIX
SITUATIONS DESCRIBING THE BIGNESS OF THE BOY'S
DAD. THE NEXT SIX ELEMENTS DEAL WITH FATHER/SON
COOPERATIVE RELATIONSHIPS, USING THE LAWN MOWER,
BIKE, AND JUNGLE GYM, ENDING WITH THE INTERESTING
STATEMENT THAT "FATHER CAN EVEN MAKE ME BIGGER
THAN HE IS." THE PICTURE OPPOSITE SHOWS THE BOY
ON HIS FATHER'S SHOULDERS. THE FAMILY SHOWN IS
DARK SKINNED. (FAM--FATHERS, FATHERS)

RAYNOR, DORKA. THIS IS MY FATHER AND ME.
WHITMAN, A., 1973. ILLUSTRATED BY DORKA RAYNOR.
(BL)

  STRIKING BLACK AND WHITE PHOTOGRAPHS FROM ALL
OVER THE WORLD SHOW VARYING RELATIONSHIPS OF
FATHERS TO THEIR CHILDREN. WHILE NOT A BOOK WHICH
WILL BE READILY PICKED UP BY CHILDREN, IT
REVEALS THE ROLE OF LOVE, COOPERATION,
PROTECTION, CARE, DEVOTION, WORK, PLAY, AND PRIDE
WHICH CAN EXIST BETWEEN PARENT AND CHILD IN A
UNIVERSAL WAY. (EMOTIONS--LOVE, FAM--FATHERS,
FATHERS, LOVE)

SONNEBORN, RUTH. FRIDAY NIGHT IS PAPA NIGHT.
VIKING, 1970. ILLUSTRATED BY EMILY MC CULLY.
(BCB, CC)

  A SYMPATHETIC PICTURE OF PUERTO RICAN LIFE IN
A CROWDED APARTMENT, WHERE PEDRO'S BED IS IN THE
KITCHEN, AND FATHER WORKS TWO JOBS TO PROVIDE FOR
HIS FAMILY. BROWN TONES COMPLEMENT THE WARMTH
AND SKIN COLOR OF THE CHARACTERS, AND LEND A
HARMONIOUS TONE TO THE THEME, WHICH IS THE
SPECIAL FEELING IN PEDRO'S MIND WHEN HIS FATHER
COMES HOME ON FRIDAY NIGHT. (EMOTIONS--LOVE,
FAM--FATHERS, FATHERS, LOVE)

STEWART, ROBERT. DADDY BOOK. AMERICAN, 1972.
ILLUSTRATED BY DON MADDEN. (CCB-B, LJ)

  ACCORDING TO THE AUTHOR, HE WROTE THIS BOOK
BECAUSE THERE WEREN'T VERY MANY DADDIES IN THE
CHILDREN'S BOOKS HE READ, AND HE HAS PROCEEDED TO
PRESENT AN ARRAY OF TALL, FAT, YELLOW, SHORT
DADDIES WHO HAVE ALL KINDS OF HOBBIES, DO ALL
KINDS OF JOBS, BUT WHO, MOST OF ALL, SHARE MANY,
MANY ACTIVITIES WITH THEIR CHILDREN, INCLUDING
SOME OF THE TASKS THAT MOMMIES DO. A THOROUGHLY
CONTEMPORARY, HELPFUL BOOK WHICH GIVES AN
EXCELLENT VIEW OF THE MANY-FACETED ROLES OF
FATHERS. (FAM--FATHERS, FATHERS)

ZOLOTOW, CHARLOTTE. A FATHER LIKE THAT. HARPER,
1971. ILLUSTRATED BY BEN SHECTER. (BCB)

  HOME WITHOUT A FATHER IS PICTURED AS A LITTLE
BOY PAINTS AN IMAGINARY PORTRAIT OF THE PERFECT
DAD. WE SEE A MOTHER WHO MAKES THE CHILD GO TO
BED AT BEDTIME, WHO READS WHEN THE BOY WOULD LIKE

TO PLAY CHECKERS. SHE IS A MOTHER WHO CAN'T
UNDERSTAND BECAUSE SHE NEVER WAS A BOY, AND WHO
SAYS THE BASEBALL GAME ON TV IS TOO LOUD. IT IS
THE MOTHER WHO, NERVOUSLY SEWING FASTER AND
FASTER BECAUSE OF THE GLOWING PICTURE HE
DESCRIBES OF THE MYTHICAL FATHER, SAYS THE
REALISTIC WORDS OF WISDOM: "IF HE NEVER COMES, "
TRYING TO MAKE THE CHILD UNDERSTAND THAT THIS
PARAGON IS PERHAPS EXAGGERATED. IN THE END,
MOTHER SAYS THAT HE CAN TRY TO BE THAT KIND OF
FATHER WHEN HE GROWS UP. USEFUL BECAUSE OF THE
EXEMPLAR ROLE OF THE FATHER. SOME CHILDREN MAY
NEED TO BE SHOWN WHAT THE ABSENCE OF THE FATHER
IN THE FAMILY MEANS. (DIFF SIT--ONE PARENT,
FAM--FATHERS, FAM--MOTHERS, FATHERS, MOTHERS, ONE
PARENT)

FEAR

COHEN, MIRIAM. WILL I HAVE A FRIEND?. MACMILLAN,
1967.   ILLUSTRATED BY LILLIAN HOBAN.   (BCB)

A REALISTIC FEAR IN A YOUNG CHILD IS SHOWN IN
A TYPICAL PICTURE OF THE FIRST DAY OF
KINDERGARTEN. CHILDREN MILL ABOUT, EACH INTENT ON
HIS OWN BUSINESS, AND JIM DOESN'T FEEL INCLUDED
UNTIL AFTER REST TIME WHEN PAUL SHOWS HIM HIS
TINY TRUCK. THIS CHARACTER PAUL ALSO APPEARS IN
"BEST FRIEND" BY THE SAME AUTHOR.
(EMOTIONS--FEAR, FEAR, FRIENDSHIP, NEW
SIT--SCHOOL)

HOBAN, RUSSELL. BEDTIME FOR FRANCES. HARPER,
1960.   ILLUSTRATED BY GARTH WILLIAMS.   (CC)

FATHER BADGER PLAYS AN IMPORTANT ROLE IN
HANDLING THE BEDTIME PROBLEMS OF HIS DAUGHTER
FRANCES WITH AN IMAGINATIVE EXPLANATION OF HER
FEARS. WHEN FRANCES, AN ENTRANCING LITTLE GIRL
WHO ONLY INCIDENTALLY HAPPENS TO BE A BADGER,
GOES THROUGH THE FAMILIAR BEDTIME ROUTINE OF
MILK, HUGS, KISSES, AND TEDDY BEAR, BUT STILL
DOES NOT FALL ASLEEP, FATHER GIVES REASSURING
ADVICE ABOUT THE IMAGINARY GIANTS AND THE
SOMETHING SCARY THAT MIGHT COME OUT OF THE CRACK
IN THE CEILING. HIS MOST CREATIVE SOLUTION,
HOWEVER, COMES WHEN FRANCES COMPLAINS OF THE
CURTAINS MOVING AT THE WINDOW--HE TELLS HER THAT
THE WIND'S JOB IS TO GO AROUND AND BLOW ALL THE
CURTAINS, THAT EVERYBODY HAS A JOB, AND THAT

FURTHERMORE, HER JOB IS TO GO TO SLEEP.
THROUGHOUT THE BOOK, FATHER IS THE PARENT WHO
RELATES TO THE CHILD, ALTHOUGH THE MOTHER IS
VISIBLE. (BEHAVIOR--DISLIKES--SLEEP,
DISLIKES--SLEEP, EMOTIONS--FEAR, FAM--FATHERS,
FATHERS, FEAR)

IWASAKI, CHIHIRO. STAYING HOME ALONE ON A RAINY
DAY. MC GRAW, 1968. ILLUSTRATED BY CHIHIRO
IWASAKI. (LJ)

   LONELINESS IS A SHARP PAIN FOR A CHILD LEFT
ALONE FOR THE FIRST TIME, AND ALLISON TRIES MANY
WAYS TO MAKE THOSE FEELINGS GO AWAY. SHE WANTS TO
HOLD HER KITTEN, SHE ENVIES THE BABY FISH
SWIMMING WITH ITS MOTHER, AND WHEN SHE TOUCHES
THE KEYS OF THE PIANO, IT ONLY REMINDS HER OF HER
MOTHER. AUTHOR-ARTIST IWASAKI HAS COMPLEMENTED
THESE FEELINGS OF FRUSTRATION WITH EXQUISITE,
WATERY, FREE-FORM WATERCOLORS, SUITING THE BROWN
AND GRAY TONES TO THE GRAY RAINY DAY SEEN THROUGH
THE WINDOW. CHILDREN IDENTIFY WITH THESE
SITUATIONS, ESPECIALLY THE TERROR OF THE PHONE
RINGING AND BEING AFRAID TO ANSWER IT. USEFUL
BECAUSE IT HELPS THE CHILD SEE THAT OTHER
CHILDREN ARE ALSO AFRAID, BUT THAT MOTHER DOES
RETURN, WHEN THE SUNSHINE RETURNS AT THE END OF
THE AFTERNOON. (EMOTIONS--FEAR,
EMOTIONS--LONELINESS, FEAR, LONELINESS)

KRAUS, ROBERT. GOOD NIGHT, RICHARD RABBIT.
SPRINGFELLOW, 1972. ILLUSTRATED BY N.M.
BODECKER. (CCB-B)

   TINY FORMAT MAKES THIS A CHARMING BEDTIME
STORY FOR THE VERY YOUNG, AS MOST YOUNGSTERS WILL
IDENTIFY WITH RICHARD RABBIT. A MIX OF REAL AND
IMAGINARY FEARS, AND A LITTLE OF DOWNRIGHT
TEASING ARE SEEN AS THE YOUNG RABBIT PRETENDS
THERE IS A FACE LOOKING IN THE WINDOW. EVERY
OTHER PAGE DEALS WITH A QUESTION OR COMMENT, THE
FACING PAGE WITH MOTHER'S ANSWER. IN ALL OF THE
ILLUSTRATIONS, RICHARD IS VERY SMALL, AND MOTHER
LOOMS VERY LARGE AND SOLID, TRULY A SECURITY
FIGURE, AND ON THE FINAL PAGE RICHARD DRIFTS OFF
TO SLEEP. (BEHAVIOR--DISLIKES--SLEEP,
DISLIKES--SLEEP, EMOTIONS--FEAR,
EMOTIONS--SECURITY, FEAR, SECURITY)

MAHY, MARGARET. A LION IN THE MEADOW. WATTS,

1969. ILLUSTRATED BY JENNY WILLIAMS. (BCB)

FEARFUL THAT THERE IS A LION IN THE MEADOW,
THE LITTLE BOY TELLS HIS MOTHER. HER SOLUTION:
SHE SAYS HE IS MAKING UP STORIES, GIVES HIM A
LITTLE MATCH BOX, AND TELLS HIM THAT THERE IS A
TINY DRAGON IN IT WHICH WILL GROW BIG AND CHASE
THE LION AWAY. THE DRAGON MATERIALIZES AND CHASES
THE LION INTO THE HOUSE, WHERE HE AND THE BOY
BECOME FRIENDS. A CROSS BETWEEN FANTASY AND FAIRY
TALE, THE STORY CAN BE USED TO DEVELOP
IMAGINATION IN CHILDREN, AS WELL AS TO DISPEL
FEARS. HANDSOME, COLORFUL ILLUSTRATIONS TEND TO
DE-EMPHASIZE ANY FEARFUL ASPECTS OF THE BOOK.
(EMOTIONS--FEAR, FEAR)

MAYER, MERCER. YOU'RE THE SCAREDY-CAT. PARENTS'
MAG, 1974. ILLUSTRATED BY MERCER MAYER. (BL)

OLDER BROTHER CONVINCES YOUNGER BROTHER TO
SLEEP OUT IN THE BACK YARD. THINKING TO SCARE THE
SMALLER YOUTH, HE TELLS STORIES OF THE GREEN
GARBAGE CAN MONSTER, WITH BEAUTIFULLY MONSTERISH
ILLUSTRATIONS. TURNS OUT HE'S THE ONE WHO HAS THE
NIGHTMARES, BUT WON'T ADMIT HE'S SCARED.
(BRAVERY, EMOTIONS--BRAVERY, EMOTIONS--FEAR, FEAR)

RESSNER, PHILIP. AT NIGHT. DUTTON, 1967.
ILLUSTRATED BY CHARLES PRATT. (ESLC)

A SERIES OF BLACK AND WHITE PHOTOGRAPHS,
APPROPRIATELY ENOUGH, LEAD THE READER'S EYE
THROUGH A NIGHT IN THE CITY. USEFUL BECAUSE IT
WILL GIVE THE READER A FEELING OF SECURITY,
KNOWING THAT THERE IS NOTHING TO FEAR FROM
DARKNESS IN ITSELF. IT SHOWS A LIFE THE CHILD
RARELY SEES, AND MAY NOT BE ABLE TO IMAGINE: THE
EMPTY SCHOOL ROOM, THE BUMPS IN THE SIDEWALK. AS
DAWN BREAKS, THE CHILD SEES THE MIRACLE OF A NEW
DAY, AS THE CIRCLE OF THE EARTH TURNS.
(EMOTIONS--FEAR, EMOTIONS--SECURITY, FEAR,
SECURITY)

ROCKWELL, HARLOW. MY DENTIST. MORROW, 1975.
ILLUSTRATED BY HARLOW ROCKWELL. (BL)

FEAR OF THE DENTIST IS NOT CONFINED TO
CHILDREN, FOR MANY ADULTS GO THROUGH LIFE WITH AN
IRRATIONAL STATE OF APPREHENSION ABOUT SUCH
VISITS. EARLY EXPOSURE TO NON-THREATENING

SITUATIONS SUCH AS THE ONES PICTURED HERE SHOULD
DO MUCH TO REDUCE THESE FEARS, FOR THE ATTRACTIVE
PIG-TAILED YOUNGSTER IS SHOWN AS INTERESTED,
SMILING AT TIMES, AND THOROUGHLY COMFORTABLE
THROUGHOUT THE PROCESS OF TEETH CLEANING. WHILE
THE INSTRUMENTS (I.E., THE PICKS AND PROBES) MAY
LOOK MENACING, THERE IS MUCH TO BE SAID FOR
SHOWING THEM IN DETAIL ALONG WITH THE X-RAY
CAMERA AND THE DRILLS. FEAR OF THE UNKNOWN IS
PERHAPS MORE THREATENING THAN FEAR OF THE KNOWN.
(DENTIST, DIFF SIT--DENTIST, EMOTIONS--FEAR, FEAR)

ROCKWELL, HARLOW. MY DOCTOR. MACMILLAN, 1973.
ILLUSTRATED BY HARLOW ROCKWELL. (BL)

    FOR A CHILD WHO IS APPREHENSIVE ABOUT A VISIT
TO THE DOCTOR, THIS PICTURE BOOK MAY PROVE TO BE
A DE-SENSITIZING INSTRUMENT. LIKE THE OBSERVABLE
DETAIL ON THE THERMOMETER AND THE SYRINGE, THE
CALM, UNEMOTIONAL CLIMATE IN THE DOCTOR'S OFFICE
IS ALSO TANGIBLE, VISIBLE PROOF THAT THE OCCASION
IS NOT ONE TO FEAR. BY BRINGING OUT INTO THE
OPEN THE SECRETS OF THE JARS OF MEDICINE, AND BY
EXPLAINING VARIOUS INSTRUMENTS AND THEIR USES IN
A COLORFUL, FRIENDLY ATMOSPHERE, THE AUTHOR HAS
PROVIDED A NEEDED MEANS OF REDUCING TENSION IN
THE MIND OF A CHILD. (DIFF SIT--DOCTOR, DOCTOR,
EMOTIONS--FEAR, FEAR)

ROCKWELL, HARLOW. MY NURSERY SCHOOL. MORROW,
1976. ILLUSTRATED BY HARLOW ROCKWELL. (BL)

    WHILE THIS BOOK DOES NOT DEAL WITH THE
ADJUSTMENT TO THE NEWNESS OF NURSERY SCHOOL, THE
PLEASANT ENVIRONMENT OF BUILDING BLOCKS AND CLAY,
PETS AND PLANTS, AND EXCITING DRESS-UP CLOTHES
SETS A POSITIVE MOOD FOR ANY CHILD WHO MIGHT FEEL
APPREHENSIVE ABOUT GOING TO NURSERY SCHOOL.
CHILDREN OF DIFFERENT RACES ARE PICTURED IN THE
COLORFUL ACTIVITIES, AS IS MR. PAUL, A MALE
TEACHER. CLEAR, FRESH COLORS GIVE THE BOOK AN
UPBEAT FEELING, AND IT IS A PLUS FOR THOSE
PERSONS LOOKING FOR EXAMPLES OF NON-TRADITIONAL
ROLES FOR CHILDREN AND ADULTS. (EMOTIONS--FEAR,
FEAR, NEW SIT--SCHOOL)

SOBOL, HARRIET. JEFF'S HOSPITAL BOOK. WALCK,
1975. ILLUSTRATED BY PATRICIA AGRE. (BL)

    PHYSICIANS FROM TWO MAJOR MEDICAL INSTITUTIONS

WERE USED AS CONSULTANTS FOR THIS HELPFUL,
ACCURATE BOOK WHICH DESCRIBES A YOUNG BOY'S
EXPERIENCE AS HE UNDERGOES SURGERY TO CORRECT
CROSSED EYES. LARGE BLACK AND WHITE PHOTOGRAPHS
GIVE A STEP-BY-STEP NO NONSENSE APPROACH TO THIS
STORY BUT, THROUGHOUT, THE HUMAN ELEMENT IS
THERE, TOO, AS WE SEE JEFF FEELING SCARED AND
WORRIED BEFORE THE OPERATION. REASSURING PICTURES
OF MOTHER AND FATHER WITH HIM AFTERWARD, AND
HORSEPLAY WITH THE NEIGHBORHOOD KIDS LEND AN
UPBEAT FEELING TO THE BOOK. (DIFF SIT--HANDICAPS,
EMOTIONS--FEAR, FEAR, HANDICAPS, HOSPITAL, NEW
SIT--HOSPITAL)

SONNEBORN, RUTH. THE LOLLIPOP PARTY. VIKING,
1967. ILLUSTRATED BY BRINTON TURKLE. (ESLC)

ONE DAY TOMAS IS LEFT ALONE IN THE APARTMENT
FOR THE FIRST TIME. HIS SISTER ANA, WHO USUALLY
CARED FOR HIM BEFORE GOING TO HER JOB, HAD TO
LEAVE HIM ALONE. STEP-BY-STEP THE READER
PARTICIPATES IN THE LITTLE BOY'S FEAR. HE WAS
CONCERNED ABOUT THE SOUND OF FOOTSTEPS ON THE
STAIRS, AND WISHED ONLY TO SIT QUIETLY AND HOLD
HIS CAT GATTO. WHEN HIS NURSERY SCHOOL TEACHER
COMES TO THE DOOR ON A VISIT, HOWEVER, THE
EMOTIONAL TONE OF THE BOOK CHANGES IMMEDIATELY.
HE IS HAPPY TO SEE HER, ACTS THE ROLE OF THE HOST
BY OFFERING HER A LOLLIPOP, AND THE STORY ENDS
WITH TOMAS FEELING A BIT GROWN-UP.
(EMOTIONS--FEAR, EMOTIONS--LONELINESS,
FAM--MOTHERS WORKING, FEAR, LONELINESS, MOTHERS
WORKING, SELF-RELIANCE)

TAMBURINE, JEAN. I THINK I WILL GO TO THE
HOSPITAL. ABINGDON, 1965. ILLUSTRATED BY JEAN
TAMBURINE. (CCB-B, LJ)

AN EXCELLENT BOOK FOR A CHILD AND HIS PARENT
TO PREPARE FOR A HOSPITAL VISIT. WHEN SUSY
DECIDES SHE DOES NOT WANT TO GO TO THE HOSPITAL,
HER MOTHER TAKES HER TO THE WAITING ROOM OF THE
HOSPITAL, AND ON THE WAY SHE STOPS WITH GET-WELL
PRESENTS FOR PEOPLE JUST OUT OF THE HOSPITAL.
THESE ARE POSITIVE CONTACTS, AND SUSY ALSO MEETS
A FRIENDLY NURSE WHO TAKES TIME TO TALK ABOUT
WHAT WILL HAPPEN TO HER. AT HOME, SHE PLAYS
HOSPITAL WITH HER PETS, AND BY THE TIME SHE
ARRIVES AT THE HOSPITAL, SHE IS RELAXED AND READY
TO HAVE HER PARENTS LEAVE. THIS IS ONE OF THE

LONGEST STORIES ON THIS SUBJECT, AND IS A FUN
BOOK FOR READING ALOUD. (EMOTIONS--FEAR, FEAR,
HOSPITAL, NEW SIT--HOSPITAL)

VIORST, JUDITH. MY MOMMA SAYS THERE AREN'T ANY
ZOMBIES, GHOSTS, VAMPIRES, CREATURES, DEMONS,
MONSTERS, FIENDS, GOBLINS, OR THINGS. ATHENEUM,
1973. ILLUSTRATED BY KAY CHORAO. (CC)

   THE FEARSOME, SCARY PICTURES IN THIS PICTURE
BOOK WILL INTRIGUE CHILDREN WHO ARE LOOKING FOR A
SCARY BOOK, EVEN THOUGH THERE ARE REASSURING
LINES OF TEXT ON EVERY PAGE. DEMONSTRATES SOME OF
THE VERY REAL FEARS THAT CHILDREN HAVE IN THE
NIGHT ABOUT IMAGINARY THINGS. (EMOTIONS--FEAR,
FEAR)

WABER, BERNARD. IRA SLEEPS OVER. HOUGHTON, 1972.
   ILLUSTRATED BY BERNARD WABER. (ESLC)

   IRA IS THE YOUNG CHILD IN A FAMILY WITH
UNDERSTANDING PARENTS, AND A SISTER FOND OF
PUT-DOWNS. WHEN HIS MOTHER AND FATHER TELL HIM
THAT IT WILL BE OK IF HE TAKES HIS TEDDY BEAR ON
HIS FIRST SLEEPOVER AT HIS FRIEND'S HOUSE, HIS
SISTER INSISTS THAT HIS FRIEND WILL LAUGH AND
THINK HE'S A BABY. HOW WILL HE FEEL SLEEPING
WITHOUT HIS TEDDY BEAR FOR THE VERY FIRST TIME?
LUCKILY IRA NEVER NEEDS TO FACE THAT SITUATION,
FOR THE CAPPER TO THE STORY IS THAT REGGIE SLEEPS
WITH HIS TEDDY BEAR, TOO, SO IRA FEELS CONFIDENT
ENOUGH TO MARCH OVER TO HIS OWN HOUSE, UP THE
STAIRS, WITH A SMUG EXPRESSION ON HIS FACE, TO
PICK UP TAH-TAH, HIS TEDDY BEAR. NOTABLE FOR ITS
RECOGNITION OF THE FACT THAT CHILDREN ENJOY
MILDLY SCARY SITUATIONS IF THERE IS AN UNDERLYING
BOLSTERING OF SECURITY, THE BOOK IS ALSO LIKELY
TO BE AROUND FOR AWHILE BECAUSE IT PICTURES AN
URBAN, CONTEMPORARY FAMILY WITH A FATHER COOKING
AT THE STOVE AND, IN ONE SCENE, A MOTHER CURLED
UP ON THE COUCH IN HER PAJAMAS. (EMOTIONS--FEAR,
EMOTIONS--SECURITY, FEAR, SECURITY)

WILLIAMS, GWENEIRA. TIMID TIMOTHY. Y. SCOTT,
1944. ILLUSTRATED BY LEONARD WEISGARD. (CC)

   A LITTLE KITTEN IS TAUGHT BY HIS MOTHER TO BE
BRAVE, AND HOW TO SCARE OTHER ANIMALS. SHE TELLS
HIM TO ARCH HIS BACK, STICK OUT HIS WHISKERS, AND
GO P-SSS-T. TO BE SURE, MOST OF THE ANIMALS HE

SCARES ARE STUFFED ANIMALS, UNTIL HE MEETS UP
WITH A PUPPY. WHEN THE PUPPY RUNS AWAY, TIMOTHY
KNOWS HOW IT FEELS TO BE BRAVE. USEFUL BECAUSE IT
SHOWS THAT MANY YOUNG ANIMALS ARE AFRAID AT
TIMES. (BRAVERY, EMOTIONS--BRAVERY,
EMOTIONS--FEAR, FEAR)

WOLDE, GUNILLA. BETSY'S FIRST DAY AT NURSERY
SCHOOL. RANDOM, 1976. ILLUSTRATED BY GUNILLA
WOLDE. (BL)

THIS SMALL, CHILD-SIZE BOOK STRIKES JUST THE
RIGHT NOTE TO DISPEL FEARS ABOUT GOING OFF TO
NURSERY SCHOOL FOR THE FIRST TIME. MOTHER WISELY
SCHEDULES A SHORT VISIT WHICH BEGINS WITH ROBERT,
ONE OF THE TEACHERS, SHOWING THEM AROUND. BETSY
IS RELUCTANT TO JOIN IN THE ACTIVITIES, AND KEEPS
HER SNOWSUIT ON, BUT A LITTLE LATER FINDS A
FRIEND. BY THE TIME MOTHER GATHERS UP THE TWO
CHILDREN TO GO HOME, BETSY FEELS MORE RELAXED,
AND IS LOOKING FORWARD TO RETURNING THE NEXT DAY.
USEFUL BECAUSE IT SHOWS THE CHILD THAT OTHER
CHILDREN ARE ALSO A LITTLE CONCERNED ABOUT BEING
LEFT AT SCHOOL. SWEDISH AUTHOR WOLDE IS
CONSISTENT IN SHOWING MALES IN NON-TRADITIONAL
ROLES IN THIS SERIES ABOUT BETSY.
(EMOTIONS--FEAR, FEAR, NEW SIT--SCHOOL)

ZOLOTOW, CHARLOTTE. MY FRIEND JOHN. HARPER,
1960. ILLUSTRATED BY BEN SHECTER. (CC)

A STUDY IN FRIENDSHIP WHICH HIGHLIGHTS THE
DIFFERENCES AS WELL AS THE WAY THE BOYS ARE
ALIKE. ONE SLEEPS WITH THE LIGHT ON AT NIGHT, THE
OTHER IS AFRAID OF CATS. FRIENDSHIP IS KNOWING A
PERSON'S FAULTS AS WELL AS INTIMATE THOUGHTS,
AND THE AUTHOR HAS CAPTURED THIS PERFECTLY AS SHE
LETS US SEE THE SECRET CRUSHES THEY BOTH HAVE ON
GIRLS. (EMOTIONS--FEAR, FEAR, FRIENDSHIP)

FRIENDSHIP

BEHRENS, JUNE. HOW I FEEL. CHILDRENS, 1973.
ILLUSTRATED BY VINCE STREANO. (CCB-B)

A BOOK TO BE USED BY A PARENT OR TEACHER, WITH
ONE CHILD OR A GROUP. THE SIMPLE SENTENCES ARE
NOT DIFFICULT TO FOLLOW, AND CHILDREN WILL EASILY
COMPREHEND THE SEVERAL LINES DEVOTED TO VARIOUS
EMOTIONS: ANGER AND HATE, AS WELL AS PRIDE AND

HAPPINESS. EACH PAGE OF TEXT FACES A FULL-PAGE
COLOR PHOTOGRAPH SHOWING YOUNG CHILDREN IN THE
CLASSROOM, ON THE PLAYGROUND, AND AT HOME,
CAREFULLY CHOSEN TO INCLUDE CHILDREN OF VARIOUS
MINORITIES. (EMOTIONS, FRIENDSHIP,
SELF-UNDERSTANDING)

BEHRENS, JUNE. TOGETHER. CHILDRENS, 1975.
ILLUSTRATED BY VINCE STREANO. (LJ)

   REALISTIC COLOR PHOTOGRAPHS ARE USED WITH
LARGE PRINT AND FAIRLY EASY-TO-READ TEXT TO SHOW
THE DIFFERENT RAMIFICATIONS OF FRIENDSHIP. IN
ADDITION TO AGE-MATES, A TEACHER, MOTHER,
GRANDMOTHER, AND A DOG NAMED CHARLIE ARE SHOWN IN
THE ROLE OF FRIENDS. AT THE END, THE BOOK ASKS
THE QUESTION, "WHO IS YOUR BEST FRIEND?" USEFUL
BECAUSE OF THE INTRODUCTION OF ADULTS, AND ALSO
BECAUSE OF THE WAY THE BOOK SHOWS THE THINGS
FRIENDS CAN SHARE. (FRIENDSHIP,
FRIENDSHIP--ADULTS)

BERSON, HAROLD. I'M BORED, MA!. CROWN, 1976.
ILLUSTRATED BY HAROLD BERSON. (BL)

   AN ENGAGING, OVERPRIVILEGED RABBIT IS THE
CHARACTER WHO IS BORED, AS THE READER SEES HIM
KICK HIS TEDDY BEAR, THROW HIS TOY HORSE IN THE
CORNER, AND FINALLY THROW HIS LOVELY YELLOW
AIRPLANE IN THE TRASH CAN. STEVE RABBIT AND HIS
MOTHER ARE A COLORFUL PAIR IN AN URBAN APARTMENT
SETTING. MOTHER WEARS AN ANKLE LENGTH COAT AND A
HEAD SCARF TIED IN THE NEW LIFE-STYLE FASHION.
HER SON WEARS A PEAKED CAP IN THE FASHION OF TV'S
CAPTAIN AND TENNILLE AND A RAKISH LONG SCARF.
PARENTS WILL NOT FEEL SORRY FOR STEVE RABBIT, BUT
MANY CHILDREN WILL IDENTIFY WITH HIM. PACK RAT,
WHO SALVAGES THE YELLOW AIRPLANE FROM THE
GARBAGE, IS DRESSED JUST AS OUTRAGEOUSLY, AND
BETWEEN THE TWO FRIENDS THE PROBLEM OF BEING
BORED IS SOLVED IN A SATISFYING WAY. (BOREDOM,
EMOTIONS--BOREDOM, FRIENDSHIP)

BONSALL, CROSBY. IT'S MINE!--A GREEDY BOOK.
HARPER, 1964. ILLUSTRATED BY CROSBY BONSALL.
(ESLC)

   MABEL ANN AND PATRICK ARE TWO PRESCHOOLERS WHO
PLAY TOGETHER EVERY DAY, WITH THEIR ASSORTED
FAVORITE TOYS. THEY REFUSE TO SHARE, AND GO HOME

MAD. BUT AT A PICNIC, WHILE THEY ARE QUARRELING
OVER A CARROT, A GOAT EATS THEIR LUNCH, AND WHAT
FOLLOWS IS AN AMAZING TURNABOUT. THE STORY ENDS
WITH "MINE" STILL THE MOST IMPORTANT WORD IN THE
STORY, BUT PATRICK IS PLAYING WITH MABEL ANN'S
RUBBER DUCK AND MABEL ANN IS WEARING PATRICK'S
FEATHER. DELICIOUS CHILD-APPEALING DRAWINGS MAKE
THE BOOK VERY ATTRACTIVE TO CHILDREN.
(BEHAVIOR--SHARING, EMOTIONS--GREED, FRIENDSHIP,
GREED, SHARING)

CARLE, ERIC. DO YOU WANT TO BE MY FRIEND?.
CROWELL, T., 1971. ILLUSTRATED BY ERIC CARLE.
(BCB, CC)

   A NOTE AT THE BEGINNING OF THIS COLORFUL
PICTURE BOOK EXPLAINS THAT THE PICTURES CAN BE
READ FROM LEFT TO RIGHT, THUS MAKING THE STORY
USEFUL FOR A YOUNG CHILD DEVELOPING READING
READINESS SKILLS. CARLE HAS TOLD A FUNNY STORY,
ALMOST WITHOUT WORDS, ABOUT A LITTLE MOUSE
SEARCHING FOR A FRIEND. HE MEETS, IN TURN, AN
ALLIGATOR, A LION, A HIPPOPOTAMUS, WHO THEN SEEM
TO BE PURSUING HIM. ALL THE WHILE HE IS TRAVELING
ALONG THE LENGTH OF A GREAT LONG GREEN SNAKE.
THE HUMOR, THE IMAGINATIVENESS, AND THE ENDEARING
QUALITIES OF THE MOUSE, MAKE IT A BOOK WHICH CAN
BE USED TO SHOW THAT FRIENDSHIP SOMETIMES BLOOMS
WHEN TWO PEOPLE ARE AFRAID. (FRIENDSHIP)

CARLSON, NATALIE. MARIE LOUISE AND CHRISTOPHE.
SCRIBNER, 1974. ILLUSTRATED BY JOSE ARUEGO. (BL)

   IN THIS STORY OF FRIENDS WHO LIKE TO PLAY
TRICKS, A MONGOOSE AND A SPOTTED GREEN SNAKE GET
INTO BIG TROUBLE WHEN THEY ARE TRAPPED. AFTER
THEY ARE FREE, CHRISTOPHE, THE LITTLE GREEN
SNAKE, PROMISES NEVER TO PLAY TRICKS AGAIN.
ALTHOUGH THE SETTING IS THE ISLAND OF MARTINIQUE,
THE THEME IS UNIVERSAL. (BEHAVIOR--TEASING,
FRIENDSHIP, TEASING)

COHEN, MIRIAM. BEST FRIENDS. MACMILLAN, 1971.
ILLUSTRATED BY LILLIAN HOBAN. (BCB)

   THE SCENE TAKES PLACE IN AN EARLY PRIMARY
CLASSROOM, AND DEMONSTRATES THE CHANGING
RELATIONSHIPS BETWEEN YOUNG CHILDREN. JIM THINKS
PAUL IS HIS BEST FRIEND, BUT DURING THE DAY OTHER
CHILDREN CLAIM THIS POSITION, AND

MISUNDERSTANDINGS DEVELOP. WHEN JIM AND PAUL
RESCUE THE EGGS IN THE INCUBATOR IN A JOINT
EFFORT, THEY RECOGNIZE THAT TRULY THEY ARE "BEST
FRIENDS." (FRIENDSHIP)

COHEN, MIRIAM. WILL I HAVE A FRIEND?. MACMILLAN,
1967.   ILLUSTRATED BY LILLIAN HOBAN.   (BCB)

   A REALISTIC FEAR IN A YOUNG CHILD IS SHOWN IN
A TYPICAL PICTURE OF THE FIRST DAY OF
KINDERGARTEN. CHILDREN MILL ABOUT, EACH INTENT ON
HIS OWN BUSINESS, AND JIM DOESN'T FEEL INCLUDED
UNTIL AFTER REST TIME WHEN PAUL SHOWS HIM HIS
TINY TRUCK. THIS CHARACTER PAUL ALSO APPEARS IN
"BEST FRIEND" BY THE SAME AUTHOR.
(EMOTIONS--FEAR, FEAR, FRIENDSHIP, NEW
SIT--SCHOOL)

DAUGHERTY, JAMES. ANDY AND THE LION. VIKING,
1938.   ILLUSTRATED BY JAMES DAUGHERTY.   (CC)

   IN ROLLICKING, RHYTHMICAL DRAWINGS, JAMES
DAUGHERTY HAS SYNTHESIZED FEELINGS OF JOY IN
LIVING AND JOY IN HELPING OTHER PEOPLE. ANDY, WHO
BEFRIENDS A LION AND REMOVES A BIG THORN FROM
HIS PAW, LATER IS THE BENEFICIARY OF THE KIND
ACT. THE LION, WHO HAS ESCAPED FROM THE CIRCUS,
RECOGNIZES ANDY AND IS IMMEDIATELY FRIENDLY.
USEFUL BECAUSE IT DEMONSTRATES IN A VERY SIMPLE
WAY HOW ONE KIND ACT MAY BE REPAID, BUT FAR
BEYOND THAT, THE AFFECTIVE ASPECTS OF LIVING ARE
STRESSED--THE SENSUOUS EFFECT OF THE EXPRESSIONS
ON FACES, THE SUBTLE HUMOR IN THE DAILY FAMILY
LIFE, AND THE VIGOROUS FEELINGS DEPICTING THE JOY
OF LIVING. (BEHAVIOR--CONSIDERATION,
BEHAVIOR--KINDNESS, CONSIDERATION,
EMOTIONS--HAPPINESS, FAM, FRIENDSHIP, HAPPINESS,
KINDNESS)

DE PAOLA, TOMIE. WATCH OUT FOR THE CHICKEN FEET
IN YOUR SOUP. PRENTICE, 1974.   ILLUSTRATED BY
TOMIE DE PAOLA.   (CC)

   LUSH COLORS MAKE THIS BOOK AN ATTRACTIVE
SETTING FOR INTRODUCING JOEY'S ITALIAN
GRANDMOTHER. JOEY BRINGS HIS FRIEND TO VISIT,
THINKING HE MAY BE EMBARRASSED BY OLD-COUNTRY
CUSTOMS, AND IS A LITTLE PUT OUT WHEN EUGENE IS
INVITED TO BAKE THE BREAD WITH GRANDMA.
DELICIOUS-SOUNDING RECIPE IS ALSO INCLUDED FOR

THE BRAIDED BREAD DOLLS. USEFUL BECAUSE OF THE
INTERACTION BETWEEN YOUNG AND OLD.
(FAM--GRANDMOTHERS, FRIENDSHIP, GRANDMOTHERS)

DUVOISIN, ROGER. LONELY VERONICA. KNOPF, 1963.
ILLUSTRATED BY ROGER DUVOISIN. (CC)

   WHEN VERONICA THE HIPPOPOTAMUS IS MAROONED IN
NEW YORK CITY IN AN ELEVATOR SHAFT FOR AN ENTIRE
WEEKEND WITHOUT FOOD, SHE LEARNS THE MEANING OF
LONELINESS, AND SHE YEARNS FOR THE PEACEFUL RIVER
COUNTRY OF HER BIRTH. LONELY VERONICA
APPRECIATES THE CONSIDERATION SHOWN HER BY A
YOUNG PIGEON, WHO BRINGS HER FOOD, AND WHO
PROMISES TO VISIT VERONICA'S NEW HOME, A PEACEFUL
POND IN THE COUNTRY. (EMOTIONS--LONELINESS,
FRIENDSHIP, LONELINESS)

HALLINAN, P.K.. WE'RE VERY GOOD FRIENDS.
CHILDRENS, 1973. ILLUSTRATED BY P.K. HALLINAN.
(CCB-B)

   TWO BROTHERS WHO REALLY ARE FRIENDS, WHO ENJOY
PLAYING TOGETHER, "ACTING CREEPY" TOGETHER,
BEING MAD AND SAD, ARE STILL GLAD TO BE BROTHERS,
AND THAT'S THE BEST REASON WHY "WE'RE VERY GOOD
FRIENDS, MY BROTHER AND I." SLIGHT STORY AND TEXT
USEFUL TO SEE THE RELATIONSHIP OF BROTHERHOOD
AND FRIENDSHIP. (BROTHERS, FAM--BROTHERS,
FRIENDSHIP)

HAWKINS, QUAIL. ANDROCLES AND THE LION. COWARD,
1970. ILLUSTRATED BY ROCCO NEGRI. (ESLC)

   A SIMPLE RETELLING OF THIS AGE-OLD STORY
ILLUSTRATES FOR THE CHILDREN OF TODAY THE MORAL
THAT ONE SHOULD BE KIND TO PEOPLE IN NEED. WHEN
THE SLAVE ANDROCLES REMOVES A THORN FROM THE
LION'S PAW, AND THE LION LEADS HIM TO FOOD AND
DRINK, THERE IS A VIVID EXAMPLE OF THE BEGINNING
OF FRIENDSHIP. LATER ON WHEN THE LION MEETS
ANDROCLES IN THE ARENA AND REFUSES TO FIGHT HIM,
THE REWARDS OF FRIENDSHIP ARE SHOWN. A STORY FOR
OLDER CHILDREN RATHER THAN YOUNGER BECAUSE OF THE
CRUELTY IMPLIED IN THE COLOSSEUM.
(BEHAVIOR--CONSIDERATION, BEHAVIOR--KINDNESS,
CONSIDERATION, FRIENDSHIP, KINDNESS)

HAZEN, BARBARA. WHY COULDN'T I BE AN ONLY KID
LIKE YOU, WIGGER. ATHENEUM, 1975. ILLUSTRATED BY

LEIGH GRANT.   (HB)

PLEASANT CLUTTER IN A LARGE FAMILY HOUSEHOLD
WHICH HAS SIX CHILDREN KEYNOTES THE FRUSTRATION
OF THE YOUNG BOY WHO TELLS THE STORY. WIGGER, HIS
FRIEND, DOESN'T HAVE TO MOP UP THE MILK THE BABY
SPILLED, OR STAND IN LINE FOR THE BATHROOM IN
THE MORNING, AND HE, THE NARRATOR, IS FRANKLY
QUITE JEALOUS. DURING HIS TIRADE HOWEVER, THE
ILLUSTRATIONS GIVE A DIFFERENT PICTURE OF WIGGER
WHO SEEMS TO LIKE WHEELING THE BABY CARRIAGE AND
BEING A PART OF THE ROUGH AND TUMBLE OF A LARGE
FAMILY. THE NARRATOR IS SURPRISED AT THE FACT
THAT AN ONLY CHILD CAN BE A LONELY CHILD. USEFUL
FOR THE CONTRASTING POINTS OF VIEW.
(EMOTIONS--JEALOUSY, FAM--ONLY CHILD, FRIENDSHIP,
JEALOUSY, ONLY CHILD)

HOBAN, RUSSELL. A BARGAIN FOR FRANCES. HARPER,
1970.   ILLUSTRATED BY LILLIAN HOBAN.   (BCB)

THELMA IS SUPPOSED TO BE THE BEST FRIEND OF
FRANCES, BUT IN THE PAST FRANCES HAS GOTTEN THE
WORST OF THE BARGAIN. ONCE AGAIN, THELMA ENDS UP
WITH THE PRIZED TEA SET THAT FRANCES WANTED, BUT
THIS TIME FRANCES PLAYS A TRICK ON THELMA, AND
SHE GETS THE BEST OF THE BARGAIN. THEY END UP
FRIENDS, NEVERTHELESS. USEFUL TO SHOW
ASSERTIVENESS CAN BE A GOOD QUALITY IN A
RELATIONSHIP. (FRIENDSHIP, SELF-DEVELOPMENT)

HOBAN, RUSSELL. BEST FRIENDS FOR FRANCES.
HARPER, 1969.   ILLUSTRATED BY LILLIAN HOBAN.
(BCB)

THE LITTLE BADGERS IN THIS STORY DEMONSTRATE
THE POIGNANCY OF A LITTLE SISTER BEING LEFT OUT
WHEN OLDER BOYS AND GIRLS ARE PLAYING. A NO-GIRLS
AND NO-BOYS SITUATION FOLLOWS, BUT ALL IS
HAPPINESS WHEN FRANCES PACKS UP A SCRUMPTIOUS
PICNIC FOR ALBERT AND THE YOUNGER SISTER GLORIA.
(BEHAVIOR--SHARING, FAM--SISTERS, FRIENDSHIP,
SHARING, SISTERS)

HOBAN, RUSSELL. TOM AND THE TWO HANDLES. HARPER,
1965.   ILLUSTRATED BY LILLIAN HOBAN.   (ESLC)

KENNY AND TOM ARE ALWAYS FIGHTING, AND TOM
ALWAYS GETS A BLOODY NOSE. HIS DAD TELLS HIM THAT
THERE IS MORE THAN ONE WAY TO SOLVE THE PROBLEM.

YOU CAN FIGHT AGAIN, OR YOU CAN MAKE UP WITH
YOUR BEST FRIEND. TOM TRIES TO BE FRIENDS, BUT
THEY CONTINUE TO FIGHT UNTIL TOM'S FATHER GIVES
HIM SOME BOXING LESSONS. WHEN TOM WINS THE FIGHT,
THEN THEY MAKE UP, AND TOM FINDS THAT THERE WAS
ANOTHER WAY TO LOOK AT IT. (ANGER,
BEHAVIOR--QUARRELING, EMOTIONS--ANGER,
FRIENDSHIP, QUARRELING)

HOFF, SYD. WHO WILL BE MY FRIENDS?. HARPER,
1960. ILLUSTRATED BY SYD HOFF. (ESLC)

FREDDY MOVES TO A NEW NEIGHBORHOOD AND HAS NO
ONE TO PLAY WITH. HE FINALLY COMES TO A GROUP OF
BOYS WHO ARE PLAYING BALL. HE THROWS HIS BALL UP
IN THE AIR AND CATCHES IT SEVERAL TIMES. THEN THE
BOYS ASK HIM TO JOIN THEIR GAME. THIS
EASY-TO-READ BOOK EXEMPLIFIES THE FACT THAT YOU
NEED TO GO OUT AND SEARCH FOR FRIENDS, AND SHOW
PEOPLE THAT YOU CAN DO SOMETHING COMPETENTLY.
(FRIENDSHIP, MOVING, NEW SIT--MOVING,
SELF-RELIANCE)

JOHNSTON, TONY. MOLE AND TROLL TRIM THE TREE.
PUTNAM, 1974. ILLUSTRATED BY WALLACE TRIPP. (BL)

CHRISTMASY RED AND GREEN COLORS SET THE STAGE
FOR THIS STORY OF TWO FRIENDS WHO WANTED TO SHARE
THEIR CHRISTMAS TREE BUT WHO FOUND IT VERY
DIFFICULT TO DECIDE SUCH THINGS AS WHETHER A STAR
OR ANGEL WAS BETTER FOR THE TOP OF THE TREE.
DIFFERENCES ARE RESOLVED AFTER A QUARREL AND THE
BOOK ENDS ON A POSITIVE NOTE OF SHARING, WITH THE
DECORATED TREE BEING TRANSPORTED OUT INTO THE
FOREST. OBSERVANT CHILDREN WILL WONDER HOW THE
ELECTRIC LIGHTS CAN FUNCTION OUT IN THE WOODS.
(BEHAVIOR--SHARING, FRIENDSHIP, SHARING)

JUSTUS, MAY. NEW BOY IN SCHOOL. HASTINGS, 1963.
ILLUSTRATED BY JOAN PAYNE. (CC)

A BOOK FOR THIRD-GRADE READERS, THIS STORY OF
LENNIE, THE ONLY NEGRO IN HIS FIRST-GRADE
CLASSROOM, IS SOMEWHAT ARTIFICIAL IN ITS DIALOG
YET PRESENTS A REASSURING PICTURE TO CHILDREN WHO
MIGHT BE IN THE SAME SITUATION. HE IS WELCOMED
BY A SPECIAL FRIEND WHO MAKES HIM FEEL AT HOME,
AND THE STORY ENDS WITH BOTH OF THEM IN THE
SCHOOL PROGRAM SINGING A SONG LENNIE'S DADDY SANG
TO HIM AT NIGHT. (FRIENDSHIP, NEW SIT--SCHOOL)

JUSTUS, MAY. A NEW HOME FOR BILLY. HASTINGS,
1966. ILLUSTRATED BY JOAN PAYNE. (BCB)

WHEN SIX-YEAR-OLD BILLY MOVES TO A NEW
NEIGHBORHOOD HE FINDS OUT THAT NOT ALL PEOPLE
WILL RENT TO NEGROES, AT LEAST NOT AT THE TIME
THIS BOOK WAS WRITTEN. A USEFUL FACT FOR ALL
CHILDREN TO KNOW. THE NEW HOUSE, THOUGH IN NEED
OF REPAIR, HAS AN APPLE TREE IN THE YARD AND IS A
GREAT IMPROVEMENT OVER THE DIRTY SLUM AREA HE
MOVED FROM. AFTER AN INITIAL PERIOD OF
LONELINESS, BILLY MAKES FRIENDS BECAUSE OF THE
SWING, A SLIDE, A JUMPING BAR, AND A SEESAW
CONSTRUCTED BY HIS FATHER. THE BOOK ENDS WITH
FRIENDS, BLACK AND WHITE, HELPING TO PAINT THE
HOUSE. (EMOTIONS--LONELINESS, FRIENDSHIP,
LONELINESS, MOVING, NEW SIT--MOVING)

KAFKA, SHERRY. I NEED A FRIEND. PUTNAM, 1971.
ILLUSTRATED BY EROS KEITH. (BL)

EXPLORES THE DIFFERENT ROLES A FRIEND CAN
PLAY, AS LISTED BY A LITTLE GIRL PLAYING ALONE IN
HER BACK YARD WITH TWO KITTENS. THE STORY HAS A
SATISFACTORY ENDING AS WE SEE A GIRL JUST HER AGE
AND THE MOVING VAN UNLOADING NEXT DOOR. THEY
SHARE A PICNIC ON THE LAST PAGE OF THE BOOK.
UNUSUAL IN THAT IT CATALOGS THE PERSONAL NEEDS AS
FELT BY THE CHILD. (FRIENDSHIP,
SELF-UNDERSTANDING)

KANTROWITZ, MILDRED. GOOD-BYE KITCHEN. PARENTS'
MAG, 1972. ILLUSTRATED BY MERCER MAYER. (CCB-B)

AN ORIGINAL APPROACH TO MOVING DAY, AS EMILY
AND HER FRIEND RUFIE SIT ON THE STEPS AND WATCH
THE MOVING VAN. AS THEY SIT AND MUNCH ON A BAG
LUNCH, EMILY RECOUNTS IN HER IMAGINATION THE
MEMORIES OF THE FURNITURE--"GOOD-BYE, WHITE
DISHES WITH YOUR YELLOW BORDERS"--AND THE
MEMORIES OF HER BEST FRIEND JUNIE. UP UNTIL THIS
POINT THE READER THINKS IT IS EMILY WHO IS
MOVING, BUT NO, IT IS SHE WHO IS LEFT BEHIND. AS
EMILY STARTS TO LEAVE HER VANTAGE POINT, ANOTHER
MOVING VAN PULLS UP, AND SHE IS DELIGHTED TO SEE
A GIRL'S BICYCLE JUST HER SIZE, AND IS HAPPY IN
ANTICIPATION OF THE NEW FRIEND IN THE OFFING.
(FRIENDSHIP, MOVING, NEW SIT--MOVING)

KANTROWITZ, MILDRED. I WONDER IF HERBIE'S HOME

YET. PARENTS' MAG, 1971.   ILLUSTRATED BY TONY
DELUNA.   (BCB)

   WHEN SMOKEY THINKS HIS BEST FRIEND HAS
DESERTED HIM FOR LESTER PINKNEY, HE BEGINS TO
THINK ABOUT ALL THE FAVORS HE HAS DONE FOR
HERBIE, GETTING ANGRIER AND ANGRIER. WHEN SMOKEY
FINDS OUT THAT IT WAS JUST A MISUNDERSTANDING, HE
SITS AND THINKS OF ALL OF HERBIE'S GOOD POINTS.
(FRIENDSHIP)

KEATS, EZRA. LOUIE. GREENWILLOW, 1975.
ILLUSTRATED BY EZRA KEATS.   (CCB-B, CSM, HB, SLJ)

   LOUIE, A YOUNG BOY IN A SLUM NEIGHBORHOOD WHO
DOES NOT SPEAK, COMES ALIVE WHEN HE SEES A PUPPET
NAMED GUSSIE AT A PUPPET SHOW. THE READER SENSES
THE LONELINESS OF LOUIE IN A BEAUTIFUL DREAM
SEQUENCE, AND ALL CHILDREN WILL APPRECIATE THE
ENDING, WHEN LOUIE RECEIVES GUSSIE AS A GENEROUS
GIFT FROM THE CHILDREN WHO MADE HER.
(BEHAVIOR--SHARING, EMOTIONS--LONELINESS,
FRIENDSHIP, LONELINESS, SHARING)

LOBEL, ARNOLD. FROG AND TOAD ARE FRIENDS.
HARPER, 1970.   ILLUSTRATED BY ARNOLD LOBEL.   (BCB)

   AN EASY-TO-READ FORMAT IS USED FOR FIVE
STORIES OF GENTLE RELATIONSHIPS BETWEEN TWO GOOD
FRIENDS: FROG HELPS TOAD LOOK FOR THE LOST
BUTTONS ON HIS JACKET, ROUSES TOAD FROM HIS LONG
WINTER SLEEP, AND LAUGHS AT HIS OLD-FASHIONED
STRIPED BATHING SUIT. THE QUALITIES OF FRIENDSHIP
ARE ILLUMINATED WELL: LOVING CARE FOR ANOTHER
PERSON, YET A HEALTHY HUMOR WHICH ALLOWS ONE
FRIEND TO LAUGH AT ANOTHER WITHOUT HARMING THE
FRIENDSHIP. (EMOTIONS--LOVE, FRIENDSHIP, LOVE)

MARSHALL, JAMES. GEORGE AND MARTHA. HOUGHTON,
1972.   ILLUSTRATED BY JAMES MARSHALL.   (CC)

   FIVE VERY SHORT STORIES FOR THE VERY YOUNG
ABOUT GEORGE AND MARTHA, HUGE HIPPOS WHO LIVE
LIKE HUMANS, GIVE THE READER SOME GOOD HUMAN
ADVICE: ALWAYS TELL THE TRUTH TO YOUR BEST
FRIEND, SO YOU DON'T HAVE TO POUR YOUR UNWANTED
SPLIT PEA SOUP IN YOUR SNEAKERS. ALSO, YOU MAY
GET THE BATHTUB DUMPED ON YOUR HEAD IF YOU PEEK
IN THE BATHROOM WINDOW WHEN YOU SHOULDN'T. BEING
TRUTHFUL, RESPECTING PRIVACY, LOOKING ON THE

BRIGHT SIDE OF THINGS, CHEERING YOU UP, THESE ARE
SOME OF THE THINGS THAT GOOD FRIENDS DO FOR ONE
ANOTHER. (BEHAVIOR--CONSIDERATION, CONSIDERATION,
FRIENDSHIP)

MARSHALL, JAMES. GEORGE AND MARTHA ENCORE.
HOUGHTON, 1973. ILLUSTRATED BY JAMES MARSHALL.
(CC)

   GOOD FRIENDS MARTHA AND GEORGE APPEAR IN FIVE
SHORT STORIES WHICH EXTOL THE BLESSINGS OF A GOOD
RELATIONSHIP: GEORGE DOESN'T SAY "I TOLD YOU SO"
WHEN MARTHA GETS SUNBURNED. WHEN MARTHA IS
FRUSTRATED OVER THE WEEDS IN HER GARDEN, GEORGE
IN A TRULY THOUGHTFUL ACT RUSHES OUT TO THE
FLORIST TO BUY TULIPS TO STICK IN THE GROUND AS A
SURPRISE. THOUGHTFULNESS AND PROTECTING THE
FEELINGS OF THE OTHER PERSON ARE TWO OF THE
IMPORTANT ELEMENTS IN THE BOOK.
(BEHAVIOR--CONSIDERATION, CONSIDERATION,
FRIENDSHIP)

PRATHER, RAY. NEW NEIGHBORS. MC GRAW, 1975.
ILLUSTRATED BY RAY PRATHER. (CCB-B)

   WHEN RICHY MOVES TO A NEW, UNFRIENDLY SUBURBAN
NEIGHBORHOOD, HE TRIES TO MAKE FRIENDS BY
SELLING SOME OLD TOYS HE FINDS IN THE HOUSE. THIS
DRAWS THE OTHER BLACK CHILDREN INTO HIS YARD. AT
FIRST THEY TRY TO PLAY TRICKS ON HIM, BUT
LUCKILY RICHY LAUGHS, AND IS ASKED TO JOIN THE
GANG. DEMONSTRATES HOW ONE CHILD OVERCAME THE
DIFFICULTY OF FINDING NEW FRIENDS. (FRIENDSHIP,
MOVING, NEW SIT--MOVING)

SHARMAT, MARJORIE. GLADYS TOLD ME TO MEET HER
HERE. HARPER, 1970. ILLUSTRATED BY EDWARD
FRASCINO. (BCB)

   IRVING IS A SMALL BOY WHO REMINISCES ABOUT HIS
UNIQUE FRIENDSHIP WITH GLADYS. AS HE WALKS
AROUND LOOKING FOR HER, HIS ATTITUDE CHANGES WITH
THE DEGREE OF HIS FATIGUE--HE SOON IS
BAD-MOUTHING HER. WHEN HE FINALLY MEETS HER AT
THE APPOINTED MEETING PLACE, ALL IS FORGIVEN. THE
LESSON MAY BE TO WAIT IN ONE PLACE WHEN MEETING
SOMEONE BUT, NEVERTHELESS, THE MANY WAYS OF
FRIENDSHIP ARE EXPLORED. (FRIENDSHIP)

SHARMAT, MARJORIE. SOPHIE AND GUSSIE. MACMILLAN,

1973.   ILLUSTRATED BY LILLIAN HOBAN.   (HB, LJ, TLS)

TWO SQUIRRELS ARE FEATURED IN FOUR SEPARATE STORIES OF FRIENDLY ACTIVITIES SUCH AS COOKING AND BAKING, VISITING FOR THE WEEKEND, ENTERTAINING AT PARTIES, AND EXCHANGING HATS. NOT MUCH FOR BOYS IN THIS ONE, BUT IT DOES ILLUSTRATE THE KINDS OF INTERPLAY THAT MAKE UP ADULT FRIENDSHIPS. (FRIENDSHIP)

STEIG, WILLIAM. AMOS AND BORIS. FARRAR, 1971. ILLUSTRATED BY WILLIAM STEIG. (BCB)

IN A BEAUTIFUL SEA GREEN BOOK, STEIG HAS TOLD A STORY SIMILAR TO ANDROCLES AND THE LION, WHEREIN A WHALE SAVES THE LIFE OF AMOS THE MOUSE WHEN HE IS SHIPWRECKED. LATER, BORIS THE WHALE IS WASHED ASHORE DURING A HURRICANE, AND THE MOUSE BRINGS TWO ELEPHANTS TO PUSH THE WHALE BACK INTO THE WATER. POINTS OUT THE FACT THAT FRIENDSHIP CAN BE BASED ON MUTUAL HELP--EVEN THOUGH THE FRIENDS MIGHT NOT SEE EACH OTHER IN THE FUTURE. (BEHAVIOR--CONSIDERATION, CONSIDERATION, FRIENDSHIP)

TURKLE, BRINTON. THY FRIEND OBADIAH. VIKING, 1969.   ILLUSTRATED BY BRINTON TURKLE.   (BCB)

OBADIAH, A YOUNG QUAKER BOY, IS ANGRY WHEN A SEA GULL TRIES TO BE HIS FRIEND BY TAGGING ALONG BEHIND HIM IN THIS EXCELLENT PORTRAYAL OF QUAKER FAMILY LIFE. AS THE STORY PROGRESSES, THE GULL GETS A LARGE RUSTY FISHHOOK CAUGHT IN HIS BEAK, OBADIAH TAKES IT OUT, AND THE SEA GULL FLIES AWAY. WHEN THE GULL RETURNS, OBADIAH REASONS: "SINCE I HELPED HIM, I'M HIS FRIEND, TOO." TURKLE'S WATERCOLORS EVOKE A POWERFUL FEELING OF A COZY, SECURE LIFE IN THE DAYS WHEN THE FAMILY GATHERED AROUND THE FIREPLACE WHILE THE BREAD WAS BAKING. (EMOTIONS--LOVE, EMOTIONS--SECURITY, FAM, FRIENDSHIP, LOVE, SECURITY)

UDRY, JANICE. LET'S BE ENEMIES. HARPER, 1961. ILLUSTRATED BY MAURICE SENDAK. (CC)

DELICATE PINK AND GREEN WATERCOLORS BELIE SENDAK'S VIGOROUS, BLOCKY LITTLE BOYS, BUT SOMEHOW ARE HARMONIOUS WITH THE TEXT. THIS IS THE STORY OF A FRIENDSHIP SO ENDURING THAT THE BOYS'

EVEN HAVE CHICKEN POX TOGETHER--IN THE SAME BED.
BUT IN THE DAY-TO-DAY CONTACTS, THE BOYS END UP
IN SOME ABRASIVE SITUATIONS, AND THE NARRATOR
GROUSES ABOUT JAMES: HE ALWAYS WANTS TO BE BOSS.
IN THE CONCLUDING PAGES, HOWEVER, THE SUN BEGINS
TO SHINE, THE ARTIST'S BOYS BEGIN TO WALK INTO
THE FRAMES INSTEAD OF OUT OF THEM, AND THEY SKATE
OFF TOGETHER, JOINED BY A PRETZEL AND ONE PAIR
OF SKATES BETWEEN THEM. A COMFORTING STORY WHICH
IS APPEALING IN ITS REALISTIC VIEW OF THE
LOVE/HATE RELATIONSHIP WHICH CAN EXIST IN THE
BEST OF FRIENDSHIPS. (BEHAVIOR--QUARRELING,
BEHAVIOR--SHARING, FRIENDSHIP, QUARRELING,
SHARING)

VIORST, JUDITH. ROSIE AND MICHAEL. ATHENEUM,
1974. ILLUSTRATED BY LORNA TOMEI. (CC)

   ILLUSTRATED IN EXTREMELY REALISTIC BLACK AND
WHITE DRAWINGS WHICH ARE OCCASIONALLY GROTESQUE,
THIS BOOK IS NEVERTHELESS FULL OF FUNNY,
ENTERTAINING SITUATIONS WHICH ILLUSTRATE THE
DEPTHS OF THE FRIENDSHIP. EXAMPLE: "JUST BECAUSE
I CALL HER A GORILLA FACE DOESN'T MEAN THAT
ROSIE'S NOT MY FRIEND." ROSIE IS DEPICTED WITH A
GORILLA'S FACE. (FRIENDSHIP)

ZOLOTOW, CHARLOTTE. THE HATING BOOK. HARPER,
1969. ILLUSTRATED BY BEN SHECTER. (RLHR)

   A SMALL GIRL KNOWS SHE HATES HER FRIEND, BUT
CAN'T MUSTER UP HER COURAGE TO ASK HER WHY SHE IS
ACTING IN A MEAN WAY. WHEN SHE FINALLY DOES ASK,
SHE FINDS OUT THAT IT REALLY WAS A
MISUNDERSTANDING THAT STARTED ALL OF THE
UNFRIENDLINESS. MORAL IS THAT IT IS BETTER TO TRY
TO FIND OUT THE FACTS WHEN YOU FACE A PROBLEM.
(EMOTIONS--HATE, FRIENDSHIP, HATE)

ZOLOTOW, CHARLOTTE. JANEY. HARPER, 1973.
ILLUSTRATED BY RONALD HIMLER. (CC)

   A PERCEPTIVE STORY OF THE LONELINESS THAT A
LITTLE GIRL FEELS AFTER HER FRIEND MOVES AWAY.
TOLD IN A MONOLOG, CATALOGING THE WAYS IN WHICH
SHE MISSES HER FRIEND JANEY, THE BOOK SHOWS
INCIDENTS IN THE PRESENT WHICH REMIND THE LITTLE
GIRL OF THE IMPORTANT MEMORIES IN THE PAST,
WALKING HOME TOGETHER FROM SCHOOL, CHRISTMAS
PRESENTS. THE SITUATIONS DESCRIBED ARE OFTEN

SENSUOUS. THE MEMORIES OF JANEY TOUCHING
EVERYTHING AS SHE WALKED ALONG THE STREET, THE
SOUND OF HER VOICE, THE MEMORIES OF THE SOUND OF
THE WIND BLOWING THROUGH THE TREES. IT IS A BOOK
WHICH ENDS ON A POSITIVE NOTE, AND ONE FEELS
GOOD, NOT SAD, ABOUT THE SHARED MEMORIES.
(EMOTIONS--LONELINESS, FRIENDSHIP, LONELINESS)

ZOLOTOW, CHARLOTTE. MY FRIEND JOHN. HARPER,
1960. ILLUSTRATED BY BEN SHECTER. (CC)

A STUDY IN FRIENDSHIP WHICH HIGHLIGHTS THE
DIFFERENCES AS WELL AS THE WAY THE BOYS ARE
ALIKE. ONE SLEEPS WITH THE LIGHT ON AT NIGHT, THE
OTHER IS AFRAID OF CATS. FRIENDSHIP IS KNOWING A
PERSON'S FAULTS AS WELL AS INTIMATE THOUGHTS,
AND THE AUTHOR HAS CAPTURED THIS PERFECTLY AS SHE
LETS US SEE THE SECRET CRUSHES THEY BOTH HAVE ON
GIRLS. (EMOTIONS--FEAR, FEAR, FRIENDSHIP)

ZOLOTOW, CHARLOTTE. THE NEW FRIEND. ABELARD,
1968. ILLUSTRATED BY ARVIS STEWART. (ESLC)

STRONG WATERCOLOR PAINTINGS IN DEEP PURPLES,
YELLOWS, AND GREENS COMPETE WITH THE RATHER QUIET
STORY OF FRIENDSHIP AND, SUBSEQUENTLY, A LOST
FRIEND. THE LITTLE GIRL CRIES ALL DAY, THEN
DREAMS OF A NEW FRIEND, AND CONSOLES HERSELF AS
SHE THINKS THAT SHE MIGHT FORGET, AND NOT CARE
ABOUT THE OLD FRIEND, THUS SOMEWHAT RESOLVING HER
HURT FEELINGS. (EMOTIONS--LONELINESS,
FRIENDSHIP, LONELINESS)

ZOLOTOW, CHARLOTTE. A TIGER CALLED THOMAS.
LOTHROP, 1963. ILLUSTRATED BY KURT WERTH. (CC)

SHY THOMAS SITS ON THE PORCH OF HIS NEW HOUSE
AND REFUSES TO TRY TO MAKE NEW FRIENDS. HE IS
VERY OBSERVANT, HOWEVER, AND IS AWARE OF GERALD,
WHO PLAYS BALL ALONE, AND OF MARIE, AND OTHER
PEOPLE IN THE NEIGHBORHOOD. GIVEN CONFIDENCE BY
DRESSING UP IN A TIGER SUIT ON HALLOWEEN, HE
TAKES ON SOME OF THE COURAGE OF THE BEAST, AND
VISITS ALL OF THE HOUSES IN THE NEIGHBORHOOD.
WHEN PEOPLE ASK HIM TO VISIT AND PLAY, HE
REALIZES THAT THEY ALL LIKE HIM, AND HE DECIDES
THAT HE ALSO LIKES THEM. (EMOTIONS--SHYNESS,
FRIENDSHIP, MOVING, NEW SIT--MOVING,
SELF-CONFIDENCE, SHYNESS)

ZOLOTOW, CHARLOTTE. THE UNFRIENDLY BOOK. HARPER,
1975. ILLUSTRATED BY WILLIAM DU BOIS. (CCB-B)

AFTER HEARING BERTHA BA)-MOUTH ALL HER
FRIENDS, JUDY DECIDES THAT SHE REALLY DOESN'T
LIKE BERTHA. ILLUSTRATES THE WAYS IN WHICH PEOPLE
JUDGE ONLY ONE SIDE OF A PERSON. BERTHA SAID
THAT MARILYN WAS UGLY BECAUSE HER TEETH STUCK
OUT. JUDY COUNTERS WITH THE STATEMENT: "SHE KNOWS
MORE POETRY BY HEART THAN ANYONE I EVER KNEW."
(FRIENDSHIP)

FRIENDSHIP--ADULTS

ARDIZONNE, EDWARD. LUCY BROWN AND MR. GRIMES.
WALCK, 1971. ILLUSTRATED BY EDWARD ARDIZONNE.
(CC)

THIS BOOK HAS A FAIRY-TALE QUALITY WHICH MAKES
IT SOMETHING OF A FANTASY: A LONELY LITTLE
ORPHAN GIRL MEETS A LONELY OLD MAN AND THEY
BECOME GREAT FRIENDS. WHEN MR. GRIMES FALLS ILL
AND MUST MOVE TO THE COUNTRY, HE ASKS LUCY TO GO
WITH HIM, WITH LUCY'S AUNT'S PERMISSION. MR.
GRIMES, WHO IS VERY WEALTHY, IS GENEROUS WITH HIS
MONEY, AND LUCY BUYS NEW CLOTHING. ILLUSTRATES
THE POINT THAT THERE ARE THINGS IN COMMON FOR THE
YOUNG AND THE OLD. THE OLD MAN AND THE LITTLE
GIRL WALK TOGETHER, HAVE TEA TOGETHER, AND NEVER
FEEL LONELY. (DIFF SIT--OLD AGE,
EMOTIONS--LONELINESS, FRIENDSHIP--ADULTS,
LONELINESS, OLD AGE)

BEHRENS, JUNE. TOGETHER. CHILDRENS, 1975.
ILLUSTRATED BY VINCE STREANO. (LJ)

REALISTIC COLOR PHOTOGRAPHS ARE USED WITH
LARGE PRINT AND FAIRLY EASY-TO-READ TEXT TO SHOW
THE DIFFERENT RAMIFICATIONS OF FRIENDSHIP. IN
ADDITION TO AGE-MATES, A TEACHER, MOTHER,
GRANDMOTHER, AND A DOG NAMED CHARLIE ARE SHOWN IN
THE ROLE OF FRIENDS. AT THE END, THE BOOK ASKS
THE QUESTION, "WHO IS YOUR BEST FRIEND?" USEFUL
BECAUSE OF THE INTRODUCTION OF ADULTS, AND ALSO
BECAUSE OF THE WAY THE BOOK SHOWS THE THINGS
FRIENDS CAN SHARE. (FRIENDSHIP,
FRIENDSHIP--ADULTS)

SHARMAT, MARJORIE. REX. HARPER, 1967.
ILLUSTRATED BY EMILY MC CULLY. (HB)

IN THIS HANDSOMELY ILLUSTRATED PICTURE BOOK,
REX GOES TO VISIT A NEIGHBOR, UNBEKNOWN TO HIS
MOTHER. THE OLD GENTLEMAN WELCOMES THE LITTLE BOY
(WHO PRETENDS HE IS A DOG) AND THE BEGINNINGS OF
A FINE FRIENDSHIP ARE SEEN. USEFUL BECAUSE OF
THE PLEASURE BOTH MAN AND BOY RECEIVE AS THEY
JOIN IN THE MAKE-BELIEVE PLAY. (DIFF SIT--OLD
AGE, FRIENDSHIP--ADULTS, OLD AGE)

FRUSTRATION

KLIMOWICZ, BARBARA. FRED, FRED, USE YOUR HEAD.
ABINGDON, 1966. ILLUSTRATED BY FRANK ALOISE.
(CCB-B)

AN OVERLY DIDACTIC BOOK WHICH NEVERTHELESS MAY
PROVE USEFUL TO SOME PARENTS AND SOME CHILDREN.
FRED LEARNS TO USE HIS HEAD TO HELP HIMSELF
RATHER THAN RELY ON HIS PARENTS TO FIND HIS TOYS,
TO OPEN THE DOOR, TO GET A DRINK. THE ULTIMATE
IN LEARNING IS PROVEN WHEN FRED SUGGESTS TO HIS
FRIEND MELISSA: "USE YOUR HEAD," IN ORDER TO
SOLVE THE PROBLEM OF HOW TO MAKE A SWING.
(EMOTIONS--FRUSTRATION, FRUSTRATION,
SELF-RELIANCE)

KRAUS, ROBERT. LEO THE LATE BLOOMER. WINDMILL,
1971. ILLUSTRATED BY JOSE ARUEGO. (BCB)

IMAGINATIVE ILLUSTRATIONS CARRY THE MESSAGE
AND EXTEND IT MIGHTILY IN THIS STORY OF A YOUNG
TIGER, WHO STILL HAS HIS BABY FAT, MAKING HIM A
VERY APPEALING PROTAGONIST. LEO HAS A GAGGLE OF
FRIENDS--OWL, ELEPHANT, SNAKE, BIRD, AND
CROCODILE--ALL OF WHOM CAN READ, WRITE, DRAW, EAT
NEATLY, AND HE FEELS VERY INADEQUATE. BUT,
BECAUSE LEO IS A LATE BLOOMER, HE EVENTUALLY
MAKES IT, AND GIVES REASSURANCE TO TEACHERS,
PARENTS, AND ALL "LATE BLOOMERS."
(EMOTIONS--FRUSTRATION, FRUSTRATION,
SELF-CONFIDENCE, SELF-CONSCIOUSNESS)

VIORST, JUDITH. ALEXANDER AND THE TERRIBLE,
HORRIBLE, NO GOOD, VERY BAD DAY. ATHENEUM, 1972.
ILLUSTRATED BY RAY CRUZ. (BCB)

ALEXANDER KNOWS HE'S GOING TO FEEL BAD ALL DAY
BECAUSE FROM THE TIME HE GETS OUT OF BED WITH
GUM IN HIS HAIR, PAST LUNCHTIME WHEN HIS FRIEND
GETS TWO CUPCAKES IN HIS LUNCH BUT ALEXANDER'S

MOM FORGETS HIS DESSERT ENTIRELY, THINGS GO
WRONG. BY EVENING HIS FRUSTRATIONS HAVE
MULTIPLIED, BUT HE SEEMS TO SETTLE DOWN TO SLEEP
WHEN HIS MOM TELLS HIM THAT "SOME DAYS ARE LIKE
THAT." A LITTLE HOMILY ON MAKING THE BEST OF
THINGS WHEN LIFE DOESN'T GO SMOOTHLY.
(EMOTIONS--FRUSTRATION, FRUSTRATION)

WILDSMITH, BRIAN. THE LITTLE WOOD DUCK. WATTS,
1973. ILLUSTRATED BY BRIAN WILDSMITH. (CC)

   LITTLE WOOD DUCK LIVES IN A THICKET WITH HIS
MOTHER AND FIVE BROTHERS AND SISTERS. THE FIRST
TIME HE JUMPED IN THE WATER HE FOUND HE COULD
SWIM ONLY IN CIRCLES, AND HIS MOTHER BECAME
ANGRY, AND THE ANIMALS OF THE FOREST TEASED HIM.
WHEN WISE OLD OWL DIAGNOSED THE TROUBLE (ONE FOOT
WAS LARGER THAN THE OTHER), HE TOLD THE LITTLE
DUCKLING TO PAY NO ATTENTION TO THE TEASING.
LATER, WHEN WOOD DUCK'S EFFORTS AT SWIMMING IN
CIRCLES DIVERTED THE FOX, EVERYONE DECLARED HIM A
HERO, AND THEY PROMISED NEVER TO TEASE HIM
AGAIN. USEFUL BECAUSE IT ILLUMINATES THE WAY IN
WHICH A HANDICAP MAY BECOME A BLESSING, AND
DEMONSTRATES THAT MINDLESS TEASING IS
UNDESIRABLE. (BEHAVIOR--TEASING, DIFF
SIT--HANDICAPS, EMOTIONS--FRUSTRATION,
FRUSTRATION, HANDICAPS, TEASING)

GRANDFATHERS

   BORACK, BARBARA. GRANDPA. HARPER, 1967.
   ILLUSTRATED BY BEN SHECTER. (BCB, BL)

   THIS GRANDPA SEEMS ALMOST TOO GOOD TO BE TRUE.
WE'RE NOT SURE OF THE VINTAGE, BECAUSE HE
LISTENS TO THE RADIO AND RUNS A TINY STORE, BUT
WHATEVER THE VINTAGE, IT IS A LOVING PICTURE OF
THE RELATIONSHIP BETWEEN GRANDDAUGHTER, ABOUT AGE
FOUR, AND GRANDDAD, WHO IS A YOUNG OLDSTER. HE
ALWAYS HAS TIME TO PLAY HIDE-AND-SEEK, TO MAKE A
NOISE LIKE A CHICKEN, AND TO GIVE HER SYMPATHY
WHEN SHE NEEDS IT. USEFUL BECAUSE IT DEFINES THE
ROLE OF GRANDPARENTS, I.E., THEY DO PERFORM
FUNCTIONS THAT ARE DIFFERENT FROM PARENTS.
(FAM--GRANDFATHERS, GRANDFATHERS)

   BUCKLEY, HELEN. GRANDFATHER AND I. LOTHROP,
   1959. ILLUSTRATED BY PAUL GALDONE. (CC)

HELEN BUCKLEY WROTE FAMILY STORIES ABOUT
GRANDPARENTS IN THE 1950'S AND THEY ARE AS VALID
NOW AS IN 1959. IN LARGE TYPE, AND LARGE COLORFUL
ILLUSTRATIONS, THE STORY IS TOLD OF THE JOYS OF
NOT HURRYING, OF A BOY AND HIS GRANDFATHER WHO
TAKE WALKS AND TAKE TIME TO LOOK FOR THINGS SUCH
AS BIRDS AND SQUIRRELS AND EVEN SNAILS.
CONTRASTING ARE EXAMPLES OF THE HUSTLE AND BUSTLE
OF HURRYING MOTHERS, DADS, TRAFFIC, AND OLDER
CHILDREN. "EVERYONE ELSE IS ALWAYS IN A HURRY BUT
WHEN A BOY AND HIS GRANDFATHER GO WALKING THEY
HAVE TIME TO STOP AND LOOK." (FAM--GRANDFATHERS,
FAM--OLD AGE, GRANDFATHERS, OLD AGE)

FLORA, JAMES. GRANDPA'S FARM. HARCOURT, 1965.
ILLUSTRATED BY JAMES FLORA. (CC)

ALTHOUGH THIS IS A TALE ABOUT A GRANDPA WHO
TELLS STORIES, IT IS MORE A BOOK OF TALL TALES
THAN A BOOK ABOUT GRANDFATHER. THE SETTING IS
GRANDPA'S FARM, HOWEVER, AND THE READER LEARNS
STORIES OF HOW HE GOT HIS BLUE BARN, THE COW
SALVE THAT MADE EVERYTHING GROW, THE TERRIBLE
WINTER WHEN EVEN WORDS FROZE AND HAD TO BE THAWED
OUT IN THE FRYING PAN, AND LITTLE HATCHY HEN,
WHO HATCHED OUT WRISTWATCHES FROM ALARM CLOCKS.
ITS VALUE LIES IN THE CASTING OF GRANDPA IN THE
ROLE OF STORYTELLER, AND HIS RELATIONSHIP WITH
THE YOUNG CHILD LISTENING ON HIS LAP.
(FAM--GRANDFATHERS, GRANDFATHERS)

GAUCH, PATRICIA. GRANDPA AND ME. COWARD, 1972.
ILLUSTRATED BY SYMEON SHIMIN. (CC)

THE ILLUSTRATIONS ARE PARAMOUNT IN THIS STORY
OF A BOY, PERHAPS TEN OR ELEVEN, AND THE
COMPANIONSHIP HE AND HIS GRANDFATHER SHARE, AS
THE DELICATE WATERCOLORS WASH ACROSS THE PAGES IN
PASTELS OF SAND, SUN, AND WATER. SYMEON SHIMIN'S
ARTISTRY DOMINATES THE BOOK, YET IN A SUPPORTIVE
WAY, AND THE READER COMES AWAY FROM THE BOOK
WITH A FEELING OF CONTENTMENT, PEACE, AND
THOUGHTFUL REFLECTIONS ON THE VALUES OF GETTING
BACK TO NATURE AND BEING ALONE, AWAY FROM PEOPLE.
(EMOTIONS--SERENITY, FAM--GRANDFATHERS,
GRANDFATHERS, SERENITY)

HORVATH, BETTY. JASPER MAKES MUSIC. WATTS, 1967.
ILLUSTRATED BY FERMIN ROCKER. (CCB-B)

JASPER WAS WILLING TO SHOVEL SNOW ALL WINTER
IN ORDER TO MAKE ENOUGH MONEY TO BUY A GUITAR.
BUT IT WAS GRANDPA WHO TOLD HIM ABOUT THE MAGIC
SHOVEL, AND THAT PART OF THE MAGIC DEPENDED UPON
THE PERSON WHO OWNED IT. CHILDREN WILL APPRECIATE
JASPER'S EFFORT TO LINE UP CUSTOMERS, AND HIS
DETERMINATION TO SAVE HIS MONEY IN A BAKING
POWDER CAN. (FAM--GRANDFATHERS, GRANDFATHERS,
SELF-RELIANCE)

LUNDGREN, MAX. MATT'S GRANDFATHER. PUTNAM, 1972.
  ILLUSTRATED BY FIBBEN HALD. (CC)

WRITTEN IN SWEDEN, THIS REFRESHINGLY HONEST
BOOK ABOUT AN OLD MAN IN AN OLD FOLKS' HOME
PRESENTS A POINT OF VIEW VERY DIFFERENT FROM
OTHER BOOKS ON THIS SUBJECT. WE SEE LIFE FROM THE
POINT OF VIEW OF THE GRANDFATHER: HE THINKS HE
LOOKS YOUNGER THAN HIS SON, AND HE THINKS THE SON
TALKS AS IF HE WERE THE FATHER. HE MAKES A GREAT
DEAL OF SENSE, AND IS FOXY ENOUGH TO MASQUERADE
IN A LINEN JACKET, SUNGLASSES, AND A BIG FLOPPY
STRAW HAT IN ORDER TO ESCAPE INTO THE OUTSIDE
WORLD FOR A FEW HOURS. THE BOOK DOES INCLUDE SOME
OF THE FOIBLES OF OLDER PEOPLE, SUCH AS
FORGETFULNESS AND SECRETIVENESS (HE HIDES HIS
SNUFF IN THE FLOWER POT), BUT TO THE LITTLE BOY
WHO IS VISITING, THESE MILD ABERRATIONS ARE TAKEN
IN STRIDE. LOVELY PASTEL ILLUSTRATIONS ACCENTING
HORIZONTAL LINES CONTRIBUTE TO A SENSE OF
PEACEFULNESS. A SENSE OF WELL-BEING PERMEATES THE
BOOK, AND THE READER HAS A FEELING OF PLEASURE
IN KNOWING THAT THE OLD GENTLEMAN IS BEING CARED
FOR IN A BUILDING AS BIG AS A CASTLE WITH TOWERS
AND SPIRES. PARTICULARLY USEFUL TO GIVE A CHILD A
POSITIVE, ALBEIT MINORITY REPORT ON OLDER
CITIZENS, MANY OF WHOM REMAIN CHIPPER AND IN
CHARGE OF THEIR SENSES. (DIFF SIT--OLD AGE,
FAM--GRANDFATHERS, GRANDFATHERS, OLD AGE)

STEIN, SARA. ABOUT DYING. WALKER, 1974.
ILLUSTRATED BY DICK FRANK. (BL)

DRAWING THE ANALOGY BETWEEN THE DEATH OF A PET
PIGEON AND THE DEATH OF GRANDFATHER, THIS SIMPLY
WRITTEN BOOK PRESENTS DEATH IN A REALISTIC WAY,
YET IN A WAY THE YOUNG CHILD CAN UNDERSTAND,
SHOWING THAT THE BODY OF SNOW, THE PIGEON, WAS
COLD AND STIFF. BURIAL RITES FOR BOTH THE PET AND
GRANDFATHER ARE COMPARED. THE REACTION TO THE

DEATH OF THE GRANDFATHER IS EMPHASIZED, HOWEVER:
MOTHER CRIES AND JANE, A SIX-YEAR-OLD, IS ANGRY,
TEARS THINGS UP, AND CRIES. THE AUTHOR STATES
THAT ONE OF EVERY 20 CHILDREN WILL FACE THE DEATH
OF A PARENT DURING CHILDHOOD. THE BOOK GIVES
INSIGHT INTO WHAT CHILDREN MAY BE THINKING AND
FEELING, AND THROUGHOUT STRESSES HONESTY AND
COMPASSION. (DEATH, DEATH--PET, DIFF SIT--DEATH,
DIFF SIT--DEATH--PET, FAM--GRANDFATHERS,
GRANDFATHERS)

ZOLOTOW, CHARLOTTE. MY GRANDSON LEW. HARPER,
1974. ILLUSTRATED BY WILLIAM DU BOIS. (CC)

   A SMALL BOY WAKES UP IN THE NIGHT, AND TELLS
HIS MOTHER HE MISSES HIS GRANDFATHER. THEY CHAT,
AND THE LITTLE BOY RECALLS HOW HE WENT TO THE
MUSEUM WHEN HIS GRANDFATHER BABY-SAT HIM. THE
LITTLE BOY'S MOTHER IS TOUCHED BY THE MEMORIES,
AND SHE TOO REMEMBERS, GRATEFULLY, THE TIMES WHEN
GRANDPA WOULD COME TO VISIT. (DEATH, DIFF
SIT--DEATH, FAM--GRANDFATHERS, GRANDFATHERS)

GRANDMOTHERS

ALEXANDER, MARTHA. THE STORY GRANDMOTHER TOLD.
DIAL, 1969. ILLUSTRATED BY MARTHA ALEXANDER.
(BCB)

   A PRESCHOOL GIRL NAMED LISA BEGS "GRAMMA" FOR
A STORY AS SHE AND HER GRANDMOTHER FIX SUPPER IN
THE COZY KITCHEN WITH AN OLD-FASHIONED STOVE.
THEN FOR THE REST OF THE BOOK, LISA PROCEEDS TO
TELL THE STORY HERSELF, ABOUT HER CAT IVAN AND
THE BALLOON THEY BOUGHT. TOUCHES OF HUMOR IN THE
ILLUSTRATIONS MAKE THIS A BOOK THAT YOUNG
CHILDREN WILL ENJOY. (FAM--GRANDMOTHERS,
GRANDMOTHERS)

BALDWIN, ANNE. SUNFLOWERS FOR TINA. FOUR, 1970.
ILLUSTRATED BY ANN GRIFALCONI. (CCB-B)

   IN SUNFLOWER COLORS, THE ILLUSTRATOR HAS SHOWN
A CORNER OF A DIRTY CITY NEIGHBORHOOD WHERE THE
LAUNDRY HANGS BETWEEN THE BUILDINGS, WHERE TINA
TRIES TO GROW A GARDEN BY PLANTING CARROTS SHE
FINDS IN THE REFRIGERATOR. WHEN SHE DISCOVERS
SUNFLOWERS GROWING A FEW BLOCKS FROM HOME, SHE
DELIGHTS IN THEIR FRESHNESS AND THINKS OF HER
AGING GRANDMOTHER AT HOME IN HER DARK CORNER.

LATER SHE DANCES IN HER YELLOW DRESS, AND EVOKES
LAUGHTER FROM THE OLD WOMAN. A STORY OF CONTRASTS
BETWEEN OLD AND YOUNG, BEAUTY AND RUBBLE, THIS
IS A POSITIVE STATEMENT FOR THE NECESSITY OF
AESTHETIC PLEASURE IN LIFE. (FAM--GRANDMOTHERS,
FAM--OLD AGE, GRANDMOTHERS, OLD AGE)

BARTOLI, JENNIFER. NONNA. HARVEY, 1975.
ILLUSTRATED BY JOAN DRESCHER. (BL)

   AN INTERESTING, NON-THREATENING BOOK ABOUT THE
DEATH OF GRANDMOTHER TREATED FROM THE POINT OF
VIEW OF MEMORIES OF LIFE BEFORE HER DEATH AND
LIFE SEVERAL MONTHS LATER. NONNA'S COOKIES ARE
ONE MOTIF THAT REPEATS THROUGHOUT THE BOOK. IN
MEMORY, THE CHILDREN THINK ABOUT SOUP AND COOKIES
WITH NONNA ON SATURDAYS. ON THE DAY OF THE
FUNERAL, MOTHER BAKES NONNA'S COOKIES AND THE
CHILDREN EAT THEM FOR BREAKFAST, AND SIX MONTHS
LATER AT CHRISTMAS TIME, THE YOUNGEST DAUGHTER
BAKES THEM FOR THE ENTIRE FAMILY. USEFUL BECAUSE
ALTHOUGH IT SHOWS THE FUNERAL AND THE GRAVESIDE
SERVICE, IT ALSO USES A DEVICE TO SHOW HOW THE
LIVING COPE BY PERFORMING DAILY ROUTINES OF LIFE.
(DEATH, DIFF SIT--DEATH, FAM--GRANDMOTHERS,
GRANDMOTHERS)

BLUE, ROSE. GRANDMA DIDN'T WAVE BACK. WATTS,
1972. ILLUSTRATED BY TED LEWIN. (CC)

   DEBBIE, TEN YEARS OLD, REALIZES THAT HER
BELOVED GRANDMOTHER IS CHANGING. SHE NO LONGER
WAVES AT DEBBIE FROM THE WINDOW, NOR DOES SHE
HAVE COOKIES FROM THE OVEN READY FOR HER. GRANDMA
EXHIBITS LOSS OF MEMORY, CONFUSION OVER NAMES,
AND OTHER EVIDENCE OF SENILITY, SUCH AS STAYING
IN HER NIGHT DRESS ALL DAY. AS THE GRANDMOTHER
DECLINES, DEBBIE MATURES, AND IS UPSET BY THE
RELATIVES' DECISION TO ENTER THE GRANDMOTHER IN A
NURSING HOME. THE BOOK ENDS ON A POSITIVE NOTE,
HOWEVER, AS THE OLDER WOMAN SPEAKS ENCOURAGINGLY
OF THE COMING OF SPRING. A USEFUL BOOK BECAUSE IT
DEALS WITH A PROBLEM FACING MANY FAMILIES TODAY.
APPROPRIATE FOR THIRD GRADERS TO READ
INDEPENDENTLY. (DIFF SIT--OLD AGE,
FAM--GRANDMOTHERS, GRANDMOTHERS, OLD AGE,
SELF-UNDERSTANDING)

BUCKLEY, HELEN. GRANDMOTHER AND I. LOTHROP,
1961. ILLUSTRATED BY PAUL GALDONE. (CC)

LARGE PRINT AND SHORT, RHYTHMIC SENTENCES
WHICH ECHO THE ROCKING CHAIR CHARACTERIZE THIS
BOOK OF OVERSIZE PICTURES. THE ILLUSTRATIONS,
WHICH ARE BRIGHT AND HOMEY IN THE FIRELIGHT, SET
THE SCENE FOR PEACE AND COMFORT AT THE BEGINNING
OF THE BOOK, PROGRESS TO A DRAMATIC PURPLE PAGE
WHEN THE LITTLE GIRL IS SECURE FROM THE LIGHTNING
OUTSIDE, AND END ON A CHEERFUL NOTE AFTER
GRANDMOTHER'S LAP HAS BEEN COMPARED TO THOSE
BELONGING TO MOTHER, FATHER, BROTHER, AND SISTER.
USEFUL BECAUSE THE UNIQUE ROLE OF GRANDMOTHER'S
LAP IS REINFORCED AGAIN AND AGAIN.
(EMOTIONS--SECURITY, FAM--GRANDMOTHERS,
GRANDMOTHERS, SECURITY)

DE PAOLA, TOMIE. NANA UPSTAIRS AND NANA
DOWNSTAIRS. PUTNAM, 1973. ILLUSTRATED BY TOMIE
DE PAOLA. (BL)

IN AN EASY BOOK FORMAT WITH LARGE PRINT AND
PICTURES ON EVERY PAGE, LITTLE TOMMY IS SHOWN IN
A CHARMING RELATIONSHIP WITH HIS 94-YEAR-OLD
GREAT-GRANDMOTHER, WHO IS NANA UPSTAIRS. HE
LEARNED THE MEANING OF DEATH ON THE DAY HIS
MOTHER TOLD HIM THAT NANA UPSTAIRS WOULD NOT BE
HERE ANY MORE, EXCEPT IN HIS MEMORY. TOMMY THINKS
OF HER WHEN HE SEES A FALLING STAR, AND THE BOOK
ENDS WITH HIM AS A YOUNG MAN, AGAIN SEEING A
FALLING STAR, AND THINKING OF BOTH GRANDMOTHERS.
A GENTLE, THOUGHTFUL WAY TO EXPLAIN DEATH TO THE
VERY YOUNG. (DEATH, DIFF SIT--DEATH,
FAM--GRANDMOTHERS, FAM--GREAT-GRANDMOTHERS,
GRANDMOTHERS, GREAT-GRANDMOTHERS)

DE PAOLA, TOMIE. WATCH OUT FOR THE CHICKEN FEET
IN YOUR SOUP. PRENTICE, 1974. ILLUSTRATED BY
TOMIE DE PAOLA. (CC)

LUSH COLORS MAKE THIS BOOK AN ATTRACTIVE
SETTING FOR INTRODUCING JOEY'S ITALIAN
GRANDMOTHER. JOEY BRINGS HIS FRIEND TO VISIT,
THINKING HE MAY BE EMBARRASSED BY OLD-COUNTRY
CUSTOMS, AND IS A LITTLE PUT OUT WHEN EUGENE IS
INVITED TO BAKE THE BREAD WITH GRANDMA.
DELICIOUS-SOUNDING RECIPE IS ALSO INCLUDED FOR
THE BRAIDED BREAD DOLLS. USEFUL BECAUSE OF THE
INTERACTION BETWEEN YOUNG AND OLD.
(FAM--GRANDMOTHERS, FRIENDSHIP, GRANDMOTHERS)

GILL, JOAN. SARA'S GRANNY AND THE GROODLE.

DOUBLEDAY, 1969. ILLUSTRATED BY SEYMOUR CHWAST. (LJ)

NONSENSICAL TEXT WHICH LOOKS LIKE PROSE, BUT RHYMES, WITH SUCH AMUSING WORDS AS STRUDEL, NOODLE, AND GROODLE, MAKE THIS A VERY ATTRACTIVE BOOK TO READ ALOUD. IT SHOWS GRANNY AND YOUNG SARA IN AN ADVENTURE WHICH MAY OR MAY NOT BE A DREAM. THE PICTURE IT PORTRAYS OF GRANDMA IS A VERY UNCONVENTIONAL ONE. ALTHOUGH SHE WEARS LONG SKIRTS AND HIGH BUTTON BOOTS, SHE SHOUTS "OLE" AS THEY RIDE DOWN THE STREET IN THE OYSTER SHELL WHICH IS BEING DRAWN ALONG BY THE GOOSE. ITS VALUE LIES PERHAPS IN THE VIEW IT GIVES OF OLD AGE--THAT OLDER PEOPLE DON'T NEED TO SIT IN A ROCKER AT HOME. (FAM--GRANDMOTHERS, FAM--OLD AGE, GRANDMOTHERS, OLD AGE)

LEXAU, JOAN. BENJIE. DIAL, 1964. ILLUSTRATED BY DON BOLOGNESE. (CC)

A LIGHT GRAY WATERCOLOR WASH MATCHES THE GRUBBY STREET SETTING OF THIS REALISTIC STORY. ACTION TAKES PLACE ON THE STOOP, STREETS, AND SHOPS OF THE INNER CITY, INCLUDING THE ONE ROOM IN WHICH GRANNY AND BENJIE LIVE. HE IS A SMALL BOY SO SHY THAT HE HIDES BEHIND HIS GRANNY'S SKIRTS, AND IS TEASED BY THE NEIGHBORS. WHEN HIS GRANDMOTHER LOSES A FAVORITE EARRING, BENJIE OVERCOMES HIS SHYNESS TO HELP LOOK FOR IT, AND IN ASSERTING HIMSELF MAKES PROGRESS TOWARD INDEPENDENCE. USEFUL ALSO TO DEMONSTRATE A LOVING, CARING RELATIONSHIP BETWEEN YOUNG AND OLD. (EMOTIONS--SHYNESS, FAM--GRANDMOTHERS, GRANDMOTHERS, SELF-CONFIDENCE, SHYNESS)

LEXAU, JOAN. BENJIE ON HIS OWN. DIAL, 1970. ILLUSTRATED BY DON BOLOGNESE. (BCB)

WHEN YOUNG BENJIE'S GRANDMOTHER IS SICK BENJIE MUST WALK HOME FROM SCHOOL BY HIMSELF FOR THE FIRST TIME. HE MEETS SOME TOUGH-LOOKING BOYS, BUT FINALLY FINDS HIS WAY HOME. THIS IS THE STORY OF HOW A GHETTO CHILD FUNCTIONS: NO PHONE IN THEIR PLACE, SO HE USES THE POLICE BOX, EXCEPT THAT HE'S TOO SHORT. PEOPLE AT FIRST DO NOT WISH TO HELP, AND HE DOES NOT HAVE CLOSE FRIENDS TO CALL UPON. WHEN HIS GRANDMOTHER GOES TO THE HOSPITAL, HE WORRIES THAT NO ONE WILL BE AROUND TO TAKE HIM TO SCHOOL, BUT IS HAPPY WHEN HE FINDS THAT RAY,

A NEIGHBOR HE'S STAYING WITH, WILL WALK HIM TO
SCHOOL. (FAM--GRANDMOTHERS, GRANDMOTHERS,
SELF-RELIANCE)

MILES, MISKA. ANNIE AND THE OLD ONE. LITTLE,
1971. ILLUSTRATED BY PETER PARNALL. (ESLC)

   GOLDEN DESERT COLORS SPIKED WITH BLACK AND
WHITE LINE DRAWINGS CONTRIBUTE TO THE STARK
FEELINGS OF IMPENDING DEATH IN THIS DIALOG
BETWEEN A NAVAJO GRANDMOTHER AND HER SMALL
GRANDCHILD. ONE EVENING WHEN, SYMBOLICALLY, THE
FIRE IS DYING IN THE HOGAN, THE OLD ONE ANNOUNCED
THAT SHE WOULD GO TO MOTHER EARTH WHEN THE RUG
ON THE LOOM WAS FINISHED. ANNIE UNDERSTOOD,
ALTHOUGH SHE DID NOT UNDERSTAND WHY HER
GRANDMOTHER KNEW SHE WAS GOING TO DIE. IN THE
DAYS THAT FOLLOWED ANNIE DREAMED UP SCHEMES TO
DELAY THE COMPLETION OF THE RUG, AND IT IS ONLY
WHEN GRANDMOTHER EXPLAINS THE INEVITABILITY OF
DEATH IN ALL OF NATURE THAT ANNIE ACCEPTS THE
CONCEPT. INTERESTING VIEW OF DEATH FOR, WHILE A
VERY REALISTIC BOOK, IT RETAINS THE MYSTICAL
OUTLOOK OF THE NAVAJO WAY OF LIFE. (DEATH, DIFF
SIT--DEATH, FAM--GRANDMOTHERS, GRANDMOTHERS)

MINARIK, ELSE. A KISS FOR LITTLE BEAR. HARPER,
1968. ILLUSTRATED BY MAURICE SENDAK. (BCB)

   AMUSING STORY BECAUSE OF THE HUMOROUS INCIDENT
IN WHICH LITTLE BEAR'S KISS ALMOST GETS LOST
WHEN LITTLE SKUNK GIVES IT TO HIS LADY FRIEND
INSTEAD OF PASSING IT ON, BUT THE UNDERLYING
MESSAGE IS THERE. LITTLE BEAR MAKES A PRESENT FOR
HIS GRANDMOTHER AND SHE, IN A LOVING GESTURE,
SENDS HIM A KISS. THE DELICATE ROUNDED LINES IN
THE ILLUSTRATIONS, FRAMED ON EACH PAGE, FURTHER
THE GENTLE, CARING MESSAGE. (EMOTIONS--LOVE,
FAM--GRANDMOTHERS, GRANDMOTHERS, LOVE)

SKORPEN, LIESEL. MANDY'S GRANDMOTHER. DIAL,
1975. ILLUSTRATED BY MARTHA ALEXANDER. (BL)

   MANDY THINKS GRANDMOTHERS ARE PRETTY
BORING--ESPECIALLY WHEN HER GRANDMOTHER 1) BRINGS
HER A FUSSY YELLOW DRESS FOR A PRESENT, 2)
DOESN'T LIKE HER PET TOAD, AND 3) WANTS TO GIVE
HER EGGS FOR BREAKFAST. MANDY BEGINS TO
APPRECIATE HER GRANDMOTHER AFTER A SESSION OF
LAP-SITTING. THEY DID MANY THINGS TOGETHER: THEY

TOLD STORIES, MANDY LEARNED TO KNIT. SYMBOLIC OF
THEIR RAPPORT IS THE FACT THAT MANDY IS WEARING
THE YELLOW DRESS WHEN GRANDMOTHER SAYS GOOD-BYE.
(FAM--GRANDMOTHERS, GRANDMOTHERS)

SONNEBORN, RUTH. I LOVE GRAM. VIKING, 1971.
ILLUSTRATED BY LEO CARTY. (ESLC)

   A THIRD GRADER COULD READ THIS PICTURE-STORY
BOOK WHICH IS MORE TEXT THAN PICTURES, BUT IT CAN
BE ENJOYED BY YOUNGER CHILDREN AS A READ-ALOUD.
ELLIE'S GRANDMOTHER CARES FOR HER, AND COOKS FOR
THE FAMILY WHILE ELLIE'S MOTHER WORKS. WHEN GRAM
GOES TO THE HOSPITAL, ELLIE IS VERY LONELY, AND
INDEED EXPERIENCES A FEELING OF THE FORESHADOWING
OF DEATH. THE POSITIVE THINGS SHE DOES TO
PREPARE FOR GRAM'S HOMECOMING SHOW HER LOVE: A
PICTURE SHE DRAWS AND THE PARTY TABLE SHE
PREPARES. WE KNOW AT THE END OF THE STORY THE
STRONG BOND OF LOVE BETWEEN GRAM AND HER FAMILY.
(FAM--GRANDMOTHERS, FAM--MOTHERS WORKING,
FAM--OLD AGE, GRANDMOTHERS, MOTHERS WORKING, OLD
AGE)

UDRY, JANICE. MARY JO'S GRANDMOTHER. WHITMAN,
A., 1970. ILLUSTRATED BY ELEANOR MILL. (BCB)

   A SELF-RELIANT WOMAN WHO LIVES ALONE IN THE
COUNTRY GIVES A POSITIVE PICTURE OF AN OLDER
PERSON. RAISING CHICKENS AND MAKING GARDEN OCCUPY
THIS LADY'S TIME, AND MARY JO LOVES TO VISIT
HER. RESOURCEFUL MARY JO GOES FOR HELP WHEN
GRANDMA TAKES A FALL, BUT THE MAIN EMPHASIS IS ON
THE INDEPENDENT HOUSEHOLD OF THIS SPRIGHTLY
OLDSTER. (DIFF SIT--OLD AGE, FAM--GRANDMOTHERS,
GRANDMOTHERS, OLD AGE)

WAHL, JAN. GRANDMOTHER TOLD ME. LITTLE, 1972.
ILLUSTRATED BY MERCER MAYER. (LJ)

   AN IMAGINATIVE GRANDMOTHER WHO SEES DANCING
ALLIGATORS, MERMAIDS, AND TROLLS IN FAMILIAR
COUNTRYSIDE SCENES ENLIVENS HER GRANDSON'S
VISITS. THROUGH THE COMPANIONSHIP OF BAKING
BREAD, WASHING DISHES TOGETHER, AND SWEEPING THE
PORCH, GRANDMOTHER AND GRANDSON PROCEED THROUGH
THE DAYS WHICH END IN A CLIMACTIC VISION WHEN THE
LITTLE BOY SEES, OR DREAMS, OR IMAGINES ALL OF
THE THINGS HIS GRANDMOTHER HAS BEEN DESCRIBING.
ONE COMMENT: CHILDREN WILL NOT FORGIVE MERCER

MAYER FOR SHOWING PANCAKES ON A PAGE THAT REFERS
TO WAFFLES. (FAM--GRANDMOTHERS, GRANDMOTHERS)

WILLIAMS, BARBARA. ALBERT'S TOOTHACHE. DUTTON,
1974. ILLUSTRATED BY KAY CHORAO. (CC)

   APPROPRIATE AS A BEDTIME STORY FOR YOUNGER
CHILDREN, THIS SLOWLY-PACED STORY ILLUSTRATED IN
SOFT PENCIL TONES STRIKES A SYMPATHETIC CHORD IN
CHILDREN WHO HAVE TRIED TO MAKE GROWN-UPS
UNDERSTAND THEM AND BELIEVE THEM. NO ONE BELIEVED
THAT ALBERT TURTLE WAS SICK WITH A TOOTHACHE
UNTIL HIS GRANDMOTHER CAME OVER THAT NIGHT. TURNS
OUT A GOPHER BIT HIM ON HIS LEFT TOE, BUT NO ONE
HAD BEEN WISE ENOUGH TO ASK HIM WHERE HIS
TOOTHACHE WAS. (DIFF SIT--ILLNESS,
FAM--GRANDMOTHERS, GRANDMOTHERS, ILLNESS)

WILLIAMS, BARBARA. KEVIN'S GRANDMA. DUTTON,
1975. ILLUSTRATED BY KAY CHORAO. (BL)

   SPARKLY-EYED KEVIN MAY BE STRETCHING THE TRUTH
A BIT WHEN HE TELLS ABOUT HIS HONDA-RIDING
GRANDMOTHER, A VERY MUCH "WITH IT" LADY WHO IS
CONTRASTED WITH THE TRADITIONAL VIEW OF THE
NARRATOR'S GRANDMOTHER. A REFRESHING LOOK AT TWO
DIFFERENT CULTURES IN A BOOK WHICH REALLY DOESN'T
TAKE SIDES--AND AS SUCH IS A GOOD FORUM FOR
DISCUSSION. (FAM--GRANDMOTHERS, FAM--OLD AGE,
GRANDMOTHERS, OLD AGE)

GRANDPARENTS

CHARLIP, REMY. HOORAY FOR ME!. PARENTS' MAG,
1975. ILLUSTRATED BY VERA WILLIAMS. (LJ, NYTBR)

   IN WATERY, EVOCATIVE WATERCOLORS, THE
ILLUSTRATOR SETS THE TONE FOR THE THEME OF
INTERRELATEDNESS OF THE HUMAN FAMILY. THE BOOK,
WHILE STRESSING THAT THE INDIVIDUAL IS A "ME,"
EXPLORES THE RELATIONSHIP OF NIECES TO UNCLES,
AND COUSINS TO COUSINS, AND DEVELOPS
UNDERSTANDING OF GREAT-GRANDPARENTS TO
GREAT-GREAT-GRANDPARENTS IN A SEQUENCE WITH A
KITTEN WHICH CHILDREN WILL LIKE. A BOOK WHICH
DEFIES DESCRIPTION, IT IS LIKELY TO BE ONE WHICH
WILL BE ENDURINGLY USEFUL IN HELPING TO DEVELOP
THE CONCEPT OF SELF. (FAM, FAM--GRANDPARENTS,
FAM--GREAT-GRANDPARENTS, GRANDPARENTS,
GREAT-GRANDPARENTS, SELF-IDENTITY)

CHILD, LYDIA. OVER THE RIVER AND THROUGH THE
WOOD. COWARD, 1974. ILLUSTRATED BY BRINTON
TURKLE. (CC)

   WRITTEN IN 1844, MS. CHILD'S POEM GIVES AN
AUTHENTIC PICTURE OF THANKSGIVING DAYS OF THE
PAST, AND MANY OF THE VERSES WILL BE NEW TO
CHILDREN. THE WORDS AND MUSIC, INCLUDING GUITAR
ACCOMPANIMENT, ARE FOUND AT THE END. THE DETAILS
WHICH ARTIST BRINTON TURKLE INCLUDES ARE VALUABLE
DOCUMENTATION. PICTURED ARE AN OLD WOOD
COOKSTOVE, AN INDOOR PUMP IN THE SINK, THE DUST
CAP WORN BY GRANDMOTHER, AND OTHER VALUABLE
ARTIFACTS OF THE PAST. (FAM--GRANDPARENTS,
GRANDPARENTS)

GREAT-GRANDMOTHERS

DE PAOLA, TOMIE. NANA UPSTAIRS AND NANA
DOWNSTAIRS. PUTNAM, 1973. ILLUSTRATED BY TOMIE
DE PAOLA. (BL)

   IN AN EASY BOOK FORMAT WITH LARGE PRINT AND
PICTURES ON EVERY PAGE, LITTLE TOMMY IS SHOWN IN
A CHARMING RELATIONSHIP WITH HIS 94-YEAR-OLD
GREAT-GRANDMOTHER, WHO IS NANA UPSTAIRS. HE
LEARNED THE MEANING OF DEATH ON THE DAY HIS
MOTHER TOLD HIM THAT NANA UPSTAIRS WOULD NOT BE
HERE ANY MORE, EXCEPT IN HIS MEMORY. TOMMY THINKS
OF HER WHEN HE SEES A FALLING STAR, AND THE BOOK
ENDS WITH HIM AS A YOUNG MAN, AGAIN SEEING A
FALLING STAR, AND THINKING OF BOTH GRANDMOTHERS.
A GENTLE, THOUGHTFUL WAY TO EXPLAIN DEATH TO THE
VERY YOUNG. (DEATH, DIFF SIT--DEATH,
FAM--GRANDMOTHERS, FAM--GREAT-GRANDMOTHERS,
GRANDMOTHERS, GREAT-GRANDMOTHERS)

HEIN, LUCILLE. MY VERY SPECIAL FRIEND. JUDSON,
1974. ILLUSTRATED BY JOAN ORFE. (CCB-B)

   A FIVE-YEAR-OLD STAYS WITH HER GRANDMOTHER AND
GRANDFATHER WHILE HER MOTHER IS IN THE HOSPITAL,
BUT IT IS REALLY HER GREAT-GRANDMOTHER WITH WHOM
SHE SPENDS HER TIME. A HEALTHY RELATIONSHIP
DEVELOPS BETWEEN THE VERY OLD (85) AND THE VERY
YOUNG (5). THE CHILD HELPS THE OLD ONE, DOES
ERRANDS, AND IS A GENTLE COMPANION.
GREAT-GRANDMOTHER TEACHES THE CHILD TO TIE HER
SHOES, TO WHISTLE, AND SHARES OLD FAMILY
PHOTOGRAPHS TO GIVE THE CHILD A SENSE OF HISTORY

AND A SENSE OF BELONGING TO A FAMILY.
(FAM--GREAT-GRANDMOTHERS, FAM--OLD AGE,
GREAT-GRANDMOTHERS, OLD AGE)

GREAT-GRANDPARENTS

CHARLIP, REMY. HOORAY FOR ME!. PARENTS' MAG,
1975. ILLUSTRATED BY VERA WILLIAMS. (LJ, NYTBR)

IN WATERY, EVOCATIVE WATERCOLORS, THE
ILLUSTRATOR SETS THE TONE FOR THE THEME OF
INTERRELATEDNESS OF THE HUMAN FAMILY. THE BOOK,
WHILE STRESSING THAT THE INDIVIDUAL IS A "ME,"
EXPLORES THE RELATIONSHIP OF NIECES TO UNCLES,
AND COUSINS TO COUSINS, AND DEVELOPS
UNDERSTANDING OF GREAT-GRANDPARENTS TO
GREAT-GREAT-GRANDPARENTS IN A SEQUENCE WITH A
KITTEN WHICH CHILDREN WILL LIKE. A BOOK WHICH
DEFIES DESCRIPTION, IT IS LIKELY TO BE ONE WHICH
WILL BE ENDURINGLY USEFUL IN HELPING TO DEVELOP
THE CONCEPT OF SELF. (FAM, FAM--GRANDPARENTS,
FAM--GREAT-GRANDPARENTS, GRANDPARENTS,
GREAT-GRANDPARENTS, SELF-IDENTITY)

GREED

BONSALL, CROSBY. IT'S MINE!--A GREEDY BOOK.
HARPER, 1964. ILLUSTRATED BY CROSBY BONSALL.
(ESLC)

MABEL ANN AND PATRICK ARE TWO PRESCHOOLERS WHO
PLAY TOGETHER EVERY DAY, WITH THEIR ASSORTED
FAVORITE TOYS. THEY REFUSE TO SHARE, AND GO HOME
MAD. BUT AT A PICNIC, WHILE THEY ARE QUARRELING
OVER A CARROT, A GOAT EATS THEIR LUNCH, AND WHAT
FOLLOWS IS AN AMAZING TURNABOUT. THE STORY ENDS
WITH "MINE" STILL THE MOST IMPORTANT WORD IN THE
STORY, BUT PATRICK IS PLAYING WITH MABEL ANN'S
RUBBER DUCK AND MABEL ANN IS WEARING PATRICK'S
FEATHER. DELICIOUS CHILD-APPEALING DRAWINGS MAKE
THE BOOK VERY ATTRACTIVE TO CHILDREN.
(BEHAVIOR--SHARING, EMOTIONS--GREED, FRIENDSHIP,
GREED, SHARING)

HOBAN, RUSSELL. A BIRTHDAY FOR FRANCES. HARPER,
1968. ILLUSTRATED BY LILLIAN HOBAN. (BCB)

USEFUL FOR DEMONSTRATING THE CONCEPT OF THE
BASIC FEELING OF SELFISHNESS THAT MAY BE IN ALL
OF US, THIS ATTRACTIVE VOLUME PRESENTS A HUMOROUS

PICTURE OF FRANCES NOT WANTING TO GIVE HER
SISTER A BIRTHDAY PRESENT, THEN ALMOST EATING IT
UP WHEN SHE DOES BUY IT. AFTER ONE LAST SQUEEZE
ON THE CHOMPO BAR, SHE PRESENTS IT TO HER SISTER
GLORIA, AND TELLS HER SHE "CAN EAT IT ALL."
(EMOTIONS--GREED, EMOTIONS--JEALOUSY, GREED,
JEALOUSY)

KUSKIN, KARLA. WHAT DID YOU BRING ME?. HARPER,
1973. ILLUSTRATED BY KARLA KUSKIN. (LJ)

EDWINA MOUSE WAS VERY GREEDY AND WANTED
SOMETHING NEW EVERY DAY. IF SHE WENT TO THE STORE
WITH HER MOTHER, SHE BEGGED FOR A NEW TOY, AND
SHE WAS VERY ANGRY AT HER FATHER IF HE DIDN'T
BRING HER A NEW TRINKET. A HELPFUL WITCH TURNS
THE TABLES, AND EDWINA PLAYS THE ROLE OF HER
MOTHER FOR A DAY, WITH HER MOTHER AS THE CHILD. A
HELPFUL BOOK WHICH NOT ONLY SHOWS EXCESSIVE
GREEDINESS, BUT THE ROLE REVERSAL GIVES THE
READER PERSPECTIVE ON A COMMON SITUATION.
(EMOTIONS--GREED, GREED, SELF-UNDERSTANDING)

MAYER, MERCER. MINE!. SIMON, 1970. ILLUSTRATED
BY MERCER MAYER. (LJ, PBC)

A VERY FUNNY STORY OF GREEDINESS AND
POSSESSIVENESS, WHICH MOVES THROUGH SEVEN
EPISODES OF A LITTLE BOY CLAIMING THINGS WHICH
BELONG TO SOMEONE ELSE: SHOVEL, FISHING POLE, A
DOG'S BONE. HE IS RATHER A BULLY--GIVING GROUND
ONLY WHEN THE LITTLE GIRL HITS HIM OVER THE HEAD
WITH HER DOLL, AND GRUDGINGLY GIVING BACK THE
FISHLINE AFTER THE FISH HAS BEEN LOST. THE READER
FEELS THAT HE REALLY GETS HIS JUST DUES WHEN HE
FINDS HE MUST CLEAN HIS ROOM, WHICH HE ALSO
CLAIMED AS "MINE"--AND HIS MOTHER HANDS HIM THE
BROOM AND DUSTPAN WITH THE WORD "YOURS."
(BEHAVIOR--POSSESSIVENESS, EMOTIONS--GREED,
GREED, POSSESSIVENESS)

GUILT

GOFF, BETH. WHERE IS DADDY?. BEACON, 1969.
ILLUSTRATED BY SUSAN PERL. (CCB-B, JMF)

ALTHOUGH THE CHILD PORTRAYED IN THIS STORY IS
A VERY YOUNG PRESCHOOLER, AND A GIRL, A
FIFTH-GRADE BOY TUCKED THE COPY OF THIS BOOK IN
HIS DESK BECAUSE IT APPARENTLY FILLED A NEED IN

HIS LIFE. AT ONE POINT THE TEXT SAYS "THE ANGER
BETWEEN THEM (HER PARENTS) MADE A PAIN INSIDE
HER, AND SHE CRIED AND CRIED." IN THE CLASSIC
ATTITUDE OF MANY CHILDREN ABOUT DIVORCE, JANIE
FEELS THAT HER OCCASIONAL ANGER TOWARD HER DAD
CAUSED THE DIVORCE. AND SHE IS AFRAID TO SAY
ANYTHING UNPLEASANT TO HER MOTHER, WHO TAKES A
JOB, FOR FEAR HER MOTHER MIGHT ALSO ABANDON HER.
HAS AN EXCELLENT PAGE OF EXPLANATION BY AN M.D.
FROM THE CHILDREN'S PSYCHIATRIC HOSPITAL AT THE
UNIVERSITY OF MICHIGAN. (DIFF SIT--DIVORCE,
DIVORCE, EMOTIONS--GUILT, GUILT)

HANDICAPS

FASSLER, JOAN. HOWIE HELPS HIMSELF. WHITMAN, A.,
1975.   ILLUSTRATED BY JOE LASKER.   (BL)

   IN A FOREWORD, THE AUTHOR LISTS THREE GROUPS
OF PEOPLE WHO MAY BE HELPED BY THIS BOOK: A CHILD
IN A WHEELCHAIR, THE SIBLINGS OF A HANDICAPPED
CHILD, AND NORMAL CHILDREN. THE AUTHOR HAS
ACHIEVED A VERY FINE PORTRAIT OF THE EFFORT HOWIE
MAKES TO PUSH HIS WHEELCHAIR, AND THE READER
REALLY WILL UNDERSTAND WHEN HE LOOKS AT THE SWEAT
RUNNING DOWN HOWIE'S FOREHEAD. AN EXCELLENT BOOK
WHICH WILL HELP ALL READERS DISCOVER THAT
HANDICAPPED PERSONS ARE REAL PEOPLE. (DIFF
SIT--HANDICAPS, HANDICAPS)

HEIDE, FLORENCE. SOUND OF SUNSHINE, SOUND OF
RAIN. PARENTS' MAG, 1970.   ILLUSTRATED BY KENNETH
LONGTEMPS.

   THE BLIND CHILD WHO TELLS THIS STORY AND HIS
SISTER ARE NAMELESS, AND ONLY ABRAM, THE FRIENDLY
ICE CREAM MAN IN THE PARK, HAS A NAME.
NEVERTHELESS THE STORY IS ONE OF A DEVELOPING
SELF-AWARENESS IN A LITTLE BOY. HIS IS A WORLD OF
A TACTILE ENVIRONMENT, PERCEIVED AS BEING SMOOTH
OR ROUGH, AND OF SOUNDS, SOFT AND LOUD, AND OF
COLORS IMAGINED. IN THE TELLING, MANY THINGS ARE
LEARNED ABOUT THE WORLD OF THE BLIND, AND A CHILD
HEARING THIS STORY WILL HAVE AN UNDERSTANDING OF
THE GROWING INDEPENDENCE IN THIS SMALL DEPENDENT
CHILD. (BROTHERS & SISTERS, DIFF SIT--HANDICAPS,
FAM--BROTHERS & SISTERS, HANDICAPS,
SELF-IDENTITY, SELF-UNDERSTANDING)

KEATS, EZRA. APT. 3. MACMILLAN, 1971.

ILLUSTRATED BY EZRA KEATS. (ESLC)

TWO BROTHERS, SAM AND BEN, ARE LONELY AND
DECIDE TO INVESTIGATE THE SOURCE OF SOMEONE
PLAYING A HARMONICA. THE SETTING IS A GRIM GHETTO
APARTMENT BUILDING, AND VARIOUS MOODS ARE FELT
AS THE BOYS GO DOWN THE HALL. WHEN THEY FIND THE
BLIND MAN PLAYING THE HARMONICA IN APT. 3, HE
SHARES WITH THEM THE SECRETS HE KNOWS AND PLAYS
STRANGE MUSIC WHICH CONJURES UP SIGHTS, SOUNDS,
AND COLORS TO SAM. THE BOOK ENDS WITH SAM ASKING
THE OLD MAN TO TAKE A WALK WITH THEM. EVOCATIVE
ART WORK AND PROSE SHOW THE POWER OF MUSIC ON THE
EMOTIONS. (DIFF SIT--HANDICAPS, DIFF SIT--OLD
AGE, EMOTIONS--LONELIVESS, HANDICAPS, LONELINESS,
OLD AGE)

KLEIN, GERDA. THE BLUE ROSE. HILL, 1974.
ILLUSTRATED BY NORMA HOLT.

MADE IN COOPERATION WITH THE KENNEDY CHILD
STUDY CENTER, THE BOOK IS A SYMPATHETIC VIEW OF
MENTAL RETARDATION. BLACK AND WHITE PHOTOGRAPHS
SHOW JENNY PLAYING, TRYING TO TIE HER SHOES.
CLOSES WITH JENNY BEING UNHAPPY BECAUSE OTHER
CHILDREN HAVE CALLED HER RETARDED, AND LAUGHED AT
HER. (DIFF SIT--HANDICAPS, EMOTIONS--REJECTION,
HANDICAPS, REJECTION)

LASKER, JOE. HE'S MY BROTHER. WHITMAN, A., 1974.
ILLUSTRATED BY JOE LASKER. (BL)

IN A PERCEPTIVE NOTE AT THE BACK OF THIS BOOK,
MILDRED AND JOE LASKER GIVE A DESCRIPTION OF
THIS "INVISIBLE HANDICAP," AS THEY TERM IT, WHERE
A CHILD MAY NOT BE RETARDED, BUT SUFFERS
DIFFICULTY IN LEARNING AND SOCIAL SITUATIONS.
WRITTEN SO THAT OTHER FAMILIES WILL BE ABLE TO
IDENTIFY WITH THE EXPERIENCES SHOWN AND THEREBY
TAKE COMFORT, THE BOOK IS DIVIDED INTO HALF, WITH
THE SECOND PART SHOWING THE POSITIVE QUALITIES
OF JAMIE: HIS RHYTHM ON HIS DRUM SET, AND HIS
INSIGHTFUL STATEMENTS ABOUT ANIMALS. THE FIRST
HALF SHOWS, WITH REALISTIC PICTURES, THE TRIALS
OF SUCH A CHILD BEING SHUNNED IN GAMES, THE
TRAVAILS THAT TEACHERS AND PARENTS FACE, AND THE
COMPASSION AND UNDERSTANDING HE IS SOMETIMES
SHOWN. ABOVE ALL, IT IS A HELPFUL BOOK, AND A
POSITIVE BOOK, SHOWING A CHILD, IF NOT LIVING
COMFORTABLY WITH HIS PEERS, AT LEAST INTEGRATED

INTO NORMAL FAMILY LIFE. (DIFF SIT--HANDICAPS,
HANDICAPS)

LITCHFIELD, ADA. A BUTTON IN HER EAR. WHITMAN,
A., 1976.   ILLUSTRATED BY ELEANOR MILL.   (BL)

   DR. BROWN CALLED IT A MAGIC BUTTON BUT ANGELA
WEARS A HEARING AID TO HELP HER HEAR BETTER.
ANGELA NOT ONLY WEARS A HEARING AID, BUT WEARS IT
VERY VISIBLY, CARRYING A BACKPACK TYPE HARNESS
WHICH HOLDS HER BATTERIES. IN THE END, THE JAUNTY
HARNESS BECOMES A STATUS SYMBOL, A POSITIVE
ADDITION TO HER LIFE. ON THE LAST PAGE ANGELA
SAYS THAT SHE THINKS SOME OF THE OTHER CHILDREN
IN HER CLASS WISHED THEY COULD TRY A HEARING AID,
TOO. HANDSOME ILLUSTRATIONS SHOWING ANGELA TO BE
AN ACTIVE GIRL IN BLUE JEANS AND PONY TAIL MAKE
THIS A LANDMARK BOOK ON A SUBJECT NOT DEALT WITH
PREVIOUSLY FOR THIS AGE GROUP. (DIFF
SIT--HANDICAPS, HANDICAPS)

SOBOL, HARRIET. JEFF'S HOSPITAL BOOK. WALCK,
1975.   ILLUSTRATED BY PATRICIA AGRE.   (BL)

   PHYSICIANS FROM TWO MAJOR MEDICAL INSTITUTIONS
WERE USED AS CONSULTANTS FOR THIS HELPFUL,
ACCURATE BOOK WHICH DESCRIBES A YOUNG BOY'S
EXPERIENCE AS HE UNDERGOES SURGERY TO CORRECT
CROSSED EYES. LARGE BLACK AND WHITE PHOTOGRAPHS
GIVE A STEP-BY-STEP NO NONSENSE APPROACH TO THIS
STORY BUT, THROUGHOUT, THE HUMAN ELEMENT IS
THERE, TOO, AS WE SEE JEFF FEELING SCARED AND
WORRIED BEFORE THE OPERATION. REASSURING PICTURES
OF MOTHER AND FATHER WITH HIM AFTERWARD, AND
HORSEPLAY WITH THE NEIGHBORHOOD KIDS LEND AN
UPBEAT FEELING TO THE BOOK. (DIFF SIT--HANDICAPS,
EMOTIONS--FEAR, FEAR, HANDICAPS, HOSPITAL, NEW
SIT--HOSPITAL)

STEIN, SARA. ABOUT HANDICAPS. WALKER, 1974.
ILLUSTRATED BY DICK FRANK.   (BL)

   ILLUSTRATED WITH LIVELY PHOTOGRAPHS, SOME IN
COLOR, THIS BOOK ATTEMPTS TO BRING OUT INTO THE
OPEN A CHILD'S FEELINGS TOWARD HANDICAPPED
PEOPLE. SIGNIFICANT INCLUSION IS A PICTURE AND
EXPLANATION OF A MAN WITH AN ARTIFICIAL ARM WHICH
HAS A HOOK. ANOTHER USEFUL ASPECT OF THE BOOK IS
ITS VERY LARGE TYPE, AS WELL AS SECTIONS IN
SMALLER TYPE, FOR THE ADULT READER. THE BOOK

CONCLUDES WITH THE TWO YOUNG BOYS, JOE AND
MATTHEW, WORKING TOGETHER ON A BUILDING PROJECT.
(DIFF SIT--HANDICAPS, HANDICAPS)

WILDSMITH, BRIAN. THE LITTLE WOOD DUCK. WATTS,
1973.   ILLUSTRATED BY BRIAN WILDSMITH. (CC)

   LITTLE WOOD DUCK LIVES IN A THICKET WITH HIS
MOTHER AND FIVE BROTHERS AND SISTERS. THE FIRST
TIME HE JUMPED IN THE WATER HE FOUND HE COULD
SWIM ONLY IN CIRCLES, AND HIS MOTHER BECAME
ANGRY, AND THE ANIMALS OF THE FOREST TEASED HIM.
WHEN WISE OLD OWL DIAGNOSED THE TROUBLE (ONE FOOT
WAS LARGER THAN THE OTHER), HE TOLD THE LITTLE
DUCKLING TO PAY NO ATTENTION TO THE TEASING.
LATER, WHEN WOOD DUCK'S EFFORTS AT SWIMMING IN
CIRCLES DIVERTED THE FOX, EVERYONE DECLARED HIM A
HERO, AND THEY PROMISED NEVER TO TEASE HIM
AGAIN. USEFUL BECAUSE IT ILLUMINATES THE WAY IN
WHICH A HANDICAP MAY BECOME A BLESSING, AND
DEMONSTRATES THAT MINDLESS TEASING IS
UNDESIRABLE. (BEHAVIOR--TEASING, DIFF
SIT--HANDICAPS, EMOTIONS--FRUSTRATION,
FRUSTRATION, HANDICAPS, TEASING)

HAPPINESS

DAUGHERTY, JAMES. ANDY AND THE LION. VIKING,
1938.   ILLUSTRATED BY JAMES DAUGHERTY. (CC)

   IN ROLLICKING, RHYTHMICAL DRAWINGS, JAMES
DAUGHERTY HAS SYNTHESIZED FEELINGS OF JOY IN
LIVING AND JOY IN HELPING OTHER PEOPLE. ANDY, WHO
BEFRIENDS A LION AND REMOVES A BIG THORN FROM
HIS PAW, LATER IS THE BENEFICIARY OF THE KIND
ACT. THE LION, WHO HAS ESCAPED FROM THE CIRCUS,
RECOGNIZES ANDY AND IS IMMEDIATELY FRIENDLY.
USEFUL BECAUSE IT DEMONSTRATES IN A VERY SIMPLE
WAY HOW ONE KIND ACT MAY BE REPAID, BUT FAR
BEYOND THAT, THE AFFECTIVE ASPECTS OF LIVING ARE
STRESSED--THE SENSUOUS EFFECT OF THE EXPRESSIONS
ON FACES, THE SUBTLE HUMOR IN THE DAILY FAMILY
LIFE, AND THE VIGOROUS FEELINGS DEPICTING THE JOY
OF LIVING. (BEHAVIOR--CONSIDERATION,
BEHAVIOR--KINDNESS, CONSIDERATION,
EMOTIONS--HAPPINESS, FAM, FRIENDSHIP, HAPPINESS,
KINDNESS)

HOBAN, RUSSELL. LITTLE BRUTE FAMILY. MACMILLAN,
1966.   ILLUSTRATED BY LILLIAN HOBAN. (CC)

THE LITTLE BRUTE FAMILY IS NOT A FAMILY WHICH
LOVES, NOR IS IT A FAMILY ONE COULD LOVE, AT
LEAST IN THE BEGINNING. THEY QUARREL, THEY NEVER
SAY THANK-YOU, THEY EAT STONES AND ARE THOROUGHLY
DISAGREEABLE, AS WELL AS BEING UGLY. BUT THE
POWER OF ONE LITTLE GOOD FEELING UPON THIS FAMILY
WORKS A MIRACLE. THEY CHANGE SO MUCH THAT IN THE
END THE LITTLE BRUTE FAMILY CHANGES ITS NAME TO
NICE. THIS IS A DRAMATIC WAY TO SHOW A CHILD THE
IMPORTANCE OF GOOD FEELINGS.
(EMOTIONS--HAPPINESS, EMOTIONS--LOVE, HAPPINESS,
LOVE)

SIMON, NORMA. I KNOW WHAT I LIKE. WHITMAN, A.,
1971. ILLUSTRATED BY DORA LEDER. (CCB-B)

LISTING MANY BEHAVIOR PREFERENCES IN SUCH
AREAS AS FOOD, PLAY, AND CERTAIN HOUSEHOLD
CHORES, THE BOOK ALSO GIVES INSIGHT INTO THE
DISLIKES OF INDIVIDUAL CHILDREN. AUTHOR SIMON IS
PARTICULARLY EFFECTIVE IN PRESENTING SITUATIONS
WHERE THE READER CAN EMPATHIZE, THUS GAINING IN
SELF-UNDERSTANDING IN THE AFFECTIVE AREAS SUCH AS
APPRECIATION OF BEAUTY IN THE STARS, AND THE
PLEASURES OF MUSIC. (BEHAVIOR--DISLIKES,
DISLIKES, EMOTIONS--HAPPINESS, HAPPINESS,
SELF-UNDERSTANDING)

HATE

ZOLOTOW, CHARLOTTE. THE HATING BOOK. HARPER,
1969. ILLUSTRATED BY BEN SHECTER. (RLHR)

A SMALL GIRL KNOWS SHE HATES HER FRIEND, BUT
CAN'T MUSTER UP HER COURAGE TO ASK HER WHY SHE IS
ACTING IN A MEAN WAY. WHEN SHE FINALLY DOES ASK,
SHE FINDS OUT THAT IT REALLY WAS A
MISUNDERSTANDING THAT STARTED ALL OF THE
UNFRIENDLINESS. MORAL IS THAT IT IS BETTER TO TRY
TO FIND OUT THE FACTS WHEN YOU FACE A PROBLEM.
(EMOTIONS--HATE, FRIENDSHIP, HATE)

HOSPITAL

COLLIER, JAMES. DANNY GOES TO THE HOSPITAL.
NORTON, 1970. ILLUSTRATED BY YALE JOEL. (CC,
ESLC)

MANY BEHIND-THE-SCENES VIEWS ARE PICTURED,
INCLUDING A REPAIR SHOP, A SEWING ROOM, AND A

DRUGSTORE, WHICH WILL PROBABLY BE OF INTEREST TO
A YOUNG READER. A REALISTIC BUT REASSURING LOOK
AT A BOY'S STAY IN THE HOSPITAL FOR MINOR SURGERY
ON HIS EYE, GENEROUSLY ILLUSTRATED WITH BLACK
AND WHITE PHOTOGRAPHS. (HOSPITAL, NEW
SIT--HOSPITAL)

KAY, ELEANOR. LET'S FIND OUT ABOUT THE HOSPITAL.
WATTS, 1971. ILLUSTRATED BY WILLIAM BROOKS.
(CC)

   SIMPLE SENTENCES WITH SIMPLE EXPLANATIONS
DEFINE THE OPERATIONS OF A HOSPITAL--THE
PERSONNEL, EQUIPMENT, AND THE SPECIAL DEPARTMENTS
SUCH AS PEDIATRICS--IN SUCH A WAY THAT A YOUNG
CHILD WILL BE ABLE TO UNDERSTAND. THE CHILD IN
THE ILLUSTRATIONS IS ENJOYING HIMSELF, AND THE
PLEASANT ASPECTS OF HOSPITALIZATION ARE
EMPHASIZED, AND THERE IS NO REALISTIC MENTION OF
PAIN OR UNPLEASANTNESS. (HOSPITAL, NEW
SIT--HOSPITAL)

REY, MARGRET. CURIOUS GEORGE GOES TO THE
HOSPITAL. HOUGHTON, 1966. ILLUSTRATED BY MARGRET
REY. (BCB)

   WRITTEN IN COLLABORATION WITH THE CHILDREN'S
HOSPITAL MEDICAL CENTER IN BOSTON, THIS ADVENTURE
HAS THE ADVANTAGE OF A CENTRAL CHARACTER WITH
WHOM ALL CHILDREN WILL IDENTIFY. LOVABLE GEORGE
LANDS IN THE HOSPITAL WITH AN AILMENT WHICH COULD
PLAGUE ANY CHILD, AND HIS TRIP THROUGH X-RAY AND
ADMISSIONS TO THE CHILDREN'S WARD IS COLORFULLY
REASSURING. ALTHOUGH THE TEXT DESCRIBES SOME OF
THE PAIN, AND THE PICTURES REALISTICALLY DEPICT
THE OPERATING ROOM, THERE IS A HAPPY, POSITIVE
NOTE THROUGHOUT, AND IRREPRESSIBLE GEORGE ENDS
HIS HOSPITAL VISIT WITH A WILD ADVENTURE IN A
RUNAWAY GO-CART. (DIFF SIT--HOSPITAL, HOSPITAL,
NEW SIT--HOSPITAL)

SHARMAT, MARJORIE. I WANT MAMA. HARPER, 1974.
ILLUSTRATED BY EMILY MC CULLY. (CCB-B, NYTBR)

   A LITTLE GIRL'S MOTHER GOES TO THE HOSPITAL
FOR AN OPERATION. IN CHILDLIKE PICTURES AND
DIALOG, THE READER LEARNS OF THE LONELINESS AND
CONCERN WITHIN THE LITTLE GIRL. USEFUL BECAUSE IT
SHOWS WHAT A CHILD CAN DO TO SPELL THE
LONELINESS, SUCH AS MAKE PRESENTS AND CLEAN THE

HOUSE. AN ESPECIALLY MOVING ILLUSTRATION AT THE
END OF THE BOOK SHOWS THE PEACE AND CONTENTMENT
IN THE HOUSEHOLD WHEN MOTHER COMES HOME.
(EMOTIONS--LONELINESS, FAM--MOTHERS, HOSPITAL,
LONELINESS, MOTHERS, NEW SIT--HOSPITAL)

SHAY, ARTHUR. WHAT HAPPENS WHEN YOU GO TO THE
HOSPITAL. REILLY, 1969.   (CC)

   KAREN'S SHINY, SMILING FACE ON THE COLORFUL
COVER SETS THE TONE FOR A NON-THREATENING
EXPERIENCE IN THE HOSPITAL FOR ANY CHILD READER.
ALTHOUGH KAREN IS TEARFULLY APPREHENSIVE AT
TIMES, CHILDREN WILL UNDERSTAND THAT IT IS NORMAL
TO MISS YOUR PARENTS AND THAT YOU MIGHT BE A
LITTLE AFRAID OF THE X-RAY MACHINE. AUTHOR SHAY
HAS SAID THAT HIS PURPOSE IS TO SHOW THE JOBS AND
SERVICES THAT GO ON IN A HOSPITAL, AND TO HELP
CHILDREN UNDERSTAND IN ADVANCE WHAT WILL HAPPEN
TO THEM. HE HAS SUCCEEDED IN PRODUCING A VERY
USEFUL, SUCCESSFUL BOOK. (BRAVERY, DIFF
SIT--HOSPITAL, EMOTIONS--BRAVERY, HOSPITAL, NEW
SIT--HOSPITAL)

SOBOL, HARRIET. JEFF'S HOSPITAL BOOK. WALCK,
1975. ILLUSTRATED BY PATRICIA AGRE. (BL)

   PHYSICIANS FROM TWO MAJOR MEDICAL INSTITUTIONS
WERE USED AS CONSULTANTS FOR THIS HELPFUL,
ACCURATE BOOK WHICH DESCRIBES A YOUNG BOY'S
EXPERIENCE AS HE UNDERGOES SURGERY TO CORRECT
CROSSED EYES. LARGE BLACK AND WHITE PHOTOGRAPHS
GIVE A STEP-BY-STEP NO NONSENSE APPROACH TO THIS
STORY BUT, THROUGHOUT, THE HUMAN ELEMENT IS
THERE, TOO, AS WE SEE JEFF FEELING SCARED AND
WORRIED BEFORE THE OPERATION. REASSURING PICTURES
OF MOTHER AND FATHER WITH HIM AFTERWARD, AND
HORSEPLAY WITH THE NEIGHBORHOOD KIDS LEND AN
UPBEAT FEELING TO THE BOOK. (DIFF SIT--HANDICAPS,
EMOTIONS--FEAR, FEAR, HANDICAPS, HOSPITAL, NEW
SIT--HOSPITAL)

STEIN, SARA. A HOSPITAL STORY. WALKER, 1974.
ILLUSTRATED BY DORIS PINNEY. (BL)

   LARGE REALISTIC PHOTOGRAPHS, SOME IN COLOR,
SET THE TONE FOR THIS HELPFUL BOOK. ACKNOWLEDGING
THAT SOME THINGS ARE SCARY, AND SOMETIMES
PAINFUL, THE AUTHOR, IN COOPERATION WITH STAFF AT
THE CENTER FOR PREVENTIVE PSYCHIATRY, HAS

ATTEMPTED TO HELP BOTH PARENT AND CHILD. VERY
LARGE PRINT IS USED IN THE TEXT FOR THE CHILD
WHILE, ON THE SAME PAGE, THERE IS AN EXTENSIVE
SECTION DIRECTED TO THE ADULT WHICH CONTAINS
EXCELLENT PRACTICAL ADVICE, SUCH AS TAKING A
CAMERA TO RECORD WHAT THE HOSPITAL IS REALLY
LIKE, AND ASKING ALL SORTS OF QUESTIONS IN
ADVANCE. (DIFF SIT--HOSPITAL, HOSPITAL, NEW
SIT--HOSPITAL)

TAMBURINE, JEAN. I THINK I WILL GO TO THE
HOSPITAL. ABINGDON, 1965. ILLUSTRATED BY JEAN
TAMBURINE. (CCB-B, LJ)

   AN EXCELLENT BOOK FOR A CHILD AND HIS PARENT
TO PREPARE FOR A HOSPITAL VISIT. WHEN SUSY
DECIDES SHE DOES NOT WANT TO GO TO THE HOSPITAL,
HER MOTHER TAKES HER TO THE WAITING ROOM OF THE
HOSPITAL, AND ON THE WAY SHE STOPS WITH GET-WELL
PRESENTS FOR PEOPLE JUST OUT OF THE HOSPITAL.
THESE ARE POSITIVE CONTACTS, AND SUSY ALSO MEETS
A FRIENDLY NURSE WHO TAKES TIME TO TALK ABOUT
WHAT WILL HAPPEN TO HER. AT HOME, SHE PLAYS
HOSPITAL WITH HER PETS, AND BY THE TIME SHE
ARRIVES AT THE HOSPITAL, SHE IS RELAXED AND READY
TO HAVE HER PARENTS LEAVE. THIS IS ONE OF THE
LONGEST STORIES ON THIS SUBJECT, AND IS A FUN
BOOK FOR READING ALOUD. (EMOTIONS--FEAR, FEAR,
HOSPITAL, NEW SIT--HOSPITAL)

ILLNESS

BRANDENBERG, FRANZ. I WISH I WAS SICK, TOO!.
MORROW, 1976. ILLUSTRATED BY ALIKI. (BL)

   THIS IS A BOOK IN WHICH ALL OF THE ACTION CAN
BE TRACED IN THE EXPRESSIONS IN THE EYES OF
EDWARD AND ELIZABETH, TWO ENDEARING CAT
PROTAGONISTS WITH ALL TOO HUMAN FOIBLES. EDWARD'S
EYES ARE AT HALF-MAST AS WE SEE HIM IN THE
SICKBED, AND ELIZABETH SHOOTS SIDEWISE GLANCES OF
ENVIOUS RAGE AS SHE RELUCTANTLY DOES HER CHORES
AND PRACTICES PIANO. CONCERN AND LOVE ARE
EXPRESSED IN THE EYES OF MOTHER AND FATHER AS
THEY MINISTER TO THE CHILDREN, FOR YES, ELIZABETH
ALSO BECOMES ILL. HER EYES ARE EVEN MORE
HELPLESSLY DROOPED, AND ONCE AGAIN SHE IS ENVIOUS
OF THE WELL BROTHER, WHOSE EYES ARE BY NOW ROUND
AND SPARKLY. THE STORY ENDS WITH EVERYONE
PROPERLY ROUND-EYED AND HAPPY. (BROTHERS &

SISTERS, DIFF SIT--ILLNESS, FAM--BROTHERS &
SISTERS, EMOTIONS--JEALOUSY, ILLNESS, JEALOUSY)

TOBIAS, TOBI. A DAY OFF. PUTNAM, 1973.
ILLUSTRATED BY RAY CRUZ.   (CC)

   ALL CHILDREN WILL IMMEDIATELY RECOGNIZE THE
PREMISE IN THIS BOOK, THAT IT'S NICE TO STAY AT
HOME IF YOU DON'T FEEL WELL, AND ESPECIALLY IF
YOU'RE NOT ALL THAT SICK. CRUZ' ILLUSTRATIONS ARE
UNPRETTIFIED, YET MANAGE TO GIVE THE EFFECT OF A
SOLICITOUS FAMILY HOVERING AROUND, WILLING TO
CLOSE AN EYE TO BEHAVIOR WHICH MIGHT NOT NORMALLY
BE APPROVED. (DIFF SIT--ILLNESS, ILLNESS)

VIGNA, JUDITH. GREGORY'S STITCHES. WHITMAN, A.,
1974. ILLUSTRATED BY JUDITH VIGNA. (CC3-B, LJ)

   A HUMOROUS BOOK WHICH MAY BE USEFUL FOR A
CHILD WHO HAS HAD "STITCHES." WHILE ONE MAY FEEL
SORRY FOR GREGORY AT THE BEGINNING OF THE STORY,
BY THE END, WHEN HIS ACCIDENT IS MAGNIFIED AND
MAKES HIM OUT TO BE A HERO, RESCUING HIS PARENTS
FROM A LION, THE READER DOESN'T FEEL SORRY FOR
GREGORY. (DIFF SIT--ILLNESS, ILLNESS)

WILLIAMS, BARBARA. ALBERT'S TOOTHACHE. DUTTON,
1974. ILLUSTRATED BY KAY CHORAO. (CC)

   APPROPRIATE AS A BEDTIME STORY FOR YOUNGER
CHILDREN, THIS SLOWLY-PACED STORY ILLUSTRATED IN
SOFT PENCIL TONES STRIKES A SYMPATHETIC CHORD IN
CHILDREN WHO HAVE TRIED TO MAKE GROWN-UPS
UNDERSTAND THEM AND BELIEVE THEM. NO ONE BELIEVED
THAT ALBERT TURTLE WAS SICK WITH A TOOTHACHE
UNTIL HIS GRANDMOTHER CAME OVER THAT NIGHT. TURNS
OUT A GOPHER BIT HIM ON HIS LEFT TOE, BUT NO ONE
HAD BEEN WISE ENOUGH TO ASK HIM WHERE HIS
TOOTHACHE WAS. (DIFF SIT--ILLNESS,
FAM--GRANDMOTHERS, GRANDMOTHERS, ILLNESS)

WOLDE, GUNILLA. BETSY AND THE CHICKEN POX.
RANDOM, 1976. ILLUSTRATED BY GUNILLA WOLDE. (BL)

   WHEN BETSY'S BABY BROTHER BECOMES ILL AND
PARENTAL ATTENTION TURNS TOWARD HIM, BETSY'S
THUMB GOES IN HER MOUTH AS SHE WATCHES ROUND-EYED
IN THE BACKGROUND. BABY'S TEMPERATURE IS TAKEN,
THE DOCTOR IS CALLED AND, AMID ALL THE BUSTLE,
BETSY IS IGNORED. SHE PAINTS SPOTS ON HER FACE,

AND EVEN HER TONGUE, BUT STILL NO ONE NOTICES HER
AND WHEN SHE ERUPTS IN A TEMPER, BOTH PARENTS
ARE ANGRY. WHEN SHE HERSELF BREAKS OUT IN CHICKEN
POX, BETSY REALIZES SHE REALLY DOESN'T WANT THE
RED SPOTS AFTER ALL. A REALISTIC STORY WHICH IS
SIGNIFICANT FOR A NUMBER OF REASONS, IT WILL BE
USEFUL FOR PARENT AND CHILD BECAUSE IT DETAILS
THE TYPICALLY JEALOUS FEELINGS IN A CHILD WHO
FEELS NEGLECTED. A NO NONSENSE WOMAN DOCTOR, A
VIEW OF DADDY TAKING THE BABY'S TEMPERATURE WITH
A RECTAL THERMOMETER, AND LOW-KEY PASTEL AND
CRAYON DRAWINGS MAKE THIS A BOOK WHICH
DEMONSTRATES NON-STEREOTYPED SEX ROLES AS WELL AS
A RELEVANT FAMILY SITUATION. (DIFF SIT--ILLNESS,
FAM--SIBLING RIVALRY, ILLNESS, SIBLING RIVALRY)

JEALOUSY

ALEXANDER, MARTHA. NOBODY ASKED ME IF I WANTED A
BABY SISTER. DIAL, 1971.   ILLUSTRATED BY MARTHA
ALEXANDER.   (BCB)

   THE STORY OPENS WITH A SOUR-FACED LITTLE BOY
OVERHEARING GUSHY COMPLIMENTS ABOUT HIS NEW BABY
SISTER. HIS NEXT MOVE IS TO LOAD HER IN A WAGON
AND TRY TO GIVE HER AWAY. AFTER SEVERAL ABORTED
ATTEMPTS, HE ENDS UP AT HIS FRIEND'S HOUSE. BABY
BONNIE MISBEHAVES, HOWEVER, AND IN THE END IT IS
THE BROTHER WHO CAN PACIFY HER. WICKED THOUGHTS
GO THROUGH HIS HEAD AS HE IMAGINES HER GROWING UP
AND PULLING HIM IN THE WAGON. (BROTHERS &
SISTERS, EMOTIONS--JEALOUSY, FAM--BROTHERS &
SISTERS, JEALOUSY, NEW SIT--BABY)

BRANDENBERG, FRANZ. I WISH I WAS SICK, TOO!.
MORROW, 1976.   ILLUSTRATED BY ALIKI.   (BL)

   THIS IS A BOOK IN WHICH ALL OF THE ACTION CAN
BE TRACED IN THE EXPRESSIONS IN THE EYES OF
EDWARD AND ELIZABETH, TWO ENDEARING CAT
PROTAGONISTS WITH ALL TOO HUMAN FOIBLES. EDWARD'S
EYES ARE AT HALF-MAST AS WE SEE HIM IN THE
SICKBED, AND ELIZABETH SHOOTS SIDEWISE GLANCES OF
ENVIOUS RAGE AS SHE RELUCTANTLY DOES HER CHORES
AND PRACTICES PIANO. CONCERN AND LOVE ARE
EXPRESSED IN THE EYES OF MOTHER AND FATHER AS
THEY MINISTER TO THE CHILDREN, FOR YES, ELIZABETH
ALSO BECOMES ILL. HER EYES ARE EVEN MORE
HELPLESSLY DROOPED, AND ONCE AGAIN SHE IS ENVIOUS
OF THE WELL BROTHER, WHOSE EYES ARE BY NOW ROUND

AND SPARKLY. THE STORY ENDS WITH EVERYONE
PROPERLY ROUND-EYED AND HAPPY. (BROTHERS &
SISTERS, DIFF SIT--ILLNESS, FAM--BROTHERS &
SISTERS, EMOTIONS--JEALOUSY, ILLNESS, JEALOUSY)

HAZEN, BARBARA. WHY COULDN'T I BE AN ONLY KID
LIKE YOU, WIGGER. ATHENEUM, 1975. ILLUSTRATED BY
LEIGH GRANT. (HB)

   PLEASANT CLUTTER IN A LARGE FAMILY HOUSEHOLD
WHICH HAS SIX CHILDREN KEYNOTES THE FRUSTRATION
OF THE YOUNG BOY WHO TELLS THE STORY. WIGGER, HIS
FRIEND, DOESN'T HAVE TO MOP UP THE MILK THE BABY
SPILLED, OR STAND IN LINE FOR THE BATHROOM IN
THE MORNING, AND HE, THE NARRATOR, IS FRANKLY
QUITE JEALOUS. DURING HIS TIRADE HOWEVER, THE
ILLUSTRATIONS GIVE A DIFFERENT PICTURE OF WIGGER
WHO SEEMS TO LIKE WHEELING THE BABY CARRIAGE AND
BEING A PART OF THE ROUGH AND TUMBLE OF A LARGE
FAMILY. THE NARRATOR IS SURPRISED AT THE FACT
THAT AN ONLY CHILD CAN BE A LONELY CHILD. USEFUL
FOR THE CONTRASTING POINTS OF VIEW.
(EMOTIONS--JEALOUSY, FAM--ONLY CHILD, FRIENDSHIP,
JEALOUSY, ONLY CHILD)

HOBAN, RUSSELL. A BIRTHDAY FOR FRANCES. HARPER,
1968. ILLUSTRATED BY LILLIAN HOBAN. (BCB)

   USEFUL FOR DEMONSTRATING THE CONCEPT OF THE
BASIC FEELING OF SELFISHNESS THAT MAY BE IN ALL
OF US, THIS ATTRACTIVE VOLUME PRESENTS A HUMOROUS
PICTURE OF FRANCES NOT WANTING TO GIVE HER
SISTER A BIRTHDAY PRESENT, THEN ALMOST EATING IT
UP WHEN SHE DOES BUY IT. AFTER ONE LAST SQUEEZE
ON THE CHOMPO BAR, SHE PRESENTS IT TO HER SISTER
GLORIA, AND TELLS HER SHE "CAN EAT IT ALL."
(EMOTIONS--GREED, EMOTIONS--JEALOUSY, GREED,
JEALOUSY)

KEATS, EZRA. PETER'S CHAIR. HARPER, 1967.
ILLUSTRATED BY EZRA KEATS. (BCB)

   POOR PETER! HE WAS SO JEALOUS OF THE NEW BABY,
HE DECIDED TO RUN AWAY FROM HOME. WHEN HIS DAD
BEGAN TO PAINT ALL OF PETER'S FURNITURE, HE
GRABBED HIS LITTLE CHAIR, AND RAN OUTSIDE THE
DOOR. HE WAS VERY SURPRISED TO FIND THAT HE COULD
NOT FIT INTO IT ANYMORE BECAUSE HE HAD GROWN
BIGGER. USEFUL BECAUSE IT SHOWS THE RESOLVING OF
THE JEALOUS FEELINGS: PETER AND HIS FATHER PAINT

THE LITTLE CHAIR. ADDITIONALLY USEFUL BECAUSE IT
SHOWS A PRACTICAL EXAMPLE OF GROWTH IN A CHILD.
(EMOTIONS--JEALOUSY, FAM--SIBLING RIVALRY,
JEALOUSY, NEW SIT--BABY, SIBLING RIVALRY)

KLEIN, NORMA. IF I HAD MY WAY. PANTHEON, 1974.
ILLUSTRATED BY RAY CRUZ. (BL)

   ELLIE IS A LITTLE GIRL WHO GOES TO SCHOOL, BUT
IS YOUNG ENOUGH TO FEEL JEALOUS OF HER BABY
BROTHER--TO THE POINT WHERE SHE ASKS FOR A BOTTLE
HERSELF. SHE FEELS VERY PUT UPON, AND DREAMS ONE
NIGHT THAT THE ROLES ARE REVERSED, AND IT IS
SHE, THE CHILD, WHO HAS POWER OVER HER PARENTS.
IN THE INCIDENTS WHICH SHOW THIS URGE FOR
DOMINATION, ONE SEES THE ISSUES THAT MAKE
CHILDREN FEEL SO POWERLESS: HAVING TO GO TO BED
BEFORE THE GROWN-UPS, HAVING TO EAT CHILDREN'S
FOOD WHILE ADULTS HAVE SPECIAL ITEMS. HUMOR IS
PERVASIVE, AND ELLIE IS QUITE INGENIOUS IN
ORDERING UP A NEW BABY PERIODICALLY, ON APPROVAL,
TO BE KEPT ONLY IF HE'S "PERFECT," THAT IS, IF
HE DOESN'T CRY, ISN'T TOO FAT, AND DOESN'T EAT
TOO MUCH. THE NAKED BABY MAY BE THE ONE NOTE OF
UNREALITY IN THE STORY. EVERYONE ELSE IS DRESSED
WARMLY, BUT THE IRREPRESSIBLE FAT BABY NEVER
APPEARS WITH ONE STITCH OF CLOTHING.
(EMOTIONS--JEALOUSY, JEALOUSY, NEW SIT--BABY)

VIORST, JUDITH. I'LL FIX ANTHONY. HARPER, 1969.
ILLUSTRATED BY ARNOLD LOBEL. (BL)

   A CLASSIC RECITAL OF THE VENGEFUL JEALOUSY
SEETHING INSIDE A LITTLE BOY, WHO IS NOT YET
QUITE SIX. WE SEE A PORTRAIT OF THE OLDER BROTHER
THROUGH THE EYES OF THE ABUSED YOUNGER BROTHER:
THE OLDER BROTHER WHO IS CONSISTENTLY BIGGER AND
STRONGER, PHYSICALLY AND MENTALLY, BUT SELFISH,
PRIVILEGED, AND RATHER HORRID. ANTHONY ANNOUNCES
THAT HE'S GOING TO CLOBBER YOUNGER BROTHER, AND
SAYS, "YOU STINK." LITTLE BROTHER SAYS, "I'LL FIX
ANTHONY." (WHEN I'M SIX.) (ANGER,
EMOTIONS--ANGER, EMOTIONS--JEALOUSY, FAM--SIBLING
RIVALRY, JEALOUSY, SIBLING RIVALRY)

WABER, BERNARD. LYLE AND THE BIRTHDAY PARTY.
HOUGHTON, 1966. ILLUSTRATED BY BERNARD WABER.
(CC)

   HELPFUL LYLE STEPS OUT OF HIS ROLE AS HE FINDS

HIMSELF BEING VERY JEALOUS OF JOSHUA'S BIRTHDAY
CELEBRATION. IN FACT HE BECOMES SO VERY JEALOUS
THAT HE MAKES HIMSELF SICK AND MOPES ABOUT THE
HOUSE, FINALLY LANDING IN THE HOSPITAL. HELPING
OTHER PATIENTS IS GOOD THERAPY FOR HIM, AND SOON
HE'S HOME--TO FIND THAT THE FAMILY IS PLANNING
HIS BIRTHDAY PARTY. LYLE'S FEELINGS OF JEALOUSY,
AND THE WAY THEY MADE HIM FEEL MEAN, ARE VERY
REAL AND WILL HELP CHILDREN KNOW THAT EVERYONE
HAS THESE KINDS OF FEELINGS--EVEN CROCODILES.
(BEHAVIOR--CONSIDERATION, CONSIDERATION,
EMOTIONS--JEALOUSY, JEALOUSY)

WELLS, ROSEMARY. NOISY NORA. DIAL, 1973.
ILLUSTRATED BY ROSEMARY WELLS. (CC, ESLC)

POOR NORA--SHE'S THE LEFT-OUT SISTER, AND
THREATENS TO RUN AWAY TO MAKE HER FAMILY FEEL
SORRY FOR HER AND GIVE HER SOME ATTENTION. WHEN
SHE SHOWS UP IN THE BROOM CLOSET, ALL IS WELL. A
CLEVER, FUNNY BOOK ABOUT A BUMPTIOUS LITTLE
MOUSE-GIRL WHICH WILL DELIGHT YOUNG CHILDREN AS
THEY CATALOG HER MISDEMEANORS. MANY CHILDREN MAY
SEE THEMSELVES. (BROTHERS & SISTERS,
EMOTIONS--JEALOUSY, FAM--BROTHERS & SISTERS,
FAM--SIBLING RIVALRY, JEALOUSY, SIBLING RIVALRY)

KINDNESS

DAUGHERTY, JAMES. ANDY AND THE LION. VIKING,
1938. ILLUSTRATED BY JAMES DAUGHERTY. (CC)

IN ROLLICKING, RHYTHMICAL DRAWINGS, JAMES
DAUGHERTY HAS SYNTHESIZED FEELINGS OF JOY IN
LIVING AND JOY IN HELPING OTHER PEOPLE. ANDY, WHO
BEFRIENDS A LION AND REMOVES A BIG THORN FROM
HIS PAW, LATER IS THE BENEFICIARY OF THE KIND
ACT. THE LION, WHO HAS ESCAPED FROM THE CIRCUS,
RECOGNIZES ANDY AND IS IMMEDIATELY FRIENDLY.
USEFUL BECAUSE IT DEMONSTRATES IN A VERY SIMPLE
WAY HOW ONE KIND ACT MAY BE REPAID, BUT FAR
BEYOND THAT, THE AFFECTIVE ASPECTS OF LIVING ARE
STRESSED--THE SENSUOUS EFFECT OF THE EXPRESSIONS
ON FACES, THE SUBTLE HUMOR IN THE DAILY FAMILY
LIFE, AND THE VIGOROUS FEELINGS DEPICTING THE JOY
OF LIVING. (BEHAVIOR--CONSIDERATION,
BEHAVIOR--KINDNESS, CONSIDERATION,
EMOTIONS--HAPPINESS, FAM, FRIENDSHIP, HAPPINESS,
KINDNESS)

HAWKINS, QUAIL. ANDROCLES AND THE LION. COWARD,
1970.   ILLUSTRATED BY ROCCO NEGRI.   (ESLC)

   A SIMPLE RETELLING OF THIS AGE-OLD STORY
ILLUSTRATES FOR THE CHILDREN OF TODAY THE MORAL
THAT ONE SHOULD BE KIND TO PEOPLE IN NEED. WHEN
THE SLAVE ANDROCLES REMOVES A THORN FROM THE
LION'S PAW, AND THE LION LEADS HIM TO FOOD AND
DRINK, THERE IS A VIVID EXAMPLE OF THE BEGINNING
OF FRIENDSHIP. LATER ON WHEN THE LION MEETS
ANDROCLES IN THE ARENA AND REFUSES TO FIGHT HIM,
THE REWARDS OF FRIENDSHIP ARE SHOWN. A STORY FOR
OLDER CHILDREN RATHER THAN YOUNGER BECAUSE OF THE
CRUELTY IMPLIED IN THE COLOSSEUM.
(BEHAVIOR--CONSIDERATION, BEHAVIOR--KINDNESS,
CONSIDERATION, FRIENDSHIP, KINDNESS)

LAZINESS

DU BOIS, WILLIAM. LAZY TOMMY PUMPKINHEAD.
HARPER, 1966.   ILLUSTRATED BY WILLIAM DU BOIS.
(BCB)

   TOMMY WAS SO LAZY THAT HE HAD AN ELECTRIC
HOUSE WHICH GOT HIM UP IN THE MORNING, BATHED
HIM, AND FED HIM HIS BREAKFAST. HIS ELECTRIC
GADGETS GO HAYWIRE ONE DAY, AND EVERYTHING WORKS
BACKWARD, WITH TOOTHPASTE AND TOOTHBRUSH RUBBING
AWAY AT HIS TOES. TOMMY CONCLUDES BY SAYING "I
MUST TURN OVER A NEW LEAF...." A SPOOF ON THE
CHARACTERISTIC OF LAZINESS, THE HUMOR OF WHICH
WILL NOT BE LOST ON YOUNG READERS.
(BEHAVIOR--LAZINESS, LAZINESS)

LONELINESS

ARDIZONNE, EDWARD. LUCY BROWN AND MR. GRIMES.
WALCK, 1971.   ILLUSTRATED BY EDWARD ARDIZONNE.
(CC)

   THIS BOOK HAS A FAIRY-TALE QUALITY WHICH MAKES
IT SOMETHING OF A FANTASY: A LONELY LITTLE
ORPHAN GIRL MEETS A LONELY OLD MAN AND THEY
BECOME GREAT FRIENDS. WHEN MR. GRIMES FALLS ILL
AND MUST MOVE TO THE COUNTRY, HE ASKS LUCY TO GO
WITH HIM, WITH LUCY'S AUNT'S PERMISSION. MR.
GRIMES, WHO IS VERY WEALTHY, IS GENEROUS WITH HIS
MONEY, AND LUCY BUYS NEW CLOTHING. ILLUSTRATES
THE POINT THAT THERE ARE THINGS IN COMMON FOR THE
YOUNG AND THE OLD. THE OLD MAN AND THE LITTLE

GIRL WALK TOGETHER, HAVE TEA TOGETHER, AND NEVER
FEEL LONELY. (DIFF SIT--OLD AGE,
EMOTIONS--LONELINESS, FRIENDSHIP--ADULTS,
LONELINESS, OLD AGE)

CLIFTON, LUCILLE. EVERETT ANDERSON'S YEAR. HOLT,
1974. ILLUSTRATED BY ANN GRIFALCONI. (CC)

"WALK TALL IN THE WORLD," HIS MOTHER TELLS
HIM. ALTHOUGH THIS IS, IN THE MAIN, A STORY OF A
SEVEN-YEAR-OLD BOY, THE INFLUENCE OF HIS MOTHER
SHINES THROUGH ON EVERY PAGE. EVERETT ANDERSON
REMEMBERS HIS DADDY ALTHOUGH HE DOES NOT KNOW
WHERE HE IS, AND READING THIS SERIES OF VERSES
ABOUT THE MONTHS OF THE YEAR, A CHILD CAN SHARE
THE SPECIAL LOVE THE YOUNG BOY FEELS FOR HIS
MOTHER. (DIFF SIT--ONE PARENT,
EMOTIONS--LONELINESS, FAM--MOTHERS WORKING,
LONELINESS, MOTHERS WORKING, ONE PARENT)

DEAN, LEIGH. LOOKING DOWN GAME. FUNK, 1968.
ILLUSTRATED BY PAUL GIOVANOPOULOS. (BECB)

A LONELY BOY SPENDS ALMOST A YEAR IN A NEW
NEIGHBORHOOD, LOOKING DOWN INSTEAD OF UP, TO
AVOID MAKING NEW FRIENDS. WHILE THE BONUSES ARE
MANY--THE DISCOVERY THAT HE LIKES ANTS, AND THE
BIRD'S NEST HE FOUND--THE READER IS RELIEVED WHEN
HE DISCOVERS A FRIEND UP IN A TREE AND DECIDES
TO FIND OUT "WHAT BEING UP WAS LIKE." THE SOMBER
BLACK AND WHITE DRAWINGS LEND THEMSELVES WELL TO
THE QUIET, INTROSPECTIVE MOOD OF THE STORY, AND
EDGAR IS SEEN AS A BASICALLY SHY PERSON, FAIRLY
CONTENT TO EXPLORE HIS LONELY WORLD. WHILE THE
READER IS GLAD TO SEE HIM MAKE A FRIEND, ONE ALSO
SENSES THIS IS A BOY WHO WILL ALWAYS BE A GOOD
OBSERVER OF LIFE. (EMOTIONS--LONELINESS,
EMOTIONS--SHYNESS, LONELINESS, SHYNESS)

DUVOISIN, ROGER. LONELY VERONICA. KNOPF, 1963.
ILLUSTRATED BY ROGER DUVOISIN. (CC)

WHEN VERONICA THE HIPPOPOTAMUS IS MAROONED IN
NEW YORK CITY IN AN ELEVATOR SHAFT FOR AN ENTIRE
WEEKEND WITHOUT FOOD, SHE LEARNS THE MEANING OF
LONELINESS, AND SHE YEARNS FOR THE PEACEFUL RIVER
COUNTRY OF HER BIRTH. LONELY VERONICA
APPRECIATES THE CONSIDERATION SHOWN HER BY A
YOUNG PIGEON, WHO BRINGS HER FOOD, AND WHO
PROMISES TO VISIT VERONICA'S NEW HOME, A PEACEFUL

POND IN THE COUNTRY. (EMOTIONS--LONELINESS, FRIENDSHIP, LONELINESS)

DUVOISIN, ROGER. TWO LONELY DUCKS. KNOPF, 1955. ILLUSTRATED BY ROGER DUVOISIN. (CC)

A LOVELY COUNTING BOOK FOR YOUNG CHILDREN. THE LITTLE WHITE DUCK AND THE LITTLE WHITE DRAKE WERE LONELY IN THE POND. THEY DECIDED TO RAISE A FAMILY, SO THE LITTLE DUCK BUILT A NEST, AND LAID TEN EGGS IN ALL, SITTING ON THE EGGS FOR DAYS AND WEEKS, AND ONE BY ONE HATCHED OUT TEN BABY DUCKLINGS, AND NO ONE WAS LONELY ANY MORE. UNDERSCORES COMPANIONSHIP IN FAMILY LIVING. (EMOTIONS--LONELINESS, FAM, LONELINESS)

GORDON, SELMA. AMY LOVES GOODBYES. PLATT, 1966. ILLUSTRATED BY JUNE GOLDSBOROUGH. (CCB-B)

AMY PLAYS THE GAME OF MAKING GOODBYES A VERY FUN THING UNTIL HER PARENTS LEAVE FOR A SHORT TRIP. WHEN THEY RETURN, SHE KNOWS HOW MUCH A "HELLO" CAN MEAN. (EMOTIONS--LONELINESS, LONELINESS)

IWASAKI, CHIHIRO. STAYING HOME ALONE ON A RAINY DAY. MC GRAW, 1968. ILLUSTRATED BY CHIHIRO IWASAKI. (LJ)

LONELINESS IS A SHARP PAIN FOR A CHILD LEFT ALONE FOR THE FIRST TIME, AND ALLISON TRIES MANY WAYS TO MAKE THOSE FEELINGS GO AWAY. SHE WANTS TO HOLD HER KITTEN, SHE ENVIES THE BABY FISH SWIMMING WITH ITS MOTHER, AND WHEN SHE TOUCHES THE KEYS OF THE PIANO, IT ONLY REMINDS HER OF HER MOTHER. AUTHOR-ARTIST IWASAKI HAS COMPLEMENTED THESE FEELINGS OF FRUSTRATION WITH EXQUISITE, WATERY, FREE-FORM WATERCOLORS, SUITING THE BROWN AND GRAY TONES TO THE GRAY RAINY DAY SEEN THROUGH THE WINDOW. CHILDREN IDENTIFY WITH THESE SITUATIONS, ESPECIALLY THE TERROR OF THE PHONE RINGING AND BEING AFRAID TO ANSWER IT. USEFUL BECAUSE IT HELPS THE CHILD SEE THAT OTHER CHILDREN ARE ALSO AFRAID, BUT THAT MOTHER DOES RETURN, WHEN THE SUNSHINE RETURNS AT THE END OF THE AFTERNOON. (EMOTIONS--FEAR, EMOTIONS--LONELINESS, FEAR, LONELINESS)

JUSTUS, MAY. A NEW HOME FOR BILLY. HASTINGS, 1966. ILLUSTRATED BY JOAN PAYNE. (BCB)

WHEN SIX-YEAR-OLD BILLY MOVES TO A NEW
NEIGHBORHOOD HE FINDS OUT THAT NOT ALL PEOPLE
WILL RENT TO NEGROES, AT LEAST NOT AT THE TIME
THIS BOOK WAS WRITTEN. A USEFUL FACT FOR ALL
CHILDREN TO KNOW. THE NEW HOUSE, THOUGH IN NEED
OF REPAIR, HAS AN APPLE TREE IN THE YARD AND IS A
GREAT IMPROVEMENT OVER THE DIRTY SLUM AREA HE
MOVED FROM. AFTER AN INITIAL PERIOD OF
LONELINESS, BILLY MAKES FRIENDS BECAUSE OF THE
SWING, A SLIDE, A JUMPING BAR, AND A SEESAW
CONSTRUCTED BY HIS FATHER. THE BOOK ENDS WITH
FRIENDS, BLACK AND WHITE, HELPING TO PAINT THE
HOUSE. (EMOTIONS--LONELINESS, FRIENDSHIP,
LONELINESS, MOVING, NEW SIT--MOVING)

KANTROWITZ, MILDRED. MAXIE. PARENTS' MAG, 1970.
ILLUSTRATED BY EMILY MC CULLY. (ESLC)

AN INTERESTING THEME FOR A CHILDREN'S
BOOK--THE LONELINESS OF A WHITE-HAIRED OLD WOMAN
WHO LIVES ALONE AND THINKS NO ONE NEEDS HER. ALL
THIS IS CHANGED ONE DAY WHEN SHE STAYS IN BED
INSTEAD OF GOING THROUGH HER USUAL ROUTINE. SHE
FINDS OUT THAT INDEED MANY PEOPLE WERE DEPENDING
ON HER: HER CANARY BIRD WOKE UP ONE FAMILY, HER
WHISTLING TEAKETTLE ANOTHER. ALTOGETHER THERE
WERE 53 PEOPLE WHO CAME TO HER DOOR LATER THAT
DAY...AND SHE SERVED THEM ALL A CUP OF TEA. (DIFF
SIT--OLD AGE, EMOTIONS--LONELINESS, LONELINESS,
OLD AGE)

KEATS, EZRA. APT. 3. MACMILLAN, 1971.
ILLUSTRATED BY EZRA KEATS. (ESLC)

TWO BROTHERS, SAM AND BEN, ARE LONELY AND
DECIDE TO INVESTIGATE THE SOURCE OF SOMEONE
PLAYING A HARMONICA. THE SETTING IS A GRIM GHETTO
APARTMENT BUILDING, AND VARIOUS MOODS ARE FELT
AS THE BOYS GO DOWN THE HALL. WHEN THEY FIND THE
BLIND MAN PLAYING THE HARMONICA IN APT. 3, HE
SHARES WITH THEM THE SECRETS HE KNOWS AND PLAYS
STRANGE MUSIC WHICH CONJURES UP SIGHTS, SOUNDS,
AND COLORS TO SAM. THE BOOK ENDS WITH SAM ASKING
THE OLD MAN TO TAKE A WALK WITH THEM. EVOCATIVE
ART WORK AND PROSE SHOW THE POWER OF MUSIC ON THE
EMOTIONS. (DIFF SIT--HANDICAPS, DIFF SIT--OLD
AGE, EMOTIONS--LONELINESS, HANDICAPS, LONELINESS,
OLD AGE)

KEATS, EZRA. LOUIE. GREENWILLOW, 1975.

ILLUSTRATED BY EZRA KEATS. (CCB-B, CSM, HB, SLJ)

LOUIE, A YOUNG BOY IN A SLUM NEIGHBORHOOD WHO
DOES NOT SPEAK, COMES ALIVE WHEN HE SEES A PUPPET
NAMED GUSSIE AT A PUPPET SHOW. THE READER SENSES
THE LONELINESS OF LOUIE IN A BEAUTIFUL DREAM
SEQUENCE, AND ALL CHILDREN WILL APPRECIATE THE
ENDING, WHEN LOUIE RECEIVES GUSSIE AS A GENEROUS
GIFT FROM THE CHILDREN WHO MADE HER.
(BEHAVIOR--SHARING, EMOTIONS--LONELINESS,
FRIENDSHIP, LONELINESS, SHARING)

MC GOVERN, ANN. SCRAM, KID!. VIKING, 1974.
ILLUSTRATED BY NOLA LANGNER. (BL)

IN AN INTERESTING ARRANGEMENT OF ILLUSTRATIONS
ON THE PAGE, PART BLACK AND WHITE AND PART
SEPIA, THE ILLUSTRATOR OF THIS BOOK HAS MANAGED
TO CAPTURE THE SIMULTANEITY OF REALITY AND
DAYDREAM. THE STORY OF A LITTLE BOY WHO FEELS
LEFT OUT AND HAS ANGRY FEELINGS ABOUT IT SHOULD
STRIKE A FEELING OF EMPATHY IN MANY READERS.
DON'T WE ALL WISH WE WERE BRAVE ENOUGH TO SAY,
"I'LL FIX YOUR WAGON!" AFTER VENTING HIS ANGER IN
THE DAYDREAM, JOE FINDS A FRIEND WHO WILL SAIL A
BOAT WITH HIM AND, TEMPORARILY AT LEAST, FORGETS
ABOUT THE KIDS WHO WON'T LET HIM PLAY BASEBALL.
(ANGER, EMOTIONS--ANGER, EMOTIONS--LONELINESS,
LONELINESS)

NESS, EVALINE. SAM, BANGS, AND MOONSHINE. HOLT,
1966. ILLUSTRATED BY EVALINE NESS. (BCB)

DESPITE HER FATHER'S CAUTIONS, SAMANTHA IS NOT
ABLE TO KEEP STRAIGHT HER IMAGINARY LIFE FROM
HER REAL LIFE, AND TELLS PRETTY BIG WHOPPERS
TRIGGERED BY HER LONELINESS AND AN INSPIRED
IMAGINATION. WHEN SHE TELLS HER FRIEND THOMAS
THAT HER PET KANGAROO LIVES OUT IN A CAVE, THOMAS
BECOMES MAROONED AND ALMOST LOSES HIS LIFE. SAM
IS DISTRAUGHT WHEN SHE REALIZES THAT HER LIE, FOR
THAT IS WHAT IT IS, IS RESPONSIBLE. HER FATHER
TELLS HER TO THINK ABOUT THE DIFFERENCE BETWEEN
REAL AND MOONSHINE AND, AT THE END, HE ALSO TELLS
HER THAT THERE ARE TWO KINDS OF MOONSHINE: THE
GOOD KIND, WHICH IS HEALTHY IMAGINATIVE PLAY, AND
THE BAD KIND, THAT WHICH CAN BE HARMFUL.
(BEHAVIOR--MISBEHAVIOR, DIFF SIT--ONE PARENT,
EMOTIONS--LONELINESS, FAM--ONE PARENT,
LONELINESS, MISBEHAVIOR, ONE PARENT)

SENDAK, MAURICE. WHERE THE WILD THINGS ARE.
HARPER, 1963. ILLUSTRATED BY MAURICE SENDAK.
(BC, BESL, CC, CCB-B, GBC)

   MAX MISBEHAVES ONE NIGHT, NAILING A SPIKE INTO
THE WALL AND CRACKING THE PLASTER, CHASING THE
DOG WITH A FORK, AND HIS MOTHER SENDS HIM TO HIS
ROOM, TO BED WITHOUT ANY SUPPER. MAX DREAMS A
FANTASTIC DREAM, IN WHICH HE TURNS THE SITUATION
AROUND, AND HE IS THE BOSS. WHEN HE TELLS THE
WILD ANIMALS TO "BE STILL"--THEY OBEY, AND WHEN
HE IS CROWNED KING, HE REVELS IN HIS CONTROL OVER
THE BEASTS. OVERCOME WITH LONELINESS, THE SMELL
OF FOOD, AND WANTING TO BE SAFE AT HOME, MAX ENDS
UP IN HIS ROOM, WHERE HIS SUPPER IS WAITING. THE
AMBIVALENCE OF INDEPENDENCE/DEPENDENCE, THE
QUALITIES OF SECURITY AND LOVE ARE STRESSED IN
THIS BOOK. (BEHAVIOR--MISBEHAVIOR,
EMOTIONS--LONELINESS, EMOTIONS--LOVE,
EMOTIONS--SECURITY, LONELINESS, LOVE,
MISBEHAVIOR, SECURITY)

SHARMAT, MARJORIE. I WANT MAMA. HARPER, 1974.
ILLUSTRATED BY EMILY MC CULLY. (CCB-B, NYTBR)

   A LITTLE GIRL'S MOTHER GOES TO THE HOSPITAL
FOR AN OPERATION. IN CHILDLIKE PICTURES AND
DIALOG, THE READER LEARNS OF THE LONELINESS AND
CONCERN WITHIN THE LITTLE GIRL. USEFUL BECAUSE IT
SHOWS WHAT A CHILD CAN DO TO SPELL THE
LONELINESS, SUCH AS MAKE PRESENTS AND CLEAN THE
HOUSE. AN ESPECIALLY MOVING ILLUSTRATION AT THE
END OF THE BOOK SHOWS THE PEACE AND CONTENTMENT
IN THE HOUSEHOLD WHEN MOTHER COMES HOME.
(EMOTIONS--LONELINESS, FAM--MOTHERS, HOSPITAL,
LONELINESS, MOTHERS, NEW SIT--HOSPITAL)

SONNEBORN, RUTH. THE LOLLIPOP PARTY. VIKING,
1967. ILLUSTRATED BY BRINTON TURKLE. (ESLC)

   ONE DAY TOMAS IS LEFT ALONE IN THE APARTMENT
FOR THE FIRST TIME. HIS SISTER ANA, WHO USUALLY
CARED FOR HIM BEFORE GOING TO HER JOB, HAD TO
LEAVE HIM ALONE. STEP-BY-STEP THE READER
PARTICIPATES IN THE LITTLE BOY'S FEAR. HE WAS
CONCERNED ABOUT THE SOUND OF FOOTSTEPS ON THE
STAIRS, AND WISHED ONLY TO SIT QUIETLY AND HOLD
HIS CAT GATTO. WHEN HIS NURSERY SCHOOL TEACHER
COMES TO THE DOOR ON A VISIT, HOWEVER, THE
EMOTIONAL TONE OF THE BOOK CHANGES IMMEDIATELY.

HE IS HAPPY TO SEE HER, ACTS THE ROLE OF THE HOST
BY OFFERING HER A LOLLIPOP, AND THE STORY ENDS
WITH TOMAS FEELING A BIT GROWN-UP.
(EMOTIONS--FEAR, EMOTIONS--LONELINESS,
FAM--MOTHERS WORKING, FEAR, LONELINESS, MOTHERS
WORKING, SELF-RELIANCE)

THOMPSON, VIVIAN. SAD DAY, GLAD DAY. HOLIDAY,
1962. ILLUSTRATED BY LILIAN OBLIGADO. (RLHR)

   THE LARGE PRINT IS JUST RIGHT IN THIS BOOK FOR
NEW READERS WHO ARE BEGINNING TO PROGRESS TO
MORE DIFFICULT THINGS. KATHY MOVES TO A NEW
APARTMENT IN THE CITY FROM THE COUNTRY WHERE SHE
HAD A SWING ON AN APPLE TREE, AND FEELS VERY
LONELY. LUCKILY SHE FINDS A DOLL IN THE CLOSET OF
THE NEW HOUSE WHICH GOES A LONG WAY TOWARD
MAKING HER FEEL GOOD. EXPLAINS CHANGE AND HOW
PEOPLE ADJUST TO NEW PLACES.
(EMOTIONS--LONELINESS, LONELINESS, MOVING, NEW
SIT--MOVING)

ZINDEL, PAUL. I LOVE MY MOTHER. HARPER, 1975.
ILLUSTRATED BY JOHN MELO. (CCB-B)

   STRIKING FULL-COLOR ILLUSTRATIONS EXPAND THE
LIMITED TEXT OF THIS STORY OF A BOY AND HIS
MOTHER, PRESUMABLY LIVING ALONE BECAUSE OF
DIVORCE OR SEPARATION. THE REASON IS NOT
EXPLICITLY STATED. COMPANIONSHIP AT THE ZOO, IN
THE KITCHEN, AND LATE AT NIGHT WHEN THE BAD
DREAMS COME, MAKES UP ONE PART OF THE BOOK. THERE
IS ALSO DEPICTED THE REALISM OF VULNERABLE
FEELINGS WHEN THE BOY WANTS TO RUN AWAY FROM
HOME, WHEN HIS MOTHER TRIES NOT TO LET HIM KNOW
WHEN THEY ARE SHORT OF MONEY, BUT THE MOST MOVING
SCENES ARE WHEN MOTHER ADMITS THAT SHE IS LONELY
AND WHEN THE BOY MISSES HIS FATHER. (DIFF
SIT--DIVORCE, DIVORCE, EMOTIONS--LONELINESS,
EMOTIONS--LOVE, FAM--MOTHERS, FAM--ONE PARENT,
LONELINESS, LOVE, MOTHERS, ONE PARENT)

ZOLOTOW, CHARLOTTE. JANEY. HARPER, 1973.
ILLUSTRATED BY RONALD HIMLER. (CC)

   A PERCEPTIVE STORY OF THE LONELINESS THAT A
LITTLE GIRL FEELS AFTER HER FRIEND MOVES AWAY.
TOLD IN A MONOLOG, CATALOGING THE WAYS IN WHICH
SHE MISSES HER FRIEND JANEY, THE BOOK SHOWS
INCIDENTS IN THE PRESENT WHICH REMIND THE LITTLE

GIRL OF THE IMPORTANT MEMORIES IN THE PAST,
WALKING HOME TOGETHER FROM SCHOOL, CHRISTMAS
PRESENTS. THE SITUATIONS DESCRIBED ARE OFTEN
SENSUOUS. THE MEMORIES OF JANEY TOUCHING
EVERYTHING AS SHE WALKED ALONG THE STREET, THE
SOUND OF HER VOICE, THE MEMORIES OF THE SOUND OF
THE WIND BLOWING THROUGH THE TREES. IT IS A BOOK
WHICH ENDS ON A POSITIVE NOTE, AND ONE FEELS
GOOD, NOT SAD, ABOUT THE SHARED MEMORIES.
(EMOTIONS--LONELINESS, FRIENDSHIP, LONELINESS)

ZOLOTOW, CHARLOTTE. THE NEW FRIEND. ABELARD,
1968. ILLUSTRATED BY ARVIS STEWART. (ESLC)

   STRONG WATERCOLOR PAINTINGS IN DEEP PURPLES,
YELLOWS, AND GREENS COMPETE WITH THE RATHER QUIET
STORY OF FRIENDSHIP AND, SUBSEQUENTLY, A LOST
FRIEND. THE LITTLE GIRL CRIES ALL DAY, THEN
DREAMS OF A NEW FRIEND, AND CONSOLES HERSELF AS
SHE THINKS THAT SHE MIGHT FORGET, AND NOT CARE
ABOUT THE OLD FRIEND, THUS SOMEWHAT RESOLVING HER
HURT FEELINGS. (EMOTIONS--LONELINESS,
FRIENDSHIP, LONELINESS)

LOVE

ADOFF, ARNOLD. BLACK IS BROWN IS TAN. HARPER,
1973. ILLUSTRATED BY EMILY MC CULLY. (CC)

   DESCRIBING THIS FAMILY IN TERMS OF FREE VERSE
AND BEAUTIFUL WATERCOLORS DOES NOT BEGIN TO
INCLUDE THE NUANCES OF LOVE PORTRAYED AS THESE
CONTEMPORARY FAMILY MEMBERS CHOP THEIR OWN WOOD,
MAKE THEIR OWN MUSIC, COOK ON A BIG BLACK
COOKSTOVE. ALTHOUGH COLOR, THE VARYING SHADES OF
SKIN, IS THE THEME, CERTAINLY THE WARMTH OF
FAMILY LOVE IS THE MORE IMPORTANT MESSAGE.
(EMOTIONS--LOVE, FAM, LOVE)

ANGLUND, JOAN. LOVE IS A SPECIAL WAY OF FEELING.
HARCOURT, 1960. ILLUSTRATED BY JOAN ANGLUND.
(ESLC)

   SUBTLE ASPECTS OF LOVE ARE DEALT WITH IN THIS
TINY VOLUME--THE GOOD FEELINGS THAT COME WITH
HELPING AND SHARING, AND WITH THE SECURITY OF A
MOTHER'S LAP AND THE PEACEFULNESS OF HOME. A
WHOLESOME WAY TO EXPLORE THE FACETS OF LOVE
WITHOUT DEALING WITH ROMANTIC LOVE.
(EMOTIONS--LOVE, LOVE)

BROWNSTONE, CECILY. ALL KINDS OF MOTHERS. MC
KAY, 1969. ILLUSTRATED BY MIRIAM BROFSKY. (CSM,
LJ)

THE ILLUSTRATIONS AND TEXT ILLUSTRATE THAT
MOTHERS COME IN ALL SHAPES AND SIZES, THAT SOME
ARE NEAT AND SOME MAY BE SLOPPY, BUT THE MAIN
MESSAGE THAT COMES THROUGH IS THAT "MOTHERS KEEP
RIGHT ON LOVING THEM"--THOSE MISBEHAVING
CHILDREN. WHEN THE BOOK DISCUSSES WHERE SOME
MOTHERS MIGHT WORK, THE LIST IS RATHER LIMITED,
AND WOULD SUGGEST A RATHER NARROW ROLE FOR WOMEN
OUTSIDE THE HOME. (EMOTIONS--LOVE, FAM--MOTHERS,
LOVE, MOTHERS)

EHRLICH, AMY. ZEEK SILVER MOON. DIAL, 1972.
ILLUSTRATED BY ROBERT PARKER. (ESLC)

NOTABLE BECAUSE IT SHOWS AN ALTERNATIVE LIFE
STYLE OF A MUSICIAN, HIS WIFE, AND THEIR CHILD,
ZEEK SILVER MOON, THE BOOK IS GREATLY ENHANCED BY
STUNNINGLY BEAUTIFUL WATERCOLORS EVOKING THE
SOFTNESS OF LOVE. THIS IS A STORY OF
NON-CONFORMING, ALIVE, NEW LIFE-STYLE PEOPLE:
FATHER MADE THE BABY A CRADLE OF WOOD AFTER HE
WAS BORN AND LATER, WHEN ZEEK WAS FOUR YEARS OLD,
HIS FATHER, IN AN INCIDENT CALLED THE CARPET
RAISING, STAPLED THEIR LIVING ROOM RUG TO THE
CEILING BECAUSE A NEIGHBOR COMPLAINED OF NOISE.
WITHIN THE FRAMEWORK OF A FAMILY WHICH PLACES A
HIGH VALUE ON NATURAL FOODS, HOME-BAKED BREAD,
AND ENTERTAINMENT OTHER THAN TELEVISION, ZEEK IS
SHOWN TO BE A LOVED CHILD, ONE WHO RECEIVES
GENTLE LOVING CARE, IS TUCKED IN AT NIGHT AND
TOLD STORIES. (EMOTIONS--LOVE,
EMOTIONS--SECURITY, FAM, LOVE, SECURITY)

FLACK, MARJORIE. ASK MR. BEAR. MACMILLAN, 1932.
ILLUSTRATED BY MARJORIE FLACK. (CC)

THIS CLASSIC PICTURE BOOK WHICH PORTRAYS THE
DILEMMA OF WHAT TO GIVE MOTHER FOR HER BIRTHDAY
SUSTAINS THE BELIEF THAT AN EXPRESSION OF LOVE,
LIKE A BIG BEAR HUG, IS JUST AS GOOD, OR PERHAPS
BETTER, THAN ANY MATERIAL GIFT A CHILD COULD
GIVE. (EMOTIONS--LOVE, FAM, LOVE)

HOBAN, RUSSELL. LITTLE BRUTE FAMILY. MACMILLAN,
1966. ILLUSTRATED BY LILLIAN HOBAN. (CC)

THE LITTLE BRUTE FAMILY IS NOT A FAMILY WHICH
LOVES, NOR IS IT A FAMILY ONE COULD LOVE, AT
LEAST IN THE BEGINNING. THEY QUARREL, THEY NEVER
SAY THANK-YOU, THEY EAT STONES AND ARE THOROUGHLY
DISAGREEABLE, AS WELL AS BEING UGLY. BUT THE
POWER OF ONE LITTLE GOOD FEELING UPON THIS FAMILY
WORKS A MIRACLE. THEY CHANGE SO MUCH THAT IN THE
END THE LITTLE BRUTE FAMILY CHANGES ITS NAME TO
NICE. THIS IS A DRAMATIC WAY TO SHOW A CHILD THE
IMPORTANCE OF GOOD FEELINGS.
(EMOTIONS--HAPPINESS, EMOTIONS--LOVE, HAPPINESS,
LOVE)

LOBEL, ARNOLD. FROG AND TOAD ARE FRIENDS.
HARPER, 1970. ILLUSTRATED BY ARNOLD LOBEL. (BCB)

AN EASY-TO-READ FORMAT IS USED FOR FIVE
STORIES OF GENTLE RELATIONSHIPS BETWEEN TWO GOOD
FRIENDS: FROG HELPS TOAD LOOK FOR THE LOST
BUTTONS ON HIS JACKET, ROUSES TOAD FROM HIS LONG
WINTER SLEEP, AND LAUGHS AT HIS OLD-FASHIONED
STRIPED BATHING SUIT. THE QUALITIES OF FRIENDSHIP
ARE ILLUMINATED WELL: LOVING CARE FOR ANOTHER
PERSON, YET A HEALTHY HUMOR WHICH ALLOWS ONE
FRIEND TO LAUGH AT ANOTHER WITHOUT HARMING THE
FRIENDSHIP. (EMOTIONS--LOVE, FRIENDSHIP, LOVE)

MILES, BETTY. AROUND AND AROUND--LOVE. KNOPF,
1975. ILLUSTRATED BY BETTY MILES. (BL)

BLACK AND WHITE PHOTOGRAPHS OF LOVE IN AN
INFINITE VARIETY DOMINATE THIS PICTURE BOOK. THE
BRIEF TEXT READS LIKE POETRY, AND SERVES TO TIE
THE PICTURES TOGETHER IN A LOOSE MANNER, AS IN
THE ONE SEQUENCE OF FIVE PICTURES WHICH
ILLUSTRATE "WORKING AND SHARING ARE LOVE."
RELATIONSHIPS BETWEEN PETS AND CHILDREN, THE OLD
AND THE YOUNG, PARENT AND CHILD, GIRL/BOY LOVE,
INCLUDING ETHNIC GROUPS OTHER THAN WHITE, ARE
ONLY SOME OF THE WAYS LOVE IS DEPICTED. "IT'S
HARD TO TELL ABOUT, EASY TO SHOW."
(EMOTIONS--LOVE, LOVE)

MINARIK, ELSE. A KISS FOR LITTLE BEAR. HARPER,
1968. ILLUSTRATED BY MAURICE SENDAK. (BCB)

AMUSING STORY BECAUSE OF THE HUMOROUS INCIDENT
IN WHICH LITTLE BEAR'S KISS ALMOST GETS LOST
WHEN LITTLE SKUNK GIVES IT TO HIS LADY FRIEND
INSTEAD OF PASSING IT ON, BUT THE UNDERLYING

MESSAGE IS THERE. LITTLE BEAR MAKES A PRESENT FOR
HIS GRANDMOTHER AND SHE, IN A LOVING GESTURE,
SENDS HIM A KISS. THE DELICATE ROUNDED LINES IN
THE ILLUSTRATIONS, FRAMED ON EACH PAGE, FURTHER
THE GENTLE, CARING MESSAGE. (EMOTIONS--LOVE,
FAM--GRANDMOTHERS, GRANDMOTHERS, LOVE)

RAYNOR, DORKA. THIS IS MY FATHER AND ME.
WHITMAN, A., 1973.   ILLUSTRATED BY DORKA RAYNOR.
(BL)

   STRIKING BLACK AND WHITE PHOTOGRAPHS FROM ALL
OVER THE WORLD SHOW VARYING RELATIONSHIPS OF
FATHERS TO THEIR CHILDREN. WHILE NOT A BOOK WHICH
WILL BE READILY PICKED UP BY CHILDREN, IT
REVEALS THE ROLE OF LOVE, COOPERATION,
PROTECTION, CARE, DEVOTION, WORK, PLAY, AND PRIDE
WHICH CAN EXIST BETWEEN PARENT AND CHILD IN A
UNIVERSAL WAY. (EMOTIONS--LOVE, FAM--FATHERS,
FATHERS, LOVE)

SCOTT, ANN. ON MOTHER'S LAP. MC GRAW, 1972.
ILLUSTRATED BY GLO COALSON. (BCB)

   A LOVING STORY OF A LAP WITH UNLIMITED ROOM.
FIRST IT HAS MICHAEL, THEN HIS DOLL, THEN HIS
BOAT, THEN HIS PUPPY, THEN HIS REINDEER BLANKET.
THEY ALL ROCKED TOGETHER. WHEN THE BABY WAKES UP,
MICHAEL PUTS ON A SOUR FACE, AND SAYS THERE
ISN'T ANY ROOM. BUT MOTHER MAKES ROOM FOR ALL,
AND GIVES A SENSE OF SECURITY TO THE READER THAT
ONLY A LAP AND A ROCKING CHAIR CAN PROVIDE.
(EMOTIONS--LOVE, EMOTIONS--SECURITY,
FAM--MOTHERS, FAM--SIBLING RIVALRY, LOVE,
MOTHERS, SECURITY, SIBLING RIVALRY)

SEGAL, LORE. TELL ME A MITZI. FARRAR, 1970.
ILLUSTRATED BY HARRIET PINCUS. (BCB)

   MARTHA IS A VERY LUCKY LITTLE GIRL: HER MOTHER
AND FATHER AND GRANDMOTHER ARE WONDERFUL
STORYTELLERS. THEY TELL HER "MITZIES," WHICH ARE
REALLY STORIES ABOUT HER AND HER BROTHER, SUCH AS
THE TIME SHE WOKE UP EARLY, GOT HER BABY BROTHER
UP AND DRESSED, AND PLANNED TO TAKE A TAXI TO
SEE HER GRANDPARENTS. EXCEPT THAT SHE DIDN'T KNOW
THE ADDRESS. SO THE TAXI DRIVER LET HER OUT AND
SHE AND JACOB WENT UPSTAIRS AND WENT BACK TO BED,
JUST AS MOTHER'S ALARM CLOCK WENT OFF. TWO OTHER
STORIES COMPLETE THE BOOK: ONE IS A HILARIOUS

ACCOUNT OF THE FAMILY FALLING ILL, ONE BY ONE,
THE OTHER AN IMAGINATIVE TALE OF THE PRESIDENT OF
THE UNITED STATES GIVING A PIECE OF GUM TO
JACOB. ILLUSTRATIONS ARE IN RICH, VIBRANT COLORS
WHICH REFLECT THE VIGOR OF THE FAMILY.
(EMOTIONS--LOVE, FAM, LOVE)

SENDAK, MAURICE. WHERE THE WILD THINGS ARE.
HARPER, 1963. ILLUSTRATED BY MAURICE SENDAK.
(BC, BESL, CC, CCB-B, GBC)

   MAX MISBEHAVES ONE NIGHT, NAILING A SPIKE INTO
THE WALL AND CRACKING THE PLASTER, CHASING THE
DOG WITH A FORK, AND HIS MOTHER SENDS HIM TO HIS
ROOM, TO BED WITHOUT ANY SUPPER. MAX DREAMS A
FANTASTIC DREAM, IN WHICH HE TURNS THE SITUATION
AROUND, AND HE IS THE BOSS. WHEN HE TELLS THE
WILD ANIMALS TO "BE STILL"--THEY OBEY, AND WHEN
HE IS CROWNED KING, HE REVELS IN HIS CONTROL OVER
THE BEASTS. OVERCOME WITH LONELINESS, THE SMELL
OF FOOD, AND WANTING TO BE SAFE AT HOME, MAX ENDS
UP IN HIS ROOM, WHERE HIS SUPPER IS WAITING. THE
AMBIVALENCE OF INDEPENDENCE/DEPENDENCE, THE
QUALITIES OF SECURITY AND LOVE ARE STRESSED IN
THIS BOOK. (BEHAVIOR--MISBEHAVIOR,
EMOTIONS--LONELINESS, EMOTIONS--LOVE,
EMOTIONS--SECURITY, LONELINESS, LOVE,
MISBEHAVIOR, SECURITY)

SONNEBORN, RUTH. FRIDAY NIGHT IS PAPA NIGHT.
VIKING, 1970. ILLUSTRATED BY EMILY MC CULLY.
(BCB, CC)

   A SYMPATHETIC PICTURE OF PUERTO RICAN LIFE IN
A CROWDED APARTMENT, WHERE PEDRO'S BED IS IN THE
KITCHEN, AND FATHER WORKS TWO JOBS TO PROVIDE FOR
HIS FAMILY. BROWN TONES COMPLEMENT THE WARMTH
AND SKIN COLOR OF THE CHARACTERS, AND LEND A
HARMONIOUS TONE TO THE THEME, WHICH IS THE
SPECIAL FEELING IN PEDRO'S MIND WHEN HIS FATHER
COMES HOME ON FRIDAY NIGHT. (EMOTIONS--LOVE,
FAM--FATHERS, FATHERS, LOVE)

STEPTOE, JOHN. STEVIE. HARPER, 1969.
ILLUSTRATED BY JOHN STEPTOE. (BCB)

   BRILLIANT PAINTINGS ENHANCE THIS INTERESTING
BOOK WRITTEN AND ILLUSTRATED BY A YOUNG BLACK
MAN. THE STORY OF STEVIE, WHO COMES TO STAY WITH
THE NARRATOR, BEGINS WHEN ROBERT'S MOTHER TAKES A

PRESCHOOLER INTO HER HOME FOR DAY CARE. ROBERT,
AN ONLY CHILD, IS BOTHERED BY HAVING A TAG-ALONG
WHEREVER HE GOES AND ONE WHO ALWAYS BREAKS THE
TOYS. ROBERT THINKS STEVIE IS SPOILED AND HE
THINKS HIS MOTHER ISN'T STRICT ENOUGH. BUT WHEN
STEVIE'S FAMILY MOVES AWAY, ROBERT REALIZES THE
VOID IN HIS LIFE AND, AS HE MUSES OVER THIS
THOUGHT, HE REALIZES HE ALMOST HAD A REAL-LIFE
LITTLE BROTHER. (EMOTIONS--LOVE, LOVE,
SELF-UNDERSTANDING)

TURKLE, BRINTON. THY FRIEND OBADIAH. VIKING,
1969. ILLUSTRATED BY BRINTON TURKLE. (BCB)

   OBADIAH, A YOUNG QUAKER BOY, IS ANGRY WHEN A
SEA GULL TRIES TO BE HIS FRIEND BY TAGGING ALONG
BEHIND HIM IN THIS EXCELLENT PORTRAYAL OF QUAKER
FAMILY LIFE. AS THE STORY PROGRESSES, THE GULL
GETS A LARGE RUSTY FISHHOOK CAUGHT IN HIS BEAK,
OBADIAH TAKES IT OUT, AND THE SEA GULL FLIES
AWAY. WHEN THE GULL RETURNS, OBADIAH REASONS:
"SINCE I HELPED HIM, I'M HIS FRIEND, TOO."
TURKLE'S WATERCOLORS EVOKE A POWERFUL FEELING OF
A COZY, SECURE LIFE IN THE DAYS WHEN THE FAMILY
GATHERED AROUND THE FIREPLACE WHILE THE BREAD WAS
BAKING. (EMOTIONS--LOVE, EMOTIONS--SECURITY,
FAM, FRIENDSHIP, LOVE, SECURITY)

YOLEN, JANE. IT ALL DEPENDS. FUNK, 1969.
ILLUSTRATED BY DON BOLOGNESE. (LJ)

   IN A ROUNDABOUT WAY, THIS IS A POETICAL STORY
OF THE VALUE OF LOVE. DAVID IS A LITTLE BOY WHO
QUESTIONS HIS MOTHER ABOUT A NUMBER OF THINGS.
"HOW TALL AM I?" AND SHE ANSWERS BY SAYING THAT
IT ALL DEPENDS UPON THE RELATIONSHIP OF THINGS.
THAT TO AN ANT, HE IS VERY LARGE, BUT THAT TO A
WHALE, HE IS VERY SMALL. IN AN IMAGINATIVE SERIES
OF ILLUSTRATIONS, BOLOGNESE HAS PRODUCED A BOOK
USEFUL TO TEACHERS AND PARENTS WHICH TEACHES
DIFFERING SIZE RELATIONSHIPS. IT IS NOT UNTIL
ALMOST THE END THAT DAVID ASKS, "WHAT IF I GROW,
AND CHANGE," AND SHE ANSWERS THAT HE WILL ALWAYS
BE JUST RIGHT, BECAUSE HIS PARENTS LOVE HIM.
(EMOTIONS--LOVE, FAM--MOTHERS, LOVE, MOTHERS,
SELF-CONSCIOUSNESS--SIZE)

ZINDEL, PAUL. I LOVE MY MOTHER. HARPER, 1975.
ILLUSTRATED BY JOHN MELO. (CCB-B)

STRIKING FULL-COLOR ILLUSTRATIONS EXPAND THE
LIMITED TEXT OF THIS STORY OF A BOY AND HIS
MOTHER, PRESUMABLY LIVING ALONE BECAUSE OF
DIVORCE OR SEPARATION. THE REASON IS NOT
EXPLICITLY STATED. COMPANIONSHIP AT THE ZOO, IN
THE KITCHEN, AND LATE AT NIGHT WHEN THE BAD
DREAMS COME, MAKES UP ONE PART OF THE BOOK. THERE
IS ALSO DEPICTED THE REALISM OF VULNERABLE
FEELINGS WHEN THE BOY WANTS TO RUN AWAY FROM
HOME, WHEN HIS MOTHER TRIES NOT TO LET HIM KNOW
WHEN THEY ARE SHORT OF MONEY, BUT THE MOST MOVING
SCENES ARE WHEN MOTHER ADMITS THAT SHE IS LONELY
AND WHEN THE BOY MISSES HIS FATHER. (DIFF
SIT--DIVORCE, DIVORCE, EMOTIONS--LONELINESS,
EMOTIONS--LOVE, FAM--MOTHERS, FAM--ONE PARENT,
LONELINESS, LOVE, MOTHERS, ONE PARENT)

ZOLOTOW, CHARLOTTE. DO YOU KNOW WHAT I'LL DO?.
HARPER, 1958. ILLUSTRATED BY GARTH WILLIAMS.
(CC)

A LOVING PICTURE OF A GIRL ABOUT SEVEN YEARS
OLD, DREAMING ABOUT ALL OF THE WAYS SHE WILL BE
GOOD TO HER BABY BROTHER. GARTH WILLIAMS HAS
DRAWN LARGE FULL-PAGE ILLUSTRATIONS FILLED IN
WITH A DELICATE WATERCOLOR WASH TO ACCENTUATE THE
DREAMY QUALITY OF THE LITTLE GIRL'S THOUGHTS.
SHE PROMISES CONCRETE THINGS, SUCH AS BRINGING
HOME A PIECE OF BIRTHDAY CAKE, AND SHE PROMISES
THINGS THAT ARE IN THE AFFECTIVE DOMAIN: SHE
TELLS HIM THAT SHE'LL GET RID OF HIS NIGHTMARES
FOR HIM. IN DOING THIS, OF COURSE, SHE
DEMONSTRATES THE THINGS THAT ARE IMPORTANT AND
PROMINENT IN CHILDREN'S LIVES, THEIR EXPECTATIONS
AND FEARS. (BROTHERS & SISTERS, EMOTIONS--LOVE,
FAM--BROTHERS & SISTERS, LOVE)

MANNERS

SLOBODKIN, LOUIS. THANK YOU--YOU'RE WELCOME.
VANGUARD, 1957. ILLUSTRATED BY LOUIS SLOBODKIN.
(CC)

IN SLOBODKIN'S SPARE STYLE, A LITTLE BOY IS
SHOWN HAPPILY SAYING THANK YOU IN THE PROPER
CIRCUMSTANCES. HE LEARNS THAT TO SAY "YOU'RE
WELCOME," HE MUST DO SOMETHING FOR SOMEONE ELSE.
A SIMPLE, HONEST STORY OF BASIC COURTESY.
(BEHAVIOR--MANNERS, MANNERS)

VIPONT, ELFRIDA. THE ELEPHANT AND THE BAD BABY.
COWARD, 1969. ILLUSTRATED BY RAYMOND BRIGGS.
(BCB)

EARLY RAYMOND BRIGGS ILLUSTRATIONS ADD TO THE
LIVELY VIGOR OF THIS STORY OF A BAD BABY WHO
NEVER SAID "PLEASE." MUCH PLEASING REPETITION IN
THE WAY THEY WENT RUNNING AROUND THE TOWN:
"RUMPETA, RUMPETA." BABY REALLY WAS BAD, BUT HE
TOO SHARED IN THE PANCAKES AT THE END, BEING SENT
TO BED ONLY AFTER THE FESTIVITIES WERE OVER.
RATHER A JOYOUS WAY TO LEARN MANNERS!
(BEHAVIOR--MANNERS, BEHAVIOR--MISBEHAVIOR,
MANNERS, MISBEHAVIOR)

ZOLOTOW, CHARLOTTE. WHEN I HAVE A SON. HARPER,
1967. ILLUSTRATED BY HILARY KNIGHT. (BCB)

IN AN IMAGINATIVE PROJECTION INTO THE FUTURE,
JOHN TELLS HOW HIS SON WOULD BE PERMITTED TO
BEHAVE AND, IN DOING SO, THE READER SEES A PARADE
OF FORBIDDEN BEHAVIOR: NOT SAYING THANK YOU FOR
PRESENTS HE HATES, AND HAVING A TRIPLE MALTED
JUST BEFORE DINNER. THE IDEAS THAT JOHN IS
REJECTING FALL INTO THE AREAS OF ETIQUETTE,
GROOMING, PARENTAL CONTROL, COMMON COURTESY, FOOD
DESIRES, AND HEALTH. SOME SEEM QUITE HARMLESS,
SUCH AS STAYING DOWN AT THE RAILROAD STATION ALL
DAY TO WATCH THE TRAINS. IN GENERAL, A MILD
GROUSING AGAINST RULES SET DOWN BY GROWN-UPS. IN
THE END, WE REALIZE JOHN IS ONLY DAYDREAMING OUT
LOUD TO HIS FRIEND: HE DUTIFULLY GOES IN THE
HOUSE FOR THE HATED PIANO LESSON.
(BEHAVIOR--DISLIKES, BEHAVIOR--MANNERS,
BEHAVIOR--MISBEHAVIOR, DISLIKES, MANNERS,
MISBEHAVIOR)

MISBEHAVIOR

ETS, MARIE. BAD BOY, GOOD BOY!. CROWELL, T.,
1967. ILLUSTRATED BY MARIE ETS. (BCB)

ALTHOUGH THE STORY IS TOLD THROUGH THE
DESTRUCTIVE ACTIVITIES OF ROBERTO, A LITTLE
PRESCHOOLER ON HIS OWN AS HE ROAMS THE
NEIGHBORHOOD UNSUPERVISED, IT IS REALLY A
PORTRAIT OF A TROUBLED FAMILY, SEVEN SLEEPING IN
ONE BEDROOM, WITH A YOUNG INEXPERIENCED MOTHER
INCAPABLE OF COPING WITH THE FAMILY. WHEN ROBERTO
GOES TO DAY SCHOOL AT THE CHILDREN'S CENTER,

THINGS GET BETTER: HE LEARNS SOME ENGLISH BUT,
MORE IMPORTANTLY, PRINTS THE LETTER TO HIS MOTHER
WHICH BRINGS HER HOME. MOST CHILDREN WILL
UNDERSTAND THE "BAD" BEHAVIOR WHICH CAME ABOUT
BECAUSE ROBERTO NEEDED ATTENTION. THE TEXT IS
QUITE LONG, AND IT IS NOT PARTICULARLY EASY TO
READ. THEREFORE THIS IS PROBABLY MORE USEFUL AS A
BOOK TO BE SHARED. (BEHAVIOR--MISBEHAVIOR, DIFF
SIT--SEPARATION, MISBEHAVIOR, SEPARATION)

GAEDDERT, LOU. NOISY NANCY NORRIS. DOUBLEDAY,
1965. ILLUSTRATED BY GIOIA FIAMMENGHI. (CC)

NOT A MODEL GIRL, NANCY IS ABOUT THE NOISIEST
CHILD IMAGINABLE. WHEN THE NEIGHBOR COMPLAINS,
NANCY BECOMES SO VERY QUIET THAT EVERYONE THINKS
SHE IS ILL. THE LAST PICTURE IN THE BOOK IS TRULY
FUNNY, FOR NANCY HAS TIED A BIG SOFT RAG AROUND
HER STICK HORSE SO SHE WILL NOT BANG ON THE
FLOOR. USEFUL TO PRESENT A NON-STEREOTYPED LOOK
AT A LITTLE GIRL'S BEHAVIOR.
(BEHAVIOR--CONSIDERATION, BEHAVIOR--MISBEHAVIOR,
CONSIDERATION, MISBEHAVIOR)

MC LEOD, EMILIE. THE BEAR'S BICYCLE. LITTLE,
1975. ILLUSTRATED BY DAVID MC PHAIL. (BL)

AN IMAGINATIVE STORY IN WHICH AN ENORMOUS
BEAR, ON A MINIATURE BICYCLE, BREAKS ALL THE
RULES. AS THE LITTLE BOY IN THE STORY
DEMONSTRATES THE CORRECT WAY TO STAY ON THE RIGHT
WHEN MEETING ANOTHER BIKER, THE LUMBERING BEAR
TAKES A SPILL IN THE MIDDLE OF THE PATH, CROWDING
A YOUNG BOY, CAUSING HIM TO CRASH. BEAUTIFUL
ILLUSTRATIONS AND HUMOROUS SITUATIONS TEACH A
LESSON OF SAFETY IN A PAINLESS WAY.
(BEHAVIOR--CONSIDERATION, BEHAVIOR--MISBEHAVIOR,
BEHAVIOR--SAFETY, CONSIDERATION, MISBEHAVIOR,
SAFETY)

NESS, EVALINE. SAM, BANGS, AND MOONSHINE. HOLT,
1966. ILLUSTRATED BY EVALINE NESS. (BCB)

DESPITE HER FATHER'S CAUTIONS, SAMANTHA IS NOT
ABLE TO KEEP STRAIGHT HER IMAGINARY LIFE FROM
HER REAL LIFE, AND TELLS PRETTY BIG WHOPPERS
TRIGGERED BY HER LONELINESS AND AN INSPIRED
IMAGINATION. WHEN SHE TELLS HER FRIEND THOMAS
THAT HER PET KANGAROO LIVES OUT IN A CAVE, THOMAS
BECOMES MAROONED AND ALMOST LOSES HIS LIFE. SAM

IS DISTRAUGHT WHEN SHE REALIZES THAT HER LIE, FOR
THAT IS WHAT IT IS, IS RESPONSIBLE. HER FATHER
TELLS HER TO THINK ABOUT THE DIFFERENCE BETWEEN
REAL AND MOONSHINE AND, AT THE END, HE ALSO TELLS
HER THAT THERE ARE TWO KINDS OF MOONSHINE: THE
GOOD KIND, WHICH IS HEALTHY IMAGINATIVE PLAY, AND
THE BAD KIND, THAT WHICH CAN BE HARMFUL.
(BEHAVIOR--MISBEHAVIOR, DIFF SIT--ONE PARENT,
EMOTIONS--LONELINESS, FAM--ONE PARENT,
LONELINESS, MISBEHAVIOR, ONE PARENT)

SENDAK, MAURICE. WHERE THE WILD THINGS ARE.
HARPER, 1963. ILLUSTRATED BY MAURICE SENDAK.
(BC, BESL, CC, CCB-B, GBC)

   MAX MISBEHAVES ONE NIGHT, NAILING A SPIKE INTO
THE WALL AND CRACKING THE PLASTER, CHASING THE
DOG WITH A FORK, AND HIS MOTHER SENDS HIM TO HIS
ROOM, TO BED WITHOUT ANY SUPPER. MAX DREAMS A
FANTASTIC DREAM, IN WHICH HE TURNS THE SITUATION
AROUND, AND HE IS THE BOSS. WHEN HE TELLS THE
WILD ANIMALS TO "BE STILL"--THEY OBEY, AND WHEN
HE IS CROWNED KING, HE REVELS IN HIS CONTROL OVER
THE BEASTS. OVERCOME WITH LONELINESS, THE SMELL
OF FOOD, AND WANTING TO BE SAFE AT HOME, MAX ENDS
UP IN HIS ROOM, WHERE HIS SUPPER IS WAITING. THE
AMBIVALENCE OF INDEPENDENCE/DEPENDENCE, THE
QUALITIES OF SECURITY AND LOVE ARE STRESSED IN
THIS BOOK. (BEHAVIOR--MISBEHAVIOR,
EMOTIONS--LONELINESS, EMOTIONS--LOVE,
EMOTIONS--SECURITY, LONELINESS, LOVE,
MISBEHAVIOR, SECURITY)

VIPONT, ELFRIDA. THE ELEPHANT AND THE BAD BABY.
COWARD, 1969. ILLUSTRATED BY RAYMOND BRIGGS.
(BCB)

   EARLY RAYMOND BRIGGS ILLUSTRATIONS ADD TO THE
LIVELY VIGOR OF THIS STORY OF A BAD BABY WHO
NEVER SAID "PLEASE." MUCH PLEASING REPETITION IN
THE WAY THEY WENT RUNNING AROUND THE TOWN:
"RUMPETA, RUMPETA." BABY REALLY WAS BAD, BUT HE
TOO SHARED IN THE PANCAKES AT THE END, BEING SENT
TO BED ONLY AFTER THE FESTIVITIES WERE OVER.
RATHER A JOYOUS WAY TO LEARN MANNERS!
(BEHAVIOR--MANNERS, BEHAVIOR--MISBEHAVIOR,
MANNERS, MISBEHAVIOR)

WABER, BERNARD. NOBODY IS PERFICK. HOUGHTON,
1971. ILLUSTRATED BY BERNARD WABER. (CCB-B)

A HARD-TO-DESCRIBE BOOK BECAUSE OF ITS
UNCONVENTIONAL FORMAT. IT IS DIVIDED INTO SEVEN
SECTIONS DEALING WITH IMPERFECTNESS: THE CHILD
WHO CAN'T SIT UP STRAIGHT, ONE WHO DAYDREAMS,
ANOTHER WHO SQUEALS THE CONTENTS OF SOMEONE'S
DIARY, AND ENDING WITH A PORTRAIT OF A PERFECT
BOY (WHO TURNS OUT TO BE A ROBOT WITH A WIND-UP
KEY IN HIS BACK). (BEHAVIOR--MISBEHAVIOR,
MISBEHAVIOR, SELF-EVALUATION)

WILLARD, BARBARA. HULLABALOO!. MEREDITH, 1969.
ILLUSTRATED BY FRITZ WAGNER.   (ESLC)

A BEAUTIFUL COLLECTION OF POETRY AND STORIES
WHICH IS DIFFICULT TO CATEGORIZE OR DESCRIBE, BUT
THE EDITOR SAYS ONE OF THE GOOD THINGS ABOUT IT
IS THAT WE OUGHT TO BE GLAD WE ARE LIVING TODAY,
BECAUSE MANY OF THE OLDER POEMS INCLUDED SHOW
DIRE CONSEQUENCES OF MISBEHAVIOR, SUCH AS MAY, A
WISP OF A "FLIBBETIGIBBET," WHO WAS SWALLOWED UP
WHOLE BY THE GIANT NAMED MUST. NOT EVERYONE'S CUP
OF TEA, THIS ANTHOLOGY NEEDS TO BE PERUSED
LEISURELY BY THE READER, AND WILL PROBABLY REWARD
HIM/HER WITH A JUST RIGHT STORY. MANY OF THE
SELECTIONS ARE HUMOROUS. TRY THE LAST SELECTION
IN THE BOOK, "NURSE MATILDA," FOR A SPLENDID
EXAMPLE OF MISBEHAVING CHILDREN.
(BEHAVIOR--MISBEHAVIOR, MISBEHAVIOR)

WINN, MARIE. SHIVER, GOBBLE AND SNORE. SIMON,
1971.   ILLUSTRATED BY WHITNEY DARROW JR..   (ESLC)

A BOOK FOR VERY YOUNG CHILDREN ABOUT WHY
PEOPLE NEED LAWS. THREE FRIENDS WHO DON'T LIKE
ALL OF THE LAWS WHICH THE KING MAKES DECIDE TO
MOVE AWAY AND NOT HAVE ANY LAWS. CHAOS REIGNS
HOWEVER--SHIVER MADE FIRES WHICH BOTHERED GOBBLE,
AND THE SNORING OF SNORE BOTHERED SHIVER. WHEN
THEY DECIDE THAT LIFE LIKE THIS IS NOT GOOD
EITHER, THEY SET UP NEW RULES. A GOOD WAY TO
INTRODUCE CHILDREN TO THE NECESSITY FOR LAWS.
THERE ARE FOUR PAGES AT THE END DEVOTED TO
ACTIVITIES TO REINFORCE THE CONCEPT.
(BEHAVIOR--CONSIDERATION, BEHAVIOR--MISBEHAVIOR,
BEHAVIOR--RESPONSIBILITY, CONSIDERATION,
MISBEHAVIOR, RESPONSIBILITY)

ZOLOTOW, CHARLOTTE. WHEN I HAVE A SON. HARPER,
1967.   ILLUSTRATED BY HILARY KNIGHT.   (BCB)

IN AN IMAGINATIVE PROJECTION INTO THE FUTURE,
JOHN TELLS HOW HIS SON WOULD BE PERMITTED TO
BEHAVE AND, IN DOING SO, THE READER SEES A PARADE
OF FORBIDDEN BEHAVIOR: NOT SAYING THANK YOU FOR
PRESENTS HE HATES, AND HAVING A TRIPLE MALTED
JUST BEFORE DINNER. THE IDEAS THAT JOHN IS
REJECTING FALL INTO THE AREAS OF ETIQUETTE,
GROOMING, PARENTAL CONTROL, COMMON COURTESY, FOOD
DESIRES, AND HEALTH. SOME SEEM QUITE HARMLESS,
SUCH AS STAYING DOWN AT THE RAILROAD STATION ALL
DAY TO WATCH THE TRAINS. IN GENERAL, A MILD
GROUSING AGAINST RULES SET DOWN BY GROWN-UPS. IN
THE END, WE REALIZE JOHN IS ONLY DAYDREAMING OUT
LOUD TO HIS FRIEND: HE DUTIFULLY GOES IN THE
HOUSE FOR THE HATED PIANO LESSON.
(BEHAVIOR--DISLIKES, BEHAVIOR--MANNERS,
BEHAVIOR--MISBEHAVIOR, DISLIKES, MANNERS,
MISBEHAVIOR)

MOTHER-DAUGHTER

TOBIAS, TOBI. THE QUITTING DEAL. VIKING, 1975.
ILLUSTRATED BY TRINA HYMAN. (BL)

IN REALISTIC DRAWINGS AND TEXT DEALING WITH A
CONTEMPORARY MOTHER AND DAUGHTER, EACH WEARING
LONG HAIR AND JEANS, THE AUTHOR AND ILLUSTRATOR
HAVE PRESENTED A SITUATION IN WHICH EACH
CHARACTER WISHES TO CONQUER A BAD HABIT: THUMB
SUCKING ON THE PART OF THE DAUGHTER, AND SMOKING
CIGARETTES ON THE PART OF THE MOTHER. THEY
PROGRESS THROUGH SEVERAL CURES, SUCH AS HOLDING
HANDS, AND THE CANDY CURE--EACH HAS ITS
DRAWBACKS. WHILE THEY SUCCEED FOR AWHILE, IN THE
END BOTH MOTHER AND DAUGHTER FIND THEY CANNOT
QUIT COLD. NOT THE USUAL ENDING FOR A CHILDREN'S
BOOK. (BEHAVIOR--THUMB SUCKING,
FAM--MOTHER-DAUGHTER, MOTHER-DAUGHTER, THUMB
SUCKING)

MOTHERS

BROWN, MARGARET. THE RUNAWAY BUNNY. HARPER,
1942. ILLUSTRATED BY CLEMENT HURD. (CC)

A THOROUGHLY SATISFYING STORY FOR A YOUNG
CHILD, FOR ALL CHILDREN DREAM OF RUNNING AWAY
FROM HOME. THIS MOTHER RABBIT, WHO ALWAYS THINKS
OF A WAY TO INTERCEPT HER YOUNG ONE, IS A PERFECT
PORTRAIT OF THE MOTHER WHO IS ALWAYS THERE, AND

WILL ALWAYS BE THERE, THE ULTIMATE IN SECURITY
AND LOVE. (EMOTIONS--SECURITY, FAM--MOTHERS,
MOTHERS, SECURITY)

BROWNSTONE, CECILY. ALL KINDS OF MOTHERS. MC
KAY, 1969. ILLUSTRATED BY MIRIAM BROFSKY. (CSM,
LJ)

   THE ILLUSTRATIONS AND TEXT ILLUSTRATE THAT
MOTHERS COME IN ALL SHAPES AND SIZES, THAT SOME
ARE NEAT AND SOME MAY BE SLOPPY, BUT THE MAIN
MESSAGE THAT COMES THROUGH IS THAT "MOTHERS KEEP
RIGHT ON LOVING THEM"--THOSE MISBEHAVING
CHILDREN. WHEN THE BOOK DISCUSSES WHERE SOME
MOTHERS MIGHT WORK, THE LIST IS RATHER LIMITED,
AND WOULD SUGGEST A RATHER NARROW ROLE FOR WOMEN
OUTSIDE THE HOME. (EMOTIONS--LOVE, FAM--MOTHERS,
LOVE, MOTHERS)

LEXAU, JOAN. EMILY AND THE KLUNKY BABY AND THE
NEXT DOOR DOG. DIAL, 1972. ILLUSTRATED BY MARTHA
ALEXANDER. (CE)

   CHARMINGLY ILLUSTRATED, THE BOOK IS A SLIGHT
EPISODE OF A SMALL GIRL ATTEMPTING TO RUN AWAY TO
HER FATHER, WHO LIVES IN AN APARTMENT NEAR BY.
EMILY FEELS HER MOTHER WAS IGNORING HER WHEN
DOING HER INCOME TAXES AND DIDN'T WANT TO BE
BOTHERED. EMILY TAKES THE BABY AND ALMOST GETS
LOST BUT INSTEAD GOES AROUND THE BLOCK (BECAUSE
SHE'S NOT ALLOWED TO CROSS THE STREET)--AND MAKES
IT HOME TO A LOVING MOTHER WHO THINKS SHE'S OUT
PLAYING. (DIFF SIT--DIVORCE, DIFF SIT--ONE
PARENT, DIVORCE, FAM--MOTHERS, FAM--ONE PARENT,
MOTHERS, ONE PARENT)

MARINO, DOROTHY. WHERE ARE THE MOTHERS?.
LIPPINCOTT, 1959. ILLUSTRATED BY DOROTHY MARINO.
(ESLC)

   DIFFERENT ROLES OF MOTHERS ARE EXPLORED, AND A
VARIETY OF ROLES OUTSIDE THE HOME ARE DEPICTED:
OFFICE WORKER, SCHOOL TEACHER, AND CHECK-OUT
PERSON IN A GROCERY STORE. SINCE THE BOOK WAS
WRITTEN IN 1959, THE ROLES TEND TO BE
TRADITIONAL. A BONUS TO THE BOOK IS THE SECTION
WHICH DEALS WITH THE FAMILY. IT INCLUDES
SIBLINGS, FATHERS, AND GRANDPARENTS INVOLVED IN
SUCH ACTIVITIES AS SWIMMING, PICNICKING, AND
GOING TO THE ZOO. (FAM--MOTHERS, MOTHERS)

SCOTT, ANN. ON MOTHER'S LAP. MC GRAW, 1972.
ILLUSTRATED BY GLO COALSON. (BCB)

A LOVING STORY OF A LAP WITH UNLIMITED ROOM.
FIRST IT HAS MICHAEL, THEN HIS DOLL, THEN HIS
BOAT, THEN HIS PUPPY, THEN HIS REINDEER BLANKET.
THEY ALL ROCKED TOGETHER. WHEN THE BABY WAKES UP,
MICHAEL PUTS ON A SOUR FACE, AND SAYS THERE
ISN'T ANY ROOM. BUT MOTHER MAKES ROOM FOR ALL,
AND GIVES A SENSE OF SECURITY TO THE READER THAT
ONLY A LAP AND A ROCKING CHAIR CAN PROVIDE.
(EMOTIONS--LOVE, EMOTIONS--SECURITY,
FAM--MOTHERS, FAM--SIBLING RIVALRY, LOVE,
MOTHERS, SECURITY, SIBLING RIVALRY)

SHARMAT, MARJORIE. I WANT MAMA. HARPER, 1974.
ILLUSTRATED BY EMILY MC CULLY. (CCB-B, NYTBR)

A LITTLE GIRL'S MOTHER GOES TO THE HOSPITAL
FOR AN OPERATION. IN CHILDLIKE PICTURES AND
DIALOG, THE READER LEARNS OF THE LONELINESS AND
CONCERN WITHIN THE LITTLE GIRL. USEFUL BECAUSE IT
SHOWS WHAT A CHILD CAN DO TO SPELL THE
LONELINESS, SUCH AS MAKE PRESENTS AND CLEAN THE
HOUSE. AN ESPECIALLY MOVING ILLUSTRATION AT THE
END OF THE BOOK SHOWS THE PEACE AND CONTENTMENT
IN THE HOUSEHOLD WHEN MOTHER COMES HOME.
(EMOTIONS--LONELINESS, FAM--MOTHERS, HOSPITAL,
LONELINESS, MOTHERS, NEW SIT--HOSPITAL)

WELBER, ROBERT. THE WINTER PICNIC. PANTHEON,
1970. ILLUSTRATED BY DEBORAH RAY. (CC)

A YOUNG PRESCHOOLER CAN'T WAIT FOR SUMMER TO
COME IN ORDER TO HAVE A PICNIC. DESPITE HIS
MOTHER'S DISINTEREST, ADAM MAKES CUPS AND PLATES
OUT OF FROZEN SNOW, AND FILLS THEM WITH PEANUT
BUTTER SANDWICHES AND LEMONADE. HIS SURPRISED
MOTHER AGREES IN THE END THAT ONE CAN INDEED HAVE
A WINTER PICNIC. INTERESTING IN THAT THE CHILD'S
POINT OF VIEW IS ALLOWED TO PREVAIL OVER THAT OF
HIS MOTHER. (FAM--MOTHERS, MOTHERS)

YOLEN, JANE. IT ALL DEPENDS. FUNK, 1969.
ILLUSTRATED BY DON BOLOGNESE. (LJ)

IN A ROUNDABOUT WAY, THIS IS A POETICAL STORY
OF THE VALUE OF LOVE. DAVID IS A LITTLE BOY WHO
QUESTIONS HIS MOTHER ABOUT A NUMBER OF THINGS.
"HOW TALL AM I?" AND SHE ANSWERS BY SAYING THAT

IT ALL DEPENDS UPON THE RELATIONSHIP OF THINGS.
THAT TO AN ANT, HE IS VERY LARGE, BUT THAT TO A
WHALE, HE IS VERY SMALL. IN AN IMAGINATIVE SERIES
OF ILLUSTRATIONS, BOLOGNESE HAS PRODUCED A BOOK
USEFUL TO TEACHERS AND PARENTS WHICH TEACHES
DIFFERING SIZE RELATIONSHIPS. IT IS NOT UNTIL
ALMOST THE END THAT DAVID ASKS, "WHAT IF I GROW,
AND CHANGE," AND SHE ANSWERS THAT HE WILL ALWAYS
BE JUST RIGHT, BECAUSE HIS PARENTS LOVE HIM.
(EMOTIONS--LOVE, FAM--MOTHERS, LOVE, MOTHERS,
SELF-CONSCIOUSNESS--SIZE)

ZINDEL, PAUL. I LOVE MY MOTHER. HARPER, 1975.
ILLUSTRATED BY JOHN MELO. (CCB-B)

   STRIKING FULL-COLOR ILLUSTRATIONS EXPAND THE
LIMITED TEXT OF THIS STORY OF A BOY AND HIS
MOTHER, PRESUMABLY LIVING ALONE BECAUSE OF
DIVORCE OR SEPARATION. THE REASON IS NOT
EXPLICITLY STATED. COMPANIONSHIP AT THE ZOO, IN
THE KITCHEN, AND LATE AT NIGHT WHEN THE BAD
DREAMS COME, MAKES UP ONE PART OF THE BOOK. THERE
IS ALSO DEPICTED THE REALISM OF VULNERABLE
FEELINGS WHEN THE BOY WANTS TO RUN AWAY FROM
HOME, WHEN HIS MOTHER TRIES NOT TO LET HIM KNOW
WHEN THEY ARE SHORT OF MONEY, BUT THE MOST MOVING
SCENES ARE WHEN MOTHER ADMITS THAT SHE IS LONELY
AND WHEN THE BOY MISSES HIS FATHER. (DIFF
SIT--DIVORCE, DIVORCE, EMOTIONS--LONELINESS,
EMOTIONS--LOVE, FAM--MOTHERS, FAM--ONE PARENT,
LONELINESS, LOVE, MOTHERS, ONE PARENT)

ZOLOTOW, CHARLOTTE. A FATHER LIKE THAT. HARPER,
1971. ILLUSTRATED BY BEN SHECTER. (BCB)

   HOME WITHOUT A FATHER IS PICTURED AS A LITTLE
BOY PAINTS AN IMAGINARY PORTRAIT OF THE PERFECT
DAD. WE SEE A MOTHER WHO MAKES THE CHILD GO TO
BED AT BEDTIME, WHO READS WHEN THE BOY WOULD LIKE
TO PLAY CHECKERS. SHE IS A MOTHER WHO CAN'T
UNDERSTAND BECAUSE SHE NEVER WAS A BOY, AND WHO
SAYS THE BASEBALL GAME ON TV IS TOO LOUD. IT IS
THE MOTHER WHO, NERVOUSLY SEWING FASTER AND
FASTER BECAUSE OF THE GLOWING PICTURE HE
DESCRIBES OF THE MYTHICAL FATHER, SAYS THE
REALISTIC WORDS OF WISDOM: "IF HE NEVER COMES, "
TRYING TO MAKE THE CHILD UNDERSTAND THAT THIS
PARAGON IS PERHAPS EXAGGERATED. IN THE END,
MOTHER SAYS THAT HE CAN TRY TO BE THAT KIND OF
FATHER WHEN HE GROWS UP. USEFUL BECAUSE OF THE

EXEMPLAR ROLE OF THE FATHER. SOME CHILDREN MAY
NEED TO BE SHOWN WHAT THE ABSENCE OF THE FATHER
IN THE FAMILY MEANS. (DIFF SIT--ONE PARENT,
FAM--FATHERS, FAM--MOTHERS, FATHERS, MOTHERS, ONE
PARENT)

MOTHERS WORKING

BALDWIN, ANNE. JENNY'S REVENGE. FOUR, 1974.
ILLUSTRATED BY EMILY MC CULLY. (CCB-B)

JENNY HATES HER BABY-SITTER, AND EXPRESSES
HIDDEN ANGER TOWARD HER WORKING MOTHER WHO
APPARENTLY HAS WORKED ONLY SINCE A RECENT
DIVORCE. AFTER TRYING A NUMBER OF PLOYS TO FORCE
THE BABY-SITTER TO QUIT, SHE FINDS COMRADESHIP
WITH MRS. CRAMIE WHEN THEY DISCOVER A COMMON
INTEREST IN THE CIRCUS. A REALISTIC LOOK AT A
CHILD WHO NEEDS AND WANTS ATTENTION FROM HER
MOTHER. (ANGER, DIFF SIT--DIVORCE, DIFF SIT--ONE
PARENT, DIVORCE, EMOTIONS--ANGER, FAM--MOTHERS
WORKING, MOTHERS WORKING, ONE PARENT)

BLAINE, MARGE. THE TERRIBLE THING THAT HAPPENED
AT OUR HOUSE. PARENTS' MAG, 1975. ILLUSTRATED BY
JOHN WALLNER. (BL)

A DEVASTATINGLY FUNNY/SAD BOOK ABOUT MOTHER
GOING BACK TO WORK AS A SCIENCE TEACHER. THE
ILLUSTRATIONS ARE VERY REALISTIC WHEN THEY
PORTRAY CHAOS IN THE MORNING AS ALL THE FAMILY
HAS TO DRESS AND LEAVE AT THE SAME TIME.
ACCUSTOMED TO COMING HOME FOR LUNCH, THE
BESPECTACLED LITTLE GIRL WHO NOW EATS IN THE
SCHOOL LUNCHROOM IS APPALLED AT THE NOISE AND
MESSINESS. WHILE THE FAMILY FINALLY ADJUSTS
SOMEWHAT, AND SOME VALUABLE LESSONS IN
COOPERATION ARE LEARNED, THE READER MAY BE LEFT
WITH THE FEELING THAT PERHAPS THERE ARE SOME VERY
POSITIVE VALUES IN HAVING A FULL-TIME MOTHER AT
HOME. (FAM--MOTHERS, FAM--MOTHERS WORKING,
MOTHERS WORKING)

CLIFTON, LUCILLE. EVERETT ANDERSON'S YEAR. HOLT,
1974. ILLUSTRATED BY ANN GRIFALCONI. (CC)

"WALK TALL IN THE WORLD," HIS MOTHER TELLS
HIM. ALTHOUGH THIS IS, IN THE MAIN, A STORY OF A
SEVEN-YEAR-OLD BOY, THE INFLUENCE OF HIS MOTHER
SHINES THROUGH ON EVERY PAGE. EVERETT ANDERSON

REMEMBERS HIS DADDY ALTHOUGH HE DOES NOT KNOW
WHERE HE IS, AND READING THIS SERIES OF VERSES
ABOUT THE MONTHS OF THE YEAR, A CHILD CAN SHARE
THE SPECIAL LOVE THE YOUNG BOY FEELS FOR HIS
MOTHER. (DIFF SIT--ONE PARENT,
EMOTIONS--LONELINESS, FAM--MOTHERS WORKING,
LONELINESS, MOTHERS WORKING, ONE PARENT)

MERRIAM, EVE. MOMMIES AT WORK. KNOPF, 1961.
ILLUSTRATED BY BENI MONTRESOR. (ESLC)

  ROLES OF MOTHERS PROFUSELY ILLUSTRATED WITH
STRIKING PICTURES ACCOMPANIED BY A SPARSE TEXT.
MOMMIES ARE SHOWN IN TRADITIONAL AND
NON-TRADITIONAL ROLES, NOTABLE BEING THOSE OF
TELEVISION DIRECTOR, DOCTOR, AND ARCHITECT.
(FAM--MOTHERS WORKING, MOTHERS WORKING)

SONNEBORN, RUTH. I LOVE GRAM. VIKING, 1971.
ILLUSTRATED BY LEO CARTY. (ESLC)

  A THIRD GRADER COULD READ THIS PICTURE-STORY
BOOK WHICH IS MORE TEXT THAN PICTURES, BUT IT CAN
BE ENJOYED BY YOUNGER CHILDREN AS A READ-ALOUD.
ELLIE'S GRANDMOTHER CARES FOR HER, AND COOKS FOR
THE FAMILY WHILE ELLIE'S MOTHER WORKS. WHEN GRAM
GOES TO THE HOSPITAL, ELLIE IS VERY LONELY, AND
INDEED EXPERIENCES A FEELING OF THE FORESHADOWING
OF DEATH. THE POSITIVE THINGS SHE DOES TO
PREPARE FOR GRAM'S HOMECOMING SHOW HER LOVE: A
PICTURE SHE DRAWS AND THE PARTY TABLE SHE
PREPARES. WE KNOW AT THE END OF THE STORY THE
STRONG BOND OF LOVE BETWEEN GRAM AND HER FAMILY.
(FAM--GRANDMOTHERS, FAM--MOTHERS WORKING,
FAM--OLD AGE, GRANDMOTHERS, MOTHERS WORKING, OLD
AGE)

SONNEBORN, RUTH. THE LOLLIPOP PARTY. VIKING,
1967. ILLUSTRATED BY BRINTON TURKLE. (ESLC)

  ONE DAY TOMAS IS LEFT ALONE IN THE APARTMENT
FOR THE FIRST TIME. HIS SISTER ANA, WHO USUALLY
CARED FOR HIM BEFORE GOING TO HER JOB, HAD TO
LEAVE HIM ALONE. STEP-BY-STEP THE READER
PARTICIPATES IN THE LITTLE BOY'S FEAR. HE WAS
CONCERNED ABOUT THE SOUND OF FOOTSTEPS ON THE
STAIRS, AND WISHED ONLY TO SIT QUIETLY AND HOLD
HIS CAT GATTO. WHEN HIS NURSERY SCHOOL TEACHER
COMES TO THE DOOR ON A VISIT, HOWEVER, THE
EMOTIONAL TONE OF THE BOOK CHANGES IMMEDIATELY.

HE IS HAPPY TO SEE HER, ACTS THE ROLE OF THE HOST
BY OFFERING HER A LOLLIPOP, AND THE STORY ENDS
WITH TOMAS FEELING A BIT GROWN-UP.
(EMOTIONS--FEAR, EMOTIONS--LONELINESS,
FAM--MOTHERS WORKING, FEAR, LONELINESS, MOTHERS
WORKING, SELF-RELIANCE)

MOVING

HICKMAN, MARTHA. I'M MOVING. ABINGDON, 1974.
ILLUSTRATED BY LEIGH GRANT. (BL)

LARGE, COLORFUL PICTURE BOOK, WITH MANY "NOW"
ELEMENTS. FATHER SPORTS LONGER HAIR AND A
MUSTACHE, AND THE FAMILY DRIVES A V.W. BUG.
WILLIAM, THE SMALL BOY WHO TELLS THE STORY, GIVES
A VERY POSITIVE VIEW ABOUT MOVING. THE
ILLUSTRATIONS ARE SHOWN FROM VARYING
PERSPECTIVES, AS AT THE TOP OF THE STAIRS LOOKING
DOWN, AND THE VIEWS FROM THE BOY'S BEDROOM
WINDOW. USEFUL BECAUSE OF ITS CONTRAST TO THE
NEGATIVE ASPECT OF MOVING. (MOVING, NEW
SIT--MOVING)

HOFF, SYD. WHO WILL BE MY FRIENDS?. HARPER,
1960. ILLUSTRATED BY SYD HOFF. (ESLC)

FREDDY MOVES TO A NEW NEIGHBORHOOD AND HAS NO
ONE TO PLAY WITH. HE FINALLY COMES TO A GROUP OF
BOYS WHO ARE PLAYING BALL. HE THROWS HIS BALL UP
IN THE AIR AND CATCHES IT SEVERAL TIMES. THEN THE
BOYS ASK HIM TO JOIN THEIR GAME. THIS
EASY-TO-READ BOOK EXEMPLIFIES THE FACT THAT YOU
NEED TO GO OUT AND SEARCH FOR FRIENDS, AND SHOW
PEOPLE THAT YOU CAN DO SOMETHING COMPETENTLY.
(FRIENDSHIP, MOVING, NEW SIT--MOVING,
SELF-RELIANCE)

ILSLEY, VELMA. M IS FOR MOVING. WALCK, 1966.
ILLUSTRATED BY VELMA ILSLEY. (LJ)

IN AN ALPHABET BOOK WHICH EMPHASIZES THE
BUSTLING ROUTINE OF PACKING WITH UPBEAT COLORS OF
ORANGE AND YELLOW, THE AUTHOR-ILLUSTRATOR HAS
PRODUCED A REASSURING LOOK AT THE PROCESS OF
MOVING. A BOOK WHICH CAN BE USED TO DISPEL FEARS
IN THE VERY YOUNG, IT CAN ALSO BE USED BY A
FAMILY IN ADVANCE OF THE MOVE TO ACTIVELY INVOLVE
THE CHILD, AS YOUNG CHILDREN ARE SHOWN ON EVERY
PAGE EMPTYING DRAWERS AND PACKING BOXES AND, AT

THE END, THEY LOOK ON THE MAP TO SEE WHERE THE NEW HOUSE IS LOCATED. (MOVING, NEW SIT--MOVING)

JUSTUS, MAY. A NEW HOME FOR BILLY. HASTINGS, 1956. ILLUSTRATED BY JOAN PAYNE. (BCB)

WHEN SIX-YEAR-OLD BILLY MOVES TO A NEW NEIGHBORHOOD HE FINDS OUT THAT NOT ALL PEOPLE WILL RENT TO NEGROES, AT LEAST NOT AT THE TIME THIS BOOK WAS WRITTEN. A USEFUL FACT FOR ALL CHILDREN TO KNOW. THE NEW HOUSE, THOUGH IN NEED OF REPAIR, HAS AN APPLE TREE IN THE YARD AND IS A GREAT IMPROVEMENT OVER THE DIRTY SLUM AREA HE MOVED FROM. AFTER AN INITIAL PERIOD OF LONELINESS, BILLY MAKES FRIENDS BECAUSE OF THE SWING, A SLIDE, A JUMPING BAR, AND A SEESAW CONSTRUCTED BY HIS FATHER. THE BOOK ENDS WITH FRIENDS, BLACK AND WHITE, HELPING TO PAINT THE HOUSE. (EMOTIONS--LONELINESS, FRIENDSHIP, LONELINESS, MOVING, NEW SIT--MOVING)

KANTROWITZ, MILDRED. GOOD-BYE KITCHEN. PARENTS' MAG, 1972. ILLUSTRATED BY MERCER MAYER. (CCB-B)

AN ORIGINAL APPROACH TO MOVING DAY, AS EMILY AND HER FRIEND RUFIE SIT ON THE STEPS AND WATCH THE MOVING VAN. AS THEY SIT AND MUNCH ON A BAG LUNCH, EMILY RECOUNTS IN HER IMAGINATION THE MEMORIES OF THE FURNITURE--"GOOD-BYE, WHITE DISHES WITH YOUR YELLOW BORDERS"--AND THE MEMORIES OF HER BEST FRIEND JUNIE. UP UNTIL THIS POINT THE READER THINKS IT IS EMILY WHO IS MOVING, BUT NO, IT IS SHE WHO IS LEFT BEHIND. AS EMILY STARTS TO LEAVE HER VANTAGE POINT, ANOTHER MOVING VAN PULLS UP, AND SHE IS DELIGHTED TO SEE A GIRL'S BICYCLE JUST HER SIZE, AND IS HAPPY IN ANTICIPATION OF THE NEW FRIEND IN THE OFFING. (FRIENDSHIP, MOVING, NEW SIT--MOVING)

PRATHER, RAY. NEW NEIGHBORS. MC GRAW, 1975. ILLUSTRATED BY RAY PRATHER. (CCB-B)

WHEN RICHY MOVES TO A NEW, UNFRIENDLY SUBURBAN NEIGHBORHOOD, HE TRIES TO MAKE FRIENDS BY SELLING SOME OLD TOYS HE FINDS IN THE HOUSE. THIS DRAWS THE OTHER BLACK CHILDREN INTO HIS YARD. AT FIRST THEY TRY TO PLAY TRICKS ON HIM, BUT LUCKILY RICHY LAUGHS, AND IS ASKED TO JOIN THE GANG. DEMONSTRATES HOW ONE CHILD OVERCAME THE DIFFICULTY OF FINDING NEW FRIENDS. (FRIENDSHIP,

MOVING, NEW SIT--MOVING)

THOMPSON, VIVIAN. SAD DAY, GLAD DAY. HOLIDAY, 1962. ILLUSTRATED BY LILIAN OBLIGADO. (RLHR)

THE LARGE PRINT IS JUST RIGHT IN THIS BOOK FOR NEW READERS WHO ARE BEGINNING TO PROGRESS TO MORE DIFFICULT THINGS. KATHY MOVES TO A NEW APARTMENT IN THE CITY FROM THE COUNTRY WHERE SHE HAD A SWING ON AN APPLE TREE, AND FEELS VERY LONELY. LUCKILY SHE FINDS A DOLL IN THE CLOSET OF THE NEW HOUSE WHICH GOES A LONG WAY TOWARD MAKING HER FEEL GOOD. EXPLAINS CHANGE AND HOW PEOPLE ADJUST TO NEW PLACES.
(EMOTIONS--LONELINESS, LOVELINESS, MOVING, NEW SIT--MOVING)

ZOLOTOW, CHARLOTTE. A TIGER CALLED THOMAS. LOTHROP, 1963. ILLUSTRATED BY KURT WERTH. (CC)

SHY THOMAS SITS ON THE PORCH OF HIS NEW HOUSE AND REFUSES TO TRY TO MAKE NEW FRIENDS. HE IS VERY OBSERVANT, HOWEVER, AND IS AWARE OF GERALD, WHO PLAYS BALL ALONE, AND OF MARIE, AND OTHER PEOPLE IN THE NEIGHBORHOOD. GIVEN CONFIDENCE BY DRESSING UP IN A TIGER SUIT ON HALLOWEEN, HE TAKES ON SOME OF THE COURAGE OF THE BEAST, AND VISITS ALL OF THE HOUSES IN THE NEIGHBORHOOD. WHEN PEOPLE ASK HIM TO VISIT AND PLAY, HE REALIZES THAT THEY ALL LIKE HIM, AND HE DECIDES THAT HE ALSO LIKES THEM. (EMOTIONS--SHYNESS, FRIENDSHIP, MOVING, NEW SIT--MOVING, SELF-CONFIDENCE, SHYNESS)

NEW SIT--BABY

ALEXANDER, MARTHA. NOBODY ASKED ME IF I WANTED A BABY SISTER. DIAL, 1971. ILLUSTRATED BY MARTHA ALEXANDER. (BCB)

THE STORY OPENS WITH A SOUR-FACED LITTLE BOY OVERHEARING GUSHY COMPLIMENTS ABOUT HIS NEW BABY SISTER. HIS NEXT MOVE IS TO LOAD HER IN A WAGON AND TRY TO GIVE HER AWAY. AFTER SEVERAL ABORTED ATTEMPTS, HE ENDS UP AT HIS FRIEND'S HOUSE. BABY BONNIE MISBEHAVES, HOWEVER, AND IN THE END IT IS THE BROTHER WHO CAN PACIFY HER. WICKED THOUGHTS GO THROUGH HIS HEAD AS HE IMAGINES HER GROWING UP AND PULLING HIM IN THE WAGON. (BROTHERS & SISTERS, EMOTIONS--JEALOUSY, FAM--BROTHERS &

SISTERS, JEALOUSY, NEW SIT--BABY)

ANDRY, ANDREW. HI, NEW BABY. SIMON, 1970.
ILLUSTRATED BY DI, THOMAS GRAZIA. (ESLC)

   IN WHAT APPEARS TO BE DARK CHARCOAL DRAWINGS
SUPERIMPOSED ON COLORED BACKGROUNDS, DI GRAZIA
HAS ACHIEVED AN ALMOST PHOTOGRAPHIC QUALITY IN
THIS BOOK TRACING THE MANY FACETS OF BABYHOOD.
BATHING, FEEDING, AND SLEEPING ARE SHOWN TO BE
ACTIVITIES WHICH ENCROACH ON THE OLDER SIBLING,
BUT WAYS OF HELPING ARE EXPLORED, AND THE BABY IS
SHOWN GROWING UP TO BE A COMPANION. POSITIVE
NOTE THROUGHOUT WILL MAKE THIS A USEFUL VOLUME.
(FAM--SIBLING RIVALRY, NEW SIT--BABY, SIBLING
RIVALRY)

BORACK, BARBARA. SOMEONE SMALL. HARPER, 1969.
ILLUSTRATED BY ANITA LOBEL. (BCB)

   WHEN A NEW BABY ENTERS THE HOUSEHOLD, THE
YOUNG GIRL IN THE STORY ASKS FOR A BIRD. FLUFFY
BECOMES A GREAT FRIEND AND COMPANION, AND AS THE
NEW BABY JOYCE GROWS OLDER, FLUFFY GROWS OLDER,
TOO. THEN ONE DAY HE CATCHES A COLD AND DIES. THE
LITTLE GIRL AND HER SISTER BURY HIM UNDER A
TREE, SAY A LITTLE PRAYER, THEN GO INSIDE TO SEE
IF THEIR FATHER WILL TAKE THEM OUT FOR A RIDE IN
THEIR PAJAMAS AFTER SUPPER. ILLUSTRATES THE EBB
AND FLOW OF LIFE, BIRTH AND DEATH, IN A NATURAL
NON-TRAUMATIC WAY. (DEATH--PET, DIFF
SIT--DEATH--PET, NEW SIT--BABY)

BROWN, MYRA. AMY AND THE NEW BABY. WATTS, 1965.
ILLUSTRATED BY HARRIET HUREWITZ. (RLHR)

   MOTHER WISELY BRINGS A PRESENT FOR AMY WHEN
NEW BROTHER RICKY COMES HOME. ALTHOUGH PALE BLUE
ILLUSTRATIONS ENHANCE THE SOFT TONE OF THE STORY,
JEALOUSY CREEPS IN TO SPOIL THE FAMILY
RELATIONSHIP. DADDY TAKES AMY TO THE PARK, JUST
THE TWO OF THEM, FOR A PONY RIDE AND AN ICE CREAM
CONE, TWO THINGS THE BABY CANNOT HAVE.
(FAM--SIBLING RIVALRY, NEW SIT--BABY, SIBLING
RIVALRY)

BURNINGHAM, JOHN. THE BABY. CROWELL, T., 1974.
ILLUSTRATED BY JOHN BURNINGHAM. (BL)

   IN NINE SHORT SENTENCES, THIS BRITISH AUTHOR

CAPTURES THE ESSENCE OF B-A-B-Y AND WHAT IT MEANS
TO A SLIGHTLY OLDER CHILD. THE FRONT COVER
DRAWING, CRAYONED IN A CHILDLIKE MANNER, CAPTURES
THE TONE OF THE BOOK: THE RATHER LARGE BABY WITH
THE RATHER LARGE HEAD IS ALMOST AS LARGE AS THE
BOY UPON WHOSE LAP IT SITS. YET THIS BABY CANNOT
DO ANYTHING TO GIVE THE YOUNG BOY REAL
COMPANIONSHIP, AND INDEED DEPRIVES HIM OF THE
COMPANY OF HIS MOTHER. AN EASY-TO-READ BOOK, AS
WELL AS ONE TO BE SHARED. (FAM--SIBLING RIVALRY,
NEW SIT--BABY, SIBLING RIVALRY)

BYARS, BETSY. GO AND HUSH THE BABY. VIKING,
1971.   ILLUSTRATED BY EMILY MC CULLY.   (3CB, CC)

   WHILE MOTHER IS BUSY PAINTING AT HER EASEL,
AND BAKING COOKIES, WILL IS ASKED TO PACIFY THE
BABY: "SING HIM A LITTLE SONG." WILL IS
INTRIGUED, THE BABY IS AMUSED, AND THE BASEBALL
GAME FORGOTTEN, AS WILL PLAYS GAMES AND TICKLES
THE BABY. WHEN AT LAST MOTHER COMES WITH THE
BABY'S MILK, THE BOY IS ALMOST RELUCTANT TO
LEAVE, AND THE READER SENSES THAT WILL HAD A FINE
INTERLUDE. (NEW SIT--BABY)

GORDON, SOL. DID THE SUN SHINE BEFORE YOU WERE
BORN?. OKPAKU, 1974.   ILLUSTRATED BY VIVIEN
COHEN.   (BL)

   SEPIA ILLUSTRATIONS GIVE A LOW-KEY TONE TO
THIS GENTLE EXPLANATION OF CONCEPTION AND BIRTH.
USEFUL BECAUSE THE BOOK BEGINS WITH THE STORY
MUCH EARLIER THAN MOST BOOKS ON THE SUBJECT, AND
EXPLAINS A LITTLE ABOUT A FAMILY TREE, AND
DIFFERENT FAMILIES. THERE IS ONE PAGE EXPLICITLY
EXPLAINING HOW INTERCOURSE TAKES PLACE, AND A
DIAGRAM OF THE UTERUS AND THE BABY IN THE WOMB,
PLUS AN ILLUSTRATION OF THE WOMAN ON THE DELIVERY
TABLE JUST AFTER THE BIRTH. A USEFUL BOOK WHICH
SETS FACTUAL MATERIAL IN A COMFORTABLE SETTING.
(NEW SIT--BABY, SELF-UNDERSTANDING)

GREENFIELD, ELOISE. SHE COME BRINGING ME THAT
LITTLE BABY GIRL. LIPPINCOTT, 1974.   ILLUSTRATED
BY JOHN STEPTOE.   (CC)

   "I DIDN'T LIKE THE WAY MAMA AND DADDY LOOKED
AT HER, LIKE SHE WAS THE ONLY BABY IN THE WORLD."
THIS WAS THE FEELING THAT KEVIN HAD WHEN THE NEW
BABY CAME HOME--AND RELATIVES AND NEIGHBORS CAME

TO CALL WITH PRESENTS FOR THE BABY BUT NOTHING
FOR KEVIN. WHEN HIS MOTHER TOLD HIM THAT SHE HAD
ONCE BEEN A BABY GIRL, KEVIN FELT MUCH BETTER,
AND WAS SATISFIED, AT THE END, TO SHARE ONE OF
HIS MOTHER'S ARMS WITH THE BABY. (FAM--SIBLING
RIVALRY, NEW SIT--BABY, SIBLING RIVALRY)

HOLLAND, VIKI. WE ARE HAVING A BABY. SCRIBNER,
1972. ILLUSTRATED BY VIKI HOLLAND. (RLHR)

   REALISTIC BLACK AND WHITE PHOTOGRAPHS
UNDERLINE THE AUTHENTICITY OF THIS VOLUME FOR
PARENTS AND SIBLINGS. THE BOOK OPENS WITH THE
CHILD AT HOME FEELING THE SIZE OF MOTHER'S
ABDOMEN, AND PROGRESSES THROUGH THE DAY MOTHER
LEAVES FOR THE HOSPITAL. AFTER DANA STRUGGLES TO
DRESS HERSELF, THE BOOK GIVES A STEP-BY-STEP
PICTURE OF WHAT IS HAPPENING TO THE MOTHER, MUCH
AS A FATHER MIGHT DESCRIBE IT TO THE CHILD AT
HOME. DANA HAS SOME FEELINGS OF REJECTION AFTER
THE BABY COMES HOME AND SHE REFUSES TO EAT LUNCH.
WHEN HER FATHER RETURNS IN THE EVENING THEY HAVE
A SHARING TIME TOGETHER AND SHE HELPS TO FEED
THE BABY. THERE IS A VERY SATISFIED EXPRESSION ON
DANA'S FACE IN THE LAST ILLUSTRATION AS SHE
SAYS: "HE'S MY BROTHER." (FAM--SIBLING RIVALRY,
NEW SIT--BABY, SIBLING RIVALRY)

IWASAKI, CHIHIRO. NEW BABY IS COMING TO MY
HOUSE. MC GRAW, 1970. ILLUSTRATED BY CHIHIRO
IWASAKI. (LJ)

   EXQUISITE WATERCOLORS EMPHASIZE THE HAPPINESS
THAT SISTER FEELS BECAUSE HER NEW BROTHER JOHN IS
COMING HOME FROM THE HOSPITAL TODAY. SIMPLE TEXT
MAKES THE BOOK VERY USEFUL FOR A PRESCHOOL
CHILD'S PREPARATION FOR A NEW BABY IN THE
HOUSEHOLD. (BROTHERS & SISTERS, FAM--BROTHERS &
SISTERS, NEW SIT--BABY)

JORDAN, JUNE. NEW LIFE, NEW ROOM. CROWELL, T.,
1975. ILLUSTRATED BY RAY CRUZ. (BL)

   AN EXTENDED FORMAT TAKES THIS BOOK OUT OF THE
TRUE PICTURE-BOOK CATEGORY, AND THIRD GRADERS
WILL ENJOY READING IT ALONE, BUT THE
ILLUSTRATIONS AND STORY MAKE IT ENJOYABLE FOR
YOUNGER CHILDREN ALSO. A VERY REAL PROBLEM IS
DEALT WITH HERE--THAT OF REARRANGING A FAMILY'S
SLEEPING QUARTERS TO ACCOMMODATE A NEW BABY. A

PICTURE OF A WARM, FRIENDLY FAMILY DEALING
REALISTICALLY WITH AN EVERYDAY PROBLEM PROVIDES A
REASSURING, POSITIVE APPROACH. (BROTHERS &
SISTERS, FAM--BROTHERS & SISTERS, NEW SIT--BABY)

KEATS, EZRA. PETER'S CHAIR. HARPER, 1967.
ILLUSTRATED BY EZRA KEATS. (BCB)

   POOR PETER! HE WAS SO JEALOUS OF THE NEW BABY,
HE DECIDED TO RUN AWAY FROM HOME. WHEN HIS DAD
BEGAN TO PAINT ALL OF PETER'S FURNITURE, HE
GRABBED HIS LITTLE CHAIR, AND RAN OUTSIDE THE
DOOR. HE WAS VERY SURPRISED TO FIND THAT HE COULD
NOT FIT INTO IT ANYMORE BECAUSE HE HAD GROWN
BIGGER. USEFUL BECAUSE IT SHOWS THE RESOLVING OF
THE JEALOUS FEELINGS: PETER AND HIS FATHER PAINT
THE LITTLE CHAIR. ADDITIONALLY USEFUL BECAUSE IT
SHOWS A PRACTICAL EXAMPLE OF GROWTH IN A CHILD.
(EMOTIONS--JEALOUSY, FAM--SIBLING RIVALRY,
JEALOUSY, NEW SIT--BABY, SIBLING RIVALRY)

KLEIN, NORMA. IF I HAD MY WAY. PANTHEON, 1974.
ILLUSTRATED BY RAY CRUZ. (BL)

   ELLIE IS A LITTLE GIRL WHO GOES TO SCHOOL, BUT
IS YOUNG ENOUGH TO FEEL JEALOUS OF HER BABY
BROTHER--TO THE POINT WHERE SHE ASKS FOR A BOTTLE
HERSELF. SHE FEELS VERY PUT UPON, AND DREAMS ONE
NIGHT THAT THE ROLES ARE REVERSED, AND IT IS
SHE, THE CHILD, WHO HAS POWER OVER HER PARENTS.
IN THE INCIDENTS WHICH SHOW THIS URGE FOR
DOMINATION, ONE SEES THE ISSUES THAT MAKE
CHILDREN FEEL SO POWERLESS: HAVING TO GO TO BED
BEFORE THE GROWN-UPS, HAVING TO EAT CHILDREN'S
FOOD WHILE ADULTS HAVE SPECIAL ITEMS. HUMOR IS
PERVASIVE, AND ELLIE IS QUITE INGENIOUS IN
ORDERING UP A NEW BABY PERIODICALLY, ON APPROVAL,
TO BE KEPT ONLY IF HE'S "PERFECT," THAT IS, IF
HE DOESN'T CRY, ISN'T TOO FAT, AND DOESN'T EAT
TOO MUCH. THE NAKED BABY MAY BE THE ONE NOTE OF
UNREALITY IN THE STORY. EVERYONE ELSE IS DRESSED
WARMLY, BUT THE IRREPRESSIBLE FAT BABY NEVER
APPEARS WITH ONE STITCH OF CLOTHING.
(EMOTIONS--JEALOUSY, JEALOUSY, NEW SIT--BABY)

KRASILOVSKY, PHYLLIS. THE VERY LITTLE GIRL.
DOUBLEDAY, 1953. ILLUSTRATED BY NINON. (CC)

   ABOUT HALFWAY THROUGH THIS STORY, THE LITTLE
GIRL WHO HAS BEEN SMALLER THAN EVERYTHING AROUND

HER BEGINS TO GROW, AND SUDDENLY SHE IS BIGGER
THAN THE ROSEBUSH, AND SHE GETS A NEW BED TO
SLEEP IN. THE CULMINATING EXPERIENCE IS THAT SHE
CAN BE A BIG SISTER TO HER BRAND NEW BABY
BROTHER. AN EXCELLENT EXAMPLE TO USE IN
EXPLAINING GROWTH TO THE YOUNG CHILD. (NEW
SIT--BABY, SELF-CONSCIOUSNESS--SIZE)

SAMSON, JOAN. WATCHING THE NEW BABY. ATHENEUM,
1974. ILLUSTRATED BY GARY GLADSTONE. (CC)

    FOR AN OLDER CHILD OF SEVEN OR EIGHT, THIS
BOOK WILL BE A FASCINATING VOLUME OF INFORMATION
ABOUT THE NEW BABY, FACTS ABOUT DEVELOPMENT
BEFORE AND AFTER BIRTH. MOST CHILDREN WILL BE
SURPRISED TO LEARN THAT THE UNBORN BABY SWALLOWED
THE AMNIOTIC FLUID WHILE IN THE MOTHER'S WOMB,
AND THAT HE MAY HAVE SUCKED HIS THUMB BEFORE
BIRTH. THE INFORMATIVE TONE OF THE BOOK IS
EXCELLENT, FOR NEW PARENTS AS WELL AS CHILDREN,
ALTHOUGH IT DOES NOT FALL INTO THE STRICT
CATEGORY OF THE PICTURE BOOK. ESPECIALLY USEFUL
IN ITS DESCRIPTION OF THE NEW BABY'S NEEDS FOR
BEING LOVED AND TOUCHED. (NEW SIT--BABY)

SCHICK, ELEANOR. PEGGY'S NEW BROTHER. MACMILLAN,
1970. ILLUSTRATED BY ELEANOR SCHICK. (ESLC)

    STORY OPENS WITH PEGGY'S MOTHER TELLING HER
THEY ARE GOING TO HAVE A BABY AND PEGGY SAYING
SHE'D RATHER HAVE A DOG. SHE ISN'T MUCH GOOD AT
HELPING WITH THE CHORES OF THE NEW BABY BUT SHE
IS VERY GOOD AT MAKING THE BABY LAUGH. THUS
FINDING THAT SHE IS NEEDED, SHE DOESN'T MIND
WAITING FOR A DOG. (NEW SIT--BABY)

SCHLEIN, MIRIAM. LAURIE'S NEW BROTHER. ABELARD,
1961. ILLUSTRATED BY ELIZABETH DONALD. (RLHR)

    MOTHER IS ALWAYS BUSY WITH THE NEW BABY AND
LAURIE THINKS IT WOULD BE FUN TO BE A BABY AND
CREEP ON THE FLOOR TO GET HER MOTHER'S ATTENTION,
BUT SOON MOTHER SPENDS MORE TIME WITH HER.
LAURIE DRESSES HER DOLL WHEN MOTHER DRESSES THE
BABY, AND SOON DISCOVERS SHE WANTS TO PLAY ALONE
ONCE AGAIN. (NEW SIT--BABY)

STEIN, SARA. MAKING BABIES. WALKER, 1974.
ILLUSTRATED BY DORIS PINNEY. (BL)

SEPARATE TEXTS FOR THE ADULT AND CHILD MAKE
THIS BOOK EMINENTLY USEFUL, AS DOES THE
INTRODUCTORY SECTION. IT IS IN FACT AN EXCELLENT
BOOK FOR ADULTS: IT GIVES INFORMATION, AND ALSO
GIVES GUIDANCE ON HOW TO ANSWER THEIR CHILD'S
NEED TO KNOW. ESSENTIALLY THE BOOK IS DESIGNED AS
A PRIVATE BOOK TO BE SHARED BY ONE CHILD AND AN
ADULT. EXCELLENT COLOR PHOTOGRAPHS SHOW A
PREGNANT MOTHER, CHILDREN OF BOTH SEXES IN THE
NUDE, A MOTHER CAT GIVING BIRTH TO KITTENS, AND A
MALE AND FEMALE DOG MATING. THE PHOTOS ARE
REALISTIC BUT NOT PRURIENT, AND THE EXPLANATIONS
CAN BE USED BY DEGREES, ACCORDING TO THE NEEDS OF
AN INDIVIDUAL CHILD. (NEW SIT--BABY)

STEIN, SARA. THAT NEW BABY. WALKER, 1974.
ILLUSTRATED BY DICK FRANK. (BL)

THIS HELPFUL VOLUME IS CHOCK-FULL OF PRACTICAL
SUGGESTIONS TO EASE THE TRAUMA OF A NEW BABY IN
THE HOUSEHOLD. IN THIS CASE, CHARLES AND MELISSA
ARE ABOUT FOUR AND SEVEN, RESPECTIVELY, AND THE
AUTHOR, WHO WRITES FOR THE STAFF OF THE CENTER
FOR PREVENTIVE PSYCHIATRY, SHOWS THEM
ANTICIPATING THE BABY'S BIRTH BY FEELING THE
MOTHER'S ABDOMEN. THIS ENTIRE SERIES, WHILE VERY
USEFUL TO THE CHILD, ESPECIALLY WITH ITS
REALISTIC PHOTOGRAPHS, IS EXTREMELY HELPFUL TO
PARENTS, WITH POSITIVE SUGGESTIONS ON HOW TO VIEW
THE NEW BABY THROUGH THE CHILD'S EYES. (NEW
SIT--BABY)

NEW SIT--EYEGLASSES

GOODSELL, JANE. KATIE'S MAGIC GLASSES. HOUGHTON,
1965. ILLUSTRATED BY BARBARA COONEY. (ESLC)

KATIE IS A YOUNG GIRL WHO DISCOVERS SHE NEEDS
GLASSES WHEN SHE IS SIX YEARS OLD, BUT THINKS SHE
DOES NOT WANT TO HAVE GLASSES. THE DOCTOR TELLS
HER SHE'LL SEE "MAGIC." WHEN THEY FINALLY ARRIVE,
SHE PUTS THEM ON, AND HOCUS-POCUS--THE BLUR IS
GONE! AND SHE SEES EVERYTHING "JUST RIGHT."
(EYEGLASSES, NEW SIT--EYEGLASSES)

RASKIN, ELLEN. SPECTACLES. ATHENEUM, 1968.
ILLUSTRATED BY ELLEN RASKIN. (BCB)

IMAGINATIVE ILLUSTRATIONS SHOW THE READER THE
FUNNY BUT CONFUSING IMAGES IRIS SEES IN HER

NEARSIGHTED CONDITION: THE BIG FRIENDLY-LOOKING
BULL DOG IN MRS. SCHMIDLAP'S PARLOR IS REALLY A
VICTORIAN SOFA WITH LEGS WHICH RESEMBLE THE PAWS
OF A DOG. IRIS DOES NOT WANT TO WEAR EYEGLASSES,
BUT SHE IS EXAMINED, SHE TRIES ON MANY KINDS OF
FRAMES, AND WHEN SHE WEARS THEM FOR THE FIRST
TIME NO ONE NOTICES, EXCEPT HER FRIEND CHESTER.
THE DRAMATIC DIFFERENCE IN WHAT SHE SEES IS
EVIDENT ON THE LAST PAGE WHERE THE BOOK ENDS ON
THE HUMOROUS NOTE IT HAS MAINTAINED THROUGHOUT.
AN EXCELLENT NON-PREACHY BOOK. (EYEGLASSES, NEW
SIT--EYEGLASSES)

SANDS, GEORGE. WHY GLASSES?. LERNER, 1960.
ILLUSTRATED BY ROV ANDRE. (ESLC)

   SOME THIRD GRADERS WILL BE ABLE TO ASSIMILATE
THE RATHER TECHNICAL INFORMATION IN THIS VOLUME,
AND FOR THE FACTUALLY-MINDED CHILD, IT WILL BE
HELPFUL TO KNOW TERMS SUCH AS RETINA, REFRACTION,
AND ASTIGMATISM. THIS STRAIGHTFORWARD APPROACH
MAY BE VERY USEFUL FOR THE CHILD WHO NEEDS, OR
ALREADY WEARS, EYEGLASSES, FOR IT REMOVES THE
DISCUSSION FROM THE AFFECTIVE DOMAIN INTO THE
COGNITIVE ASPECT OF THE SOMETIMES UNPLEASANT
EXPERIENCE OF WEARING EYEGLASSES. (EYEGLASSES,
NEW SIT--EYEGLASSES)

WOLFF, ANGELIKA. MOM! I NEED GLASSES!. LION,
1970. ILLUSTRATED BY DOROTHY HILL. (CC)

   SECOND-GRADER SUSAN KNOWS SHE NEEDS GLASSES
BECAUSE THE NUMBERS ON THE BLACKBOARD IN SCHOOL
ARE BLURRED, BUT SHE HAS VAGUE FEARS OF HAVING
HER EYES EXAMINED. SHE IS EXAMINED BY A VERY
BREEZY OCULIST. THERE IS A GREAT DEAL OF TEXT AND
A COMPLEX DIAGRAM OF HOW THE HUMAN EYE WORKS
(FAR TOO COMPLICATED FOR A SEVEN-YEAR-OLD). SUSAN
IS HAPPY WHEN SHE RECEIVES HER FASHIONABLE BLUE
SHADES AND CAN SEE ONCE AGAIN. (EYEGLASSES, NEW
SIT--EYEGLASSES)

NEW SIT--HOSPITAL

COLLIER, JAMES. DANNY GOES TO THE HOSPITAL.
NORTON, 1970. ILLUSTRATED BY YALE JOEL. (CC,
ESLC)

   MANY BEHIND-THE-SCENES VIEWS ARE PICTURED,
INCLUDING A REPAIR SHOP, A SEWING ROOM, AND A

DRUGSTORE, WHICH WILL PROBABLY BE OF INTEREST TO
A YOUNG READER. A REALISTIC BUT REASSURING LOOK
AT A BOY'S STAY IN THE HOSPITAL FOR MINOR SURGERY
ON HIS EYE, GENEROUSLY ILLUSTRATED WITH BLACK
AND WHITE PHOTOGRAPHS. (HOSPITAL, NEW
SIT--HOSPITAL)

KAY, ELEANOR. LET'S FIND OUT ABOUT THE HOSPITAL.
WATTS, 1971. ILLUSTRATED BY WILLIAM BROOKS.
(CC)

   SIMPLE SENTENCES WITH SIMPLE EXPLANATIONS
DEFINE THE OPERATIONS OF A HOSPITAL--THE
PERSONNEL, EQUIPMENT, AND THE SPECIAL DEPARTMENTS
SUCH AS PEDIATRICS--IN SUCH A WAY THAT A YOUNG
CHILD WILL BE ABLE TO UNDERSTAND. THE CHILD IN
THE ILLUSTRATIONS IS ENJOYING HIMSELF, AND THE
PLEASANT ASPECTS OF HOSPITALIZATION ARE
EMPHASIZED, AND THERE IS NO REALISTIC MENTION OF
PAIN OR UNPLEASANTNESS. (HOSPITAL, NEW
SIT--HOSPITAL)

REY, MARGRET. CURIOUS GEORGE GOES TO THE
HOSPITAL. HOUGHTON, 1966. ILLUSTRATED BY MARGRET
REY. (BCB)

   WRITTEN IN COLLABORATION WITH THE CHILDREN'S
HOSPITAL MEDICAL CENTER IN BOSTON, THIS ADVENTURE
HAS THE ADVANTAGE OF A CENTRAL CHARACTER WITH
WHOM ALL CHILDREN WILL IDENTIFY. LOVABLE GEORGE
LANDS IN THE HOSPITAL WITH AN AILMENT WHICH COULD
PLAGUE ANY CHILD, AND HIS TRIP THROUGH X-RAY AND
ADMISSIONS TO THE CHILDREN'S WARD IS COLORFULLY
REASSURING. ALTHOUGH THE TEXT DESCRIBES SOME OF
THE PAIN, AND THE PICTURES REALISTICALLY DEPICT
THE OPERATING ROOM, THERE IS A HAPPY, POSITIVE
NOTE THROUGHOUT, AND IRREPRESSIBLE GEORGE ENDS
HIS HOSPITAL VISIT WITH A WILD ADVENTURE IN A
RUNAWAY GO-CART. (DIFF SIT--HOSPITAL, HOSPITAL,
NEW SIT--HOSPITAL)

SHARMAT, MARJORIE. I WANT MAMA. HARPER, 1974.
ILLUSTRATED BY EMILY MC CULLY. (CCB-B, NYTBR)

   A LITTLE GIRL'S MOTHER GOES TO THE HOSPITAL
FOR AN OPERATION. IN CHILDLIKE PICTURES AND
DIALOG, THE READER LEARNS OF THE LONELINESS AND
CONCERN WITHIN THE LITTLE GIRL. USEFUL BECAUSE IT
SHOWS WHAT A CHILD CAN DO TO SPELL THE
LONELINESS, SUCH AS MAKE PRESENTS AND CLEAN THE

HOUSE. AN ESPECIALLY MOVING ILLUSTRATION AT THE
END OF THE BOOK SHOWS THE PEACE AND CONTENTMENT
IN THE HOUSEHOLD WHEN MOTHER COMES HOME.
(EMOTIONS--LONELINESS, FAM--MOTHERS, HOSPITAL,
LONELINESS, MOTHERS, NEW SIT--HOSPITAL)

SHAY, ARTHUR. WHAT HAPPENS WHEN YOU GO TO THE
HOSPITAL. REILLY, 1969.   (CC)

   KAREN'S SHINY, SMILING FACE ON THE COLORFUL
COVER SETS THE TONE FOR A NON-THREATENING
EXPERIENCE IN THE HOSPITAL FOR ANY CHILD READER.
ALTHOUGH KAREN IS TEARFULLY APPREHENSIVE AT
TIMES, CHILDREN WILL UNDERSTAND THAT IT IS NORMAL
TO MISS YOUR PARENTS AND THAT YOU MIGHT BE A
LITTLE AFRAID OF THE X-RAY MACHINE. AUTHOR SHAY
HAS SAID THAT HIS PURPOSE IS TO SHOW THE JOBS AND
SERVICES THAT GO ON IN A HOSPITAL, AND TO HELP
CHILDREN UNDERSTAND IN ADVANCE WHAT WILL HAPPEN
TO THEM. HE HAS SUCCEEDED IN PRODUCING A VERY
USEFUL, SUCCESSFUL BOOK. (BRAVERY, DIFF
SIT--HOSPITAL, EMOTIONS--BRAVERY, HOSPITAL, NEW
SIT--HOSPITAL)

SOBOL, HARRIET. JEFF'S HOSPITAL BOOK. WALCK,
1975.   ILLUSTRATED BY PATRICIA AGRE.   (BL)

   PHYSICIANS FROM TWO MAJOR MEDICAL INSTITUTIONS
WERE USED AS CONSULTANTS FOR THIS HELPFUL,
ACCURATE BOOK WHICH DESCRIBES A YOUNG BOY'S
EXPERIENCE AS HE UNDERGOES SURGERY TO CORRECT
CROSSED EYES. LARGE BLACK AND WHITE PHOTOGRAPHS
GIVE A STEP-BY-STEP NO NONSENSE APPROACH TO THIS
STORY BUT, THROUGHOUT, THE HUMAN ELEMENT IS
THERE, TOO, AS WE SEE JEFF FEELING SCARED AND
WORRIED BEFORE THE OPERATION. REASSURING PICTURES
OF MOTHER AND FATHER WITH HIM AFTERWARD, AND
HORSEPLAY WITH THE NEIGHBORHOOD KIDS LEND AN
UPBEAT FEELING TO THE BOOK. (DIFF SIT--HANDICAPS,
EMOTIONS--FEAR, FEAR, HANDICAPS, HOSPITAL, NEW
SIT--HOSPITAL)

STEIN, SARA. A HOSPITAL STORY. WALKER, 1974.
ILLUSTRATED BY DORIS PINNEY.   (BL)

   LARGE REALISTIC PHOTOGRAPHS, SOME IN COLOR,
SET THE TONE FOR THIS HELPFUL BOOK. ACKNOWLEDGING
THAT SOME THINGS ARE SCARY, AND SOMETIMES
PAINFUL, THE AUTHOR, IN COOPERATION WITH STAFF AT
THE CENTER FOR PREVENTIVE PSYCHIATRY, HAS

ATTEMPTED TO HELP BOTH PARENT AND CHILD. VERY
LARGE PRINT IS USED IN THE TEXT FOR THE CHILD
WHILE, ON THE SAME PAGE, THERE IS AN EXTENSIVE
SECTION DIRECTED TO THE ADULT WHICH CONTAINS
EXCELLENT PRACTICAL ADVICE, SUCH AS TAKING A
CAMERA TO RECORD WHAT THE HOSPITAL IS REALLY
LIKE, AND ASKING ALL SORTS OF QUESTIONS IN
ADVANCE. (DIFF SIT--HOSPITAL, HOSPITAL, NEW
SIT--HOSPITAL)

TAMBURINE, JEAN. I THINK I WILL GO TO THE
HOSPITAL. ABINGDON, 1965. ILLUSTRATED BY JEAN
TAMBURINE. (CCB-B, LJ)

   AN EXCELLENT BOOK FOR A CHILD AND HIS PARENT
TO PREPARE FOR A HOSPITAL VISIT. WHEN SUSY
DECIDES SHE DOES NOT WANT TO GO TO THE HOSPITAL,
HER MOTHER TAKES HER TO THE WAITING ROOM OF THE
HOSPITAL, AND ON THE WAY SHE STOPS WITH GET-WELL
PRESENTS FOR PEOPLE JUST OUT OF THE HOSPITAL.
THESE ARE POSITIVE CONTACTS, AND SUSY ALSO MEETS
A FRIENDLY NURSE WHO TAKES TIME TO TALK ABOUT
WHAT WILL HAPPEN TO HER. AT HOME, SHE PLAYS
HOSPITAL WITH HER PETS, AND BY THE TIME SHE
ARRIVES AT THE HOSPITAL, SHE IS RELAXED AND READY
TO HAVE HER PARENTS LEAVE. THIS IS ONE OF THE
LONGEST STORIES ON THIS SUBJECT, AND IS A FUN
BOOK FOR READING ALOUD. (EMOTIONS--FEAR, FEAR,
HOSPITAL, NEW SIT--HOSPITAL)

NEW SIT--MOVING

HICKMAN, MARTHA. I'M MOVING. ABINGDON, 1974.
ILLUSTRATED BY LEIGH GRANT. (BL)

   LARGE, COLORFUL PICTURE BOOK, WITH MANY "NOW"
ELEMENTS. FATHER SPORTS LONGER HAIR AND A
MUSTACHE, AND THE FAMILY DRIVES A V.W. BUG.
WILLIAM, THE SMALL BOY WHO TELLS THE STORY, GIVES
A VERY POSITIVE VIEW ABOUT MOVING. THE
ILLUSTRATIONS ARE SHOWN FROM VARYING
PERSPECTIVES, AS AT THE TOP OF THE STAIRS LOOKING
DOWN, AND THE VIEWS FROM THE BOY'S BEDROOM
WINDOW. USEFUL BECAUSE OF ITS CONTRAST TO THE
NEGATIVE ASPECT OF MOVING. (MOVING, NEW
SIT--MOVING)

HOFF, SYD. WHO WILL BE MY FRIENDS?. HARPER,
1960. ILLUSTRATED BY SYD HOFF. (ESLC)

FREDDY MOVES TO A NEW NEIGHBORHOOD AND HAS NO
ONE TO PLAY WITH. HE FINALLY COMES TO A GROUP OF
BOYS WHO ARE PLAYING BALL. HE THROWS HIS BALL UP
IN THE AIR AND CATCHES IT SEVERAL TIMES. THEN THE
BOYS ASK HIM TO JOIN THEIR GAME. THIS
EASY-TO-READ BOOK EXEMPLIFIES THE FACT THAT YOU
NEED TO GO OUT AND SEARCH FOR FRIENDS, AND SHOW
PEOPLE THAT YOU CAN DO SOMETHING COMPETENTLY.
(FRIENDSHIP, MOVING, NEW SIT--MOVING,
SELF-RELIANCE)

ILSLEY, VELMA. M IS FOR MOVING. WALCK, 1966.
ILLUSTRATED BY VELMA ILSLEY. (LJ)

IN AN ALPHABET BOOK WHICH EMPHASIZES THE
BUSTLING ROUTINE OF PACKING WITH UPBEAT COLORS OF
ORANGE AND YELLOW, THE AUTHOR-ILLUSTRATOR HAS
PRODUCED A REASSURING LOOK AT THE PROCESS OF
MOVING. A BOOK WHICH CAN BE USED TO DISPEL FEARS
IN THE VERY YOUNG, IT CAN ALSO BE USED BY A
FAMILY IN ADVANCE OF THE MOVE TO ACTIVELY INVOLVE
THE CHILD, AS YOUNG CHILDREN ARE SHOWN ON EVERY
PAGE EMPTYING DRAWERS AND PACKING BOXES AND, AT
THE END, THEY LOOK ON THE MAP TO SEE WHERE THE
NEW HOUSE IS LOCATED. (MOVING, NEW SIT--MOVING)

JUSTUS, MAY. A NEW HOME FOR BILLY. HASTINGS,
1966. ILLUSTRATED BY JOAN PAYNE. (BCB)

WHEN SIX-YEAR-OLD BILLY MOVES TO A NEW
NEIGHBORHOOD HE FINDS OUT THAT NOT ALL PEOPLE
WILL RENT TO NEGROES, AT LEAST NOT AT THE TIME
THIS BOOK WAS WRITTEN. A USEFUL FACT FOR ALL
CHILDREN TO KNOW. THE NEW HOUSE, THOUGH IN NEED
OF REPAIR, HAS AN APPLE TREE IN THE YARD AND IS A
GREAT IMPROVEMENT OVER THE DIRTY SLUM AREA HE
MOVED FROM. AFTER AN INITIAL PERIOD OF
LONELINESS, BILLY MAKES FRIENDS BECAUSE OF THE
SWING, A SLIDE, A JUMPING BAR, AND A SEESAW
CONSTRUCTED BY HIS FATHER. THE BOOK ENDS WITH
FRIENDS, BLACK AND WHITE, HELPING TO PAINT THE
HOUSE. (EMOTIONS--LONELINESS, FRIENDSHIP,
LONELINESS, MOVING, NEW SIT--MOVING)

KANTROWITZ, MILDRED. GOOD-BYE KITCHEN. PARENTS'
MAG, 1972. ILLUSTRATED BY MERCER MAYER. (CCB-B)

AN ORIGINAL APPROACH TO MOVING DAY, AS EMILY
AND HER FRIEND RUFIE SIT ON THE STEPS AND WATCH
THE MOVING VAN. AS THEY SIT AND MUNCH ON A BAG

LUNCH, EMILY RECOUNTS IN HER IMAGINATION THE
MEMORIES OF THE FURNITURE--"GOOD-BYE, WHITE
DISHES WITH YOUR YELLOW BORDERS"--AND THE
MEMORIES OF HER BEST FRIEND JUNIE. UP UNTIL THIS
POINT THE READER THINKS IT IS EMILY WHO IS
MOVING, BUT NO, IT IS SHE WHO IS LEFT BEHIND. AS
EMILY STARTS TO LEAVE HER VANTAGE POINT, ANOTHER
MOVING VAN PULLS UP, AND SHE IS DELIGHTED TO SEE
A GIRL'S BICYCLE JUST HER SIZE, AND IS HAPPY IN
ANTICIPATION OF THE NEW FRIEND IN THE OFFING.
(FRIENDSHIP, MOVING, NEW SIT--MOVING)

PRATHER, RAY. NEW NEIGHBORS. MC GRAW, 1975.
ILLUSTRATED BY RAY PRATHER. (CCB-B)

   WHEN RICHY MOVES TO A NEW, UNFRIENDLY SUBURBAN
NEIGHBORHOOD, HE TRIES TO MAKE FRIENDS BY
SELLING SOME OLD TOYS HE FINDS IN THE HOUSE. THIS
DRAWS THE OTHER BLACK CHILDREN INTO HIS YARD. AT
FIRST THEY TRY TO PLAY TRICKS ON HIM, BUT
LUCKILY RICHY LAUGHS, AND IS ASKED TO JOIN THE
GANG. DEMONSTRATES HOW ONE CHILD OVERCAME THE
DIFFICULTY OF FINDING NEW FRIENDS. (FRIENDSHIP,
MOVING, NEW SIT--MOVING)

THOMPSON, VIVIAN. SAD DAY, GLAD DAY. HOLIDAY,
1962. ILLUSTRATED BY LILIAN OBLIGADO. (RLHR)

   THE LARGE PRINT IS JUST RIGHT IN THIS BOOK FOR
NEW READERS WHO ARE BEGINNING TO PROGRESS TO
MORE DIFFICULT THINGS. KATHY MOVES TO A NEW
APARTMENT IN THE CITY FROM THE COUNTRY WHERE SHE
HAD A SWING ON AN APPLE TREE, AND FEELS VERY
LONELY. LUCKILY SHE FINDS A DOLL IN THE CLOSET OF
THE NEW HOUSE WHICH GOES A LONG WAY TOWARD
MAKING HER FEEL GOOD. EXPLAINS CHANGE AND HOW
PEOPLE ADJUST TO NEW PLACES.
(EMOTIONS--LONELINESS, LONELINESS, MOVING, NEW
SIT--MOVING)

ZOLOTOW, CHARLOTTE. A TIGER CALLED THOMAS.
LOTHROP, 1963. ILLUSTRATED BY KURT WERTH. (CC)

   SHY THOMAS SITS ON THE PORCH OF HIS NEW HOUSE
AND REFUSES TO TRY TO MAKE NEW FRIENDS. HE IS
VERY OBSERVANT, HOWEVER, AND IS AWARE OF GERALD,
WHO PLAYS BALL ALONE, AND OF MARIE, AND OTHER
PEOPLE IN THE NEIGHBORHOOD. GIVEN CONFIDENCE BY
DRESSING UP IN A TIGER SUIT ON HALLOWEEN, HE
TAKES ON SOME OF THE COURAGE OF THE BEAST, AND

VISITS ALL OF THE HOUSES IN THE NEIGHBORHOOD.
WHEN PEOPLE ASK HIM TO VISIT AND PLAY, HE
REALIZES THAT THEY ALL LIKE HIM, AND HE DECIDES
THAT HE ALSO LIKES THEM. (EMOTIONS--SHYNESS,
FRIENDSHIP, MOVING, NEW SIT--MOVING,
SELF-CONFIDENCE, SHYNESS)

NEW SIT--SCHOOL

AMOSS, BERTHE. THE VERY WORST THING. PARENTS'
MAG, 1972. ILLUSTRATED BY BERTHE AMOSS. (CCB-B)

THE VERY BEST THING IS THE END OF THE FIRST
DAY. AND THE VERY WORST THING IS THE FIRST DAY
WHEN TOM IS 1) ELECTED SANITATION CHIEF, WHICH
MEANS HE SWEEPS THE FLOOR, AND 2) WHEN HE WALKS
INTO THE GIRLS' REST ROOM BY MISTAKE. VARIOUS
OTHER INDIGNITIES ARE ENDURED, BUT THE HUMOROUS
APPROACH TO A TRYING SITUATION HELPS ALLEVIATE
TOM'S TROUBLES. (NEW SIT--SCHOOL)

BREINBURG, PETRONELLA. SHAWN GOES TO SCHOOL.
CROWELL, T., 1973. ILLUSTRATED BY ERROL LLOYD.
(BL)

ESPECIALLY LARGE PRINT MAKES THIS A BOOK FOR
YOUNGER READERS, THOUGH SOME WORDS ARE DIFFICULT,
SUCH AS "SMILED" AND "DONKEY." SPLASHY PAINTINGS
CREATE REALISTIC SCENES: SHAWN'S HOWLING FACE IS
A GRAPHIC EXAMPLE OF HIS REACTION TO NURSERY
SCHOOL. BY THE END OF THE BOOK, SHAWN AND THE
READER HAVE ENTERED INTO THE COLORFUL, INTRIGUING
WORLD OF A HAPPY NURSERY SCHOOL SETTING. (NEW
SIT--SCHOOL)

COHEN, MIRIAM. WILL I HAVE A FRIEND?. MACMILLAN,
1967. ILLUSTRATED BY LILLIAN HOBAN. (BCB)

A REALISTIC FEAR IN A YOUNG CHILD IS SHOWN IN
A TYPICAL PICTURE OF THE FIRST DAY OF
KINDERGARTEN. CHILDREN MILL ABOUT, EACH INTENT ON
HIS OWN BUSINESS, AND JIM DOESN'T FEEL INCLUDED
UNTIL AFTER REST TIME WHEN PAUL SHOWS HIM HIS
TINY TRUCK. THIS CHARACTER PAUL ALSO APPEARS IN
"BEST FRIEND" BY THE SAME AUTHOR.
(EMOTIONS--FEAR, FEAR, FRIENDSHIP, NEW
SIT--SCHOOL)

JUSTUS, MAY. NEW BOY IN SCHOOL. HASTINGS, 1963.
ILLUSTRATED BY JOAN PAYNE. (CC)

A BOOK FOR THIRD-GRADE READERS, THIS STORY OF
LENNIE, THE ONLY NEGRO IN HIS FIRST-GRADE
CLASSROOM, IS SOMEWHAT ARTIFICIAL IN ITS DIALOG
YET PRESENTS A REASSURING PICTURE TO CHILDREN WHO
MIGHT BE IN THE SAME SITUATION. HE IS WELCOMED
BY A SPECIAL FRIEND WHO MAKES HIM FEEL AT HOME,
AND THE STORY ENDS WITH BOTH OF THEM IN THE
SCHOOL PROGRAM SINGING A SONG LENNIE'S DADDY SANG
TO HIM AT NIGHT. (FRIENDSHIP, NEW SIT--SCHOOL)

ROCKWELL, HARLOW. MY NURSERY SCHOOL. MORROW,
1976. ILLUSTRATED BY HARLOW ROCKWELL. (BL)

WHILE THIS BOOK DOES NOT DEAL WITH THE
ADJUSTMENT TO THE NEWNESS OF NURSERY SCHOOL, THE
PLEASANT ENVIRONMENT OF BUILDING BLOCKS AND CLAY,
PETS AND PLANTS, AND EXCITING DRESS-UP CLOTHES
SETS A POSITIVE MOOD FOR ANY CHILD WHO MIGHT FEEL
APPREHENSIVE ABOUT GOING TO NURSERY SCHOOL.
CHILDREN OF DIFFERENT RACES ARE PICTURED IN THE
COLORFUL ACTIVITIES, AS IS MR. PAUL, A MALE
TEACHER. CLEAR, FRESH COLORS GIVE THE BOOK AN
UPBEAT FEELING, AND IT IS A PLUS FOR THOSE
PERSONS LOOKING FOR EXAMPLES OF NON-TRADITIONAL
ROLES FOR CHILDREN AND ADULTS. (EMOTIONS--FEAR,
FEAR, NEW SIT--SCHOOL)

WOLDE, GUNILLA. BETSY'S FIRST DAY AT NURSERY
SCHOOL. RANDOM, 1976. ILLUSTRATED BY GUNILLA
WOLDE. (BL)

THIS SMALL, CHILD-SIZE BOOK STRIKES JUST THE
RIGHT NOTE TO DISPEL FEARS ABOUT GOING OFF TO
NURSERY SCHOOL FOR THE FIRST TIME. MOTHER WISELY
SCHEDULES A SHORT VISIT WHICH BEGINS WITH ROBERT,
ONE OF THE TEACHERS, SHOWING THEM AROUND. BETSY
IS RELUCTANT TO JOIN IN THE ACTIVITIES, AND KEEPS
HER SNOWSUIT ON, BUT A LITTLE LATER FINDS A
FRIEND. BY THE TIME MOTHER GATHERS UP THE TWO
CHILDREN TO GO HOME, BETSY FEELS MORE RELAXED,
AND IS LOOKING FORWARD TO RETURNING THE NEXT DAY.
USEFUL BECAUSE IT SHOWS THE CHILD THAT OTHER
CHILDREN ARE ALSO A LITTLE CONCERNED ABOUT BEING
LEFT AT SCHOOL. SWEDISH AUTHOR WOLDE IS
CONSISTENT IN SHOWING MALES IN NON-TRADITIONAL
ROLES IN THIS SERIES ABOUT BETSY.
(EMOTIONS--FEAR, FEAR, NEW SIT--SCHOOL)

NEW SIT--TEACHER

COHEN, MIRIAM. NEW TEACHER. MACMILLAN, 1972.
ILLUSTRATED BY LILLIAN HOBAN.   (ESLC)

JIM'S APPREHENSIONS ABOUT HIS NEW TEACHER LEAD
HIM TO MAKE SOME UNCOMPLIMENTARY REMARKS ABOUT
HER ON THE PLAYGROUND. THE CREATORS OF THE BOOK
HAVE SHOWN A VERY REALISTIC GROUP OF CHILDREN
TEASING THE GIRLS, CHECKING OUT THE CONTENTS OF
LUNCH BAGS, AND TELLING RIDDLES IN A TYPICAL
FIRST-GRADE CLASSROOM. ALL OF THE CHILDREN ARE
REASSURED WHEN THEY SEE THE NEW TEACHER--YES, SHE
IS BIG, AND YES, SHE SHOUTS, BUT ONLY TO SAY "HI
EVERYBODY, I'M GLAD TO SEE YOU." (NEW
SIT--TEACHER)

NEW SIT--TYING SHOELACES

KLIMOWICZ, BARBARA. WHEN SHOES EAT SOCKS.
ABINGDON, 1971. ILLUSTRATED BY GLORIA KAMEN.
(BECB)

PROBABLY ONE OF THE MOST USEFUL BOOKS EVER
WRITTEN, IN THE EYES OF WEARY PARENTS AND
TEACHERS, THIS STORY OF BARNABY AND HIS ELUSIVE
SOCKS WILL GO A LONG WAY IN DEMONSTRATING A
PRACTICAL, IMAGINATIVE WAY TO TEACH CHILDREN HOW
TO TIE THEIR SHOELACES. BONUS ITEMS IN THE STORY
ARE A RACIALLY-MIXED NEIGHBORHOOD, GENUINE LOVE
AND CARINGNESS ON THE PART OF THE PARENTS, AND A
LOVING TOLERANCE ON THE PART OF PLAYMATES. (NEW
SIT--TYING SHOELACES, TYING SHOELACES)

NEW SIT--WHISTLING

KEATS, EZRA. WHISTLE FOR WILLIE. VIKING, 1964.
ILLUSTRATED BY EZRA KEATS.   (CC)

THE UNDERSTANDING PARENTS OF YOUNG PETER
SUPPORT HIS EFFORTS TO TRY TO BE GROWN-UP. HE
WANTS TO LEARN TO WHISTLE, HE TRIES ON HIS
FATHER'S HAT, HE TRIES TO CATCH HIS SHADOW. HIS
MOTHER DOES NOT DEMEAN HIM, AND BOTH HIS PARENTS
PRAISE PETER WHEN HE LEARNS TO WHISTLE. THE SMILE
THAT PETER HAS ON HIS FACE TELLS THE WHOLE STORY
OF PRIDE IN ACCOMPLISHMENT. AS MOTHER AND FATHER
APPLAUD IN THE BACKGROUND, HIS DOG WILLIE SITS
UP ON HIS HIND LEGS. (FAM, NEW SIT--WHISTLING,
SELF-DEVELOPMENT, WHISTLING)

OLD AGE

ARDIZONNE, EDWARD. LUCY BROWN AND MR. GRIMES.
WALCK, 1971. ILLUSTRATED BY EDWARD ARDIZONNE.
(CC)

   THIS BOOK HAS A FAIRY-TALE QUALITY WHICH MAKES
IT SOMETHING OF A FANTASY: A LONELY LITTLE
ORPHAN GIRL MEETS A LONELY OLD MAN AND THEY
BECOME GREAT FRIENDS. WHEN MR. GRIMES FALLS ILL
AND MUST MOVE TO THE COUNTRY, HE ASKS LUCY TO GO
WITH HIM, WITH LUCY'S AUNT'S PERMISSION. MR.
GRIMES, WHO IS VERY WEALTHY, IS GENEROUS WITH HIS
MONEY, AND LUCY BUYS NEW CLOTHING. ILLUSTRATES
THE POINT THAT THERE ARE THINGS IN COMMON FOR THE
YOUNG AND THE OLD. THE OLD MAN AND THE LITTLE
GIRL WALK TOGETHER, HAVE TEA TOGETHER, AND NEVER
FEEL LONELY. (DIFF SIT--OLD AGE,
EMOTIONS--LONELINESS, FRIENDSHIP--ADULTS,
LONELINESS, OLD AGE)

BALDWIN, ANNE. SUNFLOWERS FOR TINA. FOUR, 1970.
ILLUSTRATED BY ANN GRIFALCONI. (CCB-B)

   IN SUNFLOWER COLORS, THE ILLUSTRATOR HAS SHOWN
A CORNER OF A DIRTY CITY NEIGHBORHOOD WHERE THE
LAUNDRY HANGS BETWEEN THE BUILDINGS, WHERE TINA
TRIES TO GROW A GARDEN BY PLANTING CARROTS SHE
FINDS IN THE REFRIGERATOR. WHEN SHE DISCOVERS
SUNFLOWERS GROWING A FEW BLOCKS FROM HOME, SHE
DELIGHTS IN THEIR FRESHNESS AND THINKS OF HER
AGING GRANDMOTHER AT HOME IN HER DARK CORNER.
LATER SHE DANCES IN HER YELLOW DRESS, AND EVOKES
LAUGHTER FROM THE OLD WOMAN. A STORY OF CONTRASTS
BETWEEN OLD AND YOUNG, BEAUTY AND RUBBLE, THIS
IS A POSITIVE STATEMENT FOR THE NECESSITY OF
AESTHETIC PLEASURE IN LIFE. (FAM--GRANDMOTHERS,
FAM--OLD AGE, GRANDMOTHERS, OLD AGE)

BLUE, ROSE. GRANDMA DIDN'T WAVE BACK. WATTS,
1972. ILLUSTRATED BY TED LEWIN. (CC)

   DEBBIE, TEN YEARS OLD, REALIZES THAT HER
BELOVED GRANDMOTHER IS CHANGING. SHE NO LONGER
WAVES AT DEBBIE FROM THE WINDOW, NOR DOES SHE
HAVE COOKIES FROM THE OVEN READY FOR HER. GRANDMA
EXHIBITS LOSS OF MEMORY, CONFUSION OVER NAMES,
AND OTHER EVIDENCE OF SENILITY, SUCH AS STAYING
IN HER NIGHT DRESS ALL DAY. AS THE GRANDMOTHER
DECLINES, DEBBIE MATURES, AND IS UPSET BY THE

RELATIVES' DECISION TO ENTER THE GRANDMOTHER IN A
NURSING HOME. THE BOOK ENDS ON A POSITIVE NOTE,
HOWEVER, AS THE OLDER WOMAN SPEAKS ENCOURAGINGLY
OF THE COMING OF SPRING. A USEFUL BOOK BECAUSE IT
DEALS WITH A PROBLEM FACING MANY FAMILIES TODAY.
APPROPRIATE FOR THIRD GRADERS TO READ
INDEPENDENTLY. (DIFF SIT--OLD AGE,
FAM--GRANDMOTHERS, GRANDMOTHERS, OLD AGE,
SELF-UNDERSTANDING)

BUCKLEY, HELEN. GRANDFATHER AND I. LOTHROP,
1959. ILLUSTRATED BY PAUL GALDONE. (CC)

   HELEN BUCKLEY WROTE FAMILY STORIES ABOUT
GRANDPARENTS IN THE 1950'S AND THEY ARE AS VALID
NOW AS IN 1959. IN LARGE TYPE, AND LARGE COLORFUL
ILLUSTRATIONS, THE STORY IS TOLD OF THE JOYS OF
NOT HURRYING, OF A BOY AND HIS GRANDFATHER WHO
TAKE WALKS AND TAKE TIME TO LOOK FOR THINGS SUCH
AS BIRDS AND SQUIRRELS AND EVEN SNAILS.
CONTRASTING ARE EXAMPLES OF THE HUSTLE AND BUSTLE
OF HURRYING MOTHERS, DADS, TRAFFIC, AND OLDER
CHILDREN. "EVERYONE ELSE IS ALWAYS IN A HURRY BUT
WHEN A BOY AND HIS GRANDFATHER GO WALKING THEY
HAVE TIME TO STOP AND LOOK." (FAM--GRANDFATHERS,
FAM--OLD AGE, GRANDFATHERS, OLD AGE)

GILL, JOAN. SARA'S GRANNY AND THE GROODLE.
DOUBLEDAY, 1969. ILLUSTRATED BY SEYMOUR CHWAST.
(LJ)

   NONSENSICAL TEXT WHICH LOOKS LIKE PROSE, BUT
RHYMES, WITH SUCH AMUSING WORDS AS STRUDEL,
NOODLE, AND GROODLE, MAKE THIS A VERY ATTRACTIVE
BOOK TO READ ALOUD. IT SHOWS GRANNY AND YOUNG
SARA IN AN ADVENTURE WHICH MAY OR MAY NOT BE A
DREAM. THE PICTURE IT PORTRAYS OF GRANDMA IS A
VERY UNCONVENTIONAL ONE. ALTHOUGH SHE WEARS LONG
SKIRTS AND HIGH BUTTON BOOTS, SHE SHOUTS "OLE" AS
THEY RIDE DOWN THE STREET IN THE OYSTER SHELL
WHICH IS BEING DRAWN ALONG BY THE GOOSE. ITS
VALUE LIES PERHAPS IN THE VIEW IT GIVES OF OLD
AGE--THAT OLDER PEOPLE DON'T NEED TO SIT IN A
ROCKER AT HOME. (FAM--GRANDMOTHERS, FAM--OLD AGE,
GRANDMOTHERS, OLD AGE)

HEIN, LUCILLE. MY VERY SPECIAL FRIEND. JUDSON,
1974. ILLUSTRATED BY JOAN ORFE. (CCB-B)

   A FIVE-YEAR-OLD STAYS WITH HER GRANDMOTHER AND

GRANDFATHER WHILE HER MOTHER IS IN THE HOSPITAL,
BUT IT IS REALLY HER GREAT-GRANDMOTHER WITH WHOM
SHE SPENDS HER TIME. A HEALTHY RELATIONSHIP
DEVELOPS BETWEEN THE VERY OLD (85) AND THE VERY
YOUNG (5). THE CHILD HELPS THE OLD ONE, DOES
ERRANDS, AND IS A GENTLE COMPANION.
GREAT-GRANDMOTHER TEACHES THE CHILD TO TIE HER
SHOES, TO WHISTLE, AND SHARES OLD FAMILY
PHOTOGRAPHS TO GIVE THE CHILD A SENSE OF HISTORY
AND A SENSE OF BELONGING TO A FAMILY.
(FAM--GREAT-GRANDMOTHERS, FAM--OLD AGE,
GREAT-GRANDMOTHERS, OLD AGE)

KANTROWITZ, MILDRED. MAXIE. PARENTS' MAG, 1970.
ILLUSTRATED BY EMILY MC CULLY. (ESLC)

   AN INTERESTING THEME FOR A CHILDREN'S
BOOK--THE LONELINESS OF A WHITE-HAIRED OLD WOMAN
WHO LIVES ALONE AND THINKS NO ONE NEEDS HER. ALL
THIS IS CHANGED ONE DAY WHEN SHE STAYS IN BED
INSTEAD OF GOING THROUGH HER USUAL ROUTINE. SHE
FINDS OUT THAT INDEED MANY PEOPLE WERE DEPENDING
ON HER: HER CANARY BIRD WOKE UP ONE FAMILY, HER
WHISTLING TEAKETTLE ANOTHER. ALTOGETHER THERE
WERE 53 PEOPLE WHO CAME TO HER DOOR LATER THAT
DAY...AND SHE SERVED THEM ALL A CUP OF TEA. (DIFF
SIT--OLD AGE, EMOTIONS--LONELINESS, LONELINESS,
OLD AGE)

KEATS, EZRA. APT. 3. MACMILLAN, 1971.
ILLUSTRATED BY EZRA KEATS. (ESLC)

   TWO BROTHERS, SAM AND BEN, ARE LONELY AND
DECIDE TO INVESTIGATE THE SOURCE OF SOMEONE
PLAYING A HARMONICA. THE SETTING IS A GRIM GHETTO
APARTMENT BUILDING, AND VARIOUS MOODS ARE FELT
AS THE BOYS GO DOWN THE HALL. WHEN THEY FIND THE
BLIND MAN PLAYING THE HARMONICA IN APT. 3, HE
SHARES WITH THEM THE SECRETS HE KNOWS AND PLAYS
STRANGE MUSIC WHICH CONJURES UP SIGHTS, SOUNDS,
AND COLORS TO SAM. THE BOOK ENDS WITH SAM ASKING
THE OLD MAN TO TAKE A WALK WITH THEM. EVOCATIVE
ART WORK AND PROSE SHOW THE POWER OF MUSIC ON THE
EMOTIONS. (DIFF SIT--HANDICAPS, DIFF SIT--OLD
AGE, EMOTIONS--LONELINESS, HANDICAPS, LONELINESS,
OLD AGE)

LUNDGREN, MAX. MATT'S GRANDFATHER. PUTNAM, 1972.
 ILLUSTRATED BY FIBBEN HALD. (CC)

WRITTEN IN SWEDEN, THIS REFRESHINGLY HONEST
BOOK ABOUT AN OLD MAN IN AN OLD FOLKS' HOME
PRESENTS A POINT OF VIEW VERY DIFFERENT FROM
OTHER BOOKS ON THIS SUBJECT. WE SEE LIFE FROM THE
POINT OF VIEW OF THE GRANDFATHER: HE THINKS HE
LOOKS YOUNGER THAN HIS SON, AND HE THINKS THE SON
TALKS AS IF HE WERE THE FATHER. HE MAKES A GREAT
DEAL OF SENSE, AND IS FOXY ENOUGH TO MASQUERADE
IN A LINEN JACKET, SUNGLASSES, AND A BIG FLOPPY
STRAW HAT IN ORDER TO ESCAPE INTO THE OUTSIDE
WORLD FOR A FEW HOURS. THE BOOK DOES INCLUDE SOME
OF THE FOIBLES OF OLDER PEOPLE, SUCH AS
FORGETFULNESS AND SECRETIVENESS (HE HIDES HIS
SNUFF IN THE FLOWER POT), BUT TO THE LITTLE BOY
WHO IS VISITING, THESE MILD ABERRATIONS ARE TAKEN
IN STRIDE. LOVELY PASTEL ILLUSTRATIONS ACCENTING
HORIZONTAL LINES CONTRIBUTE TO A SENSE OF
PEACEFULNESS. A SENSE OF WELL-BEING PERMEATES THE
BOOK, AND THE READER HAS A FEELING OF PLEASURE
IN KNOWING THAT THE OLD GENTLEMAN IS BEING CARED
FOR IN A BUILDING AS BIG AS A CASTLE WITH TOWERS
AND SPIRES. PARTICULARLY USEFUL TO GIVE A CHILD A
POSITIVE, ALBEIT MINORITY REPORT ON OLDER
CITIZENS, MANY OF WHOM REMAIN CHIPPER AND IN
CHARGE OF THEIR SENSES. (DIFF SIT--OLD AGE,
FAM--GRANDFATHERS, GRANDFATHERS, OLD AGE)

SHARMAT, MARJORIE. REX. HARPER, 1967.
ILLUSTRATED BY EMILY MC CULLY. (HB)

IN THIS HANDSOMELY ILLUSTRATED PICTURE BOOK,
REX GOES TO VISIT A NEIGHBOR, UNBEKNOWN TO HIS
MOTHER. THE OLD GENTLEMAN WELCOMES THE LITTLE BOY
(WHO PRETENDS HE IS A DOG) AND THE BEGINNINGS OF
A FINE FRIENDSHIP ARE SEEN. USEFUL BECAUSE OF
THE PLEASURE BOTH MAN AND BOY RECEIVE AS THEY
JOIN IN THE MAKE-BELIEVE PLAY. (DIFF SIT--OLD
AGE, FRIENDSHIP--ADULTS, OLD AGE)

SHECTER, BEN. ACROSS THE MEADOW. DOUBLEDAY,
1973. ILLUSTRATED BY BEN SHECTER. (LJ, NYTBR,
PRC)

IN A STORY WHICH DOES NOT MENTION DEATH OR
DYING, THE CONCEPT IS CARRIED FORWARD BY AN OLD
CAT WHO JOURNEYS INTO THE FOREST, SAYING GOOD-BYE
TO HIS FRIENDS, AND CURLING UP TO SLEEP IN AN
OLD ABANDONED CAR. THE FEELING OF DEATH IS
FINALIZED WHEN WE SEE THE OLD CAR COMPLETELY
COVERED BY CREEPING VINES, MUCH AS THE CASTLE IN

"SLEEPING BEAUTY." A SUBTLE WAY OF INDICATING
DEATH AND DECAY IS THE USE OF DEAD TWIGS IN THE
FRAMING MOTIF OF EACH PAGE, THOUGH ONE WHICH
CHILDREN MAY NOT RECOGNIZE. THE INTRODUCTION OF A
YOUNG KITTEN WHO IS SENT BACK TO THE FARM AS HIS
REPLACEMENT EMPHASIZES THE BIRTH/DEATH CYCLE.
(DEATH--PET, DIFF SIT--DEATH--PET, DIFF SIT--OLD
AGE, OLD AGE)

SONNEBORN, RUTH. I LOVE GRAM. VIKING, 1971.
ILLUSTRATED BY LEO CARTY. (ESLC)

   A THIRD GRADER COULD READ THIS PICTURE-STORY
BOOK WHICH IS MORE TEXT THAN PICTURES, BUT IT CAN
BE ENJOYED BY YOUNGER CHILDREN AS A READ-ALOUD.
ELLIE'S GRANDMOTHER CARES FOR HER, AND COOKS FOR
THE FAMILY WHILE ELLIE'S MOTHER WORKS. WHEN GRAM
GOES TO THE HOSPITAL, ELLIE IS VERY LONELY, AND
INDEED EXPERIENCES A FEELING OF THE FORESHADOWING
OF DEATH. THE POSITIVE THINGS SHE DOES TO
PREPARE FOR GRAM'S HOMECOMING SHOW HER LOVE: A
PICTURE SHE DRAWS AND THE PARTY TABLE SHE
PREPARES. WE KNOW AT THE END OF THE STORY THE
STRONG BOND OF LOVE BETWEEN GRAM AND HER FAMILY.
(FAM--GRANDMOTHERS, FAM--MOTHERS WORKING,
FAM--OLD AGE, GRANDMOTHERS, MOTHERS WORKING, OLD
AGE)

UDRY, JANICE. MARY JO'S GRANDMOTHER. WHITMAN,
A., 1970. ILLUSTRATED BY ELEANOR MILL. (BCB)

   A SELF-RELIANT WOMAN WHO LIVES ALONE IN THE
COUNTRY GIVES A POSITIVE PICTURE OF AN OLDER
PERSON. RAISING CHICKENS AND MAKING GARDEN OCCUPY
THIS LADY'S TIME, AND MARY JO LOVES TO VISIT
HER. RESOURCEFUL MARY JO GOES FOR HELP WHEN
GRANDMA TAKES A FALL, BUT THE MAIN EMPHASIS IS ON
THE INDEPENDENT HOUSEHOLD OF THIS SPRIGHTLY
OLDSTER. (DIFF SIT--OLD AGE, FAM--GRANDMOTHERS,
GRANDMOTHERS, OLD AGE)

WILLIAMS, BARBARA. KEVIN'S GRANDMA. DUTTON,
1975. ILLUSTRATED BY KAY CHORAO. (BL)

   SPARKLY-EYED KEVIN MAY BE STRETCHING THE TRUTH
A BIT WHEN HE TELLS ABOUT HIS HONDA-RIDING
GRANDMOTHER, A VERY MUCH "WITH IT" LADY WHO IS
CONTRASTED WITH THE TRADITIONAL VIEW OF THE
NARRATOR'S GRANDMOTHER. A REFRESHING LOOK AT TWO
DIFFERENT CULTURES IN A BOOK WHICH REALLY DOESN'T

TAKE SIDES--AND AS SUCH IS A GOOD FORUM FOR
DISCUSSION. (FAM--GRANDMOTHERS, FAM--OLD AGE,
GRANDMOTHERS, OLD AGE)

OLD AGE--PET

SKORPEN, LIESEL. OLD ARTHUR. HARPER, 1972.
ILLUSTRATED BY WALLACE TRIPP. (CC)

   AS THE STORY OPENS, THE OLD DOG ARTHUR IS
HELPING TO BRING THE COWS HOME, AND HELPING THE
FARMER HUNT RABBITS, EXCEPT THAT HE IS SLOW AND
FORGETFUL. WHEN HE SENSES THAT THE FARMER IS
GOING TO GET RID OF HIM, HE SLIPS AWAY IN THE
NIGHT, AND ENDS UP IN THE POUND. WHEN HE IS
CLAIMED BY A LITTLE BOY, HIS LIFE TAKES A TURN
FOR THE BETTER, AND A SPLENDID RELATIONSHIP
DEVELOPS BETWEEN OLD ARTHUR AND THE BOY WILLIAM.
USEFUL BECAUSE OF HUMAN PARALLELS: OLD PEOPLE WHO
NO LONGER FEEL USEFUL ARE APT TO SLIP AWAY, OR
BE PUT AWAY, YET CAN LEAD HAPPY LIVES DOING
THINGS WITHIN THEIR ABILITIES. (DIFF SIT--OLD
AGE--PET, OLD AGE--PET)

ONE PARENT

BALDWIN, ANNE. JENNY'S REVENGE. FOUR, 1974.
ILLUSTRATED BY EMILY MC CULLY. (CCB-B)

   JENNY HATES HER BABY-SITTER, AND EXPRESSES
HIDDEN ANGER TOWARD HER WORKING MOTHER WHO
APPARENTLY HAS WORKED ONLY SINCE A RECENT
DIVORCE. AFTER TRYING A NUMBER OF PLOYS TO FORCE
THE BABY-SITTER TO QUIT, SHE FINDS COMRADESHIP
WITH MRS. CRAMIE WHEN THEY DISCOVER A COMMON
INTEREST IN THE CIRCUS. A REALISTIC LOOK AT A
CHILD WHO NEEDS AND WANTS ATTENTION FROM HER
MOTHER. (ANGER, DIFF SIT--DIVORCE, DIFF SIT--ONE
PARENT, DIVORCE, EMOTIONS--ANGER, FAM--MOTHERS
WORKING, MOTHERS WORKING, ONE PARENT)

BLUE, ROSE. A MONTH OF SUNDAYS. WATTS, 1972.
ILLUSTRATED BY TED LEWIN. (CC)

   IT WAS HARD HAVING A DAD WHO LOVED YOU ON
SUNDAYS WHEN HE USED TO LOVE YOU EVERY DAY. THIS
COMMENT EPITOMIZES THE UNHAPPY FEELINGS JEFFREY
HAS WHEN HE AND HIS MOTHER MOVE INTO AN APARTMENT
IN THE CITY. WHEN JEFF AND HIS DAD GET TOGETHER
IN THE OLD NEIGHBORHOOD, THINGS REALLY DON'T WORK

OUT. THE RELATIVES TALK AROUND HIM AS IF HE
WEREN'T PRESENT IN THE ROOM. THE MOTHER OF JEFF'S
BEST FRIEND MATTHEW TURNS OUT TO BE A GOOD
STRONG FRIEND WHO EXPLAINS SOME OF THE PROBLEMS
THAT JEFF'S MOM IS HAVING. GETTING INVOLVED IN A
GROUP PROJECT AT SCHOOL AND PARTICIPATING IN A
BIG BLOCK PARTY OVERFLOWING WITH DELICIOUS ETHNIC
FOODS, MUSIC, AND PEOPLE SEEM TO BE THE TWO
THINGS THAT BODE WELL FOR JEFF'S FUTURE. (DIFF
SIT--DIVORCE, DIVORCE, FAM--ONE PARENT, ONE
PARENT)

CLIFTON, LUCILLE. EVERETT ANDERSON'S YEAR. HOLT,
1974. ILLUSTRATED BY ANN GRIFALCONI. (CC)

  "WALK TALL IN THE WORLD," HIS MOTHER TELLS
HIM. ALTHOUGH THIS IS, IN THE MAIN, A STORY OF A
SEVEN-YEAR-OLD BOY, THE INFLUENCE OF HIS MOTHER
SHINES THROUGH ON EVERY PAGE. EVERETT ANDERSON
REMEMBERS HIS DADDY ALTHOUGH HE DOES NOT KNOW
WHERE HE IS, AND READING THIS SERIES OF VERSES
ABOUT THE MONTHS OF THE YEAR, A CHILD CAN SHARE
THE SPECIAL LOVE THE YOUNG BOY FEELS FOR HIS
MOTHER. (DIFF SIT--ONE PARENT,
EMOTIONS--LONELINESS, FAM--MOTHERS WORKING,
LONELINESS, MOTHERS WORKING, ONE PARENT)

KINDRED, WENDY. LUCKY WILMA. DIAL, 1973.
ILLUSTRATED BY WENDY KINDRED. (LJ)

  BEGINNING WITH A SERIES OF SATURDAYS WILMA AND
"CHARLIE," HER DAD, WALK TO MUSEUMS AND ZOOS,
AND FATHER AND DAUGHTER HAVE A UNIFORMLY GLUM
EXPRESSION. THE NEXT EIGHTEEN PAGES DEAL WITH
JOYOUS PICTURIZATION OF CLIMBING, JUMPING,
PIGGYBACKING, DANCING, AND REVELRY WITH THE
PIGEONS IN THE PARK. OBVIOUSLY THIS WAS THE
NEATEST SATURDAY THEY HAD SPENT TOGETHER, AND
THEY HUG AS THEY SEPARATE AND DAD SAYS: "WE'VE
GOT ALL THE SATURDAYS IN THE WORLD." CURIOUSLY
ENOUGH THE WORD DIVORCE IS NOT MENTIONED. WITH
VERY LITTLE TEXT, THIS BOOK CONVEYS THAT INDEED
WILMA IS LUCKY TO HAVE A WONDERFUL RELATIONSHIP
WITH HER FATHER. (DIFF SIT--DIVORCE, DIFF
SIT--ONE PARENT, DIVORCE, FAM--FATHERS, FATHERS,
ONE PARENT)

LEXAU, JOAN. EMILY AND THE KLUNKY BABY AND THE
NEXT DOOR DOG. DIAL, 1972. ILLUSTRATED BY MARTHA
ALEXANDER. (CC)

CHARMINGLY ILLUSTRATED, THE BOOK IS A SLIGHT
EPISODE OF A SMALL GIRL ATTEMPTING TO RUN AWAY TO
HER FATHER, WHO LIVES IN AN APARTMENT NEAR BY.
EMILY FEELS HER MOTHER WAS IGNORING HER WHEN
DOING HER INCOME TAXES AND DIDN'T WANT TO BE
BOTHERED. EMILY TAKES THE BABY AND ALMOST GETS
LOST BUT INSTEAD GOES AROUND THE BLOCK (BECAUSE
SHE'S NOT ALLOWED TO CROSS THE STREET)--AND MAKES
IT HOME TO A LOVING MOTHER WHO THINKS SHE'S OUT
PLAYING. (DIFF SIT--DIVORCE, DIFF SIT--ONE
PARENT, DIVORCE, FAM--MOTHERS, FAM--ONE PARENT,
MOTHERS, ONE PARENT)

LEXAU, JOAN. ME DAY. DIAL, 1971. ILLUSTRATED BY
ROBERT WEAVER. (BCB)

"ME DAY" IS RAFER'S BIRTHDAY, BUT IN A SLUM
FAMILY WHERE THERE IS NO MONEY FOR PRESENTS AND
THE TV IS BROKEN, WHAT MAKES A BOY HAPPY? THROUGH
THE TEXT WE LEARN THAT THE FATHER IS NOT AT
HOME, THE PARENTS BEING DIVORCED, APPARENTLY
BECAUSE THE FATHER COULD NOT FIND WORK. RAFER'S
DAY IS MADE PERFECT WHEN HIS FATHER SHOWS UP TO
SPEND THE ENTIRE DAY WITH HIM IN THE PARK, WITH
ICE CREAM AND HOT DOGS. (DIFF SIT--DIVORCE,
DIVORCE, FAM--FATHERS, FAM--ONE PARENT, FATHERS,
ONE PARENT, SELF-IDENTITY)

NESS, EVALINE. SAM, BANGS, AND MOONSHINE. HOLT,
1966. ILLUSTRATED BY EVALINE NESS. (BCB)

DESPITE HER FATHER'S CAUTIONS, SAMANTHA IS NOT
ABLE TO KEEP STRAIGHT HER IMAGINARY LIFE FROM
HER REAL LIFE, AND TELLS PRETTY BIG WHOPPERS
TRIGGERED BY HER LONELINESS AND AN INSPIRED
IMAGINATION. WHEN SHE TELLS HER FRIEND THOMAS
THAT HER PET KANGAROO LIVES OUT IN A CAVE, THOMAS
BECOMES MAROONED AND ALMOST LOSES HIS LIFE. SAM
IS DISTRAUGHT WHEN SHE REALIZES THAT HER LIE, FOR
THAT IS WHAT IT IS, IS RESPONSIBLE. HER FATHER
TELLS HER TO THINK ABOUT THE DIFFERENCE BETWEEN
REAL AND MOONSHINE AND, AT THE END, HE ALSO TELLS
HER THAT THERE ARE TWO KINDS OF MOONSHINE: THE
GOOD KIND, WHICH IS HEALTHY IMAGINATIVE PLAY, AND
THE BAD KIND, THAT WHICH CAN BE HARMFUL.
(BEHAVIOR--MISBEHAVIOR, DIFF SIT--ONE PARENT,
EMOTIONS--LONELINESS, FAM--ONE PARENT,
LONELINESS, MISBEHAVIOR, ONE PARENT)

PEARSON, SUSAN. MONNIE HATES LYDIA. DIAL, 1975.

ILLUSTRATED BY DIANE PATERSON.   (BL)

INTERESTING BECAUSE A FATHER HEADS THIS
ONE-PARENT FAMILY CONSISTING OF MONNIE AND HER
THOROUGHLY OBNOXIOUS SISTER LYDIA. DADDY IS AN
IMPARTIAL ARBITER IN THE FAMILY SQUABBLE WHICH
ERUPTS ON LYDIA'S BIRTHDAY, SUPPORTIVE OF
MONNIE'S HURT FEELINGS, BUT NOT WILLING TO PUNISH
LYDIA. HE IS AN ATTRACTIVE, BEARDED CONTEMPORARY
FATHER WHO CAN BE ADMIRED FOR HIS COOL WHEN
MONNIE DUMPS THE BIRTHDAY CAKE IN LYDIA'S FACE.
ONE FEELS HE SHOULD BE CHEERING, BUT INSTEAD HE
HANDS LYDIA A TOWEL AND KISSES HER ON THE CHEEK.
USEFUL AS A PORTRAIT OF A NEW LIFE-STYLE FAMILY
COPING WITH OLD LIFE-STYLE PROBLEMS. (ANGER, DIFF
SIT--ONE PARENT, EMOTIONS--ANGER, FAM--FATHERS,
FAM--ONE PARENT, FAM--SIBLING RIVALRY, FATHERS,
ONE PARENT, SIBLING RIVALRY)

STANEK, MURIEL. I WON'T GO WITHOUT A FATHER.
WHITMAN, A., 1972.   ILLUSTRATED BY ELEANOR MILL.
(CCB-B, LJ)

THE READER IS NOT TOLD WHY STEVE DOESN'T HAVE
A FATHER. THE REASON MAY BE DEATH, DESERTION, OR
DIVORCE, BUT WHAT WE ARE SHOWN IS THE JEALOUSY
AND LONELINESS THAT STEVE FEELS WHEN HE SEES
SOMEONE ELSE WITH A FATHER. WHEN PARENTS ARE
INVITED TO AN OPEN-HOUSE AT SCHOOL, STEVE DOES
NOT WANT TO GO BECAUSE HE BELIEVES EVERYONE WILL
THINK HE'S A MAMA'S BOY, AND HE THINKS THEN
EVERYONE WILL SEE THAT HE DOES NOT HAVE A FATHER.
MANY VARIATIONS ON THE KINDS OF PARENTHOOD SERVE
TO GIVE STEVE SOME PERSPECTIVE: FIRST OF ALL,
ONE BOY'S FATHER WORKED NIGHTS AND HIS MOTHER WAS
ILL, SO A SISTER FILLED IN. ANOTHER BOY WAS
BRINGING TWO SETS OF PARENTS: HIS PARENTS WERE
DIVORCED. IN STEVE'S CASE, HIS GRANDPA, HIS
UNCLE, AND A NEIGHBOR SAT WITH HIM AND HIS
MOTHER. BUT WHAT STEVE REALLY FOUND OUT WAS THAT
NO ONE WAS LOOKING AT HIM. HE FINALLY LEARNS TO
ACCEPT THE STATEMENT HIS MOTHER MADE: "LOTS OF
CHILDREN DON'T HAVE BOTH PARENTS...THEY MUST
LEARN TO GET ALONG WITH THE FAMILY AND FRIENDS
THEY HAVE." (DIFF SIT--ONE PARENT, FAM--ONE
PARENT, ONE PARENT)

ZINDEL, PAUL. I LOVE MY MOTHER. HARPER, 1975.
ILLUSTRATED BY JOHN MELO. (CCB-B)

STRIKING FULL-COLOR ILLUSTRATIONS EXPAND THE
LIMITED TEXT OF THIS STORY OF A BOY AND HIS
MOTHER, PRESUMABLY LIVING ALONE BECAUSE OF
DIVORCE OR SEPARATION. THE REASON IS NOT
EXPLICITLY STATED. COMPANIONSHIP AT THE ZOO, IN
THE KITCHEN, AND LATE AT NIGHT WHEN THE BAD
DREAMS COME, MAKES UP ONE PART OF THE BOOK. THERE
IS ALSO DEPICTED THE REALISM OF VULNERABLE
FEELINGS WHEN THE BOY WANTS TO RUN AWAY FROM
HOME, WHEN HIS MOTHER TRIES NOT TO LET HIM KNOW
WHEN THEY ARE SHORT OF MONEY, BUT THE MOST MOVING
SCENES ARE WHEN MOTHER ADMITS THAT SHE IS LONELY
AND WHEN THE BOY MISSES HIS FATHER. (DIFF
SIT--DIVORCE, DIVORCE, EMOTIONS--LONELINESS,
EMOTIONS--LOVE, FAM--MOTHERS, FAM--ONE PARENT,
LONELINESS, LOVE, MOTHERS, ONE PARENT)

ZOLOTOW, CHARLOTTE. A FATHER LIKE THAT. HARPER,
1971. ILLUSTRATED BY BEN SHECTER. (BCB)

HOME WITHOUT A FATHER IS PICTURED AS A LITTLE
BOY PAINTS AN IMAGINARY PORTRAIT OF THE PERFECT
DAD. WE SEE A MOTHER WHO MAKES THE CHILD GO TO
BED AT BEDTIME, WHO READS WHEN THE BOY WOULD LIKE
TO PLAY CHECKERS. SHE IS A MOTHER WHO CAN'T
UNDERSTAND BECAUSE SHE NEVER WAS A BOY, AND WHO
SAYS THE BASEBALL GAME ON TV IS TOO LOUD. IT IS
THE MOTHER WHO, NERVOUSLY SEWING FASTER AND
FASTER BECAUSE OF THE GLOWING PICTURE HE
DESCRIBES OF THE MYTHICAL FATHER, SAYS THE
REALISTIC WORDS OF WISDOM: "IF HE NEVER COMES, "
TRYING TO MAKE THE CHILD UNDERSTAND THAT THIS
PARAGON IS PERHAPS EXAGGERATED. IN THE END,
MOTHER SAYS THAT HE CAN TRY TO BE THAT KIND OF
FATHER WHEN HE GROWS UP. USEFUL BECAUSE OF THE
EXEMPLAR ROLE OF THE FATHER. SOME CHILDREN MAY
NEED TO BE SHOWN WHAT THE ABSENCE OF THE FATHER
IN THE FAMILY MEANS. (DIFF SIT--ONE PARENT,
FAM--FATHERS, FAM--MOTHERS, FATHERS, MOTHERS, ONE
PARENT)

ONLY CHILD

HAZEN, BARBARA. WHY COULDN'T I BE AN ONLY KID
LIKE YOU, WIGGER. ATHENEUM, 1975. ILLUSTRATED BY
LEIGH GRANT. (HB)

PLEASANT CLUTTER IN A LARGE FAMILY HOUSEHOLD
WHICH HAS SIX CHILDREN KEYNOTES THE FRUSTRATION
OF THE YOUNG BOY WHO TELLS THE STORY. WIGGER, HIS

FRIEND, DOESN'T HAVE TO MOP UP THE MILK THE BABY
SPILLED, OR STAND IN LINE FOR THE BATHROOM IN
THE MORNING, AND HE, THE NARRATOR, IS FRANKLY
QUITE JEALOUS. DURING HIS TIRADE HOWEVER, THE
ILLUSTRATIONS GIVE A DIFFERENT PICTURE OF WIGGER
WHO SEEMS TO LIKE WHEELING THE BABY CARRIAGE AND
BEING A PART OF THE ROUGH AND TUMBLE OF A LARGE
FAMILY. THE NARRATOR IS SURPRISED AT THE FACT
THAT AN ONLY CHILD CAN BE A LONELY CHILD. USEFUL
FOR THE CONTRASTING POINTS OF VIEW.
(EMOTIONS--JEALOUSY, FAM--ONLY CHILD, FRIENDSHIP,
JEALOUSY, ONLY CHILD)

OVERWEIGHT

PINKWATER, MANUS. FAT ELLIOT AND THE GORILLA.
FOUR, 1974.   ILLUSTRATED BY MANUS PINKWATER.   (BL)

ELLIOT WAS A COMPULSIVE OVEREATER. HE WAS VERY
FAT. HIS DOCTOR GAVE HIM A DIET AND A LOLLIPOP
AND HIS FAMILY GAVE HIM ALL SORTS OF
RATIONALIZATIONS FOR BEING FAT. A PENNY SCALE
WHICH TALKED TO HIM AND GAVE OUT A MAGIC FORTUNE,
AND A BOOK ELLIOT BOUGHT FOR TEN CENTS, CHANGED
HIS LIFE. THE FORTUNE TOLD HIM HE DIDN'T HAVE TO
BE WHAT HE DIDN'T WANT TO BE, AND THE BOOK
SUGGESTED THAT HE CONJURE UP THE IMAGE OF
SOMETHING HE'D REALLY LIKE TO BE. A GORILLA?
ELLIOT'S GORILLA WAS HIS FRIEND AND CONSTANT
COMPANION. THE GORILLA SHOOK HIS HEAD WHEN ELLIOT
WANTED TO FINISH HIS EIGHTH DOUGHNUT, AND THE
GORILLA ALLOWED HIM ONLY GRAPEFRUIT AND EGG FOR
BREAKFAST THE NEXT DAY. WHEN ELLIOT STARTED
RUNNING ON THE TRACK, THE GORILLA GRABBED HIM BY
THE SHIRT AND HELPED HIM ALONG. IN A LONG,
COMPLEX STORY WHICH EXPLORES ALL OF THE PITFALLS
AND FRUSTRATION OF A DIETER, AUTHOR PINKWATER HAS
CREATED A CREDIBLE STORY WITH IMAGINATIVE
PICTURES FOR CHILDREN ON A SUBJECT NOT TACKLED
BEFORE. (DIFF SIT--OVERWEIGHT, OVERWEIGHT,
SELF-CONSCIOUSNESS--SIZE)

POSSESSIVENESS

MAYER, MERCER. MINE!. SIMON, 1970.   ILLUSTRATED
BY MERCER MAYER.   (LJ, PBC)

A VERY FUNNY STORY OF GREEDINESS AND
POSSESSIVENESS, WHICH MOVES THROUGH SEVEN
EPISODES OF A LITTLE BOY CLAIMING THINGS WHICH

BELONG TO SOMEONE ELSE: SHOVEL, FISHING POLE, A
DOG'S BONE. HE IS RATHER A BULLY--GIVING GROUND
ONLY WHEN THE LITTLE GIRL HITS HIM OVER THE HEAD
WITH HER DOLL, AND GRUDGINGLY GIVING BACK THE
FISHLINE AFTER THE FISH HAS BEEN LOST. THE READER
FEELS THAT HE REALLY GETS HIS JUST DUES WHEN HE
FINDS HE MUST CLEAN HIS ROOM, WHICH HE ALSO
CLAIMED AS "MINE"--AND HIS MOTHER HANDS HIM THE
BROOM AND DUSTPAN WITH THE WORD "YOURS."
(BEHAVIOR--POSSESSIVENESS, EMOTIONS--GREED,
GREED, POSSESSIVENESS)

MC KEAN, ELLY. IT'S MINE. VANGUARD, 1951.
ILLUSTRATED BY ELLY MC KEAN. (GBC)

   THOUGH PEDANTIC IN TONE AT TIMES, A USEFUL
VOLUME FOR PARENTS OF CHILDREN WHO ARE FINDING IT
DIFFICULT TO SHARE POSSESSIONS. ALSO INCLUDES A
PREFACE DIRECTED TO ADULTS, BUT THE CHILD READER
OR LISTENER WILL UNDERSTAND HOW OTHER PEOPLE FEEL
ABOUT THEIR OWN TOYS, AND IN TURN MAY UNDERSTAND
THE DIFFICULT BUT REWARDING PATH TOWARD LEARNING
TO SHARE. (BEHAVIOR--POSSESSIVENESS,
BEHAVIOR--SHARING, POSSESSIVENESS, SHARING)

QUARRELING

BRONIN, ANDREW. GUS AND BUSTER WORK THINGS OUT.
COWARD, 1975. ILLUSTRATED BY CYNDY SZEKERES.
(BL)

   BROTHER RACCOONS ARE SHOWN IN FOUR STORIES OF
BROTHERLY SQUABBLES. GUS, WHO MAY BE A LITTLE
OLDER, TRICKS HIS SIBLING IN MANY
SITUATIONS--TRYING TO GET THE LOWER BUNK BED,
TRYING TO GET ALL THE BEST TOYS ON A RAINY DAY.
USEFUL FOR DISCUSSION BECAUSE SYMPATHY TENDS TO
LIE WITH BUSTER, THE PUT-UPON BROTHER, AND HE
SOMETIMES GETS THE BEST OF HIS WILY BIG BROTHER.
(BEHAVIOR--QUARRELING, BROTHERS, FAM--BROTHERS,
FAM--SIBLING RIVALRY, QUARRELING, SIBLING RIVALRY)

HOBAN, RUSSELL. THE SORELY TRYING DAY. HARPER,
1964. ILLUSTRATED BY LILLIAN HOBAN. (CC)

   ALTHOUGH THIS IS A TONGUE-IN-CHEEK SPOOF, IT
WILL BE VALUABLE FOR POINTING OUT HOW ONE THING
LEADS TO ANOTHER IN A QUARREL, AND SHOWS IN A
VERY FUNNY WAY WHAT HAPPENS WHEN EVERYBODY
ACCEPTS THE BLAME. SHOWS THE BEAUTY OF THE PHRASE

"I AM SORRY." (BEHAVIOR--CONSIDERATION,
BEHAVIOR--QUARRELING, CONSIDERATION, FAM,
QUARRELING)

HOBAN, RUSSELL. TOM AND THE TWO HANDLES. HARPER,
1965.   ILLUSTRATED BY LILLIAN HOBAN.   (ESLC)

   KENNY AND TOM ARE ALWAYS FIGHTING, AND TOM
ALWAYS GETS A BLOODY NOSE. HIS DAD TELLS HIM THAT
THERE IS MORE THAN ONE WAY TO SOLVE THE PROBLEM.
YOU CAN FIGHT AGAIN, OR YOU CAN MAKE UP WITH
YOUR BEST FRIEND. TOM TRIES TO BE FRIENDS, BUT
THEY CONTINUE TO FIGHT UNTIL TOM'S FATHER GIVES
HIM SOME BOXING LESSONS. WHEN TOM WINS THE FIGHT,
THEN THEY MAKE UP, AND TOM FINDS THAT THERE WAS
ANOTHER WAY TO LOOK AT IT. (ANGER,
BEHAVIOR--QUARRELING, EMOTIONS--ANGER,
FRIENDSHIP, QUARRELING)

UDRY, JANICE. LET'S BE ENEMIES. HARPER, 1961.
ILLUSTRATED BY MAURICE SENDAK. (CC)

   DELICATE PINK AND GREEN WATERCOLORS BELIE
SENDAK'S VIGOROUS, BLOCKY LITTLE BOYS, BUT
SOMEHOW ARE HARMONIOUS WITH THE TEXT. THIS IS THE
STORY OF A FRIENDSHIP SO ENDURING THAT THE BOYS
EVEN HAVE CHICKEN POX TOGETHER--IN THE SAME BED.
BUT IN THE DAY-TO-DAY CONTACTS, THE BOYS END UP
IN SOME ABRASIVE SITUATIONS, AND THE NARRATOR
GROUSES ABOUT JAMES: HE ALWAYS WANTS TO BE BOSS.
IN THE CONCLUDING PAGES, HOWEVER, THE SUN BEGINS
TO SHINE, THE ARTIST'S BOYS BEGIN TO WALK INTO
THE FRAMES INSTEAD OF OUT OF THEM, AND THEY SKATE
OFF TOGETHER, JOINED BY A PRETZEL AND ONE PAIR
OF SKATES BETWEEN THEM. A COMFORTING STORY WHICH
IS APPEALING IN ITS REALISTIC VIEW OF THE
LOVE/HATE RELATIONSHIP WHICH CAN EXIST IN THE
BEST OF FRIENDSHIPS. (BEHAVIOR--QUARRELING,
BEHAVIOR--SHARING, FRIENDSHIP, QUARRELING,
SHARING)

ZOLOTOW, CHARLOTTE. THE QUARRELING BOOK. HARPER,
1963.   ILLUSTRATED BY ARNOLD LOBEL. (CC)

   THE GRAYNESS OF A RAINY DAY IS ECHOED IN THE
BLACK AND WHITE DRAWINGS OF ARNOLD LOBEL, AND THE
SLANTY LINES OF THE DRIVING RAIN ADD TENSION
THROUGHOUT. BEGINNING WITH A FATHER WHO FORGETS
HIS GOOD-BYE KISS, THE BOOK PROGESSES TO A CRANKY
MOTHER, A TEASING BOY CHILD, AND A SISTER SALLY

WITH HURT FEELINGS. IT TOOK THE DOG, WHO WASN'T
AFFECTED BY THE DEPRESSIVE DAY, TO SWEETEN UP
EVERYONE'S SPIRITS, AND IT IS A LESSON IN THE
CONTAGIOUSNESS OF FEELINGS, BOTH GOOD AND BAD.
(BEHAVIOR--QUARRELING, FAM, QUARRELING)

REJECTION

KLEIN, GERDA. THE BLUE ROSE. HILL, 1974.
ILLUSTRATED BY NORMA HOLT.

MADE IN COOPERATION WITH THE KENNEDY CHILD
STUDY CENTER, THE BOOK IS A SYMPATHETIC VIEW OF
MENTAL RETARDATION. BLACK AND WHITE PHOTOGRAPHS
SHOW JENNY PLAYING, TRYING TO TIE HER SHOES.
CLOSES WITH JENNY BEING UNHAPPY BECAUSE OTHER
CHILDREN HAVE CALLED HER RETARDED, AND LAUGHED AT
HER. (DIFF SIT--HANDICAPS, EMOTIONS--REJECTION,
HANDICAPS, REJECTION)

SCOTT, ANN. SAM. MC GRAW, 1967. ILLUSTRATED BY
SYMEON SHIMIN. (BCB)

THE ILLUSTRATIONS ARE PARAMOUNT IN THIS STORY
OF A LEFT-OUT BROTHER WHO IS REJECTED FIRST BY
MOTHER, BIG BROTHER GEORGE, SISTER MARCIA, AND
THEN HIS FATHER, WHO FORBIDS HIM TO TOUCH HIS
TYPEWRITER. THE BLACK, SEPIA, AND GOLDEN BROWN
WATERCOLORS INTENSIFY THE FEELINGS OF SADNESS IN
SAM'S HEART. SUDDENLY THE WHOLE FAMILY REALIZES
THAT HE NEEDS ATTENTION: HIS MOTHER HOLDS HIM AND
ROCKS HIM, AND AS EVERYONE RALLIES AROUND TO
KEEP HIM COMPANY, SAM HELPS BAKE A RASPBERRY
TART. (BROTHERS & SISTERS, EMOTIONS--REJECTION,
FAM--BROTHERS & SISTERS, REJECTION)

RESPONSIBILITY

WINN, MARIE. SHIVER, GOBBLE AND SNORE. SIMON,
1971. ILLUSTRATED BY WHITNEY DARROW JR.. (ESLC)

A BOOK FOR VERY YOUNG CHILDREN ABOUT WHY
PEOPLE NEED LAWS. THREE FRIENDS WHO DON'T LIKE
ALL OF THE LAWS WHICH THE KING MAKES DECIDE TO
MOVE AWAY AND NOT HAVE ANY LAWS. CHAOS REIGNS
HOWEVER--SHIVER MADE FIRES WHICH BOTHERED GOBBLE,
AND THE SNORING OF SNORE BOTHERED SHIVER. WHEN
THEY DECIDE THAT LIFE LIKE THIS IS NOT GOOD
EITHER, THEY SET UP NEW RULES. A GOOD WAY TO
INTRODUCE CHILDREN TO THE NECESSITY FOR LAWS.

THERE ARE FOUR PAGES AT THE END DEVOTED TO
ACTIVITIES TO REINFORCE THE CONCEPT.
(BEHAVIOR--CONSIDERATION, BEHAVIOR--MISBEHAVIOR,
BEHAVIOR--RESPONSIBILITY, CONSIDERATION,
MISBEHAVIOR, RESPONSIBILITY)

SAFETY

MC LEOD, EMILIE. THE BEAR'S BICYCLE. LITTLE,
1975.   ILLUSTRATED BY DAVID MC PHAIL.   (BL)

AN IMAGINATIVE STORY IN WHICH AN ENORMOUS
BEAR, ON A MINIATURE BICYCLE, BREAKS ALL THE
RULES. AS THE LITTLE BOY IN THE STORY
DEMONSTRATES THE CORRECT WAY TO STAY ON THE RIGHT
WHEN MEETING ANOTHER BIKER, THE LUMBERING BEAR
TAKES A SPILL IN THE MIDDLE OF THE PATH, CROWDING
A YOUNG BOY, CAUSING HIM TO CRASH. BEAUTIFUL
ILLUSTRATIONS AND HUMOROUS SITUATIONS TEACH A
LESSON OF SAFETY IN A PAINLESS WAY.
(BEHAVIOR--CONSIDERATION, BEHAVIOR--MISBEHAVIOR,
BEHAVIOR--SAFETY, CONSIDERATION, MISBEHAVIOR,
SAFETY)

SECURITY

BROWN, MARGARET. THE RUNAWAY BUNNY. HARPER,
1942.   ILLUSTRATED BY CLEMENT HURD.   (CC)

A THOROUGHLY SATISFYING STORY FOR A YOUNG
CHILD, FOR ALL CHILDREN DREAM OF RUNNING AWAY
FROM HOME. THIS MOTHER RABBIT, WHO ALWAYS THINKS
OF A WAY TO INTERCEPT HER YOUNG ONE, IS A PERFECT
PORTRAIT OF THE MOTHER WHO IS ALWAYS THERE, AND
WILL ALWAYS BE THERE, THE ULTIMATE IN SECURITY
AND LOVE. (EMOTIONS--SECURITY, FAM--MOTHERS,
MOTHERS, SECURITY)

BUCKLEY, HELEN. GRANDMOTHER AND I. LOTHROP,
1961.   ILLUSTRATED BY PAUL GALDONE.   (CC)

LARGE PRINT AND SHORT, RHYTHMIC SENTENCES
WHICH ECHO THE ROCKING CHAIR CHARACTERIZE THIS
BOOK OF OVERSIZE PICTURES. THE ILLUSTRATIONS,
WHICH ARE BRIGHT AND HOMEY IN THE FIRELIGHT, SET
THE SCENE FOR PEACE AND COMFORT AT THE BEGINNING
OF THE BOOK, PROGRESS TO A DRAMATIC PURPLE PAGE
WHEN THE LITTLE GIRL IS SECURE FROM THE LIGHTNING
OUTSIDE, AND END ON A CHEERFUL NOTE AFTER
GRANDMOTHER'S LAP HAS BEEN COMPARED TO THOSE

BELONGING TO MOTHER, FATHER, BROTHER, AND SISTER.
USEFUL BECAUSE THE UNIQUE ROLE OF GRANDMOTHER'S
LAP IS REINFORCED AGAIN AND AGAIN.
(EMOTIONS--SECURITY, FAM--GRANDMOTHERS,
GRANDMOTHERS, SECURITY)

CHALMERS, MARY. BE GOOD, HARRY. HARPER, 1967.
ILLUSTRATED BY MARY CHALMERS. (BCB)

A USEFUL BOOK, WITH SUBTLE HUMOR, FOR THE
SMALL CHILD WHO WILL EMPATHIZE WITH HARRY AS HE
GOES TO A BABY-SITTER FOR THE FIRST TIME, AND
SITS ON MRS. BREWSTER'S LAP ALL OF THE TIME WITH
ALL OF HIS TOYS AND BOOKS. PARTICULARLY
REASSURING FOR A CHILD WHO NEEDS THE SECURITY OF
HIS OWN THINGS, SUCH AS A BLANKET, SO THAT HE
KNOWS HE'S NOT THE ONLY ONE WITH NEEDS SUCH AS
THESE. (EMOTIONS--SECURITY, SECURITY)

EHRLICH, AMY. ZEEK SILVER MOON. DIAL, 1972.
ILLUSTRATED BY ROBERT PARKER. (ESLC)

NOTABLE BECAUSE IT SHOWS AN ALTERNATIVE LIFE
STYLE OF A MUSICIAN, HIS WIFE, AND THEIR CHILD,
ZEEK SILVER MOON, THE BOOK IS GREATLY ENHANCED BY
STUNNINGLY BEAUTIFUL WATERCOLORS EVOKING THE
SOFTNESS OF LOVE. THIS IS A STORY OF
NON-CONFORMING, ALIVE, NEW LIFE-STYLE PEOPLE:
FATHER MADE THE BABY A CRADLE OF WOOD AFTER HE
WAS BORN AND LATER, WHEN ZEEK WAS FOUR YEARS OLD,
HIS FATHER, IN AN INCIDENT CALLED THE CARPET
RAISING, STAPLED THEIR LIVING ROOM RUG TO THE
CEILING BECAUSE A NEIGHBOR COMPLAINED OF NOISE.
WITHIN THE FRAMEWORK OF A FAMILY WHICH PLACES A
HIGH VALUE ON NATURAL FOODS, HOME-BAKED BREAD,
AND ENTERTAINMENT OTHER THAN TELEVISION, ZEEK IS
SHOWN TO BE A LOVED CHILD, ONE WHO RECEIVES
GENTLE LOVING CARE, IS TUCKED IN AT NIGHT AND
TOLD STORIES. (EMOTIONS--LOVE,
EMOTIONS--SECURITY, FAM, LOVE, SECURITY)

KRAUS, ROBERT. GOOD NIGHT, RICHARD RABBIT.
SPRINGFELLOW, 1972. ILLUSTRATED BY N.M.
BODECKER. (CCB-B)

TINY FORMAT MAKES THIS A CHARMING BEDTIME
STORY FOR THE VERY YOUNG, AS MOST YOUNGSTERS WILL
IDENTIFY WITH RICHARD RABBIT. A MIX OF REAL AND
IMAGINARY FEARS, AND A LITTLE OF DOWNRIGHT
TEASING ARE SEEN AS THE YOUNG RABBIT PRETENDS

THERE IS A FACE LOOKING IN THE WINDOW. EVERY
OTHER PAGE DEALS WITH A QUESTION OR COMMENT, THE
FACING PAGE WITH MOTHER'S ANSWER. IN ALL OF THE
ILLUSTRATIONS, RICHARD IS VERY SMALL, AND MOTHER
LOOMS VERY LARGE AND SOLID, TRULY A SECURITY
FIGURE, AND ON THE FINAL PAGE RICHARD DRIFTS OFF
TO SLEEP. (BEHAVIOR--DISLIKES--SLEEP,
DISLIKES--SLEEP, EMOTIONS--FEAR,
EMOTIONS--SECURITY, FEAR, SECURITY)

RESSNER, PHILIP. AT NIGHT. DUTTON, 1967.
ILLUSTRATED BY CHARLES PRATT. (ESLC)

A SERIES OF BLACK AND WHITE PHOTOGRAPHS,
APPROPRIATELY ENOUGH, LEAD THE READER'S EYE
THROUGH A NIGHT IN THE CITY. USEFUL BECAUSE IT
WILL GIVE THE READER A FEELING OF SECURITY,
KNOWING THAT THERE IS NOTHING TO FEAR FROM
DARKNESS IN ITSELF. IT SHOWS A LIFE THE CHILD
RARELY SEES, AND MAY NOT BE ABLE TO IMAGINE: THE
EMPTY SCHOOL ROOM, THE BUMPS IN THE SIDEWALK. AS
DAWN BREAKS, THE CHILD SEES THE MIRACLE OF A NEW
DAY, AS THE CIRCLE OF THE EARTH TURNS.
(EMOTIONS--FEAR, EMOTIONS--SECURITY, FEAR,
SECURITY)

SCHULZ, CHARLES. SECURITY IS A THUMB AND A
BLANKET. DETERMINED, 1963. ILLUSTRATED BY
CHARLES SCHULZ.

THE EXEMPLAR OF DEFINITIONS OF SECURITY IN A
CHILD'S MIND, ALTHOUGH, AS IN MANY CHILDREN'S
BOOKS, THE PHILOSPHY IS UNIVERSAL. "SECURITY IS
RETURNING HOME AFTER A VACTION" IS A TRUISM FOR
GROWN-UPS, TOO, AS IS SNOOPY'S LINE THAT
"SECURITY IS OWNING YOUR OWN HOME," EVEN IF IT IS
ONLY A DOG HOUSE, BUT THE MORE TRULY CHILD-LIKE
EXPRESSIONS OF SECURITY ARE TO BE FOUND IN THOSE
RELATING TO FINDING YOUR MOTHER IN THE HOUSE WHEN
YOU COME HOME FROM SCHOOL, AND SALLY SAYING AS
SHE WALKS ALONG A HIGH CHAIN-LINK FENCE:
"SECURITY IS KNOWING THAT BIG DOG CAN'T REALLY
GET OUT." CURIOUSLY, THUMB SUCKING AND SECURITY
BLANKETS ARE MENTIONED ONLY IN THE TITLE, BUT
SERVE TO TUNE IN THE READER TO THE SUBJECT.
(BEHAVIOR--THUMB SUCKING, EMOTIONS--SECURITY,
SECURITY, THUMB SUCKING)

SCOTT, ANN. ON MOTHER'S LAP. MC GRAW, 1972.
ILLUSTRATED BY GLO COALSON. (BCB)

A LOVING STORY OF A LAP WITH UNLIMITED ROOM.
FIRST IT HAS MICHAEL, THEN HIS DOLL, THEN HIS
BOAT, THEN HIS PUPPY, THEN HIS REINDEER BLANKET.
THEY ALL ROCKED TOGETHER. WHEN THE BABY WAKES UP,
MICHAEL PUTS ON A SOUR FACE, AND SAYS THERE
ISN'T ANY ROOM. BUT MOTHER MAKES ROOM FOR ALL,
AND GIVES A SENSE OF SECURITY TO THE READER THAT
ONLY A LAP AND A ROCKING CHAIR CAN PROVIDE.
(EMOTIONS--LOVE, EMOTIONS--SECURITY,
FAM--MOTHERS, FAM--SIBLING RIVALRY, LOVE,
MOTHERS, SECURITY, SIBLING RIVALRY)

SENDAK, MAURICE. WHERE THE WILD THINGS ARE.
HARPER, 1963. ILLUSTRATED BY MAURICE SENDAK.
(BC, BESL, CC, CCB-B, GBC)

MAX MISBEHAVES ONE NIGHT, NAILING A SPIKE INTO
THE WALL AND CRACKING THE PLASTER, CHASING THE
DOG WITH A FORK, AND HIS MOTHER SENDS HIM TO HIS
ROOM, TO BED WITHOUT ANY SUPPER. MAX DREAMS A
FANTASTIC DREAM, IN WHICH HE TURNS THE SITUATION
AROUND, AND HE IS THE BOSS. WHEN HE TELLS THE
WILD ANIMALS TO "BE STILL"--THEY OBEY, AND WHEN
HE IS CROWNED KING, HE REVELS IN HIS CONTROL OVER
THE BEASTS. OVERCOME WITH LONELINESS, THE SMELL
OF FOOD, AND WANTING TO BE SAFE AT HOME, MAX ENDS
UP IN HIS ROOM, WHERE HIS SUPPER IS WAITING. THE
AMBIVALENCE OF INDEPENDENCE/DEPENDENCE, THE
QUALITIES OF SECURITY AND LOVE ARE STRESSED IN
THIS BOOK. (BEHAVIOR--MISBEHAVIOR,
EMOTIONS--LONELINESS, EMOTIONS--LOVE,
EMOTIONS--SECURITY, LONELINESS, LOVE,
MISBEHAVIOR, SECURITY)

TURKLE, BRINTON. THY FRIEND OBADIAH. VIKING,
1969. ILLUSTRATED BY BRINTON TURKLE. (BCB)

OBADIAH, A YOUNG QUAKER BOY, IS ANGRY WHEN A
SEA GULL TRIES TO BE HIS FRIEND BY TAGGING ALONG
BEHIND HIM IN THIS EXCELLENT PORTRAYAL OF QUAKER
FAMILY LIFE. AS THE STORY PROGRESSES, THE GULL
GETS A LARGE RUSTY FISHHOOK CAUGHT IN HIS BEAK,
OBADIAH TAKES IT OUT, AND THE SEA GULL FLIES
AWAY. WHEN THE GULL RETURNS, OBADIAH REASONS:
"SINCE I HELPED HIM, I'M HIS FRIEND, TOO."
TURKLE'S WATERCOLORS EVOKE A POWERFUL FEELING OF
A COZY, SECURE LIFE IN THE DAYS WHEN THE FAMILY
GATHERED AROUND THE FIREPLACE WHILE THE BREAD WAS
BAKING. (EMOTIONS--LOVE, EMOTIONS--SECURITY,
FAM, FRIENDSHIP, LOVE, SECURITY)

WABER, BERNARD. IRA SLEEPS OVER. HOUGHTON, 1972.
ILLUSTRATED BY BERNARD WABER. (ESLC)

IRA IS THE YOUNG CHILD IN A FAMILY WITH
UNDERSTANDING PARENTS, AND A SISTER FOND OF
PUT-DOWNS. WHEN HIS MOTHER AND FATHER TELL HIM
THAT IT WILL BE OK IF HE TAKES HIS TEDDY BEAR ON
HIS FIRST SLEEPOVER AT HIS FRIEND'S HOUSE, HIS
SISTER INSISTS THAT HIS FRIEND WILL LAUGH AND
THINK HE'S A BABY. HOW WILL HE FEEL SLEEPING
WITHOUT HIS TEDDY BEAR FOR THE VERY FIRST TIME?
LUCKILY IRA NEVER NEEDS TO FACE THAT SITUATION,
FOR THE CAPPER TO THE STORY IS THAT REGGIE SLEEPS
WITH HIS TEDDY BEAR, TOO, SO IRA FEELS CONFIDENT
ENOUGH TO MARCH OVER TO HIS OWN HOUSE, UP THE
STAIRS, WITH A SMUG EXPRESSION ON HIS FACE, TO
PICK UP TAH-TAH, HIS TEDDY BEAR. NOTABLE FOR ITS
RECOGNITION OF THE FACT THAT CHILDREN ENJOY
MILDLY SCARY SITUATIONS IF THERE IS AN UNDERLYING
BOLSTERING OF SECURITY, THE BOOK IS ALSO LIKELY
TO BE AROUND FOR AWHILE BECAUSE IT PICTURES AN
URBAN, CONTEMPORARY FAMILY WITH A FATHER COOKING
AT THE STOVE AND, IN ONE SCENE, A MOTHER CURLED
UP ON THE COUCH IN HER PAJAMAS. (EMOTIONS--FEAR,
EMOTIONS--SECURITY, FEAR, SECURITY)

SELF-CONFIDENCE

ALEXANDER, MARTHA. BLACKBOARD BEAR. DIAL, 1969.
ILLUSTRATED BY MARTHA ALEXANDER. (BCB)

A SMALL BOY, FRUSTRATED BECAUSE THE OLDER BOYS
WILL NOT LET HIM PLAY COWBOYS AND INDIANS OR
COPS AND ROBBERS, AND TIRED OF PLAYING ALONE WITH
HIS TEDDY BEAR, THROWS IT OUT THE WINDOW AND
DRAWS ON HIS BLACKBOARD A HUGE BEAR, WHICH
OBLIGINGLY STEPS DOWN INTO THE ROOM. THE LITTLE
BOY GAINS STATUS WITH THE OLDER BOYS AS HE
PARADES HIM AROUND, AND HAS A THOROUGHLY
SATISFACTORY EXPERIENCE WHICH IS VERY
EGO-ENHANCING. (SELF-CONFIDENCE)

BUCKLEY, HELEN. MICHAEL IS BRAVE. LOTHROP, 1971.
ILLUSTRATED BY EMILY MC CULLY. (ESLC)

AN EXCELLENTLY REALISTIC STORY CONCERNING THE
FEAR THAT MICHAEL HAD ABOUT GOING DOWN THE SLIDE.
WHEN A NEW GIRL IN SCHOOL TRIES IT, AND FINDS
HERSELF IN TEARS, THE TEACHER SUGGESTS THAT
MICHAEL CLIMB THE LADDER AND STAND BEHIND HER.

THROUGH THIS ACT OF HELPING, MICHAEL IS ABLE TO
GO DOWN THE SLIDE ALONE. ILLUSTRATES THE POINT
THAT WHEN YOU HELP SOMEONE ELSE, YOU BECOME MORE
BRAVE YOURSELF. (BRAVERY, EMOTIONS--BRAVERY,
SELF-CONFIDENCE)

COHEN, MIRIAM. TOUGH JIM. MACMILLAN, 1974.
ILLUSTRATED BY LILLIAN HOBAN. (CCB-B)

JIM IS THE RATHER QUIET, SELF-EFFACING FIRST
GRADER IN A MULTI-ETHNIC CLASSROOM WHO HAS
APPEARED IN EARLIER COHEN BOOKS, AND WE SEE HIS
INNER THOUGHTS IN THIS STORY OF A COSTUME PARTY.
HE WANTS TO BE "SOMEONE VERY STRONG, SOMEONE VERY
TOUGH." HE DRESSES AS THE STRONGEST MAN IN THE
WORLD AND, IN A VERY SUPPORTIVE CIRCLE OF
FRIENDS, GETS THE BEST OF AN OLDER BOY WHO WANTS
TO FIGHT. (BRAVERY, EMOTIONS--BRAVERY,
SELF-CONFIDENCE, SELF-IDENTITY)

CONFORD, ELLEN. IMPOSSIBLE POSSUM. LITTLE, 1971.
ILLUSTRATED BY ROSEMARY WELLS. (CC, ESLC)

AN EXAMPLE OF SELF-FULFILLING PROPHECY OF
FAILURE. RANDOLPH, WHO COULDN'T HANG BY HIS TAIL
LIKE OTHER POSSUMS, BEGAN TO FEEL HE NEVER COULD
LEARN, AND THOSE AROUND HIM THOUGHT SO TOO.
GERALDINE, HIS INGENIOUS SISTER, FOUND THAT SAP
HELPED HIS TAIL STAY ON THE BRANCH, AND ALL WENT
WELL UNTIL THE SAP DRIED UP. SHE ALSO IS
INSTRUMENTAL IN PROVING TO HIM THAT HE REALLY
DOESN'T NEED THE SAP TO HANG UPSIDE DOWN.
(BROTHERS & SISTERS, FAM--BROTHERS & SISTERS,
SELF-CONFIDENCE)

KRASILOVSKY, PHYLLIS. THE SHY LITTLE GIRL.
HOUGHTON, 1970. ILLUSTRATED BY TRINA HYMAN.
(LJ, TLS)

ANNE WAS A LONER WHO SPOKE IN A VOICE NO ONE
COULD HEAR, WHO OFTEN PLAYED ALONE, AND WHO, WHEN
SHE DID PLAY, FOUND PLAYMATES YOUNGER THAN
HERSELF. WHEN CLAUDIA, A NEW GIRL, COMES TO
SCHOOL, THEY IMMEDIATELY STRIKE UP A FRIENDSHIP.
ANNE'S SELF-CONFIDENCE GROWS AS THE FRIENDSHIP
GROWS, AND WE SEE HER BLOSSOM INTO A
PARTICIPATING, SHARING YOUNG GIRL.
(EMOTIONS--SHYNESS, SELF-CONFIDENCE, SHYNESS)

KRAUS, ROBERT. LEO THE LATE BLOOMER. WINDMILL,

1971. ILLUSTRATED BY JOSE ARUEGO. (BCB)

IMAGINATIVE ILLUSTRATIONS CARRY THE MESSAGE
AND EXTEND IT MIGHTILY IN THIS STORY OF A YOUNG
TIGER, WHO STILL HAS HIS BABY FAT, MAKING HIM A
VERY APPEALING PROTAGONIST. LEO HAS A GAGGLE OF
FRIENDS--OWL, ELEPHANT, SNAKE, BIRD, AND
CROCODILE--ALL OF WHOM CAN READ, WRITE, DRAW, EAT
NEATLY, AND HE FEELS VERY INADEQUATE. BUT,
BECAUSE LEO IS A LATE BLOOMER, HE EVENTUALLY
MAKES IT, AND GIVES REASSURANCE TO TEACHERS,
PARENTS, AND ALL "LATE BLOOMERS."
(EMOTIONS--FRUSTRATION, FRUSTRATION,
SELF-CONFIDENCE, SELF-CONSCIOUSNESS)

LEXAU, JOAN. BENJIE. DIAL, 1964. ILLUSTRATED BY
DON BOLOGNESE. (CC)

A LIGHT GRAY WATERCOLOR WASH MATCHES THE
GRUBBY STREET SETTING OF THIS REALISTIC STORY.
ACTION TAKES PLACE ON THE STOOP, STREETS, AND
SHOPS OF THE INNER CITY, INCLUDING THE ONE ROOM
IN WHICH GRANNY AND BENJIE LIVE. HE IS A SMALL
BOY SO SHY THAT HE HIDES BEHIND HIS GRANNY'S
SKIRTS, AND IS TEASED BY THE NEIGHBORS. WHEN HIS
GRANDMOTHER LOSES A FAVORITE EARRING, BENJIE
OVERCOMES HIS SHYNESS TO HELP LOOK FOR IT, AND IN
ASSERTING HIMSELF MAKES PROGRESS TOWARD
INDEPENDENCE. USEFUL ALSO TO DEMONSTRATE A
LOVING, CARING RELATIONSHIP BETWEEN YOUNG AND
OLD. (EMOTIONS--SHYNESS, FAM--GRANDMOTHERS,
GRANDMOTHERS, SELF-CONFIDENCE, SHYNESS)

ZOLOTOW, CHARLOTTE. A TIGER CALLED THOMAS.
LOTHROP, 1963. ILLUSTRATED BY KURT WERTH. (CC)

SHY THOMAS SITS ON THE PORCH OF HIS NEW HOUSE
AND REFUSES TO TRY TO MAKE NEW FRIENDS. HE IS
VERY OBSERVANT, HOWEVER, AND IS AWARE OF GERALD,
WHO PLAYS BALL ALONE, AND OF MARIE, AND OTHER
PEOPLE IN THE NEIGHBORHOOD. GIVEN CONFIDENCE BY
DRESSING UP IN A TIGER SUIT ON HALLOWEEN, HE
TAKES ON SOME OF THE COURAGE OF THE BEAST, AND
VISITS ALL OF THE HOUSES IN THE NEIGHBORHOOD.
WHEN PEOPLE ASK HIM TO VISIT AND PLAY, HE
REALIZES THAT THEY ALL LIKE HIM, AND HE DECIDES
THAT HE ALSO LIKES THEM. (EMOTIONS--SHYNESS,
FRIENDSHIP, MOVING, NEW SIT--MOVING,
SELF-CONFIDENCE, SHYNESS)

SELF-CONSCIOUSNESS

KRAUS, ROBERT. LEO THE LATE BLOOMER. WINDMILL,
1971. ILLUSTRATED BY JOSE ARUEGO. (BCB)

IMAGINATIVE ILLUSTRATIONS CARRY THE MESSAGE
AND EXTEND IT MIGHTILY IN THIS STORY OF A YOUNG
TIGER, WHO STILL HAS HIS BABY FAT, MAKING HIM A
VERY APPEALING PROTAGONIST. LEO HAS A GAGGLE OF
FRIENDS--OWL, ELEPHANT, SNAKE, BIRD, AND
CROCODILE--ALL OF WHOM CAN READ, WRITE, DRAW, EAT
NEATLY, AND HE FEELS VERY INADEQUATE. BUT,
BECAUSE LEO IS A LATE BLOOMER, HE EVENTUALLY
MAKES IT, AND GIVES REASSURANCE TO TEACHERS,
PARENTS, AND ALL "LATE BLOOMERS."
(EMOTIONS--FRUSTRATION, FRUSTRATION,
SELF-CONFIDENCE, SELF-CONSCIOUSNESS)

SELF-CONSCIOUSNESS--NAME

ALEXANDER, MARTHA. SABRINA. DIAL, 1971.
ILLUSTRATED BY MARTHA ALEXANDER. (ESLC)

A SLIGHT STORY ABOUT A LITTLE GIRL WHO IS
EMBARRASSED BY HER NAME ON THE FIRST DAY OF
SCHOOL. WHEN SHE UNDERSTANDS THAT THE OTHER GIRLS
IN THE CLASS REALLY WANT HER NAME, SHE REALIZES
THE VALUE OF HAVING A UNIQUE NAME.
(SELF-CONSCIOUSNESS--NAME)

SELF-CONSCIOUSNESS--SIZE

HUTCHINS, PAT. TITCH. MACMILLAN, 1971.
ILLUSTRATED BY PAT HUTCHINS. (ESLC)

TITCH WAS TOO LITTLE, A PREDICAMENT COMMON TO
MANY PRESCHOOLERS. IN THIS LOVELY PICTURE BOOK
WITH LARGE COLORFUL PICTURES AND A SMALL AMOUNT
OF TEXT, PAT HUTCHINS HAS OUTLINED ALL OF THE
INEQUITIES--THE OLDER SIBLINGS HAVE BIGGER BIKES
AND TOYS. BUT JUSTICE PREVAILS IN THE END, FOR IT
IS TITCH WHO HAS THE TINY SEED, WHICH GROWS INTO
AN ENORMOUS PLANT, LARGER THAN ANYTHING HIS BIG
BROTHER PETE AND SISTER MARY OWN. (BROTHERS &
SISTERS, FAM--BROTHERS & SISTERS,
SELF-CONSCIOUSNESS--SIZE)

KOHN, BERNICE. EVERYTHING HAS A SHAPE AND
EVERYTHING HAS A SIZE. PRENTICE, 1964.
ILLUSTRATED BY ALIKI. (ESLC)

AN IMAGINATIVE STORY DEALING WITH SHAPES, AND
SIZES, AND THE IDEA THAT EACH THING HAS A SHAPE
AND SIZE THAT SUITS IT. ALSO STRESSES THE
RELATIVE SIZE OF OBJECTS AND PEOPLE. IT IS THE
SMALL SECTION OF THE BOOK WHICH DEALS WITH TWO
BOYS AND THEIR COMPARATIVE SIZES, BIG FOR FIVE
YEARS OLD OR VERY SMALL FOR SEVEN YEARS OLD,
WHICH CAN BE USEFUL FOR DEMONSTRATING THE
DIFFERENT RATES OF GROWTH OF CHILDREN.
(SELF-CONSCIOUSNESS--SIZE)

KRASILOVSKY, PHYLLIS. THE VERY LITTLE GIRL.
DOUBLEDAY, 1953. ILLUSTRATED BY NINON. (CC)

ABOUT HALFWAY THROUGH THIS STORY, THE LITTLE
GIRL WHO HAS BEEN SMALLER THAN EVERYTHING AROUND
HER BEGINS TO GROW, AND SUDDENLY SHE IS BIGGER
THAN THE ROSEBUSH, AND SHE GETS A NEW BED TO
SLEEP IN. THE CULMINATING EXPERIENCE IS THAT SHE
CAN BE A BIG SISTER TO HER BRAND NEW BABY
BROTHER. AN EXCELLENT EXAMPLE TO USE IN
EXPLAINING GROWTH TO THE YOUNG CHILD. (NEW
SIT--BABY, SELF-CONSCIOUSNESS--SIZE)

KRASILOVSKY, PHYLLIS. THE VERY TALL LITTLE GIRL.
DOUBLEDAY, 1969. ILLUSTRATED BY OLIVIA COLE.
(CC)

A LITTLE GIRL WHO IS SIX INCHES TALLER THAN
HER CONTEMPORARIES FEELS VERY SELF-CONSCIOUS, AND
WISHES SHE COULD PLAY THE ROLE OF THE TINY
KITTEN OR THE LITTLEST ANGEL IN THE SCHOOL PLAY.
WHEN SHE NOTICES THAT ALL THE MEMBERS OF HER
FAMILY ARE TALL, AND THAT NO ONE SEEMS TO MIND,
SHE BEGINS TO THINK OF ALL THE GOOD THINGS THERE
ARE ABOUT BEING TALL, THE MOST IMPORTANT BEING,
TO HER, THAT SHE IS DIFFERENT, AND SHE IS
SPECIAL. (SELF-CONSCIOUSNESS--SIZE, SELF-IDENTITY)

PINKWATER, MANUS. FAT ELLIOT AND THE GORILLA.
FOUR, 1974. ILLUSTRATED BY MANUS PINKWATER. (BL)

ELLIOT WAS A COMPULSIVE OVEREATER. HE WAS VERY
FAT. HIS DOCTOR GAVE HIM A DIET AND A LOLLIPOP
AND HIS FAMILY GAVE HIM ALL SORTS OF
RATIONALIZATIONS FOR BEING FAT. A PENNY SCALE
WHICH TALKED TO HIM AND GAVE OUT A MAGIC FORTUNE,
AND A BOOK ELLIOT BOUGHT FOR TEN CENTS, CHANGED
HIS LIFE. THE FORTUNE TOLD HIM HE DIDN'T HAVE TO
BE WHAT HE DIDN'T WANT TO BE, AND THE BOOK

SUGGESTED THAT HE CONJURE UP THE IMAGE OF
SOMETHING HE'D REALLY LIKE TO BE. A GORILLA?
ELLIOT'S GORILLA WAS HIS FRIEND AND CONSTANT
COMPANION. THE GORILLA SHOOK HIS HEAD WHEN ELLIOT
WANTED TO FINISH HIS EIGHTH DOUGHNUT, AND THE
GORILLA ALLOWED HIM ONLY GRAPEFRUIT AND EGG FOR
BREAKFAST THE NEXT DAY. WHEN ELLIOT STARTED
RUNNING ON THE TRACK, THE GORILLA GRABBED HIM BY
THE SHIRT AND HELPED HIM ALONG. IN A LONG,
COMPLEX STORY WHICH EXPLORES ALL OF THE PITFALLS
AND FRUSTRATION OF A DIETER, AUTHOR PINKWATER HAS
CREATED A CREDIBLE STORY WITH IMAGINATIVE
PICTURES FOR CHILDREN ON A SUBJECT NOT TACKLED
BEFORE. (DIFF SIT--OVERWEIGHT, OVERWEIGHT,
SELF-CONSCIOUSNESS--SIZE)

SCHLEIN, MIRIAM. BILLY THE LITTLEST ONE.
WHITMAN, A., 1966. ILLUSTRATED BY LUCY
HAWKINSON. (CCB-B, TLS)

   TOLD IN FIRST PERSON BY A LITTLE BOY, THIS
BOOK EMPHASIZES SOME OF THE GOOD THINGS ABOUT
BEING LITTLE, SUCH AS GETTING TO BE FIRST ON THE
SLED, AND HAVING A CHAIR JUST THE RIGHT SIZE.
BESIDES, BILLY REALIZES THAT HE IS GROWING, AND
WON'T BE THE LITTLEST ONE FOREVER.
(SELF-CONSCIOUSNESS--SIZE)

YOLEN, JANE. IT ALL DEPENDS. FUNK, 1969.
ILLUSTRATED BY DON BOLOGNESE. (LJ)

   IN A ROUNDABOUT WAY, THIS IS A POETICAL STORY
OF THE VALUE OF LOVE. DAVID IS A LITTLE BOY WHO
QUESTIONS HIS MOTHER ABOUT A NUMBER OF THINGS.
"HOW TALL AM I?" AND SHE ANSWERS BY SAYING THAT
IT ALL DEPENDS UPON THE RELATIONSHIP OF THINGS.
THAT TO AN ANT, HE IS VERY LARGE, BUT THAT TO A
WHALE, HE IS VERY SMALL. IN AN IMAGINATIVE SERIES
OF ILLUSTRATIONS, BOLOGNESE HAS PRODUCED A BOOK
USEFUL TO TEACHERS AND PARENTS WHICH TEACHES
DIFFERING SIZE RELATIONSHIPS. IT IS NOT UNTIL
ALMOST THE END THAT DAVID ASKS, "WHAT IF I GROW,
AND CHANGE," AND SHE ANSWERS THAT HE WILL ALWAYS
BE JUST RIGHT, BECAUSE HIS PARENTS LOVE HIM.
(EMOTIONS--LOVE, FAM--MOTHERS, LOVE, MOTHERS,
SELF-CONSCIOUSNESS--SIZE)

SELF-DEVELOPMENT

   HOBAN, RUSSELL. A BARGAIN FOR FRANCES. HARPER,

1970. ILLUSTRATED BY LILLIAN HOBAN. (BCB)

THELMA IS SUPPOSED TO BE THE BEST FRIEND OF
FRANCES, BUT IN THE PAST FRANCES HAS GOTTEN THE
WORST OF THE BARGAIN. ONCE AGAIN, THELMA ENDS UP
WITH THE PRIZED TEA SET THAT FRANCES WANTED, BUT
THIS TIME FRANCES PLAYS A TRICK ON THELMA, AND
SHE GETS THE BEST OF THE BARGAIN. THEY END UP
FRIENDS, NEVERTHELESS. USEFUL TO SHOW
ASSERTIVENESS CAN BE A GOOD QUALITY IN A
RELATIONSHIP. (FRIENDSHIP, SELF-DEVELOPMENT)

KEATS, EZRA. WHISTLE FOR WILLIE. VIKING, 1964.
ILLUSTRATED BY EZRA KEATS. (CC)

THE UNDERSTANDING PARENTS OF YOUNG PETER
SUPPORT HIS EFFORTS TO TRY TO BE GROWN-UP. HE
WANTS TO LEARN TO WHISTLE, HE TRIES ON HIS
FATHER'S HAT, HE TRIES TO CATCH HIS SHADOW. HIS
MOTHER DOES NOT DEMEAN HIM, AND BOTH HIS PARENTS
PRAISE PETER WHEN HE LEARNS TO WHISTLE. THE SMILE
THAT PETER HAS ON HIS FACE TELLS THE WHOLE STORY
OF PRIDE IN ACCOMPLISHMENT. AS MOTHER AND FATHER
APPLAUD IN THE BACKGROUND, HIS DOG WILLIE SITS
UP ON HIS HIND LEGS. (FAM, NEW SIT--WHISTLING,
SELF-DEVELOPMENT, WHISTLING)

SELF-EVALUATION

BERGER, TERRY. I HAVE FEELINGS. BEHAVIORAL,
1971. ILLUSTRATED BY HOWARD SPIVAK. (CCB-B)

ONE LARGE BROWN TONE PHOTOGRAPH ACCOMPANIES
EACH EMOTION WHICH IS EXPLORED IN THIS VOLUME.
UNFORTUNATELY MOST OF THE EMOTIONS ARE NEGATIVE
ONES, AND THE SOMBER PHOTOGRAPHS CONTRIBUTE TO
THE ATMOSPHERE OF DOWNNESS, WHICH IS NOT
NECESSARILY STRESSED IN THE EXPLANATORY TEXT.
FACING EACH PHOTOGRAPH IS A POSSIBLE SOLUTION, OR
EXPLANATION, AS WHEN THE BABY-SITTER TELLS THE
BOY THAT BREAKING HIS MOTHER'S PLANT DOES NOT
MEAN HE IS BAD, ONLY THAT HE HAS MADE A MISTAKE.
OF LIMITED APPEAL TO CHILDREN, THE BOOK WILL BE
ESPECIALLY USEFUL WITH AN OLDER CHILD OF SEVEN OR
EIGHT CONFRONTING A SPECIFIC PROBLEM. (EMOTIONS,
SELF-EVALUATION)

NESS, EVALINE. DO YOU HAVE THE TIME, LYDIA?.
DUTTON, 1971. ILLUSTRATED BY EVALINE NESS. (CC,
ESLC)

LYDIA IS A LITTLE GIRL WHO NEVER "HAS TIME" TO
FINISH ALL OF THE MANY THINGS IN WHICH SHE'S
INTERESTED. WHEN SHE NEGLECTS TO FINISH A RACING
CAR FOR HER YOUNGER BROTHER, HE IS DISAPPOINTED,
AND SHE BEGINS TO MAKE AMENDS. THE LESSON IS "IF
YOU TAKE TIME, YOU'LL HAVE TIME."
(BEHAVIOR--CONSIDERATION, BROTHERS & SISTERS,
CONSIDERATION, FAM--BROTHERS & SISTERS,
SELF-EVALUATION)

WABER, BERNARD. NOBODY IS PERFICK. HOUGHTON,
1971. ILLUSTRATED BY BERNARD WABER. (CCB-B)

A HARD-TO-DESCRIBE BOOK BECAUSE OF ITS
UNCONVENTIONAL FORMAT. IT IS DIVIDED INTO SEVEN
SECTIONS DEALING WITH IMPERFECTNESS: THE CHILD
WHO CAN'T SIT UP STRAIGHT, ONE WHO DAYDREAMS,
ANOTHER WHO SQUEALS THE CONTENTS OF SOMEONE'S
DIARY, AND ENDING WITH A PORTRAIT OF A PERFECT
BOY (WHO TURNS OUT TO BE A ROBOT WITH A WIND-UP
KEY IN HIS BACK). (BEHAVIOR--MISBEHAVIOR,
MISBEHAVIOR, SELF-EVALUATION)

SELF-IDENTITY

CHARLIP, REMY. HOORAY FOR ME!. PARENTS' MAG,
1975. ILLUSTRATED BY VERA WILLIAMS. (LJ, NYTBR)

IN WATERY, EVOCATIVE WATERCOLORS, THE
ILLUSTRATOR SETS THE TONE FOR THE THEME OF
INTERRELATEDNESS OF THE HUMAN FAMILY. THE BOOK,
WHILE STRESSING THAT THE INDIVIDUAL IS A "ME,"
EXPLORES THE RELATIONSHIP OF NIECES TO UNCLES,
AND COUSINS TO COUSINS, AND DEVELOPS
UNDERSTANDING OF GREAT-GRANDPARENTS TO
GREAT-GREAT-GRANDPARENTS IN A SEQUENCE WITH A
KITTEN WHICH CHILDREN WILL LIKE. A BOOK WHICH
DEFIES DESCRIPTION, IT IS LIKELY TO BE ONE WHICH
WILL BE ENDURINGLY USEFUL IN HELPING TO DEVELOP
THE CONCEPT OF SELF. (FAM, FAM--GRANDPARENTS,
FAM--GREAT-GRANDPARENTS, GRANDPARENTS,
GREAT-GRANDPARENTS, SELF-IDENTITY)

COHEN, MIRIAM. TOUGH JIM. MACMILLAN, 1974.
ILLUSTRATED BY LILLIAN HOBAN. (CCB-B)

JIM IS THE RATHER QUIET, SELF-EFFACING FIRST
GRADER IN A MULTI-ETHNIC CLASSROOM WHO HAS
APPEARED IN EARLIER COHEN BOOKS, AND WE SEE HIS
INNER THOUGHTS IN THIS STORY OF A COSTUME PARTY.

HE WANTS TO BE "SOMEONE VERY STRONG, SOMEONE VERY
TOUGH." HE DRESSES AS THE STRONGEST MAN IN THE
WORLD AND, IN A VERY SUPPORTIVE CIRCLE OF
FRIENDS, GETS THE BEST OF AN OLDER BOY WHO WANTS
TO FIGHT. (BRAVERY, EMOTIONS--BRAVERY,
SELF-CONFIDENCE, SELF-IDENTITY)

CRETAN, GLADYS. ME, MYSELF AND I. MORROW, 1969.
ILLUSTRATED BY DON BOLOGNESE. (ESLC)

   DON BOLOGNESE HAS SAID THAT THIS BOOK REMINDS
HIM OF HIS CHILDHOOD AND THE DREAMS HE HAD. AND
THE ILLUSTRATIONS ARE EVOCATIVE OF THE FANTASY
LIFE THE YOUNG BOY IMAGINES: A BRAVE LION TAMER
IN BOLD BLACK AND WHITE, AND A BRILLIANT RACING
HORSE IN SURREALISTIC BLUES AND GREENS. IN ONE
ILLUSTRATION, THE TEXT SPEAKS OF THE BOY'S
FEELING FOR COLOR AS HE PAINTS, AND HE WONDERS IF
HE COULD BE A COLOR, OR BE IN THE COLOR. NOT A
BOOK OF EASY ANSWERS, OR CUT-AND-DRIED
STATEMENTS, THIS VOLUME IS ONE TO MAKE A CHILD
THINK, AND EXPAND HIS IMAGINATION. (SELF-IDENTITY)

FLORA, JAMES. FISHING WITH DAD. HARCOURT, 1967.
ILLUSTRATED BY JAMES FLORA. (ESLC)

   EXPLORES THE CONCEPT OF A LITTLE BOY GROWING
OLD ENOUGH TO PARTICIPATE IN AN ADULT'S WORLD,
AND IS A REALISTIC LOOK AT LIFE ON A DEEP-SEA
FISHING BOAT. THE FISHING NET PICKS UP A TORPEDO
WHICH MUST BE DISPOSED OF BY THE COAST GUARD, AND
THIS, PLUS THE DANGER OF FOG AND COLLISION WITH
LARGE SHIPS, GIVES AN UNUSUAL SENSE OF ADVENTURE.
A LONGER STORY THAN MANY, THE READING LEVEL
FALLS AT THE HIGH RANGE OF THIRD GRADE, BUT THE
BOOK WILL APPEAL TO A MUCH YOUNGER AUDIENCE.
(FAM--FATHERS, FATHERS, SELF-IDENTITY)

HEIDE, FLORENCE. SOUND OF SUNSHINE, SOUND OF
RAIN. PARENTS' MAG, 1970. ILLUSTRATED BY KENNETH
LONGTEMPS.

   THE BLIND CHILD WHO TELLS THIS STORY AND HIS
SISTER ARE NAMELESS, AND ONLY ABRAM, THE FRIENDLY
ICE CREAM MAN IN THE PARK, HAS A NAME.
NEVERTHELESS THE STORY IS ONE OF A DEVELOPING
SELF-AWARENESS IN A LITTLE BOY. HIS IS A WORLD OF
A TACTILE ENVIRONMENT, PERCEIVED AS BEING SMOOTH
OR ROUGH, AND OF SOUNDS, SOFT AND LOUD, AND OF
COLORS IMAGINED. IN THE TELLING, MANY THINGS ARE

LEARNED ABOUT THE WORLD OF THE BLIND, AND A CHILD
HEARING THIS STORY WILL HAVE AN UNDERSTANDING OF
THE GROWING INDEPENDENCE IN THIS SMALL DEPENDENT
CHILD. (BROTHERS & SISTERS, DIFF SIT--HANDICAPS,
FAM--BROTHERS & SISTERS, HANDICAPS,
SELF-IDENTITY, SELF-UNDERSTANDING)

KENT, JACK. JUST ONLY JOHN. PARENTS' MAG, 1968.
ILLUSTRATED BY JACK KENT. (CC)

   A FOUR-YEAR-OLD BOY FINDS OUT WHAT IT'S LIKE
TO WANT TO BE SOMETHING HE'S NOT. IN THIS
FANTASY, HE BECOMES A LAMB, A PIG, AND A LITTLE
OLD MAN WITH A PIG AFTER HE EATS SOME CANDY WHICH
CASTS A MAGIC SPELL. THE MORAL IS "YOU ARE YOU,"
AND WHILE A RATHER WEAK ILLUSTRATION OF THIS
AXIOM, THIS BOOK MAY PROVE USEFUL. (SELF-IDENTITY)

KESSLER, ETHEL. DO BABY BEARS SIT IN CHAIRS?.
DOUBLEDAY, 1961. ILLUSTRATED BY ETHEL KESSLER.
(ESLC)

   FATHER CATS DON'T SWING BATS, MOTHER CATS
DON'T WEAR FANCY HATS, LITTLE KITTENS DON'T WEAR
KNITTED MITTENS, BUT THEY ALL LIKE MILK, JUST AS
THE LITTLE BOY IN THE STORY. MANY COMPARISONS
BETWEEN ANIMALS AND HUMANS ARE MADE, ENDING WITH
THE WAY IN WHICH THE LITTLE BOY GETS A HUG AND
GOOD NIGHT KISS FROM HIS MOTHER. AN AMUSING AND
INSTRUCTIVE BOOK TO HELP A CHILD SEE HIS
UNIQUENESS AS A HUMAN AS WELL AS HIS RESEMBLANCE
TO OTHER ANIMALS IN THE UNIVERSE. (SELF-IDENTITY)

KRASILOVSKY, PHYLLIS. THE VERY TALL LITTLE GIRL.
DOUBLEDAY, 1969. ILLUSTRATED BY OLIVIA COLE.
(CC)

   A LITTLE GIRL WHO IS SIX INCHES TALLER THAN
HER CONTEMPORARIES FEELS VERY SELF-CONSCIOUS, AND
WISHES SHE COULD PLAY THE ROLE OF THE TINY
KITTEN OR THE LITTLEST ANGEL IN THE SCHOOL PLAY.
WHEN SHE NOTICES THAT ALL THE MEMBERS OF HER
FAMILY ARE TALL, AND THAT NO ONE SEEMS TO MIND,
SHE BEGINS TO THINK OF ALL THE GOOD THINGS THERE
ARE ABOUT BEING TALL, THE MOST IMPORTANT BEING,
TO HER, THAT SHE IS DIFFERENT, AND SHE IS
SPECIAL. (SELF-CONSCIOUSNESS--SIZE, SELF-IDENTITY)

LEXAU, JOAN. ME DAY. DIAL, 1971. ILLUSTRATED BY
ROBERT WEAVER. (BCB)

"ME DAY" IS RAFER'S BIRTHDAY, BUT IN A SLUM
FAMILY WHERE THERE IS NO MONEY FOR PRESENTS AND
THE TV IS BROKEN, WHAT MAKES A BOY HAPPY? THROUGH
THE TEXT WE LEARN THAT THE FATHER IS NOT AT
HOME, THE PARENTS BEING DIVORCED, APPARENTLY
BECAUSE THE FATHER COULD NOT FIND WORK. RAFER'S
DAY IS MADE PERFECT WHEN HIS FATHER SHOWS UP TO
SPEND THE ENTIRE DAY WITH HIM IN THE PARK, WITH
ICE CREAM AND HOT DOGS. (DIFF SIT--DIVORCE,
DIVORCE, FAM--FATHERS, FAM--ONE PARENT, FATHERS,
ONE PARENT, SELF-IDENTITY)

SIMON, NORMA. WHAT DO I SAY?. WHITMAN, A., 1967.
   ILLUSTRATED BY JOE LASKER. (ESLC)

   THE AUTHOR'S NOTE IN THE PREFACE TELLS THE
ADULT READER THAT CHILDREN WANT TO LET PEOPLE
KNOW WHO THEY ARE, AND SHE HAS GIVEN AMPLE
OPPORTUNITY FOR CHILD RESPONSE. ON EACH PAGE
THERE IS A QUESTION, AND THE CHILD AUDIENCE WILL
LIKELY RESPOND, AS IN THE CASE OF PLAYING
PEEK-A-BOO WITH THE BABY. ALTHOUGH MANUEL IS
PUERTO RICAN AND MAY HAVE LIMITED ENGLISH, THE
SITUATIONS HE FACES ARE NORMAL FOR MOST CHILDREN.
THUS THE BOOK WILL BE USEFUL FOR ALL, AS A
PARTICIPATORY PICTURE BOOK. (SELF-IDENTITY)

SOLBERT, RONNI. THIRTY-TWO FEET OF INSIDES.
PANTHEON, 1970. ILLUSTRATED BY RONNI SOLBERT.
(LJ)

   HIDDEN AMONG THE IMAGINATIVE POEMS AND
ILLUSTRATIONS ARE ELEMENTS TO ENCOURAGE A CHILD'S
LOOK AT HIMSELF OR HERSELF. THE INTRIGUING TITLE
IS A REALISTIC ONE AS THE LITTLE GIRL SAYS THAT
IF SHE HAS 32 FEET OF INSIDES, THAT'S A TIGHT
PACKAGE, BECAUSE SHE'S ONLY THREE FEET TALL. MANY
OF THE POEMS ARE "I" POEMS, SO THE CHILD CAN
IDENTIFY WITH THEM: "I THINK HEAVY THOUGHTS WITH
LONG TRUNKS WHEN THE SKY IS GRAY LIKE AN
ELEPHANT." THE BOOK CAN BE ENJOYED BY AN
INTROSPECTIVE CHILD, OR ENJOYED WITH AN ADULT
WILLING TO TAKE THE TIME TO HELP A CHILD THINK
THROUGH SOME OF THE DEEP PROBLEMS, AS WELL AS
SOME OF THE IMAGISTIC LANGUAGE OF POETRY.
(SELF-IDENTITY)

SELF-RELIANCE

   HOBAN, RUSSELL. NOTHING TO DO. HARPER, 1964.

ILLUSTRATED BY LILLIAN HOBAN.   (CC)

   WALTER, AN OPOSSUM, ALWAYS SAYS THERE IS
NOTHING TO DO UNTIL HIS FATHER GIVES HIM A
SOMETHING-TO-DO-STONE. WALTER USES HIS
SOMETHING-TO-DO-STONE VERY WELL, AND THINKS OF A
LOT OF WAYS FOR KENNETH AND HIMSELF TO PLAY. HE
LOSES THE STONE, BUT WHEN HIS PESTY SISTER
CHARLOTTE COMES AROUND BOTHERING HIM, HE GIVES
HER A PLAY-RIGHT-HERE STICK, WHICH WORKS MAGIC,
JUST THE WAY THE STONE WORKED FOR HIM. (BOREDOM,
EMOTIONS--BOREDOM, SELF-RELIANCE)

HOFF, SYD. WHO WILL BE MY FRIENDS?. HARPER,
1960. ILLUSTRATED BY SYD HOFF. (ESLC)

   FREDDY MOVES TO A NEW NEIGHBORHOOD AND HAS NO
ONE TO PLAY WITH. HE FINALLY COMES TO A GROUP OF
BOYS WHO ARE PLAYING BALL. HE THROWS HIS BALL UP
IN THE AIR AND CATCHES IT SEVERAL TIMES. THEN THE
BOYS ASK HIM TO JOIN THEIR GAME. THIS
EASY-TO-READ BOOK EXEMPLIFIES THE FACT THAT YOU
NEED TO GO OUT AND SEARCH FOR FRIENDS, AND SHOW
PEOPLE THAT YOU CAN DO SOMETHING COMPETENTLY.
(FRIENDSHIP, MOVING, NEW SIT--MOVING,
SELF-RELIANCE)

HORVATH, BETTY. JASPER MAKES MUSIC. WATTS, 1967.
 ILLUSTRATED BY FERMIN ROCKER. (CCB-B)

   JASPER WAS WILLING TO SHOVEL SNOW ALL WINTER
IN ORDER TO MAKE ENOUGH MONEY TO BUY A GUITAR.
BUT IT WAS GRANDPA WHO TOLD HIM ABOUT THE MAGIC
SHOVEL, AND THAT PART OF THE MAGIC DEPENDED UPON
THE PERSON WHO OWNED IT. CHILDREN WILL APPRECIATE
JASPER'S EFFORT TO LINE UP CUSTOMERS, AND HIS
DETERMINATION TO SAVE HIS MONEY IN A BAKING
POWDER CAN. (FAM--GRANDFATHERS, GRANDFATHERS,
SELF-RELIANCE)

KLIMOWICZ, BARBARA. FRED, FRED, USE YOUR HEAD.
ABINGDON, 1966. ILLUSTRATED BY FRANK ALOISE.
(CCB-B)

   AN OVERLY DIDACTIC BOOK WHICH NEVERTHELESS MAY
PROVE USEFUL TO SOME PARENTS AND SOME CHILDREN.
FRED LEARNS TO USE HIS HEAD TO HELP HIMSELF
RATHER THAN RELY ON HIS PARENTS TO FIND HIS TOYS,
TO OPEN THE DOOR, TO GET A DRINK. THE ULTIMATE
IN LEARNING IS PROVEN WHEN FRED SUGGESTS TO HIS

FRIEND MELISSA: "USE YOUR HEAD," IN ORDER TO
SOLVE THE PROBLEM OF HOW TO MAKE A SWING.
(EMOTIONS--FRUSTRATION, FRUSTRATION,
SELF-RELIANCE)

LEXAU, JOAN. BENJIE ON HIS OWN. DIAL, 1970.
ILLUSTRATED BY DON BOLOGNESE. (BCB)

   WHEN YOUNG BENJIE'S GRANDMOTHER IS SICK BENJIE
MUST WALK HOME FROM SCHOOL BY HIMSELF FOR THE
FIRST TIME. HE MEETS SOME TOUGH-LOOKING BOYS, BUT
FINALLY FINDS HIS WAY HOME. THIS IS THE STORY OF
HOW A GHETTO CHILD FUNCTIONS: NO PHONE IN THEIR
PLACE, SO HE USES THE POLICE BOX, EXCEPT THAT
HE'S TOO SHORT. PEOPLE AT FIRST DO NOT WISH TO
HELP, AND HE DOES NOT HAVE CLOSE FRIENDS TO CALL
UPON. WHEN HIS GRANDMOTHER GOES TO THE HOSPITAL,
HE WORRIES THAT NO ONE WILL BE AROUND TO TAKE HIM
TO SCHOOL, BUT IS HAPPY WHEN HE FINDS THAT RAY,
A NEIGHBOR HE'S STAYING WITH, WILL WALK HIM TO
SCHOOL. (FAM--GRANDMOTHERS, GRANDMOTHERS,
SELF-RELIANCE)

SONNEBORN, RUTH. THE LOLLIPOP PARTY. VIKING,
1967. ILLUSTRATED BY BRINTON TURKLE. (ESLC)

   ONE DAY TOMAS IS LEFT ALONE IN THE APARTMENT
FOR THE FIRST TIME. HIS SISTER ANA, WHO USUALLY
CARED FOR HIM BEFORE GOING TO HER JOB, HAD TO
LEAVE HIM ALONE. STEP-BY-STEP THE READER
PARTICIPATES IN THE LITTLE BOY'S FEAR. HE WAS
CONCERNED ABOUT THE SOUND OF FOOTSTEPS ON THE
STAIRS, AND WISHED ONLY TO SIT QUIETLY AND HOLD
HIS CAT GATTO. WHEN HIS NURSERY SCHOOL TEACHER
COMES TO THE DOOR ON A VISIT, HOWEVER, THE
EMOTIONAL TONE OF THE BOOK CHANGES IMMEDIATELY.
HE IS HAPPY TO SEE HER, ACTS THE ROLE OF THE HOST
BY OFFERING HER A LOLLIPOP, AND THE STORY ENDS
WITH TOMAS FEELING A BIT GROWN-UP.
(EMOTIONS--FEAR, EMOTIONS--LONELINESS,
FAM--MOTHERS WORKING, FEAR, LONELINESS, MOTHERS
WORKING, SELF-RELIANCE)

SELF-UNDERSTANDING

BEHRENS, JUNE. HOW I FEEL. CHILDRENS, 1973.
ILLUSTRATED BY VINCE STREANO. (CCB-B)

   A BOOK TO BE USED BY A PARENT OR TEACHER, WITH
ONE CHILD OR A GROUP. THE SIMPLE SENTENCES ARE

NOT DIFFICULT TO FOLLOW, AND CHILDREN WILL EASILY
COMPREHEND THE SEVERAL LIVES DEVOTED TO VARIOUS
EMOTIONS: ANGER AND HATE, AS WELL AS PRIDE AND
HAPPINESS. EACH PAGE OF TEXT FACES A FULL-PAGE
COLOR PHOTOGRAPH SHOWING YOUNG CHILDREN IN THE
CLASSROOM, ON THE PLAYGROUND, AND AT HOME,
CAREFULLY CHOSEN TO INCLUDE CHILDREN OF VARIOUS
MINORITIES. (EMOTIONS, FRIENDSHIP,
SELF-UNDERSTANDING)

BLUE, ROSE. GRANDMA DIDN'T WAVE BACK. WATTS,
1972. ILLUSTRATED BY TED LEWIN. (CC)

   DEBBIE, TEN YEARS OLD, REALIZES THAT HER
BELOVED GRANDMOTHER IS CHANGING. SHE NO LONGER
WAVES AT DEBBIE FROM THE WINDOW, NOR DOES SHE
HAVE COOKIES FROM THE OVEN READY FOR HER. GRANDMA
EXHIBITS LOSS OF MEMORY, CONFUSION OVER NAMES,
AND OTHER EVIDENCE OF SENILITY, SUCH AS STAYING
IN HER NIGHT DRESS ALL DAY. AS THE GRANDMOTHER
DECLINES, DEBBIE MATURES, AND IS UPSET BY THE
RELATIVES' DECISION TO ENTER THE GRANDMOTHER IN A
NURSING HOME. THE BOOK ENDS ON A POSITIVE NOTE,
HOWEVER, AS THE OLDER WOMAN SPEAKS ENCOURAGINGLY
OF THE COMING OF SPRING. A USEFUL BOOK BECAUSE IT
DEALS WITH A PROBLEM FACING MANY FAMILIES TODAY.
APPROPRIATE FOR THIRD GRADERS TO READ
INDEPENDENTLY. (DIFF SIT--OLD AGE,
FAM--GRANDMOTHERS, GRANDMOTHERS, OLD AGE,
SELF-UNDERSTANDING)

GORDON, SOL. DID THE SUN SHINE BEFORE YOU WERE
BORN?. OKPAKU, 1974. ILLUSTRATED BY VIVIEN
COHEN. (BL)

   SEPIA ILLUSTRATIONS GIVE A LOW-KEY TONE TO
THIS GENTLE EXPLANATION OF CONCEPTION AND BIRTH.
USEFUL BECAUSE THE BOOK BEGINS WITH THE STORY
MUCH EARLIER THAN MOST BOOKS ON THE SUBJECT, AND
EXPLAINS A LITTLE ABOUT A FAMILY TREE, AND
DIFFERENT FAMILIES. THERE IS ONE PAGE EXPLICITLY
EXPLAINING HOW INTERCOURSE TAKES PLACE, AND A
DIAGRAM OF THE UTERUS AND THE BABY IN THE WOMB,
PLUS AN ILLUSTRATION OF THE WOMAN ON THE DELIVERY
TABLE JUST AFTER THE BIRTH. A USEFUL BOOK WHICH
SETS FACTUAL MATERIAL IN A COMFORTABLE SETTING.
(NEW SIT--BABY, SELF-UNDERSTANDING)

HEIDE, FLORENCE. SOUND OF SUNSHINE, SOUND OF
RAIN. PARENTS' MAG, 1970. ILLUSTRATED BY KENNETH

LONGTEMPS.

   THE BLIND CHILD WHO TELLS THIS STORY AND HIS
SISTER ARE NAMELESS, AND ONLY ABRAM, THE FRIENDLY
ICE CREAM MAN IN THE PARK, HAS A NAME.
NEVERTHELESS THE STORY IS ONE OF A DEVELOPING
SELF-AWARENESS IN A LITTLE BOY. HIS IS A WORLD OF
A TACTILE ENVIRONMENT, PERCEIVED AS BEING SMOOTH
OR ROUGH, AND OF SOUNDS, SOFT AND LOUD, AND OF
COLORS IMAGINED. IN THE TELLING, MANY THINGS ARE
LEARNED ABOUT THE WORLD OF THE BLIND, AND A CHILD
HEARING THIS STORY WILL HAVE AN UNDERSTANDING OF
THE GROWING INDEPENDENCE IN THIS SMALL DEPENDENT
CHILD. (BROTHERS & SISTERS, DIFF SIT--HANDICAPS,
FAM--BROTHERS & SISTERS, HANDICAPS,
SELF-IDENTITY, SELF-UNDERSTANDING)

HILL, ELIZABETH. EVAN'S CORNER. HOLT, 1967.
ILLUSTRATED BY NANCY GROSSMAN.   (BCB)

   EVAN, WHO WANTED A CORNER OF HIS OWN IN THE
TWO-ROOM APARTMENT HE SHARED WITH FIVE OTHER
CHILDREN AND HIS PARENTS, WAS SATISFIED TO FIND A
CORNER BY THE WINDOW WHICH HE FIXED UP WITH A
PICTURE HE PAINTED, AND A TURTLE. WHEN HE STILL
FELT UNHAPPY HIS MOTHER SUGGESTED HE HELP HIS
YOUNGER BROTHER ADAM, AND IMMEDIATELY HE FELT
BETTER AT THE THOUGHT OF HELPING ADAM FIX UP HIS
OWN CORNER. (BEHAVIOR--SHARING, BROTHERS &
SISTERS, FAM--BROTHERS & SISTERS,
SELF-UNDERSTANDING, SHARING)

KAFKA, SHERRY. I NEED A FRIEND. PUTNAM, 1971.
ILLUSTRATED BY EROS KEITH.   (BL)

   EXPLORES THE DIFFERENT ROLES A FRIEND CAN
PLAY, AS LISTED BY A LITTLE GIRL PLAYING ALONE IN
HER BACK YARD WITH TWO KITTENS. THE STORY HAS A
SATISFACTORY ENDING AS WE SEE A GIRL JUST HER AGE
AND THE MOVING VAN UNLOADING NEXT DOOR. THEY
SHARE A PICNIC ON THE LAST PAGE OF THE BOOK.
UNUSUAL IN THAT IT CATALOGS THE PERSONAL NEEDS AS
FELT BY THE CHILD. (FRIENDSHIP,
SELF-UNDERSTANDING)

KUSKIN, KARLA. WHAT DID YOU BRING ME?. HARPER,
1973.   ILLUSTRATED BY KARLA KUSKIN.   (LJ)

   EDWINA MOUSE WAS VERY GREEDY AND WANTED
SOMETHING NEW EVERY DAY. IF SHE WENT TO THE STORE

WITH HER MOTHER, SHE BEGGED FOR A NEW TOY, AND
SHE WAS VERY ANGRY AT HER FATHER IF HE DIDN'T
BRING HER A NEW TRINKET. A HELPFUL WITCH TURNS
THE TABLES, AND EDWINA PLAYS THE ROLE OF HER
MOTHER FOR A DAY, WITH HER MOTHER AS THE CHILD. A
HELPFUL BOOK WHICH NOT ONLY SHOWS EXCESSIVE
GREEDINESS, BUT THE ROLE REVERSAL GIVES THE
READER PERSPECTIVE ON A COMMON SITUATION.
(EMOTIONS--GREED, GREED, SELF-UNDERSTANDING)

LE SHAN, EDA. WHAT MAKES ME FEEL THIS WAY?.
MACMILLAN, 1972. ILLUSTRATED BY LISL WEIL. (CC)

   IN A BOOK WHICH IS DIRECTED TOWARD CHILDREN,
BUT IS VERY, VERY HELPFUL FOR PARENTS AND
TEACHERS, THERE IS SOME PLAIN TALK REGARDING SOME
OF THE THINGS ABOUT WHICH CHILDREN ARE SHY AND
EMBARRASSED. THEREFORE ONE WOULD USE DISCRETION
WITH THE BOOK, EVEN WITH UPPER THIRD GRADERS, FOR
IT TOUCHES ON THE SUBJECTS OF MASTURBATION AND
OTHER MORE GROWN-UP MATTERS. THE VARIOUS CHAPTERS
ARE HELPFUL IN A MUCH BROADER SENSE, HOWEVER,
AND OFFER INSIGHTS INTO FEARS, TEACHERS' AND
PARENTS' BEHAVIOR, AND KNOWLEDGE OF SELF.
(EMOTIONS, SELF-UNDERSTANDING)

PRESTON, EDNA. THE TEMPER TANTRUM BOOK. VIKING,
1969. ILLUSTRATED BY RAINEY BENNETT. (HB)

   AN IMAGINATIVE WAY TO PORTRAY ALL OF THE
THINGS THAT BOTHER LITTLE KIDS--MOM GETS SOAP IN
YOUR EYES IN THE SHOWER, SHE HURTS YOU TRYING TO
GET SNARLS OUT OF YOUR HAIR--EXCEPT THAT ANIMALS
HUMOROUSLY ACT OUT ALL OF THESE HUMAN TEMPER
TANTRUMS. LIONS, TURTLES, AND PIGGISH PIGS MARCH
ACROSS THE PAGES, AND LEND A CERTAIN PERSPECTIVE
TO THE CHILD WHO MAY BE ABLE TO PUT HIMSELF INTO
THE BOOK. (ANGER, EMOTIONS--ANGER,
SELF-UNDERSTANDING)

SIMON, NORMA. I KNOW WHAT I LIKE. WHITMAN, A.,
1971. ILLUSTRATED BY DORA LEDER. (CCB-B)

   LISTING MANY BEHAVIOR PREFERENCES IN SUCH
AREAS AS FOOD, PLAY, AND CERTAIN HOUSEHOLD
CHORES, THE BOOK ALSO GIVES INSIGHT INTO THE
DISLIKES OF INDIVIDUAL CHILDREN. AUTHOR SIMON IS
PARTICULARLY EFFECTIVE IN PRESENTING SITUATIONS
WHERE THE READER CAN EMPATHIZE, THUS GAINING IN
SELF-UNDERSTANDING IN THE AFFECTIVE AREAS SUCH AS

APPRECIATION OF BEAUTY IN THE STARS, AND THE
PLEASURES OF MUSIC. (BEHAVIOR--DISLIKES,
DISLIKES, EMOTIONS--HAPPINESS, HAPPINESS,
SELF-UNDERSTANDING)

SIMON, NORMA. I WAS SO MAD!. WHITMAN, A., 1974.
ILLUSTRATED BY DORA LEDER.   (CCB-B)

   THE AUTHOR'S NOTE IN THE FOREWORD SPELLS OUT
THE INTENTION OF THIS BOOK: TO PICTURE SITUATIONS
WHICH PRODUCE ANGER AND SHOW THAT THIS HAPPENS
TO MANY PEOPLE. PERHAPS ONE OF THE STRENGTHS OF
THE BOOK IS THAT A DIFFERENT PERSON IS SHOWN IN
EACH SITUATION, INCLUDING A MOTHER. ENDS WITH A
FUNNY SONG ABOUT A MAN WHO WAS SO MAD HE "JUMPED
INTO A PUDDING BOG"--AND LEAVES THE READER WITH A
GOOD TASTE IN HIS MOUTH. (ANGER,
EMOTIONS--ANGER, SELF-UNDERSTANDING)

STEPTOE, JOHN. STEVIE. HARPER, 1969.
ILLUSTRATED BY JOHN STEPTOE.   (BCB)

   BRILLIANT PAINTINGS ENHANCE THIS INTERESTING
BOOK WRITTEN AND ILLUSTRATED BY A YOUNG BLACK
MAN. THE STORY OF STEVIE, WHO COMES TO STAY WITH
THE NARRATOR, BEGINS WHEN ROBERT'S MOTHER TAKES A
PRESCHOOLER INTO HER HOME FOR DAY CARE. ROBERT,
AN ONLY CHILD, IS BOTHERED BY HAVING A TAG-ALONG
WHEREVER HE GOES AND ONE WHO ALWAYS BREAKS THE
TOYS. ROBERT THINKS STEVIE IS SPOILED AND HE
THINKS HIS MOTHER ISN'T STRICT ENOUGH. BUT WHEN
STEVIE'S FAMILY MOVES AWAY, ROBERT REALIZES THE
VOID IN HIS LIFE AND, AS HE MUSES OVER THIS
THOUGHT, HE REALIZES HE ALMOST HAD A REAL-LIFE
LITTLE BROTHER. (EMOTIONS--LOVE, LOVE,
SELF-UNDERSTANDING)

SELFISHNESS

ZOLOTOW, CHARLOTTE. IF IT WEREN'T FOR YOU.
HARPER, 1966. ILLUSTRATED BY BEN SHECTER.   (BCB)

   BIG BROTHER COMPLAINS THROUGHOUT THE BOOK
ABOUT THE THINGS HE MIGHT HAVE IF HE WERE AN ONLY
CHILD--HE'D GET ALL THE PRESENTS, THE TREE HOUSE
WOULD BE HIS ALONE, AND HE COULD ALWAYS SIT IN
THE FRONT SEAT OF THE CAR. A BASICALLY SELFISH
ATTITUDE IS EXPOSED, ALBEIT A NATURAL ONE. AT THE
END, HOWEVER, BIG BROTHER CONCEDES THAT IF IT
WEREN'T FOR LITTLE BROTHER, HE'D HAVE TO BE WITH

THE GROWN-UPS ALL THE TIME, AND THAT SEEMS A
WORSE FATE. (BEHAVIOR--SELFISHNESS, BROTHERS,
FAM--BROTHERS, SELFISHNESS)

SEPARATION

ETS, MARIE. BAD BOY, GOOD BOY!. CROWELL, T.,
1967. ILLUSTRATED BY MARIE ETS. (BCB)

ALTHOUGH THE STORY IS TOLD THROUGH THE
DESTRUCTIVE ACTIVITIES OF ROBERTO, A LITTLE
PRESCHOOLER ON HIS OWN AS HE ROAMS THE
NEIGHBORHOOD UNSUPERVISED, IT IS REALLY A
PORTRAIT OF A TROUBLED FAMILY, SEVEN SLEEPING IN
ONE BEDROOM, WITH A YOUNG INEXPERIENCED MOTHER
INCAPABLE OF COPING WITH THE FAMILY. WHEN ROBERTO
GOES TO DAY SCHOOL AT THE CHILDREN'S CENTER,
THINGS GET BETTER: HE LEARNS SOME ENGLISH BUT,
MORE IMPORTANTLY, PRINTS THE LETTER TO HIS MOTHER
WHICH BRINGS HER HOME. MOST CHILDREN WILL
UNDERSTAND THE "BAD" BEHAVIOR WHICH CAME ABOUT
BECAUSE ROBERTO NEEDED ATTENTION. THE TEXT IS
QUITE LONG, AND IT IS NOT PARTICULARLY EASY TO
READ. THEREFORE THIS IS PROBABLY MORE USEFUL AS A
BOOK TO BE SHARED. (BEHAVIOR--MISBEHAVIOR, DIFF
SIT--SEPARATION, MISBEHAVIOR, SEPARATION)

SERENITY

GAUCH, PATRICIA. GRANDPA AND ME. COWARD, 1972.
ILLUSTRATED BY SYMEON SHIMIN. (CC)

THE ILLUSTRATIONS ARE PARAMOUNT IN THIS STORY
OF A BOY, PERHAPS TEN OR ELEVEN, AND THE
COMPANIONSHIP HE AND HIS GRANDFATHER SHARE, AS
THE DELICATE WATERCOLORS WASH ACROSS THE PAGES IN
PASTELS OF SAND, SUN, AND WATER. SYMEON SHIMIN'S
ARTISTRY DOMINATES THE BOOK, YET IN A SUPPORTIVE
WAY, AND THE READER COMES AWAY FROM THE BOOK
WITH A FEELING OF CONTENTMENT, PEACE, AND
THOUGHTFUL REFLECTIONS ON THE VALUES OF GETTING
BACK TO NATURE AND BEING ALONE, AWAY FROM PEOPLE.
(EMOTIONS--SERENITY, FAM--GRANDFATHERS,
GRANDFATHERS, SERENITY)

SHARING

BONSALL, CROSBY. IT'S MINE!--A GREEDY BOOK.
HARPER, 1964. ILLUSTRATED BY CROSBY BONSALL.
(ESLC)

MABEL ANN AND PATRICK ARE TWO PRESCHOOLERS WHO
PLAY TOGETHER EVERY DAY, WITH THEIR ASSORTED
FAVORITE TOYS. THEY REFUSE TO SHARE, AND GO HOME
MAD. BUT AT A PICNIC, WHILE THEY ARE QUARRELING
OVER A CARROT, A GOAT EATS THEIR LUNCH, AND WHAT
FOLLOWS IS AN AMAZING TURNABOUT. THE STORY ENDS
WITH "MINE" STILL THE MOST IMPORTANT WORD IN THE
STORY, BUT PATRICK IS PLAYING WITH MABEL ANN'S
RUBBER DUCK AND MABEL ANN IS WEARING PATRICK'S
FEATHER. DELICIOUS CHILD-APPEALING DRAWINGS MAKE
THE BOOK VERY ATTRACTIVE TO CHILDREN.
(BEHAVIOR--SHARING, EMOTIONS--GREED, FRIENDSHIP,
GREED, SHARING)

HILL, ELIZABETH. EVAN'S CORNER. HOLT, 1967.
ILLUSTRATED BY NANCY GROSSMAN. (BCB)

EVAN, WHO WANTED A CORNER OF HIS OWN IN THE
TWO-ROOM APARTMENT HE SHARED WITH FIVE OTHER
CHILDREN AND HIS PARENTS, WAS SATISFIED TO FIND A
CORNER BY THE WINDOW WHICH HE FIXED UP WITH A
PICTURE HE PAINTED, AND A TURTLE. WHEN HE STILL
FELT UNHAPPY HIS MOTHER SUGGESTED HE HELP HIS
YOUNGER BROTHER ADAM, AND IMMEDIATELY HE FELT
BETTER AT THE THOUGHT OF HELPING ADAM FIX UP HIS
OWN CORNER. (BEHAVIOR--SHARING, BROTHERS &
SISTERS, FAM--BROTHERS & SISTERS,
SELF-UNDERSTANDING, SHARING)

HOBAN, RUSSELL. BEST FRIENDS FOR FRANCES.
HARPER, 1969. ILLUSTRATED BY LILLIAN HOBAN.
(BCB)

THE LITTLE BADGERS IN THIS STORY DEMONSTRATE
THE POIGNANCY OF A LITTLE SISTER BEING LEFT OUT
WHEN OLDER BOYS AND GIRLS ARE PLAYING. A NO-GIRLS
AND NO-BOYS SITUATION FOLLOWS, BUT ALL IS
HAPPINESS WHEN FRANCES PACKS UP A SCRUMPTIOUS
PICNIC FOR ALBERT AND THE YOUNGER SISTER GLORIA.
(BEHAVIOR--SHARING, FAM--SISTERS, FRIENDSHIP,
SHARING, SISTERS)

JOHNSTON, TONY. MOLE AND TROLL TRIM THE TREE.
PUTNAM, 1974. ILLUSTRATED BY WALLACE TRIPP. (BL)

CHRISTMASY RED AND GREEN COLORS SET THE STAGE
FOR THIS STORY OF TWO FRIENDS WHO WANTED TO SHARE
THEIR CHRISTMAS TREE BUT WHO FOUND IT VERY
DIFFICULT TO DECIDE SUCH THINGS AS WHETHER A STAR
OR ANGEL WAS BETTER FOR THE TOP OF THE TREE.

DIFFERENCES ARE RESOLVED AFTER A QUARREL AND THE
BOOK ENDS ON A POSITIVE NOTE OF SHARING, WITH THE
DECORATED TREE BEING TRANSPORTED OUT INTO THE
FOREST. OBSERVANT CHILDREN WILL WONDER HOW THE
ELECTRIC LIGHTS CAN FUNCTION OUT IN THE WOODS.
(BEHAVIOR--SHARING, FRIENDSHIP, SHARING)

KEATS, EZRA. LOUIE. GREENWILLOW, 1975.
ILLUSTRATED BY EZRA KEATS.   (CCB-B, CSM, HB, SLJ)

   LOUIE, A YOUNG BOY IN A SLUM NEIGHBORHOOD WHO
DOES NOT SPEAK, COMES ALIVE WHEN HE SEES A PUPPET
NAMED GUSSIE AT A PUPPET SHOW. THE READER SENSES
THE LONELINESS OF LOUIE IN A BEAUTIFUL DREAM
SEQUENCE, AND ALL CHILDREN WILL APPRECIATE THE
ENDING, WHEN LOUIE RECEIVES GUSSIE AS A GENEROUS
GIFT FROM THE CHILDREN WHO MADE HER.
(BEHAVIOR--SHARING, EMOTIONS--LONELINESS,
FRIENDSHIP, LONELINESS, SHARING)

MC KEAN, ELLY. IT'S MINE. VANGUARD, 1951.
ILLUSTRATED BY ELLY MC KEAN.   (GBC)

   THOUGH PEDANTIC IN TONE AT TIMES, A USEFUL
VOLUME FOR PARENTS OF CHILDREN WHO ARE FINDING IT
DIFFICULT TO SHARE POSSESSIONS. ALSO INCLUDES A
PREFACE DIRECTED TO ADULTS, BUT THE CHILD READER
OR LISTENER WILL UNDERSTAND HOW OTHER PEOPLE FEEL
ABOUT THEIR OWN TOYS, AND IN TURN MAY UNDERSTAND
THE DIFFICULT BUT REWARDING PATH TOWARD LEARNING
TO SHARE. (BEHAVIOR--POSSESSIVENESS,
BEHAVIOR--SHARING, POSSESSIVENESS, SHARING)

UDRY, JANICE. LET'S BE ENEMIES. HARPER, 1961.
ILLUSTRATED BY MAURICE SENDAK.   (CC)

   DELICATE PINK AND GREEN WATERCOLORS BELIE
SENDAK'S VIGOROUS, BLOCKY LITTLE BOYS, BUT
SOMEHOW ARE HARMONIOUS WITH THE TEXT. THIS IS THE
STORY OF A FRIENDSHIP SO ENDURING THAT THE BOYS
EVEN HAVE CHICKEN POX TOGETHER--IN THE SAME BED.
BUT IN THE DAY-TO-DAY CONTACTS, THE BOYS END UP
IN SOME ABRASIVE SITUATIONS, AND THE NARRATOR
GROUSES ABOUT JAMES: HE ALWAYS WANTS TO BE BOSS.
IN THE CONCLUDING PAGES, HOWEVER, THE SUN BEGINS
TO SHINE, THE ARTIST'S BOYS BEGIN TO WALK INTO
THE FRAMES INSTEAD OF OUT OF THEM, AND THEY SKATE
OFF TOGETHER, JOINED BY A PRETZEL AND ONE PAIR
OF SKATES BETWEEN THEM. A COMFORTING STORY WHICH
IS APPEALING IN ITS REALISTIC VIEW OF THE

LOVE/HATE RELATIONSHIP WHICH CAN EXIST IN THE
BEST OF FRIENDSHIPS. (BEHAVIOR--QUARRELING,
BEHAVIOR--SHARING, FRIENDSHIP, QUARRELING,
SHARING)

SHYNESS

DEAN, LEIGH. LOOKING DOWN GAME. FUNK, 1968.
ILLUSTRATED BY PAUL GIOVANOPOULOS. (BECB)

A LONELY BOY SPENDS ALMOST A YEAR IN A NEW
NEIGHBORHOOD, LOOKING DOWN INSTEAD OF UP, TO
AVOID MAKING NEW FRIENDS. WHILE THE BONUSES ARE
MANY--THE DISCOVERY THAT HE LIKES ANTS, AND THE
BIRD'S NEST HE FOUND--THE READER IS RELIEVED WHEN
HE DISCOVERS A FRIEND UP IN A TREE AND DECIDES
TO FIND OUT "WHAT BEING UP WAS LIKE." THE SOMBER
BLACK AND WHITE DRAWINGS LEND THEMSELVES WELL TO
THE QUIET, INTROSPECTIVE MOOD OF THE STORY, AND
EDGAR IS SEEN AS A BASICALLY SHY PERSON, FAIRLY
CONTENT TO EXPLORE HIS LONELY WORLD. WHILE THE
READER IS GLAD TO SEE HIM MAKE A FRIEND, ONE ALSO
SENSES THIS IS A BOY WHO WILL ALWAYS BE A GOOD
OBSERVER OF LIFE. (EMOTIONS--LONELINESS,
EMOTIONS--SHYNESS, LONELINESS, SHYNESS)

KRASILOVSKY, PHYLLIS. THE SHY LITTLE GIRL.
HOUGHTON, 1970. ILLUSTRATED BY TRINA HYMAN.
(LJ, TLS)

ANNE WAS A LONER WHO SPOKE IN A VOICE NO ONE
COULD HEAR, WHO OFTEN PLAYED ALONE, AND WHO, WHEN
SHE DID PLAY, FOUND PLAYMATES YOUNGER THAN
HERSELF. WHEN CLAUDIA, A NEW GIRL, COMES TO
SCHOOL, THEY IMMEDIATELY STRIKE UP A FRIENDSHIP.
ANNE'S SELF-CONFIDENCE GROWS AS THE FRIENDSHIP
GROWS, AND WE SEE HER BLOSSOM INTO A
PARTICIPATING, SHARING YOUNG GIRL.
(EMOTIONS--SHYNESS, SELF-CONFIDENCE, SHYNESS)

LEXAU, JOAN. BENJIE. DIAL, 1964. ILLUSTRATED BY
DON BOLOGNESE. (CC)

A LIGHT GRAY WATERCOLOR WASH MATCHES THE
GRUBBY STREET SETTING OF THIS REALISTIC STORY.
ACTION TAKES PLACE ON THE STOOP, STREETS, AND
SHOPS OF THE INNER CITY, INCLUDING THE ONE ROOM
IN WHICH GRANNY AND BENJIE LIVE. HE IS A SMALL
BOY SO SHY THAT HE HIDES BEHIND HIS GRANNY'S
SKIRTS, AND IS TEASED BY THE NEIGHBORS. WHEN HIS

GRANDMOTHER LOSES A FAVORITE EARRING, BENJIE
OVERCOMES HIS SHYNESS TO HELP LOOK FOR IT, AND IN
ASSERTING HIMSELF MAKES PROGRESS TOWARD
INDEPENDENCE. USEFUL ALSO TO DEMONSTRATE A
LOVING, CARING RELATIONSHIP BETWEEN YOUNG AND
OLD. (EMOTIONS--SHYNESS, FAM--GRANDMOTHERS,
GRANDMOTHERS, SELF-CONFIDENCE, SHYNESS)

ZOLOTOW, CHARLOTTE. A TIGER CALLED THOMAS.
LOTHROP, 1963. ILLUSTRATED BY KURT WERTH. (CC)

SHY THOMAS SITS ON THE PORCH OF HIS NEW HOUSE
AND REFUSES TO TRY TO MAKE NEW FRIENDS. HE IS
VERY OBSERVANT, HOWEVER, AND IS AWARE OF GERALD,
WHO PLAYS BALL ALONE, AND OF MARIE, AND OTHER
PEOPLE IN THE NEIGHBORHOOD. GIVEN CONFIDENCE BY
DRESSING UP IN A TIGER SUIT ON HALLOWEEN, HE
TAKES ON SOME OF THE COURAGE OF THE BEAST, AND
VISITS ALL OF THE HOUSES IN THE NEIGHBORHOOD.
WHEN PEOPLE ASK HIM TO VISIT AND PLAY, HE
REALIZES THAT THEY ALL LIKE HIM, AND HE DECIDES
THAT HE ALSO LIKES THEM. (EMOTIONS--SHYNESS,
FRIENDSHIP, MOVING, NEW SIT--MOVING,
SELF-CONFIDENCE, SHYNESS)

SIBLING RIVALRY

AMOSS, BERTHE. TOM IN THE MIDDLE. HARPER, 1968.
ILLUSTRATED BY BERTHE AMOSS. (CCB-B)

THE VERY REAL PLIGHT OF HAVING A YOUNGER
BROTHER WHO BUGS YOU AND AN OLDER BROTHER WHO
THINKS YOU'RE A PEST IS DEPICTED IN THIS
ATTRACTIVE LITTLE PICTURE BOOK. TOM THINKS HE
WILL RUN AWAY, BUT ALSO THINKS THAT HOME AND THE
SAFETY OF BREAD AND BUTTER AT BEDTIME IS THE
BETTER IDEA. (BROTHERS, FAM--BROTHERS,
FAM--SIBLING RIVALRY, SIBLING RIVALRY)

ANDRY, ANDREW. HI, NEW BABY. SIMON, 1970.
ILLUSTRATED BY DI, THOMAS GRAZIA. (ESLC)

IN WHAT APPEARS TO BE DARK CHARCOAL DRAWINGS
SUPERIMPOSED ON COLORED BACKGROUNDS, DI GRAZIA
HAS ACHIEVED AN ALMOST PHOTOGRAPHIC QUALITY IN
THIS BOOK TRACING THE MANY FACETS OF BABYHOOD.
BATHING, FEEDING, AND SLEEPING ARE SHOWN TO BE
ACTIVITIES WHICH ENCROACH ON THE OLDER SIBLING,
BUT WAYS OF HELPING ARE EXPLORED, AND THE BABY IS
SHOWN GROWING UP TO BE A COMPANION. POSITIVE

NOTE THROUGHOUT WILL MAKE THIS A USEFUL VOLUME.
(FAM--SIBLING RIVALRY, NEW SIT--BABY, SIBLING
RIVALRY)

BRONIN, ANDREW. GUS AND BUSTER WORK THINGS OUT.
COWARD, 1975. ILLUSTRATED BY CYNDY SZEKERES.
(BL)

   BROTHER RACCOONS ARE SHOWN IN FOUR STORIES OF
BROTHERLY SQUABBLES. GUS, WHO MAY BE A LITTLE
OLDER, TRICKS HIS SIBLING IN MANY
SITUATIONS--TRYING TO GET THE LOWER BUNK BED,
TRYING TO GET ALL THE BEST TOYS ON A RAINY DAY.
USEFUL FOR DISCUSSION BECAUSE SYMPATHY TENDS TO
LIE WITH BUSTER, THE PUT-UPON BROTHER, AND HE
SOMETIMES GETS THE BEST OF HIS WILY BIG BROTHER.
(BEHAVIOR--QUARRELING, BROTHERS, FAM--BROTHERS,
FAM--SIBLING RIVALRY, QUARRELING, SIBLING RIVALRY)

BROWN, MYRA. AMY AND THE NEW BABY. WATTS, 1965.
ILLUSTRATED BY HARRIET HUREWITZ. (RLHR)

   MOTHER WISELY BRINGS A PRESENT FOR AMY WHEN
NEW BROTHER RICKY COMES HOME. ALTHOUGH PALE BLUE
ILLUSTRATIONS ENHANCE THE SOFT TONE OF THE STORY,
JEALOUSY CREEPS IN TO SPOIL THE FAMILY
RELATIONSHIP. DADDY TAKES AMY TO THE PARK, JUST
THE TWO OF THEM, FOR A PONY RIDE AND AN ICE CREAM
CONE, TWO THINGS THE BABY CANNOT HAVE.
(FAM--SIBLING RIVALRY, NEW SIT--BABY, SIBLING
RIVALRY)

BURNINGHAM, JOHN. THE BABY. CROWELL, T., 1974.
ILLUSTRATED BY JOHN BURNINGHAM. (BL)

   IN NINE SHORT SENTENCES, THIS BRITISH AUTHOR
CAPTURES THE ESSENCE OF B-A-B-Y AND WHAT IT MEANS
TO A SLIGHTLY OLDER CHILD. THE FRONT COVER
DRAWING, CRAYONED IN A CHILDLIKE MANNER, CAPTURES
THE TONE OF THE BOOK: THE RATHER LARGE BABY WITH
THE RATHER LARGE HEAD IS ALMOST AS LARGE AS THE
BOY UPON WHOSE LAP IT SITS. YET THIS BABY CANNOT
DO ANYTHING TO GIVE THE YOUNG BOY REAL
COMPANIONSHIP, AND INDEED DEPRIVES HIM OF THE
COMPANY OF HIS MOTHER. AN EASY-TO-READ BOOK, AS
WELL AS ONE TO BE SHARED. (FAM--SIBLING RIVALRY,
NEW SIT--BABY, SIBLING RIVALRY)

ELLENTUCK, SHAN. MY BROTHER BERNARD. ABELARD,
1968. ILLUSTRATED BY SHAN ELLENTUCK. (CCB-B)

TOLD BY A NAMELESS LITTLE SISTER, THIS IS A
PORTRAIT OF A KOOKY BROTHER WHO WANTS EVERYONE TO
THINK HE IS A PRINCE. IN ONE SENSE, HE BULLIES
HIS SISTER, AND THREATENS TO HIT HER IF SHE
DOESN'T PLAY AT THE GAME OF MAKE-BELIEVE. SHE,
HOWEVER, SECRETLY ADMIRES HIM AND HIS IMAGINARY
KINGDOM, AND IN THE END IS FLATTERED BY BEING
MADE A PRINCESS. THIS BOOK IS NOT A TRACT FOR
PERSONS LOOKING FOR BOOKS WITH STRONG IMAGES OF
WOMEN. (BROTHERS & SISTERS, FAM--BROTHERS &
SISTERS, FAM--SIBLING RIVALRY, SIBLING RIVALRY)

FRIEDMAN, AILEEN. CASTLES OF THE TWO BROTHERS.
HOLT, 1972. ILLUSTRATED BY STEVEN KELLOGG.
(ESLC)

AILEEN FRIEDMAN WAS INSPIRED TO WRITE THIS
STORY AFTER SHE VISITED TWO REAL CASTLES SITUATED
ON THE RHINE RIVER. IT HAS A FOLKTALE QUALITY
ABOUT IT WHICH IS MATCHED BY MEDIEVAL
ILLUSTRATIONS. BASICALLY IT IS THE STORY OF TWO
BROTHERS WHO WERE ORPHANED. HUBERT, THE OLDER
BROTHER, LOOKS AFTER HIS YOUNGER BROTHER KLAUS TO
SUCH AN EXTENT THAT THE YOUNGER BROTHER FINALLY
REBELS. AFTER BUILDING HIS OWN CASTLE AND A HUGE
WALL TO SEPARATE IT FROM HUBERT'S, KLAUS NARROWLY
AVOIDS DISASTER WHEN THE WALL CRUMBLES.
ILLUSTRATES VERY WELL THAT TOO MUCH "MOTHERING"
CAN BE BAD. (BROTHERS, FAM--BROTHERS,
FAM--SIBLING RIVALRY, SIBLING RIVALRY)

GREENFIELD, ELOISE. SHE COME BRINGING ME THAT
LITTLE BABY GIRL. LIPPINCOTT, 1974. ILLUSTRATED
BY JOHN STEPTOE. (CC)

"I DIDN'T LIKE THE WAY MAMA AND DADDY LOOKED
AT HER, LIKE SHE WAS THE ONLY BABY IN THE WORLD."
THIS WAS THE FEELING THAT KEVIN HAD WHEN THE NEW
BABY CAME HOME--AND RELATIVES AND NEIGHBORS CAME
TO CALL WITH PRESENTS FOR THE BABY BUT NOTHING
FOR KEVIN. WHEN HIS MOTHER TOLD HIM THAT SHE HAD
ONCE BEEN A BABY GIRL, KEVIN FELT MUCH BETTER,
AND WAS SATISFIED, AT THE END, TO SHARE ONE OF
HIS MOTHER'S ARMS WITH THE BABY. (FAM--SIBLING
RIVALRY, NEW SIT--BABY, SIBLING RIVALRY)

HOLLAND, VIKI. WE ARE HAVING A BABY. SCRIBNER,
1972. ILLUSTRATED BY VIKI HOLLAND. (RLHR)

REALISTIC BLACK AND WHITE PHOTOGRAPHS

UNDERLINE THE AUTHENTICITY OF THIS VOLUME FOR
PARENTS AND SIBLINGS. THE BOOK OPENS WITH THE
CHILD AT HOME FEELING THE SIZE OF MOTHER'S
ABDOMEN, AND PROGRESSES THROUGH THE DAY MOTHER
LEAVES FOR THE HOSPITAL. AFTER DANA STRUGGLES TO
DRESS HERSELF, THE BOOK GIVES A STEP-BY-STEP
PICTURE OF WHAT IS HAPPENING TO THE MOTHER, MUCH
AS A FATHER MIGHT DESCRIBE IT TO THE CHILD AT
HOME. DANA HAS SOME FEELINGS OF REJECTION AFTER
THE BABY COMES HOME AND SHE REFUSES TO EAT LUNCH.
WHEN HER FATHER RETURNS IN THE EVENING THEY HAVE
A SHARING TIME TOGETHER AND SHE HELPS TO FEED
THE BABY. THERE IS A VERY SATISFIED EXPRESSION ON
DANA'S FACE IN THE LAST ILLUSTRATION AS SHE
SAYS: "HE'S MY BROTHER." (FAM--SIBLING RIVALRY,
NEW SIT--BABY, SIBLING RIVALRY)

KEATS, EZRA. PETER'S CHAIR. HARPER, 1967.
ILLUSTRATED BY EZRA KEATS. (BCB)

POOR PETER! HE WAS SO JEALOUS OF THE NEW BABY,
HE DECIDED TO RUN AWAY FROM HOME. WHEN HIS DAD
BEGAN TO PAINT ALL OF PETER'S FURNITURE, HE
GRABBED HIS LITTLE CHAIR, AND RAN OUTSIDE THE
DOOR. HE WAS VERY SURPRISED TO FIND THAT HE COULD
NOT FIT INTO IT ANYMORE BECAUSE HE HAD GROWN
BIGGER. USEFUL BECAUSE IT SHOWS THE RESOLVING OF
THE JEALOUS FEELINGS: PETER AND HIS FATHER PAINT
THE LITTLE CHAIR. ADDITIONALLY USEFUL BECAUSE IT
SHOWS A PRACTICAL EXAMPLE OF GROWTH IN A CHILD.
(EMOTIONS--JEALOUSY, FAM--SIBLING RIVALRY,
JEALOUSY, NEW SIT--BABY, SIBLING RIVALRY)

PEARSON, SUSAN. MONNIE HATES LYDIA. DIAL, 1975.
ILLUSTRATED BY DIANE PATERSON. (BL)

INTERESTING BECAUSE A FATHER HEADS THIS
ONE-PARENT FAMILY CONSISTING OF MONNIE AND HER
THOROUGHLY OBNOXIOUS SISTER LYDIA. DADDY IS AN
IMPARTIAL ARBITER IN THE FAMILY SQUABBLE WHICH
ERUPTS ON LYDIA'S BIRTHDAY, SUPPORTIVE OF
MONNIE'S HURT FEELINGS, BUT NOT WILLING TO PUNISH
LYDIA. HE IS AN ATTRACTIVE, BEARDED CONTEMPORARY
FATHER WHO CAN BE ADMIRED FOR HIS COOL WHEN
MONNIE DUMPS THE BIRTHDAY CAKE IN LYDIA'S FACE.
ONE FEELS HE SHOULD BE CHEERING, BUT INSTEAD HE
HANDS LYDIA A TOWEL AND KISSES HER ON THE CHEEK.
USEFUL AS A PORTRAIT OF A NEW LIFE-STYLE FAMILY
COPING WITH OLD LIFE-STYLE PROBLEMS. (ANGER, DIFF
SIT--ONE PARENT, EMOTIONS--ANGER, FAM--FATHERS,

FAM--ONE PARENT, FAM--SIBLING RIVALRY, FATHERS,
ONE PARENT, SIBLING RIVALRY)

SCOTT, ANN. ON MOTHER'S LAP. MC GRAW, 1972.
ILLUSTRATED BY GLO COALSON. (BCB)

A LOVING STORY OF A LAP WITH UNLIMITED ROOM.
FIRST IT HAS MICHAEL, THEN HIS DOLL, THEN HIS
BOAT, THEN HIS PUPPY, THEN HIS REINDEER BLANKET.
THEY ALL ROCKED TOGETHER. WHEN THE BABY WAKES UP,
MICHAEL PUTS ON A SOUR FACE, AND SAYS THERE
ISN'T ANY ROOM. BUT MOTHER MAKES ROOM FOR ALL,
AND GIVES A SENSE OF SECURITY TO THE READER THAT
ONLY A LAP AND A ROCKING CHAIR CAN PROVIDE.
(EMOTIONS--LOVE, EMOTIONS--SECURITY,
FAM--MOTHERS, FAM--SIBLING RIVALRY, LOVE,
MOTHERS, SECURITY, SIBLING RIVALRY)

VIORST, JUDITH. I'LL FIX ANTHONY. HARPER, 1969.
ILLUSTRATED BY ARNOLD LOBEL. (BL)

A CLASSIC RECITAL OF THE VENGEFUL JEALOUSY
SEETHING INSIDE A LITTLE BOY, WHO IS NOT YET
QUITE SIX. WE SEE A PORTRAIT OF THE OLDER BROTHER
THROUGH THE EYES OF THE ABUSED YOUNGER BROTHER:
THE OLDER BROTHER WHO IS CONSISTENTLY BIGGER AND
STRONGER, PHYSICALLY AND MENTALLY, BUT SELFISH,
PRIVILEGED, AND RATHER HORRID. ANTHONY ANNOUNCES
THAT HE'S GOING TO CLOBBER YOUNGER BROTHER, AND
SAYS, "YOU STINK." LITTLE BROTHER SAYS, "I'LL FIX
ANTHONY." (WHEN I'M SIX.) (ANGER,
EMOTIONS--ANGER, EMOTIONS--JEALOUSY, FAM--SIBLING
RIVALRY, JEALOUSY, SIBLING RIVALRY)

WELLS, ROSEMARY. NOISY NORA. DIAL, 1973.
ILLUSTRATED BY ROSEMARY WELLS. (CC, ESLC)

POOR NORA--SHE'S THE LEFT-OUT SISTER, AND
THREATENS TO RUN AWAY TO MAKE HER FAMILY FEEL
SORRY FOR HER AND GIVE HER SOME ATTENTION. WHEN
SHE SHOWS UP IN THE BROOM CLOSET, ALL IS WELL. A
CLEVER, FUNNY BOOK ABOUT A BUMPTIOUS LITTLE
MOUSE-GIRL WHICH WILL DELIGHT YOUNG CHILDREN AS
THEY CATALOG HER MISDEMEANORS. MANY CHILDREN MAY
SEE THEMSELVES. (BROTHERS & SISTERS,
EMOTIONS--JEALOUSY, FAM--BROTHERS & SISTERS,
FAM--SIBLING RIVALRY, JEALOUSY, SIBLING RIVALRY)

WOLDE, GUNILLA. BETSY AND THE CHICKEN POX.
RANDOM, 1976. ILLUSTRATED BY GUNILLA WOLDE. (BL)

WHEN BETSY'S BABY BROTHER BECOMES ILL AND
PARENTAL ATTENTION TURNS TOWARD HIM, BETSY'S
THUMB GOES IN HER MOUTH AS SHE WATCHES ROUND-EYED
IN THE BACKGROUND. BABY'S TEMPERATURE IS TAKEN,
THE DOCTOR IS CALLED AND, AMID ALL THE BUSTLE,
BETSY IS IGNORED. SHE PAINTS SPOTS ON HER FACE,
AND EVEN HER TONGUE, BUT STILL NO ONE NOTICES HER
AND WHEN SHE ERUPTS IN A TEMPER, BOTH PARENTS
ARE ANGRY. WHEN SHE HERSELF BREAKS OUT IN CHICKEN
POX, BETSY REALIZES SHE REALLY DOESN'T WANT THE
RED SPOTS AFTER ALL. A REALISTIC STORY WHICH IS
SIGNIFICANT FOR A NUMBER OF REASONS, IT WILL BE
USEFUL FOR PARENT AND CHILD BECAUSE IT DETAILS
THE TYPICALLY JEALOUS FEELINGS IN A CHILD WHO
FEELS NEGLECTED. A NO NONSENSE WOMAN DOCTOR, A
VIEW OF DADDY TAKING THE BABY'S TEMPERATURE WITH
A RECTAL THERMOMETER, AND LOW-KEY PASTEL AND
CRAYON DRAWINGS MAKE THIS A BOOK WHICH
DEMONSTRATES NON-STEREOTYPED SEX ROLES AS WELL AS
A RELEVANT FAMILY SITUATION. (DIFF SIT--ILLNESS,
FAM--SIBLING RIVALRY, ILLNESS, SIBLING RIVALRY)

SISTERS

HOBAN, RUSSELL. BEST FRIENDS FOR FRANCES.
HARPER, 1969. ILLUSTRATED BY LILLIAN HOBAN.
(BCB)

THE LITTLE BADGERS IN THIS STORY DEMONSTRATE
THE POIGNANCY OF A LITTLE SISTER BEING LEFT OUT
WHEN OLDER BOYS AND GIRLS ARE PLAYING. A NO-GIRLS
AND NO-BOYS SITUATION FOLLOWS, BUT ALL IS
HAPPINESS WHEN FRANCES PACKS UP A SCRUMPTIOUS
PICNIC FOR ALBERT AND THE YOUNGER SISTER GLORIA.
(BEHAVIOR--SHARING, FAM--SISTERS, FRIENDSHIP,
SHARING, SISTERS)

ZOLOTOW, CHARLOTTE. BIG SISTER AND LITTLE
SISTER. HARPER, 1966. ILLUSTRATED BY MARTHA
ALEXANDER. (ESLC)

FRETTING BECAUSE OF AN OVERLY SOLICITOUS BIG
SISTER WHO HOLDS HER HAND AND WATCHES OVER HER,
LITTLE SISTER DECIDES TO SLIP AWAY INTO THE
MEADOW TO BE ALONE. WHEN BIG SISTER CRIES BECAUSE
LITTLE SISTER IS LOST, LITTLE SISTER PUTS HER
ARMS AROUND BIG SISTER AND HELPS HER BLOW HER
NOSE, AND COMFORTS HER. THE LESSON IS THAT LITTLE
SISTER NEEDED TO LEARN TO GIVE AS WELL AS
RECEIVE, AND IN FACT BIG SISTER NEEDED TO LEARN

TO RECEIVE. (FAM--SISTERS, SISTERS)

TEASING

CARLSON, NATALIE. MARIE LOUISE AND CHRISTOPHE.
SCRIBNER, 1974. ILLUSTRATED BY JOSE ARUEGO. (BL)

IN THIS STORY OF FRIENDS WHO LIKE TO PLAY
TRICKS, A MONGOOSE AND A SPOTTED GREEN SNAKE GET
INTO BIG TROUBLE WHEN THEY ARE TRAPPED. AFTER
THEY ARE FREE, CHRISTOPHE, THE LITTLE GREEN
SNAKE, PROMISES NEVER TO PLAY TRICKS AGAIN.
ALTHOUGH THE SETTING IS THE ISLAND OF MARTINIQUE,
THE THEME IS UNIVERSAL. (BEHAVIOR--TEASING,
FRIENDSHIP, TEASING)

WILDSMITH, BRIAN. THE LITTLE WOOD DUCK. WATTS,
1973. ILLUSTRATED BY BRIAN WILDSMITH. (CC)

LITTLE WOOD DUCK LIVES IN A THICKET WITH HIS
MOTHER AND FIVE BROTHERS AND SISTERS. THE FIRST
TIME HE JUMPED IN THE WATER HE FOUND HE COULD
SWIM ONLY IN CIRCLES, AND HIS MOTHER BECAME
ANGRY, AND THE ANIMALS OF THE FOREST TEASED HIM.
WHEN WISE OLD OWL DIAGNOSED THE TROUBLE (ONE FOOT
WAS LARGER THAN THE OTHER), HE TOLD THE LITTLE
DUCKLING TO PAY NO ATTENTION TO THE TEASING.
LATER, WHEN WOOD DUCK'S EFFORTS AT SWIMMING IN
CIRCLES DIVERTED THE FOX, EVERYONE DECLARED HIM A
HERO, AND THEY PROMISED NEVER TO TEASE HIM
AGAIN. USEFUL BECAUSE IT ILLUMINATES THE WAY IN
WHICH A HANDICAP MAY BECOME A BLESSING, AND
DEMONSTRATES THAT MINDLESS TEASING IS
UNDESIRABLE. (BEHAVIOR--TEASING, DIFF
SIT--HANDICAPS, EMOTIONS--FRUSTRATION,
FRUSTRATION, HANDICAPS, TEASING)

THUMB SUCKING

SCHULZ, CHARLES. SECURITY IS A THUMB AND A
BLANKET. DETERMINED, 1963. ILLUSTRATED BY
CHARLES SCHULZ.

THE EXEMPLAR OF DEFINITIONS OF SECURITY IN A
CHILD'S MIND, ALTHOUGH, AS IN MANY CHILDREN'S
BOOKS, THE PHILOSPHY IS UNIVERSAL. "SECURITY IS
RETURNING HOME AFTER A VACTION" IS A TRUISM FOR
GROWN-UPS, TOO, AS IS SNOOPY'S LINE THAT
"SECURITY IS OWNING YOUR OWN HOME," EVEN IF IT IS
ONLY A DOG HOUSE, BUT THE MORE TRULY CHILD-LIKE

EXPRESSIONS OF SECURITY ARE TO BE FOUND IN THOSE
RELATING TO FINDING YOUR MOTHER IN THE HOUSE WHEN
YOU COME HOME FROM SCHOOL, AND SALLY SAYING AS
SHE WALKS ALONG A HIGH CHAIN-LINK FENCE:
"SECURITY IS KNOWING THAT BIG DOG CAN'T REALLY
GET OUT." CURIOUSLY, THUMB SUCKING AND SECURITY
BLANKETS ARE MENTIONED ONLY IN THE TITLE, BUT
SERVE TO TUNE IN THE READER TO THE SUBJECT.
(BEHAVIOR--THUMB SUCKING, EMOTIONS--SECURITY,
SECURITY, THUMB SUCKING)

TOBIAS, TOBI. THE QUITTING DEAL. VIKING, 1975.
ILLUSTRATED BY TRINA HYMAN. (BL)

IN REALISTIC DRAWINGS AND TEXT DEALING WITH A
CONTEMPORARY MOTHER AND DAUGHTER, EACH WEARING
LONG HAIR AND JEANS, THE AUTHOR AND ILLUSTRATOR
HAVE PRESENTED A SITUATION IN WHICH EACH
CHARACTER WISHES TO CONQUER A BAD HABIT: THUMB
SUCKING ON THE PART OF THE DAUGHTER, AND SMOKING
CIGARETTES ON THE PART OF THE MOTHER. THEY
PROGRESS THROUGH SEVERAL CURES, SUCH AS HOLDING
HANDS, AND THE CANDY CURE--EACH HAS ITS
DRAWBACKS. WHILE THEY SUCCEED FOR AWHILE, IN THE
END BOTH MOTHER AND DAUGHTER FIND THEY CANNOT
QUIT COLD. NOT THE USUAL ENDING FOR A CHILDREN'S
BOOK. (BEHAVIOR--THUMB SUCKING,
FAM--MOTHER-DAUGHTER, MOTHER-DAUGHTER, THUMB
SUCKING)

TYING SHOELACES

KLIMOWICZ, BARBARA. WHEN SHOES EAT SOCKS.
ABINGDON, 1971. ILLUSTRATED BY GLORIA KAMEN.
(BECB)

PROBABLY ONE OF THE MOST USEFUL BOOKS EVER
WRITTEN, IN THE EYES OF WEARY PARENTS AND
TEACHERS, THIS STORY OF BARNABY AND HIS ELUSIVE
SOCKS WILL GO A LONG WAY IN DEMONSTRATING A
PRACTICAL, IMAGINATIVE WAY TO TEACH CHILDREN HOW
TO TIE THEIR SHOELACES. BONUS ITEMS IN THE STORY
ARE A RACIALLY-MIXED NEIGHBORHOOD, GENUINE LOVE
AND CARINGNESS ON THE PART OF THE PARENTS, AND A
LOVING TOLERANCE ON THE PART OF PLAYMATES. (NEW
SIT--TYING SHOELACES, TYING SHOELACES)

WHISTLING

KEATS, EZRA. WHISTLE FOR WILLIE. VIKING, 1964.

ILLUSTRATED BY EZRA KEATS.   (CC)

THE UNDERSTANDING PARENTS OF YOUNG PETER
SUPPORT HIS EFFORTS TO TRY TO BE GROWN-UP. HE
WANTS TO LEARN TO WHISTLE, HE TRIES ON HIS
FATHER'S HAT, HE TRIES TO CATCH HIS SHADOW. HIS
MOTHER DOES NOT DEMEAN HIM, AND BOTH HIS PARENTS
PRAISE PETER WHEN HE LEARNS TO WHISTLE. THE SMILE
THAT PETER HAS ON HIS FACE TELLS THE WHOLE STORY
OF PRIDE IN ACCOMPLISHMENT. AS MOTHER AND FATHER
APPLAUD IN THE BACKGROUND, HIS DOG WILLIE SITS
UP ON HIS HIND LEGS. (FAM, NEW SIT--WHISTLING,
SELF-DEVELOPMENT, WHISTLING)

Title Index

Author Index

Illustrator Index